Frommer's®
Las Vegas

My Las Vegas

by Mary Herczog

SOME PEOPLE SAY, "I'M NOT GOING TO LAS VEGAS. IT'S JUST NOT my kind of place." And I think, "What does that have to do with anything?"

The Grand Canyon is a wonder of the natural world, but Vegas is a wonder of the artificial world. It is, at once, everyone's kind of town and no one's kind of town. It has a little bit of a lot of places, recreated in meticulous, scale detail and then covered in neon and lights. As a visitor, I feel both at home and out of this world. It's loud and gaudy, it's heartbreaking and ridiculous, and it exists for one reason only: to take your money. And to make sure you have a ball doing it.

I don't like to gamble—except when I win, in which case I like it a lot—but I remain fascinated. Vegas is glamorous; remember, a "glamour" is a type of hypnotic, magic spell. Something is always new in a town that periodically tears everything down to start again. So, I will always come back. Because my brother can eat a steak at 3am, my sister can gamble on the penny slots, my niece can dance all night at a club, my parents can marvel at Mystère, and my husband and I can giggle and enjoy the spectacle.

You have to go. At least once. Okay, maybe twice. In a few years, the town will be all new, yet again. You can't say that about the Grand Canyon.

© Siegfried & Roy's Secret Garden at The Mirage

They may not strut their stuff on the Strip any more, but you can still coo at **SIEGFRIED & ROY'S WHITE TIGERS (left)** at the Secret Garden, a mini-zoo behind the Mirage hotel—a visit with them and the playful mammals of the adjacent Dolphin Habitat are about the most un-Vegas thing to do in Vegas.

This **MGM GRAND (above)** kitty isn't real (unlike his tiger pals over at the Mirage). But the hotel is—real big, that is, with the most rooms in Vegas (over 5,000) and the largest casino in town. Translation: this cat has a big appetite for your money…

OOH, LA, LA! A perfect two-thirds scale replica of the Eiffel Tower stands at the front of the **PARIS HOTEL (left)**. Inside, the casino is set amid a Parisian street scene—just the right mix of class and gimmick. Move over to Egypt and behold the wonders of **LUXOR'S (below)** glass pyramid and a spiffed-up Sphinx. Locals will tell you that the beam of light that emanates from the pyramid's top can be seen from outer space. Personal experience in a 747 puts that claim in serious doubt.

The best free show on the Strip is the **WATER FOUNTAINS OUTSIDE THE BELLAGIO (above, right)** that dance, dip, and sway in time to tunes ranging from Sinatra to opera. Sound cheesy? It's actually delightful. And also complex; set on a 22-million-gallon lake, the show involves 5,000 lights and a sound system cranking up 56,000 watts.

In other cities, hotels are built near the attractions. In Las Vegas, hotels are the attractions. Here, the skyline of New York City is replicated—not to mention seriously compacted—to create **THE NEW YORK–NEW YORK HOTEL (below, right)**.

Taste. Subtlety. Neither word applies to the late, great Liberace, which is why we love him so much. See this understated garment, and so much more, at the **LIBERACE MUSEUM (left).**

We all need constants in an everchanging world. In Vegas, that means the over-the-top production shows, complete with topless feathered showgirls like the ones here, at *JUBILEE!* **(above).** Good taste and class are all well and good, but sometimes, one just wants to look at a bunch of pretty girls. Preferably in Bob Mackie–designed headdresses.

Slot machines, like the ones pictured here at **NEW YORK–NEW YORK (left),** will be happy to take your money. And maybe, just maybe, they might give some of it back.

The otherworldly landscape of **VALLEY OF FIRE (above)** is the perfect natural-world accompaniment to the artificial weirdness of Vegas. Clear your head for a day and take a tour of this gorgeous state park.

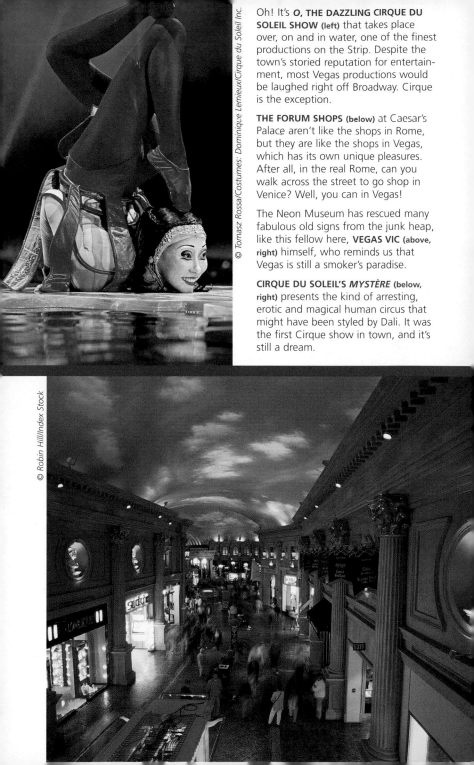

Oh! It's *O, THE DAZZLING CIRQUE DU SOLEIL SHOW* (left) that takes place over, on and in water, one of the finest productions on the Strip. Despite the town's storied reputation for entertainment, most Vegas productions would be laughed right off Broadway. Cirque is the exception.

THE FORUM SHOPS (below) at Caesar's Palace aren't like the shops in Rome, but they are like the shops in Vegas, which has its own unique pleasures. After all, in the real Rome, can you walk across the street to go shop in Venice? Well, you can in Vegas!

The Neon Museum has rescued many fabulous old signs from the junk heap, like this fellow here, **VEGAS VIC** (above, right) himself, who reminds us that Vegas is still a smoker's paradise.

CIRQUE DU SOLEIL'S *MYSTÈRE* (below, right) presents the kind of arresting, erotic and magical human circus that might have been styled by Dali. It was the first Cirque show in town, and it's still a dream.

Las Vegas
at a Glance

Blackjack

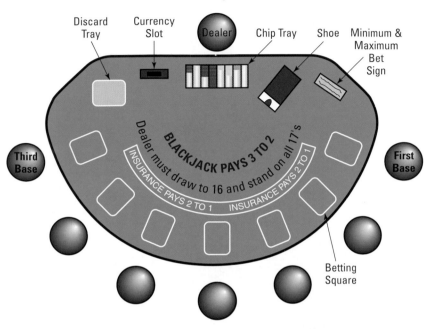

The Dealer Is Showing:	2	3	4	5	6	7	8	9	10	Ace
Your Total Is: 4–11	H	H	H	H	H	H	H	H	H	H
12	H	H	S	S	S	H	H	H	H	H
13	S	S	S	S	S	H	H	H	H	H
14	S	S	S	S	S	H	H	H	H	H
15	S	S	S	S	S	H	H	H	H	H
16	S	S	S	S	S	H	H	H	H	H

Poker Hands

Royal Flush

ACE · KING · QUEEN · JACK · TEN

Straight Flush

THREE · FOUR · FIVE · SIX · SEVEN

Four-of-a-Kind

EIGHT · EIGHT · EIGHT · EIGHT · ACE

Full House

KING · KING · THREE · THREE · THREE

Flush

FOUR · SIX · SEVEN · JACK · ACE

Straight

SIX · SEVEN · EIGHT · NINE · TEN

Three-of-a-Kind

QUEEN · QUEEN · QUEEN · FIVE · SEVEN

Two Pair

FIVE · FIVE · THREE · THREE · KING

One Pair

ACE · ACE · FOUR · NINE · TWO

The Craps Layout

Roulette:
The American Wheel

Frommer's®

Las Vegas

2006

by Mary Herczog

Here's what the critics say about Frommer's:

"Amazingly easy to use. Very portable, very complete."
—*Booklist*

"Detailed, accurate, and easy-to-read information for all price ranges."
—*Glamour Magazine*

"Hotel information is close to encyclopedic."
—*Des Moines Sunday Register*

"Frommer's Guides have a way of giving you a real feel for a place."
—*Knight Ridder Newspapers*

WILEY
Wiley Publishing, Inc.

About the Author

Mary Herczog lives in Los Angeles and works in the film industry. She is the author of *Frommer's New Orleans, California For Dummies, Frommer's Portable Las Vegas for Non-Gamblers,* and *Las Vegas For Dummies,* and has contributed to *Frommer's Los Angeles*. She still isn't sure when to hit and when to hold in blackjack.

Published by:

Wiley Publishing, Inc.

111 River St.
Hoboken, NJ 07030-5774

ISBN-13: 978-0-7645-9767-1
ISBN-10: 0-7645-9767-1

Editor: John Vorwald
Production Editor: Melissa S. Bennett
Cartographer: Elizabeth Puhl
Photo Editor: Richard Fox
Production by Wiley Indianapolis Composition Services

Front cover photo: Kevin Miller/Getty Images
Back cover photo: Mark & Audrey Gibson/Lonely Planet Images

For information on our other products and services or to obtain technical support, please contact our Customer Care Department within the U.S. at 800/762-2974, outside the U.S. at 317/572-3993 or fax 317/572-4002.

Wiley also publishes its books in a variety of electronic formats. Some content that appears in print may not be available in electronic formats.

Manufactured in the United States of America

5 4 3 2

Contents

List of Maps

An Invitation to the Reader

An Additional Note

Other Great Guides for Your Trip:

Frommer's Portable Las Vegas

Frommer's Portable Las Vegas for Non-Gamblers

Las Vegas For Dummies

The Unofficial Guide to Las Vegas

Frommer's Irreverent Guide to Las Vegas

Frommer's Arizona

Frommer's Star Ratings, Icons & Abbreviations

Every hotel, restaurant, and attraction listing in this guide has been ranked for quality, value, service, amenities, and special features using a **star-rating system.** In country, state, and regional guides, we also rate towns and regions to help you narrow down your choices and budget your time accordingly. Hotels and restaurants are rated on a scale of zero (recommended) to three stars (exceptional). Attractions, shopping, nightlife, towns, and regions are rated according to the following scale: zero stars (recommended), one star (highly recommended), two stars (very highly recommended), and three stars (must-see).

In addition to the star-rating system, we also use **seven feature icons** that point you to the great deals, in-the-know advice, and unique experiences that separate travelers from tourists. Throughout the book, look for:

Finds	Special finds—those places only insiders know about
Fun Fact	Fun facts—details that make travelers more informed and their trips more fun
Kids	Best bets for kids and advice for the whole family
Moments	Special moments—those experiences that memories are made of
Overrated	Places or experiences not worth your time or money
Tips	Insider tips—great ways to save time and money
Value	Great values—where to get the best deals

The following **abbreviations** are used for credit cards:

AE	American Express	DISC	Discover	V	Visa
DC	Diners Club	MC	MasterCard		

Frommers.com

Now that you have the guidebook to a great trip, visit our website at **www.frommers.com** for travel information on more than 3,000 destinations. With features updated regularly, we give you instant access to the most current trip-planning information available. At Frommers.com, you'll also find the best prices on airfares, accommodations, and car rentals—and you can even book travel online through our travel booking partners. At Frommers.com, you'll also find the following:

- Online updates to our most popular guidebooks
- Vacation sweepstakes and contest giveaways
- Newsletter highlighting the hottest travel trends
- Online travel message boards with featured travel discussions

What's New in Las Vegas

Gee, what *isn't* new in Las Vegas? That they want to take your money and will do so by any means necessary. Cynical? Hardly. That is, after all, why this town was built, and don't, for a minute, think anything else.

Otherwise, everything is new in Las Vegas. This town is afflicted with terminal restlessness and must keep finding new ways of attracting visitors who can then be relieved of their money. Heck, by the time we've finished writing this, everything we've written, everything in the whole town, will be outdated, changed, or somehow different.

Perhaps we exaggerate. But really, only a little. Hotels are routinely renovating, upgrading, redecorating their rooms, and changing their themes (because everyone knows that a Spanish theme will bring in more tourist dollars than a Mardi Gras theme—that is, until they decide it's been long enough with the Spanish theme and then switch to an Asian one), and that's only if they aren't blowing up the hotel and starting over from scratch. New restaurants with celebrity chefs and big prices open, and longtime stalwarts with comfort food for the ages close. Shows that have been touted with enormous billboards and bigger budgets close in the blink of an eye. Please remember this and think kindly of us if anything in this book is inaccurate. Because that's why.

So, as we write this, what's new? Or even, what's going to be new?

EVERYTHING OLD IS NEW AGAIN May 15, 2005, was the 100th anniversary of Las Vegas. (We aren't sure exactly how they calculated it, but it has something to do with when land leases were signed.) A Vegas-style blowout (and we mean that in terms of both size and absurdity) never quite materialized, though there were parades and fireworks, and the city brought back Helldorado, the Wild West–themed day that was observed for 60 years but dropped some time ago. Various 100-year-themed exhibits are still on display; check www.lasvegas2005.org for details.

The **monorail,** months after its original opening date, finally launched in July 2004, only to close minutes later when a piece fell off, only to reopen, only to close, only to reopen, only to . . . well, you get the idea. When it works, it works swell—who doesn't love a monorail—but the fees are ridiculous—$3 each time you get on. Though it is a much nicer (and cooler) way of traveling up and down the Strip, one that could relieve the horrible traffic problems to some extent, the monorail is simply not yet popular enough to make a difference. If it doesn't get enough patronage, local government will take it over. For now, any extensions to Downtown are on hold.

PLANNING YOUR TRIP "What happens here, stays here." (If only that applied to damage done to our hips and liver!) If you didn't know that the Disneyfication of Vegas was dead and gone, this new city motto, which pretty much encourages visitors to go forth and sin freely, should confirm it. Vegas has reclaimed its adult roots with glee, and that whole Britney minute-marriage was just the kind of publicity the motto needed. The point is, this is not a city that is "great for families," as people still apparently think. It's a city loaded with topless revues, nekkid shows, bars, and other glorious adult pursuits. Go ahead, get married to a stranger if you must, but do think twice about dragging Junior along with you to Sin City.

With the economy in flux, continuing concerns about security during travel, and all sorts of world-shaking events occurring, tourism for Vegas is up and down and up and down, and what you are going to face is unpredictable. Conventions are still coming to town—not as huge, perhaps, as in the past, but enough to make hotel bookings impossible during their staging. The rest of the time, you might well find a bargain, especially if that time lands Sunday through Thursday. Or you might find that all the hotels are handling their losses by charging up the wazoo for a room even during a slow period. We can't quite figure it out. For cost-cutting tips and other useful planning advice, see chapter 2.

ACCOMMODATIONS All kinds of thrilling news here. The most obvious to you will be that new gleaming resort toward the north end of the Strip, the one that has put Steve Wynn's name literally at the top of the town. That's right, his brand-new resort hotel, **Wynn Las Vegas,** 3131 Las Vegas Blvd. S., at the corner of Sands Dr., Las Vegas, NV 89109 (© **888/ 320-9966** or 702/770-7100; fax 702/770-1571; www.wynnlasvegas.com), is the tallest regular building in the city (the Stratosphere is taller, but that's a needle, so it's sort of cheating). The $2.7 billion state-of-the-art hotel gives the city another 4,000 rooms, plus high-end shopping, celebrity chef–run restaurants, a new 18-hole golf course (not sure what was wrong with the old Desert Inn one it

replaced, but what do we know?), an art gallery, a Ferrari dealership, a couple popular shows, and much, much more. That this was a big deal was apparent when *Vanity Fair* did a spread on the hotel's opening. The reviews were mixed, mostly along the lines of "Though it certainly is swell, we aren't sure what makes it all that different from Bellagio, and did it really need to cost that much?"

This being Vegas, "top this" is the mantra, and some take that literally. Wynn himself already has plans for **Encore,** another billion-dollar-plus addition with 1,500 more rooms, more casino, more restaurants, more everything. But that's not until 2008, at the earliest. Meanwhile, right next door, at The Venetian, there is a very big hole in the ground that, by 2007, will hold up its new tower, **Palazzo,** 3355 Las Vegas Blvd. S., Las Vegas, NV 89109 (© **888/2-VENICE** or 702/414-1000; fax 702/414-4805; www. venetian.com), which will, in turn, contain another 3,000 rooms and will be 53 stories tall. That's two stories taller, you see, than Wynn, which is, as we said, right next door. Bigger is, of course, better, and taller better still, and so Donald Trump has decided he can't possibly be outdone in such matters, and therefore *his* Trump International, two towers of hotel rooms and condos, will be 60-something stories. This hasn't even broken ground yet (though there is a sales office, built to the tune of $3 million, taking offers on the condos, which allegedly are already sold out). This news only prompted an Australian group, partnered with a certain ex–Mrs. Trump, to announce that *their* condo tower, farther north up the Strip, will be 75 stories high, the tallest in Vegas, and will be dubbed, of course, the Ivana. Take that, Donald! The town giggles delightedly over all this display of architectural macho.

Less obvious to the naked eye, Mandalay Resorts agreed to a $4.8-billion takeover by MGM MIRAGE. The new giant will own more than half the hotel rooms on the Strip. That's great news for shareholders, but lousy news for visitors, who will find even fewer bargains on Strip rooms as competition dries up— especially now that Harrah's and Caesars have also joined forces, leaving pretty much all the hotels on the Strip in about two sets of corporate hands. The newly combined MGM MIRAGE–Mandalay Group is starting off with a bang, announcing the destruction of the old Boardwalk Hotel, to be replaced by 2010 by the most ambitious project yet in a town full of 'em: Project CityCenter. Get this: It will contain, if it all comes to fruition, not just a 4,000-room megaresort and casino and all that goes with it (shops, restaurants, clubs), but also three 400-room boutique hotels (hot rumor: one of those will be a **Ritz-Carlton;** either way, excellent news, as boutique hotels are the one kind of lodging this town is lacking), plus a couple thousand condo units and even more shopping, clubs, and restaurants separate from those belonging to the hotel complex.

Three other hotels will also be open by the time you read this, but we bet you won't even notice the new **Sun Coast** (so far down south on the Strip, it will be the first hotel there, and will include a world-class equestrian center), the **Red Rock Station** (way out west on the way to Red Rock Canyon), or the **Conrad,** the new four-star (or is it five?) hotel resort going up next to The Rivera on the site of the former El Concho.

Other hotels aren't stopping either; the **Bellagio,** 3600 Las Vegas Blvd. S. at the corner of Flamingo Road, Las Vegas, NV 89109 (© **888/987-6667** or 702/693-7111; fax 702/693-8546; www.bellagio.com), just opened its new **Spa Tower** and has given all original rooms makeovers to match the new accommodations. Caesars will be opening its new **Augustus Tower,**

3570 Las Vegas Blvd. S. just north of Flamingo Road, Las Vegas, NV 89109 (© **877/427-7243** or 702/731-7110; www.caesars.com), with 900 new rooms, by the time you read this. The **Hard Rock,** 4455 Paradise Rd. at Harmon Avenue, Las Vegas, NV 89109 (© **800/473-ROCK** or 702/693-5000; fax 702/693-5588; www.hardrockhotel.com), is building new sets of rooms and even condos, though they aren't adding to their casino space. And Lowes hotels is building a 400-room facility at the end of the Ponte Vecchio Bridge in Lake Las Vegas, on the other side of the water from the Ritz-Carlton. And MGM Grand just announced plans to redo all their rooms as well.

For complete details on the lodging scene in Las Vegas, see chapter 5.

DINING   Lotsa fun going on here, mostly due to Steve Wynn, who really does know how to woo a chef. **American Iron Chef Alex Strada** left Renoir at The Mirage (which closed) to follow his old boss over to Wynn Las Vegas, and opened up his eponymous Alex restaurant, Las Vegas Blvd. S., in Wynn Las Vegas hotel (© **888/320-7110** or 702/770-9966; www.wynnlasvegas.com). James Beard Award–winning Paul Bartolotta moved his authentic Italian cooking to his own self-named establishment at 3131 Las Vegas Blvd. S. in the Wynn Las Vegas hotel (© **888/320-7110** or 702/770-9966; www.wynnlasvegas.com). Master French chef Alain Ducasse is behind **Mix,** 3950 Las Vegas Blvd. S., in THEhotel (© **877/632-1766**). And Jean-Philippe Patissere has the world's tallest chocolate fountain, at 3600 Las Vegas Blvd. S., in Bellagio (© **702/693-8788**). Oh, and a World Champion Gold Medal–winning pastry chef is running the joint, too.

For more dining options in Las Vegas, see chapter 6.

ABOUT CASINO GAMBLING   There is a big change quietly happening all over town—and actually, the key word here is *quiet.* Like us, perhaps you thrill to that distinct sound of coins dropping, *clinkclinkclinkclinkclink,* as you cash out on your slot (or poker) machine. That sound will always be with us, but very soon it's just going to be a programmed audio track because all the major casinos (and maybe all of them, period) are changing their machines over to a cashless system, wherein the payouts will come in the form of printed slips you take to exchange at the cages. And many slots and other machines won't even take coins at all. Gone are the days when one could dump that pocket full of loose change in a slot as one passed by. Meanwhile, many casinos, especially the ones belonging to "resort hotels," are easing up on the noise factor; there is considerably less "bing-bingdingdingdingdingding" going on in the casinos, which is fine in terms of noise pollution, but still. Gambling will never be the same again.

For tips on maximizing your wins and choosing a casino, see chapter 8.

SHOPPING The Esplanade at Wynn

Las Vegas is another high-end shopping dream, with all sorts of famous-maker labels, from Dior to Chanel, Gaultier to Blahnik, Vuitton to de la Renta, and more. Never one to stop with the expansion, the **Forum Shops** in Caesars have undergone yet another huge expansion, this one with a three-story glass entrance right near the Strip. While the Esplanade is pretty much like the shopping area at Bellagio, this new area is unlike any other one in Vegas, with all kinds of natural light pouring into an overblown, suitably Caesars' affair (expect many large and gaudy statues, fountains, and more assaults on good taste—we adore it). Shops include Agent Provacateur lingerie, Vosages chocolates, Juicy Couture, Kiehl's cosmetics, Brooks Brothers, Harry Winston, and more.

LAS VEGAS AFTER DARK   It's clear that everyone is open to putting the "sin" back in Sin City, as more adult-oriented shows make a comeback. Still more fancy new strip joints made the scene around the time we wrote this, and, of course, Cirque du Soleil's ode to human sexuality and the gullibility of theatergoers (nope, we didn't care for it), *Zumanity,* opened.

Céline Dion's show continues to look like a hit (it seems to be selling very well), and when she's got days off, **Elton John** has brought his own combination production show and concert act to Caesars. Unlike Miss Dion's, Mr. John's show has received critical raves for its construction and use of multimedia, and was just renewed through 2008. Elton's example has inspired other musical luminaries; Barry Manilow is pleasing his fanilows with his residency at the Hilton, while **Stevie Nicks** is sometimes filling in gaps between Elton and Céline at Caesars.

Just as there can't be enough hotel rooms in Vegas, there can't be enough Cirque, and so MGM Grand got one of its own. We rolled our eyes, but *KA* (in the MGM Grand, 3799 Las Vegas Blvd. S.; ✆ **877/880-0880**) is not only terrific, but it completely sold us on the idea that, yes, Vegas *does* need more Cirque shows. Consequently, we look forward to their Beatles-themed extravaganza, opening sometime in 2006 at The Mirage, in the old Siegfried and Roy theater. Then again, *Le Rêve,* 3131 Las Vegas Blvd. S.; ✆ **888/320-7110**), a Cirque-like production at Wynn Las Vegas, proved there can be a bit too much of a good thing, especially if all one is doing is fulfilling a tried-and-true formula without attempting a new vision. But Wynn Las Vegas is making up for that with the Tony Award–winning musical *Avenue Q* (which, as a result, unlike other Broadway block-busters, will not have a road tour at all) in a custom-built, $40-million, 1,200-seat theater that should be open fall 2005.

Given that the production is based around puppets, this is a bigger risk than one might think. Also opening at The Venetian is a slightly revamped **Blue Man Group,** shifting over from the Luxor, which in its place will mount a production of the Tony-winning musical **Hairspray.** Also at The Venetian will be that perennial fave **Phantom of the Opera.** Look for both, in somewhat shortened forms, to open around mid-2006.

For the scoop on after-dark activities in Las Vegas, see chapter 10.

RUMORS Vegas just loves gossiping about big plans and changes. None of this is confirmable—we can't even get most hotels to confirm their rates—but this gives you an idea of the dreams this city dreams.

The hot-off-the-press rumor has the newly conjoined Harrah's and Caesars setting their sights on Bally's; it will be either remodeled and rebranded as Harrah's Horseshoe (the company bought the name from the venerable Binion's Downtown) or torn down entirely.

Several other Strip hotels continue to be the subject of speculation. An announcement is supposed to be imminent about the Tropicana, but at this point, we are celebrating the 2-year anniversary of that imminent announcement, so even though something has to be done soon, we are no longer holding our breath. The Riveria seems to have gotten a reprieve, which, given Vegas history, probably means it will be under the wrecking ball by the time you read this. Already gone is water park Wet 'n Wild, to make room for a water-themed resort called Voyagers, which will feature a lakefront, complete with yachts, on which will be the resort's nicest rooms. The owners of the Stardust have bought up parcels of surrounding land, apparently with an eye toward another Project City-Center–type development. The clock continues to tick on the Frontier, with the owner continuing to make plans to knock it down and start over. And there is gossip that a W Hotel will be going up on Harmon, west of the freeway. Much of this probably will happen, but it could be tomorrow or 6 years from now.

Meanwhile, there are also entertainment rumors, with the most recurring featuring Michael Jackson in some kind of Céline-style residency. The most excellent such rumor, however, is that Planet Hollywood, once it properly takes over Aladdin, is building a special theater just for Mötley Crüe!

1

The Best of Las Vegas

The point about [Las Vegas], which both its critics and its
admirers overlook, is that it's wonderful and awful simultaneously.
So one loves it and detests it at the same time.

—David Spanier, *Welcome to the*
Pleasure Dome: Inside Las Vegas

As often as you might have seen it on TV or in a movie, there is nothing that prepares you for that first sight of Las Vegas. The skyline is hyperreality, a mélange of the Statue of Liberty, a giant lion, a pyramid, and a Sphinx, and preternaturally glittering buildings. At night, it's so bright you can actually get disoriented—and suffer from a sensory overload that can reduce you to hapless tears or fits of giggles. And that's without setting foot inside a casino, where the shouts from the craps tables, the crash of coins from the slots, and the general roar combine into either the greatest adrenaline rush of your life or the ninth pit of hell.

Las Vegas is a true original; there is nothing like it in America or arguably the world. In other cities, hotels are built near the major attractions. Here, the hotels *are* the major attractions. For that matter, what other city has a skyline made up almost entirely of buildings from other cities' skylines? Instead of historical codes to follow, builders in Vegas have to worry about the height of the roller coaster in their hotel.

Once you get to Vegas, you'll want to come back again, if only to make sure you didn't dream it all. It's not just the casinos with their nonstop action and sound, the almost-blinding lights, or the buildings that seek to replicate some other reality (Paris, Venice, New York, and ancient Egypt). It's not the mountains of shrimp at the buffets, the wedding chapels that will gladly unite two total strangers in holy wedlock, or the promise of free money. It's the whole package. It's the Megabucks slots. It's Frank and Dino and Sammy. It's Elvis—the Fat Years. It's volcanoes and white tigers and cocktail waitresses dressed in Roman togas. It's cheesy and sleazy and artificial and wholly, completely unique. It's wonderful. It's awful. It's wonderfully awful and awfully wonderful. Love it, loathe it, or both, no one has ambivalent feelings about Vegas.

Las Vegas can be whatever a visitor wants, and for a few days, a visitor can be whatever he or she wants. Just be prepared to leave all touchstones with reality behind. Here, you will rise at noon and gorge on endless amounts of rich food at 3am. You will watch your money grow or (more likely) shrink. You will watch a volcano explode and pirates fight sexy showgirls. And after a while, it will all seem pretty normal. This is not a cultural vacation, okay? Save the thoughts of museums and historical sights for the real New York, Egypt, Paris, and Venice. Vegas is about fun. Go have some. Go have too much. It won't be hard.

The Vegas of the Rat Pack years, classic Old Las Vegas, does not exist anymore. Even as ancient civilizations are replicated, "old" in Vegas terms is anything over a decade.

Las Vegas & Environs

Indeed, thanks to teardowns and renovations, there is virtually nothing original left on the Strip. In a way, that is both admirable and ghastly, and also part of what makes Vegas so *Vegas*. What other city can completely shed its skin in such a short amount of time?

But as much as one might mourn the loss of such landmarks as the Sands, one has to admit that time marches on, and Vegas has to keep pace. Nostalgia for the vanished does not mean you can't enjoy what turns up in its place. Even as you might sneer at the sheer gaudy tastelessness of it all, you have to admit that what's out there is undeniably remarkable.

And when it's all lit up at night . . . well, even those who have lived here for years agree there is nothing like the sight of the Strip in all its evening glory. "It still takes my breath away, even after all this time," says one longtime resident. Everything is in lights in Vegas: hotels, casinos, 7-Elevens, the airport parking garage. Stand still long enough, and they'll probably cover you in neon.

Oh, the gambling? Yep, there's plenty of that. Which is much like saying there's plenty of sand at the beach. Let's not kid ourselves: Gambling is the main attraction of Vegas. The rest—the buffets, the shows, the cartoonish buildings—is so much window dressing to lure you and your money to the city. But even a nongambler can have a perfectly fine time in Vegas, though the lure of countless slot machines has tempted even the most Puritan of souls in their day.

Unfortunately, the days of an inexpensive Las Vegas vacation are gone. The cheap buffets and meal deals still exist, as do some cut-rate rooms, but both are likely to prove the old adage about getting what you pay for. If all you're looking for is fuel and a place to catch a quick nap, they'll do just fine. Be prepared to pay if you want glamour and fine dining.

However, free drinks are still handed to anyone lurking near a slot, and even if show tickets aren't in your budget, you won't lack for entertainment. Free lounge shows abound, and the people-watching opportunities never disappoint. From the Armani-clad high rollers in the baccarat rooms to the polyester-sporting couples at the nickel slots, Vegas attracts a cross section of America.

Yes, it's noisy and chaotic. Yes, it's gotten more and more like Disneyland for adults. Yes, it's a shrine to greed and the love of filthy lucre. Yes, there is little ambience and even less "culture." Yes, someone lacking self-discipline can come to great grief.

But in its own way, Vegas is every bit as amazing as the nearby Grand Canyon, and every bit as much a must-see. It's one of the Seven Wonders of the Artificial World. And everyone should experience it at least once—you might find yourself coming back for more.

1 Frommer's Favorite Las Vegas Experiences

- **A Stroll on the Strip After Dark:** You haven't really seen Las Vegas until you've seen it at night. This neon wonderland is the world's greatest sound-and-light show. Begin at Luxor and work your way down past the incredible hotels and their attractions. You'll pass the amazing New York–New York on your way, and if your strength holds out, you will end at Circus Circus, where live acrobat acts take place overhead while you gamble. Make plenty of stops en route to take in the *Sirens* show at Treasure Island, see The Mirage volcano erupt, take a photo of the full moon over the Eiffel Tower, and, most of all, marvel at the choreographed water-fountain ballet at Bellagio.

- **Casino-Hopping on the Strip:** The interior of each lavish new hotel-casino is more outrageous and giggle-inducing than the last. Just when you think they can't possibly top themselves, they do. From Venice to ancient Egypt, from a rainforest to a pirate's lair, from King Arthur's castle to New York City, to the brand-new Wynn Las Vegas, it is still all, totally, completely, and uniquely Las Vegas.

- **An Evening in Glitter Gulch:** Set aside an evening to tour the Downtown hotels and take in the overhead light show of the **Fremont Street Experience** (p. 193). Unlike the lengthy and exhausting Strip, you can hit 17 casinos in about 5 minutes.

- **Buffets:** They may no longer be the very best of bargains, as the cheaper ones do not provide the quality of the more pricey ones, but there is something about the endless mounds of food that just screams "Vegas" to us. Our choices for the best in town are listed in the dining section later in this chapter.

- **A Creative Adventures Tour:** Char Cruze of **Creative Adventures** (© **702/361-5565;** www.creative adventuresltd.com) provides personalized tours unlike anything offered by a commercial tour company, full of riveting stories and incredible facts about both natural and artificial local wonders. See p. 216.

- **The Liberace Museum:** It's not the Smithsonian, but then again, the Smithsonian doesn't have rhinestones like these. Only in Vegas. See p. 195.

- **The Dolphins at The Mirage:** Actually, a most un-Vegas experience. Zone out as you watch these gorgeous mammals frolic in their cool blue pool. If you are really lucky, they'll play ball with you. See p. 200.

- **Playing Penny Slots:** Where even the most budget-conscious traveler can gamble for hours. They used to be as rare as a non-silicone-enhanced showgirl, but now they're in all the major casinos. See chapter 8.

- **Shop the Big Three Casino Arcades:** Take what Napoleon called "the greatest drawing room in Europe," replicate it, add shops, and you've got the **Grand Canal Shoppes at The Venetian** (p. 259)—it's St. Mark's Square, complete with canals and working gondolas. Then there are the **Forum Shops at Caesars Palace** (p. 257), replicating an ancient Roman streetscape, with classical piazzas and opulent fountains. Don't miss the scary audio-animatronic statues as they come to glorious, cheesy life. And not to be outdone, the **Desert Passage at Aladdin** (p. 256) re-creates the ancient trade route through Morocco, complete with a special-effects rainstorm over an indoor harbor (at least until the hotel's new owners take over).

- **Cirque du Soleil's *O, KA,* and *Mystère:*** You haven't really seen Cirque du Soleil until you've seen it performed in a showroom equipped with state-of-the-art sound-and-lighting systems and a seemingly infinite budget for sets, costumes, and high-tech special effects. It's an enchantment. See p. 269 and 270.

- **Your Favorite Headliners:** As soon as you arrive in town, pick up a show guide and see who's playing during your stay. For the top showrooms, see chapter 10.

- **Finding the Worst Lounge Shows:** Some feel this is the ultimate Vegas experience and dedicate many an evening to it. Be sure to watch out for Cook E. Jarr and the Crumbs. See chapter 10 for some ideas.

A Look Back at Vegas: No Tomorrow

Las Vegas is convention central. Orthodontists go there as well as architects. Computer geeks and gynecologists, TV preachers and township clerks, postal workers and pathologists. There's an abundance of good hotel rooms, cheap eats, agreeable weather. Coming and going is reasonably painless. There's golf and gambling and ogling girls—showgirls of unspeakable beauty—and, of course, the mountains, the desert, and the sky.

The National Funeral Directors Association advertised its 116th Annual Convention and International Exposition there in the trade press as "A Sure Bet." Debbie Reynolds was talking to the Spouse's Luncheon. Neil Sedaka was singing at the Annual Banquet. There was a golf outing, a new website, the installation of officers. I called the brother and the brother-in-law and said, "Let's get our funeral homes covered and go out to Vegas for the convention." Pat and Mike agreed. All of us are funeral directors. All of us were due for a break. Here's another coincidence: All of our wives are named Mary. The Marys all agreed to come along. They'd heard about the showgirls and high-stakes tables and figured Pat and Mike and I would need looking after. They'd heard about the great malls and the moving statues and the magic shows.

My publisher paid for my airfare and our room at the Hilton. "A Sure Bet" is what they reckoned, too. My book, *The Undertaking—Life Studies from the Dismal Trade,* was being featured in the Marketplace Booth at the exhibit hall. The association would be selling and I'd be signing as many copies as we could for a couple of days. So there I sat, behind a stack of books, glad-handing and autographing, surrounded by caskets and hearses, cremation urns and new computer software, flower stands and funeral flags and embalming supplies. Some things about this enterprise never change— the basic bias toward the horizontal, the general preference for black and blue, the arcane lexicons of loss and wonder. And some are changing every day. Like booksellers and pharmacists and oncologists, many of the small firms are being overtaken by the large consolidators and conglomerates. Custom gives way to convenience. The old becomes old, then new again.

Five thousand undertakers made it to Vegas—the biggest turnout since the last time here, in '74—and 2,300 sales reps and suppliers. It was bigger than Orlando or Kansas City or Chicago, or next year in Boston.

Las Vegas seems perfect for the mortuary crowd—a metaphor for the vexed, late-century American soul that seems these days to run between

2 Best Hotel Bets

- **Best for Conventioneers/Business Travelers:** The **Las Vegas Hilton,** 3000 Paradise Rd. (© **888/732-7117**), adjacent to the Las Vegas Convention Center and the setting for many on-premises conventions, offers extensive facilities that include a full business center. And now it's a stop on the nifty new monorail, making access to the Strip easier than extremes of fantasy and desolation. Vegas seems just such an oasis: a neon garden of earthly delights amid a moonscape of privations, abundance amid the cacti, indulgence surrounded by thirst and hunger.

Or maybe it's that we undertakers understand these games of chance—the way life is ever asking us to ante up, the way the wager's made before the deal is dealt or dice are tossed, before we pull the lever. Some people play for nickels and dimes, some for dollars, some for keeps. But whatever we play for, we win or lose according to these stakes. We cannot, once winning is certain or losing is sure, change our bet. We cannot play for dollars, then lose in dimes or win in cash when we wager matchsticks. It's much the same with love and grief. They share the same arithmetic and currency. We ante up our hearts in love, we pay our losses off in grief. Baptisms, marriages, funerals—this life's casinos—the games we play for keeps.

Oh, we can play the odds, hedge our bets, count the cards, get a system. I think of Blaise Pascal, the 17th-century French mathematician who bet on heaven thus: "Better to believe in a God who isn't than not to believe in a God who is." Figure the math of that, the odds. Pascal's Wager is what they called it. All of us play a version of this game.

I came downstairs in the middle of the night and lost 200 bucks before it occurred to me that this is how they built this city—on folks like me, on what we'd be willing to lose. The next night my Mary won $800 on one pull of the lever on the slots. They paid her off in crisp C-notes. We laughed and smiled. She tipped the woman who sold her the tokens. She went shopping the next day for a pair of extravagant shoes and came home, as they say, with money in her pockets.

We undertakers understand winners and losers. Our daily lives are lessons in the way love hurts, grief heals, and life—always a game of chance—goes on. In Vegas we get to play the game as if there's no tomorrow. And after a long night of winning or losing, it's good to have a desert close at hand into which we wander, like holy ones of old, to raise our songs of thanks or curse our luck to whatever God there is, or isn't.

—Thomas Lynch

Thomas Lynch is a poet and essayist and a funeral director in Milford, Michigan. *The Undertaking—Life Studies from the Dismal Trade* won the Heartland Prize and the American Book Award, and was a finalist for the National Book Award. His latest work is *Booking Passage: We Irish and Americans*.

ever. Be warned: New owners could make changes by the time you read this. See p. 117.

- **Best Luxury Resort:** There really is only one, and that's the **Ritz-Carlton, Lake Las Vegas,** 1610 Lake Las Vegas Pkwy. (© **800/241-3333**), perched on the edge (and over part of) Lake Las Vegas in Henderson. It's the combination of setting (gorgeous, peaceful) and experience (such service!) that wins them the prize. See

p. 128. But you might want something that's actually in town, and for that, you must go straight to the **Four Seasons,** 3960 Las Vegas Blvd. S. (© **877/632-5000**), because experience running luxury resorts around the world makes them the only true claimant to the throne within the Vegas city limits. See p. 77.

- **Best Resort for the Indecisive: Green Valley Ranch Resort,** 2300 Paseo Verde Pkwy. (at I-215), Henderson (© **866/782-9487**), somehow manages to combine the comfort of a Ritz-Carlton with the style of boutique chains such as the W, and makes it all work. Have your cake and eat it too, either in the most comfortable beds in town or by one of our favorite pools. See p. 129.

- **Best Archetypically Las Vegas Hotel:** As of press time, there weren't any. Las Vegas hotels are one and all doing such massive face-lifts that the archetype is going to be but a memory. Still, despite some major changes, including a complete exterior face-lift, **Caesars Palace,** 3570 Las Vegas Blvd. S. (© **877/427-7243**), will probably continue to embody the excess, the romance (oh, yes) and, well, downright silliness that used to characterize Vegas—and to a certain extent still does. See p. 92.

- **Best Non-Vegas Vegas Hotel:** Mandalay Bay's expansion, **THEhotel,** 3950 Las Vegas Blvd. S. (© **877/632-7000**) is as elegant and sophisticated as any lodging in Manhattan. All accommodations are true suites, complete with plasma-screen TVs and deep soaking tubs. Since it's a separate tower, you are far away from the clash and clang of Vegas—at least in spirit. In reality, it's just a medium walk down a long hallway. Quite possibly our favorite hotel in the city. See p. 86.

- **Best Swimming Pool:** Hands down, the acres of water park fun at **Mandalay Bay,** 3950 Las Vegas Blvd. S. (© **877/632-7000**)—wave pool (even if the waves never get all that big), lazy river, beach, regular swimming pools . . . no wonder they check IDs carefully to make sure only official guests enter. Everyone wants to swim and splash here. See p. 78. If you can't, you won't be disappointed by the amorphously shaped pools with water fountains and slides, plus a rather festive atmosphere at **The Mirage,** 3400 Las Vegas Blvd. S. (© **800/627-6667**). See p. 102. But if you've ever longed to swim at Hearst Castle, **Bellagio,** 3600 Las Vegas Blvd. S. (© **888/987-6667**), with six swimming pools in a neoclassical Italian garden setting (and a more hushed, chic ambience), is for you. See p. 91. Then again, the pool at the **Green Valley Ranch Resort** (p. 129), with its foliage, beach, in-water gambling, and everything else, perhaps has them both beat. But its distant location (in south Las Vegas) takes it out of the running. Only just, though.

- **Best Spa/Health Club:** We only wish our own gym was as handsomely equipped as the one at the Canyon Ranch Spa in **The Venetian,** 3355 Las Vegas Blvd. S. (© **877/883-6423;** p. 95), which also has a number of other high-priced amenities on which you can blow your blackjack winnings. We are also partial to the full complement of machines at the health club at **Bellagio** (p. 91), probably the best-equipped club of all. Attendants who soothe you with iced towels and drinks, a well-stocked locker room, and comfortable lounges in which to rest up after your workout are other pluses.

- **Best Hotel Dining:** Foodies will work up a good case of gout trying all the haute-cuisine options at **Bellagio** (p. 91), which has restaurants by Todd English (Olives) and Julian Serrano (Picasso). The hotel has seven James Beard Award–winning chefs on staff. **The Venetian** (p. 95) isn't too far behind, with restaurants from Wolfgang Puck, Emeril Lagasse, and Joachim Splichal (Pinot), plus branches of the noted Lutèce. In The Venetian's new expansion is a version of Thomas Keller's bistro **Bouchon. Wynn Las Vegas,** 3131 Las Vegas Blvd. S. (© **888/320-9966**) has brought in a number of name-brand chefs, including Alex Strada (Alex) and Paul Bartolotta (Bartolotta). See chapter 6 for reviews of these restaurants.

- **Best for 20-Somethings to Baby Boomers: Palms Resort & Casino,** 4321 W. Flamingo Rd. (© **866/942-7777**), is the single most happening hotel for the hip and hip-hop sets. No wonder Britney stayed here before, during, and through the aftermath of her quickie marriage. See p. 103. The **Hard Rock Hotel & Casino,** 4455 Paradise Rd. (© **800/473-\ROCK**), bills itself as the world's "first rock 'n' roll hotel and casino" and "Vegas for a new generation." Aficionados of headbanger clubs won't mind the noise level, but we aren't sure about everyone else. See p. 116.

- **Best Interior:** For totally different reasons, it's a tie between **New York–New York Hotel & Casino,** 3790 Las Vegas Blvd. S. (© **800/693-6763**), **The Mirage,** and **The Venetian.** The Mirage's (p. 102) tropical rainforest and massive coral-reef aquarium behind the registration desk may not provide as much relaxation as a Club Med vacation, but they're a welcome change from the general hubbub that is usual for Vegas. Speaking of hubbub, **New York–New York** (p. 84) has cornered the market on it, but its jaw-dropping interior, with its extraordinary attention to detail (re-creating virtually every significant characteristic of New York City), makes this a tough act to beat (though Big City residents may despise its realism). The Venetian's (p. 95) authentic re-creation of Venice, however, might top it.

- **Best for Families:** The **MGM Grand,** 3799 Las Vegas Blvd. S. (© **800/929-1111**), is still a hit with families, despite backing away from more child-friendly details such as its original Oz theme and eliminating its amusement park. See p. 82. Then there is also the classic choice: **Circus Circus Hotel/Casino,** 2880 Las Vegas Blvd. S. (© **800/634-3450**) with ongoing circus acts, a vast video-game arcade, a carnival midway, and a full amusement park. See p. 112. Less aged, and less hectic, **Mandalay Bay,** 3950 Las Vegas Blvd. S. at Hacienda Avenue (© **877/632-7000**) is a more modern choice, right for families because you can gain access to both the guest rooms and the pool area (itself fun for kids, with a beach, a wave pool, and a lazy river) without trotting through the casino. And grown-ups will find party-fun restaurants, bars, and clubs (including the House of Blues) for their own enjoyment. See p. 78. Those of you with bigger budgets might want to try the **Ritz-Carlton** (p. 128) because not only is it well out of range of Sin City's temptations, but it also offers a variety of healthy and fun activities (from hikes to fly-fishing to stargazing).

- **Best Rooms Off the Strip:** Again, we love the **Ritz-Carlton** (p. 128), with its perfect decor, spacious interior, and gorgeous bathrooms, but you'll probably want something closer to town.

- **Best Rooms on the Strip:** We need to break this down. If one is talking suites, then **THEhotel** wins the day, with their one-bedroom could-be-a-great-apartment-in-Manhattan sophisticated wonders. Best "suites" (because no matter how they are billed, it's really just one big room) are clearly the 700-square-foot extravaganzas at **The Venetian** (p. 95), with separate sitting and bedroom areas, full of all sorts of special details. Best "room" goes to the brand-new **Wynn Las Vegas**, where the rooms are quite big, the bathrooms not far behind, the beds are plush, the TVs (plural!) are flatscreen, the windows floor to ceiling, and the tubs are deep. The Grand Tower rooms at the **MGM Grand** (p. 82) are the best bet in the medium price range; their modern twist on 1930s curves stands out from the cookie-cutter decor found all around town. Downtown, the rooms at the **Golden Nugget,** 129 E. Fremont St. (✆ **800/634-3454**), are by far the best. See p. 123.

- **Best Bathrooms:** This honor goes to **THEhotel at Mandalay Bay** (p. 86), where the good-size marble bathrooms feature a large glass shower, a separate water closet, and a soaking tub so deep the water comes up to your chin. If only they'd angled the plasma-screen TV a bit better—it's hard to see from the tub, though it's fine for the shower. It's a wonder anyone ever leaves to go to the casino, either. But not far behind is **Wynn Las Vegas,** which offers a similar layout, including that plasma TV and the deep, long tub, plus lemon-grass-scented amenities and silky robes to cradle you afterward.

- **Best Noncasino Hotel: Four Seasons** (p. 77) used to win this category, but now it's a tie with **THEhotel.** It can't be a coincidence that both are found around **Mandalay Bay.** Once you've experienced the Four Seasons' quiet good taste, superior service and pampering, and the serenity of their non-casino property, or the sophistication and elegance of THEhotel, it's hard to go back to traditional Vegas hotels. But best of all, should you want the best of both worlds, you need only pass through one door to have access to **Mandalay Bay** (p. 78) and all its traditional Vegas hotel accouterments, including that missing casino. Coming in a close second is the **Venezia** at The Venetian; same idea as THEhotel (a separate yet equal entity, the non-casino part of the casino hotel), though we prefer the decor and gestalt of the latter.

- **Best Casinos:** Our favorite places to gamble are anywhere we might win. But we also like the casinos in **The Mirage** (lively, beautiful, and not overwhelming; p. 102), **New York–New York** (because of the aforementioned attention to detail—it almost makes losing fun; p. 84), and **Main Street Station,** 200 N. Main St. (✆ **800/465-0711**), because it's about the most smoke-free casino in town, and because it's pretty. See p. 127.

- **Best Downtown Hotel:** It's a tie. The upscale **Golden Nugget** (p. 123) is exceptionally appealing in every aspect. And **Main Street Station** (p. 127), which has done a terrific job of renovating an older space, now evokes early-20th-century San Francisco, with great Victorian details everywhere, solidly good restaurants, and surprisingly nice rooms for an inexpensive price.

- **Best Views:** From the high-floor rooms at the **Stratosphere Casino Hotel & Tower,** 2000 Las Vegas Blvd. S. (✆ **800/99-TOWER**), you can see clear to the next county (p. 112), while the Strip-side rooms at **Four Seasons** (p. 77) give you the entire Las Vegas Boulevard panorama from the southernmost end. Higher-up floors at the **Las Vegas Hilton** (p. 117) show you that same panorama from a different perspective.

3 Best Dining Bets

A number of celebrity chefs are cooking in Vegas, awakening us to the opinion that Vegas's rep for lackluster restaurants is no longer deserved. Reviews for all of the restaurants listed below can be found in chapter 6.

- **Best Restaurant to Blow Your Money On:** You could lighten your wallet at the craps table—and why not?—or you could spend that same amount, and take a lot longer doing so, exalting in the culinary work being done at Alex Strada's (© 702/770-9966) and Paul Bartolotta's (© 702/770-9966) eponymous places in Wynn Las Vegas, and Hubert Keller's Fleur de Lys (© 877/632-9200) at Mandalay Place. Meals come dear at all three places, but each is turning out works of edible art, from three different inspired sources of creation. To us, this is what Vegas indulgence is all about, and the memories make us much happier than our losses at the table.

- **Best All Around:** Given our druthers, we are hard-pressed to choose between **Alizé** (© 702/951-7000; p. 146), at the top of the Palms, where nearly flawless dishes often compete with the sparkling view for sheer delight, and **Rosemary's Restaurant** (© 702/869-2251; p. 170), a 20-minute drive off the Strip and worth twice as much effort, for some Southern-influenced cooking. Each of these may well put the work of those many high-profile chefs, so prominently featured all over town, to shame. Lastly, though, speaking of high-profile chefs, we have just sworn allegiance to Thomas Keller's **Bouchon** (© 702/414-6200; p. 154), in **The Venetian**'s expansion, **Venezia.** Keller may be the best chef in America, and while this is simply his take on classic bistro food, you should never underestimate the joys of simple food precisely prepared. We also never ever turn down a chance to eat what Julian Serrano is making over at **Picasso** (© 702/693-7223; p. 152).

- **Best Inexpensive Meal:** The beautiful, fresh, monster submarine sandwiches at **Capriotti's** (© 702/474-0229; p. 160). They roast their own beef and turkey on the premises and assemble it (or cold cuts, or even vegetables) into delicious well-stuffed submarine sandwiches, ranging in size from 9 to 20 inches, and none of them over $10. We never leave town without one . . . or two.

- **Best Buffet:** On the Strip, it's the **Paris, Le Village Buffet** (© 888/266-5687), where the stations break from standard form by adhering to regional French food specialties (from places such as Provence, Alsace, and Burgundy) and the results are much better than average. Though not cheap, this is a reasonable substitute for an even more costly fancy meal. See p. 182. If you want something a little more traditional buffet—as in, one not devoted to one particular cuisine—**Wynn Las Vegas** (© 702/770-3340) is terrific all the way, even through the usual buffet weakness, dessert. See p. 182. The **Palms Festival Market Buffet** (© 702/942-7777) offers the best of the more budget-oriented options, with an array of Middle Eastern goodies and some eccentric additions to the ubiquitous carving stations. See p. 184. Downtown, the **Main Street Station Garden Court,** 200 N. Main St. (© 702/387-1896), has an incredible buffet: all live-action stations (where the food is made in front of you, sometimes to order); wood-fired brick-oven pizzas; fresh, lovely salsas and guacamole in the Mexican section; and better-than-average desserts. See p. 186.

- **Best Sunday Champagne Brunch:** Head for Bally's, at Mid-Strip, where the lavish **Sterling Sunday Brunch** (© 702/967-7999) features tables dressed with linen and silver. The buffet itself has everything from caviar and lobster to sushi and sashimi, plus fancy entrees that include the likes of roast duckling with black-currant and blueberry sauce. See p. 181.

- **Best Group Budget Meal Deal:** **Capriotti's** (p. 160) again—a large sandwich can feed two with leftovers, for about $5 each. Or split a bowl of soup at the **Grand Wok and Sushi Bar** (© 702/891-7777), in the MGM. This pan-Asian restaurant offers a variety of soups in such generous portions that four people can make a decent meal out of one serving. See p. 141.

- **Best Bistro:** We ate nearly the entire menu at **Bouchon** (© 702/414-6200; p. 154), from Thomas Keller, in The Venetian, and didn't find a misstep, just what you might expect from one of the most critically lauded chefs in the country. But don't overlook **Mon Ami Gabi** (© 702/944-4224), in the Paris Las Vegas hotel. Offering lovely, reasonably priced bistro fare (steak and *pommes frites,* onion soup), it's also a charming spot. See p. 158.

- **Best Restaurant Interiors:** The designers ran amok in the restaurants of **Mandalay Bay.** At **Aureole** (© 877/632-1766), a four-story wine tower requires that a pretty young thing be hauled up in a harness a la *Peter Pan* to fetch your chosen vintage. See p. 135. The post-Communist party decor at **Red Square** (© 702/632-7407; p. 139) is topped only by the fire-and-water walls at neighboring **rumjungle** (© 702/632-7408; p. 295). And then there is the futuristic fantasy of **Mix** (© 877-632-1766), on top of THEhotel, where stunning sky-high views of the Strip compete with a giant beaded curtain made of hand-blown glass balls, to say nothing of silver "pods" in lieu of booths.

- **Best Spot for a Romantic Dinner:** **Alizé,** at the top of the Palms, has windows on three sides of the dining room, with no other buildings around for many blocks. You get an unobstructed view of all of Vegas, the desert, and the mountains from every part of the restaurant, not just the window seats. Seriously, aren't you in the mood already? See p. 146.

- **Best Spot for a Celebration:** Let's face it, no one parties like the Red Party, so head to **Red Square,** in Mandalay Bay, where you can have caviar and vodka in the ultimate capitalist revenge. See p. 139. If you have deep pockets, get a table atop the stairwell at Mix, and watch the Strip twinkle below.

- **Best Free Show at Dinner: Daniel Boulard Brasserie** (© 702/770-9966) at Wynn Las Vegas provides front-and-center seating of the strange yet compelling Lake of Dreams show. And then there is the vista offered by the restaurants in Bellagio (**Picasso, Le Cirque, Olives,** and **Circo**), which are grouped to take advantage of the view of the dancing water fountains. See chapter 6 for reviews of all of the Bellagio restaurants.

- **Best Wine List:** It's a competitive market in Vegas for such a title, and with sommeliers switching around, it's hard to guarantee any wine list will retain its quality. Still, you can't go wrong at Mandalay Bay's **Aureole** (© **877/632-1766**), which has the largest collection of Austrian wines outside of that country, among other surprises. See p. 135.
- **Best Beer List: Rosemary's Restaurant'** (© **702/869-2251**) offers "beer pairings" suggestions with most of its menu options, and includes some curious and fun brands, including fruity Belgian numbers. See p. 170.
- **Best View: Mix** and **Alizé** (p. 146) win with their floor-to-ceiling window views, but there is something to be said for seeing all of Vegas from the revolving **Top of the World** (© **702/380-7711**), 106 stories off the ground in the Stratosphere Casino Hotel & Tower. See p. 153.
- **Best Eclectic:** Many celebrity-chef or other high-profile restaurants in Vegas are disappointments because said chef isn't in the kitchen. But

---

Best Restaurant Booze

We could have said "best wine cellars," but that felt too exclusive—what if you don't want to swish and swirl, but do shots? The point is, Vegas is increasingly an oeniphile's delight, but other parts of the alcohol spectrum have not been neglected in the process. Some of the following is silly, meant as show-off, one-for-the-record books, as much as anything else, but even in those cases, there is a serious wine person behind the glitz, doing very good work.

Alizé has the largest "large format" collection, as in larger than a standard 750 bottle, so think magnum, double magnum, and so on. **Wynn Las Vegas** has on site a 90,000-bottle central storage for their wine—that's in addition to storage in individual restaurants. The four-story wine cellar at **Aureole,** from which choices are plucked by comely lasses hauled up and down by harnesses, is surely the most dramatic in town. Nifty little electronic gadgets containing all the choices, with recommendations for pairing just a flick of a button away, only add to the fun. **Bartolotta** has an all-Italian wine list—an extremely daring move in wine circles.

A master sommelier can be found at **Picasso,** and a third at **Delmonico Steakhouse.** And one more works magic at **Alex,** while still another, while now Alex's front of house manager, was originally sommelier at **Chef Strada's Renoir** restaurant, where he came up with the welcome idea of offering a specially priced 1-ounce pairing of Chateau D'Yquem with foie gras.

The Grand Award of Excellence, from *Wine Spectator* magazine, was created especially for **Valentino** restaurant—the one in Los Angeles admittedly, but obviously there must be sibling benefits. **Rosemary's** caters not to a tourist crowd, but a connoisseur crowd, and their list reflects it. But just for fun, they also offer beer pairings!

Charlie Palmer's **Aureole** (© 877/ 632-1766), in Mandalay Bay, hits all the right gourmet notes with its clever, sophisticated cuisine.

- **Best Italian:** You won't find anything more authentic outside of Italy than at **Bartolotta,** at Wynn Las Vegas. Given that the chef has his fish flown in daily from the Mediterranean, this also wins "best seafood." See p. 147. For Tuscan cuisine at slightly less dear prices, **Circo** (© **702/693-8150**), in Bellagio, is terrific. See p. 155.
- **Best Deli:** Wars are fought over less, so all you New Yorkers can square off between **Stage Deli** (© **702/893-4045**), in Caesars, or **Carnegie Deli** (© 702/791-7310), in The Mirage. The rest of us will find out mouths too packed with pastrami to weigh in. See p. 159.
- **Best New Orleans Cuisine:** Emeril's **Delmonico Steakhouse** (© 702/631-1000), in The Venetian, brings the celebrity chef's "Bam!" cuisine to the

other side of the Mississippi, and we are glad, while we are perhaps even gladder that Commander's Palace has an outlet in Aladdin. See p. 149 for Delmonico Steakhouse.

- **Best Red Meat: Lawry's The Prime Rib,** 4043 Howard Hughes Pkwy. (© **702/893-2223**; p. 163), has such good prime rib it's hard to imagine ever having any better. If you want cuts other than prime rib, **Charlie Palmer's** (© **702/632-5120**; p. 136), in the Four Seasons, has some of the best steaks in town, though the more budget-conscious might want to either split the enormous cuts or try the justly popular **Austins Steakhouse** (© **702/631-1033**; p. 170).

And since we have strayed from the subject of wine to other parts of the liquor world, Isla has an impressive tequila collection. Then there is Shibuya, in the MGM Grand, which has the largest sake list of any restaurant in the country.

4 Best of Vegas After Dark

- **Best Production Show:** Total deadlock tie between **Cirque du Soliel's** *KA* **and** *O.* The latter is more "traditional"—if you can call a human circus that uses a giant tank of water as a stage "traditional," but it is in that it has only a loose semblance of narrative, whereas *KA* (yet another revolutionary piece of stage craft, though we will let you be surprised as to how that plays out) actually has a plot. Both are dazzling and, given the extremely high production values, feel worth the extremely high ticket price. (*KA* © **877/880-0880** and *O* © **888/488-7111** or 702/693-7722; see p. 169 and p. 170.)
- **Best Old-Time Vegas Production:** You know: big huge stage sets, pointless production numbers, showgirls,

nipples on parade, Bob Mackie headdresses. Ah, *Jubilee!;* this world would be dreary without you (© **800/ 237-7469** or 702/739-4567). See p. 273.
- **Best Smart Show:** This town isn't good enough for either **Blue Man Group** or **Penn & Teller** (Penn & Teller © **888/746-7784** or 702/739-4567). See p. 268 and p. 277.
- **Best Local Hang:** They don't keep the same late hours as they once did, but you will still find performer friends and other in-the-know types gathering at **Jazzed Cafe & Vinoteca** (© 702/233-2859), eating Kirk's authentic Italian fare and comparing notes on the artist's life in Vegas. The more hard-core types (including, on certain nights, Blue Men sans

Tips Winning Websites

Start your online journey to Sin City at **www.vegas4visitors.com**. This small, family-run endeavor is packed full with information, unbiased reviews, contact info, maps, photos, and links to hotels, restaurants, and more.

If you want to pick the brains of the local populace—and who better to ask about life in Las Vegas—head over to **www.lasvegasweekly.com**. You'll find out where locals go for fun, and you can browse through reviews of bars, cafes, nightclubs, restaurants, and amusement parks.

For the most comprehensive Vegas dining resource on the Web, go to **www.nightonthetown.com**. The site arranges its plethora of restaurants by cuisine and location so you can find what you want, where you want it.

If you like your information with a side order of humor, head over to **www.cheapovegas.com**. This fun site offers lots of sassy reviews and unbiased opinions, especially on the Las Vegas casino hotels. There's also a small section on getting freebies while you're in town.

And, finally, for a plethora of information, including trip reports and reviews written by Vegas visitors and locals, try **www.A2Zlasvegas.com**. The site also features ratings for hotels, restaurants, and shows based on their appropriateness for kids, making this a good site for families.

makeup, doing weird percussion things) will be gathering way after hours at the **Double Down Saloon** (© 702/791-5775). See p. 283 and p. 288.

- **Best Ultra-Lounge:** That's just Vegas-speak for "fancy-pants hotel bar," but most of them are pretty nice, if trying too hard to be all-that. Still, we like the vibe at **Risque** (© 702/946-7000), and we love the lush, sexy look of **Lure**. See p. 289.

- **Best Reason to Wait in Line:** Truth be told, we never think there is a good enough reason, but **Ghost Bar** (© 702/942-7778) is a fantastic hotel bar, especially because of its outstanding view, perched high above the Strip. Meanwhile, there's a good reason **Rain** (© 702/940-7246) keeps packing them in—it's plus ne

ultra for dance clubs, but the new **Body English**'s (© 702/693-5000) style is terribly appealing to us. See chapter 10.

- **Best Burlesque:** Tough call, given the competition, but **40 Deuce** (© 702/632-7000) was the first establishment (back in Los Angeles) to cash in on the return of the high-class hoochie girl, and still does it the best. See p. 288.

- **Best Strip Club:** Ah, you know you want to know. Tie between **Sapphire** (© 702/796-0000), because of its size (so big, it goes right past intimidating into nonthreatening), and **Treasures** (© 702/257-3030), because we think all strip joints should insist on production numbers with stage effects, and look like old-fashioned English brothels. See p. 300.

2

Planning Your Trip to Las Vegas

Before any trip, you need to do a bit of advance planning. You'll need to decide whether a package tour makes sense for you, when to go, and more. In the pages that follow, you'll find everything you need to know to handle the practical details of planning your trip in advance: airlines and area airports, a calendar of events, a list of major conventions you may want to avoid, resources for those of you with special needs, and much more.

We also suggest that you check out chapter 10, "Las Vegas After Dark," before you leave home. If you want to see the most popular shows, it's a good idea to call ahead and order tickets well in advance to avoid disappointment. Ditto if you want to dine in one of the city's top restaurants: Head to chapter 6, "Where to Dine," for full reviews and contact information.

1 Visitor Information

For advance information, call or write the **Las Vegas Convention and Visitors Authority,** 3150 Paradise Rd., Las Vegas, NV 89109 (© **877/VISIT-LV** or 702/ 892-0711; www.visitlasvegas.com). They can send you a comprehensive packet containing brochures, a map, a show guide, an events calendar, and an attractions list; help you find a hotel that meets your specifications (and even make reservations); and tell you if a major convention is scheduled during the time you would like to visit Las Vegas. Or stop by when you're in town. They're open daily from 8am to 5pm.

Another excellent information source is the **Las Vegas Chamber of Commerce,** 3720 Howard Hughes Pkwy., #100, Las Vegas, NV 89109 (© **702/735-1616;** www.lvchamber.com). Ask them to send you their *Visitor's Guide,* which contains extensive information about accommodations, attractions, excursions, children's activities, and more. They can answer all your Las Vegas questions, including those about weddings and divorces. They're open Monday to Friday from 8am to 5pm.

For information on all of Nevada, including Las Vegas, contact the **Nevada Commission on Tourism** (© **800/638-2328;** www.travelnevada.com). They have a comprehensive information packet on Nevada.

There's also lots of great info on the Web. See "Planning Your Trip Online," later in this chapter, which will send you straight to the most useful sites.

2 Money

ATMs

The easiest and best way to get cash away from home is from an ATM (automated teller machine). The **Cirrus** (© **800/424-7787;** www.mastercard.com) and **PLUS** (© **800/843-7587;** www.visa.com) networks span the globe; look at the back of your bank card to see which network you're on, then call or check online for ATM locations at your destination. Be sure you know

Las Vegas Advisor

Professional gambler and longtime Las Vegas resident Anthony Curtis, author of *Bargain City: Booking, Betting, and Beating the New Las Vegas,* knows all the angles for stretching your hotel, restaurant, and, most important, gaming dollar. His 12-page monthly newsletter, the *Las Vegas Advisor,* is chock-full of insider tips on how to maximize your odds on every game, which slot tournaments to enter, casino promotions that represent money-making opportunities for the bettor, where to obtain the best Fun Books (coupon books full of freebies and discounts), which hotel offers a 12-ounce margarita for 99¢ or a steak dinner for $3, what the best buffet and show values in town are, and much, much more.

Subscribers get more than $3,400 worth of coupons for discounts on rooms, meals, show tickets, and car rentals, along with free slot plays, two-for-one bets, and other perks. A subscription is $50 a year, a single issue $5. To subscribe, call ℂ 800/244-2224 or send a check to Las Vegas Advisor, 3687 S. Procyon St., Las Vegas, NV 89103. You can also subscribe through the Las Vegas Advisor website at **www.lasvegasadvisor.com** and get everything except the mailed newsletters and reference guide for $37 per year.

your personal identification number (PIN) before you leave home and be sure to find out your daily withdrawal limit before you depart. There is an ATM within several feet of you at all times in Las Vegas; no one wants you to find yourself without cash you could lose in a slot! Beware of withdrawal charges, though, which can often run as high as $2 or $3 (the highest charges are usually for commercial machines in convenience stores, hotel lobbies, and casinos). Also be aware that your own bank may impose a fee every time a card is used at an ATM in a different city or bank. To compare banks' ATM fees within the U.S., use www.bankrate.com.

TRAVELER'S CHECKS

Traveler's checks are something of an anachronism from the days before the ATM made cash accessible at any time. Traveler's checks used to be the only sound alternative to traveling with dangerously large amounts of cash. They were as reliable as currency, but, unlike cash, could be replaced if lost or stolen.

These days, traveler's checks are less necessary because most cities have 24-hour ATMs that allow you to withdraw small amounts of cash as needed. However, keep in mind that you will likely be charged an ATM withdrawal fee if the bank is not your own, so if you're withdrawing money every day, you might be better off with traveler's checks—provided that you don't mind showing identification every time you want to cash one.

You can get traveler's checks at almost any bank. **American Express** offers denominations of $20, $50, $100, $500, and (for cardholders only) $1,000. You'll pay a service charge ranging from 1% to 4%. You can also get American Express traveler's checks over the phone by calling ℂ **800/221-7282;** Amex gold and platinum cardholders who use this number are exempt from the 1% fee.

Visa offers traveler's checks at Citibank locations nationwide, as well as at several other banks. The service charge ranges between 1.5% and 2%; checks come in denominations of $20, $50, $100, $500, and $1,000. Call ℂ **800/732-1322** for information. **MasterCard** also offers traveler's checks. Call ℂ **800/223-9920** for a location near you.

If you choose to carry traveler's checks, be sure to keep a record of their serial numbers separate from your checks in the event that they are stolen or lost. You'll get a refund faster if you know the numbers.

CREDIT CARDS

Credit cards are a safe way to carry money, they provide a convenient record of all your expenses, and they generally offer good exchange rates. You can also withdraw cash advances from your credit cards at banks or ATMs, provided you know your PIN. If you've forgotten yours, or didn't even know you had one, call the number on the back of your credit card and ask the bank to send it to you. It usually takes 5 to 7 business days, though some banks will provide the number over the phone if you tell them your mother's maiden name or some other personal information.

For tips and telephone numbers to call if your wallet is stolen or lost, go to "Lost & Found" in the "Fast Facts: Las Vegas," section of chapter 4.

3 When to Go

Most of a Las Vegas vacation is usually spent indoors, so you can have a good time here year-round. The most pleasant seasons in this area are spring and fall, especially if you want to experience the great outdoors.

Weekdays are slightly less crowded than weekends. Holidays are always a mob scene and come accompanied by high hotel prices. Hotel prices also skyrocket when big conventions and special events are taking place. The slowest times of year are June and July, the week before Christmas, and the week after New Year's.

If a major convention is to be held during your trip, you might want to change your date. Check the box on p. 24 for convention dates, and contact the **Las Vegas Convention and Visitors Authority** (ℂ **877/VISIT-LV** or 702/892-7575; www.visitlasvegas.com), as convention schedules often change.

THE WEATHER

First of all, Vegas isn't always hot, but when it is hot, it's *really* hot. One thing you'll hear again and again is that even though Las Vegas gets very hot, the dry desert heat is not unbearable. This is true. The exception is most of the hotel pool areas because they are surrounded by massive hotels covered in mirrored glass, which acts as a giant magnifying glass, focusing the sun's rays on the antlike people below. Generally, the humidity averages a low 22%, and even on very hot days, there's apt to be a breeze. Also, barring the hottest summer days, there's relief at night when temperatures often drop by at least 20°F (11°C).

⌐ *Fun Fact* **Beating the Odds**

In 1995, Don Harrington entered a satellite event at the World Series of Poker for just $220, won his way into the $10,000 buy for the Championship Event, and went on to win the $1 million prize.

Las Vegas's Average Temperatures (°F/°C) & Precipitation

	Jan	Feb	Mar	Apr	May	June	July	Aug	Sept	Oct	Nov	Dec
Avg. Temp.	47	52	58	66	75	86	91	89	81	69	55	47
	8	11	14	19	24	30	33	32	27	21	13	8
Avg. High Temp.	57	63	69	78	88	99	104	102	94	81	66	57
	14	17	21	26	31	37	40	39	34	27	19	14
Avg. Low Temp.	37	41	47	54	63	72	78	77	69	57	44	37
	3	5	8	12	17	22	26	25	21	14	7	3
Avg. Precip. (in.)	.6	.7	.6	.2	.2	.1	.4	.5	.3	.2	.3	.4

For the average, average high, and average low, temperatures are in Fahrenheit on the first line and Celsius on the following line. For the average precipitation measurements, values are in inches.

But this is the desert, and it's not hot year-round. It can get quite cold, especially in the winter, when the temperature at night can drop to 30°F (−1°C) and lower. (In Dec 2003, it actually snowed in Vegas, dropping nearly 6 in. on some parts of town and coating the Strip in a white blanket. For sheer bizarre spectacle, nothing beat the sight of the Luxor's Sphinx covered in snow.) The winter breeze can also become a cold, biting, strong wind of 40 mph or more. And so, there are entire portions of the year when you won't be using that hotel swimming pool at all (even if you want to—be aware that most of the hotels close huge chunks of those fabulous swimming pool areas for "the season," which can be as long as Labor Day to Memorial Day). If you aren't traveling in the height of summer, bring a wrap. Also, remember your sunscreen and hat—even if it's not all that hot, you can burn very easily and very fast. (You should see all the lobster-red people glowing in the casinos at night.)

LAS VEGAS CALENDAR OF EVENTS

You may be surprised that Las Vegas does not offer as many annual events as most tourist cities. The reason is Las Vegas's very raison d'être: the gaming industry. This town wants its visitors spending their money in the casinos, not at Renaissance fairs and parades.

When in town, check the local paper and contact the **Las Vegas Convention and Visitors Authority** (© 877/VISIT-LV or 702/892-7575; www.visitlasvegas.com) or the **Chamber of Commerce** (© 702/735-1616; www.lvchamber.com) to find out about other events scheduled during your visit.

March

NASCAR/Winston Cup. The **Las Vegas Motor Speedway,** 7000 N. Las Vegas Blvd. (© 800/644-4444; www.lvms.com), has become one of the premier facilities in the country, attracting races and racers of all stripes and colors. The biggest of the year are the Sam's Town 300 and the UAW–DaimlerChrysler 400 held in early March, often drawing over 150,000 race fans to town.

June

CineVegas International Film Festival. This annual event, usually held in early June, is growing in popularity and prestige, with film debuts from both independent and major studios, plus lots of celebrities hanging around for the big parties. Call © 702/992-7979 or visit their website at **www.cinevegas.com**.

World Series of Poker. When Harrah's Entertainment bought the legendary Binion's Horseshoe in Downtown Vegas out of bankruptcy, they quickly turned around and sold the hotel, but kept the hosting rights to this famed event and moved its location and place on the calendar. Now held at **The Rio All-Suite Hotel and Casino** (3700 W.

Major Convention Dates for 2006

Listed below are Las Vegas's major annual conventions with projected attendance figures for 2006; believe us, unless you're coming for one of them, you probably want to avoid the biggies. Since convention schedules frequently change, contact the **Las Vegas Convention and Visitors Authority** (© **800/VISIT-LV** or 702/892-7575; www.visitlasvegas.com) to double-check the latest info before you commit to your travel dates.

Event	Dates	Expected Attendance
Consumer Electronics Show	Jan 5–8	120,000
World of Concrete Exposition	Jan 17–20	80,000
Shooting, Hunting & Outdoor Trade Show	Feb 9–12	45,000
Associated Surplus Dealers	Mar 5–9	52,000
National Association of Broadcasters (NAB)	Apr 24–27	135,000
Associated Surplus Dealers	Aug 13–17	52,000
Specialty Equip. Mkt. Assn. (SEMA)	Oct 31–Nov 3	130,000

Flamingo Rd.; © **800/PLAY-RIO**) in June and July instead of April and May, the event features high-stakes gamblers and showbiz personalities competing for six-figure purses. There are daily events with entry stakes ranging from $125 to $5,000. To enter the World Championship Event (purse: $1 million), players must pony up $10,000. It costs nothing to go crowd around the tables and watch the action (which, in 2003, was televised for the first time on The Travel Channel). In 2005 they even added the world's first Poker convention and trade show to capitalize on the growing popularity of the game. For more information, visit the official website at www.worldseries ofpoker.com.

September

Oktoberfest. This boisterous autumn holiday is celebrated from mid-September through the end of October at the **Mount Charleston Lodge** (© **800/955-1314** or 702/872-5408; www.mtcharlestonlodge.com)   with music, folk dancers, singalongs around a roaring fire, special decorations, and Bavarian cookouts.

International Mariachi Festival. Mandalay Bay, 3950 Las Vegas Blvd. S. (at Hacienda Ave.), started hosting this worldwide Mariachi (Mexican music) festival a few years ago, and it has become one of the city's most eagerly anticipated events. Call Mandalay Bay at © **877/632-7400.** The event is usually held in early September.

October

The Championship at Las Vegas. This 5-day championship event (formerly called the PGA Tour Las Vegas Invitational), played on three local courses (the main course is TPC Summerland), is televised by ESPN. For details, call © **702/242-3000.**

December

National Finals Rodeo. This is the Super Bowl of rodeos, attended by close to 170,000 people each year and offering nearly $5 million in prize money. The top 15 male rodeo stars compete in six different events: calf roping, steer wrestling, bull riding, team roping, saddle bronco riding, and bareback riding. The top 15 women compete in barrel racing. An all-around "Cowboy of the Year" is chosen. In connection with this event, hotels book country stars in their showrooms, and there's even a cowboy shopping opportunity—the **NFR Cowboy Christmas Gift Show,** a trade show for Western gear—at Cashman Field. The NFR runs for 10 days during the first 2 weeks of December at the 17,000-seat Thomas and Mack Center of the University of Nevada, Las Vegas (UNLV). It usually begins on the first Friday in December and lasts through the following Sunday. Order tickets as far in advance as possible (© **702/895-3900**). For more information, see **www.nfrexperience. com.**

Las Vegas Bowl Week. A championship football event in mid-December pits the winners of the Mid-American Conference against the winners of the Big West Conference. The action takes place at the 32,000-seat Sam Boyd Stadium. Call © **702/895-3900** or visit www.lvbowl.com for ticket information.

Western Athletic Conference (WAC) Football Championship. This collegiate championship event takes place the first week in December in Sam Boyd Stadium. Call © **702/731-5595**

(Moments New Year's Eve in Las Vegas

Over the last couple of years, more and more people have been choosing Las Vegas as their party destination for New Year's Eve. In fact, some estimates indicate that by the time you read this, there will be more people ringing in the new year in Nevada than in New York City's Times Square.

From experience, we can tell you that there are a lot of people who come here on December 31. We mean a lot of people. Traffic is a nightmare, parking (at least legally) is next to impossible, and there is not 1 square inch of the place that isn't occupied by a human being. Las Vegas doesn't really need a reason to throw a party, but when an event like this comes along, they do it up right. It doesn't make a bit of difference to the many gamblers who remain perched at tables and in front of machines, barely looking up long enough to mumble "Happynewyear" at the key moment.

A major portion of the Strip is closed down, sending the masses and their substantial quantities of alcohol into the street. Each year's celebration is a little different but usually includes a streetside performance by a major celebrity, confetti, the obligatory countdown, and fireworks.

For New Year's 2001, the city launched a massive fireworks extravaganza entitled "America's Party." It involved blasting pyrotechnics from the roofs of 10 different hotels in succession up the Strip, with a grand finale at midnight that rivaled the worldwide millennium celebrations the year before. The event was considered such a success that the city has made it an annual event.

for ticket information. Ticket prices start around $20 and go up over $100 for the best seats.

New Year's Eve. This is a biggie (reserve your hotel room early). Downtown, on the Fremont Street Experience, there's a big block party with two dramatic countdowns to midnight (the first is at 9pm, midnight on the East Coast). The Strip is usually closed to street traffic, and hundreds of thousands of people pack the area for the festivities. There are, of course, fireworks.

4 Travel Insurance

Check your existing insurance policies and credit card coverage before you buy travel insurance. You may already be covered for lost luggage, canceled tickets, or medical expenses. The cost of travel insurance varies widely, depending on the cost and length of your trip, your age, your health, and the type of trip you're taking.

TRIP-CANCELLATION INSURANCE Trip-cancellation insurance helps you get your money back if you have to back out of a trip, if you have to go home early, or if your travel supplier goes bankrupt. Allowed reasons for cancellation can range from sickness to natural disasters to the State Department declaring your destination unsafe for travel. (Insurers usually won't cover vague fears, though, as many travelers discovered who tried to cancel their trips in Oct 2001 because they were wary of flying.) In this unstable world, trip-cancellation insurance is a good buy if you're getting tickets well in advance—who knows what the state of the world, or of your airline, will be in 9 months? Insurance policy details vary, so read the fine print—and especially make sure that your airline or cruise line is on the list of carriers covered in case of bankruptcy. For information, contact one of the following insurers: **Access America** (© 866/807-3982; www.accessamerica. com); **Travel Guard International** (© 800/826-4919; www.travelguard.com); **Travel Insured International** (© 800/ 243-3174; www.travelinsured.com); or **Travelex Insurance Services** (© 888/457-4602; www.travelex-insurance.com).

MEDICAL INSURANCE Most health insurance policies cover you if you get sick away from home—but check, particularly if you're insured by an HMO. If you require additional medical insurance, try **MEDEX Assistance** (© 410/453-6300; www.medexassist.com) or **Travel Assistance International** (© 800/821-2828; www.travelassistance.com; for general information on services, call the company's Worldwide Assistance Services Inc. at © **800/777-8710**).

LOST-LUGGAGE INSURANCE On domestic flights, checked baggage is covered up to $2,500 per ticketed passenger. If you plan to check items more valuable than the standard liability, see if your valuables are covered by your homeowner's policy, get baggage insurance as part of your comprehensive travel-insurance package, or buy Travel Guard's Bag-Trak product. Don't buy insurance at the airport, as it's usually overpriced. Be sure to take any valuables or irreplaceable items with you in your carry-on luggage, as many valuables (including books, money, and electronics) aren't covered by airline policies.

If your luggage is lost, immediately file a lost-luggage claim at the airport, detailing the luggage contents. For most airlines, you must report delayed, damaged, or lost baggage within 4 hours of arrival. The airlines are required to deliver luggage, once found, directly to your house or destination free of charge.

5 Health & Safety

THE HEALTHY TRAVELER

It can be hard to find a doctor you can trust when you're in an unfamiliar place. Try to take proper precautions the week before you depart to avoid falling ill while you're away from home. Amid the last-minute frenzy that often precedes a vacation, make an extra effort to eat and sleep well—especially if you feel an illness coming on. It's a drag to be sick on vacation, and a head cold can make a plane flight intolerable.

Limit your exposure to the sun, especially during the first few days of your trip, and from 11am to 2pm every day. Use a sunscreen with a high protection factor and apply it liberally all day, every day, even during the winter. The desert sun can be brutal. Remember that children need more protection than adults do.

WHAT TO DO IF YOU GET SICK AWAY FROM HOME

In most cases, your existing health plan will provide the coverage you need. But double-check; you may want to buy **travel medical insurance** instead. (See the section on insurance, above.) Bring your insurance ID card with you when you travel.

If you suffer from a chronic illness, consult your doctor before your departure. For conditions like epilepsy, diabetes, or heart problems, wear a **Medic Alert Identification Tag** (© **888/633-4298;** www.medicalert.org), which will immediately alert doctors to your condition and give them access to your records through Medic Alert's 24-hour hot line.

Pack **prescription medications** in your carry-on luggage, and carry prescription medications in their original containers, with pharmacy labels—otherwise, they won't make it through airport security. Also bring along copies of your prescriptions in case you lose your pills or run out. Don't forget an extra pair of contact lenses or prescription glasses.

If you do get sick, ask the concierge at your hotel to recommend a local doctor, even his or her own. See also the section "Fast Facts: Las Vegas" at the end of chapter 4, "Getting to Know Las Vegas"; there you'll find listings for hospitals, dental referrals, and even a clinic right on the Strip. For physician referrals, call **Desert Springs Hospital** (© **702/388-4888**) Monday to Friday from 8am to 8pm and Saturday from 9am to 3pm except holidays, or 24 hours a day online at www.desertspringshospital.net.

STAYING SAFE

CSI, one of the nation's top-rated TV shows, may turn up new corpses each week, but the crime rate in real-life Vegas isn't higher than any other major metropolis of its size. Predictably, with all that cash floating around town, pickpockets and thieves are active, so keep an eye on your belongings and store valuables in your in-room safe or a hotel safety-deposit box. And don't flash your cash; it might attract the wrong kind of attention and your big bucks will go bye-bye.

For more information on safety, see "Fast Facts: Las Vegas," in chapter 4, and "Safety," in chapter 3. Women should also see "Women Travelers," below.

Tips Quick Luggage ID

Tie a colorful ribbon or piece of yarn around your luggage handle, or slap a distinctive sticker on the side of your bag. This makes it less likely that someone will mistakenly appropriate it. And if your luggage gets lost, it will be easier to find.

6 Specialized Travel Resources

TRAVELERS WITH DISABILITIES

Most disabilities shouldn't stop anyone from traveling. There are more options and resources out there than ever before.

On the one hand, Las Vegas is fairly well equipped for travelers with disabilities, with virtually every hotel having accessible rooms, ramps, and other requirements. On the other hand, the distance between each hotel (particularly on the Strip) makes a vehicle of some sort virtually mandatory for most people with disabilities, and it may be extremely strenuous and time-consuming to get from place to place (even within a single hotel, because of the crowds). Additionally, the casinos can be quite difficult to maneuver in, particularly for a guest in a wheelchair. The casino floors are crowded, and the machines and tables are often laid out close together, with chairs and such blocking easy access. You should also consider that it is often a long trek through larger hotels between the entrance and the room elevators (or, for that matter, anywhere in the hotel), and then add a crowded casino to the equation.

The **Southern Nevada Center for Independent Living Program,** 6039 Eldora St., Suite F, Las Vegas, NV 89146 (© 702/889-4216; www.sncil.org), can recommend hotels and restaurants that meet your needs, help you find a personal attendant, advise about transportation, and answer all sorts of other questions.

The **Nevada Commission on Tourism** (© 800/638-2328; www.travelnevada. com) offers a free accommodations guide to Las Vegas hotels that includes access information.

Many travel agencies offer customized tours and itineraries for travelers with disabilities. **Flying Wheels Travel** (© 507/451-5005; www.flyingwheelstravel.com) offers escorted tours and cruises that emphasize sports and private tours in minivans with lifts. **Accessible Journeys** (© 800/846-4537 or 610/521-0339; www.disabilitytravel.com) caters specifically to slow walkers and wheelchair travelers and their families and friends.

Wheelchair Getaways (© 800/642-2042; www.wheelchair-getaways.com) rents specialized vans with wheelchair lifts and other features for travelers with disabilities in more than 100 cities across the U.S.

Many of the major car-rental companies now offer hand-controlled cars for drivers with disabilities. **Avis** can provide such a vehicle at any of its locations in the U.S. with 48-hour advance notice; **Hertz** requires between 24 and 72 hours of advance reservations at most of its locations.

Greyhound (© 800/752-4841; www. greyhound.com) allows a person with disabilities to travel with a companion for a single fare. Call at least 72 hours in advance to discuss this and other special needs.

Organizations that offer assistance to travelers with disabilities include the **Moss Rehab Hospital** (www.moss resourcenet.org), which provides a library of accessible-travel resources online; **SATH (Society for Accessible Travel and Hospitality)** (© 212/447-7284; www. sath.org; annual membership fees: $45 adults, $30 seniors and students), which offers a wealth of travel resources for all types of disabilities, and informed recommendations on destinations, access guides, travel agents, tour operators, vehicle rentals, and companion services; and the **American Foundation for the Blind** (© 800/232-5463; www.afb.org), which provides information on traveling with Seeing Eye dogs.

For more information specifically targeted to travelers with disabilities, the community website **iCan** (**www.ican online.net/channels/travel/index.cfm**) has destination guides and several regular columns on accessible travel. Also check out the quarterly magazine **Emerging Horizons** ($14.95 per year, $19.95 outside the U.S.; www.emerginghorizons. com); and **Open World Magazine,** published by the Society for Accessible Travel and Hospitality (see above; subscription: $13 per year, $21 outside the U.S.).

GAY & LESBIAN TRAVELERS

For such a licentious, permissive town, Las Vegas has its conservative side and is not the most gay-friendly city. This will not manifest itself in any signs of outrage toward open displays of gay affection, but it does mean that the local gay community is largely confined to the bar scene. This may be changing, with local gay pride parades and other activities gathering steam each year, including the first-ever nighttime parade through Downtown, with the mayor in attendance, in 2001. See listings for gay bars in chapter 10, "Las Vegas After Dark."

The **International Gay & Lesbian Travel Association** (IGLTA; © 800/ 448-8550 or 954/776-2626; www.iglta. org) is the trade association for the gay and lesbian travel industry, and offers an online directory of gay- and lesbian-friendly travel businesses; go to their website and click on "Members."

Many agencies offer tours and travel itineraries specifically for gay and lesbian travelers. **Above and Beyond Tours** (© 800/397-2681; www.abovebeyond tours.com) is the exclusive gay and lesbian tour operator for United Airlines. **Now, Voyager** (© 800/255-6951; www. nowvoyager.com) is a well-known San Francisco–based gay-owned and -operated travel service.

The following travel guides are available at most travel bookstores and gay and lesbian bookstores, or you can order them from **Giovanni's Room** bookstore, 1145 Pine St., Philadelphia, PA 19107

(© 215/923-2960; www.giovannisroom. com): **Gay.com** snapped up the **Out and About** guide series and is now offering them online exclusively to their members. Visit www.gay.com/travel for more info. **Spartacus International Gay Guide** and **Odysseus,** both good, annual English-language guidebooks focused on gay men; the **Damron** guides, with separate, annual books for gay men and lesbians; and **Gay Travel A to Z: The World of Gay & Lesbian Travel Options at Your Fingertips,** by Marianne Ferrari (Ferrari Publications; Box 35575, Phoenix, AZ 85069), a very good gay and lesbian guidebook series.

SENIORS

One of the benefits of age is that travel often costs less. Mention the fact that you're a senior when you make travel reservations. Although all of the major U.S. airlines except America West have canceled their senior discount and coupon book programs, many hotels still offer discounts for seniors. In most cities, people over the age of 60 qualify for reduced admission to theaters, museums, and other attractions, as well as discounted fares on public transportation.

Greyhound (© 800/231-2222; www. greyhound.com) offers seniors travel discounts. **Choice Hotels** (Clarion Hotels, Quality Inns, Comfort Inns, Sleep Inns, Econo Lodges, Friendship Inns, and Rodeway Inns) give 20% to 30% off their published rates to anyone over 60, provided you book your room through their nationwide toll-free reservations number (© 877/424-6423) instead of directly with the hotels or through a travel agent. Those over 50 receive a 10% discount. For a complete list of Choice Hotels, visit **www.hotelchoice.com**.

Members of **AARP,** 601 E St. NW, Washington, DC 20049 (© 888/687-2277 or 202/434-2277; www.aarp.org), get discounts on hotels, airfares, and car rentals. AARP offers members a wide range of benefits, including *AARP: The Magazine* and a monthly newsletter. Anyone over 50 can join.

Many reliable agencies and organizations target the 50-plus market. **Elderhostel** (© 877/426-8056; www.elder hostel.org) arranges study programs for those ages 55 and over (and a spouse or companion of any age) in the U.S. and in more than 80 countries around the world. Most courses last 5 to 7 days, and many include airfare, accommodations in modest inns or hotels, meals, and tuition. Its Las Vegas options include sessions on the city's entertainment and gaming industries.

Recommended publications offering travel resources and discounts for seniors include the quarterly magazine *Travel 50 & Beyond* (www.travel50andbeyond. com); *Travel Unlimited: Uncommon Adventures for the Mature Traveler* (Avalon); and *101 Tips for Mature Travelers,* available from Grand Circle Travel (© 800/959-0405; www.gct.com).

FAMILY TRAVEL

Family travel can be immensely rewarding, giving you new ways of seeing the world through smaller pairs of eyes. That said, Vegas is hardly an ideal place to bring the kids. For one thing, they're not allowed in casinos at all. Because most hotels are laid out so that you frequently have to walk through their casinos, you can see how this becomes a headache. Some casino hotels will not allow the children of nonguests on the premises after 6pm—and this policy is seriously enforced.

Note also that the Las Vegas Strip is often peppered with people distributing fliers and other information about decidedly adult entertainment options in the city. Sex is everywhere. Just walking down the Strip might give your kids an eyeful of items that you might prefer they avoid. (They don't call it Sin City for nothing!)

On top of everything else, there is a curfew law in Vegas: Kids under 18 are forbidden from being on the Strip without a parent after 9pm on weekends and holidays. In the rest of the county, minors can't be out without parents after 10pm on school nights and midnight on the weekends. If you choose to travel here with the children, see the "Especially for Kids" section in chapter 7, and the "Family-Friendly" boxes in chapters 5, 6, and 10 for suggested hotels, restaurants, and shows.

If you do decide to take your family vacation in Las Vegas, the good news is that children under 12, and in many cases even older, stay free in their parent's rooms in most hotels (we've noted these in chapter 5). You'll definitely want to book a place with a pool. Many hotels also have enormous video arcades and other diversions.

For great tips and suggestions for your Vegas family vacation, we strongly suggest you pick up a copy of *Frommer's Las Vegas with Kids.*

You can find good family-oriented vacation advice on the Internet from sites like the **Family Travel Network** (www. familytravelnetwork.com); **Traveling Internationally with Your Kids** (www. travelwithyourkids.com), a comprehensive site offering sound advice for long-distance and international travel with children; and **Family Travel Files** (www. thefamilytravelfiles.com), which offers an online magazine and a directory of off-the-beaten-path tours and tour operators for families.

WOMEN TRAVELERS

Las Vegas, thanks to the crowds, is as safe as any other big city for a woman traveling alone. A woman on her own should, of course, take the usual precautions and should be wary of hustlers or drunken businessmen who may mistake her for a "working girl." (Alas, million-dollar proposals a la

Robert Redford are a rarity.) Many of the big hotels (all MGM MIRAGE hotels, for example) have security guards stationed at the elevators at night to prevent anyone other than guests from going up to the room floors. Ask when you make your reservation. If you're anxious, ask a security guard to escort you to your room. *Always* double-lock your door *and* deadbolt it to prevent intruders from entering.

Check out the website **Journeywoman** (www.journeywoman.com), a lively travel resource with a free e-mail newsletter; or the travel guide *Safety and Security for Women Who Travel,* by Sheila Swan Laufer and Peter Laufer (Travelers' Tales Inc.), offering common-sense advice and tips on safe travel.

7 Planning Your Trip Online

SURFING FOR AIRFARES

The "big three" online travel agencies, **Expedia.com, Travelocity.com,** and **Orbitz.com,** sell most of the air tickets bought on the Internet. (Canadian travelers should try Expedia.ca and Travelocity.ca; U.K. residents can go for Expedia.co.uk and Opodo.co.uk.) Each has different business deals with the airlines and may offer different fares on the same flights, so it's wise to shop around. Expedia and Travelocity will also send you **e-mail notification** when a cheap fare becomes available to your favorite destination. Of the smaller travel agency websites, **SideStep** (www.sidestep.com) has gotten the best reviews from Frommer's authors. It's a browser add-on that purports to "search 140 sites at once" but in reality beats competitors' fares only as often as other sites do.

Also remember to check **airline websites,** especially those for low-fare carriers such as Southwest, JetBlue, or AirTran, whose fares are often misreported or simply missing from travel agency websites. Even with major airlines, you can often shave a few bucks from a fare by booking directly through the airline and avoiding a travel agency's transaction fee. But you'll get these discounts only by **booking online:** Most airlines now offer online-only fares that even their phone agents know nothing about. For the websites of

airlines that fly to and from your destination, go to "Getting There," below.

Great **last-minute deals** are available through free weekly e-mail services provided directly by the airlines. Most of these are announced on Tuesday or Wednesday and must be purchased online. Most are valid only for travel that weekend, but some (such as Southwest's) can be booked weeks or months in advance. Sign up for weekly e-mail alerts at airline websites or check megasites that compile comprehensive lists of last-minute specials, such as **Smarter Living** (smarterliving.com). For last-minute trips, **site59.com** in the U.S. and **lastminute.com** in Europe often have better deals than the major-label sites.

If you're willing to give up some control over your flight details, use an **opaque fare service** like **Priceline** (www.priceline.com; www.priceline.co.uk for Europeans) or **Hotwire** (www.hotwire.com). Both offer rock-bottom prices in exchange for travel on a "mystery airline" at a mysterious time of day, often with a mysterious change of planes en route. The mystery airlines are all major, well-known carriers—and the possibility of being sent from Philadelphia to Chicago via Tampa is remote; the airlines' routing computers have gotten a lot better than they used to be.

> **Tips A Web Wonder**
>
> A little-known gem, **Travelaxe** (**www.travelaxe.com**) offers a free, download-able price-comparison program that will make your Las Vegas hotel search infi-nitely easier. The program searches the hotels (including the major casino hotels' websites) and a host of discount travel websites for the best prices for your travel dates. Click on the price you like and the program will send you straight to the website offering it. And, unlike most websites, Travelaxe prices include hotel tax, so you actually see the total price of the room.

But your chances of getting a 6am or 11pm flight are pretty high. Hotwire tells you flight prices before you buy; Priceline usually has better deals than Hotwire, but you have to play their "name our price" game. If you're new at this, the helpful folks at **BiddingFor-Travel** (www.biddingfortravel.com) do a good job of demystifying Priceline's prices. Priceline and Hotwire are great for flights within North America and between the U.S. and Europe. But for flights to other parts of the world, consolidators will almost always beat their fares. *Note:* In 2004 Priceline added non-opaque service to its roster. You now have the option to pick exact flights, times, and airlines from a list of offers—or opt to bid on opaque fares as before.

For much more about airfares and savvy air-travel tips and advice, pick up a copy of *Frommer's Fly Safe, Fly Smart* (Wiley Publishing, Inc.).

SURFING FOR HOTELS

Shopping online for hotels is much easier in the U.S., Canada, and certain parts of Europe than it is in the rest of the world. Of the "big three" sites, **Expedia** may be the best choice, thanks to its long list of special deals. **Travelocity** runs a close sec-ond. Hotel specialist sites **hotels.com** and **hoteldiscounts.com** are also reliable. *Tip:* Always check the individual casino hotel websites, as they often feature deals you won't find anywhere else.

Priceline and Hotwire are even better for hotels than for airfares; with both, you're allowed to pick the neighborhood and quality level of your hotel before offering up your money. Priceline's hotel product covers several of the major casino hotels, including The Venetian, The Mirage, and MGM Grand. Be sure to do your research before putting in a bid, however, because their prices aren't always the best available in Vegas.

BiddingForTravel (www.biddingfor travel.com) has an excellent Las Vegas board in its hotel section. If you plan on bidding on Priceline, it's a must-stop. It also frequently posts hotel discount codes and available packages.

SURFING FOR RENTAL CARS

For booking rental cars online, the best deals are usually found at rental-car com-pany websites, although all the major online travel agencies also offer rental-car reservations services. Priceline and Hotwire work well for rental cars, too; the only "mystery" is which major rental company you get, and for most travelers the differ-ence between Hertz, Avis, and Budget is negligible.

ONLINE TRAVELER'S TOOLBOX

Following is a selection of online tools to bookmark and use:

- **Mapquest** (www.mapquest.com). This best of the mapping sites lets you choose a specific address or destina-tion, and in seconds it will return a map and detailed directions.

- **Cybercafes.com** (www.cybercafes. com). Locate Internet cafes at hundreds of locations around the globe. Catch up on your e-mail and log on to the Web for a few dollars per hour.

- **Universal Currency Converter** (www.xe.net/currency). See what your dollar or pound is worth in more than 100 other countries.

Anthony Zuiker's Top Seven Las Vegas Movies

A graduate of the University of Nevada at Las Vegas who's lived in Vegas for 35 years, Anthony Zuiker worked for The Mirage as a graveyard-shift tram driver, bellboy, and ad writer before he was inspired to create *CSI*, currently the number-one-rated TV show in the country.

- *Ocean's Eleven* (the remake)   It's our modern-day Rat Pack actors. Who can deny George Clooney and Brad Pitt?
- *Fear and Loathing in Las Vegas*   It epitomizes the surreal journey of coming to Las Vegas and it captured the hyper-reality very well.
- *Indecent Proposal*   I was there when they were shooting this movie. I remember seeing Demi Moore shooting the film at the Hilton, and Bruce Willis was playing blackjack at the tables while the filming was going on. She would run over to him and kiss him, and then go back and shoot the scene. That was my first taste of Hollywood glory long before I was in the business.
- *Ocean's Eleven* (the original)   It's timeless actors and classic Vegas, platinum swagger that can never be replicated. I watch it, remembering that Sinatra would do just one take and that was it. Being in the business now, I marvel at that. He was always dressed so amazingly in those sweaters, he always had a cocktail, and he was just so cool.
- *Viva Las Vegas*   To me, this was the first movie to put Las Vegas on the map, with the King of rock 'n' roll, no less, exemplifying what Vegas was all about, in its true glory days. Back then, times were good, it was all about the gambler, and it was amazing.
- *Casino*   I actually grew up in town during this era, so I remember these characters very well. It was one of the first movies that took us inside the world of the casino, not just on the floor, but also behind the scenes. It was the look of the mob era in Vegas, how it really was; and since I knew of those men, I could see both how accurate it was, and where creative license was taken.
- *Leaving Las Vegas*   It's one of my top five films of all time. The concept of an alcoholic going to Vegas because they never close the bars was a genius dramatic idea. And the way that director Mike Figgis shot Nick Cage, with Luxor in the background, with the red lights of Bally's blinking, the seedy hotel, it all just felt like the dark, surreal side of Vegas that we are used to as locals on a much more guttural and emotional level. A wonderful movie.

8 The 21st-Century Traveler

INTERNET ACCESS AWAY FROM HOME

Travelers have any number of ways to check their e-mail and access the Internet on the road. Of course, using your own laptop—or even a PDA (personal digital assistant) or electronic organizer with a modem—gives you the most flexibility. But even if you don't have a computer, you can still access your e-mail and even your office computer from cybercafes.

WITHOUT YOUR OWN COMPUTER

It's hard nowadays to find a city that *doesn't* have a few cybercafes, and Las Vegas has its share. Although there's no definitive directory for cybercafes—these are independent businesses, after all—three places to start looking are at **www. cybercaptive.com**, **www.netcafeguide. com**, and **www.cybercafe.com**.

Most major airports now have **Internet kiosks** scattered throughout their gates. These kiosks, which you'll also see in shopping malls, hotel lobbies, and tourist information offices around the world, give you basic Web access for a per-minute fee that's usually higher than cybercafe prices. The kiosks' clunkiness and high price means they should be avoided whenever possible.

Warning: There has been an upswing in identity theft occurring after sneaky, high-tech criminals capture your personal info while you use these Internet kiosks or public Wi-Fi spots. If you absolutely have to use them, make sure you do so to access only noncritical information. Never, ever purchase something online through one of these systems.

To retrieve your e-mail, ask your **Internet service provider (ISP)** if it has a Web-based interface tied to your existing e-mail account. If your ISP doesn't have such an interface, you can use the free **mail2web** service (www.mail2web.com)

to access your home e-mail. For more flexibility, you may want to open a free, Web-based e-mail account with **Yahoo! Mail** (http://mail.yahoo.com) or **Microsoft's Hotmail** (www.hotmail.com). Your home ISP may be able to forward your e-mail to the Web-based account automatically.

If you need to access files on your office computer, look into a service called **GoToMyPC** (www.gotomypc.com). The service provides a Web-based interface for you to access and manipulate a distant PC from anywhere—even a cybercafe—provided your "target" PC is on and has an always-on connection to the Internet (such as with Road Runner cable). The service offers top-quality security, but if you're worried about hackers, use your own laptop rather than a cybercafe to access the GoToMyPC system.

USING A CELLPHONE

Just because your cellphone works at home doesn't mean it'll work elsewhere in the country (thanks to our nation's fragmented cellphone system). It's a good bet that your phone will work in major cities. But take a look at your wireless company's coverage map on its website before heading out—T-Mobile, Sprint, and Nextel are particularly weak in rural areas. If you need to stay in touch at a destination where you know your phone won't work, **rent** a phone that does from **InTouch USA** (© 800/872-7626; www. intouchglobal.com) or a rental-car location, but beware that you'll pay $1 a minute or more for airtime.

If you're not from the U.S., you'll be appalled at the poor reach of our **GSM (Global System for Mobiles) wireless network,** which is used by much of the rest of the world (see below). Your phone will probably work in most major U.S. cities; it definitely won't work in many rural areas. (To see where GSM phones work in the U.S., check out **www. t-mobile.com/coverage/national_pop up.asp**.) And you may or may not be able to send SMS (text messaging) home—something Americans tend not to do anyway, for various cultural and technological reasons. (International budget travelers like to send text messages home because it's much cheaper than making international calls.) Assume nothing—call your wireless provider and get the full scoop. In a worst-case scenario, you can always rent a phone; InTouch USA delivers to hotels.

9 Getting There

BY PLANE

Given the shambles the airline industry is in, writing this section makes us wince. Just be aware that the future of many of the following airlines was in varying degrees of doubt as we went to press.

The following airlines have regularly scheduled flights into Las Vegas (some of these are regional carriers, so they may not all fly from your point of origin): **AeroMexico** (℃ 800/237-6639; www. aeromexico.com); **Air Canada** (℃ 888/ 247-2262; www.aircanada.ca); **Alaska Airlines** (℃ 800/426-0333; www.alaska air.com); **Allegiant Air** (℃ 877/202-6444; www.allegiantair.com); **Aloha Air** (℃ 800/367-5250; www.alohaairlines. com); **America West** (℃ 800/235-9292; www.americawest.com); **American/ American Eagle** (℃ 800/433-7300; www.aa.com); **American Trans Air/ Comair** (℃ 800/435-9282; www.ata.com or www.fly-comair.com); **Continental** (℃ 800/525-0280; www.continental.com); **Delta/Skywest** (℃ 800/221-1212; www. delta.com); **Frontier Airlines** (℃ 800/ 432-1359; www.flyfrontier.com); **Harmony Airways** (℃ 866/248-6789; www. hmyairways.com); **Hawaiian Airlines** (℃ 800/367-5320; www.hawaiianair. com); **Hooters Air** (℃ 888/359-4668; www.hoootersair.com), goes nicely with the new Hooters Hotel in Vegas; **Independence Air** (℃ 800/359-3594; www. flyi.com); **Japan Airlines** (℃ 800/525-3663; www.jal.co.jp/en); **JetBlue** (℃ 800/ 538-2583; www.jetblue.com); **Mexicana Airlines** (℃ 800/531-7921; www. mexicana.com); **Midwest Airlines** (℃ 800/452-2022; www.midwestairlines. com); **Northwest** (℃ 800/225-2525; www.nwa.com); **Philippine Airlines** (℃ 800/435-9725; www.philippine airlines.com); **Song,** a new low-cost airline from Delta (℃ 800/359-7664; www.fly song.com); **Southwest** (℃ 800/435-9792; www.southwest.com); **Spirit Airlines** (℃ 800/772-7117; www.spiritair.com); **Ted Airlines** (℃ 800/225-5833; www.fly ted.com); **United** (℃ 800/241-6522; www.united.com); **US Airways** (℃ 800/ 428-4322; www.usairways.com); and **Virgin Atlantic Airways** (℃ 800/862-8621; www.virgin-atlantic.com).

We've always enjoyed Southwest's relaxed attitude, and their service leaves few complaints. However, they mostly feature first-come, first-served seating, so if you want to avoid that, you can't go wrong with United—assuming, of course, that they are still in business when you read this.

Then again, now might be the time to talk about the spiffy new leather seat/ DirecTV wonder that is **JetBlue** (℃ **800/ JET-BLUE** or 800/538-2583; www.jet blue.com). First-time passengers usually turn into longtime converts. Currently, they fly to Vegas from Long Beach, California, and New York City, and often for very low prices.

With the federalization of airport security, security procedures at U.S. airports are more stable and consistent than ever. Generally, you'll be fine if you arrive at

Flying with Film & Video

Never pack film—developed or undeveloped—in checked bags, as the new, more powerful scanners in U.S. airports can fog film. The film you carry with you can be damaged by scanners as well. X-ray damage is cumulative; the slower the film, and the more times you put it through a scanner, the more likely the damage. Film under 800 ASA is usually safe for up to five scans. If you're taking your film through additional scans, U.S. regulations permit you to demand hand inspections. Keep in mind that airports are not the only places where your camera may be scanned: Highly trafficked attractions are X-raying visitors' bags with increasing frequency.

Most photo supply stores sell protective pouches designed to block damaging X-rays. The pouches fit both film and loaded cameras. They should protect your film in checked baggage, but they also may raise alarms and result in a hand inspection.

An organization called **Film Safety for Traveling on Planes (FSTOP;** ℭ **888/301-2665;** www.f-stop.org) can provide additional tips for traveling with film and equipment.

Carry-on scanners will not damage **videotape** in video cameras, but the magnetic fields emitted by the walk-through security gateways and hand-held inspection wands will. Always place your loaded camcorder on the screening conveyor belt or have it hand-inspected. Be sure your batteries are charged, as you will probably be required to turn the device on to ensure that it's what it appears to be.

the airport **1 hour** before a domestic flight and **2 hours** before an international flight; if you show up late, tell an airline employee and he or she will probably whisk you to the front of the line.

Bring a **current, government-issued photo ID** such as a driver's license or passport, and if you've got an e-ticket, print out the **official confirmation page;** you'll need to show your confirmation at the security checkpoint, and your ID at the ticket counter or the gate. (Children under 18 do not need photo IDs for domestic flights, but the adults checking in with them need them.)

Security lines are getting shorter than they were a couple of years ago, but some doozies remain. We've heard reports of security checks and gridlocks causing delays of up to 4 and 5 hours, with plenty of missed flights as a result. If it's a busy convention or holiday weekend, you might want to plan accordingly. Better a long wait at the airport than a missed flight. If you have trouble standing for long periods of time, tell an airline employee; the airline will provide a wheelchair. Speed up security by **not wearing metal objects** such as big belt buckles or clanky earrings. If you've got metallic body parts, a note from your doctor can prevent a long chat with the security screeners. Keep in mind that only **ticketed passengers** are allowed past security, except for folks escorting passengers with disabilities, or children.

Federalization has stabilized **what you can carry on** and **what you can't.** The general rule is that sharp things are out, nail clippers are okay, and food and beverages must be passed through the X-ray machine—but that security screeners can't make you drink from your coffee cup. Bring food in your carry-on rather than checking it, as explosive-detection machines used on checked luggage have been known to mistake food (especially chocolate, for some reason) for bombs. Travelers in the U.S. are allowed one carry-on bag, plus a "personal item" such as a purse, brief-case, or laptop bag. Carry-on hoarders can stuff all sorts of things into a laptop bag; as long as it has a laptop in it, it's still considered a personal item. The Transportation Security Administration (TSA) has issued a list of restricted items; check its website (**www.tsa.gov/ public/index.jsp**) for details.

In 2003 the TSA phased out **gate check-in** at all U.S. airports. Passengers with e-tickets and without checked bags can still beat the ticket-counter lines by using **electronic kiosks** or even **online check-in.** Ask your airline which alterna-tives are available, and if you're using a kiosk, bring the credit card you used to book the ticket. If you're checking bags, you will still be able to use most airlines' kiosks; again, call your airline for up-to-date information. **Curbside check-in** is also a good way to avoid lines, although a few airlines still ban curbside check-in entirely; call before you go.

At press time, the TSA is also recom-mending that you **not lock your checked luggage** so screeners can search it by hand if necessary. The agency says to use plastic "zip ties" instead, which can be bought at hardware stores and can be easily cut off.

FLYING FOR LESS: TIPS FOR GETTING THE BEST AIRFARE

Passengers sharing the same airplane cabin rarely pay the same fare. Travelers who need to purchase tickets at the last minute, change their itinerary at a moment's notice, or fly one-way often get stuck paying the premium rate. Here are some ways to keep your airfare costs down:

- Passengers who can book their ticket **long in advance,** who can **stay over Saturday night,** or who **fly midweek** or **at less-trafficked hours** will pay a fraction of the full fare. If your sched-ule is flexible, say so, and ask if you can secure a cheaper fare by changing your flight plans.

- You can also save on airfares by keep-ing an eye out in local newspapers for **promotional specials** or **fare wars,** when airlines lower prices on their most popular routes. You rarely see fare wars offered for peak travel times, but if you can travel in the off-months, you may snag a bargain.

- Search **the Internet** for cheap fares (see "Planning Your Trip Online," earlier in this chapter).

- **Consolidators,** also known as bucket shops, are great sources for interna-tional tickets, although they usually can't beat the Internet on fares within North America. Start by looking in Sunday newspaper travel sections; U.S. travelers should focus on the *New York Times, Los Angeles Times,* and *Miami Herald.* For less-developed destina-tions, small travel agencies that cater to immigrant communities in large cities often have the best deals. *Beware:* Bucket shop tickets are usually nonre-fundable or rigged with stiff cancella-tion penalties, often as high as 50% to 75% of the ticket price, and some put you on charter airlines with question-able safety records. **FlyCheap** (*©* **800/ FLY-CHEAP;** www.flycheap.com) is owned by package-holiday megalith MyTravel and so has especially good access to fares for sunny destinations. **Air Tickets Direct** (*©* **800/778-3447;** www.airticketsdirect.com) is based in Montréal and leverages the currently weak Canadian dollar for low fares. And **TravelHub** (www.travel hub.com) represents nearly 1,000 travel agencies, many of whom offer consolidator and discount fares.

- Join **frequent-flier clubs.** Accrue enough miles and you'll be rewarded with free flights and elite status. It's free, and you'll get the best choice of seats, faster response to phone inquiries, and prompter service if your luggage is stolen, if your flight is canceled or delayed, or if you want to change your seat. You don't need to fly to build frequent-flier miles— **frequent-flier credit cards** can provide thousands of miles for doing your everyday shopping.

- For many more tips about air travel, including a rundown of the major frequent-flier credit cards, pick up a copy of *Frommer's Fly Safe, Fly Smart* (Wiley Publishing, Inc.).

BY CAR

The main highway connecting Las Vegas with the rest of the country is I-15; it links Montana, Idaho, and Utah with Southern California. The drive from Los Angeles is quite popular and, thanks to the narrow two-lane highway, can get very crowded on Friday and Sunday afternoons with hopeful weekend gamblers making their way to and from Vegas. An expansion project will widen most of that stretch of road to three lanes in each direction by late 2006, but in the meantime, expect construction delays and often dangerous road conditions. (By the way, as soon as you cross the state line, there are three casinos ready to handle your immediate gambling needs, with two more about 20 min. up the road, 30 miles before you get to Las Vegas.)

From the east, take I-70 or I-80 west to Kingman, Arizona, and then U.S. 93 north to downtown Las Vegas (Fremont St.). From the south, take I-10 west to Phoenix and then U.S. 93 north to Las Vegas. From San Francisco, take I-80 east to Reno and then U.S. 95 south to Las Vegas. If you're driving to Las Vegas, be sure to read the driving precautions in "Getting Around" in chapter 4.

Vegas is 286 miles from Phoenix, 759 miles from Denver, 421 miles from Salt Lake City, 269 miles from Los Angeles, and 586 miles from San Francisco.

BY TRAIN

Amtrak (© **800/USA-RAIL;** www. amtrak.com) does not currently offer direct rail service, although plans have been in the works to restore the rails between Los Angeles and Las Vegas for years now. At press time, Amtrak wouldn't confirm a date, but various reports have indicated eventually they will restore service using the **Talgo.** This European-designed "Casino

---

Travel in the Age of Bankruptcy

At press time, two major U.S. airlines were struggling in bankruptcy court and most of the rest weren't doing very well either. To protect yourself, **buy your tickets with a credit card,** as the Fair Credit Billing Act guarantees that you can get your money back from the credit card company if a travel supplier goes under (and if you request the refund within 60 days of the bankruptcy). **Travel insurance** can also help, but make sure it covers against "carrier default" for your specific travel provider. And be aware that if a U.S. airline goes bust midtrip, a 2001 federal law requires other U.S.-based carriers to take you to your destination (albeit on a space-available basis) for a fee of no more than $25, provided you rebook within 60 days of the cancellation.

Tips **Canceled Plans**

If your flight is canceled, don't book a new fare at the ticket counter. Find the nearest phone and call the airline directly to reschedule. You'll be relaxing while other passengers are still standing in line.

Train" will complete the trip from Los Angeles in about 5½ hours, with a wholesale seat price of $99 round-trip. We've been hearing these reports for so long now they just make us roll our eyes, but believe it, if and when this ever happens, you will have to fight us for a seat.

In the meantime, you can take the train to Los Angeles or Barstow and Amtrak will get you to Vegas by bus.

10 Packages for the Independent Traveler

Before you start your search for the lowest airfare, you may want to consider booking your flight as part of a travel package. Package tours are not the same thing as escorted tours. Package tours are simply a way to buy the airfare, accommodations, and other elements of your trip (such as car rentals, airport transfers, and sometimes even activities) at the same time and often at discounted prices—kind of like one-stop shopping. Packages are sold in bulk to tour operators—who resell them to the public at a cost that usually undercuts standard rates.

Just to give you an example, at press time, **Southwest Airlines** (© **800/435-9792**; www.southwest.com) was offering round-trip airfare from Los Angeles with 2 nights at several different hotels; per person based on double occupancy, for Bellagio it was $294, and for the Golden Nugget $159 (before taxes and fees), although these prices vary dramatically depending upon when you are traveling.

One good source of package deals is the airlines themselves. Most major airlines offer air/land packages, including **American Airlines Vacations** (© **800/321-2121**; www.aavacations.com), **Delta Vacations** (© **800/221-6666**; www.deltavacations.com), **Continental Airlines Vacations** (© **800/301-3800**; www.coolvacations.com), and **United Vacations** (© 888/854-3899; www.unitedvacations.com).

Several big **online travel agencies**—Expedia, Travelocity, Orbitz, Site59, and Lastminute.com—also do a brisk business in packages.

Vacation Together (© **800/839-9851**; www.vacationtogether.com) allows you to search for and book packages offered by a number of tour operators and airlines.

The **United States Tour Operators Association**'s website (www.ustoa.com) has a search engine that allows you to look for operators that offer packages to a specific destination. Travel packages are also listed in the travel section of your local Sunday newspaper.

Reservations Plus, 2275 A Renaissance Dr., Las Vegas, NV 89119 (© **800/805-9528**; www.resplus.com), runs a free room-reservations service, but they can also arrange packages (including meals, transportation, tours, show tickets, car rentals, and other features) and group rates.

If you're unsure about the pedigree of a smaller packager, check with the Better Business Bureau in the city where the company is based, or go online to **www.bbb.org**. If a packager won't tell you where it's based, don't fly with it.

Travel packages are also listed in the travel section of your local Sunday newspaper. Or check ads in the national travel magazines such as *Arthur Frommer's Budget Travel Magazine, Travel & Leisure, National Geographic Traveler,* and *Condé Nast Traveler.*

Package tours can vary by leaps and bounds. Some offer a better class of hotels than others. Some offer the same hotels for lower prices. Some offer flights on scheduled airlines, while others book charters. Some limit your choice of accommodations and travel days. You are often required to make a large payment upfront. On the plus side, packages can save you money, offering group prices but allowing for independent travel. Some

even let you add on a few guided excursions or escorted day trips (also at prices lower than if you booked them yourself) without booking an entirely escorted tour.

Before you invest in a package tour, get some answers. Ask about the **accommodations choices** and prices for each. Then look up the hotels' reviews in a Frommer's guide and check their rates for your specific dates of travel online.

Finally, look for **hidden expenses.** Ask whether airport departure fees and taxes, for example, are included in the total cost.

11 Tips on Accommodations

For information on the various types of accommodations that you'll find in Las Vegas, and suggestions for saving on your hotel costs, see chapter 5, "Where to Stay."

LANDING THE BEST ROOM

Somebody has to get the best room in the house. It might as well be you. You can start by joining the hotel's frequent-guest program, which may make you eligible for upgrades. A hotel-branded credit card usually gives its owner "silver" or "gold" status in frequent-guest programs for free. In the case of Las Vegas, joining a casino hotel's players club may net you upgrade privileges. Always ask about a corner room. They're often larger and quieter, with more windows and light, and they often cost the same as standard rooms. When you make your reservation, ask if the hotel is renovating; if it is, request a room away from the construction. Ask about nonsmoking rooms, rooms with views, rooms with twin, queen-, or king-size beds. If you're a light sleeper, request a quiet room away from vending machines, elevators, restaurants, bars, and discos. Ask for one of the rooms that have

been most recently renovated or redecorated.

If you aren't happy with your room when you arrive, say so. If another room is available, most lodgings will be willing to accommodate you. And while it may seem hopelessly outdated, the fact is that tipping a desk clerk in Vegas—if you can do it with a straight face—can still sometimes produce results.

In Las Vegas, asking the following questions is also useful before you book a room:

- **What's the view like?** Cost-conscious travelers may be willing to pay less for a back room facing the parking lot, especially if they don't plan to spend much time in their room. A room on a higher floor with a view of the Strip can cost up to $20 a night extra at some hotels. (Paris Las Vegas, for example, charges more for rooms that overlook the Bellagio fountains.)

- **How far is the room from the main entrance, the casino, and other amenities?** We know one exercise fanatic who didn't mind skipping her workouts in Vegas because her room was almost a mile away (or felt like it), one-way, from the hotel's entrance. Most of the world's largest hotels are in Las Vegas, so make sure your room is close to the action if you don't want to hoof it too often.

12 Recommended Reading

If you believe in "reading more about it," here are a select few of our favorites you might turn to:

- McManus, James. *Positively Fifth Street: Murderers, Cheetahs, and Binion's World Series of Poker* (Farrar, 2003). The author went to write about the World Series of Poker and ended up playing in it, and going further, and not just in the sense of advancing in the tournament, than he would have thought.
- Hess, Alan. *Viva Las Vegas: After Hours Architecture* (Chronicle Books, 1993). Vegas doesn't have architecture as much as set design, and here you can learn all about how its bizarre skyline is an icon of modern American urban culture.
- McCracken, Robert D. *Las Vegas: The Great American Playground* (University of Nevada Press, 1997). A comprehensive history of Las Vegas.

- Martinez, Andrez. *24/7 Living It Up and Doubling Down in the New Las Vegas* (Villard, 1999). Wherein the author takes his $50,000 book advance to Vegas, with the specific plan to blow it all. He does while chronicling all he encounters—and it's a lot—along the way.
- Spanier, David. *Welcome to the Pleasure Dome: Inside Las Vegas* (University of Nevada Press, 1992). First-person history and analysis of the Las Vegas phenomenon.
- Thompson, Hunter S. *Fear and Loathing in Las Vegas* (Random House, 1971). A gonzo journalist and his Samoan lawyer head to Sin City for the all-time binge.
- Tronnes, Mike, ed. *Literary Las Vegas* (Henry Holt, 1995). A terrific collection of different essays and excerpts from books about Vegas.

3

For International Visitors

The pervasiveness of American culture around the world may make you feel that you know the United States pretty well, but leaving your own country still requires an additional degree of planning. This chapter will help prepare you for the more common issues you may encounter in Las Vegas.

1 Preparing for Your Trip

ENTRY REQUIREMENTS

Check at any U.S. embassy or consulate for current information and requirements. You can also obtain a visa application and other information online at the **U.S. State Department**'s website, at **www.travel.state.gov**.

VISAS The U.S. State Department has a **Visa Waiver Program** allowing citizens of certain countries to enter the United States without a visa for stays of up to 90 days. At press time these included Andorra, Australia, Austria, Belgium, Brunei, Denmark, Finland, France, Germany, Iceland, Ireland, Italy, Japan, Liechtenstein, Luxembourg, Monaco, the Netherlands, New Zealand, Norway, Portugal, San Marino, Singapore, Slovenia, Spain, Sweden, Switzerland, and the United Kingdom. Citizens of these countries need only a valid passport and a round-trip air or cruise ticket in their possession upon arrival. If they first enter the United States, they may also visit Mexico, Canada, Bermuda, and/or the Caribbean islands and return to the United States without a visa. Further information is available from any U.S. embassy or consulate. Canadian citizens may enter the United States without visas; they need only proof of residence.

Citizens of all other countries must have (1) a valid passport that expires at least 6 months later than the scheduled end of their visit to the United States, and (2) a tourist visa, which may be obtained for a minimum fee of $100 (some countries charge more) from any U.S. consulate.

To obtain a visa, the traveler must submit a completed application form (either in person or by mail) with a 1½-inch-square photo, and must demonstrate binding ties to a residence abroad. Usually you can obtain a visa at once or within 24 hours, but it may take longer during the summer rush from June through August. If you cannot go in person, contact the nearest U.S. embassy or consulate for directions on applying by mail. Your travel agent or airline office may also be able to provide you with visa applications and instructions. The U.S. consulate or embassy that issues your visa will determine whether you will be issued a multiple- or single-entry visa and any restrictions regarding the length of your stay.

British subjects can obtain up-to-date visa information by calling the **U.S. Embassy Visa Information Line** (© **0891/200-290**) or by visiting the "Consular Services" section of the American Embassy London's website at **www.usembassy.org.uk**.

Irish citizens can obtain up-to-date visa information through the **Embassy of USA Dublin,** 42 Elgin Rd., Dublin 4, Ireland (© **353/1-668-8777**), or by checking the "Consular Services" section of the website at **http://dublin.usembassy. gov.**

Australian citizens can obtain up-to-date visa information by contacting the **U.S. Embassy Canberra,** Moonah Place, Yarralumla, ACT 2600 (© **02/6214-5600**), or by checking the U.S. Diplomatic Mission's website at **http://us embassy-australia.state.gov/consular.**

Citizens of **New Zealand** can obtain up-to-date visa information by contacting the **U.S. Embassy New Zealand,** 29 Fitzherbert Terrace, Thorndon, Wellington (© **644/472-2068**), or get the information directly from the "Services to New Zealanders" section of the website at **http://usembassy.org.nz.**

MEDICAL REQUIREMENTS Unless you're arriving from an area known to be suffering from an epidemic (particularly cholera or yellow fever), inoculations or vaccinations are not required for entry into the United States. If you have a medical condition that requires **syringe-administered medication,** carry a valid signed prescription from your physician—the Transportation Security Administration (TSA) no longer allows airline passengers to pack syringes in their carry-on baggage without documented proof of medical need. If you have a disease that requires treatment with **narcotics,** you should also carry documented proof with you—smuggling narcotics aboard a plane is a serious offense that carries severe penalties in the U.S.

For **HIV-positive visitors,** requirements for entering the United States are somewhat vague and change frequently. According to the latest publication of *HIV and Immigrants: A Manual for AIDS Service Providers,* the Immigration and Naturalization Service (INS) doesn't require a medical exam for entry into the United States, but INS officials may stop individuals because they look sick or because they are carrying AIDS/HIV medicine.

If an HIV-positive noncitizen applies for a nonimmigrant visa, the question on the application regarding communicable diseases is tricky no matter which way it's answered. If the applicant checks "no," INS may deny the visa on the grounds that the applicant committed fraud. If the applicant checks "yes" or if INS suspects the person is HIV-positive, it will deny the visa unless the applicant asks for a special waiver for visitors. This waiver is for people visiting the United States for a short time, to attend a conference, for instance, to visit close relatives, or to receive medical treatment. It can be a confusing situation. For up-to-the-minute information, contact **AIDSinfo** (© **800/448-0440** or 301/519-6616 outside the U.S.; www.aidsinfo.nih.gov) or the **Gay Men's Health Crisis** (© **212/367-1000;** www.gmhc.org).

DRIVER'S LICENSES Foreign driver's licenses are mostly recognized in the U.S., although you may want to get an international driver's license if your home license is not written in English.

PASSPORT INFORMATION
FOR RESIDENTS OF CANADA

You can pick up a passport application at 1 of 28 regional passport offices or most travel agencies. Canadian children who travel must have their own passports. However, if you hold a valid Canadian passport issued before December 11, 2001, that bears the name of your child, the passport remains valid for you and your child until it expires. Passports cost C$85 for those 16 years and older (valid 5 years), C$35 for children 3 to 15 (valid 5 years), and C$20 for children under 3 (valid 3 years). Applications, which must be accompanied by two identical passport-size photographs and proof of Canadian citizenship, are available at travel agencies throughout Canada or from the central **Passport Office,** Department of Foreign Affairs and International Trade, Ottawa, ON K1A 0G3 (© 800/567-6868; www.ppt.gc.ca). Processing takes 5 to 10 days if you apply in person, or about 3 weeks by mail.

FOR RESIDENTS OF THE UNITED KINGDOM

As a member of the European Union, you need only an identity card, not a passport, to travel to other E.U. countries. However, if you already possess a passport, it's always useful to carry it. To pick up an application for a standard 10-year passport (5-year passport for children under 16), visit the nearest Passport Office, major post office, or travel agency. You can also contact the **United Kingdom Passport Service** at © 0870/571-0410 or visit its website at **www.passport.gov.uk**. Passports are £33 for adults and £19 for children under 16, with an additional £30 fee if you apply in person at a passport office. Processing takes about 2 weeks (1 week if you apply at the passport office).

FOR RESIDENTS OF IRELAND

You can apply for a 10-year passport, costing €57, at the **Passport Office,** Setanta Centre, Molesworth Street, Dublin 2 (© 01/671-1633; http://foreignaffairs. gov.ie/). Those under age 18 and over 65 must apply for a €12 3-year passport. You can also apply at 1A South Mall, Cork (© 021/272-525), or over the counter at most main post offices.

FOR RESIDENTS OF AUSTRALIA

You can pick up an application from your local post office or any branch of Passports Australia, but you must schedule an interview at the passport office to present your application materials. Call the **Australian Passport Information Service** at

© **131-232,** or visit the government website at **www.passports.gov.au**. Passports for adults are A$144 and for those under 18 are A$72.

FOR RESIDENTS OF NEW ZEALAND

You can pick up a passport application at any New Zealand Passports Office or download it from their website. Contact the **Passports Office** at © **0800/225-050** in New Zealand or 04/474-8100, or log on to **www.passports.govt.nz**. Passports for adults are NZ$80 and for children under 16, NZ$40.

CUSTOMS
WHAT YOU CAN BRING IN

Every visitor more than 21 years of age may bring in, free of duty, the following: (1) 1 liter of wine or hard liquor; (2) 200 cigarettes, 100 cigars (but not from Cuba), or 3 pounds of smoking tobacco; and (3) $200 worth of gifts. These exemptions are offered to travelers who spend at least 72 hours in the United States and who have not claimed them within the preceding 6 months. It is altogether forbidden to bring into the country foodstuffs (particularly fruit, cooked meats, and canned goods) and plants (vegetables, seeds, tropical plants, and the like). Foreign tourists may bring in or take out up to $10,000 in U.S. or foreign currency with no formalities; larger sums must be declared to U.S. Customs on entering or leaving, which includes filing form CM 4790. For more specific information regarding U.S. Customs, contact your nearest U.S. embassy or consulate, or the **U.S. Customs** office (© **202/927-1770** or www.customs.ustreas.gov).

WHAT YOU CAN TAKE HOME

U.K. citizens returning from a non-E.U. country have a Customs allowance of: 200 cigarettes; 50 cigars; 250 grams of smoking tobacco; 2 liters of still table wine; 1 liter of spirits or strong liqueurs

Impressions

For the grand debut of Monte Carlo as a resort in 1879 the architect Charles Garnier designed an opera house for the Place du Casino; and Sarah Bernhardt read a symbolic poem. For the debut of Las Vegas as a resort in 1946 Bugsy Siegel hired Abbott and Costello, and there, in a way, you have it all.

—Tom Wolfe

(over 22% volume); 2 liters of fortified wine, sparkling wine, or other liqueurs; 60 cubic centimeters (mL) of perfume; 250 cubic centimeters (mL) of toilet water; and £145 worth of all other goods, including gifts and souvenirs. People under 17 cannot have the tobacco or alcohol allowance. For more information, contact HM Customs & Excise at ℂ 0845/010-9000 (from outside the U.K., 020/8929-0152), or consult their website at www.hmce.gov.uk.

For a clear summary of **Canadian** rules, request the booklet *I Declare,* issued by the **Canada Customs and Revenue Agency** (ℂ 800/461-9999 in Canada, or 204/983-3500; www.ccra-adrc.gc.ca). Canada allows its citizens a C$750 exemption, and you're allowed to bring back duty-free one carton of cigarettes, one can of tobacco, 40 imperial ounces of liquor, and 50 cigars. In addition, you're allowed to mail gifts to Canada valued at less than C$60 a day, provided they're unsolicited and don't contain alcohol or tobacco (write on the package "Unsolicited gift, under $60 value"). All valuables should be declared on the Y-38 form before departure from Canada, including serial numbers of valuables you already own, such as expensive foreign cameras. *Note:* The C$750 exemption can be used only once a year and only after an absence of 7 days.

The duty-free allowance in **Australia** is A$400 or, for those under 18, A$200. Citizens age 18 and over can bring in 250 cigarettes or 250 grams of loose tobacco, and 1,125 milliliters of alcohol. If you're returning with valuables you already own, such as foreign-made cameras, you should file form B263. A helpful brochure available from Australian consulates or Customs offices is *Know Before You Go.* For more information, call the **Australian Customs Service** at ℂ 1300/363-263, or log on to www.customs.gov.au.

The duty-free allowance for **New Zealand** is NZ$700. Citizens over 17 can bring in 200 cigarettes, 50 cigars, or 250 grams of tobacco (or a mixture of all three if their combined weight doesn't exceed 250g); plus 4.5 liters of wine and beer, or 1.125 liters of liquor. New Zealand currency does not carry import or export restrictions. Fill out a certificate of export, listing the valuables you are taking out of the country; that way, you can bring them back without paying duty. Most questions are answered in a free pamphlet available at New Zealand consulates and Customs offices: *New Zealand Customs Guide for Travellers, Notice no. 4.* For more information, contact **New Zealand Customs,** The Customhouse, 17–21 Whitmore St., Box 2218, Wellington (ℂ 0800/428-786 or 04/473-6099; www.customs.govt.nz).

HEALTH INSURANCE

Although it's not required of travelers, health insurance is highly recommended. Unlike many European countries, the United States does not usually offer free or low-cost medical care to its citizens or visitors. Doctors and hospitals are expensive, and in most cases will require advance payment or proof of coverage before they render their services. Policies can cover everything from the loss or theft of your baggage and trip cancellation to the guarantee of bail in case you're arrested. Good policies will also cover the costs of an accident, repatriation, or death. See "Health & Safety" in chapter 2 for more information. Packages such as **Europ Assistance's "Worldwide Healthcare Plan"** are sold by European automobile clubs and travel agencies at attractive rates. **Worldwide Assistance Services Inc.** (℗ **800/821-2828;** www.worldwide assistance.com) is the agent for Europ Assistance in the United States.

Though lack of health insurance may prevent you from being admitted to a hospital in non-emergencies, don't worry about being left on a street corner to die: The American way is to fix you now and bill the living daylights out of you later.

INSURANCE FOR BRITISH TRAVELERS Most big travel agents offer their own insurance and will probably try to sell you their package when you book a holiday. Think before you sign. **Britain's Consumers' Association** recommends that you insist on seeing the policy and reading the fine print before buying travel insurance. **The Association of British Insurers** (℗ 020/7600-3333; www.abi.org.uk) gives advice by phone and publishes *Holiday Insurance,* a free guide to policy provisions and prices. You might also shop around for better deals: Try **Columbus Direct** (℗ 020/7375-0011;** www.columbusdirect.net).

INSURANCE FOR CANADIAN TRAVELERS Canadians should check with their provincial health plan offices or call **Health Canada** (℗ 613/957-2991;** www.hc-sc.gc.ca) to find out the extent of their coverage and what documentation and receipts they must take home in case they are treated in the United States.

MONEY

CURRENCY The U.S. monetary system is very simple: The most common **bills** are the $1 (colloquially, a "buck"), $5, $10, and $20 denominations. There are also $2 bills (seldom encountered), $50 bills, and $100 bills (the last two are usually not welcome as payment for small purchases). All the paper money was recently redesigned, making the famous faces adorning them disproportionately large. The old-style bills are still legal tender.

There are seven denominations of coins: 1¢ (1 cent, or a penny); 5¢ (5 cents, or a nickel); 10¢ (10 cents, or a dime); 25¢ (25 cents, or a quarter); 50¢ (50 cents, or a half dollar); the newer gold "Sacagawea" coin worth $1; and, prized by collectors, the rare, older silver dollar.

Note: The "foreign-exchange bureaus" so common in Europe are rare even at airports in the United States, and nonexistent outside major cities. It's best not to change foreign money (or traveler's checks denominated in a currency other than U.S. dollars) at a small-town bank, or even a branch in a big city; in fact, leave any currency other than U.S. dollars at home—it may prove a greater nuisance to you than it's worth.

TRAVELER'S CHECKS Though traveler's checks are widely accepted, make sure that they're denominated in U.S. dollars, as foreign-currency checks are often difficult to exchange. The three traveler's checks that are most widely recognized—and least likely to be denied—are **Visa, American Express,** and **Thomas Cook.** Be sure to record the numbers of the checks, and keep that information in a separate place in case they get lost or stolen. Most businesses are pretty good about taking traveler's checks, but you're better off cashing them in at a bank (in small amounts, of course) and paying in cash. *Remember:* You'll

SIZE CONVERSION CHART

Women's Clothing

American	4	6	8	10	12	14	16
French	34	36	38	40	42	44	46
British	6	8	10	12	14	16	18

Women's Shoes

American	5	6	7	8	9	10
French	36	37	38	39	40	41
British	4	5	6	7	8	9

Men's Suits

American	34	36	38	40	42	44	46	48
French	44	46	48	50	52	54	56	58
British	34	36	38	40	42	44	46	48

Men's Shirts

American	14½	15	15½	16	16½	17	17½
French	37	38	39	41	42	43	44
British	14½	15	15½	16	16½	17	17½

Men's Shoes

American	7	8	9	10	11	12	13
French	39½	41	42	43	44½	46	47
British	6	7	8	9	10	11	12

need identification, such as a driver's license or passport, to change a traveler's check.

CREDIT CARDS & ATMs Credit cards are the most widely used form of payment in the United States: **Visa** (Barclaycard in Britain), **MasterCard** (Euro-Card in Europe, Access in Britain, Chargex in Canada), **American Express, Diners Club, Discover,** and **Carte Blanche.** You'll also find that some Vegas vendors may also accept international cards like **enRoute, EuroCard,** and **JCB,** but not as universally as Amex, MasterCard, or Visa. There are, however, a handful of stores and restaurants that do not take credit cards, so be sure to ask in advance. Most businesses display a sticker near their entrance to let you know which cards they accept. (***Note:*** Businesses may require a minimum purchase, usually around $10, to use a credit card.)

It is strongly recommended that you bring at least one major credit card. You must have a credit or charge card to rent a car. Hotels and airlines usually require a credit card imprint as a deposit against expenses, and in an emergency a credit card can be priceless.

You'll find **automated teller machines (ATMs)** on just about every block—at least in almost every town—across the country. Some ATMs will allow you to draw U.S. currency against your bank and credit cards. Check with your bank before leaving home, and remember that you will need your personal identification number (PIN) to do so. Most accept Visa, MasterCard, and American Express, as well as ATM cards from other U.S. banks. Expect to be charged up to $3 per transaction, however, if you're not using your own bank's ATM.

One way around these fees is to ask for cash back at grocery stores that accept ATM cards and don't charge usage fees. Of course, you'll have to purchase something first.

ATM cards with major credit card backing, known as "debit cards," are now a commonly acceptable form of payment in most stores and restaurants. Debit cards draw money directly from your checking account. Some stores enable you to receive "cash back" on your debit card purchases as well.

SAFETY
GENERAL SAFETY SUGGESTIONS
While tourist areas are generally safe, crime is a national problem, and U.S. urban areas tend to be less safe than those in Europe or Japan. You should always stay alert. It's wise to ask your hotel front-desk staff if you're in doubt about which neighborhoods are safe.

Avoid carrying valuables with you on the street, and don't display expensive cameras or electronic equipment. Hold on to your pocketbook, and place your billfold in an inside pocket. In theaters, restaurants, and other public places, keep your possessions in sight.

Remember also that hotels are open to the public, and in a large hotel, security may not be able to screen everyone entering. Always lock your room door—don't assume that once inside your hotel you are automatically safe and no longer need

to be aware of your surroundings. In Las Vegas, many hotels check room keys at the elevators at night, providing some extra security. Many Las Vegas hotels also have in-room safes; if yours doesn't and you're traveling with valuables, put them in a safety-deposit box at the front desk.

DRIVING SAFETY   Driving safety is important too, and carjacking is not unprecedented. Question your rental agency about personal safety and ask for a traveler-safety brochure when you pick up your car. Obtain from the agency written directions—or a map with the route clearly marked—showing how to get to your destination. (Many agencies now offer the option of renting a cellphone for the duration of your car rental; check with the rental agent when you pick up the car. Otherwise, contact **InTouch USA** at ✆ **800/872-7626** or www.intouchusa.com for short-term cellphone rental.) And, if possible, arrive and depart during daylight hours.

If you drive off a highway and end up in a dodgy-looking neighborhood, leave the area as quickly as possible. If you have an accident, even on the highway, stay in your car with the doors locked until you assess the situation or until the police arrive. If you're bumped from behind on the street or are involved in a minor accident with no injuries, and the situation appears to be suspicious, motion to the other driver to follow you. Never get out of your car in such situations. Go directly to the nearest police precinct, well-lit service station, or 24-hour store.

Park in well-lit and well-traveled areas whenever possible—in the casino hotels,

---

Tips **Travel-Document Tip**

Be sure to keep a copy of all your travel papers separate from your wallet or purse, and leave a copy with someone at home, should you need it faxed in an emergency.

take advantage of the free valet parking. Always keep your car doors locked, whether the vehicle is attended or unattended. Never leave any packages or valuables in sight. If someone attempts to rob you or steal your car, don't try to resist the thief/carjacker. Report the incident to the police department immediately by calling © 911.

2 Getting to the United States

THE MAJOR AIRLINES A number of U.S. airlines offer service from Europe to the United States, though a number of those same airlines are having financial troubles, and may perhaps be in different shape by the time you read this. If they do not have direct flights from Europe to Las Vegas, they can book you straight through on a connecting flight. You can make reservations by calling the following numbers in the United Kingdom: **American** (© **0181/572-5555** in the U.K., 800/433-7300 in the U.S.; www.aa.com), **Continental** (© **01293/776-464** in the U.K., 800/525-0280 in the U.S.; www.continental.com), **Delta** (© **0800/414-767** in the U.K., 800/221-1212 in the U.S.; www.delta.com), and **United** (© **0845/8-444-777** in the U.K., 800/538-2929 in the U.S.; www.ual.com).

And, of course, many international carriers serve Los Angeles and/or San Francisco International Airport. From LAX or San Francisco International Airport, you can take a domestic airline to Las Vegas. Helpful numbers to know include **Virgin Atlantic** (© **01293/747-747** in the U.K., 800/862-8621 in the U.S.; www.virgin-atlantic.com), **British Airways** (© **0345/222-111** in the U.K., 800/AIRWAYS in the U.S.; www.britishairways.com), and **Aer Lingus** (© **01/886-8888** in Dublin, 800/IRISH-AIR in the U.S.; www.aerlingus.ie). **Qantas** (© **13-13-13** in Australia, 800/227-4500 in the U.S.; www.qantas.com.au) has flights from Sydney to Los Angeles and San Francisco; you can also take United from Australia to the West Coast. **Air New Zealand** (© **0800/737-000** in New Zealand, 800/262-1234 in the U.S.;

www.airnewzealand.co.nz) also offers service to LAX. Canadian readers can book flights on **Air Canada** (© **800/776-3000;** www.aircanada.ca), which offers direct service from Toronto, Montréal, Calgary, and Vancouver to San Francisco and Los Angeles, and will book your final leg on a partner airline.

JetBlue (© **800/538-2583;** www.jetblue.com) is a highly rated low-cost carrier that operates out of a number of U.S. cities, and has daily direct service to Las Vegas out of New York City and Long Beach, California.

AIRLINE DISCOUNTS The smart traveler can find numerous ways to reduce the price of a plane ticket simply by taking time to shop around. For example, overseas visitors can take advantage of the APEX (Advance Purchase Excursion) reductions offered by all major U.S. and European carriers. For more money-saving airline advice, see "Getting There" and "Planning Your Trip Online," in chapter 2. For the best rates, compare fares and be flexible with the dates and times of travel.

Operated by the European Travel Network, **http://lowestairfareshomepage. com** is a great online source for regular and discounted airfares to Las Vegas and other destinations around the world. You can also use this site to compare rates and book accommodations, car rentals, and tours. Click "Special Offers" for the latest package deals.

IMMIGRATION & CUSTOMS CLEARANCE Visitors arriving by air, no matter what the port of entry, should cultivate patience and resignation before

Impressions

A few centuries from now archaeologists, studying the ruins of our civilization, will no doubt determine that Las Vegas was an important religious center, boasting dozens of massive temples to which pilgrims from afar brought bountiful offerings.

—Andres Martinez, *24/7: Living It Up While Doubling Down in the New Las Vegas*

setting foot on U.S. soil. Getting through immigration control can take as long as 2 hours on some days, especially on summer weekends, so be sure to carry this guidebook or something else to read. This is especially true in the aftermath of the September 11, 2001, terrorist attacks, when security clearances have been considerably beefed up at U.S. airports.

People traveling by air from Canada, Bermuda, and certain countries in the Caribbean can sometimes clear Customs and Immigration at the point of departure, which is much quicker.

3 Getting Around the United States

BY PLANE Some large airlines (for example, Northwest and Delta) offer travelers on their transatlantic or transpacific flights special discount tickets under the name **Visit USA,** allowing mostly one-way travel from one U.S. destination to another at very low prices. These discount tickets are not on sale in the United States and must be purchased abroad in conjunction with your international ticket. This system is the best, easiest, and fastest way to see the United States at low cost. You should obtain information well in advance from your travel agent or the office of the airline concerned, since the conditions attached to these discount tickets can be changed without advance notice.

BY CAR Though you don't necessarily have to rent a car while in Las Vegas, the most cost-effective, convenient, and comfortable way to travel around the United States is by car. The interstate highway system connects cities and towns all over the country; in addition to these high-speed, limited-access roadways, there's an extensive network of federal, state, and local highways and roads. Some of the national car-rental companies include **Alamo** (© 800/462-5266; www.alamo.com), **Avis** (© 800/230-4898; www.avis.com), **Budget** (© 800/527-0700; www.budget.com), **Dollar** (© 800/800-3665; www.dollar.com), **Hertz** (© 800/654-3131; www.hertz.com), **National** (© 800/227-7368; www.nationalcar.com), and **Thrifty** (© 800/847-4389; www.thrifty.com).

If you plan to rent a car in the United States, you probably won't need the services of an additional automobile organization. If you're planning to buy or borrow a car, automobile-association membership is recommended. **AAA,** the **American Automobile Association** (© 800/222-4357; www.aaa.com), is the country's largest auto club and supplies its members with maps, insurance, and, most important, emergency road service. The cost of joining runs from $66 for singles to $89 for two members, but if you're a member of a foreign auto club with reciprocal arrangements, you can enjoy free AAA service in America. See "Getting Around," in chapter 4 for more information on renting a car in Las Vegas.

BY BUS   Although bus travel is often the most economical form of public transit for short hops between U.S. cities, it can also be slow and uncomfortable—certainly not an option for everyone (particularly when Amtrak, which is far more luxurious, offers similar or slightly higher rates). **Greyhound/Trailways** (© 800/231-2222; www.greyhound.com), the sole nationwide bus line, offers an **International Ameripass** that must be purchased before coming to the United States, or by phone through the Greyhound International Office at the Port Authority Bus Terminal in New York City (© 212/971-0492). The pass can be obtained from foreign travel agents and costs less than the domestic version. Costs for 2005 passes are as follows: 7 days ($219), 10 days ($269), 15 days ($319), 21 days ($379), 30 days ($419), 45 days ($479), and 60 days ($589). You can get more info on the pass at www.greyhound.com, or by calling © 212/971-0492 (2–9pm) or © 402/330-8552 (all other times). Special ticket rates are available for seniors and students. Though bus stations are often located in undesirable neighborhoods, the one in Las Vegas is conveniently located in a safe part of Downtown.

BY TRAIN   Amtrak (© 800/USA-RAIL; www.amtrak.com) does not currently offer direct rail service, although plans have been in the works to restore the rails between Los Angeles and Las Vegas for years now. At press time, Amtrak wouldn't confirm a date, but various reports have indicated that at some point they will restore service using the Talgo. This European-designed "Casino Train" completes the trip from Los Angeles in about 5½ hours, with a wholesale seat price of $99 round-trip. (There's some talk that the train's route may continue on to Salt Lake City, but this had not been finalized at press time.) We still don't believe this is going to happen in our lifetime.

Much of the train will be pre-sold to various hotels, so the final price to the traveler will depend on how you get the ticket. High rollers will probably end up with freebies, but the ticket will most likely be $99 if you purchase at the counter. In the meantime, you can take the train to Los Angeles or Barstow and Amtrak will get you to Vegas by bus.

FAST FACTS: For the International Traveler

Automobile Organizations   Auto clubs will supply maps, suggested routes, guidebooks, accident and bail-bond insurance, and emergency road service. The **American Automobile Association (AAA)** is the major auto club in the United States. If you belong to an auto club in your home country, inquire about AAA reciprocity before you leave. You may be able to join AAA even if you're not a member of a reciprocal club; to inquire, contact AAA (© 800/222-4357; www.aaa.com). AAA is actually an organization of regional auto clubs; so look under "AAA Automobile Club" in the White Pages of the telephone directory. AAA has a nationwide emergency road service telephone number (© 800/AAA-HELP).

Business Hours   Offices are usually open weekdays from 9am to 5pm. Banks are open weekdays from 9am to 3pm or later, and sometimes on Saturday morning, although there's 24-hour access to the automated teller machines (ATMs) at most banks and other outlets. In Las Vegas, money is also available around the clock at casino cages—and every casino has at least one ATM. Shops, especially those in shopping complexes, tend to stay open late: until about 9pm weekdays and until 6pm weekends (including Sun).

Climate See "When to Go," in chapter 2.

Currency & Currency Exchange See "Money" under "Preparing for Your Trip," earlier in this chapter.

Drinking Laws The legal age for purchase and consumption of alcoholic beverages is 21; proof of age is required and often requested at bars, nightclubs, and restaurants, so it's always a good idea to bring ID when you go out, especially if you look young. Do not carry open containers of alcohol in your car or any public area that isn't zoned for alcohol consumption. The police can fine you on the spot. And nothing will ruin your trip faster than getting arrested for DUI ("driving under the influence"), so don't even think about driving while you're under the influence. Beer, wine, and liquor are all sold in all kinds of stores, pretty much around the clock; trust us, you won't have a hard time finding a drink in this town.

Electricity Like Canada, the United States uses 110–120 volts AC (60 cycles), compared to 220–240 volts AC (50 cycles) in most of Europe, Australia, and New Zealand. If your small appliances use 220–240 volts, you'll need a 110-volt transformer and a plug adapter with two flat parallel pins to operate them here. Downward converters that change 220–240 volts to 110–120 volts are difficult to find in the United States, so bring one with you.

Embassies & Consulates All embassies are located in the nation's capital, Washington, D.C. Some consulates are located in major U.S. cities, and most nations have a mission to the United Nations in New York City. If your country isn't listed below, call for directory information in Washington, D.C. (© **202/ 555-1212**), or log on to **www.embassy.org/embassies**.

The embassy of **Australia** is at 1601 Massachusetts Ave. NW, Washington, DC 20036 (© **202/797-3000;** www.austemb.org). There are consulates in New York, Honolulu, Houston, Los Angeles, and San Francisco.

The embassy of **Canada** is at 501 Pennsylvania Ave. NW, Washington, DC 20001 (© **202/682-1740;** www.canadianembassy.org). Other Canadian consulates are in Buffalo (N.Y.), Detroit, Los Angeles, New York, and Seattle.

The embassy of **Ireland** is at 2234 Massachusetts Ave. NW, Washington, DC 20008 (© **202/462-3939;** www.irelandemb.org). Irish consulates are in Boston, Chicago, New York, and San Francisco.

The embassy of **Japan** is at 2520 Massachusetts Ave. NW, Washington, DC 20008 (© **202/238-6700;** www.embjapan.org). Japanese consulates are located in Atlanta, Kansas City, San Francisco, and Washington, D.C.

The embassy of **New Zealand** is at 37 Observatory Circle NW, Washington, DC 20008 (© **202/328-4800;** www.nzemb.org). New Zealand consulates are in Los Angeles, Salt Lake City, San Francisco, and Seattle.

The embassy of the **United Kingdom** is at 3100 Massachusetts Ave. NW, Washington, DC 20008 (© **202/462-1340;** www.britainusa.com). British consulates are in Atlanta, Boston, Chicago, Cleveland, Houston, Los Angeles, New York, San Francisco, and Seattle.

Emergencies Call ℂ **911** to report a fire, call the police, or get an ambulance in Las Vegas. This is a toll-free call (no coins are required at public telephones).

If you have a medical emergency that doesn't require an ambulance, you can walk into a hospital's 24-hour emergency room (usually a separate entrance). For a list of hospitals, see "Fast Facts: Las Vegas" in chapter 4.

If you encounter serious problems, contact **Traveler's Aid International** (ℂ **202/546-1127;** www.travelersaid.org) to help direct you to a local branch. This nationwide, nonprofit, social-service organization geared to helping travelers in difficult straits offers services that might include reuniting families separated while traveling, providing food and/or shelter to people stranded without cash, or even offering emotional counseling. If you're in trouble, seek them out. In Las Vegas there is an office at **McCarran International Airport** (ℂ **702/798-1742**), which is open daily from 8am to 5pm. Similar services are provided by **Help of Southern Nevada,** 953 E. Sahara Ave., Suite 208, at Maryland Parkway in the Commercial Center on the northeast corner (ℂ **702/ 369-4357**). Hours are Monday to Friday from 8am to 4pm.

Gasoline (Petrol) Petrol is known as gasoline (or simply "gas") in the United States, and petrol stations are known as both gas stations and service stations. Though prices were volatile and rising sharply throughout the first half of 2004, gasoline costs significantly less here than it does in Europe (about $2.50 per gallon in Vegas at press time), and taxes are already included in the printed price. One U.S. gallon equals 3.8 liters or .85 imperial gallons.

Holidays Banks, government offices, post offices, and many stores, restaurants, and museums are closed on the following legal national holidays: January 1 (New Year's Day), the third Monday in January (Martin Luther King, Jr., Day), the third Monday in February (Presidents' Day, Washington's Birthday), the last Monday in May (Memorial Day), July 4 (Independence Day), the first Monday in September (Labor Day), the second Monday in October (Columbus Day), November 11 (Veterans Day/Armistice Day), the fourth Thursday in November (Thanksgiving Day), and December 25 (Christmas). Also, the Tuesday following the first Monday in November is Election Day and is a federal government holiday in presidential-election years (held every 4 years, most recently in 2004).

Legal Aid If you are "pulled over" for a minor infraction (such as speeding), never attempt to pay the fine directly to a police officer; this could be construed as attempted bribery, a much more serious crime. Pay fines by mail, or directly into the hands of the clerk of the court. If accused of a more serious offense, say and do nothing before consulting a lawyer. Here the burden is on the state to prove a person's guilt beyond a reasonable doubt, and everyone has the right to remain silent, whether he or she is suspected of a crime or actually arrested. Once arrested, a person can make one telephone call to a party of his or her choice. Call your embassy or consulate.

Mail If you aren't sure what your address will be in the United States, mail can be sent to you, in your name, c/o General Delivery at the main post office of the city or region where you expect to be. (Call ℂ **800/275-8777** for information on the nearest post office.) The addressee must pick up mail in person and must produce proof of identity (driver's license, passport, and so forth). Most post offices will hold your mail for up to 1 month and are open Monday to Friday from 8am to 6pm and Saturday from 9am to 3pm.

Generally found at intersections, mailboxes are blue with a red-and-white stripe and carry the inscription U.S. MAIL. If your mail is addressed to a U.S. destination, don't forget to add the five-digit postal code (or zip code) after the two-letter abbreviation of the state to which the mail is addressed. This is essential for prompt delivery.

At press time, domestic postage rates were 23¢ for a postcard and 37¢ for a letter. For international mail, a first-class letter of up to ½ ounce costs 80¢ (60¢ to Canada and Mexico), a first-class postcard costs 70¢ (50¢ to Canada and Mexico), and a preprinted postal aerogramme costs 70¢. Point your Web browser to **www.usps.gov** for complete U.S. postal information.

In Las Vegas the closest post office to the Strip is behind the Stardust Hotel at 3100 S. Industrial Rd., between Sahara Avenue and Spring Mountain Road (℗ **800/297-5543**). The **main post office** is at 1001 E. Sunset Rd., same phone number. It's open Monday to Friday from 8:30am to 6pm. You can also mail letters and packages at your hotel, and there's a full-service U.S. Post Office in the Forum Shops in Caesars Palace.

Measurements See the chart on the inside front cover of this book for details on converting metric measurements to U.S. equivalents. See also the "Size Conversion Chart" on p. 47 in this chapter for clothing and shoe size equivalencies.

Taxes The United States has no value-added tax (VAT) or other indirect tax at the national level. Every state, county, and city has the right to levy its own local tax on all purchases, including hotel and restaurant checks, airline tickets, and so on. These taxes are not refundable and are not included in the price tags you'll see on merchandise. In Clark County (where Las Vegas is located), hotel room tax is 9% and sales tax is 7%.

Telephone, Telegraph, Telex & Fax The telephone system in the United States is run by private corporations, so rates, especially for long-distance service and operator-assisted calls, can vary widely. Generally, hotel surcharges on long-distance and local calls are astronomical, so you're usually better off using a **public pay telephone,** which you'll find clearly marked in most public buildings and private establishments as well as on the street. Convenience grocery stores and gas stations always have them. Many convenience groceries and packaging services sell **prepaid calling cards** in denominations up to $50; these can be the least expensive way to call home. Many public phones at airports now accept American Express, MasterCard, and Visa credit cards. **Local calls** made from public pay phones in most locales cost either 25¢ or 35¢. Pay phones do not accept pennies, and few will take anything larger than a quarter.

You may want to look into leasing a cellphone for the duration of your trip.

Most long-distance and international calls can be dialed directly from any phone. **For calls within the United States and to Canada,** dial 1 followed by the area code and the seven-digit number. **For other international calls,** dial 011 followed by the country code, city code, and the telephone number of the person you are calling.

Calls to area codes **800, 888, 877,** and **866** are toll-free. However, calls to numbers in area codes **700** and **900** (chat lines, bulletin boards, "dating" services, and so on) can be very expensive—usually a charge of 95¢ to $3 or more per minute, and they sometimes have minimum charges that can run as high as $15 or more.

For **reversed-charge or collect calls,** and for person-to-person calls, dial 0 (zero, not the letter O) followed by the area code and number you want; an operator will then come on the line, and you should specify that you are calling collect, or person-to-person, or both. If your operator-assisted call is international, ask for the overseas operator.

For **local directory assistance** ("information"), dial ⓒ 411; for long-distance information, dial 1, then the appropriate area code and 555-1212.

Telegraph and telex services are provided primarily by Western Union. You can bring your telegram into the nearest Western Union office (there are hundreds across the country) or dictate it over the phone (ⓒ **800/325-6000**). You can also telegraph money, or have it telegraphed to you, very quickly over the Western Union system, but this service can cost as much as 15% to 20% of the amount sent. You can find a Western Union office at 1350 E. Flamingo Rd. (ⓒ **702/732-0024**)

Most Las Vegas hotels have **fax machines** available for guest use (be sure to ask about the charge to use it, as charges tend to be very expensive), and many hotel rooms are even wired for guests' fax machines. A less-expensive way to send and receive faxes is to do it at stores such as Kinko's, a national chain offering computer and copying services. There is a Kinko's near UNLV at 4440 S. Maryland Pkwy. (ⓒ **702/735-4402**), and another branch is located Downtown at 830 4th St. (ⓒ **702/383-7022**).

There are two kinds of telephone directories in the United States. The so-called **White Pages** list private households and business subscribers in alphabetical order. The inside front cover lists emergency numbers for police, fire, ambulance, the Coast Guard, poison-control center, crime victims' hot line, and so on. The first few pages will tell you how to make long-distance and international calls, complete with country codes and area codes. Government numbers are usually printed on blue paper within the White Pages. Printed on yellow paper, the so-called **Yellow Pages** list all local services, businesses, industries, and houses of worship according to activity with an index at the front or back. (Drugstores/pharmacies and restaurants are also listed by geographic location.) The Yellow Pages also include city plans or detailed area maps, postal zip codes, and public transportation routes.

Time The continental United States is divided into four time zones, and Nevada is on **Pacific Standard Time (PST),** which is 3 hours earlier than on the U.S. East Coast. For instance, when it is noon in Las Vegas, it is 3pm in New York City (EST), 2pm in Chicago (CST), and 1pm in Denver (MST). Nevada, like most of the rest of the United States (but not all of it), observes **daylight saving time** from 1am on the first Sunday in April through 1am on the last Sunday in October.

Daylight saving time moves the clock 1 hour ahead of standard time. This results in lovely, long summer evenings, when the sun sets as late as 8:30 or 9pm.

Tipping Tipping is so ingrained in the American way of life that the annual income tax of tip-earning service personnel is based on how much they should have received in light of their employers' gross revenues. Accordingly, they may have to pay tax on a tip you didn't actually give them.

Here are some rules of thumb:

In hotels, tip **bellhops** at least $1 per bag ($2–$3 per bag if you have a lot of luggage) and tip the **chamber staff** $1 to $2 per day (more if you've left a disaster area for him or her to clean up, or if you're traveling with kids and/or pets). Tip the **doorman** or **concierge** only if he or she has provided you with some specific service (for example, calling a cab for you or obtaining difficult-to-get theater tickets). Tip the **valet-parking attendant** $1 every time you get your car.

In restaurants, bars, and nightclubs, tip **service staff** 15% to 20% of the check, tip **bartenders** 10% to 15%, tip **checkroom attendants** $1 per garment, and tip **valet-parking attendants** $1 per vehicle. Tip the **doorman** only if he has provided you with some specific service (such as calling a cab for you). Tipping is not expected in cafeterias and fast-food restaurants.

Tip **cab drivers** 15% of the fare.

As for other service personnel, tip **skycaps** at airports at least $1 per bag ($2–$3 per bag if you have a lot of luggage) and tip **hairdressers** and **barbers** 15% to 20%.

Tipping ushers at movies and theaters, and gas-station attendants, is not expected.

See chapter 10 for details on tipping showroom maitred's; casino dealers usually get a few dollars if you've had a big win.

Toilets You won't find public toilets or "restrooms" on the streets in most U.S. cities, but they can be found in hotel lobbies, bars, restaurants, museums, department stores, railway and bus stations, and service stations. Large hotels, all of the casino hotels, and fast-food restaurants are probably the best bet for good, clean facilities. If possible, avoid the toilets at parks and beaches, which tend to be dirty; some may be unsafe. Restaurants and bars in resorts or heavily visited areas may reserve their restrooms for patrons. Some establishments display a notice indicating this. You can ignore this sign or, better yet, avoid arguments by paying for a cup of coffee or a soft drink, which will qualify you as a patron.

4

Getting to Know Las Vegas

Located in the southernmost precincts of a wide, pancake-flat valley, Las Vegas is the biggest city in the state of Nevada. Treeless mountains form a scenic backdrop to hotels awash in neon glitter. Although it is one of the fastest-growing cities in America, for tourism purposes, the city is quite compact.

1 Orientation

ARRIVING AT THE LAS VEGAS AIRPORT

Las Vegas is served by **McCarran International Airport,** 5757 Wayne Newton Blvd. (*C* **702/261-5211,** TDD 702/261-3111; www.mccarran.com), just a few minutes' drive from the southern end of the Strip, where the bulk of casinos and hotels are concentrated. This big, modern airport—with a relatively new $500-million expansion—is rather unique in that it includes several casino areas with more than 1,000 slot machines. Although these are reputed to offer lower paybacks than hotel casinos (the airport has a captive audience and doesn't need to lure repeat customers), it's hard to resist throwing in a few quarters while waiting for the luggage to arrive. We actually know someone who hit a $250 jackpot there on his way out of town, thereby recouping most of his gambling losses at the last possible moment. (He was surprised, too.)

Getting to your hotel from the airport is a cinch. **Bell Trans** (*C* **702/739-7990;** www.bell-trans.com) runs 20-passenger minibuses daily between the airport and all major Las Vegas hotels and motels (7:45am–midnight). There are several other companies that run similar ventures—just stand outside on the curb and one will be flagged down for you. Buses from the airport leave about every 10 minutes. When you want to check out of your hotel and head back to the airport, call at least 2 hours in advance to be safe (though often you can just flag down one of the buses outside any major hotel). The cost is $5 per person each way to Strip- and Convention Center–area hotels, $6.50 to Downtown or other Off-Strip properties (anyplace north of the Sahara Hotel and west of I-15). Other similarly priced shuttles run 24 hours and can be found in the same place.

Even less expensive are **Citizen's Area Transit (CAT)** buses (*C* **702/CAT-RIDE;** www.rtcsouthernnevada.com/cat). The no. 108 bus departs from the airport and will take you to the Stratosphere, where you can transfer to the no. 301, which stops close to most Strip- and Convention Center–area hotels. The no. 109 bus goes from the airport to the Downtown Transportation Center at Casino Center Boulevard and Stewart Avenue. The fares for buses on Strip routes are $2 for adults, 60¢ for seniors and children. *Note:* If you have heavy luggage, you should know that you might have a long walk from the bus stop to the hotel entrance (even if the bus stop is right in front of your hotel). Vans are able to get right up to the entrance, so choose a van if you're lugging lots of baggage.

Tips **Help for Troubled Travelers**

The **Traveler's Aid Society** is a social-service organization geared to helping travelers in difficult straits. Their services might include reuniting families separated while traveling, feeding people stranded without cash, or even emotional counseling. If you're in trouble, seek them out. In Las Vegas there is a Traveler's Aid office at McCarran International Airport (℗ **702/798-1742**). It's open daily from 8am to 5pm. Similar services are provided by **Help of Southern Nevada**, 953–35B E. Sahara Ave. (Suite 208), at Maryland Parkway in the Commercial Center (℗ **702/369-4357**). Hours are Monday to Friday from 8am to 4pm.

All of the major car-rental companies are represented in Las Vegas, if you choose to rent a car while you are in town. For a list of agencies and more information on getting a good deal on a rental, see "Getting Around," below.

VISITOR INFORMATION

All major Las Vegas hotels provide comprehensive tourist information at their reception and/or sightseeing and show desks.

Other good information sources are the **Las Vegas Convention and Visitors Authority,** 3150 Paradise Rd., Las Vegas, NV 89109 (℗ **877/VISIT-LV** or 702/892-7575; www.visitlasvegas.com), open daily from 8am to 5pm; the **Las Vegas Chamber of Commerce,** 3720 Howard Hughes Pkwy., #100, Las Vegas, NV 89109 (℗ **702/735-1616;** www.lvchamber.com), open Monday to Friday from 8am to 5pm; and, for information on all of Nevada, including Las Vegas, the **Nevada Commission on Tourism** (℗ **800/638-2328;** www.travelnevada.com), open 24 hours.

CITY LAYOUT

There are two main areas of Las Vegas: the **Strip** and **Downtown.** For many people, that's all there is to Las Vegas. But there is actually more to the town than that: Although maybe not as glitzy and glamorous as the Strip and Downtown—okay, definitely not—Paradise Road and east Las Vegas are home to quite a bit of casino action, Maryland Parkway boasts mainstream and alternative-culture shopping, and there are different restaurant options all over the city. Confining yourself to the Strip and Downtown is fine for the first-time visitor, but repeat customers (and you will be) should get out there and explore. Las Vegas Boulevard South (the Strip) is the starting point for addresses; any street crossing it will start with 1 East and 1 West (and go up from there) at its intersection with the Strip.

THE STRIP

The Strip is probably the most famous 4-mile stretch of highway in the nation. Officially called Las Vegas Boulevard South, it contains most of the top hotels in town and offers almost all of the major showroom entertainment. First-time visitors will, and probably should, spend the bulk of their time on the Strip. If mobility is a problem, we suggest basing yourself in a South or Mid-Strip location.

For the purposes of organizing this book, we've divided the Strip into three sections. The **South Strip** can be roughly defined as the portion of the Strip south of Harmon Avenue, including the MGM Grand, Mandalay Bay, the Monte Carlo, New York–New York, Luxor, and many more hotels and casinos.

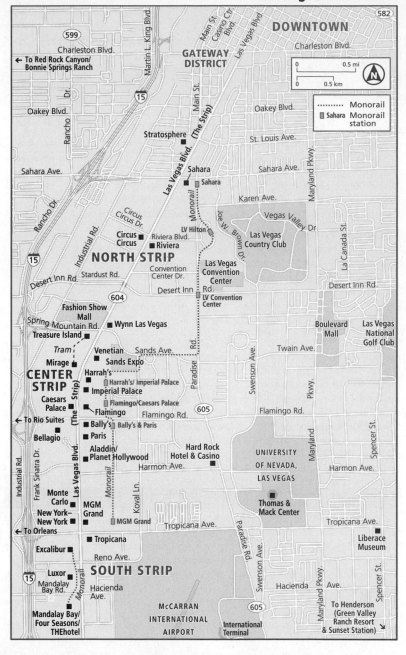

582

DOWNTOWN

599

Charleston Blvd.
Charleston Blvd.

← To Red Rock Canyon/
Bonnie Springs Ranch

GATEWAY
DISTRICT

0   0.5 mi
0   0.5 km

Oakey Blvd.
Oakey Blvd.

St. Louis Ave.

······· Monorail
▪ Sahara Monorail
station

Stratosphere

Sahara Ave.
Sahara Ave.
Sahara

Sahara Ave.

Sahara

Karen Ave.

Vegas Valley Dr.

Las Vegas
Country Club

LV Hilton

Circus
Circus Dr.

Circus
Circus

Riviera Blvd.
▪ Riviera

NORTH STRIP

Convention
Center Dr.

Las Vegas
Convention
Center

Desert Inn Rd.
Desert Inn Rd.
Stardust Rd.

Desert Inn Rd.

LV Convention
Center

604

Boulevard
Mall

Las Vegas
National
Golf Club

Fashion Show
Mall

Spring Mountain Rd.
▪ Wynn Las Vegas

Treasure Island ▪

Twain Ave.

Tram

Mirage ▪

Venetian
Sands Expo

Sands Ave.

**CENTER
STRIP**

Harrah's ▪
Harrah's/ Imperial Palace
Imperial Palace

Caesars
Palace ▪
Flamingo/Caesars Palace
▪ Flamingo
Flamingo Rd.

605

Flamingo Rd.

← To Rio Suites

▪ Bally's Bally's & Paris
Bellagio ▪ ▪ Paris

Aladdin/
▪ Planet Hollywood

Hard Rock
Hotel & Casino

Harmon Ave.

**UNIVERSITY
OF NEVADA,
LAS VEGAS**

Harmon Ave.

Monte
Carlo ▪
MGM
Grand
New York–
New York ▪

Koval Ln.

Thomas &
Mack Center

← To Orleans

MGM Grand

Tropicana Ave.

Tropicana Ave.

▪ Tropicana

Liberace
Museum

Excalibur ▪

Reno Ave.

SOUTH STRIP

15

Luxor ▪
Mandalay
Bay Rd.

Hacienda
Ave.

Hacienda   Ave.

605

To Henderson
(Green Valley
Ranch Resort
& Sunset Station)

Mandalay Bay/
Four Seasons/
THEhotel ▪

McCARRAN
INTERNATIONAL
AIRPORT

International
Terminal

Mid-Strip is a long stretch of the street between Harmon Avenue and Spring Mountain Road, including Bellagio, Caesars, The Mirage and TI at the Mirage (formerly Treasure Island), Bally's, Paris Las Vegas, The Flamingo Las Vegas, and Harrah's, among other hotels and casinos.

The **North Strip** stretches north from Spring Mountain Road all the way to the Stratosphere Casino Hotel & Tower and includes the new Wynn Las Vegas, Stardust, Sahara, The Riviera, and Circus Circus, to name a few of the accommodations and attractions.

EAST OF THE STRIP/CONVENTION CENTER

This area has grown up around the Las Vegas Convention Center. Las Vegas is one of the nation's top convention cities, attracting more than 2.9 million conventioneers each year. The major hotel in this section is the Las Vegas Hilton, but in recent years, Marriott has built Residence Inn and Courtyard properties here, and the Hard Rock Hotel is a major draw. You'll find many excellent smaller hotels and motels southward along Paradise Road. All of these hotels offer proximity to the Strip.

BETWEEN THE STRIP & DOWNTOWN

The area between the Strip and Downtown is a seedy stretch dotted with tacky wedding chapels, bail-bond operations, pawnshops, and cheap motels.

However, the area known as the **Gateway District** (roughly north and south of Charleston Blvd. to the west of Las Vegas Blvd. S.) is slowly but surely gaining a name for itself as an actual artists' colony. Studios, small cafes, and other signs of life are springing up, and we hope this movement will last.

DOWNTOWN

Also known as **"Glitter Gulch"** (narrower streets make the neon seem brighter), Downtown Las Vegas, which is centered on Fremont Street between Main and 9th streets, was the first section of the city to develop hotels and casinos. With the exception of the Golden Nugget, which looks like it belongs in Monte Carlo, this area has traditionally been more casual than the Strip. But with the advent of the **Fremont Street Experience** (p. 193), Downtown has experienced a revitalization. The area is clean, the crowds are low-key and friendly, and the light show overhead is as ostentatious as anything on the Strip. Don't overlook this area. Las Vegas Boulevard runs all the way into Fremont Street Downtown.

2 Getting Around

It shouldn't be too hard to navigate your way around. But remember, between huge hotel acreage, increased and very slow traffic, and lots and lots of people trying to explore like you, getting around takes a lot longer than you might think. Heck, it can take 15 to 20 minutes to get from your room to another part of your hotel! Always allow for plenty of time to get from point A to point B.

BY CAR

We highly recommend that visitors rent a car. The Strip is too spread out for walking (and Las Vegas is often too hot or too cold to make strolls pleasant), Downtown is too far away for a cheap cab ride, and public transportation is often ineffective in getting you from point A to point B. Plus, return visits call for exploration in more remote parts of the city, and a car brings freedom (especially if you want to do any side trips—

bus tours are available, but a car lets you explore at your own pace rather than according to a tour schedule).

You should note that places with addresses some 60 blocks east or west from the Strip are actually less than a 10-minute drive—provided there is no traffic.

That said, if you plan to confine yourself to one part of the Strip or to Downtown, your feet will suffice.

Having advocated renting a car, we should warn you that the growing population means a proportionate increase in the number of cars. Traffic is getting worse, and it's harder and harder to get around town with any certain swiftness. We've included a list of particular traffic danger zones in the "Chopper Tom's Traffic Tips" box below, but a general rule of thumb is to avoid driving on the Strip whenever you can, and avoid driving at all during peak rush hours (8–9:30am and 4:30–6pm), especially if you have to make a show curtain.

Parking is usually a pleasure because all casino hotels offer free valet service. That means that for a mere $1 to $2 tip, you can park right at the door, though the valet usually fills up on busy nights. In those cases, you can use the gigantic self-parking lot that all hotels have.

RENTING A CAR

National companies with outlets in Las Vegas include **Alamo** (© 877/227-8367; www.goalamo.com), **Avis** (© 800/230-4898; www.avis.com), **Budget** (© 800/527-0700; https://rent.drivebudget.com/Home.jsp), **Dollar** (© 800/800-3665; www.dollar.com), **Enterprise** (© 800/736-8227; www.enterprise.com), **Hertz** (© 800/654-3131; www.hertz.com), **National** (© 800/227-7368; www.nationalcar.com), **Payless** (© 800/729-5377; www.paylesscarrental.com), and **Thrifty** (© 800/847-4389; www.thrifty.com).

Car-rental rates vary even more than airline fares. The price you pay will depend on the size of the car, where and when you pick it up and drop it off, the length of the rental period, where and how far you drive it, whether you purchase insurance, and a host of other factors. A few key questions could save you hundreds of dollars:

- Are weekend rates lower than weekday rates? Ask if the rate is the same for pickup Friday morning, for instance, as it is for Thursday night.
- Is a weekly rate cheaper than the daily rate? Even if you need the car for only 4 days, it may be cheaper to keep it for 5.
- Does the agency assess a drop-off charge if you don't return the car to the same location where you picked it up? Is it cheaper to pick up the car at the airport compared to a Downtown location?
- Are special promotional rates available? If you see an advertised price in your local newspaper, be sure to ask for that specific rate; otherwise, you may be charged the standard cost. Terms change constantly, and reservations agents are notorious for not mentioning available discounts unless you ask.
- Are discounts available for members of AARP, AAA, frequent-flier programs, or trade unions? If you belong to any of these organizations, you may be entitled to discounts of up to 30%.
- How much tax will be added to the rental bill? Local tax? State use tax?
- What is the cost of adding an additional driver's name to the contract?
- How many free miles are included in the price? Free mileage is often negotiable, depending on the length of your rental.

Tips   Chopper Tom's Traffic Tips

"Chopper" Tom Hawley has watched Las Vegas grow since he was a little kid catching lizards in the desert back in the '60s. A self-described "traffic geek," Tom reports from the helicopter and from the studio most mornings and afternoons in Las Vegas on KVBC-TV/Channel 3. For further information on the following projects, tips, and much more, stop by Channel 3's website at **www.kvbc.com** and click "Traffic."

- **Monorail Mania:** After decades of abandoned plans and false starts, a commuter monorail serving the Strip is finally a reality! This 4-mile system is a larger, faster, and more modern version of the Disney hand-me-down that used to run between the MGM and Bally's. The new Las Vegas Monorail has seven stations sprinkled from the MGM to the Sahara with a one-way fare running $3 per person (discounts are available for multiple trips). You may have heard about the less than glorious opening months of the system (parts falling off, system failures, a 4-month shutdown) but we're happy to report that as of this writing things seem to be in fine working order. The bad news is that the monorail has probably scuttled planned extensions to Downtown and the airport at least for now.
- **People Movers Galore:** Las Vegas has a greater variety of independent people-mover systems than any other city in the world, and they're a great way to get around without having to get into your car. In addition to the people movers at McCarran Airport, a variety of trains will take you from hotel to hotel. The **Doppelmayr Cable Liner Shuttle** whisks you from the Tropicana Walkways to the Excalibur, Luxor, and Mandalay Bay hotels. Smaller shuttles operate between The Mirage and TI at the Mirage and between the Circus Circus Big Top and East Tower.
- **Spaghetti Bowl:** The "Spaghetti Bowl" is what locals call the mess where I-15 intersects U.S. 95. The whole thing was reconstructed in 2000, but some studies indicate that it's already carrying more traffic than it was designed for, so don't expect a congestion-free ride.
- **U.S. 95 Widening:** The west leg of U.S. 95 was designed in the early '70s, when growth at the turn of the 21st century was expected to be about one-third of what it actually turned out to be. A massive widening project is underway with a projected 2006 completion. For now, this stretch of U.S. 95 (called the **Oran K. Gragson Expwy.**, after a former Las Vegas mayor) is bulging at the seams. During rush hours, surface streets like Charleston and Lake Mead Boulevard are your best alternate routes.
- **Keep Your Feet off the Streets:** Local engineers have been trying to improve traffic on the Strip by separating the cars from the pedestrians.

- How much does the rental company charge to refill your gas tank if you return with the tank less than full? Though most rental companies claim these prices are "competitive," fuel is almost always cheaper in town. Try to allow enough time to refuel the car yourself before returning it.

The first overhead pedestrian walkways opened at Tropicana Avenue in 1995; similar bridges were completed at Flamingo Avenue by 2000. A new set of bridges connects the hotels and shopping mall at Spring Mountain.

- **Do D.I. Direct:** Most visitors seem to get a lot of mileage out of the Strip and I-15. But if you're checking out the local scene, you can bypass both of those using Desert Inn Road, which, after a recent addition, is now one of the longest streets running from one side of the valley to the other. Plus, the 2-mile "Superarterial" section between Valley View and Paradise zips you nonstop over the interstate and under the Strip. The biggest thrill ride this side of the New York–New York roller coaster!

- **Grin and Bear It:** Yes, there are ways to avoid traffic jams on the Strip. But at least these traffic jams are entertaining! If you have the time and patience, go ahead and take a ride along the Strip from Hacienda to Sahara. The 4-mile drive might take an hour, but while you're grinding along, you might see a Sphinx, an active volcano, a water ballet, and some uniquely Vegas architecture.

- **Rat Pack Back Doors:** 2004 saw the opening of Frank Sinatra Drive, a bypass road running parallel to the Strip from Russell Road north to Industrial. It's a great way to avoid the traffic jams and sneak in the back of hotels like Mandalay Bay, Luxor, Monte Carlo, and Bellagio. On the other side of Interstate 15, a bunch of high-end condo developers talked the city into rechristening a big portion of Industrial Road as Dean Martin Drive (hey, where's Sammy's road?). It's still Industrial from near Downtown to Twain, allowing back entrances to Circus Circus, TI at the Mirage, and others, but as it passes under the freeway to the west, it becomes Dean Martin and is still a terrific bypass to the busy Strip and I-15 congestion.

- **Beltway Bypass:** Started in December 2003, a 53-mile beltway (I-215) will eventually wrap around the valley, allowing for easy access to the outskirts and to bypass the city. The "ultimate facility" of six-lane, limited-access divided highway won't be complete for another decade, but the southern section is a full freeway, and a few dozen more miles of interim roads are now open as frontage roads and four-lane highways.

- **Catch the CAT:** Some locals complain about Citizens Area Transit (CAT) bus service in certain neighborhoods. But the Strip routes are frequent and well serviced, running 'round the clock from the South Strip Transfer Terminal to the Downtown Transportation Center in the north. The 301 runs every 10 minutes during busy hours, and there's also a limited-stop express bus (no. 302) every 15 minutes. Other routes go for $1.25, but the 301 and 302 are the CAT's gravy trains and will run you $2. Exact change, please.

Some companies offer "refueling packages," in which you pay for an entire tank of gas up front. The price is usually fairly competitive with local gas prices, but you don't get credit for any gas remaining in the tank. If a stop at a gas station on the way to the airport will make you miss your plane, then by all means take advantage of the fuel purchase option. Otherwise, skip it.

Many available packages include airfare, accommodations, and a rental car with unlimited mileage. Compare these prices with the cost of booking airline tickets and renting a car separately to see if these offers are good deals. See "Packages for the Independent Traveler," in chapter 2, for details on packages and where to find them.

Internet resources can make comparison-shopping easier. See "Planning Your Trip Online," in chapter 2, for tips on the best sites.

Demystifying Renter's Insurance

Before you drive off in a rental car, be sure you're insured. Hasty assumptions about your personal auto insurance or a rental agency's additional coverage could end up costing you tens of thousands of dollars—even if you are involved in an accident that was clearly the fault of another driver.

If you already hold a **private auto insurance** policy, you are most likely covered in the United States for loss of or damage to a rental car and liability in case of injury to any other party involved in an accident. Be sure to find out whether you are covered in the area you are visiting, whether your policy extends to all persons who will be driving the rental car, how much liability is covered in case an outside party is injured in an accident, and whether the type of vehicle you are renting is included under your contract. (Rental trucks, sport utility vehicles, and luxury vehicles such as the Jaguar may not be covered.)

Most **major credit cards** provide some degree of coverage as well—provided they were used to pay for the rental. Terms vary widely, however, so be sure to call your credit card company directly before you rent.

If you are **uninsured,** your credit card may provide primary coverage as long as you decline the rental agency's insurance. This means that the credit card will cover damage or theft of a rental car for the full cost of the vehicle. If you already have insurance, your credit card may provide secondary coverage—which basically covers your deductible.

Fun Fact **Did You Know?**

- Las Vegas (Sin City) has more churches per capita than any other city in America.
- Illusionists Siegfried and Roy have sawed a woman in half more times than anyone else.
- Visitors on a trail ride once brought a horse into the crowded casino of the Thunderbird Hotel. They put a pair of dice between his lips at the craps table and he threw a natural 7.
- In January, a Las Vegas visitor can ski the snowy slopes of Mount Charleston and water-ski on Lake Mead in the same day.
- Former president Ronald Reagan performed at the Last Frontier in 1954. Those who saw him said he was a pretty good song-and-dance man.
- Bandleader Xavier Cugat and Spanish bombshell singer Charo were the first couple to exchange vows at Caesars Palace, 2 days after its 1966 opening.

Credit cards will not cover liability, or the cost of injury to an outside party and/or damage to an outside party's vehicle. If you do not hold an insurance policy, you may seriously want to consider purchasing additional liability insurance from your rental company. Be sure to check the terms, however: Some rental agencies cover liability only if the renter is not at fault; even then, the rental company's obligation varies from state to state. Bear in mind that each credit card company has its own peculiarities; call your own credit card company for details before relying on a card for coverage.

The basic insurance coverage offered by most car-rental companies, known as the **Loss/Damage Waiver (LDW)** or **Collision Damage Waiver (CDW),** can cost as much as $20 per day. The former should cover everything, including the loss of income to the rental agency, should you get in an accident (normally not covered by your own insurance policy): It usually covers the full value of the vehicle with no deductible if an outside party causes an accident or other damage to the rental car. In all states but California, you will probably be covered in case of theft as well. Liability coverage varies according to the company policy and state law, but the minimum is usually at least $15,000. If you are at fault in an accident, however, you will be covered for the full replacement value of the car but not for liability. In Nevada, you can buy additional liability coverage for such cases. Most rental companies will require a police report in order to process any claims you file, but your private insurer will not be notified of the accident. Check your own policies and credit cards before you shell out money on this extra insurance because you may already be covered.

DRIVING SAFETY

Because driving on the outskirts of Las Vegas—for example, coming from California—involves desert driving, you must take certain precautions. It's a good idea to check your tires, water, and oil before leaving. Take at least 5 gallons of water in a clean container that can be used for either drinking or the radiator. Pay attention to road signs that suggest when to turn off your car's air conditioner. And don't push your luck with gas—it may be 35 miles or more between stations. If your car overheats, do not remove the radiator cap until the engine has cooled, and then remove it very slowly. Add water to within an inch of the top of the radiator.

BY TAXI

Since cabs line up in front of all major hotels, an easy way to get around town is by taxi. Cabs charge $3.20 at the meter drop and 25¢ for each additional ⅛ mile, plus an additional $1.20 fee for being picked up at the airport. A taxi from the airport to the Strip will run you $12 to $20, from the airport to Downtown $15 to $20, and between the Strip and Downtown about $10 to $15. You can often save money by sharing a cab with someone going to the same destination (up to five people can ride for the same fare). All of this implies that you have gotten a driver who is honest; many cabbies will take you the long way around, which sometimes means the shortest physical distance between two points—right down the Strip—but longest time on the clock and, thus, meter. Either way, you could end up paying a fare that . . . let's just say a new pair of shoes would have been a much more fun way to spend that jackpot. Your only recourse is to write down the cab number and call the company after and complain. They may not respond, but at least you tried.

If you want to call a taxi, any of the following companies can provide one: **Desert Cab Company** (© 702/386-9102), **Whittlesea Blue Cab** (© 702/384-6111), and **Yellow/Checker Cab/Star Company** (© 702/873-2000).

BY MONORAIL

The first leg of a high-tech monorail that will eventually become a citywide mass-transit system opened in 2004, offering riders their first and best shot of getting from one end of the Strip to the other with a minimum of frustration and expense. The 4-mile route runs from the MGM Grand at the southern end of the Strip to the Sahara at the northern end, with stops at Paris/Bally's, The Flamingo, Imperial Palace/Harrah's, the Las Vegas Convention Center, and the Las Vegas Hilton along the way.

These spiffy new trains can accommodate over 200 passengers (standing and sitting) and make the end-to-end run in about 15 minutes. They operate 7 days a week from 8am until midnight.

Fares are $3 (!!!) for a one-way ride (whether you ride from one end to the other or just to the next station), but discounts are available for round-trips and multi-ride/day passes.

Despite a very rocky start that involved a 4-month shutdown while they worked out some kinks like wheels and driveshafts falling off the trains, things seem to be running smoothly now. But don't be looking for previously announced extensions to the airport or Downtown anytime soon.

BY PUBLIC TRANSPORTATION

The no. 301 bus operated by **Citizens Area Transit** (© 702/CAT-RIDE) plies a route between the Downtown Transportation Center (at Casino Center Blvd. and Stewart Ave.) and a few miles beyond the southern end of the Strip. The fare is $2 for adults, 60¢ for seniors 62 and older and children 5 to 17, and free for those under 5. CAT buses run 24 hours a day and are wheelchair-accessible. Exact change is required, but dollar bills are accepted.

Or you can hop aboard a classic streetcar replica run by **Las Vegas Strip Trolley** (© 702/382-1404). These old-fashioned, dark-green vehicles have interior oak paneling and are comfortably air-conditioned. Like the buses, they run northward from Hacienda Avenue, stopping at all major hotels en route to the Sahara, and then loop back from the Las Vegas Hilton. They do not, however, go to the Stratosphere Casino Hotel & Tower or Downtown. Trolleys run about every 15 minutes daily between 9:30am and 2am. The fare is $1.75 (free for children under age 5), and exact change is required.

There are also a number of free transportation services, courtesy of the casinos. A free monorail connects Mandalay Bay with Luxor and Excalibur, and a free tram shuttles between The Mirage and TI at the Mirage. Given how far apart even neighboring hotels can be, thanks to their size, and how they seem even farther apart on really hot days, these are blessed additions—and the more tourists who take them, the less traffic there might be on the Strip.

FAST FACTS: Las Vegas

Area Codes The area code for Las Vegas is **702.**

Babysitters Contact **Around the Clock Child Care** (© **800/798-6768** or 702/365-1040). In business since 1987, this reputable company clears its sitters with the health department, the sheriff, and the FBI, and carefully screens references. Charges are $54 for 4 hours for one or two children, $12 for each additional hour, with surcharges for additional children and on holidays. Sitters are on call 7 days a week, 24 hours a day, and they will come to your hotel. Call at least 3 hours in advance.

Banks Banks are generally open from 9 or 10am to 5 and sometimes 6pm, and most have Saturday hours. ATMs are plentiful all around town. See also "Cash & Credit" below.

Car Rentals See "Renting a Car" under "Getting Around," earlier in this chapter.

Cash & Credit It's extremely easy, too easy, to obtain cash in Las Vegas. Most casino cashiers will cash personal checks and can exchange foreign currency, and just about every casino has a machine that will provide cash on a wide variety of credit cards.

Conventions Las Vegas is one of America's top convention destinations. Much of the action takes place at the **Las Vegas Convention Center,** 3150 Paradise Rd., Las Vegas, NV 89109 (© **702/892-7575**), which is the largest single-level convention center in the world. Its 1.3 million square feet include 89 meeting rooms. And this immense facility is augmented by the **Cashman Field Center,** 850 Las Vegas Blvd. N., Las Vegas, NV 89101 (© **702/386-7100**). Under the same auspices, Cashman provides another 98,100 square feet of convention space. Additionally, there are massive convention facilities at many of the big hotels, including the MGM Grand, The Mirage, Mandalay Bay, The Venetian, and more.

Dentists & Doctors Hotels usually have lists of dentists and doctors, should you need one. In addition, they are listed in the Centel Yellow Pages. See also "Hospitals," below.

For dentist referrals, you can also call the **Southern Nevada Dental Society** (© **702/733-8700**) weekdays from 9am to noon and 1 to 5pm; when the office is closed, a recording will tell you who to call for emergency service.

For physician referrals, call the **Desert Springs Hospital** (© **702/388-4888**). Hours are Monday to Friday from 8am to 8pm, and Saturday from 9am to 3pm.

Emergencies Dial © **911** to contact the police or fire department or to call an ambulance.

Highway Conditions For recorded information, call © **702/486-3116.** You can also tune in 970 AM for traffic news or 1610 AM for highway reports.

Hospitals Emergency services are available 24 hours a day at **University Medical Center,** 1800 W. Charleston Blvd., at Shadow Lane (© **702/383-2000**); the emergency-room entrance is on the corner of Hastings and Rose streets. **Sunrise Hospital and Medical Center,** 3186 Maryland Pkwy., between Desert Inn Road and Sahara Avenue (© **702/731-8080**), also has a 24-hour emergency room.

For more minor problems, if you are on the Strip, the Imperial Palace has a 24-hour urgent-care facility, the **Nevada Resort Medical Center,** an independently run facility on the eighth floor, with doctors and X-ray machines. It's located at 3535 Las Vegas Blvd. S., between Sands and Flamingo streets (© **702/ 893-6767**).

Hot Lines Emergency hot lines include the **Rape Crisis Center** (© **702/366-1640**), **Suicide Prevention** (© **702/731-2990**), and **Poison Emergencies** (© **800/ 446-6179**).

Liquor & Gambling Laws You must be 21 to drink or gamble; proof of age is required and often requested at bars, nightclubs, and restaurants, so it's always a good idea to bring ID when you go out, especially if you look young. There are no closing hours in Las Vegas for the sale or consumption of alcohol, even on Sunday. Don't even think about driving while you're under the influence, or having an open container of alcohol in your car. Beer, wine, and liquor are all sold in all kinds of stores pretty much around the clock; trust us, you won't have a hard time finding a drink in this town. And even though people still do it with abandon, a law was passed recently forbidding open containers on the streets, so you shouldn't be carrying that giant plastic Eiffel Tower full of strawberry margarita from Paris over to Bellagio.

Lost & Found Be sure to tell all of your credit card companies the minute you discover your wallet has been lost or stolen and file a report at the nearest police precinct. Your credit card company or insurer may require a police report number or record of the loss. Most credit card companies have an emergency toll-free number to call if your card is lost or stolen; they may be able to wire you a cash advance immediately or deliver an emergency credit card in a day or two. **Visa**'s U.S. emergency number is ✆ **800/847-2911** or 410/581-9994. **American Express** cardholders and traveler's check holders should call ✆ **800/221-7282**. **MasterCard** holders should call ✆ **800/307-7309** or 636/722-7111. For other credit cards, call the toll-free number directory at ✆ **800/555-1212**.

If you need emergency cash over the weekend when all banks and American Express offices are closed, you can have money wired to you via **Western Union** (✆ **800/325-6000**; www.westernunion.com).

Identity theft and fraud are potential complications of losing your wallet, especially if you've lost your driver's license along with your cash and credit cards. Notify the major credit-reporting bureaus immediately; placing a fraud alert on your records may protect you against liability for criminal activity. The three major U.S. credit-reporting agencies are **Equifax** (✆ **800/766-0008**; www.equifax.com), **Experian** (✆ **888/397-3742**; www.experian.com), and **TransUnion** (✆ **800/680-7289**; www.transunion.com). Finally, if you've lost all forms of photo ID, call your airline and explain the situation: They might allow you to board the plane if you have a copy of your passport or birth certificate and a copy of the police report you've filed.

Newspapers & Periodicals There are two Las Vegas dailies: the *Las Vegas Review Journal* and the *Las Vegas Sun.* The *Review Journal*'s Friday edition has a helpful "Weekend" section with a comprehensive guide to shows and buffets. There are two free alternative papers, with club listings and many unbiased restaurant and bar reviews. Both *City Life* and *Las Vegas Weekly* are published weekly. And at every hotel desk, you'll find dozens of free local magazines, such as *Vegas Visitor, What's On in Las Vegas, Showbiz Weekly,* and *Where to Go in Las Vegas,* that are chock-full of helpful information—although probably of the sort that comes from paid advertising.

Parking Free valet parking is one of the great pleasures of Las Vegas and well worth the dollar tip (given when the car is returned) to save walking a city block from the far reaches of a hotel parking lot, particularly when the temperature is over 100°F (38°C). Another summer plus: The valet will turn on your air-conditioning so that you don't have to get into an "oven on wheels."

Pharmacies There's a 24-hour **Walgreens** (which also has 1-hr. photo process-ing) at 3763 Las Vegas Blvd. S. (© **702/739-9638**), almost directly across from the Monte Carlo. **Sav-On** is a large 24-hour drugstore and pharmacy close to the Strip at 1360 E. Flamingo Rd., at Maryland Parkway (© **702/731-5373**). **White Cross Drugs,** 1700 Las Vegas Blvd. S. (© **702/382-1733**), open daily from 7am to 1am, will make pharmacy deliveries to your hotel during the day.

Police For non-emergencies, call © **702/795-3111.** For emergencies, call © **911.**

Post Office The most convenient post office is immediately behind the Stardust hotel at 3100 Industrial Rd., between Sahara Avenue and Spring Mountain Road (© **800/297-5543**). It's open Monday to Friday from 8:30am to 5pm. You can also mail letters and packages at your hotel, and there's a full-service U.S. Post Office in the Forum Shops in Caesars Palace.

Safety In Las Vegas, vast amounts of money are always on display, and crimi-nals find many easy marks. Don't be one of them. At gaming tables and slot machines, men should keep wallets well concealed and out of the reach of pickpockets, and women should keep handbags in plain sight (on laps). If you win a big jackpot, ask the pit boss or slot attendant to cut you a check rather than give you cash—the cash may look nice, but flashing it can attract the wrong kind of attention. Outside casinos, popular spots for pickpockets and thieves are restaurants and outdoor shows, such as the volcano at The Mirage or the fountains at Bellagio. Stay alert. Unless your hotel room has an in-room safe, check your valuables in a safe-deposit box at the front desk.

Show Tickets See chapter 10 for details on obtaining show tickets.

Taxes Clark County hotel room tax is 9%, and in Henderson it's 10%; the sales tax is 7%.

Time Zone Las Vegas is in the Pacific time zone, 3 hours earlier than the East Coast, 2 hours earlier than the Midwest. For exact local time, call © **702/248-4800.**

Veterinarian If Fido or Fluffy gets sick while traveling, go to the **West Flamingo Animal Hospital,** 5445 W. Flamingo Rd., near Decatur Boulevard (© **702/876-2111**). They're open 24 hours and they take Discover, MasterCard, and Visa, and have an ATM.

Weather See "When to Go" in chapter 2. For local weather information, call © **702/248-4800.** The radio station 970 FM does weather reports.

Weddings Las Vegas is one of the easiest places in the world to tie the knot. There's no blood test or waiting period, the ceremony and license are inex-pensive, chapels are open around the clock, and your honeymoon destination is right at hand. More than 101,000 marriages are performed here each year. Get a license Downtown at the **Clark County Marriage License Bureau,** 200 S. 3rd St., at Bridger Avenue (© **702/455-4415**), which is open Monday to Thurs-day from 8am to midnight, and from 8am Friday through midnight Sunday. On legal holidays, they're open 24 hours. The cost of a marriage license is $55; the cost of the ceremony varies depending on where you go to have it done. See "Getting Married" in chapter 7 for details on the local wedding chapels.

5

Where to Stay

If there's one thing Vegas has, it's hotels. Big hotels. And lots of them. You'll find the 9 of the 10 largest hotels in the United States—8 of the top 10 in the world—right here. And you'll find a whole lot of rooms: 135,000 rooms, to be exact—or at least exact as of this writing. Every 5 minutes, or so it seems, someone is putting up a new giant hotel, or adding another 1,000 rooms to an existing one. So finding a place to stay in Vegas should be the least of your worries.

Or should it?

When a convention, a fight, or some other big event is happening—and these things are always happening—darn near all of those 135,000 rooms are going to be sold out. (Over the course of a regular year—one not affected by the Sept 11, 2001, terrorist attacks—the occupancy rate for hotel rooms in Las Vegas runs at about 90%.) A last-minute Vegas vacation can turn into a housing nightmare. If possible, plan in advance so that you can have your choice: Ancient Egypt or Ancient Rome? New York or New Orleans? Strip or Downtown? Luxury or economy? Vegas has all that and way too much more.

The bottom line is that with a few, mostly subtle differences, a hotel room is a hotel room is a hotel room. After you factor in location, price, and whether you have a pirate-loving kid, there isn't that much difference between rooms, except for perhaps size and the quality of their surprisingly similar furnishings.

Hotel prices in Vegas are anything but fixed, so you will notice wild price ranges. The same room can routinely go for anywhere from $60 to $250, depending on demand, and even that range is negotiable if it's a slow time (though such times are less and less common, thanks to the influx of conventions). So use our price categories with a grain of salt, and don't rule out a hotel just because it's listed as "Very Expensive"—on any given day, you might get a great deal on a room in a pricey hotel. Just ask.

Yes, if you pay more, you'll probably (but not certainly) get a "nicer" establishment and clientele to match (perhaps not so many loud drunks in the elevators). On the other hand, if a convention is in town, the drunks will be there no matter how upscale the hotel—they'll just be wearing business suits and/or funny hats. And frankly, the big hotels, no matter how fine, have mass-produced rooms; at 3,000 rooms or more, they are the equivalent of '60s tract housing. Consequently, even in the nicest hotels, you can (and probably will) encounter plumbing noises, overhear conversations from other rooms, or be woken by the maids as they knock on the doors next to yours that don't have the DO NOT DISTURB sign up.

1 Coming Attractions

Part of the reason that we patiently tell people they haven't really been to Vegas, even if they have, is because if they haven't been by in the last, oh, week—okay, let's say 2 or 3 years—they might find several surprises awaiting them on the Strip. And if it's been more than a decade, well, forget it. All of the classic old hotels are either gone (Sands, Hacienda) or renovated virtually beyond recognition (Caesars, The Flamingo). In their place rise bigger and better and trendier resort hotels, changing the landscape and altering the welcome that Vegas visitors receive.

The new era of Vegas hotels was ushered in by The Mirage, and since then, everyone has been trying to up the ante. The year 1997 began with the opening of New York–New York, which set yet another level of stupendous excess that remained unmatched for, oh, at least 18 months.

The fall of 1998 saw the official beginning of the new era of Vegas luxury resorts (many with themes), with the opening of the opulent Bellagio, followed by Mandalay Bay and Four Seasons. And then these took a back seat (sort of) to The Venetian, which combines the jaw-dropping detail and extravagance of New York–New York (complete with canals and gondolas) with the luxury of Bellagio. Could anything top it? Possibly—hot on its heels was Paris, themed as you can imagine, and just a few months later, the new and improved Aladdin, with its desert-fantasy decor.

The last couple of years have been less about new stuff and more about old stuff getting bigger and/or better. Sure, Caesars opened its Roman Colosseum replica, built just to house Céline Dion's new show, but other than that, no grand new hotels or major expansions arrived, unless you count (and we sure do) the arrival of a true luxury resort, the Ritz-Carlton, Lake Las Vegas, over in nearby Henderson. One old hotel, The Maxim, was reborn as a swank Westin complete with their trademark "Heavenly Beds." The rest of the action was all about expansions: The Venetian added 1,000 rooms, a new pool, a fancy restaurant, and more in their new Venezia Tower; Mandalay Bay added over 1,000 rooms and other goodies in a facility they call THEhotel; Bellagio joined the fray with over 900 new rooms and a swank new spa in a new tower; and Caesars Palace added a new 700-room tower to their empire. Most notably, of course, 2005 brought the eagerly awaited Wynn Las Vegas, the latest hotel concept from Steve Wynn, the man behind Mirage Corp., at a mere cost of $2.7 billion. But that won't be the end of it, not hardly. After all, Wynn's already at work on an addition to his brand new hotel, the Encore, set to debut in 2008. Sometime during 2006, Planet Hollywood will have completely revamped the old-turned-new-turned-bankrupt Aladdin into something less Eastern-evocative and more Hollywood memorabilia–starstruck. The creaky old San Remo is going pneumatic, as it becomes a Hooters hotel and casino. (No, really.) The Palms is adding a new tower. Most intriguingly (well, apart from that Hooters, but that's different), a new Station hotel is going up out at Red Rocks. Looking farther down the road, 2007 should bring yet another Venetian expansion, the Palazzo, plus the new Conrad Majestic hotel, on the site of the old La Concha, just south of The Riviera. 2008 is supposed to bring the ambitious new Project CityCenter from the MGM MIRAGE group, on the site of the Boardwalk hotel. Somewhere in here, Donald Trump is going to enter the Vegas market with his hotel/condo combo near the Frontier, while the group behind the Turnberry condos has announced plans for a $1.5-billion 4,000-room hotel/condo near The Riviera, to be called the Fountainbleau after the venerable Miami hotel. Speaking of condos, that seems to be the property development trend right now, so if you haven't been to Vegas in a while, and you wonder what that, and that over there, and also that, really big tall tower is, it's more than likely a condo building. Finally, there remain possible wrecking balls in store for the Stardust, the Tropicana, and The Riviera. Of course, another economic downturn of even the slightest size could prevent all of it. Stay tuned.

2 Three Questions to Ask Before You Book a Room

WHERE SHOULD I STAY?

Your two main choices for location are the Strip and Downtown. The Strip, home to many of the most dazzling hotels and casinos in Vegas, is undeniably the winner, especially for first-timers, if only because of the sheer, overwhelming force of its "Vegasness." On the other hand, it is crowded, confining, and strangely claustrophobic. We say "strangely claustrophobic" because the hotels only *look* close together: In reality, they are situated on large properties, and it's a long (and often very hot or very cold) walk from one place to the next.

Contrast that with Downtown, which is nowhere near as striking, but more easily navigated on foot. Within 5 minutes you can reach about 17 different casinos. The Fremont Street upgrade and the Neonopolis entertainment-and-shopping complex have turned a rapidly declining area into a very pleasant place to be, and the crowds reflect that: They seem nicer and more relaxed, and a calmer atmosphere pervades. Hotels certainly aren't state-of-the-art down there, but the rooms at many are not just clean and acceptable, but rather pleasant. The establishments' smaller size often means friendlier, faster service than at the big 'uns uptown, and you often can't beat the rates. Since it's only a 5-minute ride by car between Downtown and Strip hotels (the Convention Center is more or less in between), there's no such thing as a bad location if you have access to a car. If money is no object, a $10 to $15 cab ride separates the Strip from Downtown.

For those of you depending on public transportation: While the bus ride between Downtown and the Strip is short in distance, it can be long in time if you get stuck in traffic. You should also be aware that the buses become quite crowded once they reach the Strip and may bypass a bus stop if no one signals to get out and the driver does not wish to take on more passengers. Without a car, your ease of movement between different areas of town is limited.

Frankly, for first-timers, there probably isn't any point to staying anywhere but the Strip—you're going to spend most (if not all) of your time there anyway. For future visits, however, we'd strongly advise you to consider Downtown.

But the Strip vs. Downtown location isn't the end of the debate; there is also the issue of where to stay on the Strip. Staying on the **South Strip** end means an easy trip (sometimes in the air-conditioned comfort of covered walkways or monorail) to Mandalay Bay, MGM Grand, New York–New York, Tropicana, Luxor, and Excalibur—all virtually on one corner. **Mid-Strip** has Caesars, The Mirage, Bellagio, TI at the Mirage (formerly Treasure Island), Paris, The Venetian, Bally's, The Flamingo, Harrah's, and so forth. The **North Strip** gets you Wynn Las Vegas, The Riviera, Sahara, Stardust, and Circus Circus, though with a bit more of a walk between them. For this reason, if mobility is a problem and you want to see more than just your own hotel casino, the South and Mid-Strip locations are probably the best bets.

Reservations Services

If you get harried when you have to haggle, use a free service offered by **Reservations Plus,** 2275 A Renaissance Dr., Las Vegas, NV 89119 (© **800/805-9528;** fax 702/795-3999). They'll find you a hotel room in your price range that meets your specific requirements. Because they book rooms in volume, they are able to get discounted rates. Not only can they book rooms, but they can arrange packages (including meals, transportation, tours, show tickets, car rentals, and other features) and group rates.

The **Las Vegas Convention and Visitors Authority** also runs a room-reservations hot line (© **877/VISIT-LV**) that can be helpful. They can apprise you of room availability, quote rates, contact a hotel for you, and tell you when major conventions will be in town.

Other reputable online reservations services that book rooms in Las Vegas are listed in "Planning Your Trip Online" in chapter 2.

A couple words of warning: Make sure they don't try to book you into a hotel you've never heard of. Try to stick with the hotels listed in this book. Always get your information in writing and then make some phone calls just to confirm that you really have the reservations that they say they've made for you.

WHAT AM I LOOKING FOR IN A HOTEL?

If gambling is not your priority, what are you doing in Vegas? Just kidding. But not 100% kidding. Vegas's new identity as a luxury resort, and very adult, destination means there are several hotels that promise to offer you all sorts of alternatives to gambling—lush pool areas, fabulous spas, incredible restaurants, lavish shopping. But if you look closely, much of this is Vegas bait and switch; the pools are often chilly (and often partially closed during nonsummer months), and it will be years before there is more foliage than concrete in these newly landscaped environments. The spas cost extra (sometimes a whole lot extra), the best restaurants are rarely cheap, and the stores are often the kinds of places where average mortals can't even afford the oxygen. So what does that leave you with? Why, that's right—gambling.

The other problem with these self-proclaimed luxury hotels is their size. True luxury hotels do not have 3,000 rooms—they have a couple of hundred, at best, because you simply can't provide first-class service and Egyptian-cotton sheets in mass quantity. But while Wynn, Bellagio, The Venetian, and, to a lesser extent, Mandalay Bay have done their best to offer sterling service and to make their rooms more attractive and luxurious than those at other Vegas hotels, there's only so much that any place that big can do. Don't get us wrong—these places are absolutely several steps up in quality from other large hotels, and compared to them, even the better older hotels really look shabby. But they are still sprawling, frequently noisy complexes.

Having said that, there is a new trend in Vegas; many of the big hotels have put up new towers or additions that function as virtually separate hotels. This began with the Four Seasons, which occupies the top floors of Mandalay Bay and has its own separate entrance. Now Mandalay Bay has added the sterling THEhotel, while The Venetian has a new tower. Each has its own check-in area and functions like a separate hotel entity. You gain some quiet (there are no casinos in these venues); in the case of THE-hotel, considerable style; and, overall, at least the illusion of better service (and probably some reality of it, too, since there are fewer rooms under the special monikers). Classier grown-ups, or well-heeled families, should make these new additions first on their list.

Sadly, it's relatively easy for both you and us to make a mistake about a hotel; either of us may experience a particular room or two in a 1,000-plus-room hotel, and from there conclude that a place is nicer than it is or more of a dump than it is. Mainte-nance, even in the best of hotels, can sometimes be running a bit behind, so if there is something wrong with your room, don't hesitate to ask for another. Of course, if it's one of those busy weekends, there may not be another room to be had, but at least this way you've registered a complaint, perhaps letting a busy hotel know that a cer-tain room needs attention. And who knows? If you are gracious and persistent enough, you may be rewarded with a deal for some future stay.

If you want a true luxury-resort hotel, there are only two options: On the Strip it's the Four Seasons, and off, way off, in nearby Henderson, it's the Ritz-Carlton. Both offer, in addition to that same service and level of comfort only found at a smaller hotel, those extra goodies that pile on the hidden charges at other hotels—health club, poolside cabanas, and so on—as part of the total package, meaning that their slightly higher prices may be more of a bargain than you'd think.

Still, if you want peace and quiet and don't land in the tax bracket that Four Sea-sons/Ritz caters to, there are other, less high-profile hotels without a casino. (And there is also the option of staying in either the casino-free new Venetian addition or THEhotel at Mandalay Bay, both of which charge higher prices than their home base but might be running an affordable special.) Make certain the hotel has a pool, how-ever, especially if you need some recreation. There is nothing as boring as a noncasino, non-pool Vegas hotel—particularly if you have kids.

Casino hotels, by the way, are not always a nice place for children. It used to be that the casino was a separate section in the hotel and children were not allowed inside (we have fond memories of standing just outside the casino line, watching our dads put quarters in a slot machine "for us"). But in almost all the new hotels, you have to walk through the casino to get anywhere—the lobby, the restaurants, the out-side world. This makes sense from the hotel's point of view; it gives you many oppor-tunities to stop and drop a quarter or $10 into a slot. But this often long, crowded trek gets wearying for adults—and it's far worse for kids. The rule is that kids can walk through the casinos, but they can't stop, even to gawk for a second at someone

---

Tips Who Kept the Kids Out?

Some hotels—notably Bellagio, which started the practice—ban children who are not staying on-site from stepping foot on the hotel premises. Childfree adults love the ban, but families who travel to Vegas (can we say yet again that this is not a family destination?) may be seriously inconvenienced by it. The pol-icy doesn't appear to be uniformly enforced (hotels don't want to offend par-ents with plenty of dough to gamble, after all), but we've seen families and teenagers get turned away from a hotel because they couldn't produce a room key. If you're traveling with your kids, or want to be free of someone else's, your best bet is to call your chosen hotel and ask what its policy is.

hitting a jackpot nearby. The casino officials who will immediately hustle the child away are just doing their job, but, boy, it's annoying.

So, take this (and what a hotel offers that kids might like) into consideration when booking a room. Again, please note that those gorgeous hotel pools are often cold (and again, sometimes closed altogether) and not very deep. They look like places you would want to linger, but often (from a kid's point of view) they are not. Plus, the pools close early. Hotels want you inside gambling, not outside swimming.

Ultimately, though, if it's a busy time, you'll have to nab any room you can, especially if you get a price you like. How much time are you going to spend in the room, anyway?

WHAT WILL I HAVE TO PAY?

The rack rate is the maximum rate that a hotel charges for a room. It's the rate you'd get if you walked in off the street and asked for a room for the night. Hardly anybody pays these prices, however, especially in Vegas, where prices fluctuate wildly with demand and there are many ways around rack rates. Here are some tips for landing a low rate:

- **Don't be afraid to bargain.** Get in the habit of asking for a lower price than the first one quoted. Always ask politely whether a less expensive room is available than the first one mentioned, or whether any special rates apply to you. If you belong to one of the players clubs at a hotel casino, you may be able to secure a better deal on a hotel room. Of course, you will also be expected to spend a certain amount of time, and money, gambling there. See below for more details on players clubs.
- **Rely on a qualified professional.** Certain hotels give travel agents discounts in exchange for steering business their way, so if you're shy about bargaining, an agent may be better equipped to negotiate discounts for you.
- **Dial direct.** When booking a room in a chain hotel (Courtyard by Marriott, for example), call the hotel's local line, as well as the toll-free number, and see where you get the best deal. A hotel makes nothing on a room that stays empty. The clerk who runs the place is more likely to know about vacancies and will often grant deep discounts in order to fill up.
- **Remember the law of supply and demand.** Las Vegas hotels are most crowded and therefore most expensive on weekends. So the best deals are offered midweek, when prices can drop dramatically. If possible, go then. You can also call the **Las Vegas Convention and Visitors Authority** (© 877/VISIT-LV) to find out if an important convention is scheduled at the time of your planned visit; if so, you might want to change your date. Some of the most popular conventions are listed under "When to Go" in chapter 2. Remember also that planning your vacation just a week before or after official peak season can mean big savings.
- **Look into group or long-stay discounts.** If you come as part of a large group, you should be able to negotiate a bargain, since the hotel can then guarantee occupancy in a number of rooms. Likewise, when you're planning a long stay in town (usually from 5 days to a week), you'll usually qualify for a discount.
- **Avoid excess phone charges.** We can't stress this enough. Virtually every hotel in Vegas charges like crazy for phone calls. At best, it will be $1 for a local call, and sky-high prices for long distance (a 7-min. call to California recently set us back $35). At worst, it's all that plus an additional charge—as much as 30¢ a minute—for all local calls lasting more than 30 minutes. This is particularly onerous if you are using a laptop with a dial-up Internet connection and stay online for any length of time.

- **Beware of hidden extras.** Almost all of the major hotels (Four Seasons is one notable exception) charge extra for things that are always free in other destinations, like health-club privileges. Expect to pay anywhere from $15 to $30 to use almost any hotel spa/health club. (We've noted these charges in the listings that follow so that you won't be taken by surprise.)
- **Watch for coupons and advertised discounts.** Scan ads in your local Sunday travel section, an excellent source for up-to-the-minute hotel deals. *The Fun Book,* available from the Las Vegas Convention and Visitors Authority (see above), offers some discounts on lodging.
- **Consider a suite.** If you are traveling with your family or another couple, you can pack more people into a suite (which usually comes with a sofa bed) and thereby reduce your per-person rate. Remember that some places charge for extra guests and some don't.
- **Investigate reservations services.** These outfits usually work as consolidators, buying up or reserving rooms in bulk and then dealing them out to customers at a profit. Most of them offer online reservations services as well. See the box on "Reservations Services," above, for outfits that operate in the Las Vegas area.

As far as prices go, keep in mind that our price categories are rough guidelines, at best. If you see a hotel that appeals to you, even if it seems out of your price range, give them a call anyway. They might be having a special, a slow week, or some kind of promotion, or they may just like the sound of your voice (we have no other explanation for it). You could end up with a hotel in the "expensive" category offering you a room for $35 a night. (Even Bellagio, which insists they will never fall below a certain three-figure price, has been quietly offering rooms for as low as $89 on certain nights). Since it's a toll-free call, it's worth a try.

Consider also, even if you think from the outset that this is your one and only trip to Vegas, joining a hotel players club—or possibly every hotel's players club. This costs you nothing, and players/members often get nifty offers in the mail for heavily discounted, and occasionally even free, rooms (plus meals, shows, and so on). Players clubs reward you with freebies and discounts when you play in their casinos, regardless of whether you win. Even as one luxury hotel was firmly insisting their prices would never, ever fall below about $149 per night, players club members were receiving invitations to stay for $89. How much you have to play to get these deals varies, but if you are going to gamble anyway, why not make it work more to your advantage? You can sign up online, which will get you e-mail-only offers. You can do this on almost every hotel's website, and it's worth it, though it does mean spontaneous Vegas vacations, to take advantage of the times the offers are valid.

We've classified all our hotel recommendations based on the average rack rate that you can expect to be quoted for a double room on an average night (not when the Consumer Electronics Show is in town, and not on New Year's Eve). Expect to pay a little less than this if you stay only Sunday to Thursday, and a little more than this if you stay Friday and Saturday.

Of course, you can expect significant savings if you book a money-saving package deal, like those described in chapter 2. And on any given night when business is slow, you might be able to stay at a "very expensive" hotel for a "moderate" price.

Note: All the casinos for the major hotels on the Strip and Downtown (and a few other ones) are reviewed in chapter 8.

3 South Strip

VERY EXPENSIVE

Four Seasons Hotel Las Vegas ★★★ *(Kids)*   Various mammoth Vegas hotels attempt to position themselves as luxury resorts, insisting that service and fine cotton sheets can be done on a mass scale. But there is only one true luxury resort—in some people's eyes, *the* luxury resort—in town (see later in this chapter for two more luxury options in Henderson), located on the top five floors of Mandalay Bay, though in many ways, the Four Seasons is light-years away. A separate driveway and portico entrance, plus an entire registration area, set you up immediately. This is one fancy hotel in town where you are not greeted, even at a distance, with the clash and clang of slots, and the general hubbub that is the soundtrack to Vegas.

Inside the hotel, all is calm and quiet. But it's really the best of both worlds—all you have to do is walk through a door and instantly you are in Mandalay Bay, with access to a casino, nightlife, and, yes, general hubbub. The difference is quite shocking, and frankly, once you've experienced Vegas this way, it's kind of hard to go back to the constant sensory overload. So let's scurry quickly back to the womblike comfort of Four Seasons.

The rooms don't look like much at first—slightly bland but in good taste—but when you sink down into the furniture, you appreciate the fine quality. Here at last is a Vegas hotel where they really don't care if you ever leave your room, so the beds have feather pillows and down comforters, robes are plush, and amenities (such as pricey L'Occitane products in the lush bathrooms, safes, irons, voice mail, hair dryers, and VCRs) are really, really nice. Since Four Seasons has the southernmost location on the Strip, its Strip-view rooms (the most expensive units) give you the whole incredible panorama.

Service is superb (if they say 20 min. for room service, you can expect your food in 19½ min.). Your needs are anticipated so quickly that you're tempted to sink to the floor in the lobby because you know someone will have a chair under your rear before you land. Children are encouraged and spoiled with welcome gifts of toys and goodies, rooms are childproofed in advance, and the list of comforts available for the asking is a yard long. Once you factor in all the freebies (gym/spa access, pool cabanas, various other amenities), not to mention the service and the blessed peace, the difference in price between Four Seasons and Bellagio (with all its hidden charges) is nothing.

3960 Las Vegas Blvd. S., Las Vegas, NV 89119. ✆ **877/632-5000** or 702/632-5000. Fax 702/632-5195. www.four seasons.com. 424 units. $200–$500 double; from $400 suite. Extra person $30. Children 17 and under stay free in parent's room. AE, DC, DISC, MC, V. Free self- and valet parking. **Amenities:** 2 restaurants; heated outdoor pool; elegant health club (free to guests) and spa; concierge; car-rental desk; courtesy car; full 24-hr. business center w/faxing, delivery, and secretarial service; 24-hr. room service; in-room massage; babysitting; overnight laundry service and dry cleaning; executive-level rooms. *In room:* A/C, TV w/pay movies, dataport, minibar, fridge, coffeemaker, hair dryer, iron/ironing board, safe, high-speed Internet access (for a fee).

EXPENSIVE

Aladdin Resort & Casino ★   *Note:* The beleaguered and bankrupt Aladdin has been bought by Planet Hollywood, which, as of now, intends to rename, remodel, and restyle the property. We still don't exactly know what this will entail, since details haven't been forthcoming, but this process should be complete by summer 2006 (though we've heard other, failed deadlines before already), so don't be confused if there is a big blue globe out front, a new name, and lots of cast-off clothes and props from various Hollywood movies enshrined inside.

It's a bit of a pity because the new Aladdin, rising on the ashes of the old Vegas stalwart, which was desperately out-of-date, is a handsome building both inside and out. The theme is generic Middle East—you know, the sort that pretends there is no significant difference between Egypt, Morocco, and Turkey, which may be news to Egyptians, Moroccans, and Turks—best characterized by one observer as "the Sahara with a billion dollars thrown at it." Details that indicate considerable thought went into the design are everywhere—what other casino has actual tile work (clearly Moroccan in origin) throughout? But all that work came at a price, hence a $700-million bankruptcy—the largest in Nevada history.

That petty detail aside, this is already what a sexy, but distinctly Vegas, hotel ought to be: a little bit of kitsch, a little bit of class, and all of it playful. And we hope that the new owners will concentrate on maintaining and building on these aspects. The rooms are not distinctive, but they are pleasing (except for the beds—the money must have run out before buying the mattresses, which are some of the most uncomfortable we've slept on), and the bathrooms can be quite large, with a deep tub and separate glass shower, plus little Aladdin-lamp-shaped faucets and exotic spice-scented amenities. Another plus is that the hotel is constructed so that guests need to see little of the casino (a plus for you, a drag for needed gambling revenue, and likely one of the first things the new owners will change), while the pool area is decent but nothing spectacular.

And then there is the **Desert Passage** shopping area (p. 256), another one to rival the capitalist ventures over at Caesars and The Venetian. This has also been sold to a new owner (separate from Planet Hollywood), so the Arabian Nights theme, all Casbah this and Sultan that, may not stay, but the plan for now is to keep this theme. As is, it's impressive, to be sure, and better still for the live-action touches such as jugglers, acrobats, and belly dancers who pop up regularly to entertain shoppers and add that hectic souk feel to the experience. Inside the Desert Passage are a number of terrific restaurants, including a branch of New Orleans's venerated **Commander's Palace** (p. 136). The hotel also has its own arena, the **Center for the Performing Arts,** which is attracting big names back to Vegas. Finally, there is the **Elemis spa** ⟨★★★⟩, maybe aesthetically our hands-down local favorite. The owners (who also run Elemis in London) sent their designers to Morocco for ideas, and it shows in this Medina-flavored facility; just looking at it is pampering, and that's before one of their attentive staff puts you in a wrap and "dry float" (a womblike water bed–style cradle). No word whether the new owners will revamp this facility like the rest of the property.

All in all, the place teeters on the brink of a higher rating, and all we can hope is that the new owners help push it over the hump rather than in the other direction. The place deserves it.

3667 Las Vegas Blvd. S., Las Vegas, NV 89109. ℂ **877/333-WISH** (9474) or 702/785-5555. Fax 702/785-5558. www.aladdincasino.com. 2,567 units. $99 and up double. Extra person $30; no discount for children. AE, DC, DISC, MC, V. Free self- and valet parking. **Amenities:** Casino; performing-arts center; showroom; 19 restaurants; 7 bars/lounges; 2 outdoor pools; health club and spa; Jacuzzi; sauna; concierge; tour desk; car-rental desk; business center; shopping arcade; 24-hr. room service; in-room massage; babysitting; laundry service; dry cleaning; nonsmoking rooms; executive-level rooms. *In room:* A/C, TV w/pay movies, dataport, hair dryer, iron/ironing board, safe, high-speed Internet access (for a fee).

Mandalay Bay ⟨★★⟩ Mandalay Bay is one of our favorite hotels. Why? Well, we love that the lobby (impossibly high ceilings, calm, gleaming with marble, and housing a

Monorail

Excalibur **5**
Four Seasons Hotel Las Vegas **8**
Luxor Las Vegas **7**
Mandalay Bay **8**
MGM Grand Hotel & Casino **4**
Monte Carlo Resort & Casino **2**

New York–New York
  Hotel & Casino **8**
Planet Hollywood **1**
THEhotel **8**
Tropicana Resort & Casino **6**

large aquarium) and the other public areas really do make this seem more like an actual resort hotel than just a Vegas version of one. You don't have to walk through the casino to get to any of these public areas or the guest-room elevators, the pool area is spiffy, and the whole complex is marginally less confusing and certainly less overwhelming than some of the neighboring behemoths.

We wouldn't say it really evokes colonial Southeast Asia—oh, maybe around the edges, if you squint, thanks to the odd bit of foliage or Balinese carving. This may well keep out the gawkers, who are looking for bigger visual thrills, but we find a place whose theme doesn't bop you over the head refreshing.

The rooms are among the most desirable on the Strip (king rooms are more attractive than doubles), spacious and subdued in decor. Tropical influence seems to be limited to faux leopard-skin chairs by the worktables, and plantation shutter doors to closets and the bathroom (unfortunately, the bathroom's shutter doors seem to not entirely join together, leaving a gap of varying size). King-size beds have large, carved headboard posts and firm mattresses. The bathrooms are the crowning glory—probably the best on the Strip—they're downright large, with impressive, slightly sunken tubs; glassed-in showers; double sinks; and separate water closets, plus fab amenities and lots of them. (Bathrobes are available on request.)

Locals' Hotels

No, not hotels where locals stay—they have that already, after all—but so-called because it's here that locals themselves often come to eat and gamble. Why? Because these places are cheap. The way Vegas used to be. See, an increasing frustration for the Vegas visitor, still under the impression that Vegas is a vacation bargain, is hotel prices, particularly those on the Strip, most of which have long left "bargain" behind. Where once rooms went for a couple of sawbucks, now rates on weekends frequently break the $200-a-night barrier. The solution is simple; give up that Strip location, and suddenly, there is a host of budget-minded options available to you, completely satisfying casino-hotels, that may not have the luxury appointments of the big Strip palaces but also don't come with the luxury price tags.

Topping the list of these so-called Locals' Hotels are those managed by the Station Casinos chain. These folks are the kings of the neighborhood joints, snapping up worn properties and turning them into nice and gratifyingly cheap accommodations. All of the following hotels are admittedly located away from the main tourist areas, but if you have a car at your disposal, you can save yourself a great deal of money by being flexible with your location. None of them is more than 20 minutes from the Strip, while several offer free shuttles to other sister properties. Most of these properties offer a variety of family-friendly entertainment—bowling alleys, multi-screen movie theaters, and more.

On the southeast side of town there are three Station Casinos properties. **Sunset Station** ⍟⍟, 1301 W. Sunset Rd., Henderson (⌖ **702/547-7777**; www.sunsetstation.com), is the newest and probably the nicest. Rooms are simple but have all of the amenities you are likely to need, such as irons and boards, high-speed Internet access (for a fee), pay-per-view movies, room service, and so on. Sure, the bathrooms may not be bigger than your apartment, and the beds may not be as plush, but if all you need is a nice room for a moderate amount of money, this is a fine option. On-site you'll find more than a dozen restaurants including a Hooters, a new (as of 2005) bowling alley, movie theaters, bars, lounges, a nightclub, an outdoor amphitheater with regular concerts, and a huge casino with much lower gaming limits than the Strip ($5 blackjack tables abound!). Prices at Sunset Station are usually well below $100 a night during the week (we've seen them as low as $59) and usually not too much above $100 on the weekends.

Just down the street a bit is **Fiesta Henderson** ⍟, 777 W. Lake Mead Dr. (⌖ **702/558-7000**; www.fiestacasino.com), a Mexican jungle–themed hotel and casino that has equally basic yet comfortable lodgings, plus plenty of gaming options, a decent and dirt-cheap buffet, other restaurants, bars, and more. Things are even cheaper here, with rooms going for as low as $29 a night during the week. You'll also find **Boulder Station** ⍟, 4111 Boulder Hwy. (⌖ **800/683-7777**; www.boulderstation.com), in this part of town, with more than 300 guest rooms, a 75,000-square-foot casino, movie theaters, a day-care facility, a big video-game arcade, restaurants and bars, and a very nice concert venue called The Railhead. Rates at Boulder Station run in the $75-to-$125-a-night range.

There are a couple of other properties in this area worth knowing about even though they aren't managed by the Station Casinos chain. **Sam's Town** (see p. 120) is listed separately in this chapter, and nearby is **Arizona Charlie's** 🏨, 4575 Boulder Hwy. (© **800/632-4040**; www.arizonacharlies.com), a sister hotel to the Stratosphere, with 300 minisuite-style rooms, a 37,000-square-foot casino, an on-site laundry facility, several restaurants, and a casino lounge. This place is also very inexpensive, with weekday rooms as low as $30 and weekends often as low as $50.

On the north and west side of town are three more Station properties. **Texas Station** 🏨, 2101 Texas Star Lane (© **800/654-8888**; www.texasstation. com), has a 91,000-square-foot casino, 200 rooms that got complete makeovers in 2004, movie theaters, a bowling alley, concert venues, bars, and a number of very fine restaurants, including the recommended and justly popular Austins Steakhouse. You can often get rooms for as low as $50 a night here.

Right across the street is **Fiesta Rancho** 🏨, 2400 N. Rancho Rd. (© **888/899-7770**; www.fiestacasino.com), another Station hotel similar in concept and execution to its sister property mentioned above. In addition to the 100 rooms (all redone in 2005), they have a big casino and a new (as of 2004) indoor, regulation-size ice skating rink, complete with equipment rentals and lessons. Prices go as low as $39 a night. Continue north on Rancho Road and you'll run into **Santa Fe Station** 🏨🏨, 4949 N. Rancho Rd. (© **866/767-7771**; www.santafestationcasinos.com), a place that used to be a really dingy affair until Station Casinos got hold of it. They redid the place from top to bottom, including an unexpectedly spiffy casino (it looks similar to their flagship Green Valley Station), brand-new rooms with stylish furnishings and all the amenities you could reasonably want or need, lots of restaurants and bars, a newly revamped bowling alley, and a new addition in 2005 that includes movie theaters, a showroom, a video game arcade, and a kids' day-care center. All this for rates as low as $35 a night and rarely over $100, even during the busiest times.

Also on the north side of town is **The Cannery** 🏨, 2121 E. Craig Rd., N. Las Vegas (© **866/999-4899**; www.cannerycasinos.com), a '40s patriotic World War II–themed hotel and casino with a couple hundred fine and very inexpensive rooms (usually well under $100 a night), a fun casino, a terrific buffet and a few other restaurants, a really cool indoor/outdoor events center that hosts regular concerts and festivals, plus a major expansion underway (in 2005) that will add still more. Keep all this up, and the Strip might start experiencing some serious competition.

Service overall is pretty good, and those pool-area employees are the tops in Vegas, though there were no security guards at the guest elevators. A monorail system connects the hotel with Luxor and Excalibur, which are located in the heart of the Strip action, and this should more than help you get over any feelings of isolation.

The restaurants in Mandalay Bay feature some of the most innovative interiors in Vegas, each one more whimsical and imaginative than the next. Even if you don't eat at the hotel, drop in and poke around the restaurants. **Aureole,** a branch of Charlie Palmer's renowned New York City restaurant; the **Border Grill; Red Square;** and the **buffet** are reviewed in chapter 6. And then there's **rumjungle,** which features a dramatically skewered all-you-can-eat multicourse Brazilian feast, which you'll enjoy while listening to world-beat drums, surrounded by walls of fire and water and other striking visual features. More casual food can be found at the **House of Blues,** whose Southern delicacies are often quite palate pleasing; HOB is probably the best place in town to see rock bands. Mandalay Bay has a showroom and a separate arena, which was inaugurated by none other than Luciano Pavarotti, and currently offers *Mamma Mia!,* the Broadway musical of ABBA songs. See chapter 10 for details on the hotel's major nightlife offerings. There's also a big, comfortable casino, airier and less claustrophobic than most, plus three bars, often featuring live music (including rock impersonator acts) at night.

There are no fewer than four pools (entering this area is like going to a water park, thanks to upgraded security—*all* guests, regardless of age, must show a room key), including the touted wave pool, which is, unfortunately, a classic example of Vegas bait-and-switch. It can't handle waves of any serious size, but bobbing in the mini-waves is delightful, as is floating happily in the lazy river (tubes are available for rental—we say save some bucks and share a tube with friends, taking turns using it). All in all, this area alone makes this resort a top choice for families, sans, perhaps, the topless swimming area.

The health club is sufficiently stocked to give you a good workout (it should be, as they charge guests $27 per day to use it—$20 for the gym only at THEhotel's facility). The spa area proper—featuring hot and warm pools, plus a cold plunge—is exotically designed, as close to those found in the Turkish spas in Eastern Europe as we've come across, though without the patina (read: weathered decay) of decades or centuries, which can be a good thing. Load up on that rich moisturizer when dressing—it costs $17 a bottle in the store outside the door.

See the separate listing later in this chapter for Mandalay Bay's new THEhotel addition.

3950 Las Vegas Blvd. S. (at Hacienda Ave.), Las Vegas, NV 89119. ℂ 877/632-7000 or 702/632-7000. Fax 702/632-7228. www.mandalaybay.com. 4,427 units. From $99 standard double; from $149 suite; from $149 House of Blues Signature Rooms. Extra person $35; no discount for children. AE, DC, DISC, MC, V. Free self- and valet parking. **Amenities:** Casino; 12,000-seat events center; 1,700-seat performing-arts theater; 22 restaurants; 4 outdoor pools; health club and spa; Jacuzzi; sauna; water sports equipment/rental; concierge; tour desk; business center; 24-hr. room service; in-room massage; babysitting; laundry service; dry cleaning; nonsmoking rooms; executive-level rooms. *In room:* A/C, TV w/pay movies, dataport, hair dryer, iron/ironing board, safe, high-speed Internet access (for a fee) in THEhotel suites only.

MGM Grand Hotel & Casino ⟨⟩⟨⟩

Vegas goes back and forth on its position on whether size does matter, and the MGM Grand is a perfect example of that. When it first opened, the massive glaring green behemoth was the largest hotel in town, with a casino to match—and its owners were mighty proud of it, boasting still further of their family appropriateness, as typified by the theme park that was originally in the back. But times and emphasis change, and with everyone else in Vegas moving away from the pseudo-family-friendly direction to the whole luxury-resort persona, the MGM Grand had no choice but to follow. So if you book here—and you should consider doing so because it's a good bargain, as you will see—thinking your kids are still the property's priority, you should think again. The amusement park in the back is gone, and so is the *Wizard of Oz* theme that originally gave the hotel its identity. Instead, there are striptease shows and a lounge called Tabu. That sort of thing certainly sends a message.

Consider also the place's size. The hotel management now downplays the once touted "hugeness," trying to pretend that the really big casino is actually several medium-big casinos. Whatever. Despite plenty of signage, it is still a lengthy, confusing schlep from anywhere to anywhere. The 80 or so 42-inch TV monitors (apprising registering guests of hotel happenings) in the vast white-marble lobby only add to the chaotic confusion a guest might feel—all the worse if you are toting kids. (At least the lobby is now immediately accessible from the outside world.)

Having said all of that, we've grown very fond of this hotel and we have to admit that they've gone to some efforts to make the ridiculous size work to its—and, thus, your—advantage. On the absolute plus side, we are just knocked out by the Grand Tower rooms. No cookie-cutter, generic, upscale-but-forgettably-bland furniture here; instead, it's a modern-day homage to 1930s modern—all clean, curvy lines; good wood; and a fun palette of colors (pale pastels or wheaty earth tones), plus black-and-white movie-star glamour photos. The results are some of the most distinctive rooms on the Strip—and even if there are a heck of a lot of them, they are the best choice in town in their price range. In addition to redoing all the rooms (naturally, since they are already so likeable), the West Wing rooms got the first go-round of face-lifts. They reflect the influence of hip hotels like the W on Vegas, starting with a new lobby downstairs, while the rooms themselves feature lots of mirrors and use frosted green glass on bathroom and shower doors, with at least two flat-screen TVs (one in the bedroom, one in the bathroom) and liberal use of electronic "gee whiz" moments like lamps that turn on and off if you touch them, while all lights in the rooms are controlled by the insertion of your room key. It's the sort of stylish trend that we are complete suckers for.

The expanded pool area is another victory, with several choices for dunking, including a lazy river (though we wish portions of it weren't closed off for nonsummer months). Overall, guests report that the staff couldn't be more friendly and helpful.

MGM houses a prestigious assemblage of dining rooms, among them **Shibuya, Wolfgang Puck Bar & Grill,** and Emeril Lagasse's **New Orleans Fish House.** These, along with buffet offerings and the **Rainforest Café,** are reviewed in chapter 6.

As befits a behemoth of this size, there's an appropriately gigantic casino. The show is *KA,* a dazzling new offering from Cirque du Soleil show. Plus, there's *La Femme,* a very adult topless show; a hot lounge, **Tabu;** nightclub **Studio 54;** a headliner showroom; and a larger events arena that hosts sporting events and bigger concerts. See chapter 10 for details on all the nightlife options.

The **Lion Habitat** is reviewed on p. 197.

The MGM Grand's spa is a Zen-Asian minimalist wonder, all natural stone and aged wood. The services offered are quite marvelous—for a romantic outing or a Mother's Day treat, try the half-day full services and private room (it's a mere $400, but for what you get, it might be worth the price). The state-of-the-art health club is larger than most, with some serious machines, including ones equipped with fancy computer video monitors (it'll cost you $25 to work up a sweat here most of the day, but you can use the gym facilities only, without the whirlpools and other amenities of the spa, for only $10 after 6pm).

The swimming pool area is a rousing success. The 6½ acres of landscaped grounds feature five pools, including the longest lazy river in town.

3799 Las Vegas Blvd. S. (at Tropicana Ave.), Las Vegas, NV 89109. © 800/929-1111 or 702/891-7777. Fax 702/891-1030. www.mgmgrand.com. 5,034 units. $99 and up standard double; $159 and up suite. Extra person $30. Children under 13 stay free in parent's room. AE, DC, DISC, MC, V. Free self- and valet parking. **Amenities:** Casino; events arena; showroom; cabaret theater; 2 wedding chapels; 15 restaurants; outdoor pool; fitness center and spa; Jacuzzi; sauna; arcade; concierge; tour desk; car-rental desk; business center; 24-hr. room service; in-room massage; babysitting; laundry service; dry cleaning; nonsmoking rooms; executive-level rooms. *In room:* A/C, TV w/pay movies, dataport, hair dryer, iron/ironing board, safe, high-speed Internet access (for a fee).

Monte Carlo Resort & Casino ♔   When it was built, the massive Monte Carlo was the world's seventh-largest hotel. It's now considerably overshadowed by its high-profile, more theme-intensive brethren. Entering it is still nice, as it comes off more as a European casino hotel alternative (before Bellagio usurped that position), replete with Corinthian colonnades, triumphal arches, and big and busy statuary, with an entranceway opening onto a bustling casino. A separate entrance in the rear of the hotel leads to a splendid marble-floored, crystal-chandeliered lobby evocative of a European grand hotel. We love that the guest rooms are accessible without going through the casino, but we hate that said rooms are somewhat dingy and badly in need of a makeover, with dinky bathrooms. The pool area, once the very last word in local pool fun, is now put to shame by better versions (including superior lazy rivers) over at Mandalay Bay and the MGM Grand. It does have a number of child-/family-/budget-friendly restaurants. All in all, just about last on our list of second-choice hotels, but a serious room redo, plus some work on the pool area, could move it up fast.

The **Monte Carlo Pub & Brewery** and **Dragon Noodle Co.** are described in chapter 6. In addition, there is a highly recommended branch of the classic Downtown French restaurant **Andre's** (p. 175). There's also a large and overly ornate casino, plus a lavish showroom that currently hosts the recommended show by magician **Lance Burton** (p. 274).

Monte Carlo's health club and spa are nothing special, but then again, it's $22 for 1 day's access, which is cheaper than the fee at most other hotels.

3770 Las Vegas Blvd. S. (between Flamingo Rd. and Tropicana Ave.), Las Vegas, NV 89109. © 800/311-8999 or 702/730-7777. Fax 702/730-7250. www.montecarlo.com. 3,002 units. $99 and up double; $149 and up suite. Extra person $25; no discount for children. AE, DC, DISC, MC, V. Free self- and valet parking. **Amenities:** Casino; showroom; wedding chapel; 7 restaurants plus a food court; large wave pool w/lazy-river ride and separate kiddie pool; 3 night-lit tennis courts w/full services and equipment rental; health club and spa; Jacuzzi; sauna; watersports equipment/rental; video arcade; concierge; tour desk; business center; 24-hr. room service; in-room massage; babysitting; laundry service; dry cleaning; nonsmoking rooms; executive-level rooms. *In room:* A/C, TV w/pay movies, dataport, hair dryer, iron/ironing board, high-speed Internet access (for a fee).

New York–New York Hotel & Casino ♔♔ *Kids*   Isn't this exactly the kind of hotel you think about—or dream about or fear—when you think "Las Vegas"? There it is, a jumbled pile mock-up of the venerable Manhattan skyline—the Empire State Building, the Chrysler Building, the Public Library—all crammed together, along with the 150-foot Statue of Liberty and Ellis Island, all built to approximately one-third scale. And as if that weren't enough, they threw in a roller coaster running around the outside and into the hotel and casino itself.

And inside, it all gets better. There are details everywhere—so many, in fact, that the typical expression on the face of casino-goers is slack-jawed wonder. If you enter the casino via the Brooklyn Bridge (the walkway from the Strip), you'll find yourself in a replica of Greenwich Village, down to the cobblestones, the manhole covers, the tenement-style buildings, and the graffiti. (Yes, they even re-created that. You should see the subway station.) The reception area and lobby are done in an Art Deco, golden-age-of-Manhattan style; you'll feel like breaking into a 1930s musical number while standing there. It's a *wow!* all right. The word *subtle* was obviously not in the lexicon of the designers. We will leave it to you to decide, based on your own aesthetic values, if all this is a good or bad thing. Let's just say that to us, it's very, very good indeed. Because . . . this is exactly what we come to Vegas for—unbridled, unrepentant, theme-gone-wild.

Upstairs—oh, yes, there's much more—is the arcade, which is Coney Island–themed (naturally), and just as crowded as the real thing. Kids play boardwalk games in the hopes of winning tickets redeemable for cheap prizes. (You're never too young to start learning about gambling.) The line for the roller coaster starts here. There are many restaurants, all housed in buildings that fit the theme of whatever New York neighborhood is represented in that particular part of the hotel.

Rooms are housed in different towers, each with a New York–inspired name. Truthfully, the place is so massive and mazelike that finding your way to your room can take a while. There are 64 different layouts of newly redecorated rooms, with the original Deco-inspired decor having made way for something they call '40s inspired. We don't see it, but we do find it a sophisticated modern color scheme of earth tones and pale pastels, with dark, rich wood furniture and even padded headboards. Overall, sufficiently urbane, for a mass-market room. The lamps and armoires reflect the skyscraper theme, TVs are now larger, the lighting is bad, the work desk is fine, and pillows and mattresses are surprisingly comfortable for this level of hotel room, while the baths are small, though done in a pleasing gray marble. Upgrades did not include better towels or water pressure. There can be a loooonnngggg walk from the elevators, so if you have ambulatory issues, you had best mention this while booking. (Rooms in the single digits seem to be in the Empire Tower, if that helps give you a clue to location.) Light sleepers should request a room away from the roller coaster. There's a small health club and spa, and the mediocre pool is right next to the parking lot.

In addition to a particularly nice food court and a number of more-than-decent restaurants, including reliable Italian chain Il Fornaio, there are several festive and beautifully decorated bars throughout the property. **Coyote Ugly** is a party-hearty bar where dancing on furniture is encouraged and the female bartenders are hired just to be sassy. At **The Bar at Times Square,** a lighted ball drops every night at midnight to re-create the famous New Year's Eve event in the real location. New Year's Eve every night: a terrific promotion or hell on earth? For a review of the topless and adults-only Cirque du Soleil production *Zumanity,* see p. 270. Chapter 10 offers more on the hotel's nightlife.

The main casino area is done as Central Park, complete with trees, babbling brooks, streetlamps, and footbridges. The change carts are little yellow cabs.

3790 Las Vegas Blvd. S. (at Tropicana Ave.), Las Vegas, NV 89109. ℂ **800/693-6763** or 702/740-6969. Fax 702/740-6920. www.nynyhotelcasino.com. 2,033 units. Sun–Thurs from $79 double; Fri–Sat from $119 double. Extra person $30; no discount for children. AE, DC, DISC, MC, V. Free self- and valet parking. **Amenities:** Casino; showrooms; 10 restaurants plus a food court; outdoor pool; fitness center and spa; Jacuzzi; sauna; video arcade w/carnival midway games; concierge; tour desk; 24-hr. room service; laundry service; dry cleaning; nonsmoking rooms; executive-level rooms. *In room:* A/C, TV w/pay movies, dataport, hair dryer, iron/ironing board, safe, high-speed Internet access (for a fee).

(Kids) Family-Friendly Hotels

We've said it before, and we'll say it again: Vegas is simply not a good place to bring your kids. Most of the major hotels are backing away from being perceived as places for families. But if you want to make it a family trip, here are our recommendations, based, if not on an overall kid-friendly attitude, at least on elements that make it appealing for families.

In addition to the suggestions below, you might consider choosing a non-casino hotel, particularly a reliable chain, and a place with kitchenettes. See "East of the Strip," later in this chapter, for details on several such options.

- **Circus Circus Hotel/Casino** (p. 112)   Centrally located on the Strip, this is our first choice if you're traveling with the kids. The hotel's mezzanine level offers ongoing circus acts daily from 11am to midnight, dozens of carnival games, and an arcade with more than 300 video and pinball games. And behind the hotel is a full amusement park.
- **Excalibur** (p. 88)   Now owned by MGM MIRAGE, Excalibur features a whole floor of midway games, a large video-game arcade, free shows for kids (puppets, jugglers, and magicians), and thrill cinemas. It also has child-oriented eateries and shows.
- **Four Seasons** (p. 77)   For free goodies, service, and general child pampering, the costly Four Seasons is probably worth the dough (your kids will be spoiled!).
- **Luxor Las Vegas** (p. 89)   Another newly acquired MGM MIRAGE property. Kids will enjoy the Games of the Gods Arcade, an 18,000-square-foot video-game arcade that showcases Sega's latest game technologies. Another big attraction here is the IMAX Ridefilm a high-tech adventure/thrill ride using motion simulators and IMAX film.
- **New York–New York** (p. 85)   Overstimulating and hectic, for sure, but between the roller coaster and the Coney Island–style midway, not to mention just looking around, this has many options for children (though going almost anywhere requires walking through the casino).
- **Ritz-Carlton, Lake Las Vegas** (p. 128)   Like the Four Seasons, it's costly, but with so many recreational activities and the Lake Las Vegas setting (well out of the way of the path of Sin City—although parents can make nighttime getaways, thanks to the hotel's babysitting services), it offers a lot over the regular Vegas resorts.

THEhotel at Mandalay Bay *(R)(R)(R)*   The rather silly nomenclature of this recent, utterly fabulous Vegas accommodation reminds us of our previous consideration regarding the Four Seasons' relationship with Mandalay Bay (located on the top floors, but operated as a separate entity)—it's part *of* the hotel, but not precisely *the* hotel. In this case, this really is *THE*hotel, in all senses, not least of which is that even though we were quite fond of Mandalay Bay prior to the opening of this conjoined twin of a property, we now think of it, if we do at all, rather as the frowzy sister from the sticks who looks tawdry and rumpled next to its sleek *Vogue* magazine editor sibling.

(Actually, we still like Mandalay Bay a great deal.) Yes, if Prada were a hotel, it would look something like THEhotel. Certainly, if there are Prada wearers in town, we bet they are going to be staying here.

The new trend in Vegas hotels seems to be hotels that allow you, if you so choose, to forget you are in Vegas. Never mind that psychology. What that translates to here is an entirely separate entrance, and an entirely different atmosphere. This is not a casino hotel—though it is connected to one by a long hallway—but a world of sleek towering walls of lighting, ambiguous modern art, and both guests and employees in head-to-toe black. Like any good Vegas hotel, it wows you from the start, but not in the usual Vegas marble-gilt-and-chandelier screaming over the top "look-how-you-can-live-if-only-you-hit-that-jackpot-over-there" way, but in a way that coolly says, "You probably already live like this, don't you?" while handing you a nicely chilled Cosmopolitan. In other words, this isn't Donald Trump's version of the best, but rather that of Mr. Big from *Sex and the City.* Don't get us wrong—everything here is still out-of-proportion large—but it's sophisticated and chic, all blacks, tans, woods, and midcentury modern sharp lines. We fell for it instantly, and that's before we went to our room. Ah, the rooms; every one is a genuine suite (not just separated living room and bedroom, but even wet bar and second WC), done in more black, tans, and gleaming woods, like your professionally decorated Manhattan dream apartment. There are plasma-screen TVs in every room, including the enormous marbled bathroom, where the tub is so deep the water came up to our chin when we sat down. Bath amenities are posh, the comforters are down, and the sheets—well, remember our complaints about how you just can't get good sheets in big hotels? Feel the soft heft of these. *That's* what we want. One complaint might be the excess of mirrors (the wall-length double closet and TV cabinet are covered in them, as is another wall), and the overall lack of good lighting. But seriously, you won't care. For once, a hotel room in Vegas designed to make you want to stay put. Not that you have to; as stated, all the amenities of Mandalay Bay (their incredible pool area, a number of terrific restaurants) are just down a long hall, though the instant you step from this grown-up world into the world of, well, noisy grown-up pursuits, which isn't the same thing at all, you might well want to turn right back around.

Having raved about it all, we do have some complaints. The staff are hardly cuddly, and service reflects that. Costs at the sleek cafes are higher than even the usual elevated hotel restaurant prices. Then again, you can use just the workout facilities at the Bathhouse Spa, its rather unfortunately named but gorgeous health club and spa, for only $20 (cheap compared to other comparable hotels, though it's $30 if you also want to use the saunas and the like). This is the place we would splash out on (and certainly would leap on any specials offered), but with the understanding that it's still, despite appearances, a Vegas hotel, though very likely the best there is.

3950 Las Vegas Blvd. S., Las Vegas, NV 89119. © 702/632-7777 or 877/632-7000. www.mandalaybay.com. 1,118 units. $189 and up double. AE, DC, DISC, MC, V. Free self- and valet parking. **Amenities:** 2 restaurants; bar; access to Mandalay Bay restaurants/pool/casino; health club; spa; tour desk; car rental; business center; sundries shop; 24-hr. room service; laundry service. *In room:* A/C, 3 flatscreen plasma TVs, CD/DVD, combo printer/fax, wet bar, minibar, hair dryer, iron/ironing board, high-speed Internet access (for a fee), robes and slippers, scale.

Tropicana Resort & Casino *⚘*   As we go to press, the Trop's future remains in doubt. No formal decision has been made, but at press time, the hotel announced it wouldn't go public with plans until about the time this book hits the stands. The rumors are it will be torn down and in its place will be erected two miniresorts of 2,000 rooms each. We'd like to say we are sorry—and in a nostalgic way we are, but really, the Trop has seen better days. Once known for its lavish tropical resort stylings, it's now more than a little worn around the edges, especially when compared with its splashy neighbors. The birds and other wildlife are gone, which makes things a little less messy, but the tacky "Garden rooms" are still around and ought to be demolished ASAP. Gone also is the outside light show.

Rooms—well, think a clean '70s motel room, but a little bit nicer. Unless you're a Jimmy Buffett fan, you are better off staying in the Trop's Paradise Tower, where the rooms are slightly bigger and much easier on the eyes—mock provincial, to be sure (check out the plaster molding and ceiling cornices—a curious and welcome little touch)—but it all appears less shabby and more fresh. Bathrooms are also bigger here, but dull, except for the ones with Jacuzzis. Even without the wildlife, the pool area is among the best around and is the place's biggest draw. Note, however, that their touted swim-up blackjack is seasonal (read: summer only).

Calypsos (p. 144), the 24-hour coffee shop, is a good value, as are the Trop's **buffet** (p. 180) offerings. The showroom currently hosts the *Folies Bergère* revue (p. 273).

3801 Las Vegas Blvd. S. (at Tropicana Ave.), Las Vegas, NV 89109. © **888/826-8767** or 702/739-2222. Fax 702/739-2469. www.tropicanalv.com. 1,878 units. $79 and up double. Extra person $20. Children under 18 stay free in parent's room. AE, DC, DISC, MC, V. Free self- and valet parking. **Amenities:** Casino; showrooms; wedding chapel; 7 restaurants; 3 outdoor pools; small health club and spa; video arcade; concierge; tour desk; car-rental desk; 24-hr. room service; laundry service; dry cleaning; nonsmoking rooms; executive-level rooms. *In room:* A/C, TV w/pay movies, dataport, minifridge in some rooms, hair dryer, iron/ironing board, safe.

MODERATE

Excalibur ⭐ (Kids) Now *this* is kitsch. One of the largest resort hotels in the world, Excalibur (aka "the Realm") is a gleaming white, turreted castle complete with moat, drawbridge, battlements, and lofty towers. And it's huger than huge.

You know, as much as we might publicly stand in favor of quiet good taste, there is a part of our soul that is secretly thrilled by overblown fantasy locations—it's so authentically Vegas. And so we just pray that the Lords of Taste never touch Excalibur, and it is allowed to forever run amok with sword and sorcery imagery. Actually, the decorating fairies have already made some quiet changes (the deep reds in the public areas have been switched to creams), but nothing that really sullies the silliness. There are some ominous rumblings in keeping with the rest of Vegas's careening away from the "family-friendly" image—gone is the animatronic dragon and wizard show out front, and inside there is a male stripper act, *Thunder from Down Under*. It's really too bad because, without the excess, this is just another hotel—a mighty big and chaotic hotel, thanks to a sprawling casino full of families and small-time gamblers, which is located smack dab in the middle of everything, including, naturally, the path between you and the elevators to your room.

Rooms are done in neutrals (a little too much brown for our tastes). They have vague heraldic overtones and, given the price, are perhaps the best bet on the Strip for the budget-minded. Note that none of the bathrooms have tubs, just showers. Guests who have stayed in Tower 2 have complained about the noise from the roller coaster across the street at New York–New York. (It runs till 11pm, so early birds should probably ask to be put in a different part of the hotel.) Frankly, we prefer stopping in for a visit rather than actually settling in here, but we know single-minded others (read: Vegas is for gambling, and so is the majority of the vacation budget) who wouldn't consider staying anywhere else.

The second floor holds the Medieval Village, where Excalibur's restaurants and shops are peppered along winding streets and alleyways, a sort of permanent Renaissance Faire, which could be reason enough to stay away (or to come). On the Village's "Jester's Stage," jugglers, puppeteers, and magicians amuse guests with free 20-minute performances throughout the day. Up here you can access the enclosed, air-conditioned, moving sidewalk that connects with the Luxor. There are plenty of restaurants, including the **Round Table Buffet** (p. 180), and a pretty good prime rib joint. Excalibur won our hearts forever by installing a branch of **Krispy Kreme Doughnuts** on the second level, on the way to the Luxor walkway. The *Tournament of Kings* (p. 278) is a medieval-style dinner show, and there's a very loud, claustrophobic casino.

3850 Las Vegas Blvd. S. (at Tropicana Ave.), Las Vegas, NV 89109. © **800/937-7777** or 702/597-7700. Fax 702/597-7163. www.excalibur.com. 4,008 units. $49 and up double. Extra person $15. Children under 13 stay free in parent's room. AE, DC, DISC, MC, V. Free self- and valet parking. **Amenities:** Casino; showrooms; wedding chapel; 5 restaurants and a food court; outdoor pool; video arcade; concierge; tour desk; car-rental desk; shopping arcade; 24-hr. room service; laundry service; dry cleaning; nonsmoking rooms. *In room:* A/C, TV w/pay movies, dataport, hair dryer, iron/ironing board.

Luxor Las Vegas ★★ *Kids*   Another hotel that thrills us to our very kitsch-worshipping souls. How happy you, who share our aesthetic taste—or lack thereof—will be when you behold the main hotel, a 30-story onyx-hued pyramid, complete with a really tall 315,000-watt light beam at the top. (Luxor says that's because the Egyptians believed their souls would travel up to heaven in a beam of light. We think it's really because it gives them something to brag about: "The most powerful beam on earth!") You'll be giddy when you spy replicas of Cleopatra's Needle and the Sphinx gracing the outside. And when you get inside and see the towering statues of Ramses and overhear the talking animatronic camels, well, you might not care that the lobby tries also to be classy, vaguely Art Deco (influenced by Egyptian Revival, remember) marble and cherrywood. No, you'll just want to ride the 39-degree high-speed *inclinators*—that's what an elevator is when it works inside a pyramid. (Really, they are part conveyance, part thrill ride—check out that jolt when they come to a halt!) Great fun, the Luxor, you can gather. Not as impressive as the real landmarks in the real Egypt, of course. But you knew that.

Once you stop laughing (or screaming) at what greets you, you should be quite pleased with this hotel. Rooms in the pyramid open onto the vast center that contains the casino—indeed, ground-level rooms open more or less right into the action (though many of these have been turned into offices), so if you want only a short drunken stumble back to your room, these are for you. Otherwise, ask for a room higher up. The pyramid rooms cross Egyptian kitsch with Art Deco stylings, including gleaming inlaid wood furniture and a hilarious hieroglyphic bedspread. Marvelous views are offered through the slanted windows (the higher up, the better, of course), but the bathrooms are shower-only, no tubs. Tower rooms (an expansion put additional rooms in a tower rather than another pyramid—drat!) are even heavier on the Egyptian motif (with huge armoires housing the TVs and closet space), pleasing in a campy way but not as aesthetically successful. The bathrooms, however, including deep tubs, are better, so it might be a worthwhile trade-off. Regardless of which room you get, these are some of the few rooms in Las Vegas that stand out. You know you are in the Luxor when you find yourself surrounded by unique, charming room design, as opposed to the cookie-cutter room decor usually found elsewhere in town. Especially desirable is a group of suites with glamorous Art Deco elements, private sitting rooms, refrigerators, and, notably, whirlpools by the window (enabling you to soak under the stars at night).

The Luxor's **Pharaoh's Pheast Buffet** (p. 181) offers a cool archaeological-dig atmosphere. The hotel's high-tech nightclub **Ra** (p. 295) is a happening nightspot. Two notable attractions here are **King Tut's Tomb & Museum** (p. 194) and the **Luxor IMAX Theater** (p. 196).

3900 Las Vegas Blvd. S. (between Reno and Hacienda aves.), Las Vegas, NV 81119. (C) 888/777-0188 or 702/262-4000. Fax 702/262-4478. www.luxor.com. 4,400 units. Sun–Thurs $59 and up double; Fri–Sat $99 and up double; $149 and up whirlpool suite, $249–$800 other suites. Extra person $25. Children under 12 stay free in parent's room. AE, DC, DISC, MC, V. Free self- and valet parking. **Amenities:** Casino; showrooms; 10 restaurants plus a food court; 5 outdoor pools; health club and spa; 18,000-sq.-ft. video arcade; concierge; tour desk; car-rental desk; business center; shopping arcade; 24-hr. room service; dry cleaning; nonsmoking rooms; executive-level rooms. *In room:* A/C, TV w/pay movies, dataport, hair dryer, iron/ironing board, high-speed Internet access (for a fee).

INEXPENSIVE

Orleans ⊛ *Value*   The Orleans is a little out of the way, and there is virtually nothing around it, but with an 18-screen movie complex, complete with a food court and day-care center, a bowling alley (that keeps ridiculously late hours; we know more than one recent guest who found a 3–4am game just the right way to wind down after a hectic clubbing night), and a new 9,000-seat arena for a minor-league hockey team (but also available for concerts and the like), this is a reasonable alternative to staying on the hectic Strip. Plus, there is a shuttle that runs continuously to the Barbary Coast on the Strip. The facade is aggressively fake New Orleans, more reminiscent of Disneyland than the actual Big Easy. Inside it's much of the same. But a bright casino (complete with Cajun and zydeco music over the loudspeakers) and a policy of handing out Mardi Gras beads at all the restaurants and bars (ask if you haven't gotten yours) make for a pleasantly festive atmosphere.

If the prices hold true (as always, they can vary), this hotel is one of the best bargains in town, despite the location, though the staff can be rotten, which can seriously sour a bargain experience. (On the other hand, room service seems fine.) The rooms are nice enough and you'll find the largest standard rooms in town, or so the hotel claims. They all have a definite New Orleans–French feel. Each is L-shaped, with a seating alcove by the windows, and comes complete with an old-fashioned, over-stuffed chair and sofa. The beds have brass headboards, the lamps (including some funky iron floor lamps) look antique, and lace curtains flutter at the windows. The one drawback is that all these furnishings, and the busy floral decorating theme, make the room seem crowded (particularly down by the seating area in front of the bathrooms). Still, it's meant to evoke a cozy, warm Victorian parlor, which traditionally is very overcrowded, so maybe it's successful after all. There are 1,400 newer rooms in a recently built tower, and these hold to the same surprisingly nice standard.

The hotel has your basic Vegas-type places to eat. Worth noting is the moderately priced Italian **Sazio** (p. 143), Big Al's Oyster Bar, a not unauthentic Creole/Cajun-themed restaurant, and **Don Miguel's,** a basic but satisfying Mexican restaurant that makes its own tortillas while you watch. There are several bars, including one with live music at night. The **Orleans Showroom** is an 827-seat theater featuring live entertainment, the **Orleans Arena** is a 9,000-plus-seat facility for concerts and sporting events, and, of course, there's a casino.

4500 W. Tropicana Ave. (west of the Strip and I-15), Las Vegas, NV 89103. (C) 800/ORLEANS (675-3267) or 702/365-7111. Fax 702/365-7505. www.orleanscasino.com. 840 units. $39 and up standard double; $175–$225 1-bedroom suite. Extra person $10. Children under 14 stay free in parent's room. AE, DC, DISC, MC, V. Free self- and valet parking.

Amenities: Casino; showroom; 12 restaurants; 2 outdoor pools; health club; 70-lane bowling center; 18 movie theaters; Kids Tyme children's center offering amusements and day care for kids 12 and under; video arcade; concierge; tour desk; car-rental desk; 24-hr. room service; laundry service; dry cleaning; nonsmoking rooms; executive-level rooms. *In room:* A/C, TV w/pay movies, dataport, hair dryer, iron/ironing board, high-speed Internet access (for a fee).

4 Mid-Strip

VERY EXPENSIVE

Bellagio ✿✿   This is the luxury resort that ushered in the new post-Vegas-is-for-families elegance epoch, and it was so successful that many of its attributes can now be found, in varying forms, up the street at the brand-new Wynn resort. It's hard not to compare the two, and which you prefer will depend on your aesthetics. We give the edge to Bellagio because even though it is not as theme-intensive as it could be, it still has some elements drawn from its charming Lake Como village namesake, and we do prefer even our resorts to have some of that Vegas silliness, however faint. In this case, it's an 8-acre Lake Como stand-in out front, complete with a dazzling choreographed water-ballet extravaganza, plus a representation of an Italian lakeside village, while the pool area is sort of Hearst Castle Romanesque. However, don't think this is not much like a getaway to a peaceful, romantic Italian village because it's not. But it is exactly like going to a big, grand, state-of-the-art Vegas hotel. To expect more probably isn't fair, but then again, they tried to set the tone with dreamy, soft-focus TV ads aired when the hotel debuted. Nothing with a casino stuck in the middle of it can be that serene and restful.

But does it work as a luxury hotel? Sort of. It certainly is much closer to a European casino hotel than a Vegas one. Fabulous touches abound, including a lobby that's unlike any other in Vegas. It's not just grand, with marble and a gaudy blown-glass flower sculpture on the ceiling (the largest of its kind in the world), but it's also brave with plants, natural lighting, and actual seating. There's also a downright lovely conservatory, complete with a 100-year-old fountain and stuffed full of gorgeous, brightly colored flowers and plants, preposterously (and delightfully) changed every few weeks to go with the season (yellows and whites for Easter, for example, though we could have done without the gianormous animatronic bald eagle chicks as part of the extremely gaudy July 4 decor)—it's one of the sweetest spots in all of Vegas.

On the downside, you still can't avoid a walk through the casino to get just about anywhere (with the inevitable ruckus shattering your blissful state every time you exit the elevators from your room). At least the casino is laid out in an easy-to-navigate grid with wide aisles. (*Tip:* Black floral carpets indicate the main casino paths.) There are hidden charges galore (a pricey fee for the spa, another one for poolside cabanas). The rooms are quite nice, better than ever thanks to a recent redo that changed the colors from the usual resort-sand to a more cosmopolitan look with handsome sage greens and dark woods, but given the relatively puny size, it may still not be enough for the price. (Having said that, you can find deals on their website for as low as $139 depending on day of week and time of year.) Furnishings are plush (good cushy beds with quality linens, comfy chairs), the roomy bathrooms even more so (marble and glass plus good-smelling soap and hair dryers—it works every time), but it's all just a busier and slightly more luxurious variation on what's found over at TI at the Mirage. Strip-side rooms, while featuring a much-desired view of the hotel's dancing water fountains (see below), don't quite muffle the booms said fountains make as they explode (although we didn't find it annoying). Rooms in the new Spa Tower are more desirable if you want a shorter walk to the pool and the gym and spa areas (guests in the original building will have a long jog around the casino perimeter instead), but only a "partial" (read: a bit set back with a parking lot in the foreground) view of the fountains. Note that a channel on the TV will play the songs as the fountains dance because you can't quite hear the music from your room. Still, service is top-notch, despite the size of the place; the staff is eager to please and nonpatronizing.

Meanwhile, many of the better restaurants are found in Bellagio. Full reviews of **Picasso, Le Cirque, Circo, Michael Mina, Fix, Sensi, Jean-Philippe Patisserie,** and **Olives** are found in chapter 6, as is a review of the buffet. And the man who brought us a free pirate show and a volcano explosion now brings us a **water ballet** ⍟⍟⍟, courtesy of a dancing fountain with jets timed to a rotating list of nine songs (everything from pop to Sinatra to Broadway to opera). This sounds cheesy, but it absolutely is not. It's really quite delightful and even witty (no, really), and is the best free show in Vegas.

Bellagio also features an upscale casino and ***O*** (p. 270), one of the most incredible shows yet from Cirque du Soleil.

The hotel's pool area has skidded to the top of our favorites list; it boasts six swimming pools (two heated year-round and two with fountains) geometrically set in a neoclassical Roman garden, with flowered, trellised archways and Italian opera piped in over the sound system. The Grand Patio could have come right off a movie set (pillars, domes, you get the idea). Arguably a more sophisticated environment than the tropical party over at The Mirage (our other favorite), it is sure to be the place where thonged model types hang out with moneyed Eurotrash—it comes off as *that* chic.

The newly redone health club is marvelous, large, and well stocked with top-of-the-line machines, with natural light coming in through windows to the outside world, but at $25 a pop, it's pretty pricey if all you want is a simple session on a treadmill (though with your fee, you are allowed to return throughout the day for additional soakings/steamings/workouts). Attendants ply you with iced towels and drinks. The also revamped spa is not quite as pretty as some others around town, but it does offer a full range of pricey treatments and has a serene soaking area, with plunge pools ranging in temperature from icy to boiling. In addition to drinks and snacks, smoothies are sometimes offered—take one.

The shopping area, called **Via Bellagio,** features all the stores that advertise in color in glossy magazines: Tiffany, Armani, Gucci, Prada, Hermès, and the like. There's also an **art gallery** (p. 190) that boasts enough highly regarded works to draw some million visitors a year.

What does all this add up to? As good as a casino-hotel can provide and perform the duties of a luxury resort experience, certainly. If it doesn't quite work, that's probably more the fault of the initial concept than the hotel itself.

3600 Las Vegas Blvd. S. (at the corner of Flamingo Rd.), Las Vegas, NV 89109. ℭ 888/987-6667 or 702/693-7111. Fax 702/693-8546. www.bellagio.com. 3,933 units. $139 and up double. Extra person $35; no discount for children. AE, DC, DISC, MC, V. Free self- and valet parking. **Amenities:** Casino; showrooms; wedding chapel; 14 restaurants; 6 outdoor pools; fitness center and spa; concierge; tour desk; car-rental desk; business center; 24-hr. room service; in-room massage; laundry service; dry cleaning; nonsmoking rooms; executive-level rooms. *In room:* A/C, TV w/pay movies, dataport, hair dryer, iron/ironing board, safe, high-speed Internet access (for a fee).

Caesars Palace ⍟⍟   Since 1966, Caesars has stood simultaneously as the ultimate in Vegas luxury and the nadir (or pinnacle, depending on your values) of Las Vegas cheese. It's the most Vegas-style hotel you'll find, covering all the bases from the tacky

Bally's Las Vegas **14**
Barbary Coast Hotel
 & Casino **10**
Bellagio **13**
Bourbon Street **11**
Caesars Palace **8**
The Flamingo Las Vegas **9**
Harrah's Las Vegas **4**

Imperial Palace **5**
The Mirage **3**
Palms Resort & Casino **6**
Paris Las Vegas Casino Resort **15**
Rio All-Suite Hotel & Casino **7**
TI at the Mirage **1**
The Venetian **2**
Westin Casuarina **12**

fabulous cheese of the recent past to the current trend in high-end luxury. And it's moving ever on, with the most over-the-top showroom in town, specially built for Miss Thang herself, Céline Dion, and yet another expansion to the Forum Shops, the first themed shopping experience on the Strip.

When Caesars was originally built to reflect Roman decadence, its designers probably had no idea how guffaw-inducing this would be some years later. It's the level of kitsch all should aspire to: Roman colonnades, Roman pillars, gigantic faux-marble Roman statues, staff attired in gladiator outfits—it's splendidly ridiculous. It's what Vegas ought to be.

But all things change, and Caesars was outshined over the years by more modern glamour. And frankly, that facade was looking dated 2 decades ago. Never one to rest on any kind of laurels, Roman or otherwise, Caesars gave itself a massive face-lift and keeps on building and expanding. Never fear, the Roman statues still remain, as do the toga-clad cocktail waitresses, and so does Caesars' giggle factor (it's still pretty campy). Past or future, Caesars remains spectacular. From the Roman temples, heroic arches, golden charioteers, and 50-foot Italian cypresses at its entrance, to the impressive interiors, it's the spectacle a good Vegas hotel should be.

But the hotel is also getting a bit too big for its own britches. The haphazard layout has become ever more confusing and hard to negotiate, and it takes forever to get anywhere—especially out to the Strip. Sometimes you feel like just surrendering and staying in, which isn't necessarily a bad thing. Caesars is also known for its luxurious rooms and service. (Long lines at the reservations desk are sometimes relieved by gratis champagne.)

Accommodations occupy four towers—and by the time you read this, yet another new tower will have been completed, adding 900 more rooms, plus additional restaurants—and there are too many decorating schemes to describe here. Art in the rooms keeps to the Greco-Roman theme (some have classical sculptures in niches); furnishings tend to neoclassic styles; Roman columns, pilasters, and pediments are common. Many rooms have four-poster beds with mirrored ceilings. The newest rooms are handsome, if not as giggle-inducingly overwhelming as the classic ones, and have floor-to-ceiling windows that offer a hypnotizing panoramic view. You'll likely enjoy a lavish bathroom with marble floor, European fixtures, and oversize marble tubs (about half are whirlpools). Some of the rooms have lavish tubs in the middle of the room, which can be uncomfortable if you wish to shower and don't want your shower to turn into a spectator sport.

Caesars has a well-deserved reputation for superior in-house restaurants. There are nine in the hotel, plus dining facilities in the Forum shopping area. All are highly recommended. The hotel's sushi restaurant, **Hyakumi,** is described in chapter 6, as are the hotel's food court and buffets. Restaurants in the Forum Shops arcade include **Spago, The Palm,** and the **Stage Deli**—all discussed in chapter 6. In the newer Atlantis section is a **Cheesecake Factory.** See also **Cleopatra's Barge Nightclub** on p. 293.

Having spent over $100 million renovating its **Garden of the Gods,** Caesars has created a tasteful, undeniably "Caesaresque" masterpiece. With three pools measuring a total of 22,000 square feet, there is plenty of space for frolicking in the hot sun. Inspired by the healing Baths of Caracalla in Rome, each of the pools is adorned with griffins or sea horses and inlaid with classic granite-and-marble mosaics. To feel even more regal, snatch one of the shaded cabanas that offer phones, TV, and air-conditioning starting at $150 a day (reserve them early). Several amenities are also available by the pool area, including massage, two whirlpools, the Neptune Bar, and, of course, a Snackus Maximus.

The **Caesars Spa** is another gorgeous facility, offering full salon services (a large range of facials, massages, wraps, and other beauty treatments). While we can't say we've tried every masseuse or facialist in town, we have tried a lot, and what we got at Caesars was the best so far. The spa also offers saunas, steam rooms, and whirlpool tubs, plus an incredibly well-supplied health club with state-of-the-art machinery, a rock-climbing wall, personal trainers, and more (it's a whopping $24 per day just to work out, though). Go work off some of that Caesars indulgence and then get a little pampered.

The **Forum Shops** (p. 257) are in the grandest mall you can imagine (think of the *La Dolce Vita* walk on the Via Veneto) and are about to get grander. A massive addition roughly doubled the size of the existing shopping areas and is even grander, and sunnier, than ever. Not content to stop paying contractors, Caesars also added the 4,000-seat Colosseum, a replica of the original building in Rome. This was built for one purpose only—to give diva Céline Dion a place to play. No kidding. She appears 200 nights a year in a ridiculously expensive production created just to showcase her vocal talents, and featuring Cirque du Soleil–type visuals. See p. 268 for a review of the production. When she's not in town, her venue is taken over by various Uber-Names, like Elton John and his *The Red Piano* production.

3570 Las Vegas Blvd. S. (just north of Flamingo Rd.), Las Vegas, NV 89109. © **877/427-7243** or 702/731-7110. www.caesars.com. 2,471 units. From $99 standard double, $109–$500 "run-of-house deluxe" double; $549–$1,000 suite. Extra person $20. Children under 18 stay free in parent's room. AE, DC, DISC, MC, V. Free self- and valet parking. **Amenities:** Casino; wedding chapel; 23 restaurants; 3 outdoor pools; health club and spa; concierge; tour desk; car-rental desk; business center; shopping arcade; 24-hr. room service; laundry service; dry cleaning; nonsmoking rooms; executive-level rooms. *In room:* A/C, TV w/pay movies, dataport, hair dryer, iron/ironing board, safe, high-speed Internet access (for a fee).

Paris Las Vegas Casino Resort 𝒜   *Sacre bleu!* The City of Light comes to Sin City in this, one of the most recent fantasy hotels to hit the Strip. It's theme-run-amok time again, and we are so happy about it. The outside reproduces various Parisian landmarks (amusing anyone familiar with Paris, as the Hotel de Ville is crammed on top of the Louvre), complete with a half-scale perfect replica of the Eiffel Tower. The interior puts you in the middle of a dollhouse version of the city. You can stroll down a mini–Rue de la Paix, ride an elevator to the top of the Eiffel Tower, stop at an over-priced bakery for a baguette, and take your photo by several very nice fountains.

You'll find signage employing the kind of dubious use of the French language that makes genuine Frenchmen really cross ("le car rental" and so forth), while all the employees are forced to dust off their high school French ("Bonjour, Madame! Merci beaucoup!") when dealing with the public. Don't worry, it's all not quite enough to make you sick to "le stomach."

Quel dommage, this attention to detail does not extend to the rooms, which are nice enough but disappointingly uninteresting, with furniture that only hints at mock French Regency. Bathrooms are small but pretty, with deep tubs. Try to get a Strip-facing room so that you can see Bellagio's fountains across the street; note also that north-facing rooms give you nice Peeping-Tom views right into neighboring Bally's. The brand-new monorail has a stop out back. Overall, not a bad place to stay but a great place to visit—*quel hoot!*

The hotel has eight more-or-less French-themed restaurants, including a highly lauded **buffet,** the **Eiffel Tower restaurant** (located guess where), and bistro **Mon Ami Gabi,** all of which are covered in chapter 6. The bread for all these restaurants is made fresh on-site at the bakery. You can buy delicious, if pricey, loaves of it at the bakery, and we have to admit that's kinda fun. There are also five lounges.

The **Eiffel Tower** attraction is covered on p. 192, and the hotel's new nightclub, **Risque,** is reviewed on p. 289.

3655 Las Vegas Blvd. S., Las Vegas, NV 89109. © **888/BONJOUR** (266-5687) or 702/946-7000. www.parislv.com. 2,916 units. $119–$269 double; $350 and up suites. Extra person $30. Children under 18 stay free in parent's room. AE, DC, DISC, MC. V. Free self- and valet parking. **Amenities:** Casino; showrooms; 2 wedding chapels; 11 restaurants; outdoor pool; health club and spa; concierge; tour desk; business center; shopping arcade; 24-hr. room service; laundry service; dry cleaning; nonsmoking rooms; executive-level rooms. *In room:* A/C, TV w/pay movies, dataport, hair dryer, iron/ironing board, safe, high-speed Internet access (for a fee).

The Venetian 𝒜𝒜   One of the most elaborate hotel spectacles in town, The Venetian falls squarely between an outright adult Disneyland experience and the luxury resort experience that many of the other recently renovated Vegas hotels offer. Its exterior, which re-creates most of the top landmarks of Venice (the Campanile, a portion of St. Mark's Square, part of the Doge's Palace, a canal or two), ranks right up there with New York–New York as a must-see, and since you can wander freely through the "sights," it even has a slight edge over New York–New York. (This may be the only hotel in Vegas where it seems inviting to wander around outside in the front.) As stern as we get about re-creations *not* being a substitute for the real thing, we have to admit

⌐Tips Staying off the Strip

First-time visitors, and even second-timers, will prefer, as they should, to stay on the Strip or Downtown, hang the cost (most of the time anyway). But if you can't get a room price to your liking, or you are a three-peater (or more), you might want to consider some alternatives. Each of the following is out of the way, relatively speaking, but each makes up for it with rack rates you just aren't going to get—well, not that often—on the Strip. We're talking as low as $49 a night. Maybe lower. The rooms aren't anything to write home about, which is why we didn't bother writing much about them, but they are clean, comfortable, and sufficiently (in some cases) easy on the eyes. And several of the hotels, particularly those that are part of the Station chain, have so many extras to offer that they really could compete with some of the big boys on the Strip. However, you trade away location; for the most part, once you leave the hotel property, you enter a vast nothingness. So what? Get in that rental car—or take the shuttle that many of the hotels provide—and drive 15 minutes to the big boys' free parking lots, and use the money you saved to see *O* (p. 270), or to eat at a fancy restaurant, or to gamble. But, hey, even gambling is cheaper out here in the vast nothingness!

Northwest Las Vegas

JW Marriott ⌖, 221 N. Rampart, Las Vegas, NV 89128 (© **877/869-8777** or 702/869-8777), was the Resort at Summerlin but was recently bought out by the Marriott chain. With a handsome Spanish Mission–style building, fabulously landscaped grounds, and tricked-out rooms, this is much more of a true resort property than any Strip destination. But then again, what you gain there you lose in location—with traffic, it could take 40 minutes to get to the Strip. **Texas Station,** 2102 Texas Star Lane, Las Vegas, NV 89130 (© **800/654-8888** or 702/631-1000), features a bowling alley, movie theaters, a dozen restaurants, child care, and a huge casino. The **Fiesta Rancho,** 2400

that the attention to detail here is impressive indeed. Stone is aged for that weathered look, statues and tiles are exact copies of their Italian counterparts, security guards wear Venetian police uniforms—all that's missing is the smell from the canals, but we are happy to let that one slide.

Inside, it's more of the same, particularly in the lobby area and the entrance to the extraordinary shops, as ceilings are covered with hand-painted re-creations of Venetian art. With plenty of marble, soaring ceilings, and impressive pillars and archways, it's less kitschy than Caesars but more theme park than Bellagio. The lobby says classy hotel, if "classy hotel on steroids." The lobby, casino, and shops can all be accessed from outside through individual entrances, which helps avoid that irritating circuitous maneuvering required by most other locations. This is all the more appreciated because the casino seems to have a most confusing layout, with poor signage; perhaps it's just our problem with spatial navigation, but we consistently got lost on the way to the guest elevators.

N. Rancho Dr., Las Vegas, NV 89130 (© **800/731-7333** or 702/631-7000), has a friendly local touch that used to be found in Downtown but is rarely seen there these days, plus a performance venue that frequently has some decent names, and a Mexican restaurant with over 300 different kinds of margaritas. **Palace Station,** 2411 W. Sahara Ave., Las Vegas, NV 89102 (© **800/634-3101** or 702/367-2411), has long been a favorite with locals for gambling. While not quite as crammed with diversions as some of the others, it makes up for it with extra friendliness.

Henderson & Boulder Highway

Boulder Station, 4111 Boulder Hwy., Las Vegas, NV 89121 (© **800/683-7777** or 702/432-7777), has an 11-screen movie theater, tons of cheap eateries, nifty child-care facilities, and a lot more—consequently, it's not always as cheap as some of the others. **Sunset Station,** 1301 W. Sunset Rd., Henderson, NV 89014 (© **888/SUNSET-9**), is more of the same, plus there's a bowling alley, an outdoor performance space that features a lot of retro (read: has-been) performers, a microbrew pub, and a Hooters just because they can. It's really more of an entertainment complex than hotel, and even has a mall across the street, so it isn't so totally isolated. **Arizona Charlie's East,** 4575 Boulder Hwy., Las Vegas, NV 89121 (© **800/362-4040** or 702/951-5900), is only a step or two above budget accommodations but still very well maintained. It has very low limits in the casino, a cheap and reliable coffee shop, and a buffet priced like buffets used to be. The Mexican pueblo–themed **Fiesta Henderson,** 777 W. Lake Mead Dr., Henderson, NV 89015 (© **888/899-7770** or 702/558-7000), has fewer facilities than some of the other options and may be a better choice for people visiting family in the neighborhood than folks looking for fun.

The rooms are among the largest and probably the most handsome in town, with a flair that's more European than Vegas. They are all "suites," with a good-size bedroom giving way to a sunken living area, complete with pullout sofa bed. The decor features just one too many patterns, but it manages to work, and nice touches abound. Rooms have somewhat stately furniture, including painted, scallop-topped armoires; thickly draped half-canopies over the beds; and crown moldings on ceilings. The marbled bathrooms rocketed virtually to the top of our list of favorites, in a tie for second place with those at Bellagio. (Mandalay Bay's THEhotel are the best.) Glassed-in showers, deep soaking tubs (though your feet can easily kick the plug out), double sinks, fluffy towels, and lots of space—that does it for us every time. Devices for the hearing-impaired (ranging from door-knock lights to vibrating alarm clocks and tele-caption decoders) are available upon request.

Despite the niceties, there is a certain amount of price gouging at this hotel that unpleasantly reminds one of the real Venice. There is a charge for that in-room faxing and printing, and the minibar is automated so that if you so much as rearrange items inside, you are charged for it.

And all this is even before the new **Venezia Tower,** with over 1,000 more rooms, with the same large and lush footprint and style as the originals. The tower has its own check-in and gestalt—somehow, it comes off even more lush than the original hotel, which is pretty frilly to start. It's like a Four Seasons on human growth hormones, with over-the-top opulence. The gas lamp–lit lobby hallway slays us, as do the flatscreen TVs in the bathrooms. Rooms here cost about $35 more a night (in theory—in practice, anything goes with hotel pricing in Vegas) and we would spend it. The new trend toward casino hotels adding additions that are away from a casino—"Nope, no slot machines here. We are just a luxury hotel. Really!"—is a disingenuous stance that is actually entirely genius. There are many who prefer their Vegas at arm's length, whose finest compliment for a hotel is "It doesn't seem like it's in Vegas." These people are willing to spend extra to stay in a grown-up atmosphere, and certainly are more inclined to want a comfortable room—and nothing says "comfortable room" like "plasma TV in the bathroom."

Many celebrity chefs and high-profile restaurants are in residence at The Venetian. Reviews of **Bouchon** (by Thomas Keller, perhaps America's top chef), **Delmonico Steakhouse, Canaletto, Valentino, Lutèce,** and **Pinot Brasserie** can be found in chapter 6. Also worth noting is that **Zeffirino's** chef, Paolo Belloni, has cooked for some of the most eminent judges of Italian food: the Pope and Sinatra. And, of course, there is an elegant but confusingly laid-out casino.

The Venetian has five pools and whirlpools, but its pool area is disappointing—sterile and bland. Pools are neoclassical (think rectangles with the corners lopped off), and the fourth-floor location probably means that more dense foliage is not going to be forthcoming. The Venezia Tower has a courtyard pool area that is amusing, but the water space is tiny.

The **Canyon Ranch SpaClub** is run by a branch of arguably the finest getaway spa in America. This is an unbelievably lavish facility, certainly the finest hotel spa in town. From the Bed Head and Bumble & Bumble products on sale in the shop to the nutritionists, physical therapists, and acupuncturists on the staff, to the vibrating massage chairs that you rest in during pedicures—geez, what more could you want? Well, we want our own home gym to be as nice as the one here, with ample equipment, racks of big TVs, and a staff eager to help you with advice and bring you bottled water. The $30-a-day fee is high, but it does include a full day's worth of classes ranging from regular aerobics to yoga, Pilates, and dance. Did we mention the rock-climbing wall?

The **Grand Canal Shoppes** rank with Caesars' shops as an absolute must-see. Like Caesars, the area is a mock Italian village with a blue, cloud-studded, painted sky overhead. But down the middle runs a canal, complete with singing gondoliers. (The 10-min. ride costs about $15, which seems steep, but trust us, it's a *lot* more in the real Venice.) The whole thing finishes up at a small re-creation of St. Mark's Square, which features glass blowers, traveling musicians, flower sellers, and the like. Expect to run into famous Venetians such as a flirty Casanova and a travel-weary Marco Polo. It's ambitious and a big step up from animatronic figures. Oh, and the stores are also probably worth a look—a decent mixture of high-end fashion and more affordable shops.

And let's not forget that this is the only hotel in town with a branch of the famed Guggenheim Museum, called the **Guggenheim/Hermitage Museum** (p. 194).

And finally, because in Vegas more is always more, in 2006 The Venetian will open an entirely new hotel, this time not Venice themed, with 3,000 more posh suites, a huge casino, and who knows what else.

3355 Las Vegas Blvd. S., Las Vegas, NV 89109. ℭ 888/2-VENICE (283-6423) or 702/414-1000. Fax 702/414-4805. www.venetian.com. 4,029 units. $125–$399 double. Extra person $35. Children under 13 stay free in parent's room. AE, DC, DISC, MC, V. Free self- and valet parking. **Amenities:** Casino; wedding chapel; showroom; 18 restaurants; 6 outdoor pools; health club and spa; video arcade; concierge; tour desk; car-rental desk; business center; shopping arcade; 24-hr. room service; laundry service; dry cleaning; nonsmoking rooms; executive-level rooms. *In room:* A/C, TV w/pay movies, fax, dataport, fridge, hair dryer, iron/ironing board, safe, high-speed Internet access (for a fee).

EXPENSIVE

Bally's Las Vegas ✿   With all the fancy-pants new hotels in town, it's so hard to keep up with the Joneses, or the Wynns, as the case may be. And here's poor Bally's, with a perfect location, and it's got no big fountain or Eiffel Tower or anything to make a passerby think "Right, gotta go gamble there," much less a tourist booking long distance to think "Right, gotta stay there." And we aren't really going to make you change your mind, though lately, we might give you a reason to consider it. After all, you can get a room for a ridiculously low rate these days, and those rooms, which are larger than average, have recently been redone to an admirable degree, with some swell touches, including modern curvy couches, big TVs, wireless Internet access, and marble this and that. The public areas still feel a little dated, but the hotel is connected to its sister property, Paris Las Vegas, which is swanky and modern enough. Also, it's a stop on the new monorail system, so you'll be able to go just about everywhere by foot or by swift train, and, thanks to those nice rooms, you've got someplace pleasant to return to.

Bally's has the usual range of dining choices and is justly renowned for its **Sterling Sunday Brunch** (p. 181). The casino is large, well lit, and colorful, and there's also a headliner showroom and the splashy *Jubilee!* revue (p. 273).

3645 Las Vegas Blvd. S. (at Flamingo Rd.), Las Vegas, NV 89109. ℭ 800/634-3434 or 702/739-4111. Fax 702/967-3890. www.ballyslv.com. 2,814 units. $69 and up double; add $35–$60 to rate for concierge floor (including breakfast); $300 and up suite. Extra person $30. Children under 18 stay free in parent's room. AE, DC, MC, V. Free self- and valet parking. **Amenities:** Casino; showrooms; 13 restaurants; outdoor pool; 8 night-lit tennis courts; health club and spa; video arcade; concierge; tour desk; car-rental desk; business center; shopping arcade; 24-hr. room service; laundry service; dry cleaning; nonsmoking rooms; executive-level rooms. *In room:* A/C, TV w/pay movies, iron/ironing board, high-speed Internet access (for a fee).

The Flamingo Las Vegas ✿   The Flamingo is the Strip's senior citizen, boasting a colorful history. It's changed a great deal since Bugsy Siegel opened his 105-room oasis "in the middle of nowhere" in 1946. It was so luxurious for its time that even the janitors wore tuxedos. (Hey, new Vegas? That's class.) Jimmy Durante was the opening headliner, and the wealthy and famous flocked to the tropical paradise of swaying palms, lagoons, and waterfalls. A relatively recent renovation and expansion isn't going to make Siegel's "real class joint" cause you to forget about, say, the rooms at the new Venetian tower, but it did freshen the joint up—including making it somewhat easier to reach the outside world, which in the past was often difficult. A recent addition is a branch of singer Jimmy Buffett's Margaritaville nightclub, a theme locale that makes us wince when it's in, say, New Orleans, but this one, here in Vegas? Not bad! So let's see how these additions continue to keep the old girl going.

Rooms occupy six towers and are variously decorated. Some are done up in soft blues and peach, and enhanced by pretty fabrics, light painted-wood furnishings, and watercolors of tropical scenes, lending a resort look. Others use soft earth tones, forest green, or coral. The **Flamingo Paradise Garden Buffet** (p. 184) is a decent choice. There are also several bars, plus a huge casino and the *Second City Improv* production show (p. 278).

For those planning some leisure time outside the casino, The Flamingo's exceptional pool area, spa, and tennis courts are a big draw. Five gorgeous swimming pools, two whirlpools, water slides, and a kiddie pool are located in a 15-acre Caribbean landscape amid lagoons, meandering streams, fountains, waterfalls, a rose garden, and islands of live flamingos and African penguins. Ponds have ducks, swans, and koi, and a grove of 2,000 palms graces an expanse of lawn. Although the water can be a little chilly, kids should be able to spend hours in the pool area.

A health club ($20 fee per day) offers a variety of Universal weight machines, treadmills, stair machines, free weights, sauna, steam, a TV lounge, and hot and cold whirlpools. Exercise tapes are available, and spa services include massage, soap rub, salt glow, tanning beds, and oxygen pep-up. And the new monorail has a stop out back.

3555 Las Vegas Blvd. S. (between Sands Ave. and Flamingo Rd.), Las Vegas, NV 89109. © **800/732-2111** or 702/733-3111. Fax 702/733-3353. www.flamingolv.com. 3,999 units. $79 and up double; $249 and up suite. Extra person $20. Children under 18 stay free in parent's room. Inquire about packages and timeshare suites. AE, DC, DISC, MC, V. Free self- and valet parking. **Amenities:** Casino; showrooms; 8 restaurants; 5 outdoor pools; 4 night-lit tennis courts; health club and spa; small video arcade; tour desk; car-rental desk; business center; shopping arcade; 24-hr. room service; in-room massage; babysitting; laundry service; dry cleaning; nonsmoking rooms; executive-level rooms. *In room:* A/C, TV w/pay movies, dataport, hair dryer, iron/ironing board, safe, high-speed Internet access (for a fee).

Harrah's Las Vegas 🏃   Here's another property that is doing its best to keep up with the pace in Vegas, to no great success. Though parts of Harrah's benefited from a reworking of the place a few years ago, the rest of it evokes Old Las Vegas in the way The Riviera does—as in, dark, dated, and claustrophobic. Still, there is much to like here, and occasional quite good rates might make the so-so bits worth overlooking. Certainly, they want to be the fun and convivial place we wish more of Vegas were (instead of pretty much catering to high rollers and simply tolerating the rest of us with normal budgets). The new monorail stop might be a draw, though, since it will now be easier to get to and from here.

Guest rooms were recently refurbished—just in time, as guests were complaining. All the rooms are larger than average; the points that emerge from both the old and the newer tower wings translate inside into an extra triangle of space for a couch and table. Some rooms also contain a kitchen. Spacious minisuites in this section, offering large sofas and comfortable armchairs, are especially desirable.

The Range (p. 152) steakhouse is one of the few hotel restaurants that overlooks the Strip, and the hotel's **buffet** (p. 183) isn't bad. The casino has a fun, festive atmosphere, complete with "party pits." Harrah's showroom was hosting singer **Clint Holmes** (p. 271) and his 12-piece band at press time. An improv comedy show, **Mac King**'s wonderful comedy/magic act (p. 276), and Greg Thompson's late-night revue *Skintight* are also on the docket here, as is weekend happy-hour karaoke time in the La Playa lounge. By the time you read this, a new Toby Keith–themed restaurant/performing venue will have opened up, along with a new food court, featuring the usual fast-food suspects.

Carnaval Court (p. 258) is a festive, palm-fringed shopping plaza where strolling entertainers perform. It's notable because it's right on the Strip but entirely outdoors; similar ventures at other hotels are inside artificial environments. Note that lounge singer legend **Cook E. Jarr** often plays here late on varying nights (p. 264).

Harrah's has an Olympic-size swimming pool and sun-deck area with waterfall and trellised garden areas, a whirlpool, and a kids' wading pool. It's a pretty underwhelming pool by Vegas standards.

The hotel's health club is one of the better facilities on the Strip, with a full-range spa and a gym with Lifecycles, treadmills, stair machines, rowing machines, lots of Universal equipment, free weights, and two TVs and a VCR for which aerobic exercise tapes are available. Its $20-a-day access charge is more reasonable than the fees in other hotels.

3475 Las Vegas Blvd. S. (between Flamingo and Spring Mountain roads), Las Vegas, NV 89109. © 800/HARRAHS (427-7247) or 702/369-5000. Fax 702/369-5283. www.harrahs.com. 2,700 units. $79 and up standard "deluxe" double, $99 and up standard "superior" double; $199 and up suite. Extra person $20; no discount for children. AE, DC, DISC, MC, V. Free self- and valet parking. **Amenities:** Casino; showrooms; 8 restaurants; outdoor pool; health club and spa; concierge; tour desk; car-rental desk; business center; shopping arcade; 24-hr. room service; laundry service; dry cleaning; nonsmoking rooms; executive-level rooms. *In room:* A/C, TV w/pay movies, dataport, hair dryer, iron/ironing board, safe.

⌒Tips So Your Trip Goes Swimmingly . . .

Part of the delight of the Vegas resort complexes is the gorgeous pools—what could be better for beating the summer heat? But there are pools and there are *pools,* so you'll need to keep several things in mind when searching for the right one for you.

During the winter, it's often too cold or windy to do much lounging, and even if the weather is amenable, the hotels often close part of their pool areas during winter and early spring. The pools are also not heated for the most part, but in fairness, they largely don't need to be.

Most hotel pools are shallow, chest-high at best, only about 3 feet deep in many spots (the hotels want you gambling, not swimming). Diving is impossible—not that a single pool allows it anyway.

And finally, during those hot days, be warned that sitting by pools next to heavily windowed buildings such as The Mirage and TI at the Mirage allows you to experience the same thing a bug does under a magnifying glass with a sun ray directed on it. Regardless of time of year, be sure to slather on the sunscreen; there's a reason you see so many unhappy lobster-red people roaming the streets. Many pool areas don't offer much in the way of shade. On the other hand, if your tan line is important to you, head for Caesars or Mandalay Bay, which both have topless sunbathing areas where you can toast even more flesh than at the other hotels.

At any of the pools, you can rent cabanas (which often include TVs, special lounge chairs, and even better poolside service), but these should be reserved as far in advance as possible, and with the exception of the Four Seasons' complimentary shaded lounging area, most cost a hefty fee. If you are staying at a chain hotel, you will most likely find an average pool, but if you want to spend some time at a better one, be aware that most of the casino-hotel pool attendants will ask to see your room key. If they are busy, you might be able to sneak in, or at least blend in with a group ahead of you.

Impressions

Supercalifragilisticexpialidocious!
—Governor Bob Miller's reaction upon first visiting The Mirage

The Mirage 𝕣𝕣   Even though it has become somewhat eclipsed by the very hotels whose presence it made possible, we still really like this place. From the moment you walk in and breathe the faintly tropically perfumed air (we think it's vanilla) and enter the lush rainforest, it's just a different experience from most Vegas hotels.

The Mirage was Steve Wynn's first project built from the ground up. It seems funny now, but back in 1989, this was considered a complete gamble that was sure to be a failure. That was before the hotel opened, mind you. On opening day, the crowds nearly tore the place down getting inside, and The Mirage soon made its money back. Now it is the model upon which all recent hotels have been based.

Occupying 102 acres, The Mirage is fronted by more than a city block of cascading waterfalls and tropical foliage centering on a "volcano," which, after dark, erupts every 15 minutes, spewing fire 100 feet above the lagoons below. To be honest, it's not very volcano-like; if you've seen any of the lava-saturated volcano movies, you'll be disappointed. Instead of lava flow, expect a really neat light show, and you won't mind a bit. (In passing, that volcano cost $30 million, which is equal to the entire original construction cost for Caesars next door.) The lobby is dominated by a 53-foot, 20,000-gallon simulated coral-reef aquarium stocked with more than 1,000 colorful tropical fish. This gives you something to look at while waiting (never for long) for check-in.

Next, you'll walk through the rainforest, which occupies a 90-foot domed atrium—a path meanders through palms, banana trees, waterfalls, and serene pools. If we must find a complaint with The Mirage, it's with the next bit, as you have to negotiate 8 miles (or so it seems) of casino mayhem to get to your room, the pool, food, or the outside world. It gets old, fast. (On the other hand, the sundries shop is located right next to the guest-room elevators, so if you forgot toothpaste, you don't have to travel miles to get more.)

The rooms have recently been redone to a strong color palette that is oddly similar to the rooms' original tropical decor scheme. Frankly, it's here most of all where The Mirage isn't holding up its end; the rooms are nice, but there are nicer—and larger—ones all over town now, and the bathrooms are a little too cramped for what's supposed to be a swanky hotel.

Off the casino is a habitat for Siegfried and Roy's white tigers—yes, still in place despite the unpleasantness, a plaster enclosure that allows for photo-taking and "aaaahhhs." Behind the pool are the **Dolphin Habitat** and Siegfried and Roy's **Secret Garden.**

The Italian food at **Onda,** and the **Mirage Cravings Buffet** are detailed in chapter 6.

The highly prominent production show by **Danny Gans** is reviewed in chapter 10, and The Mirage has one of our favorite casinos.

Out back is the pool, one of the nicest in Vegas, with a quarter-mile shoreline, a tropical paradise of waterfalls and trees, water slides, and so forth. It looks inviting, but truth be told, it's sometimes on the chilly side and isn't very deep. But it's so pretty you'll hardly care. Free swimming lessons and water-aerobics classes take place daily at the pool. The **Mirage Day Spa** teems with friendly staff anxious to pamper you, bringing you iced towels to cool you during your workout and refreshing juices and smoothies afterward. The gym is one of the largest and best stocked on the Strip.

3400 Las Vegas Blvd. S. (between Flamingo Rd. and Sands Ave.), Las Vegas, NV 89109. ℂ **800/627-6667** or 702/ 791-7111. Fax 702/791-7446. www.mirage.com. 3,044 units. $119 and up double; $249 and up suite. Extra person $30; no discount for children. AE, DC, DISC, MC, V. Free self- and valet parking. **Amenities:** Casino; showrooms; 11 restaurants; beautiful outdoor pool; fitness center and spa; concierge; tour desk; car-rental desk; business center; shopping arcade; 24-hr. room service; laundry service; dry cleaning; nonsmoking rooms; executive-level rooms. *In room:* A/C, TV w/pay movies, dataport, hair dryer, iron/ironing board, safe, high-speed Internet access (for a fee).

Palms Resort & Casino 𝕽   One of the hottest of the newer hotels, given quite the PR boost when it was Britney's base for her wedding debacle. In keeping with the tropical-foliage name, it's more or less Miami-themed (but without the pastels), with a strange aversion toward straight lines (really, check out all those curves). Inside a bland building is a pretty nice complex—which we say only because it's a puzzle that the place is such a hot spot (though we predict that the beautiful person clientele will be shifting in part to THEhotel). That's mostly due to the nightlife options—both **Ghost Bar** and the nightclub **Rain** have lines of people every night the facilities are open, offering to sell their firstborn sons for a chance to go inside. Why did those two places catch on so? Not really sure (though you can read our speculations about both in chapter 10), but you need to know that the entrances to them stand right by the elevators to your hotel room, which means on a busy weekend night, there can be upwards of 4,000 gorgeous and antsy (if not angry) people standing between you and access to your hotel room. If you are a Hilton sister, or wish to see if one will date you, this could be heaven, but if encountering the beautifully dressed and coifed, with 0% body fat and sullen expressions of entitlement, and the 19-year-olds who seek to become all of that (and usually affect a thuggish demeanor) makes you, like us, itch, this might not be the most comfortable place to stay. It won't help that a new tower, set to open by the time you read this, plus yet another addition, will mean construction around the facility for some time to come.

Having said all that, note that The Palms has perhaps some of the most comfortable beds in Vegas, thanks to fluffy pillows and duvets that make one reluctant to rise, plus big TVs and huge bathrooms. The main pool is oddly cheap looking—it's really a posing spot rather than a splash, while a second pool has a bar and mermaids swimming in the water at night. Also on the property is **Alizé** (p. 146), in competition for the title Best Restaurant in Town (and owner of the title Most Gorgeous and Romantic Restaurant), a cheap and hearty **buffet** (p. 184), movie theaters, a McDonald's, and other reliable cheap chain eateries.

4321 W. Flamingo Rd. (at I-15), Las Vegas, NV 89103. ℂ **866/942-7777** or 702/942-7777. Fax 702/942-6859. www.palms.com. 400 units. Sun–Thurs $79 and up double; Fri–Sat $119 and up double. Extra person $15; no discount for children. AE, DC, DISC, MC, V. Free self- and valet parking. **Amenities:** Casino; nightclub/showroom; 7 restaurants plus a food court; outdoor pool; health club and spa; Jacuzzi; sauna; concierge; business center; 24-hr. room service; in-room massage; laundry service; dry cleaning; nonsmoking rooms; executive-level rooms. *In room:* A/C, TV w/pay movies, dataport, coffeemaker, hair dryer, iron/ironing board, safe, high-speed Internet access (for a fee).

Rio All-Suite Hotel & Casino 𝕽   Rio bills itself as a "carnival" atmosphere hotel, which in this case means hectic, crowded, and noisy, and the recent edict requiring the already Most Scantily Clad Waitresses in Town to burst into song and dance in between delivering beers. The newer section, the Masquerade Village, is actually pretty pleasant, with a very high ceiling, but the older section's low ceilings only seem to accentuate how crowded the area is in both the number of people and the amount of stuff (slot machines, gaming tables, and so on). All this party atmosphere, by the way, is strictly for adults; the hotel actively discourages guests from bringing children.

The rooms are touted because of their size. Every one is a "suite," which does not mean two separate rooms, but rather one large room with a sectional, corner sofa, and coffee table at one end. The dressing areas are certainly larger than average and feature a number of extra amenities, such as refrigerators (unusual for a Vegas hotel room) and small snacks. Windows, running the whole length of the room, are floor to ceiling, with a pretty impressive view of the Strip, Vegas, or the mountains (depending on which way you're facing). The furniture doesn't feel like hotel-room standard, but otherwise the decor is fairly bland.

Fiore and the hotel's first-rate buffet are described in chapter 6. You might consider checking out the **Wine Cellar Tasting Room,** which bills itself as "the world's largest and most extensive collection of fine wines," and hyperbole aside, it's certainly impressive and a must-do for any wine aficionado.

Penn & Teller, the smartest show in town, is reviewed in chapter 10, as is the **Voodoo Lounge, Bikinis,** and **Club Rio.** The missable Scintas also do a regular act, while we adore the unpredictable antics produced by the improv dinner show *Tony & Tina's Wedding.* The casino, alas, is dark and claustrophobic. In case you missed the party/carnival theme, there is a rather bizarre live-action show called *The Masquerade Show in the Sky.* It is presented Thursday through Tuesday at 3:30, 4:30, 5:30, 7, 8, 9, and 10pm. Sets modeled after Mardi Gras floats (sort of) move on grids set in the ceiling, filled with costumed performers who lip-sync to music that's designed to rev up the crowd but that doesn't continue the theme (swing selections, for example). These floats are best viewed from the second floor of the village. Down below, dancers do their thing on a stage, while even stranger costumes (ostriches, dragons, and so on) prance next to them. Guests can also don costumes and ride a float, but you have to pay for the privilege.

Out back is a pool with a sandy beach, and two new pools in imaginative fish and shell shapes that seem inviting until you get up close and see how small they are. It could be especially disappointing after you have braved the long, cluttered walk (particularly from the new tower rooms) to get there. Three whirlpool spas nestle amid rocks and foliage, there are two sand-volleyball courts, and blue-and-white-striped cabanas (equipped with rafts and misting coolers) can be rented for $100 and up per day. The 18-hole championship **Rio Secco golf course** was designed by Rees Jones.

3700 W. Flamingo Rd. (at I-15), Las Vegas, NV 89103. ℂ **888/752-9746** or 702/777-7777. Fax 702/777-7611. www. playrio.com. 2,582 units. $99 and up double-occupancy suite. Extra person $30; no discount for children. Inquire about golf packages. AE, DC, MC, V. Free self- and valet parking. **Amenities:** Casino; showrooms; 13 restaurants plus additional fast-food outlets; 4 outdoor pools; golf course; health club and spa; Jacuzzi; sauna; video arcade; concierge; car-rental desk; business center; shopping arcade; 24-hr. room service; in-room massage; laundry service; dry cleaning; nonsmoking rooms; executive-level rooms. *In room:* A/C, TV w/pay movies, fridge, coffeemaker, hair dryer, iron/ironing board, safe.

TI at the Mirage 🎭🎭 Huh? What happened to Treasure Island? What happened to the pirates? Why, Vegas grew up, that's what. Or, rather, it wants the kids it once actively tried to court to grow up, or at least, not come around until they are able to drink and gamble properly.

Originally the most modern family-friendly hotel, the former Treasure Island was a blown-up version of Disneyland's *Pirates of the Caribbean.* But that's all behind them now, and the name change is there to make sure you understand this is a grown-up, sophisticated resort. There might still be the odd pirate element here and there, but only because someone absent-mindedly missed it in a recent ruthless purging of the last remnants. The latest victim is the pirate stunt show out front; it's been revamped so that the pirates, and you have no idea how much we wish we were making this up, now "battle" scantily clad "strippers"—er, "sirens."

To be fair, none of this matters a whit, unless, like us, you got a kick out of the skulls and crossbones, and treasure chests bursting with jewels and gold, that originally decorated the place. What remains, after they stripped the pirate gilt, is such a nice place to stay that in some ways, it even outranks its older sister, The Mirage. The good-size rooms pretty much follow the pattern of The Mirage's last phase of room decor—modified French Regency with a mélange of patterns, but the monochromatic color (many shades of gold) tones it down, and overall, while not distinctive, per se, they are much nicer than most in their price range. Good bathrooms feature a large soaking tub—a bather's delight. Best of all, Strip-side rooms have a view of the pirate battle—views are best from the sixth floor on up. You know, so you can see right down the sirens' dresses.

The hotel offers a premier restaurant, the **Buccaneer Bay Club,** a hotel **buffet,** and the new branch of Los Angeles's **Canter's** deli. Treasure Island is home to **Cirque du Soleil's** *Mystère* (p. 270), one of the best shows in town.

A free tram travels between I at the Mirage and The Mirage almost around the clock. For a good photo op, sit in the front of the first car: As you leave the loading dock, note how The Mirage, palm trees, and a bit of the New York–New York skyline are framed in an attractive, and surreal, manner.

There's a full-service spa and health club with a complement of machines, plus sauna, steam, whirlpool, massage, on-site trainers, TVs and stereos with headsets, and anything else you might need (including a full line of Sebastian grooming products in the women's locker room). There's a $20-per-day fee to use the facilities.

The pool is not that memorable, with none of the massive foliage and other details that make the one at The Mirage stand out (so blah is it that the staff didn't even bother to check room keys when last we swam here). It's a large, free-form swimming pool with a 230-foot loop slide and a nicely landscaped sun-deck area. It's often crawling with kids, so if that's a turn-off, go elsewhere.

3300 Las Vegas Blvd. S. (at Spring Mountain Rd.), Las Vegas, NV 89109. ℰ **800/944-7444** or 702/894-7111. Fax 702/894-7446. www.treasureisland.com. 2,885 units. From $89 double; from $129 suite. Extra person $30; no discount for children. Inquire about packages. AE, DC, DISC, MC, V. Free self- and valet parking. **Amenities:** Casino; showrooms; 11 restaurants; outdoor pool; fitness center and spa; concierge; tour desk; car-rental desk; business center; shopping arcade; 24-hr. room service; laundry service; dry cleaning; nonsmoking rooms; executive-level rooms. *In room:* A/C, TV w/pay movies, fax, dataport, hair dryer, iron/ironing board, safe, high-speed Internet access (for a fee).

The Westin Casuarina Las Vegas Hotel & Spa 🐾🐾

When the ever-more-seedy Maxim was more or less stripped to its bones and turned into a Westin, we were thrilled. What Vegas needs, we keep saying, not that anyone hears us, is a true kicky boutique hotel, one that puts real service and real style ahead of slot machines. (We still have hopes for a W, actually. Silly of us, but there it is.)

This Westin won't fill that bill—coming a lot closer would be THEhotel at Mandalay Bay—but business travelers who want a little style and don't mind if said style is just a tad generic and sterile will be pleased with this hotel. There is nothing wrong with the rooms—they are in excellent taste, done in eye-pleasing sages and wheats, complete with The Westin's self-congratulatory trademarked "Heavenly Bed," which caused one occupant to dream she was sleeping on clouds (and the other to note it has a whole lot of polyester in its make-up), and the baths are gleaming, if small—but they pale compared to some of the (admittedly occasionally lurid) fantasies around town. For the price, especially if you were looking for something Vegas-riffic, you might be disappointed. It doesn't help that the cool exec-style lobby/check-in area melds into a casino area that seems to have been missed in the renovations; it's weirdly dated. It also doesn't help that the staff says "No, that's not something we do or offer" more often than "Yes, we can do that," though they say it nicely enough. There is an adequate (and free!) gym, reached by walking right by all the business meeting areas, and a decent pool. Ultimately, it's too good a property not to give a relatively high rating to, but you need to understand that, by Vegas standards—which means different things to different people—it's boring.

160 E. Flamingo Rd., Las Vegas, NV 89109. © 702/836-9775. Fax 702/836-9776. www.starwood.com. 825 units. $139 and up standard double. AE, DC, DISC, MC, V. Free self- and valet parking. Pets allowed. **Amenities:** Casino; showroom; restaurant; Starbucks; bar; pool; health club; concierge; tour desk; business center; meeting rooms; sundries shop; 24-hr. room service; massage; laundry; dry cleaning. *In room:* A/C, TV, minibar, hair dryer, iron/ironing board, safe, high-speed Internet access, robes, newspaper.

MODERATE

Barbary Coast Hotel & Casino   You can't fault the location of this hotel. It's right on the busiest corner of the Strip, smack in the middle of the action. With all the hotel business (the itty-bitty reception desk and tiny sundries/gift shop counter) set on the fringes of the small, dark, cluttered casino, this is very old Vegas, which is sort of a good thing; but unfortunately, it's becoming harder to wrap one's mind around it in these days of megacasino complexes. Nevertheless, a small hotel is a rare thing in this town, and a face-lift would make the Barbary Coast a nice boutique hotel. Let's encourage them in that direction.

As of this writing, the rooms are being completely redone to lighten up the formerly dark Victorian affairs they used to be. That's good news: Even though furnishings and carpet were holding up well, it was time for a revamp. Regardless of the look, each has an extra corner of space for a couple of chairs or a couch alongside the very cramped bathroom. *Beware:* The very loud intersection outside can make rooms noisy.

Drai's, an upscale restaurant, is covered in detail in chapter 6. **Michael's** is the hotel's premier restaurant, with only two seatings a night in an intimate, old-fashioned room. The food gets raves, but the menu is completely dated (chops and the like), so it's best for those with deep pockets who mistrust nouvelle cuisine. Two bars serve the casino.

3595 Las Vegas Blvd. S. (at Flamingo Rd.), Las Vegas, NV 89109. © **800/634-6755** or 702/737-7111. Fax 702/894-9954. www.barbarycoastcasino.com. 200 units. $69 and up double. Extra person $15. Children under 14 stay free in parent's room. AE, DC, DISC, MC, V. Free self- and valet parking. **Amenities:** Casino; 4 restaurants; tour desk; car-rental desk; 24-hr. room service; dry cleaning; nonsmoking rooms. *In room:* A/C, TV w/pay movies, dataport, hair dryer, iron/ironing board.

Bourbon Street *(Value*   Just a few steps (well, okay, more than a few, but not by much) down from the main Strip action, Bourbon Street is a bargain. It looks like a

---

⌒Tips **Is There a Doctor in the House?**

The Imperial Palace hotel has a well-appointed 24-hour urgent-care clinic, which is open to the public. Given its location, right in the middle of the action, it's well worth knowing about.

dump, but it's not. Adequately sized rooms, while hardly comparable to those in the luxe establishments on the Strip, are surprisingly nice—brighter, cleaner, and more cheerful than you would expect, with small but sweetly attended-to bathrooms (including some nice grooming amenities). Given price and location, it's a heck of a deal overall.

120 E. Flamingo Rd. (between the Strip and Koval Lane), Las Vegas, NV 89109. © 800/634-6956 or 702/737-7200. Fax 702/794-3490. www.bourbonstreethotel.com. 167 units. $39 and up standard double; $59 and up minisuite; $69 and up executive suite. Extra person $10. Children under 12 stay free in parent's room. AE, DC, DISC, MC, V. Free self- and valet parking. **Amenities:** Small casino; restaurant; dry cleaning; nonsmoking rooms. *In room:* A/C, TV w/pay movies, safe.

Imperial Palace *(Value)* Location, location, location. And price, price, price. That's what the IP has going for it—don't think anything else. It's smack in the middle of the Strip—it doesn't get any more centrally located than this, and now there's even a monorail stop right out back—and on a weekend night when rooms at nicer hotels are running $400 (that's for a regular room), lodgings can be had here for under $60. What you get in exchange is an older, darker hotel that looks sort of sleazy in spots but really isn't. Not much, anyway. It just seems like it in comparison to the gleaming hulks across and down the street. We actually know types who prefer this, a more classic Vegas feel, to the airy new upstarts. We aren't among those, we have to admit, and you may not be as well. The standard rooms are just that, but they all have balconies, which is exceedingly rare in Vegas. A perfect Vegas hoot, the "luv tub" rooms are some of the best deals on the Strip, especially if you can get them for the cheapest end of the price range; you'll get a larger bedroom (with a mirror over the bed!) and a larger-than-usual bathroom that features a 300-gallon sunken "luv tub" (with still more mirrors).

From April to October, the hotel holds "luaus" at the pool, with a Polynesian revue and buffet. Expect Tiki torches.

The hotel is also home to the long-running *Legends in Concert* impersonator show (p. 275). The casino has relatively low (for the Strip) table limits.

A unique feature is the **Auto Collections at Imperial Palace** (p. 190), displaying more than 800 antique, classic, and special-interest vehicles spanning a century of automotive history.

3535 Las Vegas Blvd. S. (between Sands Ave. and Flamingo Rd.), Las Vegas, NV 89109. © 800/634-6441 or 702/731-3311. Fax 702/735-8578. www.imperialpalace.com. 2,700 units. $59 and up double; $99 and up "luv tub" suite, $159 and up other suites. Extra person $19. Children under 6 stay free in parent's room. Inquire about packages. AE, DC, DISC, MC, V. Free self- and valet parking. **Amenities:** Casino; showrooms; wedding chapel; 10 restaurants; outdoor pool; health club and spa; video arcade; concierge; tour desk; car-rental desk; shopping arcade; 24-hr. room service; laundry service; dry cleaning; nonsmoking rooms; executive-level rooms. *In room:* A/C, TV w/pay movies, hair dryer, iron/ironing board, high-speed wireless Internet service available throughout the hotel (for a fee).

5 North Strip

VERY EXPENSIVE

Wynn Las Vegas Because Steve Wynn is a modern-day Vegas legend, because this town almost entirely owes its present-day look and outlook to him, because this hotel (built on the site of the old Desert Inn and opened on the same day, Apr 28, that grand old dame was originally opened) came with a $2.7 billion (yes, that's with a "*b*") price tag, and because there was a great deal of hype that used words and phrases such as "like nothing you've ever seen before," there was a corresponding amount of anticipation and expectation surrounding the opening of this, Vegas's newest and perhaps most trumpeted resort. The result? Something that is at once pretty "wow" and a whole lot "It looks like Bellagio." In short, it was something many of us had, in fact, seen before, just down the street. And that is both fair and not; sure, the hotel does not live up to its *sui generis* claims, but that's obvious only if you have previous knowledge of other Vegas hotels. If you are new to town, this will look plenty spectacular. A better question might be "What's the visitor getting for that price tag?" This is especially relevant since the room rate can be upward of $300 a night (though even as soon as a month after it opened, certain e-mail-only offers went as low as $139). Just about everything here can generate sticker shock in all but those used to costly resorts, but note that costly resorts usually have one-tenth the number of rooms here.

The hotel feels a little bit cramped when you first enter—we are used to swooping Vegas lobby displays—and a reception area that is impractically proportioned, resulting in some check-in wait issues. (The suspicion is that all this makes the place seem less behemoth and more resort-size.) The hotel has no discernable theme (apart from that tendency to prompt constant comparisons to Bellagio), which may be disappointing for those looking for, say, a New York–New York style of theme-aganza. The interior has some superior moments, including considerable use of natural light (via various skylights and atriums), unusual in this town and most welcome, and a floral motif reflected in eye-catching brightly hued floor mosaics, artistic fresh flower arrangements throughout, and, best of all, the conservatory that runs down the center and, like its predecessor at Bellagio, features frequently changed displays. There are also some of the most garish lighting fixtures in a town not known for its subtlety in chandeliers. The layout is devoted to old-school Vegas "force the guests to maneuver around and through the casino to get anywhere" floor planning.

As with all Wynn hotels, there is an installation in front of the building, a 150-foot tall man-made mountain covered in trees (many mature trees taken from the old Desert Inn golf course) and waterfalls, and like the others, this comes with a "free show." The quotation marks are because said show is not viewable from the street—neither, in fact, is the mountain itself. The latter can be glimpsed only in bits and pieces, though there is a decent shot at a portion of it as you enter from the Strip across from the pedestrian walkway, while the former can be viewed only when either dining at the SW or Daniel Boulard Brasserie, or having a drink at a couple bars, where you will be required to purchase two drinks per person, starting at $12 a glass. There is one truly free viewing platform, but it is tiny.

These complaints notwithstanding, there's nothing really wrong with the place; we jut nitpick because the pre-hype invited it. In fact, there is much to like here. The rooms are the hands-down best on the Strip (at least, that aren't suites, such as at The Venetian or THEhotel). Particularly large (it's kind of ruined us for even the more spacious of other rooms), with much-appreciated floor-to-ceiling views (west side shows off the mountain and waterfalls, east side the golf course; both are choice), deeply comfortable beds with high-thread-count sheets and feather beds atop good-quality mattresses plus down comforters, a flatscreen TV, and excellent up-to-the-minute bathrooms complete with quite long and deep tubs, a second flatscreen TV, and silky lemony amenities. Take note of the silky-satiny robes (the best we've ever gotten in a hotel) and plush velour slippers. All the rooms are done in shades that happily break the recent trend toward bland parchment tones, but at least one of the palettes is some strange hybrid of salmon and terra cotta, so while we appreciate the effort, the result

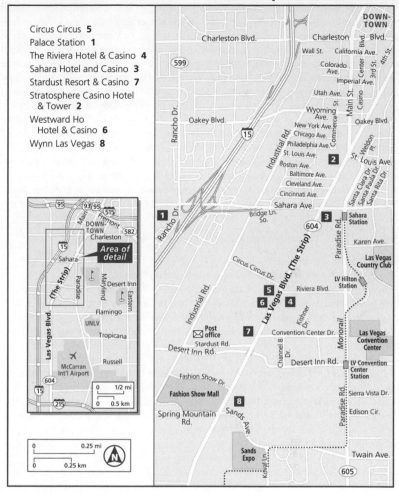

Circus Circus **5**

Palace Station **1**

The Riviera Hotel & Casino **4**

Sahara Hotel and Casino **3**

Stardust Resort & Casino **7**

Stratosphere Casino Hotel & Tower **2**

Westward Ho Hotel & Casino **6**

Wynn Las Vegas **8**

can be disconcerting. Love the Warhol flower prints, though. There is allegedly turndown service at night, but that can be spotty.

The gym is excellent, stuffed with up-to-the-minute equipment, most with individual TV screens, though we could do without the windows looking onto an interior hallway that make our workout visible to all passersby. The spa area is serene and particularly pretty, with an atrium emitting natural light into the bathing areas. The pool area has four oval-shaped numbers connected by some stretches long enough for laps, plus a "European bathing" (read: topless) area that includes outdoor blackjack tables.

Dining options are superb (though generally exceptionally pricey), including **Alex, Bartolotta, Corsa Cucina, Daniel Boulard Brasserie,** and the **buffet,** all reviewed in chapter 6. The Art Gallery is small, but every piece in it is a gem and thus just about totally worth the high admission. A shopping street features high-end choices—Chanel,

Cartier, Manolo Blahnik, Gaultier—but still seems a bit more lower-economic (that's relative, mind you) user-friendly than a similar one at Bellagio. Make special note of the apothecary-style shop next to the sundries shop; it stocks all sorts of fine lotions and potions, including, remarkably, the centuries-old, coveted (and still difficult-to-find) monk-produced line from the Santa Maria Novella Pharmacy in Florence. Products made by monks in Vegas? Well, why not? There's also a Ferrari dealership—no, really, and what's more, it's so popular that at press time, it was charging $10 (!!) for admission. (*Tip:* You can see a few cars from a slight distance from the shop, which is still free to enter.)

In the end, this is a very adult hotel, in the best sense—classy and mature, that is, and that's a good thing. But still, so was the old Desert Inn, which hit all the right resort notes even in its last days, only to be replaced by the bigger-is-better ethos.

3131 Las Vegas Blvd. S. (at the corner of Sands Dr.), Las Vegas, NV 89109. (C) **888/320-9966** or 702/770-7100. Fax 702/770-1571. www.wynnlasvegas.com. 3,933 units. $249 and up double. Extra person $50; no discount for children. AE, DC, DISC, MC, V. Free self- and valet parking. **Amenities:** Casino; showrooms; 2 wedding chapels; 13 restaurants; 5 outdoor pools; fitness center and spa; concierge; tour desk; car-rental desk; business center; 24-hr. room service; in-room massage; laundry service; dry cleaning; nonsmoking rooms; executive-level rooms. *In room:* A/C, TV w/pay movies, dataport, hair dryer, iron/ironing board, safe, high-speed Internet access (for a fee).

EXPENSIVE

The Riviera Hotel & Casino *(Overrated* Its best days long past, this former Strip star is looking awfully dumpy these days (and there are rumors, thanks to its part-owner-ship by development-happy Donald Trump, that it will soon be knocked down any-way). Between that and its promotion as an "alternative for grown-ups" and an "adult-oriented hotel," you should probably stay here only if you can get a deal and simply must be on the Strip. You certainly shouldn't bring the kids, who are actively discouraged as guests.

Opened in 1955 (Liberace cut the ribbon and Joan Crawford was the official host-ess of opening ceremonies), The Riviera was the first "high-rise" on the Strip, at nine stories. Today it tries to evoke the Vegas of the good old days—"come drink, gamble, and see a show"—and while it is appropriately dark and glitzy, it's also very crowded and has a confusing layout. Don't miss your chance to take your photo with the bronze memorial to the Crazy Girls (their premier, largely nekkid, show), and their butts, outside on the Strip. There is a pool here, but it's very dull.

Rooms are blah and not likely to improve. Half the rooms offer pool views. There is the predictable assortment of dining options—though an excellent choice for fam-ilies, ironically, is the **Mardi Gras Food Court,** which, unlike most of its genre, is extremely attractive. White-canvas umbrella tables and Toulouse-Lautrec-style murals create a comfortable, French cafe ambience. Food choices are wide ranging, including burgers, pizza, gyros, falafel, and Chinese fare. The Riviera's enormous **casino** is one of the world's largest; see chapter 10 for reviews of its production shows, *An Evening at La Cage* (female impersonators), *Crazy Girls* (sexy Las Vegas–style revue), and *Splash* (aquatic revue).

2901 Las Vegas Blvd. S. (at Riviera Blvd.), Las Vegas, NV 89109. (C) **800/634-6753** or 702/734-5110. Fax 702/794-9451. www.theriviera.com. 2,136 units. $59 and up double; $125 and up suite. Extra person $20; no discount for children. AE, DC, MC, V. Free self- and valet parking. **Amenities:** Casino; wedding chapel; showrooms; 5 restaurants plus a food court; outdoor pool; 2 night-lit tennis courts; health club and spa; concierge; tour desk; car-rental desk; business center; shop-ping arcade; 24-hr. room service; laundry service; dry cleaning; nonsmoking rooms; executive-level rooms. *In room:* A/C, TV w/pay movies, hair dryer (deluxe rooms only), iron/ironing board (deluxe rooms only), safe.

MODERATE

Sahara Hotel & Casino *(Value)*   One of the few venerable old casino hotels still standing in Vegas (it's come a long way since it opened in 1952 on the site of the old Club Bingo), how you now view the Sahara may simply depend on which direction the sun is shining. It's been a few years since a spiffy renovation really pulled in some solid Moroccan details (an arched neon dome with Moroccan detailing, plenty of marble and chandeliers, plus small tiles and other Arabian Nights decorations) and caused the loss of the landmark sign, once the tallest in Vegas. (Frankly, the new one, featuring a camel, is going to look just as dated even more quickly.) The point was not only to keep up with the Joneses (as the newer, glitzy hotels make the old ones seem not just quaint but shabby), but also to attempt to unify the theme of the hotel. Then they added a roller coaster around the outside (quite a good ride, enthusiasts assure us), you know, just because.

Unfortunately, none of this really adds up to an especially nice hotel experience. Recent guests had found the rooms, renovations notwithstanding, just a bit dreary and maybe even shabby. Again, this may simply be in comparison to the gleaming new kids in town, a comparison suffered by most of the older hotels. If you are looking for four walls and a mattress, this isn't a bad choice at all. It should be noted that the Sahara feels they are not as well equipped as other hotels for children and discourages you from bringing yours—and yet, they added a roller coaster. Go figure.

The room decor suffers from overkill, with stars and stripes assaulting the eyes and not looking terribly Moroccan. The boldly striped bedspreads on the otherwise comfortable beds are a particular mistake. The windows open, which is unusual for Vegas.

The hotel has just remodeled their **Sahara Buffet.** The casino is there, of course, and there's a headliner showroom as well.

2535 Las Vegas Blvd. S. (at E. Sahara Ave.), Las Vegas, NV 89109. © **888/696-2121** or 702/737-2111. Fax 702/791-2027. www.saharavegas.com. 1,720 units. $39 and up double. Extra person $15; no discount for children. AE, DC, DISC, MC, V. Free self- and valet parking. **Amenities:** Casino; showrooms; 5 restaurants; 2 outdoor pools (including 1 Olympic-size monster unfortunately located at the foot of a parking garage); Jacuzzi; tour desk; car-rental desk; business center; shopping arcade; limited room service; laundry service; dry cleaning; nonsmoking rooms; executive-level rooms. *In room:* A/C, TV w/pay movies, minifridge on request (free but limited availability), hair dryer, iron/ironing board.

Stardust Resort & Casino *(R)*   Opened in 1958, the Stardust is a longtime resident of the Strip, and its 188-foot starry sign is one of America's most recognized landmarks. Don't get too used to it: The owners (Boyd Gaming) have been vocal about wanting to get rid of it, through either a sale or a teardown/do-over. It's a pity, in a way; it is a likable hotel, offering on-Strip accommodations at cheap rates, but it has no personality, despite being the only star of the movie *Showgirls.* (It was probably chosen for its oh-so-Vegas light bulb–intensive facade, which turns up in just about every location-establishing shot for Vegas called for by commercials, TV, or movies. The movie *Swingers* also shot a number of scenes here.)

Rooms in the towers are perfectly adequate, nice even, but forgettable. If you must know more, the 32-story West Tower rooms are decorated in earth tones, while East Tower rooms go the floral route. You can rent an adjoining parlor room with a sofa bed, whirlpool, refrigerator, and wet bar—a good choice for families. Also quite nice are Villa rooms in two-story buildings surrounding a large swimming pool. Decorated in soft Southwestern pastels, they have private shaded patios overlooking the pool.

3000 Las Vegas Blvd. S. (at Convention Center Dr.), Las Vegas, NV 89109. © **800/634-6757** or 702/732-6111. Fax 702/732-6257. www.stardustlv.com. 1,552 units. From $60 standard double; from $250 suite. Extra person $20. Children under 13 stay free in parent's room. AE, DC, DISC, MC, V. Free self- and valet parking. **Amenities:** Casino; 2 showrooms; 5 restaurants; 2 outdoor pools; small exercise room; Jacuzzi; video arcade; concierge; tour desk; car-rental desk; shopping arcade; 24-hr. room service; dry cleaning; nonsmoking rooms; executive-level rooms. *In room:* A/C, TV w/pay movies, dataport, safe.

Stratosphere Casino Hotel & Tower *(Finds)* *(Kids)*   A really neat idea, in that Vegas way, in a really bad location. At 1,149 feet, it's the tallest building west of the Mississippi. In theory, this should have provided yet another attraction for visitors: Climb (okay, elevator) to the top and gaze at the stunning view. But despite being on the Strip, it's a healthy walk from anywhere—the nearest casino is the Sahara, which is 5 very long blocks away. This, and possibly the hefty price charged for the privilege of going up to the top of the tower, may have conspired to keep the crowds away.

And while the crowds might have been justified before, they—and by "they," we mean "you"—might reconsider, especially if you are looking for a friendly place to hang your hat, but nothing more. The smaller-size rooms here are basically motel rooms— really nice motel rooms, but with that level of comfort and style. Then again, you can often get such a room for around $29 a night. (And do join the casino's players club— they tend to offer free rooms with more or less minimal play.) Perfect if you are coming to Vegas with no plans to spend time in your room except to sleep (if even that).

That isn't to say there aren't other elements to like here, including the aforementioned casino, a midway area with kiddie-oriented rides, a pool with a view, and some of the friendliest, most accommodating staff in town. You can still ride the following incredible thrill rides (provided the wind isn't blowing too hard that day) on top of the tower: the world's highest roller coaster—aka the **High Roller**—(it careens around the outer rim of the tower 909 ft., 108 stories, above ground); the **Big Shot,** a fabulous free-fall ride that thrusts passengers up and down the tower at speeds of up to 45 mph; **X-Scream,** a giant teeter-totter-style device that gives you the sensation of falling off the side of the building; and **Insanity: the Ride,** a whirly-gig contraption that spins you around more than 900 feet above terra firma. (See p. 203 for a review of these four adrenaline pumpers.) Indoor and outdoor observation decks offer the most stunning city views you will ever see, especially at night. For the price, this might be the right place for you. Just remember you need a rental car or a lot of cash for cabs to get to the true thrills down the Strip.

In addition to the casino, the hotel sports two production shows: *American Superstars* (an impression-filled production show) and *Viva Las Vegas* (Las Vegas–style revue), which are reviewed in chapter 10.

2000 Las Vegas Blvd. S. (between St. Louis St. and Baltimore Ave.), Las Vegas, NV 89104. (C) **800/99-TOWER** (998-6937) or 702/380-7777. Fax 702/383-5334. www.stratospherehotel.com. 2,500 units. Sun–Thurs $39 and up double, Fri–Sat $59 and up double; $69 and up suite. Extra person $15. Children under 13 stay free in parent's room. AE, DC, DISC, MC, V. Free self- and valet parking. **Amenities:** Casino; showrooms; wedding chapel; 7 restaurants plus several fast-food outlets; large new pool area w/great views of the Strip; children's rides and games located at the base of the tower; concierge; tour desk; car-rental desk; shopping arcade; 24-hr. room service; laundry service; dry cleaning; nonsmoking rooms; executive-level rooms. *In room:* A/C, TV w/pay movies, dataport, hair dryer, iron/ironing board, safe.

INEXPENSIVE

Circus Circus Hotel/Casino *(Finds)* *(Kids)*   The last bastion of family-friendly Las Vegas— indeed, for years, the only hotel with such an open mind. But even *it* isn't what it ought to be, thanks to a reconfiguring a few years ago that took the pervasive (and for some, nightmare-inducing) Jumbo the Clown decorating scheme and turned it into

> ## ⟨Value⟩ Joining the Club
>
> It's worth noting that joining the players clubs at the "older hotels"—**Bally's,** the **Trop, The Flamingo, Sahara,** and **The Riviera,** among others—is something smart tourists simply must do. Watch how after rather minimal play, your mailbox is suddenly flooded with offers for $19-a-night midweek room rates.

somewhat more tasteful, more commedia dell'arte Harlequins. Like everyone else, even the venerable Circus Circus, once the epitome of kitsch, is trying to be taken more seriously.

That is not to say this is an adult atmosphere; the circus theme remains and the kid appeal along with it. (Which is also not to say that you should confuse this with a theme-park hotel. All the circus fun is still built around a busy casino.) The midway level features dozens of carnival games, a large arcade (more than 300 video and pinball games), trick mirrors, and ongoing circus acts under the big top from 11am to midnight daily. The world's largest permanent circus (according to the *Guinness Book of World Records*), it features renowned trapeze artists, stunt cyclists, jugglers, magicians, acrobats, and high-wire daredevils. Spectators can view the action from much of the midway or get up close and comfy on benches in the performance arena. There's a "be-a-clown" booth where kids can be made up with washable clown makeup and red foam-rubber noses. They can grab a bite to eat in McDonald's (also on this level), and since the mezzanine overlooks the casino action, they can also look down and wave to Mom and Dad—or, more to the point, Mom and Dad can look up and wave to the kids without having to stray too far from the blackjack table. Circus clowns wander the midway creating balloon animals and cutting up in various ways.

The thousands of rooms here occupy sufficient acreage to warrant a free Disney World–style aerial shuttle (another kid pleaser) and minibuses connecting its many components. Tower rooms have newish, just slightly better-than-average furnishings, and offer safes and TVs with in-house information and gaming-instruction stations. The Manor section comprises five white, three-story buildings out back, fronted by rows of cypresses. Manor guests can park at their doors, and a gate to the complex that can be opened only with a room key ensures security. These rooms are usually among the least expensive in town, but we've said it before and we'll say it again: You get what you pay for. A renovation of these rooms added a coat of paint and some new photos on the wall, but not much else. All sections of this vast property have their own swimming pools, additional casinos serve the main tower and sky-rise buildings, and both towers provide covered parking garages.

Adjacent to the hotel is **Circusland RV Park,** with 399 full-utility spaces and up to 50-amp hookups. It has its own 24-hour convenience store, swimming pools, saunas, whirlpools, kiddie playground, fenced pet runs, video-game arcade, and community room. The rate is $22 and up, with peak rates around $80.

The very reasonably priced **Pink Pony** is Circus Circus's cheerful bubble-gum-pink-and-bright-red 24-hour eatery, with big paintings of clowns on the walls and pink pony carpeting. It offers a wide array of coffee-shop fare, including a number of specially marked "heart-smart" (low-fat, low-cholesterol) items. For gorging, there's always the **Circus Circus Buffet** (p. 185).

In addition to the ongoing circus acts, there's also the upgraded **Adventuredome** (p. 214) indoor theme park out back. There are three full-size casinos, all crowded and noisy, where you can gamble while trapeze acts take place overhead.

2880 Las Vegas Blvd. S. (between Circus Circus Dr. and Convention Center Dr.), Las Vegas, NV 89109. ℭ **800/444-CIRC** (444-2472), 800/634-3450, or 702/734-0410. Fax 702/734-5897. www.circuscircus.com. 3,744 units. Sun–Thurs $59 and up double; Fri–Sat $79 and up double. Extra person $12. Children under 17 stay free in parent's room. AE, DC, DISC, MC, V. Free self- and valet parking. **Amenities:** Casino; circus acts; wedding chapel; 7 restaurants; 2 outdoor pools; midway-style carnival games; video arcade; tour desk; car-rental desk; shopping arcade; 24-hr. room service; laundry service; dry cleaning; nonsmoking rooms; executive-level rooms. *In room:* A/C, TV w/pay movies, hair dryer, safe.

Westward Ho Hotel & Casino   We know we referred to the Stratosphere as having motel rooms, but we did emphasize that they are nice motel rooms. These are just plain, basic motel rooms because this is, after all, a motel. Which means that it just doesn't have the facilities and other doodads that a true resort, even the Strat, offers. But the price lures. Located next door to Circus Circus, the Westward Ho is fronted by a vast casino, with rooms in two-story buildings that extend out back for several city blocks. In fact, the property is so large that a free bus shuttles regularly between the rooms and the casino 24 hours a day. Plans are in the works for a new casino and a gas station/convenience store in the back of the property. A good buy here are the two-bedroom suites, with 1½ bathrooms, living rooms with sofa beds, and refrigerators. Suites sleep up to six people. Meanwhile, around the back (by Industrial) is a new addition, the brilliantly named "The 'Ho," a combination minicasino/minimart, an oddly appealing setup that includes a cafe with some cheap, but good, basic food (sandwiches, obscenely long hot dogs).

2900 Las Vegas Blvd. S. (between Circus Circus Dr. and Convention Center Dr.), Las Vegas, NV 89109. ℭ **800/634-6803** or 702/731-2900. www.westwardho.com. 777 units. $37 and up double; $76 and up suite. Extra person $15; no discount for children. MC, V. Free parking at your room door. **Amenities:** Casino; restaurant; 3 outdoor pools; tour desk; car-rental desk; nonsmoking rooms. *In room:* A/C, TV w/pay movies.

6 East of the Strip

In this section we've covered hotels near the Convention Center, along with those farther south on Paradise Road, Flamingo Road, and Tropicana Avenue. Note that in the area around Paradise, there are over a dozen chain-style hotels—various Marriotts (Courtyard, Residence Inn), a Budget Suites, and many others—any one of which is going to provide comfortable, reliable, utterly undistinguished lodging, and all of which often go for more money than they ought to. We've singled out a few here, but they are really very interchangeable. Do some searching around online, and don't hesitate to try to play them off each other in an attempt to get a deal.

VERY EXPENSIVE

Courtyard by Marriott ℛ   A complex of three-story terra cotta–roofed stucco buildings in an attractively landscaped setting of trees, shrubbery, and flower beds, the Courtyard is a welcome link in the Marriott chain. Although the services are limited, don't picture a no-frills establishment. This is a good-looking hotel (in a chain-establishment kind of way), with a pleasant, plant-filled lobby and very nice rooms indeed. Public areas and rooms still look spanking new. Most rooms have king-size beds, and all have balconies or patios. It's also right across the street from a monorail station.

3275 Paradise Rd. (between Convention Center Dr. and Desert Inn Rd.), Las Vegas, NV 89109. ℭ **800/321-2211** or 702/791-3600. Fax 702/796-7981. www.courtyard.com. 159 units. Sun–Thurs $109 and up double, Fri–Sat $119 and

East of the Strip Accommodations

Arizona Charlie's **17**
Best Western
  Mardi Gras Inn **5**
Boulder Station **17**
Clarion Hotel & Suites—
  Emerald Springs **9**
Courtyard by Marriott **4**
Crowne Plaza **11**
Fairfield Inn by Marriott **6**

Fiesta Henderson **15**
Green Valley Ranch
  Resort **16**
Hard Rock Hotel
  & Casino **12**
Hawthorn Suites **13**
La Quinta Inn **7**
Las Vegas Hilton **1**
Marriott Suites **3**

Motel 6 **14**
Residence Inn by Marriott **2**
Ritz-Carlton,
  Lake Las Vegas **15**
Sam's Town Hotel
  & Gambling Hall **17**
Sunset Station **15**
Terrible's **8**
Tuscany Hotel & Casino **10**

up double; $119 and up suite. No charge for extra person above double occupancy. AE, DC, DISC, MC, V. Free parking at your room door. **Amenities:** Restaurant; outdoor pool; small exercise room; Jacuzzi; business center; limited room service; coin-op laundry; laundry service; dry cleaning; nonsmoking rooms; executive-level rooms. In room: A/C, TV w/pay movies, dataport, coffeemaker, hair dryer, iron/ironing board, high-speed Internet access (for a fee).

Crowne Plaza ⚿   An upscale sister of the Holiday Inn chain, this business-oriented hotel is right next to the Hard Rock but is hardly a Gen-X destination. Each room is technically a suite, but apparently after building its five-story atrium, the hotel didn't have a lot of space left for the rooms, and so each is on the small side, made more so by the sheer amount of stuff crammed into them. Expect a wet bar, a sitting area complete with convertible sofa bed, a fridge, and a desk. Summertime can find calypso bands playing by the pool, making it a party spot for the many flight crews who regularly stay here.

4255 Paradise Rd. (just north of Harmon Ave.), Las Vegas, NV 89109. © **800/2-CROWNE** (227-6963) or 702/369-4400. Fax 702/369-3770. $125 and up for up to 5 in the room. AE, DC, DISC, MC, V. Free self-parking. **Amenities:** Restaurant; outdoor pool; small exercise room w/Nautilus, weights, and treadmills; Jacuzzi; sauna; concierge; airport shuttle; business center; limited room service; dry cleaning; nonsmoking rooms; executive-level rooms. In room: A/C, TV w/pay movies, dataport, minibar, fridge, coffeemaker, hair dryer, iron/ironing board, high-speed Internet access (for a fee).

Hard Rock Hotel & Casino ⚿⚿   As soon as you check out the Hard Rock clientele, you'll know you are in a Vegas hotel that's like no other. The body-fat percentage (and median age) plummets; the percentage of black clothing skyrockets. Yep, the hip—including Hollywood and the music industry, among others—flock to the Hard Rock, drawn by the cool 'n' rockin' ambience and the goodies offered by a boutique hotel (only in Vegas could 657 rooms be considered a "boutique hotel"). Our problem is that we are not famous pop stars and we do not look enough like Pamela Anderson to warrant the kind of attention that the staff seems to reserve for those types.

It's that Boomer-meets-Gen-X sensibility that finds tacky-chic so very hip. Luckily, the "no-tell motel" look of the older rooms has been updated to more closely match the decor of the rooms in the new addition. We still aren't crazy about the decor scheme in any of them—even the newer section is too '60s-futuristic hip to come off as posh, and all of it is showing more wear than it ought to. Bathrooms are a big step forward—bigger, brighter, and shinier, though in the older section they can be cramped, spacewise, in suites. On a high note, the beds have feather pillows, and mattresses are surprisingly comfortable. Uncharacteristically large 27-inch TVs (most hotel sets are smaller, since they want you in the casino, not staring at the tube) offer special music channels.

The lobby borders on the casino (you can see how that immediately plunges you into the action, like it or not), which takes the center position in the round public area you immediately enter when arriving. On the perimeter is a collection of rock memorabilia, ranging from sad (a Kurt Cobain tribute) to cool (various guitars and outfits) to useless (various other guitars and outfits). The Hard Rock now has a permanent, if unwelcome and sad, bit of rock memorabilia for its collection: John Entwistle, bassist for the Who, died in one of its rooms on the eve of the start of a tour with the band.

There are several fine restaurants, including **AJs Steakhouse,** a tribute to owner Peter Morton's dad, who brought us the legendary Morton's. You'll also find **Nobu,** a branch of highly famed chef Nobu Matsuhisa's wildly popular Japanese restaurant. Kicky and funky Mexican food can be had at lunch and dinner in the Mexican, folk-art-filled **Cantina Pink Taco,** while three diner-type meals a day are served at the 22-seat **Counter.**

The Hard Rock's premier restaurant, **Mortoni's,** is a beauty that serves vast portions of Italian fare. **Mr. Lucky's 24/7** is the hotel's 'round-the-clock coffee shop, displaying rock memorabilia and old Las Vegas hotel signs. And the **Hard Rock Cafe** (p. 143) is adjacent to the hotel.

The **Joint** (p. 280) is a major showroom that often hosts big-name rock musicians.

If you've ever dreamed of being in a beach party movie, or on the set of one of those MTV summer beach-house shows, the reconstructed pool at the Hard Rock is for you. Multiple pools are joined by a lazy river and fringed in spots by actual sand beaches. You won't get much swimming done—the water is largely so shallow that it won't hit your knees—but there is swim-up blackjack (they give you little plastic pouches to hold your money), and a stage that features live music in the summer and is fronted by a sandy area, so you can make like Frankie, Annette, and Erik Von Zipper and do the Watusi. Or just pose in a thong bikini and new breasts. Whichever. On warm days and nights, this is *the* hangout scene.

The newly refurbished spa is smaller than its Strip counterparts but is soothing in its posh Space-Age-Zen way, and the health club is plenty large and well equipped, offering a full complement of Cybex equipment, stair machines, treadmills, massage, and steam rooms. There's a $20-per-day fee to use the health-club facilities.

4455 Paradise Rd. (at Harmon Ave.), Las Vegas, NV 89109. (℃) **800/473-ROCK** (473-7625) or 702/693-5000. Fax 702/693-5588. www.hardrockhotel.com. 657 units. Sun–Thurs $79 and up double; Fri–Sat $145 and up double; from $250 suite. Extra person $35. Children under 13 stay free in parent's room. AE, DC, MC, V. Free self- and valet parking. **Amenities:** Casino; showroom; 6 restaurants; 2 outdoor pools w/lazy-river ride and sandy-beach bottom; small health club and spa; concierge; tour desk; 24-hr. room service; laundry service; dry cleaning; nonsmoking rooms; executive-level rooms. *In room:* A/C, TV w/pay movies, dataport, hair dryer, iron/ironing board, high-speed Internet access (for a fee).

Las Vegas Hilton ☆

It's easy for us to overlook this dinosaur—look, we even called it a dinosaur. Totally unfair. It's one of the last of the dying breed of old Vegas hotels, but unlike many of its peers, it's still offering fine accommodations and even a bit more than that. Consider it even if you aren't an old-timer, and don't be put off by the distance from the Strip; the Monorail stops here, making access easier than ever. When you consider that on nights when you can't touch a room on the Strip for less than $175, the Hilton will put you in a nice room with plenty of marble (including large bathtubs) and clean, well-maintained furnishings for a decent price, then it seems silly to not make the Hilton a top choice more often. The clientele is a mix of savvy business travelers who know a good hotel deal when they see it and Trekkers lured in by the Spacequest Casino and *Star Trek: The Experience* (which got a recent fancy addition in the form of the *4-D Borg Invasion*). There are quite a few solidly good restaurants.

Those very same facilities, however, mean that even a small convention can sometimes drive the prices up at odd times—then again, since conventions are often booked for weekdays, that can also mean atypical drops in price on weekends. Just call.

A new owner recently took over the Hilton and is doing some minor spiffing up—little remodeling here, some new restaurants there, including Mistral, a new venue from Andre of Alizé and Andre's Downtown. The Hilton already has a strong showing of restaurants, including a **Benihana** and a **buffet** that's reviewed in chapter 6. *Note:* Children 12 and under can dine in any Hilton restaurant for half the listed menu prices, making this a great option for budget-conscious families.

The **Nightclub,** a first-rate casino lounge, has live entertainment nightly. It's a great place to hang out in the evening and features regular sets by local cover bands. One of

Elvis's sequined jumpsuits is enshrined in a glass case in the front, near the entrance to the lobby/casino (he played 837 sold-out shows here). In addition, Colonel Tom Parker's memorial service was held here in the hotel. There's also a major **headliner showroom** (see chapter 10).

There are also a number of shops, plus the above-mentioned *Star Trek: The Experience* (p. 202), the themed attraction, with its accompanying space-themed casino, one that is especially well designed, with some fun gimmicks.

The third-floor roof comprises a well-landscaped 8-acre recreation deck with a large swimming pool, a 24-seat whirlpool spa, six Har-Tru tennis courts lit for night play, Ping-Pong, and a putting green. Also on this level is a luxurious 17,000-square-foot state-of-the-art health club offering Nautilus equipment, Lifecycles, treadmills, rowing machines, three whirlpool spas, steam, sauna, massage, and tanning beds. There's a $20-per-day fee to use the facilities, but guests are totally pampered: All toiletries are provided; there are comfortable TV lounges; complimentary bottled waters and juices are served in the canteen; and treatments include facials and oxygen pep-ups (you inhale pure oxygen).

3000 Paradise Rd. (at Riviera Blvd.), Las Vegas, NV 89109. ℂ **888/732-7117** or 702/732-5111. Fax 702/732-5805. www.lvhilton.com. 3,174 units. $49 and up double. Extra person $30. Children under 18 stay free in parent's room. AE, DC, DISC, MC, V. Free self- and valet parking. **Amenities:** Casino; showrooms; 11 restaurants plus a food court; outdoor pool; golf course adjacent; 6 tennis courts (4 night-lit); health club and spa; Jacuzzi; car-rental desk; business center; shopping arcade; 24-hr. room service; laundry service; dry cleaning; nonsmoking rooms; executive-level rooms. *In room:* A/C, TV w/pay movies, dataport, hair dryer, iron/ironing board, high-speed Internet access (for a fee).

Marriott Suites ⭐   Oh sure, you don't lack for Marriotts in Las Vegas, but it is a reliable chain (if a tad overpriced), and you can't fault the location of this one. It's just 3 blocks off the Strip—a 10-minute walk at most, though in 100°F (38°C) heat, that may be too far—and not much farther from the Convention Center. This is a solid choice for business travelers, but families might also like the lack of casino and accompanying mayhem, not to mention the extra-large, quite comfortable rooms. Each suite has a sitting area separated from the bedroom by French doors. And there are gorgeous prints on the walls—far, far better than you would expect in a hotel, much less in one of the chain variety.

325 Convention Center Dr., Las Vegas, NV 89109. ℂ **800/228-9290** or 702/650-2000. Fax 702/650-9466. www. marriott.com. 278 units. $159 and up suite (up to 4 people). AE, DC, DISC, MC, V. Free outdoor parking. **Amenities:** Restaurant; outdoor pool; small exercise room; Jacuzzi; tour desk; car-rental desk; business center; 24-hr. room service; coin-op laundry available at Residence Inn next door; laundry service; dry cleaning; nonsmoking rooms; executive-level rooms. *In room:* A/C, TV w/pay movies, dataport, minifridge, coffeemaker, hair dryer, iron/ironing board, safe, high-speed Internet access (for a fee).

EXPENSIVE
La Quinta Inn ⭐   This is a tranquil and immediately visually appealing alternative (within the limited range of chains) to the Strip's hubbub, featuring courtyards, rustic benches, attractive pools, barbecue grills, and picnic tables. The staff is terrific— friendly and incredibly helpful. The rooms are immaculate and attractive. Executive rooms feature one queen-size bed, a small refrigerator, a wet bar, and a microwave oven—spend the extra money for it. Double queens are larger but have no kitchen facilities. And two-bedroom suites are not just spacious, they are really full apartments, with large living rooms (some with sofa beds), dining areas, and full kitchens. Ground-floor accommodations have patios, and all accommodations feature bathrooms with oversize whirlpool tubs.

3970 Paradise Rd. (between Twain Ave. and Flamingo Rd.), Las Vegas, NV 89109. © 800/531-5900 or
702/796-9000. Fax 702/796-3537. www.laquinta.com. 251 units. $79 and up standard double; $89 and up executive
queen; $115 and up suite. Rates include continental breakfast. Inquire about seasonal discounts. AE, DC, DISC, MC,
V. Free self-parking. **Amenities:** Outdoor pool; Jacuzzi; tour desk; car-rental desk; free airport/Strip shuttle; coin-op
laundry; nonsmoking rooms. *In room:* A/C, TV w/pay movies, dataport, kitchens in executive rooms and suites, coffeemaker, hair dryer, iron/ironing board.

Residence Inn by Marriott ℱ

Staying here is like having your own apartment in
Las Vegas. The property occupies 7 acres of perfectly manicured lawns with tropical
foliage and neat flower beds. It's a great choice for families and business travelers.

Accommodations, most with working fireplaces, are housed in condolike, two-story
wood-and-stucco buildings fronted by little gardens. Studios have adjoining sitting
rooms with sofas and armchairs, dressing areas, and fully equipped eat-in kitchens
complete with dishwashers. Every guest receives a welcome basket of microwave pop-
corn and coffee. TVs have DVD players (you can rent movies nearby), and all rooms
have balconies or patios. Duplex penthouses, some with cathedral ceilings, add an
upstairs bedroom (with its own bathroom, phone, TV, and radio) and a full dining
room. A station on the city's new monorail system is just across the street.

3225 Paradise Rd. (between Desert Inn Rd. and Convention Center Dr.), Las Vegas, NV 89109. © 800/331-3131 or
702/796-9300. www.marriott.com. 192 units. $119 and up studio; $149 and up penthouse. Rates include continental breakfast and free breakfast buffet, offered in lobby lounge. AE, DC, DISC, MC, V. Free self-parking. **Amenities:**
Outdoor pool; guest access to small exercise room next door at the Marriott Suites; Jacuzzi; coin-op laundry; nonsmoking rooms. *In room:* A/C, TV/DVD w/pay movies, dataport, kitchenette, coffeemaker, hair dryer, iron/ironing
board.

MODERATE

Best Western Mardi Gras Inn (Value)

This well-run little casino hotel has a lot to
offer, and is apparently popular with budget-minded Europeans (which can sometimes result in some risqué Continental-style sunbathing around the pool). A block
from the Convention Center and close to major properties, its three-story building sits
on nicely landscaped grounds. There's a gazebo out back where guests can enjoy a picnic lunch.

Accommodations are all spacious: queen-size-bedded minisuites with sofa-bedded
living-room areas and eat-in kitchens, the latter equipped with wet bars, refrigerators,
and coffeemakers. All are midlevel motel okay, but they were recently redone, so the
furnishings and so forth should be fresh. Staying here is like having your own little Las
Vegas apartment. A pleasant restaurant/bar off the lobby, open from 6:30am to 11pm
daily, serves typical coffee-shop fare.

3500 Paradise Rd. (between Sands Ave. and Desert Inn Rd.), Las Vegas, NV 89109. © 800/634-6501 or 702/731-
2020. Fax 702/731-4005. www.mardigrasinn.com. 314 units. $59 and up double. Extra person $8. Rates include free
continental breakfast. Children under 18 stay free in parent's room. AE, DC, DISC, MC, V. Free parking at your room
door. **Amenities:** Small casino; restaurant; outdoor pool; Jacuzzi; tour desk; car-rental desk; business center; free airport shuttle; limited room service; coin-op laundry; nonsmoking rooms. *In room:* A/C, TV w/pay movies, dataport,
kitchenette, fridge, coffeemaker, iron/ironing board.

Clarion Hotel & Suites—Emerald Springs ℱ (Value)

This hotel recently switched
from the Holiday Inn brand to Clarion, and we aren't sure if over time that will make
an ounce of difference. We hope that if it does, it's not for the negative. Housed in
three peach-stucco buildings, the Emerald Springs offers a friendly, low-key alternative to the usual glitz and glitter of Vegas accommodations. You'll enter via a charming marble-floored lobby with a waterfall fountain and lush, faux tropical plantings

under a domed skylight. Off the lobby is a comfortably furnished lounge with a large-screen TV and working fireplace. Typical of the inn's hospitality, there is a bowl of apples for the taking at the front desk, something we usually see only in more expensive hotels. (Why is that? It's not like the fruit is expensive.) Although your surroundings here are serene, you're only 3 blocks from the heart of the Strip.

Public areas and rooms here are notably clean and spiffy. Pristine hallways are hung with nice abstract paintings and have small seating areas on every level, and rooms are nicely decorated with bleached-oak furnishings. Even the smallest accommodations (studios) offer small sofas, desks, and armchairs with hassocks.

325 E. Flamingo Rd. (between Koval Lane and Paradise Rd.), Las Vegas, NV 89109. ℂ 800/732-7889 or 702/732-9100. Fax 702/731-9784. www.clarionlasvegas.com. 150 units. $69 and up studio; $99 and up whirlpool suite, $129 and up hospitality suite. Extra person $15. Children under 19 stay free in parent's room. AE, DC, DISC, MC, V. Free self-parking. **Amenities:** Restaurant; outdoor pool; small exercise room; Jacuzzi; concierge; tour desk; car-rental desk; courtesy limo to airport/Strip; nonsmoking rooms; executive-level rooms. *In room:* A/C, TV w/pay movies, dataport, kitchenette or minibar w/fridge, coffeemaker, hair dryer, iron/ironing board, high-speed Internet access (for a fee).

Fairfield Inn by Marriott (Value)   This pristine property is a pleasant place to stay. It has a comfortable lobby with sofas and armchairs, where coffee, tea, and hot chocolate are provided free all day. Rooms are cheerful. Units with king-size beds have convertible sofas, and all accommodations offer well-lit work areas with desks; TVs have free movie channels as well as pay-movie options. Local calls are free. Breakfast pastries, fresh fruit, juice, and yogurt are served free in the lobby each morning, and many restaurants are within easy walking distance.

3850 Paradise Rd. (between Twain Ave. and Flamingo Rd.), Las Vegas, NV 89109. ℂ 800/228-2800 or 702/791-0899. Fax 702/791-2705. www.fairfieldinn.com. 129 units. $62 and up for up to 5 people. Rates include continental breakfast. AE, DC, DISC, MC, V. Free self-parking. **Amenities:** Outdoor pool; small exercise room; Jacuzzi; tour desk; car-rental desk; airport shuttle; dry cleaning; nonsmoking rooms. *In room:* A/C, TV w/pay movies, dataport, iron/ironing board, high-speed Internet access (for a fee).

Hawthorn Suites 🔒🔒   This "all-suite" hotel has plenty of extras, making it stand out from its brethren, and is extremely appealing to families. Sure, the suites themselves are bland, but they have full kitchens (perfect for families seeking to save some money) and actual balconies, a huge relief in stuffy Vegas where the windows usually don't open. There is a full, free breakfast buffet, and an evening happy hour with snacks. The pool is large, and they've got courts for basketball and volleyball. And they take pets! All this, just a block from the corner of the Strip and the Trop! This is really a lifesaver for families looking for a nice place not too far off the beaten path (especially if said family is using Vegas as a stopping point during a family vacation with Fido)—think of the savings with the free breakfast, the snacks, and that full kitchen for other meals.

5051 Duke Ellington Way, Las Vegas, NV 89119. ℂ 800/811-2450 or 702/739-7000. Fax 702/739-9350. www. hawthorn.com. 280 units. $79–$109 1-bedroom suite (up to 4 people); $109–$169 2-bedroom suite (up to 6 people). Cribs free, no rollaways. Rates include complimentary breakfast. AE, DC, DISC, MC, V. Free outdoor parking. Pets accepted. **Amenities:** Outdoor pool; Jacuzzi; small exercise room; coin-op laundry; laundry service; dry cleaning; nonsmoking rooms. *In room:* A/C, TV w/pay movies, dataport, full kitchen, hair dryer, iron/ironing board.

Sam's Town Hotel & Gambling Hall 🔒   Just 5 miles from the Strip (which means it's not precisely near anything, but if you have a car, it's also not far), Western-themed Sam's Town is immensely popular with locals and tourists alike. This unexpectedly pleasing resort is well worth considering for the price. Off the beaten track though it may be, regular (if not exactly frequent), free shuttles to the Strip and Downtown may

help you with any feelings of isolation. The addition of a new entertainment complex (including an 18-screen movie theater and a child-care center) makes it an even more positive option, particularly for families.

Sam's Town's main draw is its centerpiece atrium, a high-rising edifice that is part park, part Western vista. With living trees and splashing fountains, plus silly animatronic animals, it's kind of goofy, but also a nice, albeit artificial (as if that's unusual for Vegas), place to wander through and sit in, which is a rare thing for this town. And if it's a bit noisy, well, we'll take the splashing sounds of the water over the ca-chinging of slots any day. The other public areas, including the casino, have gotten a facelift. If it isn't up to the impossible standards set by the new Strip hotels, everything is certainly less dated and dark.

Rooms are adequately sized, if a tad dim, thanks to the Western/Native American–themed decor, but they are clean and fine, especially for the price. All have either mountain views (higher up is much better) or inside-atrium views, which are great fun.

And bless it, the hotel has just finished yet another whole new remodeling. And while we love it when a place does not rest on its laurels but constantly seeks the improvements of change, that also means that every time we come here, some wall is up indicating that construction is going on, and every place within the hotel is subject to the whims of fortune and decor. The point being, don't totally count on anything we've mentioned above being here forever—after all, they took out a diner with the best burger in town and a large country-and-western dance hall of considerable tradition.

Sam's Town Firelight Buffet is described on p. 185. There's a variety of other dining options, including a cart in the atrium that serves homemade ice cream.

Roxy's Saloon, one of a dozen bars on the premises, offers live entertainment (country western) for dancing, daily from noon to the wee hours. There's also a deli in the race-and-sports-book area, a bowling alley snack bar, a food court, an ice-cream parlor, and the aforementioned 18-screen movie theater and entertainment complex, complete with child-care facility.

The **Sunset Stampede** is a laser-and-water show that takes place four times daily (at 2, 6, 8, and 10pm) in the Mystic Falls Park. It begins with a howl from an animatronic wolf atop the waterfall, and then water spurts in sync with orchestral themes, as lasers fire pretty colors around the room. A 10-minute show, it's not long enough or special enough to be worth the drive from the Strip (though there are free buses to transport you—call for details). But if you happen to be around, grab a seat at the bar early. This is particularly important for kids, as it gets pretty crowded, and it's tough to see the show unless you are close up.

The enormous three-floor casino has a friendly, casual atmosphere.

5111 Boulder Hwy. (at Flamingo Rd.), Las Vegas, NV 89122. © **800/634-6371** or 702/456-7777. Fax 702/454-8014. www.samstownlv.com. 650 units. $50 and up double; $140 and up suite. Extra person $10. Children under 16 stay free in parent's room. AE, DC, DISC, MC, V. Free self- and valet parking. **Amenities:** Huge casino; showrooms; 5 restaurants plus a food court; outdoor pool; day-care center for children 3–12 (charges apply); video arcade; tour desk; car-rental desk; shuttle to airport/Strip/Downtown; laundry service; nonsmoking rooms. *In room:* A/C, TV w/pay movies, dataport.

Tuscany Hotel & Casino 🏨

This may be the right kind of hybrid between chain hotel and fancier resort—not as lush as the latter, but not anywhere near as expensive, either, with far more personal detail and indulgent touches than you can find at chains. It's another "all-suite" hotel, and another where "suite" really means "very big room." The rooms aren't memorable, just like the chain rooms, but they are smart enough that you won't get depressed like you might when you see some of the rooms in similarly priced hotels. The large complex (27 acres, complete with a winding pool) isn't so much Italian as it is vaguely evoking the idea of Italian architecture, but it, too, is more stylish than most of the chains in town. And, unlike those other chains, this one comes with a large casino, roped off in such a way that this is still an appropriate place for families who want the best of all worlds (price, looks, family-friendly atmosphere, and gambling), especially as the rooms come with a separate dining area, a kitchenette, and large TVs, plus convertible couches on request. (And while the kids play, there is a large soaking tub for their folks to relax in.) There's a good Italian restaurant on the premises, plus a lounge.

255 E. Flamingo Rd., Las Vegas, NV 89109. ⓒ **877/887-2261** or 702/893-8933. www.tuscanylasvegas.com. 700 units. $79 and up suite. AE, MC, V. **Amenities:** Casino; restaurant; lounge; outdoor pool; fitness center; concierge; car rental; business center; room service; laundry service; dry cleaning. *In room:* A/C, TV, dataport, fridge, coffeemaker, hair dryer, iron/ironing board, safe, high-speed Internet access (for a fee), Nintendo.

INEXPENSIVE

Motel 6   Fronted by a big neon sign, Las Vegas's Motel 6 is the largest in the country, and it happens to be a great budget choice. Most Motel 6 properties are a little out of the way, but this one is quite close to major Strip casino hotels (the MGM is nearby). It has a big, pleasant lobby, and the rooms, in two-story, cream-stucco buildings, are clean and attractively decorated. Some rooms have showers only; others have tub/shower bathrooms. Local calls are free.

Tips   Cheap Hotel Alternatives

If you're determined to come to Vegas during a particularly busy season and you find yourself shut out of the prominent hotels, here's a list of moderate to very inexpensive alternatives.

On or Near the Strip
  Budget Suites of America, 4205 W. Tropicana Ave.; ⓒ 702/889-1700
  Budget Suites of America, 3655 W. Tropicana Ave.; ⓒ 702/739-1000
  Travelodge, 3735 Las Vegas Blvd. S.; ⓒ 800/578-7878

Paradise Road & Vicinity
  Budget Suites of America, 3684 Paradise Rd.; ⓒ 702/699-7000

Downtown & Vicinity
  Econo Lodge, 1150 S. Las Vegas Blvd.; ⓒ 800/553-2666

East Las Vegas & Vicinity
  Budget Suites of America, 4625 Boulder Hwy.; ⓒ 702/454-4625
  Budget Suites of America, 4855 Boulder Hwy.; ⓒ 702/433-3644
  Motel 6 Boulder Highway, 4125 Boulder Hwy.; ⓒ 800/466-8356
  Super 8 Motel, 5288 Boulder Hwy.; ⓒ 800/825-0880

West Las Vegas & Vicinity
  Motel 6, 5085 Dean Martin Dr. (South Las Vegas); ⓒ 800/466-8356

195 E. Tropicana Ave. (at Koval Lane), Las Vegas, NV 89109. © 800/4-MOTEL-6 (466-8356) or 702/798-0728. Fax 702/798-5657. 602 units. $49 and up single. Extra person $8. Children under 17 stay free in parent's room. AE, DC, DISC, MC, V. Free parking at your room door. **Amenities:** 2 outdoor pools; Jacuzzi; tour desk; coin-op laundry; nonsmoking rooms. *In room:* A/C, TV w/pay movies.

Terrible's (★ *(Finds* First of all, this place isn't terrible at all (the owner is Ed "Terrible" Herbst, who operates a chain of convenience stores and gas stations). Second, it isn't a bit like the hotel it took over, the rattrap known as the Continental. The Continental is gone, and good riddance. In its place is an unexpected bargain, a hotel frequently offering ridiculously low prices. Try this on for size: $29 a night! Near the Strip! Near a bunch of really good restaurants! Hot diggity! So what are we getting? Well, don't expect much in the way of memorable rooms; they are as basic as can be (despite some sweet attempts with artwork depicting European idylls), and some have views of a wall (though even those get plenty of natural light). Some, however, are considerably larger than others, so ask. The pool area is a surprise; it looks like what you might find in a nice apartment complex (which, actually, is what Terrible's resembles on the outside), with plenty of palms and other foliage. There's a small but thoroughly stocked casino (not to mention penny slots, continuing the budget theme), plus a very good 24-hour coffee shop. How could you want for anything more? Did we mention price and location? Plus a free airport shuttle? Okay, so we all wish they had used a bit more imagination with the rooms.

4100 Paradise Rd. (at Flamingo Rd.), Las Vegas, NV 89109 © 800/640-9777 or 702/733-7000. Fax 702/765-5109. www.terribleherbst.com/casinos/terriblescasinolasvegas. 374 units. Sun–Thurs $29 and up double; Fri–Sat $59 and up double. Extra person $10. Children under 13 stay free in parent's room. AE, DC, DISC, MC, V. Free self- and valet parking. **Amenities:** 3 restaurants; outdoor pool; 24-hr. room service; laundry service; nonsmoking rooms. *In room:* A/C, TV w/pay movies, dataport, coffeemaker, hair dryer, pay-per-use Nintendo.

7 Downtown

EXPENSIVE

Golden Nugget (★★ You may have seen the Golden Nugget on the short-lived reality show *The Casino*, which depicted its new hapless owners learning how to own and run a casino-hotel. You may not be surprised to learn the place recently sold again. Too bad; the place really is swell and deserves more stability. There were no plans at press time to indicate the new owners' intent towards their property, but let's hope for the best.

The Golden Nugget opened in 1946 as the first building in Las Vegas constructed specifically for casino gambling. Steve Wynn, who is basically responsible for the "new" Vegas hotel look, took the Golden Nugget over as his first major project in Vegas in 1973. He gradually transformed the Old West/Victorian interiors (typical for Downtown) into something more high rent; marble and brass gleam, and the whole package seems considerably more resortlike and genuinely luxurious, especially for downtown Vegas. The sunny interior spaces are a welcome change from the Las Vegas tradition of dim artificial lighting. Don't forget their mascot (well, it ought to be): the world's largest gold nugget. The *Hand of Faith* nugget weighs in at 61 pounds, 11 ounces, and is on display for all to see.

If the decor of The Mirage sounds appealing to you and you want to stay Downtown, come here because until recently the same people owned them and the rooms look almost identical—in fact, when The Mirage redid its rooms from a beige palette to a more vividly hued one, the Golden Nugget had the exact same remodel. In the

North Tower, the rooms are slightly larger than in the South (and also slightly larger than at The Mirage). You don't have to walk through the casino to get to your room, but you do have to walk a distance to get to the pool. During the winter, they put up a pavilion over part of the pool-deck space to allow for more interior space. The presence of the pool, and general overall quality, makes this the best hotel Downtown for families; the other Downtowners seem geared toward the much older set and/or the single-minded gambler set.

The Nugget's superb buffets and Sunday brunch are described in chapter 6. Oh, and yes, there is a casino (don't think they'd forget that!).

The Nugget's top-rated health club ($15-per-day fee to use the facilities) offers a full line of Universal equipment, Lifecycles, stair machines, treadmills, rowing machines, free weights, steam sauna, tanning beds, and massage. Salon treatments include everything from leg waxing to seaweed-mask facials. Free Sebastian products are available for sprucing up afterward. The spa's opulent Palladian-mirrored foyer is modeled after a room in New York's Frick Museum.

129 E. Fremont St. (at Casino Center Blvd.), Las Vegas, NV 89101. ℂ **800/634-3454** or 702/385-7111. Fax 702/386-8362. www.goldennugget.com. 1,907 units. $59 and up double; $275 and up suite. Extra person $20. AE, DC, DISC, MC, V. Free self- and valet parking. **Amenities:** Casino; showroom; 4 restaurants; outdoor pool; health club and spa; concierge; tour desk; car-rental desk; 24-hr. room service; laundry service; dry cleaning; nonsmoking rooms; executive-level rooms. *In room:* A/C, TV w/pay movies, dataport, hair dryer, iron/ironing board, safe.

MODERATE

Fitzgeralds Casino & Hotel ℱ   A few years ago, Fitzgeralds got a new owner, the first African American to own a Vegas casino, an interesting bit of trivia. Positive changes have come in his wake, though at this writing, mostly in the public areas. Largely gone is the luck o' the Irish theme, which makes us sad when we think about Mr. O'Lucky, the hotel's longtime mascot, but not so much when it comes to all the rest of the leprechauns and shamrocks and other bits of Blarney nonsense. The casino has been brightened up, so it's now one of the nicer places to gamble Downtown; the hallways and check-in area have been redone, and a new outdoor pool—a rare amenity for Downtown in general, and open until the unheard of (in Vegas) hour of 9pm—opened. Right now, you can expect a sort of Irish country-village walkway, complete with giant fake trees, leading to the room elevators. Fitzgeralds has the only balcony in Downtown from which you can watch the Fremont Street Experience. You can also sit in its McDonald's and gawk at the light show through the atrium windows.

The rooms are clean and comfortable, featuring standard hotel-room decor done in shades of green. Because this is the tallest building Downtown (34 stories), you get excellent views: snowcapped mountains, Downtown lights, or the Strip. Whirlpool-tub rooms are $20 more and are slightly larger, offering wraparound windows.

301 Fremont St. (at 3rd St.), Las Vegas, NV 89101. ℂ **800/274-LUCK** (274-5825) or 702/388-2400. Fax 702/388-2181. www.fitzgeralds.com. 638 units. $36 and up double; $60 and up suite. Extra person $10. Children under 19 stay free in parent's room. AE, DC, DISC, MC, V. Free self- and valet parking. **Amenities:** Casino; 5 restaurants; lounge; outdoor pool; concierge; tour desk; car-rental desk; courtesy car or limo; business center; 24-hr. room service; laundry service; dry cleaning; nonsmoking rooms. *In room:* A/C, TV w/pay movies, dataport, iron/ironing board, safe.

Four Queens ℱ   Opened in 1966 with a mere 120 rooms, the Four Queens (named for the owner's four daughters) has evolved over the decades into a major Downtown property occupying an entire city block. This property is sold so often we think it's being used as a stake in some ongoing card game—it was just sold again (yes, again), so the usual warnings about potential change still hold. The lobby is

California Hotel/
  Casino & RV Park 2
El Cortez Hotel
  & Casino 8
Fitzgeralds Casino
  & Hotel 7
Four Queens 6
Fremont Hotel
  & Casino 4
Golden Nugget 3
Lady Luck Casino
  Hotel 5
Main Street Station 1

small but elegant—in a slightly faded, slightly dated way (with mirrors and huge chandeliers). In the Four Queens, you just know you're in Old Las Vegas. And you are glad. As the staff says, this is the place to stay if you just want to gamble—or if you want to experience the *real* Old Las Vegas, and we don't just mean the clientele (though that, too—most are 50-plus and have been coming here for years). Another draw is the consistently helpful and friendly staff.

Rooms aren't going to blow you away, but note that the ones in the South Tower are a shade larger than the others, though we wouldn't hold any multiperson slumber parties in either. In most cases, rooms in the North Tower offer views of the Fremont Street Experience. The restaurant, **Hugo's Cellar** (p. 176), has a cozy lounge with a working fireplace, and two bars serve the casino.

202 Fremont St. (at Casino Center Blvd.), Las Vegas, NV 89101. © **800/634-6045** or 702/385-4011. Fax 702/387-5122. www.fourqueens.com. 690 units. $29 and up double; $119 and up suite. Extra person $15. AE, DC, DISC, MC, V. Free self- and valet parking. **Amenities:** Casino; 2 restaurants; small exercise room; limited room service; laundry service; dry cleaning; nonsmoking rooms. *In room:* A/C, TV w/pay movies, coffeemaker, hair dryer, iron/ironing board, safe.

INEXPENSIVE

California Hotel/Casino & RV Park   This is a hotel with a unique personality. California-themed, it markets itself mostly in Hawaii, and since 85% of its guests are from the Aloha State, it offers Hawaiian entrees in several of its restaurants and even has an on-premises store specializing in Hawaiian foodstuffs. You'll also notice that dealers are wearing colorful Hawaiian shirts. The rooms, however, reflect neither California nor Hawaii; they have mahogany furnishings and attractive marble bathrooms.

12 Ogden Ave. (at 1st St.), Las Vegas, NV 89101. (℃ 800/634-6255 or 702/385-1222. Fax 702/388-2660. www.the cal.com. 781 units. Sun–Thurs $50 and up double; Fri–Sat $60 and up double; holidays $70 and up double. Extra person $5. Children under 13 stay free in parent's room. AE, DC, DISC, MC, V. Free self- and valet parking. **Amenities:** Casino; 4 restaurants; small rooftop pool; video arcade; tour desk; shopping arcade; limited room service; laundry service; dry cleaning; nonsmoking rooms. *In room:* A/C, TV w/pay movies, safe.

El Cortez Hotel & Casino   This small hotel is popular with locals for its casual, oh, and let's just admit it, dated Downtown atmosphere. Rooms offer nothing except a place to rest your head and not get lice. And there is no room to swing a cat, dead or otherwise, in the bathrooms. But on the other hand, said rooms (recently renovated) supposedly do not cost more than $40 a night, so really, whaddaya want for next to nothing (by Vegas prices)? The nicest accommodations are the enormous minisuites in the 14-story tower. Some are exceptionally large king-size-bedded rooms with sofas; others have separate sitting areas with sofas, armchairs, and tables. Local calls are just 25¢. Note that although this place is but 2 blocks from Fremont Street, these are probably not 2 blocks you want to walk at night. Rumor has it that the company that bought the other hotels from the family that still owns the El Cortez has an option on it as well, and that all of them are destined for the wrecking ball.

600 Fremont St. (between 6th and 7th sts.), Las Vegas, NV 89101. (℃ 800/634-6703 or 702/385-5200. Fax 702/474-3626. www.elcortezhotelcasino.com. 428 units. $25 and up double; $40 minisuite. Extra person $5. AE, DISC, MC, V. Free self- and valet parking. **Amenities:** Casino; 2 restaurants; nonsmoking rooms. *In room:* A/C, TV.

Fremont Hotel & Casino   When it opened in 1956, the Fremont was the first high-rise in Downtown Las Vegas. Wayne Newton got his start here, singing in the now-defunct Carousel Showroom. Step just outside the front door and there you are, in the **Fremont Street Experience** (p. 193). Rooms are larger (the bathrooms, however, are the opposite of "large"), more comfortable, and more peaceful than you might expect. (Though up until midnight you can hear, sometimes all too well, music and noise from the Fremont St. Experience show. But then again, if you are in bed before midnight in Vegas, it's your own fault.) The staff is shockingly friendly, partly because you actually can have personal service with hotels this size (another advantage of staying Downtown), partly because they just are. The hotel encourages environmental awareness by changing linens only every other day; upon request, it can be more often, but why not help out the earth a bit? For that matter, why not help out your wallet a bit and stay here?

The Fremont boasts an Art Deco restaurant called the **Second Street Grill,** which is reviewed in chapter 6 along with the buffet. Guests can use the swimming pool at the nearby California Hotel, another Sam Boyd enterprise.

200 E. Fremont St. (between Casino Center Blvd. and 3rd St.), Las Vegas, NV 89101. (℃ 800/634-6182 or 702/385-3232. Fax 702/385-6229. www.fremontcasino.com. 452 units. $35 and up double. Extra person $8. Children under 12 stay free in parent's room. AE, DC, DISC, MC, V. Free valet parking; no self-parking. **Amenities:** Casino; 5 restaurants; tour desk; car-rental desk; free shuttle to Sam's Town; limited room service; laundry service; dry cleaning; nonsmoking rooms. *In room:* A/C, TV w/pay movies, fridge, coffeemaker, hair dryer, iron/ironing board.

Lady Luck Casino Hotel   Today's Lady Luck opened in 1964 as Honest John's, a 2,000-square-foot casino with five employees, five pinball machines, and 17 slots. Today that casino occupies 30,000 square feet, and the hotel, including sleek 17- and 25-story towers, is a major Downtown player, taking up an entire city block. What it retains from earlier times is a friendly atmosphere, one that has kept customers coming back for decades. Eighty percent of Lady Luck's clientele is repeat business.

A ton of dough was recently dumped into this venerable facility (by a national riverboat-owning chain), which means that while it doesn't look shockingly different, it has been given a face-lift that makes it, like a 60-year-old showgirl, a significant bit fresher. Nothing is special, but with these prices, it's well worth considering as a Downtown alternative. However, that same riverboat-owning chain sold the old gal yet again (is there no end to the indignities of time and age?), and she was sold yet one more time after that, as this book went to press, and so who knows what her fate will be by the time you read this. Until then, garden rooms are small and basic with nice motel-style furnishings, while tower rooms (the newer ones) have fresh carpeting and furnishings, and all are clean and comfy. In other words, it's good enough even before you get to the econo-prices.

206 N. 3rd St. (at Ogden Ave.), Las Vegas, NV 89101. © 800/523-9582 or 702/477-3000. Fax 702/382-2346. www. ladylucklv.com. 792 units. $40 and up double; Sun–Thurs $55 and up junior suite, Fri–Sat $70 and up junior suite. Extra person $8. AE, DC, DISC, MC, V. Free self- and valet parking. **Amenities:** Casino; small showroom; 3 restaurants; outdoor pool; tour desk; car-rental desk; free airport shuttle; limited room service; laundry service; dry cleaning; nonsmoking rooms. *In room:* A/C, TV w/pay movies, fridge, coffeemaker.

Main Street Station *★★ (Finds* Though not actually on Fremont Street, the Main Street Station is just 2 short blocks away, barely a 3-minute walk. Considering how terrific it is, this is hardly an inconvenience. Having taken over an abandoned hotel space, the Main Street Station remains, in our opinion, one of the nicest hotels in Downtown and one of the best bargains in the city.

The overall look here, typical of Downtown, is early-20th-century San Francisco. However, unlike everywhere else, the details here are outstanding, resulting in a beautiful hotel by any measure. Outside, gas lamps flicker on wrought-iron railings and stained-glass windows. Inside, you'll find hammered-tin ceilings, ornate antique-style chandeliers, and lazy ceiling fans. The small lobby is filled with wood panels, long wooden benches, and a front desk straight out of the Old West, with an old-time key cabinet with beveled-glass windows. (Check out the painting of a Victorian gambling scene to the left of the front desk.) Even the cashier cages look like antique brass bank tellers' cages. It's all very appealing and just plain pretty. An enclosed bridge connects the hotel with the California across the street, where you will find shopping and a kids' arcade.

The long and narrow rooms are possibly the largest in Downtown, though the ornate decorating downstairs does not extend up here. White-painted wood plantation shutters replace the usual curtains, each room has a very large gilt-framed mirror, and the simple but not unattractive furniture is vaguely French Provincial. It's all clean and in good taste. The bathrooms are small but well appointed. Rooms on the north side overlook the freeway, and the railroad track is nearby. The soundproofing seems quite strong—we couldn't hear anything when inside, but then again, we're from L.A. A few guests have complained about noise in these rooms, but the majority haven't had any problems. If you're concerned, request a room on the south side.

The **Pullman Grille** is the steak-and-seafood place and is much more reasonably priced than similar (and considerably less pretty) places in town. The stylish **Triple 7 Brew Pub** is described in detail in chapter 10. The excellent buffet is described in chapter 6. And the casino, thanks to some high ceilings, is one of the most smoke-free around.

200 N. Main St. (between Fremont St. and I-95), Las Vegas, NV 89101. © 800/465-0711 or 702/387-1896. Fax 702/386-4466. www.mainstreetcasino.com. 452 units. $59 and up standard double. AE, DC, DISC, MC, V. Free self- and valet parking. **Amenities:** Casino; 3 restaurants; outdoor pool next door at the California Hotel; car-rental desk; dry cleaning; nonsmoking rooms. *In room:* A/C, TV w/pay movies.

8 Henderson

VERY EXPENSIVE

Ritz-Carlton, Lake Las Vegas ☆☆☆ *Kids*   Vegas prides itself, these days, on offering all sorts of "luxury resorts." Vegas exaggerates—in some cases, by a lot. Truth be told, this is the *only* luxury resort (Four Seasons Las Vegas is a luxury hotel more than anything else because of its setup), and it's not even in Las Vegas. It's on the outskirts of next-door suburb Henderson, on the shores of Lake Las Vegas, meaning a 30-minute or so drive from the Strip.

Why on earth are we recommending it? Because to come here is to come to a gob-smackingly beautiful resort—between the sparkling water and the crisp mountains, all the better in the early evening with a warm breeze blowing, this is the serene oasis everyone dreams of when they come to the desert. Plus, it has all the pampering bells and whistles you could want. Here's the thing you have to remember: Those Strip "resorts" aren't in the hotel business, they are in the casino business. The hotel is just a sideline. Ritz-Carlton is a proper hotelier and you are the beneficiary. Certainly, the price is not cheap (though watch the website for some *great* deals), but once you realize what's included—all manner of treats that Strip "resorts" will charge you for as extras, plus impeccable service and a setting that's a dream—it's not a bad deal. Come here for a true getaway, and treat Vegas as a nearby attraction, an additional perk for your vacation.

Set right on the shores of the man-made (but so's Lake Mead and we've gotten over it) Lake Las Vegas, and styled like an Italian lakeside resort, this property couldn't be more handsome, from the lobby to the cool-palette rooms, with plump beds, comforters, and Frette linens. All bathrooms are large and fully marbled (not tile, but real marble), with deep, long soaking tubs and amenities for miles. Most rooms have water views (make sure you get one of those) either of the serpentine lake (our favorite) or of the little bay that abuts the property. Some have balconies, and all have windows that open (keep an eye on the lake for sightings of the big fish that occasionally cruise just below the surface).

The health club is the sort where all machines have flatscreen TVs, and the spa offers hot and cold plunge pools, plus a 360-degree Vichy shower. There is one basic pool and one "sandy beach" little dipping area. And the overall service? We felt like if we sneezed, three people would have rushed at us with tissues, and four would have called doctors, just to make sure we were okay. It's also quiet, a great change from the hurly-burly found at most Strip hotels. And yet, it's not at all stuffy; no one minds if you run around in a bathing suit and bare feet.

The activities are the best around, from a large array of desert and mountain hikes, both on your own and guided (including a restful evening one that includes a round of tai chi), to stargazing (you are far enough from city lights, so the looking is good), to boating on the lake, to honest-to-gosh fly-fishing. Daily yoga sessions and other physical fitness classes are also offered. And the hotel has access to three high-level golf courses.

Parents, in particular, should note that the club-level rooms offer, for an extra $100 a night, access to a lounge (complete with its own concierge and even more fabulous service), with nearly 'round-the-clock free "snacks," generous (and most of the time, rather fancy) enough to cover all your meal needs—that, plus free drinks, alcoholic and otherwise, makes this option a bargain. (Think how much you spend on meals and drinks, and tell us that it doesn't routinely go over an extra $100 a day.) Right next door is a charming faux Italian village with nearly 40 shops and restaurants (so you need not rely on the hotel's restaurant, though it is excellent), plus a large, if borderline dull, casino, if you want that kind of action but don't want to drive to the Strip. There are regular shuttles to the Strip until 2am, never fear, though why anyone would leave here is beyond us.

1610 Lake Las Vegas Pkwy., Henderson, NV 89011. (✆ **800/241-3333** or 702/567-4700. Fax 702/567-4777. www.ritzcarlton.com. 349 units. $199 and up double (additional charge for rollaway bed). AE, DC, DISC, MC, V. Pets accepted. **Amenities:** Restaurant; bar; concierge; 2 pools; health club and spa; business center; shuttle to Strip; water taxis to nearby attractions; some free exercise classes; 24-hr. room service; in-room massage; babysitting; laundry service; dry cleaning; nonsmoking rooms; club-level rooms. *In room:* A/C, TV w/pay movies, dataport, minibar, hair dryer, iron/ironing board, safe, high-speed Internet access (for a fee), Nintendo.

EXPENSIVE

Green Valley Ranch Resort ⟨★★⟩ Now, for all our heartfelt rhapsodizing above about the Ritz, do not think that we love Green Valley any less. It's not fair to this flat-out fabulous resort to compare the two—they can't quite compete on the same playing field because it doesn't have the same level of pedigree as the Ritz, nor does it have the knockout physical positioning on the lake. But it makes up for that with earnest efforts and lower prices (plus it's about half the distance back to the Strip, which is visible from the pool area), and if you can't stay at the one, you won't be unhappy staying at the other. Two different experiences, but each will make you feel like a resort should. Anyway, it seems that Green Valley's designers took careful notes on places like the Ritz-Carlton when coming up with their design—the interiors, rooms and public spaces both, feel completely influenced by same, while the exterior pool area borrowed much from hip hotel concepts such as the Standard and the W. This sounds like a potentially risky combination, but it works smashingly. You can stay here with your parents or your kids, and every age group should be happy.

Inside all is posh and stately, a dignified classy lobby, large rooms with the most comfortable beds in town (high-thread-count linens, feather beds, plump down comforters), and luxe marble bathrooms. A new expansion by the pool added more rooms, some of which have grand views. Outside is the hippest pool area this side of the aforementioned Hard Rock: part lagoon, part geometric, with shallow places for reading and canoodling, and your choice of poolside lounging equipment, ranging from teak lounge chairs to thick mattresses strewn with pillows, plus drinks served from the trendy Whiskey Beach. There is also a secluded topless bathing area for daring adults. The tiny health club is free, and the spa is also modern and hip. At night, you can hang out at the ultra-trendy Whiskey Sky as more mattresses and pillows get strewn about, all the better to attract the most beautiful bodies in town (desperate souls try to get past the velvet rope—you can pass with ease because you are staying here), or you can head over to the entirely separate (as in, an adjoining building) casino area, which offers a disappointingly old school–looking gambling area, plus a variety of restaurants and a multiscreen movie theater. And a brand-new shopping area, The District, just opened next door. A simulated street scene, you've got your usual mall and catalog favorites (Williams-Sonoma, Pottery Barn), plus still more restaurants. This addition does help alleviate the resort's somewhat isolated nature.

2300 Paseo Verde Pkwy. (at I-215), Henderson, NV 89052. (✆ **866/782-9487** or 702/782-9487. Fax 702/617-6885. www.greenvalleyranchresort.com. 200 units. Sun–Thurs $109 and up double; Fri–Sat $159 and up double. Extra person $12. Children under 12 stay free in parent's room. AE, DC, DISC, MC, V. Free self- and valet parking. **Amenities:** Casino; lounge; 7 restaurants plus a food court; outdoor pool; health club and spa; Jacuzzi; sauna; concierge; business center; 24-hr. room service; in-room massage; laundry service; dry cleaning; nonsmoking rooms; executive-level rooms. *In room:* A/C, TV w/pay movies, dataport, coffeemaker, hair dryer, iron/ironing board, safe, high-speed Internet access (for a fee).

6

Where to Dine

Among the many images that come to mind when people think of Las Vegas are cheap food deals, bargains so good the food is practically free. They think of the buffets—all a small country can eat—for only $3.99!

All that is true, but frankly, eating in Las Vegas is no longer something you don't have to worry about budgeting for. The buffets are certainly there—no good hotel would be without one—as are the cheap meal deals, but you get what you pay for. Some of the cheaper buffets, and even some of the more moderately priced ones, are mediocre at best, ghastly and inedible at worst. And we don't even want to *think* about those 69¢ beef stew specials.

However, there is some good news on the Vegas food scene. Virtually overnight, there was an explosion of new restaurants, most the creations of the so-called "celebrity chef" phenomenon. For this, we can thank those new luxury-resort hotels, whose management realized that food today is a major indulgence and obsession, and thus a significant part of the vacation experience. All of a sudden, Vegas can hold its head up alongside other big cities as a legitimate foodie destination.

Look at this partial list: Celebrity chefs Wolfgang Puck and Emeril Lagasse have half a dozen restaurants in town between them; deservedly famed chef Julian Serrano has set up shop at Bellagio's **Picasso;** Thomas Keller, the brains behind Napa Valley's French Laundry—considered by many to be the best restaurant in the United States—has opened up a branch of his **Bouchon** bistro; legendary chef Alain Ducasse is behind Mix at THEhotel; and branches of L.A., New York, San Francisco, and Boston high-profile names such as **Pinot, Le Cirque, Aqua, Aureole, Olives, Lutèce, Border Grill, Nobu,** and others have all rolled into town.

Unfortunately, this boom has affected only the very highest end of the price category. In other words, boy, can you eat well, as long as you have a trust fund. Even as dedicated foodies, we can't in good conscience tell you to eat only at places that will require taking out a small bank loan—except we just don't really have any other options. For the moment, with a few exceptions, it's hard to eat extremely well in Vegas (especially on the Strip) for a down-to-earth price. The buffets remain, certainly, but they're not the bargains they once were; the midprice-range food is, by and large, pretty forgettable; and the really low-end food found in the hotels—well, we try not to think of it as anything but fuel. Of course, this may not bother you as much as it bothers us.

If you get off the Strip, however, you can find some cheaper, more interesting alternatives, which we have listed below. If you're staying on the Strip and you don't have the mobility of a car, your food options will be severely limited. Getting outside of those enormous hotel resorts is a major proposition (and don't think that's not done on purpose), which is why visitors often settle for what the hotel has to offer—long lines and diminished quality. Walking to another hotel—on the Strip, yet another major investment of time— means probably encountering much of the same thing. But not always. Once, when faced with dismal breakfast choices, we went from The Mirage over to Caesars, landing in their Forum Shops where the Stage Deli stood, largely empty and with considerably better munchie options.

OUR BEST LAS VEGAS RESTAURANT ADVICE

GETTING IN   There are tricks to surviving dining in Vegas. If you can, make reservations in advance, particularly for the better restaurants (you might get to town planning to check out some of the better spots, only to find they are totally booked throughout your stay). Eat during off-hours when you can. Know that noon to, say, 1:30 or 2pm is going to be prime time for lunch, and 5:30 to 8:30pm (and just after the early shows get out) for dinner. Speaking of time, give yourself plenty of it, particularly if you have to catch a show. We once tried to grab a quick bite in The Riviera before running up to *La Cage*. The only choice was the food court, where long lines in front of all the stands (fast-food chains only) left us with about 5 minutes to gobble something decidedly unhealthful.

STAYING HEALTHY   *Unhealthy* is the watchword here; if you don't care about your heart or your waistline, you will do just fine in Vegas. (And really, what says "vacation" more than cream sauce?) But slowly, salads are making their way onto the menus, and some more health-conscious restaurants are opening. You just have to look for them. And we certainly don't mean to take away any enjoyment of those extravagant buffets; heck, that's a major part of the fun of Vegas! *Excess* is the other watchword here, and what better symbol is there than mounds of shrimp and unlimited prime rib?

SAVING MONEY   So you want to sample the creations of a celebrity chef, but you took a beating at the craps table? Check our listings to see which of the high-profile restaurants are open for lunch. Sure, sometimes the more interesting and exotic items are found at dinner, but the midday meal is usually no slouch and can be as much as two-thirds cheaper.

Or skip that highfalutin' stuff altogether. The late-night specials—a complete steak meal for just a couple dollars—are also an important part of a good, decadent Vegas experience (and a huge boon for insomniacs). And having complained about how prices are going up, we'll also tell you that you still can eat cheaply and decently (particularly if you are looking upon food only as fuel) all over town. The locals repeatedly say that they almost never cook because in Vegas it is always cheaper to eat out. To locate budget fare, check local newspapers (especially Fri editions) and free magazines (such as *Showbiz* and *What's On in Las Vegas*), which are given away at hotel reception desks (sometimes these sources also yield money-saving coupons).

ABOUT PRICE CATEGORIES   The restaurants in this chapter are arranged first by location, then by the following price categories (based on the average cost of a dinner entree): **Very Expensive,** more than $25; **Expensive,** $15 to $25; **Moderate,** $15 to $20; **Inexpensive,** under $15 (sometimes well under). In expensive and very expensive restaurants, expect to spend no less than twice the price of the average entree for your entire meal with a tip; you can usually get by on a bit less in moderate and inexpensive restaurants. Buffets and Sunday brunches are gathered in a separate section at the end of this chapter.

A FINAL WORD As welcome as the influx of designer chefs is—and, good lord, is it welcome—you can't help but notice that the majority are simply re-creating their best work (and sometimes not even that) from elsewhere rather than producing something new. So the Vegas food scene remains, like its architecture, a copy of something from somewhere else. And as happy as we are to encourage you to throw money at these guys, please don't forget the mom-and-pop places, which struggle not to disappear into the maw of the big hotel machines and which produce what comes the closest to true local quality. If you can, get in your car and check out some of the options listed below that are a bit off the beaten track. Show Vegas you aren't content—you want a meal you can brag about and afford, now!

1 Restaurants by Cuisine

AMERICAN

Carson Street Cafe (Downtown, $, p. 178)

Fix 𝕽𝕽 (Mid-Strip, $$$, p. 155)

Hard Rock Cafe 𝕽 (East of the Strip, $$, p. 143)

Harley Davidson Cafe 𝕽 (South Strip, $$, p. 143)

Rainforest Café 𝕽 (South Strip, $$, p. 143)

Spago 𝕽 (Mid-Strip, $$$$, p. 153)

Top of the World (North Strip, $$$$, p. 153)

ASIAN

Dragon Noodle Co. 𝕽𝕽 (South Strip, $$, p. 141)

Grand Wok and Sushi Bar 𝕽𝕽 (South Strip, $$, p. 141)

Red 8 𝕽𝕽 (North Strip, $, p. 162)

Spago 𝕽 (Mid-Strip, $$$$, p. 153)

BAGELS

Einstein Bros. Bagels 𝕽 (East of the Strip, $, p. 168)

BARBECUE

Memphis Championship Barbecue 𝕽𝕽 (East of the Strip, $$, p. 167)

BISTRO

Bouchon 𝕽𝕽𝕽 (Mid-Strip, $$$, p. 154)

Daniel Boulard Brasserie 𝕽 (Mid-Strip, $$$$, p. 148)

Mon Ami Gabi 𝕽𝕽 (Mid-Strip, $$, p. 158)

Pinot Brasserie 𝕽𝕽 (Mid-Strip, $$$, p. 156)

BUFFETS/BRUNCHES

Bally's Big Kitchen Buffet (Mid-Strip, $$, p. 183)

Bally's Sterling Sunday Brunch 𝕽𝕽 (Mid-Strip, $$$$, p. 181)

Bellagio Buffet 𝕽𝕽 (Mid-Strip, $$$$, p. 182)

The Buffet at the Las Vegas Hilton 𝕽 (East of the Strip, $$, p. 185)

Circus Circus Buffet (North Strip, $, p. 185)

Excalibur's Round Table Buffet 𝕽 (South Strip, $, p. 180)

Flamingo Paradise Garden Buffet 𝕽 (Mid-Strip, $, p. 184)

Fremont Paradise Buffet 𝕽 (Downtown, $, p. 186)

Golden Nugget Buffet 𝕽𝕽 (Downtown, $$, p. 185)

Harrah's Fresh Market Buffet 𝕽 (Mid-Strip, $$, p. 183)

Luxor's Pharaoh's Pheast Buffet 𝕽𝕽 (South Strip, $, p. 181)

Main Street Station Garden Court 𝕽𝕽𝕽 (Downtown, $, p. 186)

Mandalay Bay's Bay Side Buffet 𝕽 (South Strip, $$, p. 180)

MGM Grand Buffet 𝕽 (South Strip, $, p. 181)

Key to Abbreviations: $$$$ = Very Expensive $$$ = Expensive $$ = Moderate $ = Inexpensive

Mirage Cravings Buffet ⭐⭐
(Mid-Strip, $$, p. 183)
Monte Carlo Buffet ⭐ (South Strip,
$, p. 181)
Palms Festival Market Buffet ⭐⭐
(Mid-Strip, $, p. 184)
Paris, Le Village Buffet ⭐⭐⭐
(Mid-Strip, $$$, p. 182)
Rio's Carnival World Buffet ⭐⭐
(Mid-Strip, $$$, p. 183)
Sam's Town Firelight Buffet ⭐
(East of the Strip, $, p. 185)
Spice Market Buffet ⭐ (South Strip,
$$$, p. 133)
Treasure Island Dishes Buffet ⭐⭐
(Mid-Strip, $$, p. 184)
Tropicana Island Buffet ⭐ (South
Strip, $$, p. 180)
Wynn Las Vegas Buffet ⭐⭐⭐
(Mid-Strip, $$$$, p. 182)

CALIFORNIA

Gordon-Biersch Brewing Company ⭐
(East of the Strip, $$, p. 166)
Spago ⭐ (Mid-Strip, $$$$, p. 153)
Wolfgang Puck Bar & Grill ⭐⭐
(South Strip, $$, p. 144)

CHINESE

Cathay House (West Las Vegas, $$,
p. 174)

COFFEE SHOP

Bougainvillea ⭐⭐ (East of the Strip,
$, p. 168)

CONTEMPORARY

Mix ⭐⭐ (South Strip, $$$$, p. 138)

CONTEMPORARY CREOLE

Delmonico Steakhouse ⭐⭐
(Mid-Strip, $$$$, p. 149)
Emeril's New Orleans Fish House ⭐
(South Strip, $$$$, p. 137)

CONTINENTAL

Red Square ⭐⭐ (South Strip, $$$$,
p. 139)
Top of the World (North Strip, $$$$,
p. 153)

CREOLE

Commander's Palace ⭐⭐ (South
Strip, $$$$, p. 136)

CUBAN

Rincon Criollo (North Strip, $,
p. 162)

DELI

Stage Deli ⭐⭐ (Mid-Strip, $$,
p. 159)

DESSERTS

Freed's Bakery (East of the Strip, $,
p. 173)
Luv-It Frozen Custard (North Strip,
$, p. 173)

DINER

Burger Bar ⭐ (South Strip, $$,
p. 140)
Calypsos ⭐ (South Strip, $, p. 144)
Ice House Lounge ⭐ (Downtown, $,
p. 178)
Jillian's ⭐ (Downtown, $, p. 179)
Rainbow Bar & Grill (East of the
Strip, $$, p. 167)
Tiffany's ⭐⭐ (North Strip, $, p. 162)

DONUTS

Krispy Kreme Doughnuts (West Las
Vegas, $, p. 173)
Ronald's Donuts (West Las Vegas, $,
p. 173)

ECLECTIC

Sensi ⭐⭐ (Mid-Strip, $$, p. 159)

FOOD COURT

Cypress Street Marketplace ⭐⭐
(Mid-Strip, $$, p. 157)

FRENCH

Alizé ⭐⭐⭐ (Mid-Strip, $$$$, p. 146)
Andre's ⭐⭐ (Downtown, $$$$,
p. 175)
Le Cirque ⭐ (Mid-Strip, $$$$,
p. 150)
Lutèce ⭐ (Mid-Strip, $$$$, p. 150)
Pamplemousse ⭐ (East of the Strip,
$$$$, p. 164)

Picasso ✻✻✻ (Mid-Strip, $$$$, p. 152)

FRENCH CONTINENTAL
Fleur de Lys ✻✻✻ (South Strip, $$$$, p. 138)

GERMAN
Cafe Heidelberg German Deli and Restaurant ✻ (North Strip, $$, p. 160)

INDIAN
Shalimar (East of the Strip, $$, p. 168)

INTERNATIONAL
Hugo's Cellar ✻ (Downtown, $$$$, p. 176)

Second Street Grill ✻ (Downtown, $$$, p. 177)

IRISH
Nine Fine Irishmen ✻ (South Strip, $$, p. 142)

ITALIAN
Bartolotta ✻✻✻ (Mid-Strip, $$$$, p. 147)

Canaletto ✻✻ (Mid-Strip, $$$, p. 154)

Carluccio's Tivoli Gardens ✻ (East of the Strip, $$, p. 166)

Circo ✻✻ (Mid-Strip, $$$, p. 155)

Corsa Cucina ✻✻ (Mid-Strip, $$, p. 157)

Fiore ✻ (Mid-Strip, $$$$, p. 149)

Olives ✻✻ (Mid-Strip, $$, p. 158)

Onda ✻✻ (Mid-Strip, $$$$, p. 151)

Sazio ✻ (South Strip, $$, p. 143)

Valentino ✻ (Mid-Strip, $$$$, p. 153)

JAPANESE
Kabuki (East of the Strip, $$, p. 166)

Mizuno's ✻✻ (South Strip, $$$, p. 140)

MEDITERRANEAN
Corsa Cucina ✻✻ (Mid-Strip, $$, p. 157)

Mediterranean Cafe & Market ✻ (East of the Strip, $, p. 169)

Olives ✻✻ (Mid-Strip, $$, p. 158)

MEXICAN
Border Grill ✻✻✻ (South Strip, $$$, p. 139)

Dona Maria Tamales ✻✻ (North Strip, $, p. 162)

El Sombrero Cafe ✻✻ (Downtown, $, p. 178)

Isla ✻✻ (Mid-Strip, $$, p. 158)

Pink Taco ✻ (East of the Strip, $$, p. 167)

Toto's ✻✻ (East of the Strip, $, p. 170)

Viva Mercados ✻✻ (West Las Vegas, $$, p. 175)

NOUVEAU
Alex ✻✻✻ (Mid-Strip, $$$$, p. 146)

NOUVELLE AMERICAN
Aureole ✻✻✻ (South Strip, $$$$, p. 135)

Rosemary's Restaurant ✻✻✻ (West Las Vegas, $$$, p. 170)

PACIFIC RIM
Second Street Grill ✻ (Downtown, $$$, p. 177)

PROVENÇAL
Fiore ✻ (Mid-Strip, $$$$, p. 149)

PUB FARE
Monte Carlo Pub & Brewery ✻✻✻ (South Strip, $, p. 144)

Nine Fine Irishmen ✻ (South Strip, $$, p. 142)

RUSSIAN
Red Square ✻✻ (South Strip, $$$$, p. 139)

SANDWICHES
Capriotti's ✻✻✻ (North Strip, $, p. 160)

Jodi Maroni's Sausage Kingdom ✻✻✻ (South Strip, $, p. 144)

SEAFOOD

Austins Steakhouse ★★ (West Las
  Vegas, $$$, p. 170)
Bartolotta ★★★ (Mid-Strip, $$$$,
  p. 147)
Drai's (Mid-Strip, $$$$, p. 149)
Lawry's The Prime Rib ★★★ (East of
  the Strip, $$$$, p. 163)
Limericks ★ (Downtown, $$$,
  p. 177)
Michael Mina ★ (Mid-Strip, $$$$,
  p. 151)
Morton's of Chicago ★ (East of the
  Strip, $$$$, p. 163)
The Palm ★★ (Mid-Strip, $$$$,
  p. 151)
The Tillerman ★ (East of the Strip,
  $$$$, p. 164)

SOUTHERN

House of Blues ★★ (South Strip,
  $$$, p. 142)

STEAK

Austins Steakhouse ★★ (West Las
  Vegas, $$$, p. 170)
Charlie Palmer ★★ (South Strip,
  $$$$, p. 136)

Delmonico Steakhouse ★★ (Mid-
  Strip, $$$$, p. 148)
Drai's (Mid-Strip, $$$$, p. 149)
Lawry's The Prime Rib ★★★ (East of
  the Strip, $$$$, p. 163)
Limericks ★ (Downtown, $$$,
  p. 177)
Morton's of Chicago ★ (East of the
  Strip, $$$$, p. 163)
The Palm ★★ (Mid-Strip, $$$$,
  p. 151)
The Range ★★ (Mid-Strip, $$$$,
  p. 152)
The Tillerman ★ (East of the Strip,
  $$$$, p. 164)

SUSHI

Dragon Sushi (West Las Vegas, $,
  p. 175)
Hyakumi ★ (Mid-Strip, $$$, p. 135)

THAI

Komol (East of the Strip, $$, p. 166)
Lotus of Siam ★★★ (East of the
  Strip, $, p. 169)
Thai Spice (West Las Vegas, $$,
  p. 174)

---

2 South Strip

Note: In addition to the restaurants listed in this section, the Monte Carlo has a branch of Andre's, the French restaurant that has long been a favorite in Downtown (p. 175). The South Strip branch is just as highly recommended for fabulous food and attentive, not intimidating, service.

VERY EXPENSIVE

Aureole ★★★ NOUVELLE AMERICAN   The primary fame of this branch of a New York City fave (it's pronounced are-ree-*all*), run by Charlie Palmer, comes from their gimmicky wine tower, four stories of probably the finest wine collection in Vegas, made even more sensational thanks to catsuit-clad lovelies who are hoisted on wires to reach bottles requested from the uppermost heights. Lost in this Vegas-show glitz is one of the truly best of the fine-dining experiences around. The menu is a three-course prix fixe, though if you are winsome enough, they might send out luxurious extras like pâté on brioche topped with shaved truffles or an espresso cup of cold yellow-pepper soup with crab. Otherwise, expect marvels like a tender roasted lamb loin and braised shoulder, or a rack of venison accompanied by sweet-potato purée and chestnut crisp. Everything demonstrates the hand of a true chef in the kitchen, someone paying close attention to his work and to his customers. Service is solicitous; on a recent visit, with one diner not feeling up to an actual meal, the concerned server presented special clear consommé and mild sorbets. Desserts are playful, including a bittersweet chocolate soufflé with blood-orange sorbet and a Bartlett pear crisp with toasted cinnamon brioche and lemon-grass foam. There is also an excellent cheese plate. Oh, and that wine tower? You can navigate it from your table with the innovative and highly engrossing handheld computer that not only helps you through the vast depths of the list, but makes suggestions for you based on your meal choices.

In Mandalay Bay, 3950 Las Vegas Blvd. S. ✆ 877/632-1766. www.aureolelv.com. Reservations required. Fixed-price dinner $69; tasting menu $95. AE, DISC, MC, V. Daily 6–10pm.

Charlie Palmer 𝕬𝕬 STEAKHOUSE There are many, many steakhouses in Vegas, as if there were some additional natural law that states any hotel without one will suffer from entropy and eventually collapse into a black hole. Discerning palates know there can be a significant difference between steakhouses; discerning wallets might not care. If you find yourself among the former, do try Charlie Palmer's, probably the best of the costlier Shrines to Beef. Those with the latter can be reassured that with entrees weighing in around 22 to 45 ounces *each,* diners can legitimately, and in the name of decency ought to, share portions, which makes this a much more affordable experience. And why not? Those enormous slabs o' meat are as tender as anything because with the big bucks you do get the best cuts. We prefer the flavorful rib-eye to the other favorite, the Kansas City. Be sure to try the spinach salad topped with truffled fried egg and warm bacon vinaigrette as a starter (it gets a plus for presentation), and split sides like citrus-braised asparagus or a truffled potato purée (we are such suckers for what we call "gourmet baby food"). Desserts are stylish creations, and the whole thing is set in a generic fancy Vegas restaurant space that can be a bit noisy and crowded, so if romance is on the agenda, ask for one of the two-person tables in the back. Charlie Palmer, by the way, is the chef mind behind Aureole on the other side of Mandalay Bay; this makes two-for-two for this one celeb chef.

In the Four Seasons Hotel, 3960 Las Vegas Blvd. S. ✆ 702/632-5120. www.charliepalmersteaklv.com. Reservations suggested. Main courses $17–$35. AE, DC, DISC, MC, V. Daily 5–10:30pm.

Commander's Palace 𝕬𝕬 CREOLE This is an offshoot of the famous New Orleans restaurant, which is considered the best in that town, and sometimes even the best in the country. We did not expect quite that high a level of, well, anything, from this branch, but we did expect a lot, and they came through. It doesn't look precisely like the one in New Orleans, so it wasn't the huge shock to the system we expected (what city are we in now?), but it does have that classic, handsome old New Orleans restaurant wood paneling, big chandeliers, and that sort of thing. Service is nearly as good as at the original; no group of waiters hovering to fulfill every whim and remove every crumb, but we hardly felt neglected. And the food was, if not yet as spectacular as that of its elder cousin's, just about the best we've had in Vegas yet, with not one thing, from appetizer to dessert, disappointing our palates. On the other hand, it's interesting to see how portions shrink and prices rise when exposed to the Vegas area code. You might be best off getting the $39 three-course Creole favorite, featuring Commander's justly legendary turtle soup with sherry, Louisiana pecan-crusted fish, and signature bread pudding soufflé, three things they do very, very well indeed. Shrimp rémoulade, though, is another fine starter, and the chocolate Sheba is one of our top desserts. Overall, this is a really nice restaurant run by people who really care about the restaurant business.

RESTAURANTS
Andre's (2nd Branch) **6**
Aureole **10**
Border Grill **10**
Burger Bar **10**
Calypsos **8**
Chocolate Swan **10**
Charlie Palmer **10**
Commander's Palace **1**
Dragon Noodle Co. **3**
Emeril's New Orleans
  Fish House **6**
ESPN **1**

The Food Court
  (Monte Carlo) **3**
Grand Wok and
  Sushi Bar **7**
Harley Davidson Café **2**
House of Blues **10**
Jodi Maroni's **5**
Mizuno's **9**
Monte Carlo Pub &
  Brewery **3**
Nine Fine Irishmen **5**
New York–New York
  Food Court **5**

Rainforest Café **9**
Red Square **10**
Sazio **4**
Sherwood Forest Café **7**
Wolfgang Puck Café **6**

BUFFETS
Excalibur's Round
  Table Buffet **8**
Luxor's Pharaoh's
  Pheast Buffet **10**
Mandalay Bay's Bay Side
  Buffet **10**
MGM Grand Buffet **7**

Monte Carlo Buffet **3**
Spice Market Buffet **1**
Tropicana Island
  Buffet **8**

In the Desert Passage in the Aladdin hotel, 3663 Las Vegas Blvd. S. ✆ 702/892-8272. www.commanderspalace.com. Reservations suggested. Lunch $16–$20; dinner $28–$39. AE, DISC, MC, V. Mon–Fri breakfast 9–11am, brunch 11:30am–2pm, dinner 5:30–10pm; Sat–Sun brunch 10:30am–2pm, dinner 5:30–10pm.

Emeril's New Orleans Fish House ⍟ CONTEMPORARY CREOLE   As with Wolfgang Puck, the ubiquitous Emeril Lagasse has probably spread himself too thin. While we thoroughly enjoy his shows on the Food Network and can attest that his flagship restaurant in New Orleans remains as good as ever, this Vegas outpost seems to have slipped. Part of that may be our prejudice about seafood restaurants in the desert—yes, we know about airplanes and refrigeration, but we rarely have good fish in Vegas, so there you go. For that matter, at our last meal here, the most successful dish was the Creole-spiced aged rib-eye, drizzled with a horseradish Worchester sauce (with Emeril's famous kick that is neatly tempered by the mashed potatoes). A salad of duck comfit left us feeling the duck would be better on its own, but the sweet toasted-pecan vinaigrette was so good it reconciled one diner toward eating previously loathed spinach. A signature dish remains the foie gras–topped ahi tuna, a combination that makes no more sense to us now than it did when we first tried it (especially since they add a veal reduction sauce, though that tastes lovely with the side of spaghetti sauce). But the portions of foie gras can be generous, so you could just deconstruct it into a two-part appetizer. Still, you should try Emeril's famous lobster cheesecake appetizer, a savory delight like nothing you've tried before. The garlic-and-herb butter sauce that comes with the barbecued shrimp will have you mopping your plate with bread and asking for more of the petite rosemary biscuits that accompany it. And a slice of the banana-cream pie with banana crust and caramel drizzle is simple in its decadence.

In the MGM Grand, 3799 Las Vegas Blvd. S. ℂ 702/891-7374. www.emerils.com. Reservations required. Main courses $12–$18 at lunch, $18–$38 at dinner (more for lobster). AE, DC, DISC, MC, V. Daily 11:30am–2:30pm and 5:30–10:30pm.

Fleur de Lys ✿✿✿ FRENCH CONTINENTAL   One of the most sophisticated restaurants in Las Vegas, this is an offshoot of a highly regarded San Francisco establishment run by chef Hubert Keller. Continuing the tradition of visually show-stopping restaurant spaces in the Mandalay Bay, most tables are set in the semicircular two-story interior consisting half of '70s-style stone brick walls, half of billowing drapes, behind which are concealed a few dining booths. The tasting table is in the "wine loft" above the action, allowing fortunate diners a candle-framed view of the action below, surely the choicest table at what we consider one of the choicest restaurants in town. The whole thing is just sexy, in a grown-up way, right down to the playful, fanciful composition of the food. It's one of the few places in Vegas where you ought to dress up to dine, but in a good way. While the bustling servers do seem to know the difference between prompt care and unctuous crowding, it does feel a bit rushed, when this is food you want to linger over. At this writing, one orders from a three-, four-, or five-course tasting menu (including a well-thought-out vegetarian option), featuring seasonal choices such as delicate seared ahi tuna with a gelée of chile and garlic, a silly appearing but hearty ocean "baeckeoffe" (a collection of seafood options like a sort of seafood burger-style crab cake on a brioche), pan-seared diver scallops with parsnip fires served in a cunning mini flower pot, perfect roasted Maine lobster with an artichoke purée soup, and roasted guinea hen breast and leg confit topped with crispy basil. Our descriptions won't do these playful, sexy dishes justice. Despite the presence of a perfect white and dark chocolate mousse on the "Chocolate Feast" sampler plate, you owe it to yourself to try the fresh fruit minestrone—basic sorbet, raspberries, and poppy seed langue de chat, all strong fresh fruit flavors that harmonize beautifully, no fat, and you won't care.

3950 Las Vegas Blvd. S. (in Mandalay Place). ℂ 877/632-9200. Reservations recommended. Jacket recommended. 3- to 5-course menu $68–$88. AE, DC, DISC, MC, V. Daily 5:30–10:30pm.

Mix ✿✿ CONTEMPORARY   This is highly revered French chef Alain Ducasse's first Vegas venture, and such a Big Deal needs a Big Deal setting, in this case, on the 64th (by their counting) floor of THEhotel at Mandalay Bay. It's yet another spectacular restaurant space in a hotel full of them, this one white on white on silver, a futuristic fantasy including a set design sort of like a giant beaded curtain made of blown-glass balls that envelopes a curving stairway plopped down in the middle. Some tables are set in silver "pods" that remind one of Woody Allen's *Sleeper.* It looks like where the Jetsons might eat. It's also got drama outside, thanks to top-of-the-tall-hotel Strip views. The playful yet hip attitude is reflected in the food, which is a little self-conscious. Still, hard to resist a place that starts with bread flavors like ketchup or bacon, with a side of homemade peanut butter. But it's the sort of meal that grows progressively less "wow" as the evening wears on; early courses of melting amberjack sashimi topped with osetra and a little lemon and salt are superb, as are the lovely foie gras terrines with nifty accompaniments. The signature Ducasse pressed chicken with foie gras in black truffle sauce probably would be just that much better if Chef himself were making it. Fish dishes are solidly good but not transcendent, and by the time the meal gets to, say, the rack of lamb, you may be thinking "Well, this is excellent, certainly, but not mind-blowingly so." Which sounds like terrible nitpicking, but given the remarkable things going on in some other kitchens around town, and given the prices here, it's a fine line worth delineating. Still, the setting may make up for it.

3950 Las Vegas Blvd. S. (in THEhotel). ℂ 877/632-1766. Main courses $29–$55. AE, DISC, DC, MC, V. Daily 6–10:30pm.

Red Square 🐾🐾 CONTINENTAL/RUSSIAN The beheaded and pigeon-dropping-adorned statue of Lenin outside Red Square only hints at the near-profane delights on the interior. Inside you will find decayed posters that once glorified the Worker, cheek by jowl with a patchwork mix of remnants of Czarist trappings, as pillaged from toppled Bolsheviks and Stalinists. It is disconcerting to see the hammer and sickle so blithely and irreverently displayed, but then again, what better way to drain it of its power than to exploit it in a palace of capitalistic decadence? And then there's the ice-covered bar—all the better to keep your drinks nicely chilled. After all, they have 150 different kinds of vodka, perhaps the largest collection in the world. It's all just one big post-Communist party. (Sorry, we had to say it.)

Anyway, if you can tear your eyes away from the theme-run-amok, you might notice the menu is quite good, one of our favorites around. Blow your expense account on some caviar (we found we liked nutty osetra better than stronger beluga), properly chilled in ice, served with the correct pearl spoon. Or, more affordably, nosh on Siberian nachos—smoked salmon, citron caviar, and crème fraîche. The chef's special is a Roquefort-crusted tender filet mignon, with some soft caramelized garlic and a fine reduction sauce; it's a grand piece of meat, one of the best in town and more cheaply priced than similarly ranked places. We also very much liked the pan-seared halibut with a roasted beet vinaigrette and basil oil on a mushroom risotto. Try a silly themed drink, such as the "Cuban Missile Crisis," which is rain vodka, dark rum, sugar-cane syrup, and lime juice, or better still, take advantage of that vodka menu and try a tasting flight of four kinds, joined by theme (in our case, the "Ultimate Flight" paired Polish, Russian, Scottish, and Estonian vodkas). Desserts are not as clever but are worth saving room for, especially the warm chocolate cake with a liquid center and the strawberries Romanoff.

In Mandalay Bay, 3950 Las Vegas Blvd. S. ℂ 702/632-7407. Reservations recommended. Main courses $17–$31. AE, DC, MC, V. Daily 5:30pm–midnight.

EXPENSIVE

Border Grill 🐾🐾🐾 MEXICAN For our money, here's the best Mexican food in town. This big, cheerful space (like a Romper Room for adults) houses a branch of the much-lauded L.A. restaurant, conceived and run by the Food Network's "Two Hot Tamales," Mary Sue Milliken and Susan Feniger. This is truly authentic Mexican home cooking—the Tamales learned their craft from the real McCoy south of the border—but with a nuevo twist. So don't expect precisely the same dishes you'd encounter in your favorite corner joint, but do expect fresh and fabulous food, sitting as brightly on the plates as the decor on the walls. Stay away from the occasionally bland fish and head right toward rich and cheesy dishes like chiles rellenos (with perfect black beans) and chicken *chilaquiles* (a sister to the taco), or try nuevo items such as mushroom empanadas. Don't miss the dense but fluffy Mexican chocolate-cream pie (with a meringue crust).

In Mandalay Bay, 3950 Las Vegas Blvd. S. ⓒ 702/632-7403. www.bordergrill.com. Reservations recommended. Main courses $15–$24. AE, DC, DISC, MC, V. Sun–Thurs 11:30am–10:30pm; Fri–Sat 11:30am–11pm.

Mizuno's 𝒢𝒢 JAPANESE   Mizuno's has long had a strong reputation in town for terrific Japanese food, and while it seems like a gimmicky place, there is a good reason for those perpetually good reviews. Anyone who has eaten at a Benihana isn't going to find the concept here novel—you are seated at a grill and your own chef cooks in front of you—but we do note that the crowd is often predominantly Asian, so from that we can gather they are doing things right, gimmick or no. Yes indeedy, from our standpoint they are definitely doing things right; we told the chef what we wanted, what we didn't, and he followed instructions—with a great show, all clinging and clanging and flying utensils and even flashing Vegas strobe lights. It's hilarious even if it is schlock—and we loved everything he did for us. What we ate recently (but hey, don't limit yourself to our choices—he's *your* personal chef, remember!): crunchy and crispy deep-fried pork pot stickers *(gyoza),* filet mignon with fried rice cooked to order, and *teppanyaki,* or stir-fried, vegetables featuring perfectly spiced enormous onions. The menu options are either the Samurai dinners (one entree with all the fixings, including miso soup and salad) or the Shogun combo (all of the above but with two entrees). This is a good choice for a group or even a celebration, since it's such a giddy dining experience.

In Tropicana Resort & Casino, 3801 Las Vegas Blvd. S. ⓒ 702/739-2770. Reservations recommended. Full Samurai dinners mostly $17–$27; Shogun combination dinners $27–$45. AE, DC, DISC, MC, V. Daily 5–10:45pm.

MODERATE

Burger Bar 𝒢 DINER   See how Vegas is? They know you might be watching your budget, or just wanting something simple but not boring, so they give you a place that

---

Value **Great Meal Deals**

We've already alluded to the rock-bottom budget meals and graveyard specials available at casino hotel restaurants. Quality not assured and Pepto-Bismol not provided. As prices and deals can change without notice, we don't want to list examples, but finding a full prime-rib dinner for around $5 is not rare (pun definitely intended).

Your best bet is to keep your eyes open as you travel through town, as hotels tend to advertise their specials on their marquees. Or you can go to www.vegas.com and click **"Dining"** and then **"Dining Bargains,"** though the tips and prices may be similarly somewhat out-of-date. Following are three examples of current options for late-night munchies: **Ellis Island** offers a $4.95 10-ounce steak (plus potato and other sides), $7.77 gets you a strip steak and lobster tail at **Bourbon Street** (available 24 hours), and **Mr. Lucky's 24/7** at the Hard Rock Hotel is a particularly good coffee shop, with particularly good people-watching. Check out the blonde eating the messy nachos, and the scruffy guy eating an especially good steak. Pamela and Kid Rock? And then ask your server about the $7.77 steak, three barbequed shrimp, and sides; it's not on the menu, so you have to know about it.

gras terrines with nifty accompanim[...]
foie gras in black truffle sauce probably [...]
self were making it. Fish dishes are solidly go[...]
the meal gets to, say, the rack of lamb, you ma[...]
certainly, but not mind-blowingly so." Which so[...]
given the remarkable things going on in some other kit[...]
the prices here, it's a fine line worth delineating. Still, the se[...]

3950 Las Vegas Blvd. S. (in THEhotel). © 877/632-1766. Main courses $29–$55[...]
6–10:30pm.

Red Square ✸✸ CONTINENTAL/RUSSIAN   The beheaded and p[...]
ping-adorned statue of Lenin outside Red Square only hints at the near[...]
delights on the interior. Inside you will find decayed posters that once glorified[...]
Worker, cheek by jowl with a patchwork mix of remnants of Czarist trappings, as pi[...]
laged from toppled Bolsheviks and Stalinists. It is disconcerting to see the hammer
and sickle so blithely and irreverently displayed, but then again, what better way to
drain it of its power than to exploit it in a palace of capitalistic decadence? And then
there's the ice-covered bar—all the better to keep your drinks nicely chilled. After all,
they have 150 different kinds of vodka, perhaps the largest collection in the world. It's
all just one big post-Communist party. (Sorry, we had to say it.)

Anyway, if you can tear your eyes away from the theme-run-amok, you might
notice the menu is quite good, one of our favorites around. Blow your expense
account on some caviar (we found we liked nutty osetra better than stronger beluga),
properly chilled in ice, served with the correct pearl spoon. Or, more affordably, nosh
on Siberian nachos—smoked salmon, citron caviar, and crème fraîche. The chef's special is a Roquefort-crusted tender filet mignon, with some soft caramelized garlic and
a fine reduction sauce; it's a grand piece of meat, one of the best in town and more
cheaply priced than similarly ranked places. We also very much liked the pan-seared
halibut with a roasted beet vinaigrette and basil oil on a mushroom risotto. Try a silly
themed drink, such as the "Cuban Missile Crisis," which is rain vodka, dark rum,
sugar-cane syrup, and lime juice, or better still, take advantage of that vodka menu
and try a tasting flight of four kinds, joined by theme (in our case, the "Ultimate
Flight" paired Polish, Russian, Scottish, and Estonian vodkas). Desserts are not as
clever but are worth saving room for, especially the warm chocolate cake with a liquid
center and the strawberries Romanoff.

In Mandalay Bay, 3950 Las Vegas Blvd. S. © 702/632-7407. Reservations recommended. Main courses $17–$31.
AE, DC, MC, V. Daily 5:30pm–midnight.

EXPENSIVE

Border Grill ✸✸✸ MEXICAN   For our money, here's the best Mexican food in
town. This big, cheerful space (like a Romper Room for adults) houses a branch of the
much-lauded L.A. restaurant, conceived and run by the Food Network's "Two Hot
Tamales," Mary Sue Milliken and Susan Feniger. This is truly authentic Mexican
home cooking—the Tamales learned their craft from the real McCoy south of the border—but with a nuevo twist. So don't expect precisely the same dishes you'd encounter
in your favorite corner joint, but do expect fresh and fabulous food, sitting as brightly
on the plates as the decor on the walls. Stay away from the occasionally bland fish and
head right toward rich and cheesy dishes like chiles rellenos (with perfect black beans)
and chicken *chilaquiles* (a sister to the taco), or try nuevo items such as mushroom

ocolate-cream pie (with a

grill.com. Reservations recommended.
ri–Sat 11:30am–11pm.

strong reputation in town for
cky place, there is a good rea-
has eaten at a Benihana isn't
d at a grill and your own chef
d is often predominantly Asian,
ght, gimmick or no. Yes indeed,
gs right; we told the chef what we
ns—with a great show, all clinging
g Vegas strobe lights. It's hilarious
did for us. What we ate recently (but
personal chef, remember!): crunchy
filet mignon with fried rice cooked to
order, and *teppan* featuring perfectly spiced enormous
onions. The menu options are samurai dinners (one entree with all the fixings, including miso soup and salad) or the shogun combo (all of the above but with
two entrees). This is a good choice for a group or even a celebration, since it's such a
giddy dining experience.

In Tropicana Resort & Casino, 3801 Las Vegas Blvd. S. © **702/739-2770**. Reservations recommended. Full Samurai
dinners mostly $17–$27; Shogun combination dinners $27–$45. AE, DC, DISC, MC, V. Daily 5–10:45pm.

MODERATE

Burger Bar ⋦ DINER   See how Vegas is? They know you might be watching your
budget, or just wanting something simple but not boring, so they give you a place that

---

(Value **Great Meal Deals**

We've already alluded to the rock-bottom budget meals and graveyard specials
available at casino hotel restaurants. Quality not assured and Pepto-Bismol not
provided. As prices and deals can change without notice, we don't want to list
examples, but finding a full prime-rib dinner for around $5 is not rare (pun def-
initely intended).

Your best bet is to keep your eyes open as you travel through town, as hotels
tend to advertise their specials on their marquees. Or you can go to
www.vegas.com and click **"Dining"** and then **"Dining Bargains,"** though the
tips and prices may be similarly somewhat out-of-date. Following are three
examples of current options for late-night munchies: **Ellis Island** offers a $4.95
10-ounce steak (plus potato and other sides), $7.77 gets you a strip steak and
lobster tail at **Bourbon Street** (available 24 hours), and **Mr. Lucky's 24/7** at the
Hard Rock Hotel is a particularly good coffee shop, with particularly good people-watching. Check out the blonde eating the messy nachos, and the scruffy
guy eating an especially good steak. Pamela and Kid Rock? And then ask your
server about the $7.77 steak, three barbequed shrimp, and sides; it's not on the
menu, so you have to know about it.

specializes in hamburgers "your way," as the ads go. We love this concept, but we can't help but wince when we see how loading up a basic burger into a personalized creation turns a humble patty into a check for $15, and that's before we order fries and shakes. But we will eat at Burger Bar again because they start with Ridgefield Farm (most recommended) and Black Angus beef, and all the toppings (the usuals like bacon and avocado, but also six kinds of cheese, prosciutto, chopped scallions, and even anchovies and lobster, for Pete's sake), plus a choice of bun, adds up to a hilarious and, if you have a deft touch, delicious experience (though we have not yet gotten them to prepare the doneness of the burgers to our proper specifications, so we advise you to be very clear about your preferences of ratio of pink to gray meat). Shakes are creamy, fries aren't bad (we like the skinny ones better than the fat ones), though if you haven't before, try the sweet-potato fries. One of the most clever desserts in town lurks on this menu, a *sweet burger*—a slab of really fine chocolate pâté "burger," on a warm donut "bun," topped with cunningly crafted strawberry "tomato" slices, mint "lettuce" and translucent passion-fruit "cheese." Note the weekend late hours. And skip the highfalutin' burger options—Kobe beef is too soft to use as burger meat, while foie gras is just wasted in this context. In other words, don't show off, but do have fun.

In the Mandalay Place shopping center, 3930 Las Vegas Blvd. S. ✆ 702/632-9364. Main courses $8–$20 (burgers start at $8, depending on kind of beef; toppings start at 25¢ and go way up). AE, DISC, MC, V. Sun–Thurs 10am–11pm; Fri–Sat 10am–1am.

Dragon Noodle Co. ✰✰ ASIAN A strong choice for a reasonably priced meal, Dragon Noodle is one of the better Chinese restaurants in town. We were glad to see that in addition to the usual suspects, there are some other interesting (if not radically less commonplace) choices on the menu. Note also the many Asian clients (part of our criteria for the authenticity of a place) and that the restaurant can handle large groups. Food is served family-style and prepared in an open kitchen, so you know it's fresh. Be sure to try the very smooth house green tea. You might let your waiter choose your meal for you, but try the crispy Peking pork, the sweet pungent shrimp, the pot stickers, and perhaps the generous seafood soup. We were a little disappointed by the popular sizzling black-pepper chicken, but you may not be, so don't let us stop you. And they now have a sushi bar!

In the Monte Carlo Resort & Casino, 3770 Las Vegas Blvd. S. (between Flamingo Rd. and Tropicana Ave.). ✆ 702/730-7965. www.dragonnoodleco.com. Main courses $5.50–$17 (many under $10). AE, DC, DISC, MC, V. Sun–Thurs 11am–11pm; Fri–Sat 11am–midnight.

Grand Wok and Sushi Bar ✰✰ *Value* ASIAN A pan-Asian restaurant runs the risk of attempting to be a jack-of-all-trades and master of none, but somehow this new MGM eatery pulls it off. We didn't try every cuisine offered (Japanese, Chinese, Korean, Vietnamese, and maybe more!), but a random sampling (including lovely fresh sushi, fat dumplings, and a huge Vietnamese combo soup that was full of noodles and different kinds of meat) produced really superb and delicately prepared food. Hotel Asian restaurants are often a bit dubious, especially if they try to have too much variety, but this one really is marvelous—and the primarily Asian clientele clearly agrees. Note that soup portions are most generous; four people could easily split one order and have a nice and very cheap lunch, an unexpected bargain option for the Strip.

In the MGM Grand, 3799 Las Vegas Blvd. S. ✆ 702/891-7777. Reservations not accepted. Main courses $9–$15; sushi rolls and pieces $4.50–$12. AE, DC, DISC, MC, V. Restaurant Sun–Thurs 11am–10pm, Fri–Sat 11am–midnight; sushi bar Mon–Thurs 5–10pm, Fri–Sat 11am–midnight, Sun 11am–10pm.

You Gotta Have a Theme

It shouldn't be too surprising to learn that a town devoted to themes (what hotel worth its salt doesn't have one, at this point?) has one of virtually every theme restaurant there is. Almost all have prominent celebrity co-owners and tons of "memorabilia" on the walls, which in virtually every case means throwaway items from blockbuster movies, or some article of clothing a celeb wore once (if that) on stage or on the playing field. Almost all have virtually identical menus and have gift shops full of logo items.

This sounds cynical, and it is—but not without reason. Theme restaurants are for the most part noisy, cluttered, overpriced places that are strictly tourist traps, and, though some have their devotees, if you eat at one of these places, you've eaten at them all. We don't want to be total killjoys. Fans should have a good time checking out the stuff on the walls of the appropriate restaurant. And while the food won't be the most memorable ever, it probably won't be bad (and will be moderately priced). But that's not really what you go for.

The **House of Blues** 𝒜𝒜, in Mandalay Bay, 3950 Las Vegas Blvd. S. (© **702/ 632-7607**; daily 8am–2am on event nights and 'til midnight on non-event nights), is, for our money, food- and theme-wise, the best of the theme restaurants. The food is really pretty good (if a little more costly than it ought to be in a theme restaurant), and the mock Delta/New Orleans look works well, even if it is unavoidably commercial. You can dine here without committing to seeing whatever band is playing, as the dining room is separate from the club (note, though, that HOB gets very good bookings from nationally known acts). The gospel brunch might also be worth checking out (the food is good, though there's too much of it), but be warned: It's served inside the actual club, which can be unbelievably loud, so bring earplugs (we left with splitting headaches).

Presumably filling the hole left by the demise of the All Star Café, so that you sports fans won't feel left out in the theme restaurant race, **ESPN,** in

Nine Fine Irishmen 𝒜 IRISH/PUB Travelin' foodies swear the once-maligned food in Ireland has improved enormously, so perhaps it's justified to have an actual Irish restaurant in the pantheon of new Vegas foodie destinations, though given our not-so-secret love of insta-decor, the interior of this, mocked up to look like a rambling old Irish manor house, is enough for us. (Though once we start thinking about the complicated relationship the Irish have to New York City and vice versa, and the meta-implications of a faux Irish restaurant set in a fantasy Irish house in the middle of a Vegas casino homage to NYC, our heads begin to hurt.) We will say that the caramelized apricot and pork sausage on a bed of potatoes (of course) and veg was sweet and tangy; and the Irish stew a right honest interpretation, complete with soda bread. Protestants and monarchists might want to try the genuine British beer-battered fish and chips, served as God and Queen intended, in a newspaper cone. You'll find bacon rashers at breakfast and a large selection of Irish beer most of the time.

New York–New York, 3790 Las Vegas Blvd. S. (© **702/933-3776**; Mon–Thurs 11:30am–12:30am, Fri 11:30am–1am, Sat 11am–1:30am, and Sun 11am–12:30am), is a gigantic facility featuring rather wacky and entertaining sports memorabilia (such as Evel Knievel set up as the old "Operation" game, displaying his many broken bones), plus additions such as a rock-climbing wall/machine. It's pretty fun, actually, and the food, in a couch-potato-junk-food-junkie way, is not bad either, especially when you're sitting in one of the La-Z-Boy recliners, ordering delights such as three Krispy Kreme Doughnuts topped with ice cream, whipped cream, and syrup, and watching sports.

There are those who rave about the warm Tollhouse-cookie pie at the **Harley Davidson Cafe** ⟨*⟩, 3725 Las Vegas Blvd. S. at Harmon Avenue (© **702/740-4555**; Sun–Thurs 11am–11pm, Fri–Sat 11am–midnight).

The **Hard Rock Cafe** ⟨*⟩, 4475 Paradise Rd. at Harmon Avenue (© **702/733-8400**; Sun–Thurs 11am–11:30pm, Fri–Sat 11am–1am), has decent burgers. The serious hipster quotient at the adjacent hotel means that the people-watching opportunities are best here.

Visually, the **Rainforest Café** ⟨*⟩, in the MGM Grand, 3799 Las Vegas Blvd. S. (© **702/891-8580**; Sun–Thurs 8am–11pm, Fri–Sat 8am–midnight), with its jungle interior, complete with sound effects and animatronic animals, is the best of the bunch.

Parrot Heads like to party it up at the new **Margaritaville,** singer Jimmy Buffet's tropical-themed cafe/bar/club, at the Flamingo Hotel ("Parrot Heads" is how his fans refer to themselves). The menu runs a range from Mexican to something sort of Caribbean-themed to basic American, and it's not all that bad, considering. Lots of fruity tropical drinks doesn't hurt, either. In the Flamingo Hilton, 3555 Las Vegas Blvd. S. (© **702/733-3302**; daily 11am–2am).

Desserts are more American silliness, but when it's items like the Dunbrody Kiss, fluffy chocolate mousse on a crunchy caramel base, we don't care.

In New York–New York, 3790 Las Vegas Blvd. S. © 702/740-6969. www.ninefineirishmen.com. Reservations suggested. Dinner main courses: sandwiches $9–$12, entrees $15–$25. AE, MC, V. Daily 11am–11pm; bar Sun–Thurs 11am–3am, Fri–Sat 24 hr.

Sazio ⟨*⟩ ITALIAN   We're happy to have a place like this to recommend because this area of town is kind of shy on decent dining joints. For this spot, you have Gustav Mauler, who originally set up all the restaurants in The Mirage, to thank. He's out on his own now, creating kicky little restaurants all over town. For our tastes, his food isn't quite interesting enough and can be hit-or-miss, but when Sazio is on, the food's delicious. The menu is full of traditional Italian dishes—no, it's not just spaghetti with meat sauce, but don't look for any froufrou nouvelle cuisine here. Having said that, it's a heck of a lot better than most Vegas hotels' generic Italian food. Desserts include a knockout cheesecake. And they do takeout!

In the Orleans Hotel, 4500 W. Tropicana Ave. ⓒ **702/948-9500.** www.saziolasvegas.com. Reservations not accepted except for private parties. Lunch mostly under $10; dinner entrees $9–$17. AE, DC, DISC, MC, V. Sun–Thurs 11am–10pm; Fri–Sat 11am–10:30pm.

Wolfgang Puck Bar & Grill 🗲🗲 CALIFORNIA   This transformed Puck Café is still a desirable, if slightly less affordable, option in the MGM Grand. There is nothing surprising on the menu if you've eaten in any modern cafe in the post-Puck era; it's not his fault his influence has extended so far. Frankly, it's still a relief in Vegas and there is enough variety that everyone in your party should find something to please them, from crab cakes with basil aioli to a prime rib sandwich to homemade veal ravioli to Puck's pizzas, plus a good wine cellar. The fresh salads (we love the seasonal roasted beet) are better constructed than comparable eateries in town, while Puck's hand is still on someone's helm; witness the silly potato chips drizzled with truffle oil and melted bleu cheese. It's all set in an almost entirely open space, a minimalist art take on a country kitchen, and a bit noisy thanks to proximity to the casino floor and cheers from the nearby sports book. Expect it to be crowded right before and after *KA,* but quiet during.

In the MGM Grand, 3799 Las Vegas Blvd. S. ⓒ **702/891-3019.** www.wolfgangpuck.com. Reservations not accepted. Lunch $10–$24; dinner $10–$38 (most under $25). AE, DC, MC, V. Sun–Thurs 11:30am–10:30pm; Fri–Sat 11:30am–11:30pm.

INEXPENSIVE

Calypsos 🗲 *Value* DINER   Here's a solid, reasonably priced place to eat, which is pretty rare on the Strip. Honestly, it's kind of like a Denny's, but its traditional coffee-shop choices (including a "create your own burger") are somewhat better than you might expect. There are some eccentric items such as a chopped Mediterranean shrimp salad, a smoked-salmon plate, a rosemary-chicken sandwich on onion focaccia bread, and a strawberry cream puff swan for dessert. Note also a very good (and low-fat!) Thai shrimp satay, loaded with vegetables, which is listed under "classic American" dishes. We were amused by the fruit plate, which is actually melons and such atop poundcake. It's a dessert masquerading as a salad!

In the Tropicana Resort & Casino, 3801 Las Vegas Blvd. S. ⓒ **702/739-2222.** Reservations not accepted. Main courses $5.95–$19. AE, MC, V. Daily 24 hr.

Jodi Maroni's Sausage Kingdom 🗲🗲🗲 SANDWICHES   There are several worthy fast-food stands in the New York–New York food court, but this one deserves an individual mention. What began as a humble stand on the Venice boardwalk in Los Angeles has expanded into a sausage empire, and we are glad. You will be, too, especially if you take a chance on their menu and don't just stick with the basic hot dog (though they do offer three tempting varieties) and instead try something a little more adventurous, like the tequila chicken sausage made with jalapeños, corn, and lime. (We wish that they offered samples and an even larger menu, as the original stand still does.) Or just vary your basic sweet Italian sausage with a hotter variety. Either way, you can top it with raw or grilled onions and peppers, as it gets stuffed into a sesame-seed soft roll. Maybe some chili fries, too. Our first choice for fast food in the immediate area.

In New York–New York, 3790 Las Vegas Blvd. S. ⓒ **702/740-6969.** Reservations not accepted. $6–$11. AE, DC, MC, V. Sun–Thurs 11am–8pm; Fri–Sat 11am–10pm.

Monte Carlo Pub & Brewery 🗲🗲🗲 *Kids* *Finds* PUB FARE   Lest you think we are big, fat foodie snobs who can't appreciate a meal unless it comes drenched in truffles and caviar, we hasten to direct you to this lively, working microbrewery (with a sort of rustic factory appearance) and its hearty, not-so-highfalutin' food. No fancy French frills and, best of all, no inflated prices. Combine the general high quality with generous portions—a nachos appetizer could probably feed eight (though it was not the best nachos appetizer ever)—and this may be a better deal than most buffets. It's not, however, the place for a quiet rendezvous, with about 40 TVs spread throughout (a sports fan's dream) and music blaring.

Earning recent raves were the short ribs in a fine barbecue sauce, cooked just right; the excellent appetizer of chicken fingers and shrimp fried in beer; the garlic pizza with mounds of our favorite aromatic herb; the pizza topped with lamb, grilled eggplant, and goat cheese (well, maybe that has more frills than we promised); and the avocado-and-shrimp salad. We also highly enjoyed the double-chocolate-fudge suicide brownie, though, really, what's not to love about something like that? After 9pm, only pizza and appetizers are served.

In the Monte Carlo Resort & Casino, 3770 Las Vegas Blvd. S. (between Flamingo Rd. and Tropicana Ave.). © 702/730-7777. Reservations not accepted. Main courses $6–$15. AE, DC, DISC, MC, V. Sun–Thurs 11am–3am; Fri–Sat 11am–4am.

(Value) Quick Bites

Food courts are a dime a dozen in Vegas, but the one in **New York–New York,** 3790 Las Vegas Blvd. S. (© 702/740-6969), deserves a mention for two reasons: It's the nicest setting for this sort of thing on the Strip, sitting in the Greenwich Village section of New York–New York, which means scaled replica tenement buildings, steam rising from the manhole covers, and more than a little (faux, naturally) greenery, a nice change from unrelentingly shrill plastic mall decor. The selections are the usual, with one exception listed below (**Jodi Maroni's Sausage Kingdom**), but it's a better-than-average food court, with Chinese food and pizza (as befitting an ode to NYC), and excellent if expensive (for this situation) double-decker burgers, plus **Schraft's** ice cream. The **Monte Carlo,** 3770 Las Vegas Blvd. S., between Flamingo Road and Tropicana Avenue (© 702/730-7777), has some surprisingly good options. Sure, there's the always-reliable **McDonald's,** and for sweets there is **Häagen-Dazs,** but they also have a branch of **Nathan's Hot Dogs,** New York's finest. The **Golden Bagel** offers another New York staple, big and tasty enough to satisfy even picky natives. **Sbarro** offers enticing pizza slices. If you want a good, cheap meal on the Strip and wish to avoid some of those dubious night-owl specials, come here. It's open daily from 6am to 3am.

And if you head farther down the Strip, to the **Grande Canal Shoppes** at The Venetian, 3355 Las Vegas Blvd. S. (© 702/414-1000), you can find another decent food court, with a Panda Express, a good pizza place (despite the confusing name of **LA Italian Kitchen**), a burrito stand, a juice joint, and, best of all, a **Krispy Kreme,** where they are actually making the donuts on the premises. Plus, it's right by the canals of this faux Venice, one of our favorite places in Vegas.

3 Mid-Strip

VERY EXPENSIVE

Alex ✹✹✹ NOUVEAU   Alex Strada (possibly familiar to you from his stint on the American "Iron Chef") followed his once and present boss Steve Wynn from The Mirage, closing his Renoir venue to open this eponymous one instead. A dramatic room, all swooping drapes and inlaid wood, about two fussy steps away from true elegance but still a place where grown-ups come to dine, appreciating the venture as Occasion. Strada comes from a cosmopolitan and international background; add to that both some years working under Alain Ducasse and a general sense of food as pleasure and art, and you have one of the most special dining experiences in Vegas. This is not food as fuel, food to bolt down greedily (even though you may want to), but to slowly savor. Pay attention as you chew, and notice how many layers of interest are revealed. Great care was taken in choosing and combining ingredients, to create not fuss, but both surprise and a sense of rightness. The menu will change regularly—chef Alex is as exacting as a real chef should be, and so the readiness of seasonal ingredients will dictate any particular evening's selection. The result if in a European restaurant would almost certainly earn a Michelin star. Diners have their choice of two set tasting menus or a three-course prix-fixe choice of appetizer, main, and dessert. None of this will come cheap, but you can look at this way: You can easily lose the cost of a meal here in 15 forgettable minutes at a blackjack table (not that we did just that the very night we dined here, ahem) or you can spend 3 hours slowly enjoying a meal, storing up much more pleasurable (presumably) memories. Expect starters such as carpaccio of Santa Barbara prawn topped with osetra caviar, or roasted scallop with basil purée, and don't neglect to ponder touches like tiny vegetables ever so lightly cooked so crunch and flavor come through, the whole topped by translucent fried zucchini flower. Porcini gnocchi dissolves in the mouth, a terrine of foie gras is paired with the chef's interpretation of Waldorf salad, a main course of squab and sautéed foie gras, rhubarb and spiced pineapple is deep, rich, and bold. Even the palate cleansers are serious, such as apricot gelée topped with coconut granata ringed by passion fruit, or strawberry gelée with lemon-grass crème fraîche. Desserts are of such gorgeous complexity that we will fail to describe them adequately, but know that the construction is not served to the sacrifice of taste. You are in a master chef's hands; enjoy it.

3131 Las Vegas Blvd. S. (in Wynn Las Vegas hotel). © **888/320-7110** or 702/770-9966. www.wynnlasvegas.com. Reservations strongly recommended. Business casual attire. Three-course prix-fixe menu $110; 7-course tasting menu $145. AE, DC, DISC, MC, V. Daily 5:30–10:30pm.

Alizé ✹✹✹ FRENCH   Just a perfect restaurant, thanks to a combination of the most divine dining room and view in Vegas (situated at the top of the Palms Hotel, with three sides of full-length windows that allow a panoramic view of the night lights of Vegas; obviously, window-side tables are best, but even seats in the center of the room have a good view), and one of the best chefs in a town where many great chefs have restaurants but are rarely in their kitchens (Emeril and Wolfgang, we love them, but they can't be in 25 different places at once). Overseen by Andre, he of the eponymous (and excellent) restaurants Downtown and in the Monte Carlo, the executive chef is Jacques Van Staden, who trained with one of the world's greatest chefs, Jean-Louis Pallidin. The menu changes seasonally, but anything you order will be heavenly.

On our last visit, we had perhaps 14 different courses, and not a single one disappointed. In the appetizer department, the marinated jumbo lump crabmeat and avocado salad with heirloom tomato consommé and basil oil was a riot of freshness, while the gnocchi with sautéed wild mushrooms, black truffle, and mushroom emulsion was the kind of dish clearly created by someone thoughtful and clever. A phyllo-wrapped baked pear and Roquefort cheese with a vinegar-and-port reduction was less salad (as it was billed) and more hot appetizer. The foie gras comes in a pink-grapefruit-and-citrus-honey reduction, a tangy combination. Fish can be a little dry here, so we suggest either the stunning New York steak with summer truffle jus and potato herb pancakes, or the meltingly tender lamb chops with some shredded lamb shank wrapped in a crispy fried crepe. Desserts are similarly outstanding and often of great frivolity, such as sorbet in a case of browned marshmallow, floating in raspberry soup. Yeah, we're going over the top on this one, but we bet you won't think we're wrong.

In the Palms Hotel, 4321 W. Flamingo Rd. ℂ **702/951-7000.** Fax 702/951-7002. www.alizelv.com. Reservations strongly recommended. Entrees $28–$40. AE, MC, V. Daily 5:30–11pm.

Bartolotta ✸✸✸ ITALIAN/SEAFOOD James Beard Foundation Award–winning chef Paul Bartolotta trained in Italy under master chefs before opening up his highly acclaimed Spiaggia in Chicago. Now he's here, in this eponymous kitchen, yet more proof that celebrity chefs are all very well and good, but it's not the same as having them on the premises. In this case, the result is as authentic Italian food as one can find outside of Italy. Determined to produce just that, Bartolotta went to his boss, Steve Wynn, and insisted that his fish not just be ultra-fresh, but be flown daily straight from the Mediterranean to his Vegas kitchen, saying "I can't make authentic Italian food with American fish." Wynn's response? "Give the man his fish." (And you will be introduced to the results after you sit down!) Bartolotta is nonchalant about what goes on here; all you have to do, he claims, is know what you are doing, and then do it with the best ingredients—best olive oil, best tomatoes, and best fish. He's right. It works, and so well that this is the restaurant we are currently most likely to tout in Vegas; as in, go here, do. You can choose your whole cooked fish right from that day's batch (you can get them big enough so one can be split among several people), which may include new-to-you (they were to us) possibilities like Orata and purple snapper, each topped with a chunky "sauce" of sweet pachino tomatoes, arugula, garlic, and red onion. Pastas are perfect as well, especially the delicate sheep's milk ricotta handkerchief-style ravioli, made both sweet and savory with a veal Marsala wine-reduction glaze. Spaghetti allo Scoglio comes with large chunks of lobster, langoustines are grilled to charred smoky rightness, seared scallops with porcini mushrooms in browned butter are what scallops should be—and all because this Italian staff learned their lessons well and they are passing that knowledge on to you. The space itself is perhaps the nicest in the hotel, which has done well by all its restaurants, a multilevel construction that gives a cafe feeling on the top level, a more elegant dining area down below (accessed by a dramatic curving sweeping stairway), and, best of all, outdoor cabana seating by a small pond filled with reflecting balls, so fine for a long (as the Italians like to do it), sultry evening meal. A jewel box of a place for cooking that is a treasure.

3131 Las Vegas Blvd. S. (in Wynn Las Vegas hotel). © **888/320-7110** or 702/770-9966. www.wynnlasvegas.com. Reservations recommended. Main courses dinner $25–$42. AE, DC, DISC,, MC, V. Daily 11:30am–2:30pm and 5:30–10:30pm.

Daniel Boulard Brasserie ✦ BISTRO   Best known as the man who gave New York City the $29 hamburger (because it was filled with foie gras, short rib meat, and truffles), which is a mistake you should not make—not the hamburger itself, which is on this menu, and is fine, if extremely silly and now much imitated—but because there is more to his cuisine than burgers. This is classic French bistro food, and while Boulard himself is not in the house, he does have a superb French chef (at this writing) running the show, and very well. Still, you can always tell when someone is cooking off another master chef's menu, as opposed to working their own magic. (Especially when compared to, say, Alex or Bartolotta, here at Wynn itself.) But the cuisine here is still lovely; look at the beautifully composed salads, as roasted beets are laid out in precise order with endive and bleu cheese, or the stunning tartin du tomato, a whole reconstructed roasted tomato layered on goat cheese and puff pastry. The foie gras chaud is two fat lobes of liver on grilled pineapple, topped with a nearly see-through thin pineapple chip. Lean toward the slow-cooked dishes, such as braised short ribs Bourguignon with pomme mousseline and spring ramps—earthy and hearty. Save some room for a cheese plate and go through the evening's artisinal selections with your server. Lunch is cheaper and much the same kind of selections. But since this restaurant is one of only two that allows viewing of the Lake of Dreams show at night, dinner is more desirable. A way to get around some of the high-end cost is to work with the appetizers—cheese and charcuterie (try the duck confit terrine) are filling, whereas the entrees a little too small to split satisfyingly.

3131 Las Vegas Blvd. S. (in Wynn Las Vegas hotel). ℂ **888/320-7110** or 702/770-9966. www.wynnlasvegas.com. Reservations recommended. Main courses $18–$30 at lunch, $18–$42 at dinner. AE, DC, DISC, MC, V. Daily 11:30am–2:30pm and 5:30–10pm.

Delmonico Steakhouse ⊛⊛ CONTEMPORARY CREOLE/STEAK   Watching the Food Network, you might well feel that Emeril Lagasse is omnipresent. Slowly but surely, he's becoming as ubiquitous here in Vegas (though he has a long way to go to match Puck) as he is in New Orleans, as he brings variations on his Big Easy brand-name eateries to town. This latest is a steakhouse version of his hard-core classic Creole restaurant; this ever-so-slight twist is just enough to make it a superior choice over the more disappointing New Orleans locale. It's set in two dining rooms; the left one is '70's den ugly—choose instead the Neutra/Schindler–influenced right side.

You can try Emeril's concoctions, plus fabulous cuts of red meat. You can't go wrong with most appetizers, especially the superbly rich smoked mushrooms with home-made Tasso ham over pasta—it's enough for a meal in and of itself. The same advice holds for any of the specials, or the gumbo, particularly if it's the hearty, near-home-made country selection. If you want to experiment, definitely do it with the appetizers; you're better off steering clear of complex entrees, no matter how intriguing they sound (such as a 1-night special of foie gras–stuffed ahi tuna). We've found the entree specials to be generally disappointing, while the more deceptively simple choices are more successful. The bone-in rib-eye steak is rightly recommended (skip the gummy béarnaise sauce in favor of the fabulous homemade Worcestershire or A.O.K. sauce). Sides are hit-or-miss—the creamed spinach was too salty, but a sweet-potato purée (a special, but maybe they'll serve you a side if you ask sweetly) is most definitely a win-ner. Too full for dessert? No, you aren't. Have a chocolate soufflé, a bananas-Foster cream pie, a chocolate Sheba (a sort of dense chocolate mousse), or the lemon icebox pie, a chunk of curd that blasts tart lemon through your mouth.

In The Venetian, 3355 Las Vegas Blvd. S. ℂ **702/414-3737.** www.emerils.com. Reservations strongly recommended for dinner. Main courses $21–$40. AE, DC, DISC, MC, V. Daily 11:30am–2pm; Sun–Thurs 5:30–10:30pm; Fri–Sat 5:30–11pm.

Drai's STEAK/SEAFOOD   It's a famous Los Angeles restaurant and the place that young Hollywood execs flock to when out for a Vegas jaunt, but we can't help but notice that the food is very ordinary. It's not bad, but it may not justify the high prices. There are multiple dining rooms done in dark wood—very L.A. '70s mellow bar—with leop-ard prints on the menus and plates, and too-loud jazz music blaring throughout.

Peculiarly, the most expensive menu item is Dover sole with mashed potatoes—a cheap fish and a cheap accompaniment. The menu boasts that none of their soups is made with dairy products. But they might want to reconsider that policy because the potato-leek soup was flat and dull—it really needed cream or butter. Lake Superior whitefish in phyllo (a flaky, thin dough) with onion marmalade will please those who don't mind their appetizers on the sweet side. On the plus side, the duck was crispy and not dry. The crab cakes were also tasty, with shredded—not puréed—crab, and were served with a stiff but nice and cheesy risotto (though the lemon-caper sauce had no flavor). And it would be worth going to Drai's just for the chocolate-mousse dessert—light and delectable, and not overly sweet.

In the Barbary Coast Hotel & Casino, 3595 Las Vegas Blvd. S. ℂ **702/737-7111.** Reservations recommended. Main courses $21–$35. AE, MC, V. Daily 5:30pm–midnight.

Fiore ⊛ ITALIAN/PROVENÇAL   This is a worthwhile dining choice with a very attentive staff. Try to get a seat on the patio; outdoor dining is rare in Vegas, so it's worth taking advantage of. You can't go wrong with a perfectly done rack of lamb with roasted garlic sauce, or the appetizer of pancetta-wrapped shrimp with port-wine glaze (sure, it's just a more tony version of bacon-wrapped shrimp, but it's good!). Skip the disappointingly overdone Chilean sea bass. Save room for a cheese plate and especially the gooey chocolate desserts—Fiore has a very talented pastry chef.

In the Rio All-Suite Hotel & Casino, 3700 W. Flamingo Rd. (at I-15). ℂ 702/777-7923. Reservations recommended. Main courses $26–$38. AE, DC, DISC, MC, V. Daily 5–11pm.

Le Cirque 𝒜 FRENCH   The influx of haute-cuisine, high-profile restaurants in Vegas means there are ever so many places now where you may feel like you have to take out a bank loan in order to eat—and you may wonder why you ought to. Though generally we always feel free to spend your money for you, we actually are going to suggest that you hold on to it in the case of Le Cirque, unless someone else is doing the buying. It's not that the food is bad—quite the contrary—but it's not the very best in town, and it is among the most expensive. And remember what we said about most of Vegas being quite casual? Here, forget it. If you didn't bring your nicest black, you are going to feel very uncomfortable.

The surprisingly small dining room (you may be virtually rubbing elbows with your neighbor, so keep inflammatory secrets out of the conversation) is decorated with murals of quaint bygone circus themes and a ceiling draped with gay fabric meant to evoke the Big Top. The busy decor does add to the cramped feeling. The menu changes seasonally, but you can expect genuine French cuisine—heavy, with lots of butter, though a recent visit brought a duo of cold cucumber and heirloom tomato soups that were so refreshing, every restaurant in this desert town ought to serve them. The lobster salad is sweet and tender, with a perfect black-truffle dressing; risotto is French style, almost soupy, perfect with fresh morels (in season) and Parmesan. The filet mignon is, oddly, not as good a cut as served elsewhere, but it does come with a generous portion of foie gras. For dessert, we loved the white chocolate cream (solid but not overwhelming), layered with banana and wrapped in phyllo, along with a milk chocolate dome with crème brûlée espresso.

In Bellagio, 3600 Las Vegas Blvd. S. ℂ 877/234-6358. Reservations required. Jacket/tie required for men. Main courses $29–$45. AE, DC, DISC, MC, V. Daily 5:30–10pm.

Lutèce 𝒜 FRENCH   A branch of the highly esteemed (and now late and much-lamented) New York City establishment. When the beloved NYC original closed, we feared the worst for this, initially one of our favorite Vegas restaurants. And while those fears weren't entirely released, certainly the place isn't quite what it once was. Service is haphazard—just a touch chilly and careless, with long, long stretches between attention and, for that matter, courses. Appetizers like a silky foie gras au tor-chon and a tuna "mille feuille"—layered with Granny Smith apples—are adequate, a celery root soup amuse utterly blah, while the roasted wild salmon main course was flawless with the crispy skin laid separately on top in a geometrically pleasing way, and star anise–crusted scallops perfectly good, and no more. Desserts are unmemorable. Given the prices, it's just too much to pay for what looks very much like indifference. The minimalist decor is relieved by a modern industrial look that extends to the cut-lery and bathrooms (have a look!). It's full of style, style, style. Try to get a table in the little nook area that looks out at the Strip—it's more romantic than it sounds.

In The Venetian, 3355 Las Vegas Blvd. S. ℂ 702/414-2220. Reservations strongly recommended for dinner. Main courses $26–$38. AE, DC, DISC, MC, V. Daily 5:30–10:30pm.

Michael Mina ⚑ SEAFOOD   What is it about Vegas and fish? This is a sweeping generalization, but let's note that even this premier San Francisco piscine palace let us down. The signature lobster potpie is good, a splashy presentation that includes the wheeling of the pie to the table and the careful excising of the contents, including the broth and crusty top, which then fails to stay crusty thanks to the broth contact. Oh, well, but then again, at these prices, one cannot simply brush it off with "Oh, well." The miso-glazed sea bass in mushroom consommé tasted like nothing more than seafood sukiyaki. Really good sukiyaki, but even so. Starters of langoustine and crab ravioli are mealy and dull, while the "tasting" of foie gras, instead of multiple presentations of same, was just one serving of seared liver, with a nice parsnip Tarte Tatin. Desserts, including an actual root-beer float and a (this time genuine) chocolate tasting, are much more successful. Service is a bit too rushed, with bread and water delivered in the heedless manner of a coffee shop.

In Bellagio, 3600 Las Vegas Blvd. S. ℂ **702/693-7223**. www.michaelmina.net. Reservations recommended. Main courses $34–$59 (lobster and whole foie gras higher). AE, DISC, MC, V. Daily 5:30–10pm.

Onda ⚑⚑ ITALIAN   Onda is anything but a run-of-the-mill hotel restaurant. Chef Todd English, whose Olives cafe over at Bellagio is also well worth your dining time, offers a Mediterranean slant on Italian cooking, coming up with a menu that's full of pleasant thrills, putting most other Italian joints in town to shame. Vegetables are flown in especially for Onda, so we encourage you toward menu choices that feature them. The restaurant itself is pretty and comfortable (dress is casual chic), with a particularly good vibe later in the evening (after 9pm, say)—for some reason, the staff doesn't tire but is still ready to take care of your every wish, allowing you to linger as much as you like.

Begin with that basket of varied breads, making sure that the Gorgonzola-laced breadsticks are among them. Move on to antipasti with polenta, truffles, fresh mozzarella, onions, stuffed zucchini, roasted peppers, and goodness knows what else. Soup is good food—in particular, the fine baby-sweet-spring-pea purée with a dollop of mascarpone cheese. A foil-wrapped veggie packet (slit at the table for you) includes porcini mushrooms good enough to make even non–mushroom fans fall to their knees, reconsidering their previous conviction. By now you don't need a heavy dessert, but the chocolate-mousse cake is highly recommended if you can handle it, as is the sorbet sampler (featuring flavors such as champagne grape and caramelized grape) if you can't.

In The Mirage, 3400 Las Vegas Blvd. S. ℂ **702/791-7223**. Reservations recommended. Main courses $17–$35. AE, DC, DISC, MC, V. Daily 5:30–11pm.

The Palm ⚑⚑ STEAK/SEAFOOD   A branch of the venerable New York eatery, which has been branching ever farther afield recently, this place attracts a star-studded clientele fond of the reliable and hearty, if not terribly exciting, bill of fare. (The famous may also be hoping to find their faces among the many caricatures that cover the walls.) This is plain but filling food—at manly prices. Red-meat lovers will be happy with the high-quality steaks found here, though those on a budget will shudder in horror. The tendency is to give them a good charring, so if you don't like your meat blackened, start with it less well done and send it back for more if necessary. If you've hit a jackpot, your money will be well spent on one of The Palm's Buick-size lobsters. They're utterly succulent and outrageously priced, but given their size—they start at 3 pounds—they can easily be shared. If you're worried that all this won't be enough, add one of the delicious appetizers (plump but high-priced shrimp cocktails or a perfect prosciutto with melon) or toss in a side of crispy deep-fried onions. Desserts are similarly heavy and unspectacular.

In Caesars Palace Forum Shops, 3570 Las Vegas Blvd. S. ℂ 702/732-7256. www.thepalm.com. Reservations recommended. Main courses $10–$18 at lunch, $18–$38 at dinner. AE, DC, MC, V. Daily 11:30am–11pm.

Picasso 🕮🕮🕮 FRENCH   A Spanish chef who cooks French cuisine in an Italian-themed hotel in Vegas? Trust us, it works. This may well be the best restaurant in Vegas, and given the sudden serious competition for such a title, that says a lot. Steve Wynn spent months trying to talk Madrid-born chef Julian Serrano (whose Masa was considered the finest French restaurant in San Francisco) into coming to Bellagio. His bulldog tenacity paid off, and we should all thank him. This is an extraordinary dining experience, including the thrill of having $30 million worth of Picassos gaze down over your shoulders while you eat. It's not like dining in a stuffy museum, however—the water fountains going off outside every 15 minutes (with staid diners rushing to the windows to check it out) pretty much take care of that. Many of the furnishings were designed by one of Picasso's sons, and even the paintings themselves are challenged for beauty by the exceptional floral arrangements.

Needless to say, Serrano's cooking is a work of art that can proudly stand next to the masterpieces. The menu changes nightly and is always a choice between a four- or five-course fixed-price dinner or a tasting menu. The night we ate there, we were bowled over by roasted Maine lobster with a "trio" of corn—kernels, sauce, and a corn flan that was like eating slightly solid sunshine. Hudson Valley foie gras was crusted in truffles and went down most smoothly. A filet of roasted sea bass came with a light saffron sauce and dots of cauliflower purée. And finally, pray that they're serving the lamb rôti—it was an outstanding piece of lamb, perfectly done, tender, and crusted with truffles. Portions are dainty but so rich that you'll have plenty to eat without groaning and feeling heavy when you leave. Desserts are powerful, yet prettily constructed. A molten chocolate cake leaves any other you may have tried in the dust and comes with ice cream made with imported European chocolate. A crisp banana tart with coconut ice cream is a fine nonchocolate (foolish you) choice, while a passion-fruit flan in a citrus-soup sauce is perfect if you don't have much room left. Everything is delivered by an attentive staff that make you feel quite pampered. Can we go back soon and try it all again?

In Bellagio, 3600 Las Vegas Blvd. S. ℂ 702/693-7223. Reservations recommended. Fixed-price 4-course dinner $90; 5-course dégustation $100. AE, DC, DISC, MC, V. Wed–Mon 6–9:30pm.

The Range 🕮🕮 STEAK   This place is worth visiting if only for the spectacular view of the Strip (few Strip restaurants take advantage of this view, oddly enough) from 40-foot-high wraparound windows. Muted copper and wood tones make for a formal but not intimidating environment and a fine-looking room. The small menu features the usual steakhouse offerings—various cuts of beef and some chicken dishes, plus a few salads—but at a high-medium price. That said, the quality is better than we've found at the usual Vegas steakhouse suspects. We particularly liked the filet mignon on a Gorgonzola-onion croustade. All entrees come with family-style side dishes (they change nightly but can include such items as marinated mushrooms or horseradish mashed potatoes). Appetizers are also worth noting. The five-onion soup is thick, heavy, creamy, and served in a giant hollowed-out onion. It's delicious, as was a smoked chicken quesadilla. Don't miss the bread, which comes with a sweet and savory apricot-basil butter.

(*Moments* A Dining Room, or Two, with a View

As we keep noting, the Strip at night is a dazzling sight, which is why hotel rooms with Strip views come at such a premium. Regardless of whether you were able to get the proverbial room with a view, consider dining at either the chic **Eiffel Tower** restaurant, in Paris Las Vegas, 3655 Las Vegas Blvd. S. ((*C*) **702/ 948-6937;** daily 5:30–10:45pm), located on the 11th floor of said Mid-Strip hotel, or the **Stratosphere's Top of the World,** in the Stratosphere Casino Hotel & Tower, 2000 Las Vegas Blvd. S. ((*C*) **702/380-7711;** daily 11am–3pm, Sun–Thurs 5:30–10:30pm, Fri–Sat 5:30–11pm), which is almost at the top of the North Strip's Stratosphere Tower, the tallest structure west of the Mississippi. Both offer fantastic views. The latter even revolves 360 degrees, while the former also looks down on the Bellagio fountains. Both, however, also match sky-high views with sky-high prices, and, unfortunately, neither has food worth the price. Go for a special night out, or see if you can get away with just ordering appetizers and dessert (which are both superior to the entrees, anyway). You can also just have a drink at their respective bars, though each is set back far enough from the windows that drinkers have less-optimal views than diners.

In Harrah's, 3475 Las Vegas Blvd. S. (*C*) **702/369-5084.** Reservations highly recommended. Main courses $24–$40. AE, DC, DISC, MC, V. Daily 5–10:30pm.

Spago (*R*) (*Overrated* AMERICAN/ASIAN/CALIFORNIA   At this point in the game, Spago represents both the best and the worst of the celebrity chef phenomenon. If you eat at the Beverly Hills location, you might well have the very best meal of your life, and almost certainly something that demonstrates the reason why such a fuss is made about creative cooking. The problem is that Wolfgang Puck, the man who virtually invented the Chef as Household Name concept, and certainly had as much to do as anyone with California cuisine becoming a viable food genre, has stretched himself too thin—seven restaurants in Vegas alone. No one can keep a personal watch on that many locations, and the result is that this one, the first sign that Vegas was becoming a viable restaurant destination, is now simply not our first, nor even second, choice for you to spend your hard-won jackpot money. The inside menu changes seasonally, but the signature—and reliable—dish is a Chinese-style duck, moist but with a perfectly crispy skin. It's about as good as duck gets, served with a doughy, steamed bun and Chinese vegetables. Our other suggestion is to come here for lunch, and that's still not the worst plan. Salads, sandwiches, and pastas are all pretty and generously portioned, and the signature Puck pizzas like prosciutto and goat cheese and pear are still quite good (ask for the off-the-menu and legendary "Jewish pizza," with salmon and crème fraîche). Nothing is all that innovative, however (braised leek and ham quiche with apple-smoked bacon—good, but you've seen it before), and nothing stands out. Desserts can actually be so poor—like a dry chocolate cake—we won't even bother finishing them.

In Caesars Palace, 3570 Las Vegas Blvd. S. (*C*) **702/369-6300.** www.wolfgangpuck.com. Reservations recommended for the dining room, not accepted at the cafe. Dining room main courses $21–$45; cafe main courses $8–$25. AE, DC, DISC, MC, V. Dining room daily 5:30-10pm; cafe Sun–Thurs 11am–11pm, Fri–Sat 11am–midnight.

Valentino (*R*) ITALIAN   Valentino was long considered the best Italian restaurant in L.A., and even the best in America (per *Bon Appetit*, who we suppose oughta know).

But this branch (with generic nice restaurant decor) isn't quite as successful as its Southern California counterpart, with complicated offerings that too often just miss the mark. Quail stuffed with snails and served with white-and-yellow polenta, for example, or house-smoked shrimp with crispy veggies and an apple-balsamic sauce—they're all interesting, but the combinations don't quite work. Working entirely well, however, are the four-cheese ravioli with truffle-cream sauce and fresh truffle shavings—we shamelessly mopped our plate with our bread—and the wild-rabbit loin in rhubarb-encrusted prosciutto. Their wine list is terrific.

In The Venetian, 3355 Las Vegas Blvd. S. (C) **702/414-3000.** Reservations strongly recommended. Main courses $15–$37. AE, DC, DISC, MC, V. Daily 11am–11pm.

EXPENSIVE

Bouchon 🌟🌟🌟 BISTRO   Now here is where the whole Celebrity Chef concept bursts into full glory. Thomas Keller made his name with his Napa Valley restaurant the French Laundry, considered by many to be the best restaurant in the United States. Bouchon is a version of his Napa Valley bistro. We had mixed expectations. On the one hand, a certifiably genius chef. On the other hand, he's not going to be in the kitchen, which will be producing bistro (which is to say, not innovative) food and, what's more, based on the Napa Bouchon, rather lackluster versions of same.

Negative expectations were confounded by the right, left, and center of the menu—yeah, we've tried nearly all of it and can report that, humble though these dishes sound, in nearly every case they are gold-standard versions of classics. Someone is certainly keeping a close eye on this kitchen, and that someone has learned their lessons well. Ever wondered why people get worked up over raw oysters? The sweet and supremely fresh (kept in water until the moment they are served to you) Snow Creek oysters will enlighten you as they seem to melt on contact with your tongue. Fifty dollars seems like a lot for pâté, but here a complex multiday preparation produces a buttery whip that is so rich, it's an appropriate—and highly recommended—appetizer for four. Don't miss the bacon and poached-egg frisee salad, or the cleanly seared salmon over poached leeks, prepared to such perfection it doesn't need the accompanying sauce. Gnocchi is earthy and assertive, a peasant version of an Italian favorite, while beef bourguignon is exactly as you expect it to be, in the divine perfection sense. Leg of lamb has all chewy bits excised before cooking, leaving it a garlic-permeated bit of tenderness. This is a superlative Vegas restaurant, and while it may be hard to reconcile the prices with the apparent simplicity of the food, recall that it takes serious skill to make even the most humble of dishes correctly, as your palate will reassure you.

3355 Las Vegas Blvd. S. (C) **702/414-6200.** Reservations strongly recommended. Main courses $8–$21 at breakfast, $21–$33 at dinner. AE, DC, DISC, MC, V. Daily 7–10:30am and 5–11pm; oyster bar daily 3pm–11pm; Sat–Sun lunch 11:30am–2:30pm.

Canaletto 🌟🌟 ITALIAN   Come here for solid, true Italian fare—and that means less sauce-intensive than the red-checked-tablecloth establishments of our American youths. Here, the emphasis is on the pasta, not the accompaniments. This place is all the more enjoyable for being perched on the faux St. Mark's Square; in theory, you can pretend you are sitting on the edge of the real thing, a fantasy we don't mind admitting we briefly indulged in. A risotto of porcini, sausage, and white-truffle oil was full of strong flavors, while the wood-fired roast chicken was perfectly moist. You know, a properly roasted chicken should be a much-celebrated thing, and that alone may be a reason to come here.

In The Venetian Grand Canal Shoppes, 3377 Las Vegas Blvd. S. ℂ **702/733-0070.** Reservations recommended for dinner. Main courses $14–$35. AE, DC, MC, V. Sun–Thurs 11:30am–11pm; Fri–Sat 11:30am–midnight.

Circo ☆☆ ITALIAN   Yes, this is the less expensive offering from the same family that brings you Le Cirque, but going to one does not excuse you from going to the other. (By the way, "less expensive" is a relative term. While dinner prices for entrees other than pasta and pizza fall into our "very expensive" category, lunch prices are less high, and there are, as you will see, ways to make this fall into the "moderate" category. So we decided to split the difference and list this as "expensive." Just thought you'd like to know.)

Le Cirque's gourmet French haute cuisine does not prepare you for what to expect from Circo, or, for that matter, vice versa. Ignore the bright primary-color scheme, meant to evoke the circus but instead sadly recalling outdated hotel buffets (albeit with expensive wood grain), in favor of watching the dancing fountains outside. And then order the *mista di Campo,* a lovely little salad, both visually and in terms of taste; it's a creative construction of vegetables bound with cucumber and topped with a fab balsamic vinaigrette. Follow that with a perfect tagliatelle with rock shrimp—it comes loaded with various crustacean bits in a light sauce. Note that appetizer portions of pastas are plenty filling and cheaper than full-size servings. Nighttime brings more elaborate dishes, such as breast of Muscovy duck with dried organic fruit in port-wine sauce. Save room for desserts such as *panna cotta* (Italian cream-filled donuts) or *tutto cioccolato,* consisting of chocolate mousse, ice cream, and crumb cake.

In Bellagio, 3600 Las Vegas Blvd. S. ℂ **702/693-8150.** Reservations recommended for dinner. Main courses $12–$29 at lunch, $14–$45 at dinner. AE, DC, DISC, MC, V. Wed–Sun 11:30am–2:30pm; daily 5:30–10:30pm.

Fix ☆☆ AMERICAN   A just-right synthesis of gourmet dining, fun dining, and accessible dining, created by the people behind Bellagio's excellent Light nightclub. Looking, as one visitor described it, like a "giant clam opening up toward the casino," the menu continues this playful vibe. Look for the silly presentation called "Forks," appetizers of smoked salmon and caviar skewed on forks, served tines in the air. Or desserts like "Shake and Cake" (espresso shake and a brownie), a peanut butter and jelly crème brûlée (misconceived? Or an idea whose time has come? You decide!), and delightful banana sugared donuts with chocolate and peanut butter dipping sauce. But before those clever conclusions come particularly good (in a town not known for same) fish selections, including scallops stacked with a crust of potatoes on applewood smoked bacon, and "The Ultimate Shell," a selection of seafood (from clams to lobster) that comes in an XL size of dreamy decadence. Best of all are the steaks, which are grilled over cherrywood, giving the meat a smoky yet fruity flavor, reminding you that meat is supposed to have dimensions to its taste. From the trendy "small plates" to hamburgers, this is one complete menu, all right. All in all, a good compromise fancy location for a special occasion or just a treat of a meal: not so fou-fou that basic eaters will be dismayed, not so simplistic that foodies will feel cheated, and not in the least bit stodgy or intimidating. Given the late hours and the origins, though, expect a lively and young crowd, especially as the night wears on.

3600 Las Vegas Blvd. S. (in the Bellagio). ℂ **702/693-8400.** www.fixlasvegas.com. Reservations suggested. Main courses $25–$40. AE, MC, V. Sun–Thurs 5pm–midnight; Fri–Sat 5pm–2am.

Hyakumi ☆ SUSHI   Hyakumi (Yah-*koo*-me) is a quaint little oasis in the midst of a bustling casino. Tastefully decorated with hardwood floors in a tea-garden atmosphere, it is a relaxing respite from the madness of Vegas, as kimono-clad waitresses cater to your every need with a never-ending cup of particularly good green tea, plus hot towels, to put you in a Zenlike state.

But the setting, as serene and beautiful as it is, is not the reason for a visit to Hyakumi; it's the sushi. Supervised by executive chef Hiroji Obayashi, famed for his award-winning Hirozen Gourmet Restaurant in Los Angeles, Hyakumi offers some of the best sushi in town. It's not the cheapest, but it is well worth the extra cost. From the toro to the salmon roll, every bite melts in your mouth. The fish is shipped in daily and is prepared by friendly sushi chefs who obviously love what they do. If sushi isn't your thing, there is also a restaurant serving up traditional (but very expensive) Japanese fare in a lovely garden setting.

In Caesars Palace, 3570 Las Vegas Blvd. S. ℂ 702/731-7731. Reservations recommended. Sushi $6–$10 per roll or piece; main courses $25–$60. AE, DC, DISC, MC, V. Restaurant and sushi bar daily 5–11pm for dinner.

Pinot Brasserie 𝒜𝒜 BISTRO   This is one incarnation of a series of well-regarded Los Angeles restaurants whose mother ship, Patina, regularly tops "Best of" lists

---

(Kids) Family-Friendly Restaurants

Buffets   Cheap meals for the whole family. The kids can choose what they like, and there are sometimes make-your-own sundae machines. Section 8 of this chapter reviews all the buffets and notes which ones have reduced prices for kids.

Rainforest Café (p. 143)   This is like eating in the Jungle Book ride at Disneyland. Animals howl, thunder wails, everywhere there is something to marvel at. There is a decent kids' menu, and they might even learn a little bit about ecology and the environment.

Hard Rock Cafe (p. 143)   Kids adore this restaurant, which throbs with excitement and is filled with rock memorabilia.

Pink Pony   This bubble-gum-pink, circus-motif 24-hour coffee shop at Circus Circus will appeal to kids. Mom and Dad can linger while the kids race upstairs to watch circus acts and play carnival games.

Sherwood Forest Cafe   Kids love to climb on the lavender dragons fronting this 24-hour coffee shop at Excalibur, and they can also enjoy numerous child-oriented activities while you're on the premises.

Toto's (p. 170)   This Mexican restaurant that features enormous portions served family style is a casual place favored by locals.

Monte Carlo Pub & Brewery (p. 144)   Despite the "pub" part of the name, this noisy place in the Monte Carlo hotel has many TVs to distract short-attention kids and brooding teenagers, all of whom will like the barbecue, pizza, and chicken fingers. Parents will be pleased with the low prices.

Cypress Street Marketplace (p. 157)   Caesars Palace's food court (stylish enough to offer real plates and cloth napkins) offers a range of food (from very good hot dogs to wrap sandwiches to Vietnamese noodles) wide enough to ensure that bottomless-pit teenagers, picky grade-schoolers, and health-conscious parents will all find something that appeals, at affordable prices.

among City of Angels foodies. While the more innovative cooking is going on back in L.A., Pinot reliably delivers French and American favorites that are thoughtfully conceived and generally delicious. It's an excellent choice if you want a special meal that is neither stratospherically expensive nor too complex. And the space is highly attractive, with various props culled from French auctions and flea markets forming the archetypal, clubby bistro feel. (We particularly like the small room off the bar to the right, just perfect for a tête-à-tête.)

Salads are possibly fresher and more generous than other similar starters in town (thank that California influence), and they can come paired with various toppings for *crostini* (toasted slices of French bread) such as herbed goat cheese. Word is that they might add Patina's delightful butternut-squash soup to the menu here, and if so, you should try it. The signature dish, beloved by many, is a roasted chicken accompanied by heaping mounds of garlic fries; but if you wish to get a little more elaborate (and yet rather light), thin slices of smoked salmon with celery rémoulade could be a way to go. Desserts are lovely, and the ice cream is homemade—the chocolate alone should make you wish you'd never eaten at 31 Flavors because it was wasted calories compared to this.

In The Venetian, 3355 Las Vegas Blvd. S. (C) **702/414-8888**. Reservations recommended for dinner. Main courses $14–$18 at lunch, $19–$30 at dinner.. AE, DISC, MC, V. Mon–Thurs 7–10am, 11:30am–3pm, and 5:30–10pm; Fri 7–10am, 11:30am–3pm, and 5:30–10:30pm; Sat 7am–3pm and 5:30–10:30pm; Sun 7am–3pm and 5:30–10pm.

MODERATE

See also the listing for **Spago** (p. 153), an expensive restaurant fronted by a more moderately priced cafe.

Corsa Cucina 𝄪𝄪 ITALIAN/MEDITERRANEAN   Another talented NYC chef lured to Vegas by that clever guy Steve Wynn. Stephen Kalt is making excellent Italian- and Mediterranean-influenced food tucked just off the casino, on your way to the Ferrari dealership. (Fortunately, the management has recognized that the cheesy sports car theme decor simply did not fit Kalt's work and are giving him a more sophisticated redesign that should be in place by the time you read this.) This might be best for lunch, as dinner removes some sandwich options and ups the prices. Wood-fired pizzas come on a cracker-thin crust; we greedily consumed the mushroom and white-truffle-oil version that included a soft Italian cheese that melted into a crème fraîche consistency. For main courses, Piedmontese short ribs were an earthy, rich winner. Fra Diablo shrimp pasta was perfectly done, just the right amount of kick, while Dungeness crab–stuffed shells made us eat more than our fair share (we were supposed to split it with a friend. Sorry about that). Look for interesting wildcards like lamb tagine and bastilla, the Moroccan savory flaky pastry pie. Don't miss, for dessert, the crispy flats of dough with crème anglais. They also have a good and interesting half-bottle wine list.

3131 Las Vegas Blvd. S. (in Wynn Las Vegas hotel). (C) **888/320-7110** or 702/770-9966. www.wynnlasvegas.com. Reservations suggested. Lunch $14–$26; dinner $14–$39. AE, DC, DISC, MC, V. Daily 11:30am–10pm.

Cypress Street Marketplace 𝄪𝄪 *Kids* FOOD COURT   Often when we go to a Vegas buffet (and we are not alone in this), we sigh over all the choices, all those different kinds of pretty good, if not better, cuisines there for the taking, but, of course, we can't possibly try everything. And yet, in some of the higher-priced venues, we are charged as if we can. Here, in this modern version of the classic food court, it's sort of like being at a well-stocked buffet; there's darn fine barbecue (including North Carolina–influenced pulled pork), wrap sandwiches (grilled shrimp, for one example), Asian (including pot stickers and Vietnamese noodles), decent NY pizza, plump

Chicago hot dogs, peel-and-eat shrimp and lobster chowder, a bargain-priced salad bar, plus pastries and even wine. You get a card when you enter, and it's swiped whenever you choose something, and then you pay the total price after you eat (on real plates with real napkins and forks). It's slightly more convenient than the traditional pay-as-you-go food court, certainly more efficient than a cafeteria, and a better value (especially given how large the portions are) than many a buffet. And with the range of food, an entire family with very different tastes will all find something satisfactory.

In Caesars Palace, 3570 Las Vegas Blvd. S. ☎ 702/731-7110. Everything under $14. AE, MC, V. Mon–Thurs 7am–11pm; Fri–Sat 7am–midnight.

Isla 🐟🐟 MEXICAN   We tend to get a little snobby about Mexican restaurants, particular those in casinos, because so often they seem careless. But unless you absolutely do not consider Mexican food anything other than a specific form of Southern California burrito, you really should try this new establishment run by Richard Sandoval, who specializes in "modern Mexican cuisine." This means dishes both traditional and with potentially dangerous twists, but since the place starts with handmade tortillas and heads right to guacamole made on demand, it's all trustworthy, even if that some of that guac contains lobster and passion fruit (it's a sweet and curious take on tradition). Roast pork pipian with tamarind marinade and pumpkin-seed sauce is a lovely dish, as are the needlessly fried (though pleasantly crunching) beef empanades with dried cherries and chipolte tomato sauce—a mix of sweet and spiced. For the more timid, there is a nice assortment of particularly good tacos and burritos. They also have a charming dessert menu, with Mexican themes both culinary and visually, like a chocolate cactus stuck into a fudge hill, to complement the caramel cupcakes. The largest collection of tequila in Vegas and a slightly modern nightclub interior remind you that dining in Vegas is still a gimmick.

In TI at the Mirage, 3300 Las Vegas Blvd. S. ☎ 866/286-3809 or 702/894-7223. Main courses $10–$25. AE, DC, DISC, MC, V. Daily 11am–2am.

Mon Ami Gabi 🐟🐟 BISTRO   This charming bistro is our new favorite local restaurant. It has it all: a delightful setting, better-than-average food, and affordable prices. Sure, it goes overboard in trying to replicate a classic Parisian bistro, but the results are less cheesy than most Vegas attempts at atmosphere, and the patio seating on the Strip (no reservations taken there—first-come, first-served, but a recent addition of 70 more seats probably helps matters) actually makes you feel like you're in a real, not a pre-fab, city. You can be budget-conscious and order just the very fine onion soup, or you can eat like a real French person and order classic steak (the filet mignon is probably the best cut, if not the cheapest) and *pommes frites* (french fries). There are plenty of cheaper options (which is why we listed this place in the "moderate" category, by the way), especially at lunch. Yes, they have snails, and we loved 'em. Desserts, by the way, are massive and should be shared (another way to save). The baseball-size profiteroles (three or four to an order) filled with fine vanilla ice cream and the football-size bananas-Foster crepe are particularly recommended. Ooh la la!

In Paris Las Vegas, 3655 Las Vegas Blvd. S. ☎ 702/944-GABI (4224). www.monamigabi.com. Reservations recommended. Main courses $8.95–$27. AE, DC, DISC, MC, V. Mon–Fri lunch 11:30am–3:30pm; Sun–Thurs 5–11pm; Fri–Sat 5pm–midnight; Sat–Sun brunch 11am–3:30pm.

Olives 🐟🐟 ITALIAN/MEDITERRANEAN   If there were an Olives cafe in our neighborhood, we would eat there regularly. The less-expensive relative of The Mirage's Onda (as well as a branch of Todd English's original Boston-based restaurant), Olives

Deli Delights

It's East Coast vs. West Coast in the battle of the famous delis, here in sister properties The Mirage and TI at the Mirage. The former has brought in New York's beloved **Carnegie Deli,** home of the towering sandwich, so large no mere mortal can clamp his or her jaws around it. The latter is home to the first off-shoot of Los Angeles's **Canter's Deli,** where many a musician has whiled away many an hour, staring moodily into a bowl of matzo-ball soup. Whole families have been rent apart by stating preferences for one style over the other, so we will just say this: As much as we admit that NYC is right to claim it has superior bagels—there, we said it—and the Carnegie definitely has better hours, it smells just like the one we spent too much time in while growing up to ever swing our allegiance. Ah, just go do some pastrami taste-testing yourselves, youse. Carnegie Deli in The Mirage, daily 7am–2am. Canter's in TI at the Mirage, daily 11am–midnight.

is a strong choice for a light lunch that need not be as expensive as you might think. Here's how to enjoy a moderately priced meal here: Munch on the focaccia bread, olives, and excellent tapenade they give you at the start, have a lovely salad (maybe of Bibb lettuce, Maytag bleu cheese, and walnut dressing), and then split a flatbread. Think pizza with an ultrathin crust (like a slightly limp cracker), topped with delicious combinations such as the highly recommended Moroccan spiced lamb, eggplant purée, and feta cheese, or our other favorite, fig, prosciutto, and Gorgonzola. They are rich and wonderful—split one between two people, and you have an affordable and terrific lunch. Or try a pasta; we were steered toward the simple but marvelous spaghettini with roasted tomatoes, garlic, and Parmesan, and were happy with it. The constructed, but not too fussy, food gets more complicated and costly at night, adding an array of meats and chickens, plus pastas such as butternut squash with brown butter and sage.

In Bellagio, 3600 Las Vegas Blvd. S. ⓒ 702/693-7223. Reservations recommended. Main courses $15–$19 at lunch, $20–$34 at dinner; flatbreads $10–$15. AE, DC, DISC, MC, V. Daily 11am–10:30pm.

Sensi ⓡⓡ ECLECTIC   It's usually a truism, as far as restaurants go, "jack of all trades, master of none." Sensi seems to be an exception, given that its menu is made up of Italian (fancy pizzas and pastas), wood-grilled American options (burgers, fish, chicken), and Asian-influenced dishes (and they mean "pan-Asian," thus tandoori and sushi both). And yet, it does all it credibly, if not very well indeed. You are probably best off here at lunchtime, sampling pizza al prosciutto or wok-fried shrimp, for more moderate prices found at dinner. Best of all is the "Sensi 41," a healthy take on the bento box, featuring things like miso-glazed Chilean sea bass, some tender sashimi, piquant rice, and, disconcertingly, mozzarella salad. They finish it up with two small, cunning servings of fancy ice cream in wee cones. A fun menu in a fun-looking space, laid out to surround one very busy and versatile kitchen.

3600 Las Vegas Blvd. S (in Bellagio). ⓒ **702/693-8800.** Main courses $14–$19 at lunch, $15–$32 at dinner. AAE, MC, V. Daily 11am–2pm and 5–10:30pm.

Stage Deli ⓡⓡ DELI   New York City's Stage Deli—a legendary hangout for come-dians, athletes, and politicians—has been slapping pastrami on rye for more than half a century. Its Las Vegas branch retains the Stage's brightly lit Big Apple essence. Walls are embellished with subway graffiti and hung with Broadway theater posters, bowls of pickles grace the white Formica tables, and, in the New York tradition, comics and celebrities such as Buddy Hackett and Arnold Schwarzenegger drop by whenever they're in town.

The deli is often not crowded. In addition to being handy for Caesars guests, it's easy to pop over if you're staying next door at The Mirage, making it a satisfying breakfast alternative to the often overcrowded, overpriced, and not very good hotel breakfast joints in the area. The huge (we mean it) menu means it's easy to find something for even the pickiest of eaters.

Most of the fare—including fresh-baked pumpernickel and rye, meats, chewy bagels, lox, spicy deli mustard, and pickles—comes in daily from New York. The Stage dishes up authentic 5-inch-high sandwiches stuffed with pastrami, corned beef, brisket, or chopped liver. Maybe "overstuffed" is a better description. Unless you have a hearty appetite, are feeding two, or have a fridge in your room for leftovers, you might want to try the half-sandwich and soup or salad combos. Other specialties here include matzo-ball soup, knishes, kasha varnishkes, cheese blintzes, kreplach, pirogen, and smoked-fish platters accompanied by bagels and cream cheese. Or you might prefer a full meal consisting of pot roast and gravy, salad, homemade dinner rolls, potato pancakes, and fresh vegetables. Desserts run the gamut from rugelach cheesecake to Hungarian-style apple strudel, and available beverages include wine and beer, milkshakes, Dr. Brown's sodas, and chocolate egg creams.

In the Forum Shops at Caesars, 3570 Las Vegas Blvd. S. © **702/893-4045.** Reservations accepted for large parties only. Main courses $10–$14; sandwiches $6–$14. AE, DC, DISC, MC, V. Sun–Thurs 8am–10:30pm; Fri–Sat 8am–11:30pm (takeout stays open 30 min. later).

4 North Strip

MODERATE

Cafe Heidelberg German Deli and Restaurant ℛ GERMAN   A once-ponderous and dated German restaurant has been transformed into a German cafe already well packed (admittedly, with only six booths, not hard to do) with locals. Certainly, it's not a Vegas type of place, and because it's close enough to the Strip, it's a good place for refuge. The food is better than fine, though certainly not "lite" fare, by any means. You should feel full but not heavy when you leave; you will be moaning and holding your stomach in sorrow only if you don't share those huge portions. Recommended is the sausage sampler platter, so you can finally learn the difference between knockwurst and bratwurst, and the schnitzel sandwich of delicious breaded veal. Wash it down with a vast choice of imported beer. As you munch, enjoy traditional (or, at times, not-so-traditional) accordion music and note that the entire staff is German. This is also a full-service deli and German market, so it's a good place to pick up a picnic for sightseeing outside of the city.

604 E. Sahara. © **702/731-5310.** Reservations highly recommended for Fri–Sat nights. Main courses under $10 at lunch, $15–$20 at dinner. AE, DC, DISC, MC, V. Daily 10am–10pm.

INEXPENSIVE

Capriotti's ℛℛℛ *Finds* SANDWICHES   It looks like a dump, but there's a reason why Capriotti's is one of the fastest-growing businesses in town. They roast their own beef and turkeys on the premises and stuff them (or Italian cold cuts, or whatever) into sandwiches mislabeled "small," "medium," and "large"—the latter clocks in at 20 inches, easily feeding two for under $10 total. And deliciously so; the "Bobby" (turkey, dressing, and cranberry sauce, like Thanksgiving dinner in sandwich form) would be our favorite sandwich in the world had we not tried their "Slaw B Joe" (roast beef, coleslaw, and Russian dressing). But other combos, such as the aforementioned spicy Italian cold cuts, have their fans, too, and they even have veggie varieties. There are outlets throughout the city, but this one is not only right off the Strip, but right by the freeway. When we say Vegas needs more true budget fare, with both taste and a mom-and-pop background (as opposed to a generic chain), we mean places like Capriotti's. We never leave town without a stop here, and you shouldn't, either.

324 W. Sahara Ave. (at Las Vegas Blvd. S.). ℂ 702/474-0229. www.capriottis.com. Most sandwiches under $10. No credit cards. Mon–Fri 10am–5pm; Sat 11am–5pm.

Dona Maria Tamales 🏆🏆 MEXICAN   Decorated with Tijuana-style quilt work and calendars, this quintessential Mexican diner is convenient to both the north end of the Strip and Downtown. The cooks use lots of lard, lots of cheese, and lots of sauce. As a result, the food is really good—and really fattening. Yep, the folks who did those health reports showing how bad Mexican food can be for your heart probably did some research here. The fat just makes it all the better, in our opinion. Locals apparently agree; even at lunchtime, the place is crowded.

You will start off with homemade chips and a spicy salsa served in a mortar. Meals are so large that it shouldn't be a problem getting full just ordering off the sides, which can make this even more of a budget option. Naturally, the specialty is the fantastic tamales, which come in red, green, cheese, or sweet. They also serve up excellent enchiladas, chiles rellenos, burritos, and fajitas. All dinners include rice, beans, tortillas, and soup or salad. Sauces are heavy but oh-so-good. For dessert, they have flan, fried ice cream, and Mexican-style pumpkin pie.

910 Las Vegas Blvd. S. (corner of Charleston Blvd.). © 702/382-6538. Main courses $5.45–$8 at breakfast, $6–$13 at lunch or dinner. AE, MC, V. Daily 8am–11pm.

Red 8 🏆🏆 ASIAN   Such a relief, in the otherwise pricey Wynn, to find a dining spot that is both good and affordable. This visual standout is a small cafe—as you wander by, you think "Cool! Some of the tables overlook the casino!" Then you realize those are *all* of the tables—with a decor that screams the place's colorful name. It's probably going to be popular, given the location, size, and pricing—and the quality of the food. Covering a sort of pan-Asiatic (Southeast Asia, anyway) terrain, look for noodle dishes both wet (soup) and dry (pan-fried), rice (including porridge), dim sum, Korean barbeque, Mongolian beef, vegetarian options, and more. There are some "market price" specials that can quadruple a bill pretty fast, but otherwise, this is a more budget-friendly option.

3131 Las Vegas Blvd. S. (in Wynn Las Vegas). © 702/770-3380. Main courses $14–$20. AE, DISC, MC, V. Sun–Thurs 11am–11pm; Fri–Sat 11am–midnight.

Rincon Criollo CUBAN   Located beyond the wedding chapels on Las Vegas Boulevard, Rincon Criollo has all the right details for a good, cheap ethnic joint: It's full of locals and empty of frills. It's not the best Cuban food ever, but it gets the job done. The main courses (featuring Cuban pork and chicken specialties) are hit-or-miss; try the marinated pork leg or, better still, ask your server for a recommendation. Paella is offered, but only for parties of three or more (and starts at $20). The side-course *chorizo* (a spicy sausage) is excellent, and the Cuban sandwich (roast pork, ham, and cheese on bread, which is then pressed and flattened out) is huge and tasty. For only $3.50, the latter makes a fine change-of-pace meal.

1145 Las Vegas Blvd. S. © 702/388-1906. Reservations not accepted. Main courses $6.50–$10; paella (for 3) $20. AE, DISC, MC, V. Tues–Sun 11am–9:30pm.

Tiffany's 🏆🏆 *(Value)* DINER   Why bother with theme restaurants that pretend to be cheap diners, when the real thing is just past the end of the Strip? This decidedly unflashy soda fountain/lunch counter was Las Vegas's first 24-hour restaurant, and it has been going strong for 60 years. Plunk down at the counter and watch the cooks go nuts trying to keep up with the orders. The menu is basic comfort food: standard grill items (meatloaf, ground round steak, chops, and so on), fluffy cream pies, and classic breakfasts served "anytime"—try the biscuits and cream gravy at 3am. But the best bet is a ⅓-pound burger and "thick, creamy shake," both about as good as they get. At around $6, this is half what you would pay for a comparable meal at the Hard Rock Cafe. Places like this are a vanishing species—it's worth the short walk from the Stratosphere. Note, however, that the neighborhood remains stubbornly rough in appearance, and that can be a turnoff. Keep alert if you come here at night.

1700 Las Vegas Blvd. S. ⓒ 702/383-0196. Reservations not accepted. Most items under $7. No credit cards. Daily 24 hr.

5 East of the Strip

In this section, we cover restaurants close to the Convention Center, along with those farther south on Paradise Road, Flamingo Road, and Tropicana Avenue.

VERY EXPENSIVE

Lawry's The Prime Rib *弟弟弟* STEAK/SEAFOOD   If you love prime rib, come here. If you could take or leave prime rib, Lawry's will turn you into a believer. Lawry's does one thing, and it does it better than anyone else. Lawry's first opened in Los Angeles in 1938 and remains a popular tradition. Over the years, they have added three branches; the most recent landed in Las Vegas at the beginning of 1997. Yes, you can get prime rib all over town for under $5. But, to mix a food metaphor, that's a tuna sandwich when you can have caviar at Lawry's.

Eating at Lawry's is a ceremony, with all the parts played the same way for the last 60 years. Waitresses in brown-and-white English-maid uniforms, complete with starched white cap, take your order—for side dishes, that is. The real decision, what cut of rib you are going to have, comes later. Actually, that's the only part of the tradition that has changed. Originally, all Lawry's offered was prime rib, which they did perfectly and with tremendous style. Now they have added fresh fish (halibut, salmon, or swordfish, depending on the evening) to the menu. Anyway, you tell the waitress what side dishes you might want (sublime creamed spinach, baked potato, and so on) for an extra price. Later, she returns with a spinning salad bowl (think of salad preparation as a Busby Berkeley musical number). The bowl, resting on crushed ice, spins as she pours Lawry's special dressing in a stream from high over her head. Tomatoes garnish. Applause follows. Eventually, giant metal carving carts come to your table, bearing the meat. You name your cut (the regular Lawry's, the extra-large Diamond Jim Brady for serious carnivores, and the wimpy, thin English cut) and specify how you'd like it cooked. It comes with terrific Yorkshire pudding, nicely browned and not soggy, and some creamed horseradish that is combined with fluffy whipped cream, simultaneously sweet and tart.

Flavorful, tender, perfectly cooked, and lightly seasoned, this will be the best prime rib you will ever have. Okay, maybe that's going too far, but the rest is accurate, honest. It just has to be tasted to be believed. You can finish off with a rich dessert (English trifle is highly recommended), but it almost seems pointless. Incidentally, the other Lawry's are decorated English-manor style, but the Vegas branch has instead tried to re-create a 1930s restaurant, with Art Deco touches all around and big-band music on the sound system.

4043 Howard Hughes Pkwy. (at Flamingo Rd., between Paradise Rd. and Koval Lane). ⓒ 702/893-2223. www.lawrysonline.com. Reservations recommended. Main courses $20–$40. AE, DC, DISC, MC, V. Sun–Thurs 5–10pm; Fri–Sat 5–11pm.

Morton's of Chicago *弟* STEAK/SEAFOOD   A venerable steakhouse with branches throughout the U.S.—in fact, Mr. Morton is the proud papa of Peter Morton, he of the Hard Rock Hotel over yonder. Like **The Palm** (p. 151), this place serves "boy food"—steaks, really good steaks—and we are not prepared to say which (The Palm or Morton's) has the better hunk o' red meat because, frankly, after a while, these subtle distinctions elude us. Anyway, this is an old-time Vegas hangout (because most actual old-time Vegas hangouts have closed), even in its relatively new off-Strip location. In addition to your cut of beef, suggested sides include flavorfully fresh al dente asparagus served with hollandaise, or hash browns. And it's a good place to hang around post-dinner, drink Scotch, and smoke.

400 E. Flamingo Rd. (at Paradise Rd.). ℭ 702/893-0703. www.mortons.com. Reservations recommended. Main courses $18–$42. AE, DC, MC, V. Mon–Sat 5–11pm; Sun 5–10pm.

Pamplemousse ℛ FRENCH   A little bit off the beaten path, Pamplemousse is a long-established Vegas restaurant that shouldn't be overlooked in the crush of new high-profile eateries. Evoking a cozy French-countryside inn (at least, on the interior), it's a catacomb of low-ceilinged rooms and intimate dining nooks with rough-hewn beams. It's all very charming and un-Vegasy. There's additional seating in a small garden sheltered by a striped tent. The restaurant's name, which means "grapefruit" in French, was suggested by the late singer Bobby Darin, one of the many celebrity pals of owner Georges La Forge.

The menu, which changes nightly, is recited by your waiter. The meal always begins with a large complimentary basket of crudités (about 10 different crisp, fresh vegetables), a big bowl of olives, and, in a nice country touch, a basket of hard-boiled eggs. Recent menu offerings have included out-of-this-world soups (such as French onion and cream of asparagus) and such appetizers as shrimp in cognac-cream sauce or Maryland crab cakes with a macadamia-nut crust. Recommended entrees include a sterling veal with mushrooms and a Dijon sauce, and an even-better rack of lamb with a pistachio-nut crust and a rosemary-cream sauce (all sauces, by the way, are made with whatever the chef has on hand that evening in the kitchen). That's not to mention fabulous desserts such as homemade ice cream in a hard chocolate shell.

400 E. Sahara Ave. (between Santa Paula and Santa Rita drives, just east of Paradise Rd.). ℭ **702/733-2066.** www.pamplemousserestaurant.com. Reservations required. Main courses $18–$32. AE, DC, DISC, MC, V. Tues–Sat 5:30–10:30pm, last seating at 9:45pm; closed Mon except during major conventions and holidays.

The Tillerman ℛ STEAK/SEAFOOD   The Tillerman is often on any number of locals' "best of Vegas" lists, and while we agree the food is terrific, the high prices and somewhat snooty attitude make us feel we can spend our money better elsewhere.

Of the four main dining rooms, the center one is the best; it's filled with plants and trees, and has high ceilings and a huge circular stained-glass window. There's additional seating on the mezzanine level, where diners enjoy treetop views. The meal begins with a relish tray and a basket of delicious oven-fresh breads. Also complimentary is a Lazy Susan salad bar served at your table with a choice of homemade dressings, including a memorable chunky blue cheese. Portions are immense, so appetizers are really not necessary, but then again, they're too good to pass up. Especially notable: crab cake garnished with carrot chips or the superb filet medallions in a spicy red sauce. For entrees, regulars often order the crab legs, which are excellent. The swordfish and halibut are wonderful, too, as is the shrimp in garlic cream sauce. The wine list is huge but expensive; the cheapest glass is $8. After such a large meal, a lighter dessert such as the Bavarian crème with strawberries might be in order. Skip the carrot cake in favor of the divine chocolate éclair.

2245 E. Flamingo Rd. (at Channel 10 Dr., just west of Eastern Ave.). ℭ **702/731-4036.** www.tillerman.com. Reservations recommended. Main courses $18–$56. AE, DC, DISC, MC, V. Daily 5–11pm; bar open later.

Dining & Nightlife East of the Strip

0 — 0.5 mi
0 — 0.5 km

NIGHTLIFE
Drop Bar **30**
Icon **18**
The Beach **4**
The Buffalo **18**
Champagnes Cafe **6**
Club Monaco **21**
The Dispensary **25**
Double Down
  Saloon **19**
The Eagle **27**
Ellis Island Casino–
  Karaoke **12**
Gipsy **17**
Good Times **26**
Ice **14**
Jazzed Cafe and
  Vinoteca **28**
Whiskey Sky **30**

RESTAURANTS
Bougainvillea **13**
Carluccio's Tivoli Gardens **24**
Einstein Bros. Bagels **23**
Gordon-Biersch Brewing Company **10**
Hard Rock Café **15**
Kabuki **7**
Komol **3**
Lawry's The Prime Rib **11**
Lotus of Siam **2**
Lucille's Smokehouse Bar-B-Que **30**
Mediterranean Cafe and Market **20**
Memphis Championship Barbecue **29**
Mr. Lucky's 24/7 **15**
Morton's of Chicago **9**
Pamplemousse **1**
Pink Taco **15**
Rainbow Bar & Grill **16**

Shalimar **8**
The Tillerman **22**
Toto's **25**
BUFFETS
The Buffet at the
  Las Vegas Hilton **5**
Sam's Town Firelight Buffet **22**

MODERATE

Carluccio's Tivoli Gardens ☆ *Finds* ITALIAN   A bit of a drive, but well worth it for those seeking an authentic (read: dining in a restaurant that's been around more than 10 years) Vegas experience. This joint used to be owned by none other than the Rhinestone King himself, Liberace. See, it was formerly Liberace's Tivoli Gardens, and he designed the interior himself, so you know what that looks like (it was reopened a few years after his death and they kept the decor pretty much intact). This kind of history is more and more rare in this town with no memory, plus it's right next door to the Liberace Museum, no coincidence, so go pay your giggling respects in the late afternoon and then stop here for dinner. Expect traditional Italian food (pasta, pasta, pasta, and scampi).

1775 E. Tropicana Blvd. (at Spencer). ② 702/795-3236. Reservations recommended. Main courses $10–$25. AE, DC, DISC, MC, V. Tues–Sun 4:30–10pm.

Gordon-Biersch Brewing Company ☆ CALIFORNIA   This is a traditional brew-pub (exposed piping and ducts, but still comfortable and casual), but it's worth going to for a meal as well. The menu is pub fare meets California cuisine (kids will proba-bly find the food too complicated), and naturally, there are a lot of beers (German-style lagers) to choose from. Appetizers include satays (marinated meat on skewers served with spicy peanut sauce), pot stickers, calamari, baby back ribs, delicious beer-battered onion rings, and amazing garlic-encrusted fries. A wood-burning pizza oven turns out pies with California-type toppings: eggplant, shrimp, and so forth. For lunch, there are various pastas, stir-fries, sandwiches, and salads. The dinner menu eliminates the sand-wiches and adds rosemary chicken, steaks, fish items, and, just in case you forgot it was a brewpub-type joint, beer everything: beer-glazed ham, beer meatloaf, and beer-bar-becued glazed ribs. Doesn't that make you want to order a glass of milk?

3987 Paradise Rd. (just north of Flamingo Rd.). ② 702/312-5247. www.gordonbiersch.com. Main courses $8–$15 at lunch, $10–$21 at dinner.. AE, DISC, MC, V. Sun–Thurs 11am–10pm; Fri–Sat 11am–11pm; bar daily until midnight or later.

Kabuki JAPANESE   Primarily catering to a Japanese clientele, the Kabuki is a real taste of Japan. Rice paper covers the windows of this tastefully converted diner, while various paintings of Japanese kabuki actors grace the walls. The service is excellent, starting your meal off with a warm towel and green tea. Yes, they do have a small sushi bar, but the locals (who voted this their favorite Japanese restaurant in a recent *Las Vegas Review-Journal* poll) come back for the other Japanese dishes. *Negi ma,* a teriyaki-marinated beef rolled with onions, and *yaki gyoza* (pot stickers) are both amazing starters. For the main course, try *zarusoba* (cold Japanese buckwheat noo-dles), beef and chicken teriyaki, or *tatsuta age* (marinated chicken). They have plenty of sushi specials, including yellowtail, shrimp, and calamari, but there are other sushi places in town that do sushi better (admittedly, in some cases for a higher price).

3949 S. Maryland Pkwy. ② 702/733-0066. Reservations required on weekend nights. Main courses $7–$17. AE, DC, DISC, MC, V. Mon–Sat 11:30am–2:30pm and 5:30–11pm.

Komol THAI   This is a hole-in-the-wall dive, like most good ethnic places. The menu is pretty large, divided into different sections for poultry, beef, and pork, plus a separate section for vegetarian dishes, plus many rice and noodle selections. They'll spice the food to your specifications. Unless you know your spicy Asian food, it might be best to play it on the safe side. (While we don't want things bland, too much heat place for a morning meal, with both indoor seating and outdoor tables cooled by misters. Service is friendly, and four special-blend coffees are available each day.

Note: Bagel buffs might also want to check out the nearby **Bagelmania** at 855 E. Twain Ave. (© **702/369-3322**). The bagels are sometimes chilled for freshness, which is heresy, but you can avoid this problem by catching them early in the morning, when their extensive selection is hot and fresh.

In the University Gardens Shopping Center, 4626 S. Maryland Pkwy. (between Harmon and Tropicana aves.). © 702/795-7800. www.einsteinbros.com. All items under $6. MC, V. Mon–Fri 6am–6pm; Sat 6am–4pm; Sun 6:30am–4pm.

Lotus of Siam 🌶🌶🌶 *Finds* THAI   So we drag you out to a strip mall in the east end of nowhere and you wonder why? Because here is what critic Jonathan Gold of *Gourmet* magazine called no less than the best Thai restaurant in North America.

What makes this place so darn special? First of all, in addition to all the usual beloved Thai favorites, they have a separate menu featuring lesser-known dishes from northern Thailand—they don't routinely hand this one out (since most of the customers are there for the more pedestrian, if still excellent, $5.99 lunch buffet). Second, the owner drives at least twice a week back to Los Angeles to pick up the freshest herbs and other ingredients needed for his dishes' authenticity. That's dedication that should be rewarded with superlatives.

You might be best off letting them know you are interested in Northern food (with dried chiles and more pork, it's not un-Cajunlike, says the owner) and letting them guide you through, though you must assure them that you aren't of faint heart or palate (some customers complain the heat isn't enough, even with "well spiced" dishes, though others find even medium spice sufficient). Standouts include the Issan sausage (a grilled sour pork number), the *nam kao tod* (that same sausage, ground up with lime, green onion, fresh chile, and ginger, served with crispy rice), *nam sod* (ground pork mixed with ginger, green onion, and lime juice, served with sticky rice), jackfruit *larb* (spicy ground meat), and *sua rong hai* ("weeping tiger"), a dish of soft, sliced, and grilled marinated beef. If you insist on more conventional Thai, that's okay, in that it's unlikely you are going to have better *mee krob* noodles or *tom kah kai* (that beloved soup can also be served northern style, if asked, which is without the coconut milk). If in season, finish with mango with sticky rice, or if not, coconut ice cream with sticky rice, something you would find at many a street stall in Thailand.

953 E. Sahara Ave., #A-5. © 702/735-3033. www.saipinchutima.com. Reservations strongly suggested for dinner. Lunch buffet $5.99; other dishes $3.95–$14. AE, MC, V. Mon–Fri 11:30am–2:30pm and 5:30–9:30pm; Sat–Sun 5:30–10pm.

Mediterranean Cafe & Market 🌶 MEDITERRANEAN   The emphasis on safe mainstream food for the masses, to say nothing of the basic economy involved in running a Vegas restaurant (take your pick, either pay costly rent to a Strip hotel or get less tourist traffic with an off-Strip site), means that the kind of eateries other big cities take for granted—you know, cheap holes-in-the-wall, or charming little quirky joints, or the kind of ethnic places the chowhound folks brag about discovering—are rare indeed. And when you do find them, they are always, but always, in a strip mall.

The Mediterranean Cafe is no exception, and its main dining room has no decor worth mentioning. But it gets extra points for having a courtyard seating area full of Middle Eastern touches and an honest-to-goodness hookah lounge—it's a good break from an otherwise often stifled, insulating time in Sin City.

Plus, it's just so darn nice to find ethnic food in this town. Kabobs take, the menu warns, 25 minutes, so order an appetizer plate with various dips to while away the time. Hummus is too reminiscent of its chickpea origins, but baba ghanouj is properly smoky, and the falafel has the right crunch. Gyros may not be the most adventurous thing to order, but who cares about that when you've got a well-stuffed pocket of pita, gloopy with sweet yogurt sauce. *Fresenjan* is a dish of falling-apart chicken swimming in a tangy pomegranate sauce; ask them to ensure that the ratio of sauce to chicken is greater than 10:1.

4147 S. Maryland Pkwy. (at Flamingo Rd., in the Tiffany Sq. strip mall). ℭ 702/731-6030. www.paymons.com. Reservations not accepted. Main courses $8–$16; most sandwiches under $8. AE, DISC, MC, V. Restaurant Mon–Thurs 11am–1am, Fri–Sat 11am–3am, Sun 11am–5pm; lounge Mon–Thurs 5pm–1am, Fri–Sat 5pm–3am; market Mon–Fri 9am–8pm, Sat 10am–5pm.

Toto's 🏮🏮 (Kids) (Value) MEXICAN   A family-style Mexican restaurant favored by locals, with enormous portions and quick service, this is good value for your money. With all that food, you could probably split portions and still be satisfied. There are no surprises on the menu, though there are quite a few seafood dishes. Everything is quite tasty, and they don't skimp on the cheese. The nongreasy chips come with fresh salsa, and the nachos are terrific. Chicken tamales got a thumbs-up, while the veggie burrito was happily received by non–meat eaters (although it's not especially healthful, all the ingredients were fresh, with huge slices of zucchini and roasted bell peppers). The operative word here is *huge;* the burritos are almost the size of your arm. The generous portions continue with dessert—a piece of flan was practically pie size. The Sunday margarita brunch is quite fun, and the drinks are large (naturally) and yummy.

2055 E. Tropicana Ave. ℭ 702/895-7923. Main courses $6.25–$14. AE, DISC, MC, V. Sun–Thurs 11am–10pm; Fri–Sat 11am–11pm.

6 West Las Vegas

EXPENSIVE

Austins Steakhouse 🏮🏮 (Finds) STEAK/SEAFOOD   Now, understand that we don't send you out to nether regions such as Texas Station lightly. We do so here because, improbably, Austins Steakhouse has gained a reputation for the best steak in town. Really. Even the snooty critics at the *Las Vegas Review-Journal* agree with the hubbub about this place. And here's what has everyone, including us, raving: a 24-ounce rib-eye—yes, we know, just split it—aged and marinated, cooked over mesquite applewood, then rubbed with peppercorns and pan-seared in garlic, butter, and cilantro. A massive chunk of meat with a smoky, garlicky flavor like no other steak we can think of. Most of the dishes have a Southern twist, like the fried green tomatoes with a rémoulade dipping sauce, and for those not watching their cholesterol, or at least only watching it go up, the shrimp sautéed in garlic-butter sauce, dipped in cheese, and wrapped in bacon. The Maui onion soup is also a standout, as is, over in the desserts, the chocolate decadence cake, which actually has a molten center, sort of a semi-soufflé. Note that a comparable meal on the Strip would cost $10 to $20 more per person—yet another reason to head out to the hinterlands.

In Texas Station, 2101 Texas Star Lane. ℭ 702/631-1000. Reservations recommended. Main courses $15–$38. AE, DC, DISC, MC, V. Sun–Thurs 5–10pm; Fri–Sat 5–11pm.

Rosemary's Restaurant 🏮🏮🏮 (Finds) NOUVELLE AMERICAN   No visitor would be blamed for never leaving the Vegas Strip—it's the raison d'être of any Vegas tourist—but a true foodie should make a point of finding the nearest moving vehicle

Dining & Nightlife West of the Strip

DINING
Austins Steakhouse **1**
Cathay House **3**
Dragon Sushi **4**
Rosemary's Restaurant **2**
Thai Spice **7**
Viva Mercados **6**

NIGHTLIFE
Pink E's **8**
Sand Dollar Blues Lounge **5**
Tommy Rocker's **9**

Sweet Sensations

Plenty of opportunities exist in Vegas for satisfying your sweet tooth, but for the discriminating, here are six spots that you may have to make a detour for. We think they're worth it.

Jean-Philippe Patisserie (3600 Las Vegas Blvd. S. in Bellagio; ✆ 702/693-8788) makes us swoon, not just because it has the world's largest chocolate fountain (20 ft. high! Though only 11 ft. are on view, and they won't let us drink from it. Darn.), but perhaps, more to the point, it's the home of World Pastry Champion Jean-Philippe Maury. (Yes, you can win gold medals for pastries.) Each visit causes us to spin around distractedly trying to take in all the choices, both visually and gastronomically. From perfect gourmet chocolates to ice cream (diet-conscious folks will be relieved to learn the sorbets are excellent) to the eponymous pastries (each a little work of art), we hit greed overload. For us, this is true Vegas decadence—if only "what happens in Vegas, stays in Vegas" applied to calories. Our current favorites include a witty-looking version of lemon meringue pie that was proclaimed by one aficionado of same her favorite ever, to a chocolate hazelnut bomb with so many layers of interest we couldn't quite keep track, to brioches filled with either dolce de leche or Nutella. (You should have heard us squeal when we found the latter, oozing chocolate-hazelnut creamy goodness.) They also serve some solidly good sandwiches, which often need heating (the panini bread, in particular, gets too stiff, thanks to being premade and chilled since its assembly), which can be a problem if the ingredients are better cold (prosciutto, for example), and some adequate savory crepes. Open daily 7am–midnight.

The **Chocolate Swan** (two locations in Mandalay Place Shopping Center, 3930 Las Vegas Blvd. S., Suites 121B & 201B; ✆ 702/632-9366; www.chocolateswan.com), is here because a Mandalay Bay executive fell in love with the owners' work back at their original Midwestern shop and convinced them to close and reopen in Vegas. Patronize them so they know their decision was a good one; you will know it is as soon as you try one of their entirely-from-scratch-and-fresh products. Gorgeous elaborate baked goods, carefully created candies, and too much more to list. Have a slice of cake and homemade hot chocolate for an energy boost, and take back a few pastries and other sweets for a late-night orgy in your room. Prices aren't cheap (particularly for slices of cake), but that seems to be the way of gourmet sweet shops. The casino-level store is open daily 8am to midnight; the mall-level store open Sunday through Thursday 10am to 11pm, Friday and Saturday 10am until midnight,

There aren't lots of doughnut places around town, and most of the ones you'll find are of the chain variety—fine if you have a yen on the spot, but

that can get them to Rosemary's Restaurant. A 15-minute (or so) drive down Sahara (hardly anything) is all it takes to eat what may well be the best food in Las Vegas (certainly, it is consistently voted the best food in the *Las Vegas Review-Journal*'s annual poll, by food critics and readers alike).

in reality, you might as well be eating frosted foam rubber. If you're a connoisseur with a car or happen to be checking out the restaurants in the Chinatown area on Spring Mountain Road, go to **Ronald's Donuts,** 4600 Spring
Mountain Rd., at Decatur (© **702/873-1032**). Hours are Monday to Saturday
from 4am to 5pm, Sunday from 4am to 2pm. Some have called these doughnuts celestial. You decide.

Do a comparison taste test with **Krispy Kreme Doughnuts,** just a few more
minutes down the road at 7015 W. Spring Mountain Rd., at Rainbow Boulevard (© **702/222-2320**). There are more convenient but more crowded (and
higher-priced) Krispy Kreme locations in TI at the Mirage, Excalibur, and The
Venetian, but only the latter two make the donuts on the premises. Krispy
Kreme prompts rabid devotion in its fans—like us, who, on our first visit, ate
two of their famous glazed (don't bother with any of the other varieties)
before we even cleared the drive-through. If you've wondered what all the
fuss is about, be sure to go when the HOT DONUTS sign flashes from 5 to 11am
and 5 to 11pm. Dine-in 5am to 11pm; drive-through Sunday through Thursday between 5am and 11pm, Friday and Saturday between 5am and 1am.

Another favorite is **Freed's Bakery,** 4780 S. Eastern Ave., at Tropicana
Boulevard (© **702/456-7762**), open Monday through Saturday from 9am to
6:30pm and Sunday from 9am to 3pm. If you've got a serious sugar craving,
this is worth making the 15-minute drive from the Strip. Despite the minimalist setting, it's like walking into Grandma's kitchen (provided you had an
old-fashioned granny who felt pastries should not be fancy but should definitely be gooey, chocolaty, and buttery). The chocolate coffee cake is especially good. They also have fresh bread, napoleons, strawberry cheesecake,
cream puffs, hamantaschen, sweet rolls, Danishes, and doughnuts. Some
may find the goodies too heavy and rich, but for those of us with a powerful sweet tooth, this place hits the spot.

Hot Vegas days call for cool desserts, and frozen custard (softer than regular ice cream, but harder than soft serve) is a fine way to go. Head for **Luv-
It Frozen Custard,** 505 E. Oakey, at the Strip (© **702/384-6452**), open
Monday to Thursday from 11am to 10pm, Friday from 11am to 11pm, Saturday from noon to 11pm, and Sunday from 1 to 10pm. Since it has less fat
and sugar than premium ice cream, from which it also differs slightly in taste
and texture, you can even fool yourself into thinking this is somewhat
healthful (hah!). Made every few hours using fresh cream and eggs, Luv-It
Frozen Custard has basic flavors available for cup or cone, but more exotic
ones (maple walnut, apple spice, and more) in tubs.

The brainchild of Michael and Wendy Jordan, both veterans of the New Orleans
food scene (Michael actually opened Emeril's Seafood here in Vegas), Rosemary's
Restaurant (named for Michael's mother) shows more than a few NOLA touches,
from the food to the service, in a room that's warmer and more inviting than most

others in Vegas. Note that you can get seats at the bar overlooking the open kitchen, great fun for foodie interaction and not a bad choice for singles, or for couples looking for an unusual romantic evening.

The cuisine covers most regions of the U.S., though Southern influences dominate. Fifty local farmers help supply products. Seared foie gras with peach coulis, candied walnuts, and vanilla bean–scented arugula is like a quilt, with distinct flavors that all hang together nicely. Interesting sides include ultra-rich bleu-cheese slaw, slightly spicy crispy fried tortilla strips, and perfect cornmeal jalapeño hush puppies. A recent visit found the crispy striped bass fighting it out with the pan-seared honey-glazed salmon for "best fish dish I've ever had." Desserts are similarly Southern—lemon icebox pie!—and most pleasant.

There is a nice little wine list with a broad range, especially when it comes to half-price bottles. They also specialize, unusually, in beer suggestions to pair with courses, including some fruity Belgian numbers; this is such a rare treat, if you drink, you must try some of their suggestions.

8125 W. Sahara. $ℂ$ **702/869-2251.** www.rosemarysrestaurant.com. Reservations strongly suggested. Lunch $12–$16; dinner $18–$29. AE, MC, V. Mon–Fri 11:30am–2:30pm and 5:30–10:30pm.

MODERATE

Cathay House CHINESE　Las Vegas actually has a Chinatown—a very large strip mall (naturally) on Spring Mountain Road near Wynn. There are several Asian restaurants there, but ask locals who look like they know, and they will send you instead farther up Spring Mountain Road to the Cathay House (on the opposite side of the street). This only looks far from the Strip on a map; it's really about a 7-minute drive from TI at the Mirage

Ordering dim sum, for those of you who haven't experienced it, is sort of like being at a Chinese sushi bar, in that you order many individual, tasty little dishes. Of course, dim sum itself is nothing like sushi. Rather, it's a range of pot stickers, pan-fried dumplings, *baos* (soft, doughy buns filled with such meat as barbecued pork), translucent rice noodles wrapped around shrimp, sticky rice in lotus leaves, chicken feet, and so forth. Some of it is steamed; some is fried—for that extra-good grease! You can make your own dipping sauce by combining soy sauce, vinegar, and hot-pepper oil. The waitstaff pushes steam carts filled with little dishes; point, and they'll attempt to tell you what each one is. Better, just blindly order a bunch and dig in. Each dish ranges from approximately $1 to $3; each server makes a note of what you just received, and the total is tallied at the end. (For some reason, it almost always works out to about $9 per person.) Dim sum is usually available only until mid-afternoon.

The standout at the Cathay House was a vegetable *bao* that included Chinese glass noodles. Lightly browned and not overly doughy like many baos, it was slightly sweet and utterly delicious. The shrimp wrapped in rice noodles were big and plump, while anything that was fried was so good we decided to ignore our arteries for a while. Cathay House (which features quite a good view through the windows on one side) also has a full dinner menu, which includes the strawberry chicken invented by Chin's; it's considerably cheaper here.

In Spring Valley, 5300 W. Spring Mountain Rd. $ℂ$ **702/876-3838.** Reservations recommended. Main courses $6.75–$19. AE, DC, DISC, MC, V. Daily 10:30am–10pm.

Thai Spice *Value* THAI　Just off the Strip and across from the Rio hotel, this modern-looking, nonglitzy Thai restaurant offers decent food at reasonable prices. The subdued ambience (okay, it's a little boring, but not everything can be flashy, even in Vegas), quick service, and good food make it a local favorite. The menu is extensive and offers an array of Thai dishes and even some Chinese fare. For appetizers, the *tom kah kai* soup and pork or chicken satay (served on skewers with a spicy peanut sauce) are excellent. Skip the terrible *moo goo gai pan* in favor of terrific pad Thai and tasty lemon chicken. Lunch specials are $6.45 and include spring rolls, salad, soup, and steamed rice. Make sure you tell the waitress how spicy you want your food.

4433 W. Flamingo Rd. (at I-15). © **702/362-5308.** Main courses $6.45 at lunch, $8–$15 at dinner.. AE, DISC, MC, V. Mon–Thurs 11:30am–10pm; Fri–Sat 11:30am–10:30pm.

Viva Mercados ☆☆ MEXICAN   Ask any local about Mexican food in Vegas, and almost certainly they will point to Viva Mercados as the best in town. That recommendation, plus the restaurant's health-conscious attitude, makes this worth the roughly 10-minute drive from the Strip.

Given all those warnings lately about Mexican food and its heart-attack-inducing properties, the approach at Viva Mercados is nothing to be sniffed at. No dish is prepared with or cooked in any kind of animal fat. Nope, the lard so dear to Mexican cooking is not found here. The oil used is an artery-friendly canola. This makes the place particularly appealing to vegetarians, who will also be pleased by the regular veggie specials. Everything is quite fresh, and they do particularly amazing things with seafood. Try the *Maresco Vallarta,* which is orange roughy, shrimp, and scallops cooked in a coconut-tomato sauce, with capers and olives. They have all sorts of noteworthy shrimp dishes and 11 different salsas, ranked 1 to 10 for degree of spice. (Ask for advice first.) The staff is friendly (try to chat with owner Bobby Mercado) and the portions hearty.

6182 W. Flamingo Rd. (at Jones Blvd.). © **702/871-8826.** Reservations accepted only for large parties. Main courses $8–$17. AE, DISC, MC, V. Sun–Thurs 11am–9:30pm; Fri–Sat 11am–10:30pm.

INEXPENSIVE

Dragon Sushi SUSHI   Those used to really extraordinary sushi need to remember that you are in the middle of the desert, and so there is no way the fish you are going to eat here were swimming the ocean all that recently. This also results in less than generously sized pieces. That said, they do pretty good sushi here, with rolls that pack a wallop, such as the Tuna Tuna Roll (spicy tuna with fresh tuna wrapped around it and, unless we miss our guess, some kind of chile oil for good measure). Don't say we didn't warn you about the Hell Roll. If the incongruously named sushi chef Bruce is working, let this morose and talented man do his work for you. Better still, let him make all your choices.

4115 Spring Mountain Rd. (at Valley View Blvd.). © **702/368-4336.** Sushi $3.50–$5.50 per portion; main courses all under $20. AE, MC, V. Mon–Sat 11am–3pm and 5–10:30pm.

7 Downtown

VERY EXPENSIVE

Andre's ☆☆ FRENCH   Andre's has long been the bastion of gourmet dining in Vegas, but with all the new big boys crowding the Strip, it runs the risk of getting overlooked. It shouldn't—Andre may not have a show on the Food Network, but he ought to be a household name. Besides, his first restaurant still dominates Downtown. (This is also a celebrity haunt where you're likely to see Strip headliners. One night, Tom

Hanks, Steven Spielberg, and James Spader were all spotted joining some pals for a bachelor party. The staff played it cool, though.) In a small, converted 1930s house, you'll find an elegant French provincial atmosphere, overseen by owner-chef Andre, who brings over 40 years of experience to the table. Much of the waitstaff is also French, and they will happily lavish attention on you and guide you through the menu.

The food presentation is exquisite, and choices change seasonally. On a recent visit, an appetizer of Northwest smoked salmon *mille feuille* with cucumber salad and sevruga caviar was especially enjoyed, as was a main course of grilled veal *tournedos* with chive sauce accompanied by a mushroom and foie gras crepe. You get the idea. Desserts are similarly lovely, an exotic array of rich delights. An extensive wine list (more than 900 labels) is international in scope and includes many rare vintages; consult the sommelier.

Note: An additional branch of Andre's is in the **Monte Carlo Hotel & Casino,** 3775 Las Vegas Blvd. S. (✆ **702/798-7151**), and is also highly recommended, as is their slightly different take, **Alizé** (p. 146), in the new Palms hotel.

401 S. 6th St. (at Lewis St., 3 blocks south of Fremont St.). ✆ **702/385-5016.** www.andrelv.com. Reservations required. Main courses $24–$42. AE, DC, MC, V. Mon–Thurs 5:30–9:30pm; Fri–Sat 5:30–10:30pm.

Hugo's Cellar ✦ INTERNATIONAL   Hugo's Cellar is indeed in a cellar, or at least below street level in the Four Queens hotel. No, they aren't ashamed of it—quite the opposite. This is their pride and joy, and it is highly regarded by the locals. This is Old School Vegas Classy Dining. Each female guest is given a red rose when she enters the restaurant—the first of a series of nice touches. The restaurant proper is dimly lit, lined with dark wood and brick. It's fairly intimate, but if you really want to be cozy, ask for one of the curtained booths against the wall.

The meal is full of ceremony, perfectly delivered by a well-trained and cordial waitstaff. Salads, included in the price, are prepared at your table, from a cart full of choices. In Vegas style, though, most choices are on the calorie-intensive side, ranging from chopped egg and bleu cheese to pine nuts and bay shrimp. Still, with a honey-orange-walnut vinaigrette, it's good enough to consider paying the $14 a la carte fee and just sticking with it. Unfortunately, the main courses are not all that novel (various cuts of meat, seafood, and chicken prepared in different ways), but on a recent visit, not one of six diners was anything less than delighted. The filet of beef stuffed with crabmeat and wrapped with bacon is over the top for us, but others loved it, while the roast duckling rubbed with anise and flambéed at the table is a guilty pleasure, just the right effect for this Old School Vegas dining experience. The T-bone steak was tender enough to cut with a fork. Vegetables and excellent starchy sides are included, as is a finish of chocolate-dipped fruits with cream.

The service is impeccable (you have little to no wait between courses), and it really makes you feel pampered. The fact that salad, the small dessert, and so forth are included makes an initially hefty-seeming price tag appear a bit more reasonable, especially when compared to Strip establishments that aren't much better and can cost the same for just the entree. While it's not worth going out of your way for the food (though here we admit that well-prepared Old School is better than careless nouvelle any day), perhaps it is worth it for the whole package.

In the Four Queens hotel, 202 Fremont St. (at Casino Center Blvd.). ✆ **702/385-4011.** Reservations required. Main courses $26–$42. AE, DC, DISC, MC, V. Daily 5:30–11pm.

Downtown Dining

RESTAURANTS
Andre's **8**
Carson Street Café **2**
El Sombrero Cafe **9**
Hugo's Cellar **5**
Ice House Lounge **7**
Jillian's **4**
Limericks **6**
Second Street Grill **3**
Triple 7 Brew Pub **1**

BUFFETS
Fremont Paradise
   Buffet **3**
Golden Nugget
   Buffet **2**
Main Street Station
   Garden Court **1**

EXPENSIVE

Limericks ✵ STEAK/SEAFOOD   Decorated in the classic Olde English gentlemen's club style, Limericks is meant to be an oasis of gracious dining away from hectic casino life, and the overall effect is comforting and moderately womblike, particularly in the cozy booths at the back. Unfortunately, casino "ca-chings" still creep in, but it's not overly bothersome. The menu is classic, upscale steakhouse: beef, chops, some lobster, and chicken. The portions are Vegas-size (the small prime rib was 14 oz.), so bring an appetite (and a love of red meat), or take your leftovers back to the room to feed the kids for a couple of days. The filet mignon was tender enough to cut with a fork, and the lamb chops came with a pecan-mustard glaze. Patrons who don't eat red meat might want to try the apricot chicken. Appetizers are mostly seafood, though there is a fine-sounding baked brie with strawberry preserves. "Chef's choice" desserts change nightly, and the wine list is both good and extensive.

In Fitzgeralds Casino Holiday Inn, 301 Fremont St. (at 3rd St.). ✆ **702/388-2400.** Reservations recommended. Main courses $18–$40. AE, DISC, MC, V. Thurs–Mon 5–11pm.

Second Street Grill ✵ ⟨Finds⟩ INTERNATIONAL/PACIFIC RIM   Actually, that description above notwithstanding, they call themselves "Continental American with Euro and Asian influences." And, yes, that translates to a bit of a muddle, culinary-wise, but the portions are extremely generous (a relief in this era of dainty food), and it's hard to resist a place that plants two long potato chips in a pile of mashed potatoes, thereby creating a bunny rabbit. You are probably best off with grill dishes (various steaks and other cuts of meat), though here might be your best ratio of quality to price for lobster tail. Play around with the Hunan pork and beef lettuce wrap appetizers, and the Peking duck and shrimp tacos—don't wince, the shell was a won ton wrapper. The waist-conscious will be very pleased with the bamboo-steamed snapper in a nice broth, while others may want to try the grilled salmon with goat cheese Parmesan crust. Desserts are disappointing, unfortunately. Overall, a nice place for a family event dinner Downtown, and certainly more affordable than fancy places on the Strip.

In the Fremont Hotel & Casino, 200 E. Fremont St. © 702/385-3232. Reservations recommended. Main courses $17–$28. AE, DC, DISC, MC, V. Sun–Mon and Thurs 6–10pm; Fri–Sat 6–11pm.

INEXPENSIVE

Carson Street Cafe AMERICAN   Here's a slightly better-than-adequate hotel coffee shop, though it's a mixed bag in terms of quality of food. Sandwiches are better than ribs, burgers, and fries, all of which are merely just filling. On the other hand, the linguine with shrimp is surprisingly good, while desserts, especially pecan pie a la mode, more than earn their rep.

In the Golden Nugget, 129 E. Fremont St. (between 1st St. and Casino Center Blvd.). © 702/385-7111. Reservations not accepted. Main courses $6–$15. AE, DC, DISC, MC, V. Daily 24 hr.

El Sombrero Cafe ⋆⋆ MEXICAN   This kind of hole-in-the-wall Mexican joint can be found all over California but not always so readily elsewhere. It's also the kind of family-run (since 1950) place increasingly forced out of Vegas by giant hotel conglomerates, making it even more worth your time (it's becoming harder and harder, particularly in Downtown, to find budget options that serve food that is more than just mere fuel). Mexican-food fans, in particular, should seek out this friendly place, though it's not in an attractive part of town. Portions are generous, better than average, and unexpectedly spicy. They also cater to special requests—changing the beef burrito to a chicken one (an option that comes highly recommended), for example, without batting an eyelash. The enchilada and taco combo also won raves.

807 S. Main St. © 702/382-9234. Everything under $10. AE, MC, V. Mon–Sat 11am–9pm.

Ice House Lounge ⋆ DINER   A Downtown revitalization has been threatened probably ever since attention swung from that original center of Vegas to the constant boom that is the Strip. This eatery, part nightclub/bar, part diner, believes it's still possible, which is why the owners set up shop in a particularly grungy industrial part of the city. Don't let the dismal surroundings put you off; inside is a lively, popular modern-appearing club, with a menu full of, if not inspired, certainly reliable and well-priced menu options. The late-night hours also make this a good choice for those located near Downtown. Lunch, in particular, is a bargain, as vinyl-record-size plates are loaded with towering sandwiches or wide-reaching flatbread-style pizzas, mounds of coleslaw, or piles of crinkly fries. We like the plate of three miniburgers. None of it is thrillingly spiced or especially cleverly crafted, but it's all solidly good and, given the portions, eminently shareable. The bar borrows the "ice bar" concept from Red Square, while the walls feature historical photos from Vegas history and of the actual icehouse that once stood on the site.

650 S. Main St. (corner of Bonneville). © 702/315-2570. www.icehouselounge.com. Everything under $15. AE, MC, V. Mon–Sat 8am–2am.

Jillian's ⨍ DINER   This is a branch of a national chain, and while the fare is strictly coffee shop, it's a good representative of same. Since it's well located at the foot of Fremont Street, in the Neonopolis complex, and is open late, it should be considered for both hungry night owls and families on a budget (especially those with hungry and/or picky teens, since the large menu has something for just about everyone, except maybe those watching their diet). You will find the usual playful concept chain food starters—Buffalo wings, mozzarella sticks, plus a more clever spinach and artichoke dip with chips—and then everything from multi-burger styles (the barbecue-bacon burger oozed cheese and was piled with bacon and onion rings) to steak and seafood combos, pizzas, and some unexpected New Orleans–influenced entrees like jambalaya and even crawfish. Portions are enormous, so you can split items and save even more money, and everything is what you might expect in terms of quality—not transcendent, but solidly good. Atmosphere is lively, if not outright noisy (think T.G.I. Friday's).

450 Fremont St. (at Las Vegas Blvd. S., in the Neonopolis complex). ✆ 702/759-0450. www.jillianslasvegas.com. Main courses all under $15. AE, MC, V. Sun–Thurs 11am–1am; Fri–Sat 11am–3am.

8 Buffets & Sunday Brunches

Lavish, low-priced buffets are a Las Vegas tradition, designed to lure you to the gaming tables and to make you feel that you got such a bargain for your meal that you can afford to drop more money. They're gimmicks, and we love them. Something about filling up on too much prime rib and shrimp just says "Vegas" to us.

Unfortunately, like so much else that was Vegas tradition, the buffets are evolving. The higher-end ones no longer put out great heaping mounds o' stuff, which is probably for the best in terms of waste but is a departure from decadence that we are loathe to see go. More to the point, prices have been steadily creeping upward; the higher-end buffets are no longer a true bargain because it's unlikely you can (or should) eat enough to make you feel like you really got away with something. With the more expensive buffets, some of which have pretty good food, consider it this way: You would pay much more, per person, at one of the fancier restaurants in town, and you would be stuck ordering just one, potentially disappointing, item. Consider the higher-end recommended buffet as an alternative to a nice meal at a traditional restaurant. More variety per person means more options, less likelihood for disappointment. (Hate what you picked? Dump your plate and start all over, no financial penalty.) Not nearly as atmospheric as a proper restaurant, but then again, how else can you combine good barbecue with excellent Chinese and a cupcake or 10 on the side?

There is a lot of variety within the buffet genre. Some are just perfunctory steam-table displays and salad bars that are heavy on the iceberg lettuce, while others are unbelievably opulent spreads with caviar and free-flowing champagne. Some are quite beautifully presented as well. Some of the food is awful, some of it is decent, and some of it is memorable.

No trip to Las Vegas is complete without trying one or two buffets. Of the dozens, the most noteworthy are described below. Bear in mind that, appearance and layout aside, almost all buffets have some things in common. Unless otherwise noted, every one listed below will have a carving station, a salad bar (quality differs), and hot main courses and side dishes. We will try to point out only the more notable and original elements at the various buffets.

Also, at press time, Sahara and Stratosphere had completely remodeled their buffets. While new reviews were not to be had in time for this edition, neither was a particular standout buffet, and the new decor probably won't change that.

Note: Buffet meals are extremely popular, and reservations are usually not taken (we've indicated when they are accepted, and in all those cases, they are highly recommended). Arrive early (before opening) or late to avoid a long line, especially on weekends.

SOUTH STRIP
EXPENSIVE

Spice Market Buffet ⟨ BUFFET   A particularly good buffet, if not perhaps quite good enough to justify the price (though the range of food is large enough to please just about anyone). Come for lunch, as a more affordable compromise, and you can take advantage of the better-than-average salads (they had one with white balsamic vinegar on our last visit that was quite good), plus an especially notable Mexican station, Middle Eastern specialties, and other fun goodies.

In the Aladdin, 3667 Las Vegas Blvd. S. ⓒ **702/785-9005.** Breakfast $3; lunch $16; dinner $24; champagne brunch $21. AE, DC, DISC, MC, V. Mon–Fri 8–10:30am, 11am–2:30pm, and 4–9:30pm; Sat–Sun brunch 8:30am–2:30pm and dinner 4–9:30pm.

MODERATE

Mandalay Bay's Bay Side Buffet ⟨ BUFFET   This is a particularly pretty, not overly large buffet. Actual windows, floor to ceiling, no less, overlooking the beach part of the elaborate pool area, make it less stuffy and eliminate that closed-in feeling that so many of the other buffets in town have. The buffet itself is adequately arranged but features nothing particularly special, though there are some nice cold salads, hearty meats, and a larger and better-than-average dessert bar (they make their own desserts, and it shows).

3950 Las Vegas Blvd. S. ⓒ **702/632-7402.** Breakfast $13; lunch $16; dinner $23; Sun brunch $23. AE, DC, DISC, MC, V. Daily 7am–10pm.

Tropicana Island Buffet ⟨ BUFFET   This buffet is served in a large and delightful dining room, lushly decorated with tropical flowers and foliage. There are coral-reef aquariums at the entrance, and the appealing interior keeps to the island theme. Big semicircular booths backed by mirrored walls are separated by bead curtains, and, on the lower level, floor-to-ceiling windows overlook the Trop's stunning palm-fringed pool. Dinners here feature an extensive salad bar and peel-and-eat shrimp.

3801 Las Vegas Blvd. S. ⓒ **702/739-2222.** Breakfast $10; lunch $12; dinner $16; weekend champagne brunch $16. AE, DC, DISC, MC, V. Breakfast Mon–Fri 7:30–11am; lunch Mon–Fri 11am–1:30pm; brunch Sat–Sun 7:30am–2:30pm; dinner daily 4–10pm.

INEXPENSIVE

Excalibur's Round Table Buffet ⟨ BUFFET   This one strikes the perfect balance of cheap prices, forgettable decor (dang it, they don't have the full-on King Arthur theme going anymore), and adequate food. It's what you want in a cheap Vegas buffet—except it's just not that cheap anymore. Then again, none of them is anymore, so this still qualifies and, thus, usually has long lines.

3850 Las Vegas Blvd. S. ⓒ **702/597-7777.** Breakfast $10; lunch $11; dinner $15; Sun champagne brunch $13. AE, DC, DISC, MC, V. Sun–Thurs 6:30am–10pm; Fri–Sat 6:30am–11pm.

Luxor's Pharaoh's Pheast Buffet ★★ BUFFET Located on the lower level, where the Luxor showroom used to be, this huge buffet looks like it was set in the middle of an archaeological dig, complete with wood braces holding up the ceiling, pot shards, papyrus, and servers dressed in khaki-dig outfits. It's a unique and fun decor—be sure to avoid tripping on the mummies and their sarcophagi sticking half up out of the ground. The food is the best in its price range, and one of the top buffets in town. There's a Mexican station with some genuinely spicy food, a Chinese stir-fry station, and different Italian pastas. Desserts were disappointing, though they do offer a pretty large selection of diabetic-friendly options. A beer-and-wine cart makes the rounds. The quality-to-price ratio is no secret, and, as a result, the lines are always enormous.

3900 Las Vegas Blvd. S. (✆) **702/262-4000.** Breakfast $11; lunch $11; dinner $17. AE, DC, DISC, MC, V. Daily 6:30am–11pm.

MGM Grand Buffet ★ BUFFET This rather average buffet does feature a fresh Belgian waffle station at breakfast. Dinner also has an all-you-can-eat shrimp and prime rib option. Also available: low-fat, sugar-free desserts! And at all meals, you get a full pot of coffee on your table.

3799 Las Vegas Blvd. S. (✆) **702/891-7777.** Breakfast $12; lunch $15; Mon–Thurs dinner $22; Fri–Sat dinner $25; brunch $17. Reduced prices for children under 10, free for children under 4. AE, DC, DISC, MC, V. Mon–Thurs 7am–10pm; Fri 7am–10:30pm; Sat–Sun 10am–2:30pm and 4:30–10:30pm.

Monte Carlo Buffet ★ BUFFET A "courtyard" under a painted sky, the Monte Carlo's buffet room has a Moroccan market theme, with murals of Arab scenes, Moorish archways, Oriental carpets, and walls hung with photographs of and artifacts from Morocco. Dinner includes a rotisserie (for chicken and pork loin, or London broil), a Chinese food station, a taco/fajita bar, a baked potato bar, numerous salads, and more than a dozen desserts, plus frozen yogurt and ice-cream machines. Lunches are similar. At breakfast, the expected fare is supplemented by an omelet station, and choices include crepes, blintzes, and corned-beef hash. Fresh-baked New York–style bagels are a plus.

3770 Las Vegas Blvd. S. (✆) **702/730-7777.** Breakfast $11; lunch $12; dinner $17; Sun brunch $18 (all include tax). AE, DC, DISC, MC, V. Daily 7am–10pm.

MID-STRIP
VERY EXPENSIVE

Bally's Sterling Sunday Brunch ★★ BUFFET Now, the admittedly high cost of this brunch seems antithetical to the original purpose of a buffet, which was a lot of food for minimal money. However, if you're a dedicated buffet fan, this is probably a better spree than one of the many new high-priced restaurants. It works out to less money in the long run, and you will get, for your purposes, more bang for your buck. It's a fancy deal—linen and silver-bedecked tables, waiters to assist you, if you choose—and while the variety of food isn't as massive as at regular buffets, the quality is much higher in terms of both content and execution. We're talking unlimited champagne, broiled lobster, caviar, sushi, and rotating dishes of the day (items such as monkfish with pomegranate essence, tenderloin wrapped in porcini mushroom mousse, and even ostrich). No French toast that's been sitting out for days here! Perfect for a wedding breakfast or business brunch or just a big treat; stay a long time and eat as much as you can.

3645 Las Vegas Blvd. S. ℭ **702/967-7999.** Reservations recommended. Brunch $58. AE, DC, MC, V. Sun 9:30am–2:30pm.

Bellagio Buffet ☞☞ BUFFET   Though the priest of the buffets, the Bellagio still gets high marks from visitors. The array of food is fabulous, with one ethnic cuisine after another (Japanese, Chinese that includes unexpected buffet fare like dim sum, build-it-yourself Mexican items, and so on). There are elaborate pastas and semi-traditional Italian-style pizza from a wood-fired oven. The cold fish appetizers at each end of the line are not to be missed—scallops, smoked salmon, crab claws, shrimp, oysters, and assorted condiments. Other specialties include breast of duck and game hens. There is no carving station, but you can get the meat precarved. The salad bar is more ordinary, though prepared salads have some fine surprises, such as the eggplant-tofu salad and an exceptional Chinese chicken salad. Desserts, unfortunately, look better than they actually are.

3600 Las Vegas Blvd. S. ℭ **877/234-6358.** Breakfast $14; lunch $18; dinner Mon–Fri $26; dinner Sat–Sun $34; Sat–Sun brunch $28. AE, DC, DISC, MC, V. Breakfast Mon–Fri 8–10:30am; lunch Mon–Fri 11am–3:30pm; dinner Mon–Thurs 4–10pm, Fri–Sat 4–11pm, Sun 4:30–10pm; brunch Sat–Sun 8am–4pm.

Wynn Las Vegas Buffet ☞☞☞ BUFFET   Goodness, we do love a nice buffet, and this brand spanking new one is particularly nice, more thoughtful and artful than the average, starting with the *Alice in Wonderland*–evoking atrium styled with towers of fruit flowers and foliage and even some natural light. Don't worry if you don't score one of the few tables set there; it's a bit far from the food lines—you want to be close to the action, after all. And once there, you may get the impression that instead of the usual bunch of often gloppy dishes, someone's thinking about items not just with flavor, but that can sit for periods of time better than the usual buffet suspects, or that translate better to large-quantity preparation. Don't just take our word for it; on a visit not many weeks after it opened, we chatted with one regular buffet diner who said he had already sworn off all other buffets in favor of loyal devotion to Wynn. Look for items like jerk chicken, beef rending, wood-fired pizza, honey-glazed pork, nice little salmon rolls, five kinds of ceviche, sweet Kansas City–style barbecue, and tandoori chicken among the stations, which include Mexican, Southern, seafood, and Italian. Best of all, desserts are superior to probably all the other buffets, in construction and in taste, giving the impression that a pastry chef is active on the premises. Don't miss the mini floating islands, the unusual tiramisu, the excellent chocolate mousse and ice creams, and even a plate full of madelines.

In Wynn Las Vegas. ℭ **702/770-3340.** Breakfast $15; lunch $20; dinner $28; Sat–Sun brunch $30. AE, DC, DISC, MC, V. Breakfast Mon–Fri 8am–10:30am; lunch Mon–Fri 11:30am–3:30pm; dinner Sun–Thurs 4pm–10pm, Fri–Sat 4:30pm–10:30pm; brunch Sat–Sun 8:30am–3:30pm.

EXPENSIVE

Paris, Le Village Buffet ☞☞☞ BUFFET   One of the more ambitious buffets, with a price hike to match—still, you do get, even at the higher-priced dinner, a fine assortment of food and more value for the dollar than you are likely to find anywhere else (unless it's another buffet).

Plus, the Paris buffet is housed in the most pleasing room of the buffet bunch. It's a Disneyland-esque two-thirds replica of your classic French village clichés; it's either a charming respite from Vegas lights or it's sickening, depending on your tolerance level for such things. Buffet stations are grouped according to French regions, and though in theory entrees change daily, there do seem to be some constants, including most of the following dishes: In Brittany, you'll find things like made-to-order crepes, surprisingly good roasted duck with green peppercorn and peaches, and steamed mussels with butter and shallots. In Normandy, there's quiche and some dry bay scallops with honey cider. The carving station shows up in Burgundy but distinguishes itself by adding options of chateaubriand sauce and cherry sauce Escoffier. Lamb stew is a possibility for Alsace, while Provence has pasta to order and a solidly good braised beef. The salad station isn't strong on flavors, but the veggies are fresh, and there is even some domestic (darn it) cheese.

You can skip the dessert station in favor of heading back to Brittany for some made-to-order crepes, but you might want to try the bananas Foster.

3665 Las Vegas Blvd. S. © 888/266-5687. Breakfast $13; lunch $18; dinner $25; Sun brunch $25. AE, DC, DISC, MC, V. Sun–Thurs 7am–10pm; Fri–Sat 7am–11pm.

Rio's Carnival World Buffet 🕅🕅 BUFFET   This buffet has long been voted by locals as the best in Vegas. Qualitywise, after a makeover, it's probably as good as ever, and maybe even better. Decorwise, it's better still, since the overhaul was devoted mostly to improving the dining areas. Overall, this is simply more mainstream; an upscale food court, with "South American" cooked-to-order stir-fries, Mexican taco fixings and accompaniments, Chinese fare, a Japanese sushi bar and teppanyaki grill, a Brazilian mixed grill, Italian pasta and antipasto, and fish and chips. There's even a diner setup for hot dogs, burgers, fries, and milkshakes. (Make your own milkshakes—is there a happier concept anywhere?) All this is in addition to the usual offerings of most Las Vegas buffets. Best of all, a brand-new dessert station, featuring at least 70 kinds of pies, cakes, and pastries from an award-winning pastry chef.

3700 W. Flamingo Rd. © 702/252-7777. Breakfast $13 lunch $15; dinner $13; Sat–Sun champagne brunch $23. AE, DC, MC, V. Mon–Fri 7am–10pm; Sat–Sun 7:30am–10pm.

MODERATE

Bally's Big Kitchen Buffet *Overrated* BUFFET   Buffet buffs give the breakfast and brunch offered here a thumbs down, feeling that while there is quite a variety of food on display, breakfast features some fairly cheap stuff, and brunch has only a single item—a pretty decent prime rib—worth mentioning. Dinner fares somewhat better (it could be seafood casserole in a creamy dill sauce, baked red snapper, pork chops sautéed in Cajun spices, barbecued chicken, or broiled steak in peppercorn sauce), but overall, this is a disappointing choice for the Strip.

3645 Las Vegas Blvd. S. © 702/739-4111. Brunch $13; dinner $19. AE, DC, MC, V. Daily 7am–2pm and 4–10pm.

Harrah's Fresh Market Buffet 🕅 BUFFET   The theme here is farmers market, which means lots of big sculptures of fresh fruits and vegetables, if not actual fresh fruits and vegetables. It follows the new trend of various food stations, as opposed to one long buffet. You'll find seafood, pasta, Mexican, Asian, and American specialties ranging from meatloaf to Cajun entrees. Above-average food combined with an extremely friendly staff make this one of the better buffet choices.

3475 Las Vegas Blvd. S. © 702/369-5000. Breakfast $11; lunch $13; dinner $17; Sat–Sun champagne brunch $17. AE, DC, DISC, MC, V. Daily 7am–10pm.

Mirage Cravings Buffet 🕅🕅 BUFFET   Aesthetically, an incredible transformation from classic Vegas buffet (read: blah) style to a gleaming, streamlined look, all shining steel and up-to-the-minute high-design concept shades of green, blue, and red. A striking buffet space, instantly making all the others look tired and sad. But. It's not entirely cafeteria style, not just in layout, but in presentation. Gone are the heaping mounds of shrimp and other symbols of Vegas excess and bargain. In its place are plenty of live-action stations, but minimal offerings, just a scant few in the (admittedly inclusive) categories. This probably helps with both customer and provider waste, but if you are used to matters the other way, it does feel mingy. Seniors won't like the poor signage; kids may get tired long before completing the lengthy circuit. No worries: The line starts with excellent pizza. Look for pot stickers and Chinese barbecue pork, quite good barbecue, tangy Japanese cuke salad, slightly dry but flavorful Mexican slow-roasted pork. A trip to the made-to-order salad station is so pokey you need to find the other salads hidden with the open-faced sandwiches (where you can also find the gefilte fish). The desserts are generally disappointing.

3400 Las Vegas Blvd. S. ✆ 702/791-7111. Breakfast $13; lunch $18; dinner $21; Sat–Sun brunch $21. Reduced prices for children ages 5–10, free for children under 5. AE, DC, DISC, MC, V. Daily 7am–10pm.

Treasure Island Dishes Buffet ⋆⋆ BUFFET   Another gorgeous buffet makeover, now easily the handsomest buffet space in town, sort of contemporary diner, all dark gleaming wood, mirrors, and geometric lines. We feel mixed on the food choices; this is a smaller buffet than one might expect for such a big hotel, and while there is a reasonable range of cuisines (Italian; Japanese, with sushi chefs who will make up fresh plates just for you; Southern, including unexpected spoon bread; deli), there isn't the overwhelming bounty we've come, rightly or wrongly, to consider our right when it comes to Vegas buffets. Having said that, there are some well-considered and fine-tasting deli sandwiches (brie and honey, roast beef with goat cheese), plus better-than-decent barbecue ribs (at the carving station) and Chinese options. Best of all, some of the most charming dessert choices, focusing on such childhood tastes as (now-so-trendy) cupcakes, fresh cotton candy, quite good crème brûlée (yes, not exactly real kiddie fare, but, let's face, it's just exceptionally good vanilla custard!) and best of all, adorable minidonuts, fresh out of the fryer. We ate two dozen and we are not ashamed. Lunch is reasonably priced enough that it would be a good choice just for a light selection of savories and serious gorging on dessert.

3300 Las Vegas Blvd. S. ✆ 702/894-7111. Breakfast $12; lunch $15; dinner Sun–Thurs $20, Fri–Sat $26. AE, DC, DISC, MC, V. Daily 7am–10:30pm.

INEXPENSIVE

Flamingo Paradise Garden Buffet ⋆ BUFFET   The buffet here occupies a vast room, with floor-to-ceiling windows overlooking a verdant tropical landscape of cascading waterfalls and koi ponds. The interior, formerly one of the most pleasant in Las Vegas, is clean and tidy but showing some wear. At dinner, there is an extensive international food station (which changes monthly) presenting French, Chinese, Mexican, German, or Italian specialties. A large salad bar, fresh fruits, pastas, vegetables, potato dishes, and a vast dessert display round out the offerings. Lunch is similar, featuring a mix of international cuisines as well as a stir-fry station and a soup/salad/pasta bar. At breakfast, you'll find all the expected fare, including a made-to-order omelet station and fresh-baked breads. The seafood is dry and tough, and desserts uninspired. Drinks are unlimited, of course, but are served in small glasses, so expect to call your server for many refills.

3555 Las Vegas Blvd. S. ✆ 702/733-3111. Mon–Fri brunch $11; Sat–Sun champagne brunch $13; dinner $16. Prices may be higher on holidays. AE, DC, DISC, MC, V. Brunch daily 7:30am–2:30pm; dinner daily 4:30–10pm.

Palms Festival Market Buffet ⋆⋆ *Finds* BUFFET   As a rule, you are better off fulfilling your buffet desires (unless you demand the cheapest of prices) at one of the newer hotels, and The Palms's entry in the buffet sweepstakes bears this adage out. Not only does it look rather swell, but since the owners of the hotel are from a Middle Eastern background, that translates into some fresher concepts at the stations, most notably an emphasis on Middle Eastern fare such as gyros with warm pita bread, hummus, baba ghanouj, and kabobs of every variety. Plus, there's a huge Chinese station complete with dumplings, a Mongolian barbecue section (where they toss all your chosen ingredients in one stir-fry vat), some "Jewish" foods (knishes and kugel), an ambitious carving station with ribs and pastrami, and desserts that, as usual, aren't much of anything. And actually, all this comes for close-to-classic-buffet budget prices—while still supplying food that can be described as better than "merely edible."

4321 W. Flamingo Rd. ✆ 702/942-7777. Breakfast $6; lunch $7; dinner $12; Sun brunch $13.99. AE, DC, DISC, MC, V. Daily 8am–10pm.

NORTH STRIP
INEXPENSIVE
Circus Circus Buffet BUFFET   Here's a tradeoff: It's just about the cheapest buffet on the Strip but also what some consider the worst buffet food in town. Here you'll find 50 items of typical cafeteria fare, and none of them is all that good. Kids love it; some adults find it inedible. If food is strictly fuel for you, you can't go wrong here. Otherwise, trundle off to another buffet.

2880 Las Vegas Blvd. S. ✆ 702/734-0410. Breakfast $7; lunch $8; Sat–Sun brunch $8; dinner $10. AE, DC, DISC, MC, V. Mon–Fri 7am–2pm breakfast/lunch; Sat–Sun 7am–4pm brunch; dinner daily 4:30–10pm.

EAST OF THE STRIP
MODERATE
The Buffet at the Las Vegas Hilton ✿ BUFFET   A surprisingly stylish-looking room, with the usual suspects (salad bar, bagel bar, desserts) and a good selection of Chinese food (including Peking duck). The fare is fresh and delicious, with special mention going to the prime rib and the outstanding cream puffs and superior rice pudding (it's hard to find good desserts at Vegas buffets).

3000 Paradise Rd. ✆ 702/732-5111. Breakfast $10; lunch $11; dinner $5; Sat–Sun brunch $14 (includes unlimited champagne). Half-price for children age 12 and under. DC, DISC, MC, V. Mon–Fri 7am–2:30pm and 5–10pm; Sat–Sun 8am–2:30pm and 5–10pm.

INEXPENSIVE
Sam's Town Firelight Buffet ✿ BUFFET   This former buffet is back with a new name and a new, nicer room, with actual natural lighting and a big wall of flames— hence firelight, plus lighting that changes throughout the day according to mood requirements, and a view of the water and laser-light show in the atrium of the hotel (kind of alfresco dining, in a Vegas artificial way). The buffet now has international stations (Chinese, Mexican), a bar, and a dessert station with hand-scooped ice cream. The food is fine—for a buffet, anyway.

5111 Boulder Hwy. ✆ 702/456-7777. Lunch $8; Sat–Sun brunch $10; theme dinner nights (seafood, barbecue, and so forth) $11–$18. Discount prices for children 4–8, free for children under 4. AE, DC, DISC, MC, V. Mon–Fri 11am–3pm and 4–9pm; Sat–Sun 10am–3pm and 4–9pm.

DOWNTOWN
MODERATE
Golden Nugget Buffet ✿✿ BUFFET   This buffet has often been voted number one in Las Vegas, and it shows how Downtown is one of the last holdouts for bargains;

anywhere else in town, this quality of buffet would be at least $2 to $3 more per meal. Most of the seating is in plush booths. The buffet tables are laden with an extensive salad bar (about 50 items), fresh fruit, and marvelous desserts. Fresh seafood is featured every night. Most lavish is the all-day Sunday champagne brunch, which adds such dishes as eggs Benedict, blintzes, pancakes, creamed herring, and smoked fish with bagels and cream cheese.

129 E. Fremont St. 𝒞 702/385-7111. Breakfast $7; lunch $8; dinner $13–$17; Sun brunch $14. AE, DC, DISC, MC, V. Mon–Sat 7am–3pm and 4–10pm; Sun 7am–10pm.

INEXPENSIVE

Fremont Paradise Buffet 𝔎 BUFFET   Another buffet that makes us cross about rising Vegas prices; this was (at dinnertime) one of the cheapest buffets we could recommend, but now? Not so much. Lunchtime still brings a price that, in these days of increased inflation, is a bargain, and that's probably when you should go. The selection isn't extensive (though with some surprises in the form of a "Southwestern" station and some Chinese), but the space is adequately attractive. Because it's one of the last of the cheapie holdouts, you can expect longer lines.

200 E. Fremont St. 𝒞 702/385-3232. Breakfast $6; lunch $6; dinner $10; Sun brunch $10; various "theme" (steak or seafood) nights $10–$16. AE, DC, DISC, MC, V. Mon–Fri 7–10:30am, 11am–3pm, and 4–10pm; Sat–Sun 7am–3pm and 4–10pm.

Main Street Station Garden Court 𝔎𝔎𝔎 *Finds* BUFFET   Set in what is truly one of the prettiest buffet spaces in town (and certainly in Downtown), with very high ceilings and tall windows bringing in much-needed natural light, the Main Street Station Garden Court buffet is one of the best in town, let alone Downtown. It features nine live-action stations (meaning you can watch your food being prepared), including a wood-fired, brick-oven pizza (delicious); many fresh salsas at the Mexican station; a barbecue rotisserie; fresh sausage at the carving station; Chinese, Hawaiian, and Southern specialties (soul food and the like); and so many more we lost count. On Friday night they have all this plus nearly infinite varieties of seafood, all the way up to lobster. We ate ourselves into a stupor and didn't regret it.

200 N. Main St. 𝒞 702/387-1896. Breakfast $6; lunch $8; dinner $11–$16; Sat–Sun champagne brunch $10. Free for children 3 and under. AE, DC, DISC, MC, V. Daily 7–10:30am, 11am–3pm, and 4–10pm.

What to See & Do in Las Vegas

You aren't going to lack for things to do in Las Vegas. More than likely you've come here for the gambling, which should keep you pretty busy (we say that with some understatement). But you can't sit at a slot machine forever. (Or maybe you can.) In any event, it shouldn't be too hard to find ways to fill your time between poker hands.

Just walking on the Strip and gazing at the gaudy, garish, absurd wonder of it all can occupy quite a lot of time. This is the number-one activity we recommend in Vegas; at night, it is a mind-boggling sight. And, of course, there are shows and plenty of other nighttime entertainment. But if you need something else to do beyond resting up at your hotel's pool, or if you are trying to amuse yourself while the rest of your party gambles away, this chapter will guide you.

Don't forget to check out the **free hotel attractions,** such as Bellagio's water-fountain ballet, The Mirage's volcano and white-tiger exhibit, and the masquerade show at the Rio. Oh, yeah, and the utter piece of hooey that replaced the pirate show at TI at the Mirage. (The pirates now battle scantily clad women. Except it's even worse than that.) You can probably give that a miss.

You could also consider using a spa at a major hotel; they seem too pricey (as high as $25 a day) to fill in for your daily gym visit if you are just going to use a few machines, but spending a couple of hours working out, sweating out Vegas toxins in the steam room, and generally pampering yourself will leave you feeling relaxed, refreshed, and ready to go all night again.

There are also plenty of out-of-town sightseeing options, like **Hoover Dam** (a major tourist destination), **Red Rock Canyon,** and nexus-of-all-conspiracy-theories **Area 51,** along with excursions to the Grand Canyon. We've listed the best of these in chapter 11.

SUGGESTED ITINERARIES
The itineraries outlined here are for adults. If you're traveling with kids, incorporate some of the suggestions from "Especially for Kids," listed later in this chapter. The activities mentioned briefly here are described more fully later in this chapter.

If You Have 1 Day
Spend most of the day **casino-hopping.** These are buildings like no other (thank goodness). Each grandiose interior tops the last. You'll want to see Wynn Las Vegas, the newest thing going, but also be sure to see The Venetian, Bellagio, The Mirage (including the white tigers), TI at the Mirage (aka Treasure Island), Paris, Caesars Palace (including the Forum Shops and the talking statues), New York–New York, MGM Grand, Luxor, and Excalibur. Then at night, take a drive (if you can) down **the Strip.** As amazing as all this is during the day, you just can't believe it at night. Aside from just the Strip itself, there are Bellagio's **water fountains,** which "perform" to various musical numbers, the dreadful (and even

Going Vegas

If you're looking for a quintessential Las Vegas experience, try these suggestions from James P. Reza, Geoff Carter, and the editors of *Scope* magazine (now the *Las Vegas Weekly*).

- **Peppermill's Fireside Lounge** (p. 289). This lounge is so evocative of the Me Decade, it's impossible not to love it. Dark, cozy, sexy, and somewhat kitschy, it's a great place for romantic encounters. Try to sit by the year-round fire pit, if you can stand the heat.

- **GameWorks,** 3785 Las Vegas Blvd. S. (© **702/432-4263**). This multilevel entertainment center gives visitors a chance to wreak digitized havoc on the latest video-game creations. A few brave souls try the 75-foot climbing wall; most just hang in the lounge and shoot pool.

- **Cheetah's** (p. 297). How could you possibly visit Sin City and not sample the ubiquitous lap dance? Couples are welcome at Cheetah's, the site of Paul Verhoven's laughably overdone film *Showgirls.* More quality, less silicone, and a VIP lounge that has hosted lap dances for Wilt Chamberlain, Sting, and Drew Barrymore.

- **The Forum Shops at Caesars Palace** (p. 257). The most unique shopping experience in the world. Take Rodeo Drive, marry it to Rome, douse the whole thing in Spielberg, and you're still nowhere near this elegant retail space.

- **The Sky Lounge at the Polo Towers** (p. 290). Hidden on the 19th floor of a timeshare condominium complex, this lounge offers a far more engaging view than the Stratosphere Tower, absolutely free of charge. Watch out for kamikaze tour groups.

- **The Hard Rock Hotel & Casino** (p. 116). Everything about this hotel/casino—the bars, The Joint showroom, Mr. Lucky's 24/7—manages to evoke classic Vegas, a city that was built for young hipsters, not fanny pack–wielding families.

- **Love Shack** (check local listings for various locations). Our vote for Sin City's best lounge act. Covering the music of the '70s and '80s with tenacious fervor, Love Shack is nothing short of a funky riot in 6-inch heels and mascara.

- **Red Rock Canyon** (p. 311). Providing needed respite from the neon jungle, Red Rock is as beautiful as the desert gets. This haven for hikers and rock climbers gets a bit overrun at times, but it is still worth the trip. *Note:* Don't feed the wild burros. Unlike the entertainers at Cheetah's, they bite.

though it's free, still not worth the money) Sexy Sirens vs. **pirate battle** at Treasure Island at the Mirage, and the **volcano explosion** next door at The Mirage. Eat at a buffet (see chapter 6 for details and options) and have a drink at the top of the Stratosphere, goggling at the view from the tallest building west of the Mississippi. Oh, and maybe you should gamble a little, too.

If You Have 2 Days

Do more of the above since you may not have covered it all. Then do something really Vegasy and visit the **Liberace Museum.** The **Dolphin Habitat** at The Mirage is also worth a look, in that it's unexpectedly not Las Vegas. At night, take in a show. We think *KA, O,* and *Mystère,* the productions from the avant-garde **Cirque du Soleil,** are the finest in Vegas, but there are plenty to choose from. Though buffets are still the most Vegas-appropriate food experience, genuine haute cuisine by celebrity chefs has invaded the town and you should take advantage of it. **Fleur de Lys, Bouchon,** and **Picasso** are our top choices, but you can't go wrong with **Alex, Alizé,** or **Aureole,** plus there are branches of Onda, Olives, Circo, Pinot, and the Border Grill. Be sure to leave some time to go Downtown to check out the much more affordable casinos in the classic Glitter Gulch and to visit the **Fremont Street Experience** light show.

If You Have 3 Days

By now you've spent 2 days gambling and gawking. So take a break and drive out to **Red Rock Canyon.** The panoramic 13-mile Scenic Loop Drive is best seen early in the morning when there's little traffic. If you're so inclined, spend some time hiking here. If you want to spend the whole day out, have lunch at nearby **Bonnie Springs Ranch.** After lunch, enjoy a guided trail ride into the desert wilderness or enjoy the silliness at **Old Nevada** (see chapter 11 for details).

If You Have 4 Days or More

Plan a tour to **Hoover Dam.** Leave early in the morning, returning to Las Vegas after lunch via **Valley of Fire State Park,** stopping at the **Lost City Museum** in Overton en route (see chapter 11 for details). Alternatively, you can rest up by spending the day by the hotel pool or going to the hotel spa. At night, presumably refreshed and toxins purged, hit the casinos and/or catch another show. If you aren't tired of magic, **Lance Burton** is a wonderful show for a reasonable price, or there is the arty weirdness of the **Blue Man Group** at The Venetian, or *Jubilee!* if your trip won't be complete without a topless revue. You can also feast at dinner, since you certainly haven't tried all there is. There is some great work being done by restaurants not associated with brand-name chefs, like Rosemary's, Alizé, and Andre's.

As you plan any additional days, consider excursions to other nearby attractions such as **Lake Mead,** the **Grand Canyon,** or even **Area 51.** Inquire about interesting tours at your hotel sightseeing/tour desk.

1 The Top Attractions

See also the listings for theme parks and other fun stuff in section 4, "Especially for Kids."

The Arts Factory *Finds* Believe it or not, Las Vegas has a burgeoning art scene (what some would consider soul-crushing is what others consider inspirational), and this complex, located in the Gateway district, is the place to find proof. It features a few galleries and a number of work spaces for local artists. Several of the spaces are closed to the public. On the first Friday of each month, they have a party event (unimaginatively named "First Friday") showcasing local artists and arts-oriented businesses, with live music, street performances, and other entertainment and activities. Visit their website for further details.

101–107 E. Charleston Blvd. *C* **702/676-1111.** www.theartsfactory.com. Mon–Tues and Thurs–Fri noon–5pm and by appointment.

The Atomic Testing Museum *★★★ (Finds)* From 1951 until 1992, the Nevada Test Site was this country's primary location for testing nuclear weapons. Aboveground blasts in the early days were visible to the tourists and residents of Las Vegas, a mere 65 miles away. This well-executed museum, library, and gallery space offers visitors a fascinating glance at the test site from ancient days through modern times with memorabilia, displays, official documents, videos, interactive displays, motion-simulator theaters (like sitting in a bunker watching a blast), and emotional testimony from the people who worked there. It respectfully treads that tricky line between honoring the work done at the site and understanding its terrible implications. Not to be missed, even if it's only because of the Albert Einstein action figure in the gift shop. Seriously.

755 E. Flamingo Rd. *C* **702/794-5151.** www.ntshf.org. $10 adults; $7 seniors, military, and students with ID; free for children under 6. Mon–Sat 9am–5pm; Sun 1pm–5pm.

Auto Collections at Imperial Palace *★★* Even if you're not a car person, don't assume you won't be interested in this premier collection of antique, classic, and special-interest vehicles. Check out the graceful lines and handsome sculpture of one of the many Model J Duesenbergs (one of which Elvis Presley drove in the movie *Spinout*). The craftsmanship and attention to detail make these cars, and others here, true works of art.

Note that the vehicles on display change regularly, so there's no telling what you may see when you visit. However, the last time we were here we saw a great deal of history. Down President's Row we saw JFK's 1962 "bubbletop" Lincoln Continental, Lyndon Johnson's 1964 Cadillac, Eisenhower's 1952 Chrysler Imperial 20-foot-long parade car, Truman's 1950 Lincoln Cosmopolitan with gold-plated interior, FDR's unrestored 1936 V-16 Cadillac, and Herbert Hoover's 1929 Cadillac. There's also a 1964 Chaika that belonged to Soviet leader Nikita Krushchev.

Commercial vehicles of bygone days include antique buses, military transports, taxis (among them, the 1908 French model that appeared in the movie version of *My Fair Lady*), gasoline trucks, fire engines, delivery trucks and vans, dump trucks, and pickup trucks. Other highlights are the 1959 Cadillac Fleetwood Special 60 driven by Marilyn Monroe in *The Misfits,* Al Capone's 1930 V-16 Cadillac, a 1954 Mercedes-Benz 220 Cabriolet currently owned by Wayne Newton, the 1967 Ford Mustang Fastback driven by Nicolas Cage in *Gone in 60 Seconds,* Howard Hughes's 1954 Chrysler (because of his phobia about germs, Hughes installed a special air-purification system that cost more than the car itself!), and a 1933 Pierce-Arrow Silver Arrow, one of only three still in existence today.

In the Imperial Palace hotel, 3535 Las Vegas Blvd. S. *C* **702/794-3174.** www.autocollections.com. Admission $6.95 adults, $3 seniors and children under 12, free for children under 3. Check website for free-admission coupon. Daily 9:30am–9:30pm.

Bellagio Art Gallery *★* Everyone—ourselves not nearly least among them—scoffed when then-Bellagio owner Steve Wynn opened an art gallery on his fabulous property. Sure, Wynn's been a serious and respected fine-art collector for years, and consequently there was good stuff on display (though there are no masterpieces, there certainly are serious works by masters), but who would go see *art* in Las Vegas? Tons of tourists, as it happens, so many that they had to almost immediately relocate the gallery to a larger space.

Las Vegas Attractions

Washington Ave.
1 (8 miles)
2 3
Washington Ave.
Bonanza Rd.
93
4 (3 miles)
95
15
Bonanza Rd.
Bruce St.
Eastern Ave.
To Reno &
Mt. Charleston
Central Pkwy
Fremont St.
Experience
515
95
93
Ogden Ave.
Fremont St.
5
To Hoover Dam →
Alta Dr.
599
Bonneville
Las Vegas Blvd.
Martin L. King Blvd.
Main St.
Casino Center Blvd.
Grand
DOWNTOWN
Charleston Blvd.
To Red Rock Canyon →
Charleston Blvd.
6
**GATEWAY
DISTRICT**
7
Oakey Blvd.
Oakey Blvd.
St. Louis Ave.
15
Main St. (The Strip)
8
Sahara Ave.
Sahara Ave.
Sahara Ave.
Rancho Dr.
9 Sahara
604
Karen Ave.
Circus
Circus Dr.
LV Hilton
Riviera
Blvd.
11
Joe W. Brown Dr.
10
Las Vegas
Country Club
Maryland Pkwy.
12
**NORTH
STRIP**
Stardust Rd.
Convention
Center Dr.
Desert Inn Rd.
**Las Vegas
Convention
Center**
LV Convention
Center
13 →
Industrial Rd.
14 **Fashion
Show
Mall**
15
Sands Ave.
Paradise Rd.
**Boulevard
Mall**
Twain Ave.
**MID-
STRIP**
16 **Sands
Expo**
17
Harrah's/ Imperial Palace
18
Flamingo/Caesars Palace
605
Flamingo Rd.
Swenson Ave.
Flamingo Rd.
Maryland Pkwy.
Las Vegas Blvd. (The Strip)
19
Bally's & Paris
20
Frank Sinatra Dr.
**Hard Rock
Hotel & Casino**
Koval Ln.
Harmon Ave.
**UNIVERSITY
OF NEVADA,
LAS VEGAS**
25
Paradise Rd.
21
22 **MGM
Grand**
Tropicana
Ave.
Reno Ave.
**SOUTH
STRIP**
15
23
Mandalay
Bay Rd.
24
**McCarran
International
Airport**
605
To Henderson ↓
Tropicana Ave.
26 To Hoover Dam →

Adventuredome **11**
The Arts Factory **6**
Auto Collections
  at Imperial Palace **18**
Bellagio Art Gallery **19**
Eiffel Tower Tour **20**
Elvis-A-Rama **14**
Fremont Street Experience **5**
Gambler's Museum
  & Gift Shop **5**
GameWorks **21**
Guggenheim/Hermitage
  Museum **16**
King Tut's Tomb & Museum **23**
Las Vegas Mini Grand Prix **4**
Las Vegas Motor Speedway **1**
Las Vegas National Golf Club **13**
Las Vegas Natural History
  Museum **3**
Liberace Museum **26**
Lied Discovery
  Children's Museum **2**
Little White Chapel **7**
Luxor IMAX Theater/*Ridefilm* **23**
Madame Tussaud's
  Celebrity Encounter **16**
Marjorie Barrick Museum **25**
MGM Grand Lion Habitat **22**
Neonpolis **5**
Scandia Family Fun Center **12**
Secret Garden of Siegfried & Roy
  and Mirage Dolphin Habitat **17**
Shark Reef at Mandalay Bay **24**
Speed the Ride/Las Vegas
  Cyber Speedway **9**
Star Trek: The Experience **10**
Stratosphere Tower Thrill Rides **8**
Wynn Collection of Fine Art **15**
Wynn Conservatory **15**
Wynn Lake of Dreams **15**

········· Monorail
▪ Sahara Monorail
station

0   0.5 mi
0   0.5 km

When the MGM MIRAGE company bought Wynn's empire, the future of the gallery, which did rely on his collection (he took most of it with him), was in doubt. Surprise again, you scoffers (and that again includes us). The gallery is not only open again, it's getting written up by real art critics, thanks in part to such well-chosen shows as an exhibit from the collection of none other than Steve Martin—yes, we mean the stand-up-comedian-turned-actor-turned-playwright/author. See, he's a longtime well-respected collector, too, and, consequently, there were real-life reviewers, hushed with happy reverence, who took the whole show most seriously indeed.

Now, will there be as interesting a show when you go? Beats us. (When we wrote this, it was an acclaimed exhibit of European masterpieces—silver, gold, jewelry, furniture, and rare books on loan from England's famous Chatsworth manor.) Then there's that ticket price. Do let us point out that the Louvre and the Vatican art collections—both of which are, needless to say, quite a bit larger and both of which, one can safely say, do have some notable works—cost around $9.

In Bellagio, 3600 Las Vegas Blvd. S. (*) **702/693-7871.** www.bgfa.biz. Reservations suggested, but walk-ins taken every 15 min. Admission $15 adults; $12 seniors, students with ID, and Nevada residents. Daily 9am–9pm.

Eiffel Tower Tour *(Overrated)*   Whether this is worth the dough depends on how much you like views. An elevator operator (we refuse to call them guides) delivers a few facts about this Eiffel Tower (this is a half-size exact replica, down to the paint color of the original) during the minute or so ride to the uppermost platform, where you are welcome to stand around and look out for as long as you want, which probably isn't 2 hours, the length of the average movie, which also costs $9. Nice view, though.

In Paris Las Vegas, 3655 Las Vegas Blvd. S. (*) **702/946-7000.** Admission Mon–Thurs $9 adults, $7 seniors over 65 and children 6–12, free for children under 5; Fri–Sun $12 adults, $10 seniors over 65 and children 6–12. Daily 10am–1am, weather permitting.

Elvis-A-Rama *(★)*   Three million dollars' worth of Elvis memorabilia—we thought surely this place would give our beloved Liberace museum a run for its top spot in our camp-lovin' hearts. But alas, while this is a must for the Elvis faithful (and, admittedly, they are legion) looking to view holy relics, it's not the place for a novice to start.

The amount of cool stuff is amazing: Elvis ephemera ranging from his social security card (a $14,000 auction purchase) to his "little black book" (entries not divulged, darn it!), his Army uniform, a love letter to his hometown girlfriend, fan-club souvenirs (Elvis lipstick!), and on and on it goes. But, unfortunately, these precious (and discarded) possessions are exhibited in cases that, as of this writing, are lacking much-needed labels and identification, so all too often you have no idea what you're looking at, much less its significance. The displays also fail to give you a good overview of the King's life; the museum assumes you already know the highlights (Momma's boy, the Colonel, 'Scilla), and it's hardly complete. Despite our morbid hopes for prescription-pill bottles, there was nary a mention of Dr. Nick nor even The Death. There is, however, a whole case displaying what amounts to the contents of Vernon Presley's

---

(Fun Fact) **When Downtown Ruled**

Fremont Street was the hub of Las Vegas for almost 4 decades before the first casino hotel, El Rancho, opened on the Strip in 1941.

wallet. It's also all a little too straight-faced and reverent, though the gift shop makes up for it a bit. And they do have various Elvis impersonator shows, ranging in price from around $15 to $20. All in all, best for fans thinking, "You know, I really *should* brush up on my Elvis-iania." A while ago, the museum was hit by the kind of thieves we thought were found only in *Ocean's Eleven*. They made off with a number of items, including Elvis's high school class ring, valued at around $250,000. But they totally missed the coolest prize of all: a pair of the King's own blue suede shoes. Suckers.

3401 Industrial Rd. © **702/309-7200.** www.elvisarama.com. Admission $9.95 adults; $7.95 seniors, students with ID, and Nevada residents; free for kids under 12. Daily 10am–7pm. Call for free shuttle bus.

Fremont Street Experience 🌟🌟 Poor Downtown. For years now, it's been overlooked in favor of the Strip. And no wonder; it's so . . . small . . . by comparison. Even its once dazzling collection of hotel marquee lights seems like candles next to the klieg-light voltage of the Strip. Even a $70-million revitalization project hasn't helped give it back its mojo. That's too bad; things are cheaper down here, people, and speaking of people, if you get tired of feeling not pretty or rich enough for the Strip, you are not alone. Come join us in admiring the project that closed off the heart of "Glitter Gulch" and turned it into a much more user-friendly pedestrian mall. The Fremont Street Experience is a 5-block open-air landscaped strip of outdoor snack shops, vendor carts, and colorful kiosks purveying food and merchandise. Overhead is a 90-foot-high steel-mesh "celestial vault"; at night, it is the newly revamped **Viva Vision,** a high-tech light-and-laser show (the canopy is equipped with more than 12.5 million lights) enhanced by a concert-hall-quality sound system that takes place four times nightly. But there's music between shows as well. Not only does the canopy provide shade, it cools the area through a misting system in summer and warms you with radiant heaters in winter. It's really cool, in that Vegas over-the-top way that we love so much. Go see for yourself; you will be pleased to see how a one-time ghost town of tacky, rapidly aging buildings, in an area with more undesirables than not, is now a bustling (at least at night), friendly, safe place (they have private security guards who hustle said undesirables away). It's a place where you can stroll, eat, or even dance to the music under the lights. The crowd it attracts is more upscale than in years past, and, of course, it's a lot less crowded than the hectic Strip. Some rightly mourn the passing of cruising Glitter Gulch, gawking at the original lights. It does indeed mean the end of classic Las Vegas, but on the other hand, classic Las Vegas was dead and nearly buried anyway. This has given a second life to a deserving neighborhood.

And in a further effort to retain as much of classic Las Vegas as possible, the **Neon Museum** is installing vintage hotel and casino signs along the promenade. The first installation is the horse and rider from the old Hacienda, which presently rides the sky over the intersection of Fremont Street and Las Vegas Boulevard. Eventually, the Neon Museum hopes to have an indoor installation a couple of blocks from the Fremont Street Experience to showcase some of the smaller signs they have collected. It's uncertain when it will open, but in the meantime, the Neon Graveyard is there and it's amusing to see the (unlit, of course) old signs languishing away until they once again are lit up in their glittery glory.

Fremont St. (between Main St. and Las Vegas Blvd.), Downtown. www.vegasexperience.com. Free admission. Shows nightly every hour on the hour after dark.

GameWorks 🌟🌟 What do you get when Steven Spielberg and his DreamWorks team get in on the arcade video-game action? Grown-up state-of-the-art fun. High-tech

---

Tips **Insider Info**

A good place to view the Sky Parade light show is from the balcony at Fitzgeralds Hotel & Casino.

---

movie magic has taken over all sorts of traditional arcade games and turned them interactive, from a virtual-reality batting cage to a *Jurassic Park* game that lets you hunt dinosaurs. There are motion-simulator rides galore and even actual-motion activities like rock climbing. But classic games, from Pac-Man to pool tables, are here, too, though sometimes with surprising twists, such as air hockey where multiple pucks occasionally shoot out at once.

All this doesn't exactly come cheap. There are two routes to pricing. First is the standard version, where $15 gets you $15 in game play, $20 gets you $25, $25 gets you $35, or $35 gets you $50. Alternatively, you can purchase a block of time ($20 for 1 hr., $25 for 2 hr., $30 for 3 hr.; or if you get there at opening or closing, you get 2 hr. for $20), which goes on a debit card that you then insert into the various machines to activate them. But you do get value for your money, which makes this a viable alternative to casinos, particularly if you have children (though it's clearly geared toward a college-age-and-older demographic). Children probably should be 10 years old and up—any younger and parents will need to stand over them rather than go off and have considerable fun on their own. *Note:* If you don't like crowds, come here earlier rather than later, when it can get packed. They also have a dress code (no excessively baggy clothes, no tattoos or clothing with profanity, no chains, and so on) that they enforce occasionally, and no one under 18 is allowed without parental supervision after 9pm.

In the Showcase Mall, 3785 Las Vegas Blvd. S. © **702/432-GAME.** www.gameworks.com. See game prices listed above in the review. Sun–Thurs 10am–midnight; Fri–Sat 10am–1am. Hours may vary.

Guggenheim/Hermitage Museum ✦✦ When two branches of the famous Guggenheim opened in Vegas, it was seen as a sure sign that Vegas was on its way to, or at least had an actual chance of, becoming a real city with real culture, and not just a glittery tourist trap. No one has said much now that the first branch, the one built for special exhibits, closed after just one show. The second branch, perhaps ultimately better reviewed and regarded, remains in operation, so maybe there is hope yet for Vegas's cultural significance. That museum, the Guggenheim/Hermitage, is the first co-venture between the Guggenheim and the State Hermitage Museum in St. Petersburg. The State Hermitage in St. Petersburg has one of the finest encyclopedic collections in the world, but few have had a chance to experience any of it. The exhibit at press time was geared around ancient Egypt—still a bit light on the Hermitage collection, so we do rather hope that future exhibits feature more of those masterworks rarely, if ever, seen outside of Russia. After all, pricewise, too, we note again that both the Louvre and the Vatican come considerably cheaper (well, once you pay to fly there) and offer quite a bit more.

In The Venetian, 3355 Las Vegas Blvd. S. © **866/484-4849.** www.guggenheimlasvegas.org. $20 adults, $17 seniors and Nevada residents, $15 students with ID and children 6–12, free for children under 6. Daily 9:30am–8:30pm.

King Tut's Tomb & Museum ✦ This full-scale reproduction of King Tutankhamen's tomb includes the antechamber, annex, burial chamber, and treasury housing replicas of the glittering inventory discovered by archaeologists Howard

Carter and Lord Carnarvon in the Valley of Kings at Luxor in 1922. It was all hand-crafted in Egypt by artisans using historically correct gold leaf and linens, pigments, tools, and ancient methods, and all items have been meticulously positioned accord-ing to Carter's records. It's hardly like seeing the real thing, but if you aren't going to Egypt anytime soon, perhaps checking out reproductions isn't a bad idea—and for a Vegas fake, it's surprisingly enjoyable. A 4-minute introductory film precedes a 15-minute audio tour (available in English, French, Spanish, and Japanese).

In Luxor Las Vegas, 3900 Las Vegas Blvd. S. ℂ 702/262-4000. Admission $5. Daily 9am-11pm.

Las Vegas Mini Grand Prix 🐾🐾 (Kids) Finally, after all our yammering about how Vegas isn't for families and how most of the remaining options are really overpriced tourist traps, we can wholeheartedly recommend an actual family-appropriate enter-tainment option. Part arcade, part go-kart racetrack, this is exactly what you want to help your kids (and maybe yourselves) work their ya-ya's out. The arcade is well stocked, with a better quality of prizes than one often finds, but we suggest not spend-ing too much time in there and instead hustling outside to the slide, the little roller coaster, and best of all, the four go-kart tracks. Each offers a different thrill, from the longest road track in Vegas, full of twists and turns as you try to outrace other drivers (be a sport, let the little kids win occasionally), to a high-banked oval built just so you can try to make other drivers take spills onto the grass, to, best of all, a timed course. The latter requires a driver's license, so it's for you rather than your kids (but the wee ones will find the fourth course is just for them), and here you can live out your Le Mans or Police Chase fantasies as you blast through twisting runs one kart at a time, trying to beat your personal best. A good kind of adrenaline rush, believe us. The staff is utterly friendly, and the pizzas at the food court are triple the size and half the price of those found in your hotel. The one drawback: It's far away from main Strip action—here's where you'll need that rental car, for sure. *Note:* Kids have to be at least 36 inches tall to ride any of the attractions.

1401 N. Rainbow Rd., just off U.S. 95 N. ℂ 702/259-7000. www.lvmgp.com. Ride tickets $5.50 each, $25 for 5. Sun–Thurs 10am–10pm; Fri–Sat 10am–11pm.

Las Vegas Motor Speedway 🐾🐾 This 107,000-seat facility was the first new super-speedway to be built in the Southwest in over 2 decades. A $100-million state-of-the-art motor-sports entertainment complex, it includes a 1½-mile super-speedway, a 2½-mile FIA-approved road course, paved and dirt short-track ovals, and a 4,000-foot drag strip. Also on the property are facilities for go-kart, Legends Car, Sand Drag, and Motocross competition. The new speedway is accessible via shuttle buses to and from the Imperial Palace hotel, though some of the other major hotels have their own shuttles to the speedway.

7000 Las Vegas Blvd. N., directly across from Nellis Air Force base (take I-15 north to Speedway exit 54). ℂ 702/ 644-4443 for ticket information. www.lvms.com. Tickets $10–$75 (higher prices for major events).

Liberace Museum 🐾🐾🐾 (Moments) Forget all that stuff we said before about the great museums of the world. You can keep your Louvres and Vaticans and Smithso-nians: *This* is a museum. Housed, like everything else in Vegas, in a strip mall, this is a shrine to the glory and excess that was the art project known as Liberace. You've got your costumes (bejeweled), your many cars (bejeweled), your many pianos (bejew-eled), and many jewels (also bejeweled). Also, the entrance itself is a giant jewel. It just shows what can be bought with lots of money and no taste.

The thing is, Liberace was in on the joke (we think). The people who come here largely aren't. Many of these guests would not have liked him living next door to them if his name was, say, Bruce Smith, but they idolize the-man-the-myth. Not found here is any reference to AIDS or chauffeurs who had plastic surgery to look more like him. But you will find a Czar Nicholas uniform with 22-karat-gold braiding and a blue-velvet cape styled after the coronation robes of King George V and covered with $60,000 worth of rare chinchilla. Not to mention a 50½-pound rhinestone costing $50,000, the world's largest, presented to him by the grateful (we bet they were) Austrian firm that supplied all his costume stones.

The museum is now better than ever, thanks to a costly renovation that turned what was once a too-low-key exhibition (especially given the subject matter) into something much more gaudy and over-the-top—and, better still, properly enshrined. Expect a ridiculously outrageous entrance (three words: giant pink piano) into rooms with various exhibits that finally give detailed attention to facts and figures. Admission has been cranked up, probably to pay for the renovations, but we don't mind—this is a one-of-a-kind place. Unless you have a severely underdeveloped appreciation for camp or take your museum-going very seriously, you shouldn't miss it. The museum is 2½ miles east of the Strip on your right.

1775 E. Tropicana Ave. (at Spencer St.). © 702/798-5595. www.liberace.org. Admission $13 adults, $8.50 seniors over 64 and students, free for children under 10. Mon–Sat 10am–5pm; Sun noon–4pm. Closed Thanksgiving, Dec 25, and Jan 1.

Lost Vegas Gambler's Museum and Shop 🛝

From the same folks who brought you the late, lamented Casino Legends Hall of Fame, it's a smaller version that is only half the size of the gift shop that it accompanies. There are as many as 5,000 pieces of memorabilia associated with casino hotels of a bygone era, but those items include little gewgaws like matchbooks, a variety of old gaming chips, and even toenail clippers. Still, the videos of hotel implosions and the last days of Bugsy Siegel (the owner is particularly proud of his Siegel collection) are fun, and so is browsing among souvenirs of yesteryear—some of which are for sale in the gift shop, though we would check eBay before buying anything here, as some of the same items can be found there for less. (We found a Vegas-themed board game online for about a quarter of what it was going for at the store.)

450 Fremont St. (in Neonopolis). © 702385-1883. Admission $2.50, $1.25 seniors. Daily 10am–9pm.

Luxor IMAX Theater/IMAX Ridefilm 🛝 *Kids*

This is a state-of-the-art theater that offers both motion-simulator films and IMAX projects, some in standard two dimensions and one in 3-D. The glasses for the latter are really cool headsets (though they're a little too heavy for comfort) that include built-in speakers, bringing certain sounds right into your head. The movies change periodically but always include some extraordinary special effects. If you have a fear of heights, be sure to ask for a seat on one of the lower levels.

The IMAX Ridefilm is a motion-simulator ride with several different themed "adventures" playing at different times. You may find yourself hunting for an ancient relic in a pyramid or running from the ghoulies in Dracula's castle, among other amusements.

In Luxor Las Vegas, 3900 Las Vegas Blvd. S. © 702/262-4000. Admission $8.95 and up (prices vary depending on the movie); $6.50–7.50 for IMAX Ridefilm. Can be purchased as part of an all-attractions package for $25. Sun–Thurs 9am–11pm; Fri–Sat 9am–midnight. IMAX showtimes vary depending on the length of the film.

Madame Tussaud's Celebrity Encounter *(R)* *(Kids)*   Madame Tussaud's waxworks exhibition has been the top London attraction for nearly 2 centuries, so even if you aren't a fan of wax museums, this, its sole branch west of the Mississippi, is probably worth a stop—if you can stomach the price. Figures here are state-of-the-art, painstakingly constructed to perfectly match the original person. (Truth be told, though some are nearly identical to their living counterparts—Brad Pitt gave us a start—others look about as much like the celebrity in question as a department-store mannequin.) There's no Chamber of Horrors, but the exhibit makes up for it, since all the waxworks are free-standing, allowing, and indeed encouraging, guests to get up close and personal. (Go ahead, lay your cheek next to Elvis's or Sinatra's and have your photo taken. You know you want to.) The emphasis here is on film, television, music, and sports celebrities, plus some Vegas icons, who are housed in five themed rooms ("Sports Arena," for example). There's also a behind-the-scenes look at the lengthy process involved in creating just one of these figures.

3355 Las Vegas Blvd. S. (*C*) 702/862-7800. www.madametussaudslv.com. Admission $21 adults, $15 seniors and Nevada residents, $9.95 children 6–12, free for children 5 and under. Daily 10am–10pm, but hours vary seasonally.

Marjorie Barrick Museum *(R)*   Formerly known as the Natural History Museum (as opposed to the existing Las Vegas Natural History Museum, and now you can see why they changed the name), here's a cool place to beat the heat and noise of Vegas while examining some attractive, if not overly imaginative, displays on Native American crafts and Las Vegas history. Crafts include 19th-century Mexican religious folk art, a variety of colorful dance masks of Mexico, and Native American pottery. The first part of the hall is often the highlight, with impressive traveling art exhibits. Children won't find much that's entertaining other than some glass cases containing examples of local, usually poisonous reptiles (who, if you are lucky—or unlucky, depending on your view—will be dining on mice when you drop by). Outside is a pretty garden demonstrating how attractive desert-appropriate plants (in other words, those requiring little water) can be. You just wish the local casinos, with their lush and wasteful lawns, would take notice.

On the UNLV campus, 4505 Maryland Pkwy. (*C*) 702/895-3381. http://hrcweb.nevada.edu/museum. Free admission. Mon–Fri 8am–4:45pm; Sat 10am–2pm.

MGM Grand Lion Habitat *(R)(R)* *(Kids)*   Hit this attraction at the right time and it's one of the best freebies in town. It's a large, multilevel glass enclosure in which various lions frolic during various times of day. In addition to regular viewing spots, you can walk through a glass tunnel and get a worm's-eye view of the underside of a lion (provided one is in position); note how very big Kitty's paws are. Multiple lions share show duties (about 6 hr. on and then 2 days off at a ranch for some free-range activity, so they're never cooped up here for long). So you could see any combo—from one giant male to a pack of five females who have grown from cub to near adult size during their MGM time. Each comes with a trainer or three, who are there to keep the lions busy with play so they don't act like the big cats they are and sleep the whole time. But obviously, photo ops are more likely to occur as the more frisky younger set tussles, so what you observe is definitely going to depend on who is in residence when you drop by. (And, of course, actually seeing anything depends on how many other people think this is a two-star attraction; hordes of tourists are often pressed against the glass, preventing you, not to mention your kids, from doing the same.)

In the MGM Grand, 3799 Las Vegas Blvd. S. (*C*) 702/891-7777. Free admission. Daily 11am–10pm.

Free Vegas

Vegas used to be the land of freebies—or at least, stuff so cheap it seemed free. Those days are an increasingly dim memory, but many hotels still offer free attractions designed to lure you, the unsuspecting visitor, into their casinos, where you might well then drop far more than the cost of a day ticket to Disney World. Do not give them the satisfaction. Or do, whatever, it's your money. Meanwhile, here's a handy list of the best of the free bait, er, sights:

Bellagio Conservatory (in the Bellagio Hotel) 🐸🐸🐸. A totally preposterous idea, a larger-than-life greenhouse atrium, filled with seasonal living foliage in riotous colors and styles, changed every 6 weeks or so. From Easter to Chinese New Year, events are celebrated with carefully designed splashes of flowers, plants, and remarkable decorations—it's an incredible amount of labor for absolutely no immediate financial payoff. No wonder it's one of the most popular sights in Vegas. Open 24 hours.

Bellagio Fountains (outside the Bellagio Hotel) 🐸🐸🐸. Giant spouts of water shoot up and down and sideways, and basically dance their little aquatic hearts out, to pieces carefully choreographed to tunes ranging from show to Chopin. We tell people about this, they roll their eyes when they think we aren't looking, then they go see it for themselves . . . and end up staying for several numbers. Daily every half-hour starting early afternoon, then every 15 minutes 7pm to midnight. Closed when it's windy.

Forum Shops Fountain Shows (in the Forum Shops at Caesars) 🐸. The first of the free shows, and easily the stupidest. We love it, in theory at least, as giant "marble" Greco-Roman statues come to creaky animatronic life and deliver a largely unintelligible speech, mostly exhorting the crowds to eat, drink, and get so merry they will think nothing of dropping a bundle on the slots. Not quite so bad it's good, but one day they are going to wise up and make the thing more high tech, and a little something special will be lost. Daily every hour, starting at 10am.

Masquerade Show in the Sky (in the Rio) 🐸🐸. Think those Skyway buckets from Disneyland turned into carnival-themed floats, and you've got the basic idea of this overhead parade. Mardi Gras-by-way-of-Rio costumed extras toss beads to the cheering crowd, which probably isn't noticing how creepy cool the floating floats really are. Daily 3:30, 4:30, 5:30, 7, 8, 9, and 10pm.

Mirage Volcano (outside The Mirage) 🐸. The first curbside free attraction, and one of the reasons Wynn made it so you can't see his new mountain and lake show from the street (see below)—because that doesn't bring guests *into* the property—this remains a thrilling disappointment. It spouts flames but no lava—that's simulated by water and colored light. One show and you, too, will say "Nice try, but big whoop." Every 15 minutes after dark until midnight.

Mirage White Tigers (inside The Mirage) 🐸. Not to be confused with the Secret Garden of Siegfried and Roy, this is one, sometimes two, white tigers on display in a distressingly small glassed-in enclosure. Don't worry; the big cats rarely spend more than an hour or 2 on duty before they get to go to bigger, better places. So just enjoy a free glimpse and hope it's a cool day, and the cats might be doing something more interesting than snoozing. Open 24 hours, but cats may not be on display when you go.

Sirens of TI (outside Treasure Island at the Mirage) 🎭. We gave it the star because it has such high production values, but man, it hurt us to do even that. See, this used to be a fun, hokey stunt show, where pirates attacked a British sailing vessel. Lusty men swashed and buckled, cannons exploded, ships sank, the pirates always won. But Vegas is—repeat after us, please—*not for families anymore,* and to prove it, the British were removed (first India, now this) and now the pirates are lured by singing and dancing lingerie-clad lovelies more suited to the Victoria's Secret catalogue than Homer. Stuff happens, but no one really cares; either you like the nekkid chicks or you are so horrified by the whole spectacle because it's so appallingly bad that plot twists don't matter much. Parents, be warned: Between the gals and their undies, and the 24-foot stark raving naked female figurehead on the ship right by the Strip entrance to Treasure Island, you may be in for an interesting conversation with your children. Daily at 6pm, 8pm, and 10pm, weather permitting.

Wynn Conservatory (in the Wynn Las Vegas) 🎭. Yes, remarkably like the one at Bellagio, only we have to admit this one is better placed, situated just inside the door, and laid out so that one can stroll through it on one's way to other parts of the hotel, as opposed to the tucked-in-a-corner Bellagio version. The floral displays will change regularly, though they may reflect the striking floral mosaics on the floor below. We do hope it won't get as wacky as its Bellagio counterpart and will stick to the merely festive. Open 24 hours.

Wynn Lake of Dreams (in the Wynn Las Vegas) 🎭. The most peculiar of the "free" shows in several ways: It's not easily defined (not dancing fountains, not a parade in the sky), and it's not easily seen. The 150-foot-tall mountain, complete with mature trees saved from the old Desert Inn golf course, plus several waterfalls, cannot be seen in its entirety from anywhere other than hotel rooms facing west. The show itself can be watched only if you are dining in the Daniel Boulud Brasserie or SW Steakhouse, the Parasol or Chanel bars, or a small viewing platform set above those venues on the casino level. Nab a coveted spot there or else pay double (or more) digits to dine or drink while waiting for the shows. Should you bother? Maybe. Basically, twice an hour, the lake lights up with pretty colors, cued to tunes ranging from classical to Louis Armstrong for "interludes." At the top of the hour are bigger extravaganzas of weird hologram erotic-psychedelic images projected on the wall waterfall, while shapes and puppets pop out for even more wacky action, with some rather adult imagery at times. Not worth an overpriced drink unless you can nurse it all night, but the restaurants are good enough to try, so the shows are a bonus. Note that if you can't get a table outside, you do have to go there to see the shows properly. Shows are 7pm to midnight, at the top of hour, :20, and :40.

Neonopolis ⭐⭐ It's hard to get visitors Downtown, but if you are genuinely look-ing for activities that do not have to do with gambling, this $100-million open-air restaurant, shop, and entertainment complex (with an 11-screen movie theater) pro-vides at least some motivation. Located right at the Fremont Street Experience, where Fremont Street meets Las Vegas Boulevard South, it's basically a big open-air mall, but one that is powered by Jillian's, a national chain that specializes in creating little urban entertainment centers (they are behind the similar Metreon in San Francisco), with a state-of-the-art arcade (as well stocked, from air hockey to virtual-reality games, as we've ever seen), bowling alley, billiards, two bars, a nightclub, and a restaurant all in one tidy package. It's not a 24-hour joint, but the hours are long enough that nongam-blers can amuse themselves here while the gamblers in their party are doing their thing. The cafe has an extensive menu (from hamburgers to jambalaya), with most items in the $4-to-$10 range and as tasty as you could want from such a place. As much as we enjoy the concept of the place, it hasn't caught on with the general pub-lic, and as of this writing, most of the other storefronts are empty, pending a sale of the facility to new owners. Hopefully by the time you read this and get there, they will have found a way to make it live up to its potential.

450 Fremont St. (at Las Vegas Blvd.). © 702/678-5777. Sun–Thurs 11am–1am; Fri–Sat 11am–3am.

Secret Garden of Siegfried & Roy and Mirage Dolphin Habitat ⭐⭐⭐ (Kids)
Siegfried & Roy's famous white tigers recently became rather infamous when one of them either did what tigers all do, eventually, and attacked his beloved owner/trainer, or—depending on whether you buy this story—helped said beloved owner/trainer when the latter was having a medical emergency. Either way this story is played, it explains why this attraction is still up; no matter what, the tiger is not to blame. We hope this attraction, a gorgeous area behind the dolphin exhibit, stays put for a long time. Here, white lions, Bengal tigers, an Asian elephant, a panther, and a snow leop-ard join the white tigers (the culprit, Montecore, is not exhibited any longer). It's really just a glorified zoo featuring only the big-ticket animals; however, it is a very pretty place, with plenty of foliage and some bits of Indian- and Asian-themed archi-tecture. Zoo purists will be horrified at the smallish spaces the animals occupy, but all the animals are rotated between here and their more lavish digs at the illusionist team's home. What this does allow you to do is get very close up to a tiger, which is quite a thrill—those paws are massive indeed. Visitors are given little portable phonelike objects on which they can play a series of programs, listening to Roy and former Mirage owner Steve Wynn discuss conservation or the attributes of each animal, and deliver anecdotes.

The **Dolphin Habitat** ⭐⭐⭐ is more satisfying. It was designed to provide a healthy and nurturing environment and to educate the public about marine mammals and their role in the ecosystem. Specialists worldwide were consulted in creating the habitat, which was designed to serve as a model of a quality, man-made environment. The pool is more than eight times larger than government regulations require, and its 2.5 million gallons of man-made seawater are cycled and cleaned once every 2 hours. It must be working, as the adult dolphins here are breeding regularly. The Mirage dis-plays only dolphins already in captivity—no dolphins are taken from the wild. You can watch the dolphins frolic both above and below ground through viewing win-dows, in three different pools. (There is nothing quite like the kick you get from see-ing a baby dolphin play.) The knowledgeable staff, who surely have the best jobs in Vegas, will answer questions. If they aren't doing it already, ask them to play ball with

If I Could Talk to the Animals

Animal lovers will have a field day in Las Vegas, where a large variety of animals, including rare big cats, piranhas, penguins, flamingos, hammerhead sharks, and more are part of the attractions. Regional fauna are also well represented at local museums and zoos.

See the Feathered and Furry for Free!   Three times a day, Tiana Carroll and her avian friends delight all ages at the Tropicana, 3801 Las Vegas Blvd. S. (© **888/826-876** or 702/739-2222; www.tropicanalv.com). The big cats at the Lion Habitat at the MGM Grand, 3799 Las Vegas Blvd. S. (© **800/929-1111** or 702/891-7777; www.mgmgrand.com), sleep and frolic as you stroll through a clear tub. Look up, one might even be walking over your head. White tigers recline in their habitat at The Mirage, 3400 Las Vegas Blvd. S. (© **800/627-6667** or 702/791-7111; www.mirage.com). At The Flamingo, 3555 Las Vegas Blvd. S. (© **800/732-2111** or 702/733-3111; www.flamingolv. com), hundreds of birds, including the hotel's namesake, in addition to penguins, wander about on their own islands surrounding the pool area. All of these attractions are free.

Play with the Dolphins and Observe the Big Cats   At The Mirage, 3400 Las Vegas Blvd. S. (© **800/627-6667** or 702/791-7111; www.mirage.com), dolphins swim and frolic in a huge pool. The animals in the Secret Garden change regularly but can include black panthers, white tigers, snow leopards, and even an elephant. Admission is $12 for those over 10 years old and is free for those under 10.

Shark Reef   Along with watching sharks (including one of the world's only hammerheads in captivity), moray eels, and piranhas go about their fishy business, visitors to the Shark Reef at Mandalay Bay, 3950 Las Vegas Blvd. S. (© **877/632-7000** or 702/632-7000; www.mandalaybay.com), can participate in educational programs offered weekdays that include a 1-hour guided tour. Admission is $16 for adults, $10 for children 5 to 12; those under 4 are free. Open daily 10am to 11pm.

Meet the Locals   Check out the region's reptiles and other critters at the **Southern Nevada Zoological-Botanical Park,** 1775 N. Rancho Dr. (© **702/647-4685**), a old-fashioned zoo. Here you will find Midas and Maniac Girl, a pair of lions born in 1998, along with a family of rare Barbary apes and swamp wallabies, as well as coyotes and cougars. Admission is $7 for those over 12; admission for children 2 to 12 is $5, and children under 2 go free. It's open daily 9am to 5pm. Admission is free at the **Marjorie Barrick Museum,** at the University of Nevada, Las Vegas, 4505 Maryland Pkwy. (© **702/895-3381**), which has a collection of live local reptiles. The Wild Nevada Room at the funky **Las Vegas Museum of Natural History,** 900 Las Vegas Blvd. N. (© **702/384-3466**), displays a tableaux of different desert environments, complete with sights, sounds, and smells. It also has dioramas of taxidermied animals from around the world, a tank of live sharks, and animatronic dinosaurs. Admission is $6 for those over 18, $5 for children 11 to 18, and $2 for children 3 to 11; those under 3 get in for free.

the dolphins; they toss large beach balls into the pools, and the dolphins hit them out with their noses, leaping out of the water, cackling with dolphin glee. You catch the ball, getting nicely wet, and toss it back to them. If you have never played ball with a dolphin, shove that happy child next to you out of the way and go for it. There is also a video of a resident dolphin (Duchess) giving birth underwater; her fourth calf (30 lb. and 3 ft. long) was born just before Mother's Day in 2003. You can stay as long as you like, which might just be hours.

In The Mirage, 3400 Las Vegas Blvd. S. (C) 702/791-7111. Admission $12, free for children under 10 if accompanied by an adult. Mon–Fri 11am–5:30pm; Sat–Sun and major holidays 10am–5:30pm. Hours subject to change and vary by season.

Shark Reef at Mandalay Bay Ⓡ   Given that watching fish can lower your blood pressure, it's practically a public service for Mandalay Bay to provide this facility in a city where craps tables and other gaming areas can bring your excitement level to dangerous heights. Unfortunately, it's just a giant aquarium (though we admire the style—it's built to look like a sunken temple), which, hey, we like, but gee, not at these prices. (Though standing in the all-glass tunnel, surrounded by sharks and finny friends, was kinda cool.) Note also that it is *waaay* off in a remote part of Mandalay Bay, which might be a hassle for those with mobility problems.

In Mandalay Bay, 3950 Las Vegas Blvd. S. (C) 702/632-7000. Admission $16 adults, $9.95 children 5–12, free for children under 5. Daily 10am–11pm.

Speed: The Ride/Las Vegas Cyber Speedway ⓇⓇ   Auto racing is the fastest-growing spectator sport in America, so it's no surprise that these two attractions at the Sahara are a popular stop. The first is an 8-minute virtual-reality ride, **Cyber Speedway** ⓇⓇ, featuring a three-quarter-size replica of a NASCAR race car. Hop aboard for an animated, simulated ride—either the Las Vegas Motor Speedway or a race around the streets of Las Vegas (start with the Strip, with all the hotels flashing by, and then through the Forum Shops—whoops! There goes Versace!—and so forth). Press the gas and you lean back and feel the rush of speed; hit a bump and you go flying. Should your car get in a crash, off you go to a pit stop. At the end, a computer-generated report tells you your average speed, how many laps you made, how you did racing against the others next to you, and so forth. It's a pretty remarkable experience.

In a separate **3-D motion theater** Ⓡ, you'll don goggles to view a film that puts you right inside another race car for yet another stomach-churning ride (even more dizzying than the virtual-reality portion). Speed junkies and race-car buffs will be in heaven here, though those with tender stomachs should consider shopping at the well-stocked theme gift shop instead.

Speed: The Ride ⓇⓇ is a roller coaster that blasts riders out through a hole in the wall by the new NASCAR Cafe, then through a loop, under the sidewalk, through the hotel's marquee, and finally straight up a 250-foot tower. At the peak, you feel a moment of weightlessness, and then you do the whole thing backward! Not for the faint of heart.

In the Sahara hotel, 2535 Las Vegas Blvd. S. (C) 702/737-2111. $15 for 1 ride on each attraction, $20 for all-day pass that includes coaster. Stock-car simulator only $10 (you must be at least 48 in. tall to ride), Speed: The Ride (roller coaster) $10 for single ride, $20 for all-day pass that includes simulator. Mon–Thurs noon–9pm; Fri noon–10pm; Sat 11am–10pm; Sun 11am–9pm.

Star Trek: The Experience and Borg Invasion 4-D Ⓡ   It goes without saying that hard-core Trekkers (note use of correct term) will be delighted. On the other hand, normal, sensible fans and those who couldn't care less about *Star Trek* may find themselves saying, "I spent $35 and 2 hours in line for this?"

This is the undisputed champ in the Vegas motion-simulator ride category. You can't fault the setup and interior design; after a walk through a space-themed casino (check out those light-beam-activated slot machines!), your long wait in line will be somewhat entertaining, thanks to memorabilia (displayed as if this were the stuff of fact, not fiction) and TVs showing various *Trek* clips. As you make your way to the ride proper, you encounter actors dressed in *Trek* gear, who let you know that you've crossed the line into the *Trek* future.

There is a story line, but we won't spoil it for you. Suffice it to say it involves time travel and evil doings by the Borg, and if all doesn't work out, the very history of *Star Trek* could be affected. Do expect to be beamed aboard the *Enterprise* (that's really kind of cool), and know that if you have a sensitive stomach, you can skip the actual motion-simulator part, a wild and sometimes headache-inducing chase through space. The new *Borg Invasion 4-D* is a 3-D film starring several *Star Trek Voyager* cast members, and since it's "multimedia," there are more live actors, plus some surprises as the film plays (we don't want to give much away, but be prepared to have your anatomy unexpectedly poked). It is as well designed as the original portion and does give this attraction added value for the money. It will also send most Trekkers into orbit with happiness. In addition to the often-lengthy wait (on average, 20 min.; best shot at a slight lull would be noon–1pm on weekdays), the quality of your experience can vary depending on the quality of those *Trek*-garbed actors, whose line delivery can be awfully stilted. On the way out, through the shops selling everything *Trek*- and space-related (go ahead, get that Tribble you've always wanted), don't miss the TV showing a "news report" about some of the very things you just experienced.

In the Las Vegas Hilton, 3000 Paradise Rd. ℂ 888/GO-BOLDLY. www.startrekexp.com. Admission $35 for an all-day pass that includes both attractions and museum. Daily 11:30am–7:30pm or 9:30pm, depending on the season.

Stratosphere Thrill Rides 𝕽𝕽 (Kids)   Atop the 1,149-foot Stratosphere Tower are four marvelous thrill rides. The **High Roller** 𝕽𝕽 (the world's highest roller coaster) was recently revamped to go at even faster speeds as it zooms around a hilly track that is seemingly suspended in midair. Even more fun is the **Big Shot** 𝕽𝕽, a breathtaking free-fall ride that thrusts you 160 feet in the air along a 228-foot spire at the top of the tower, then plummets back down again. Sitting in an open car, you seem to be dangling in space over Las Vegas. We have one relative, a thrill-ride enthusiast, who said he never felt more scared than when he rode the Big Shot. After surviving, he promptly put his kids on it; they loved it. Amping up the terror factor is **X-Scream** 𝕽𝕽, a giant teeter-totter-style device that propels you in an open car off the side of the 100-story tower and lets you dangle there weightlessly before returning you to relative safety. And now they have the aptly named **Insanity: the Ride,** a spinning whirly-gig of a contraption that straps you into a seat and twirls you around 1,000 feet or so above terra firma. Insanity is right. *Note:* The rides are shut down in inclement weather and high winds.

Atop the Stratosphere Casino Hotel & Tower, 2000 Las Vegas Blvd. S. ℂ 702/380-7777. Admission: Big Shot $8; X-Scream $8; Insanity $8; High Roller $4; plus $9.95 to ascend the Tower (if you dine in the buffet room or Top of the World, there's no charge to go up to the Tower). Multiride and all-day packages also available for varying costs. Sun–Thurs 10am–midnight; Fri–Sat 10am–1am. Hours vary seasonally. Minimum height requirement for all rides is 48 in.

The Wynn Collection of Fine Art 𝕽𝕽   You know, we constantly grumble about how costly the museums on the Strip are, especially in relation to, say, the Louvre, which has a lot more than 15 pieces of art, about the total on display here. Then again, every guide to the Louvre reduces that impossibly vast collection to more or less the greatest hits—be sure to see this piece in this room, skip the rest to prevent art fatigue, that sort of thing. Now consider this: The entire Wynn Collection (which may rotate some, since it is indeed from Steve Wynn's own, but will be much like the following description) contains such all-stars as Rembrandt (*Self Portrait with Shadowed Eye*), Degas (*Dancer Taking a Bow*), van Gogh, Renoir, Monet, Matisse, Warhol (a triptych of Mr. Wynn Himself), and, best of all, not just the magnificent Picasso *Le Rêve* (which was the original name for the hotel), but a Vermeer, *Woman Seated at the Virginals*. Let us remind you that there are but 32 Vermeers extent, and so this tiny jewel is likely worth the admission alone. In other words, it is legitimate to think of this collection as a bigger one reduced to its natural highlights and, thus, unless you truly think more is more, worth the admission.

3131 S. Las Vegas Blvd. © 702/770-7000. Admission $15 adults, $6 children 6–12. Sun–Thurs 10am–11pm; Fri–Sat 10am–midnight.

2 Getting Married

This is one of the most popular things to do in Las Vegas. Just ask Britney. As she rather infamously revealed, it's very easy to get married here. Too easy. See that total stranger/"childhood friend" standing next to you? Grab him or her and head down to the **Clark Country Marriage License Bureau,** 200 S. 3rd St., at Briger Avenue (© **702/455-4415;** open Mon–Thurs 8am–midnight, Fri 8am–Sun midnight, and 24 hr. legal holidays), to get your license. Find a wedding chapel (not hard, as there are about 50 of them in town; they line the north end of the Strip, and most hotels have one) and tie the knot. Just like that. No blood test, no waiting period—heck, not even an awkward dating period. Though a potentially very awkward time explaining it afterward to your mother, your manager, and the press.

Even if you have actually known your intended for some time, Las Vegas is a great place to get married. The ease is the primary attraction, but there are a number of other appealing reasons. You can have any kind of wedding you want, from a big, traditional production number to a small, intimate affair; from a spur-of-the-moment "just-the-happy-couple-in-blue-jeans" kind of thing to an "Elvis-in-a-pink-Cadillac-at-a-drive-through-window" kind of thing. (Oh, yes. More on that later.) The wedding chapels take care of everything; usually they'll even provide a limo to take you to the license bureau and back. Most offer all the accessories, from rings to flowers to a videotaped record of the event.

We personally know several very happy couples who opted for the Vegas route. Motivations differed, with the ease factor heading the list (though the Vegas-ness of the whole thing came in a close second), but one and all reported having great fun. Really, is there a more romantic way to start off your life together than in gales of laughter?

In any event, the more than 100,000 couples who yearly take advantage of all this can't be wrong. If you want to follow in the footsteps of Elvis and Priscilla (at the first incarnation of the Aladdin Hotel), Michael Jordan, Joan Collins, Bruce Willis and Demi Moore, Dennis Rodman and Carmen Electra, and, of course, Britney and What's-His-Name, you'll want to peruse the following list of the most notable wedding chapels on or near the Strip. There are many more in town, and almost all the major hotels offer a chapel as well; though the latter are cleaner and less tacky than some of the Strip chapels, they do tend to be without any personality at all. (One exception might be the chapel at the Excalibur Hotel, where you can dress in medieval costumes, and the lovely chapel at Bellagio, which has personal wedding coordinators and a high level of customer service, holding only 8–10 weddings a day—seems like a lot, but it's nothing compared to the volume on the Strip.)

With regard to decor, there isn't a radical difference between the major places (hence, no star ratings here), though some are decidedly spiffier and less sad than others. Attitude certainly makes a difference with several and varies radically depending on who's working at any given time. Given how important your wedding is—or should be—we encourage you to give yourself time to comparison-shop and spurn anyone who doesn't seem eager enough for your business. (*Passing note:* Standing outside a wedding chapel for a couple of hours makes for interesting people-watching, as you see brides in full white gowns accompanied by a whole retinue, pregnant brides in ordinary dresses, or happy couples wearing sweats, all ready to march down that aisle.)

You can also call **Las Vegas Weddings and Rooms** (© 800/488-MATE), which offers one-stop shopping for wedding services. They'll find a chapel or outdoor garden that suits your taste (not to mention such only-in-Vegas venues as the former mansions of Elvis Presley and Liberace); book you into a hotel for the honeymoon; arrange the ceremony; and provide flowers, a photographer (or videographer), a wedding cake, a limo, car rental, music, champagne, balloons, and a garter for the bride. Basically, they can arrange anything you like. Theme weddings are a specialty. They even have a New Age minister on call who can perform a Native American ceremony. And yes, you can

---

(Fun Fact An Elvis Impersonator's Top 10 Reasons to Get Married in Las Vegas

Jesse Garon has appeared in numerous Las Vegas productions as "Young Elvis." He arrives at any special event in a 1955 pink, neon-lit Cadillac, and does weddings, receptions, birthdays, conventions, grand openings, and so on. For all your Elvis impersonator needs, call © 877/ELVIS-35 or visit his website at **www.elvis-vegas.com**.

1. It's the only place in the world where Elvis will marry you, at a drive-up window, in a pink Cadillac—24 hours a day.
2. Chances are, you'll never forget your anniversary.
3. Where else can you treat all your guests to a wedding buffet for only 99¢ a head?
4. Four words: One helluva bachelor party.
5. On wedding night, show spouse that new "watch me disappear" act you learned from Siegfried and Roy.
6. Show your parents who's boss—have your wedding your way.
7. Wedding bells ring for you everywhere you go. They just sound like slot machines.
8. You can throw dice instead of rice.
9. Easy to lie about age on the marriage certificate—just like Joan Collins did!
10. With all the money you save, it's dice clocks for everyone!

get married by an Elvis impersonator. Las Vegas Weddings can also arrange your honeymoon stay, complete with sightseeing tours, show tickets, and meals.

Weddings can be very cheap in Vegas: A license is about $55, and a basic service not much more. Even a full-blown shebang package—photos, music, some flowers, video, cake, and other doodads—will run only about $500 total. We haven't quoted any prices here, as the ultimate cost depends entirely on how much you want to spend. Go cheap, and the whole thing will set you back maybe $100, including the license (maybe even somewhat less); go elaborate, and the price is still reasonable by today's wedding-price standards. Be sure to remember that there are often hidden charges, such as expected gratuities for the minister (about $25 should do; no real need to tip anyone else), and so forth. If you're penny-pinching, you'll want to keep those in mind.

Be aware that Valentine's Day is a very popular day to get married in Vegas. Some of the chapels perform as many as 80 services on February 14.

But remember, you also don't have to plan ahead. Just show up, get your paperwork, close your eyes, and pick a chapel. And above all, have fun. Good luck and best wishes to you both.

Note: When we describe the following chapels and say "flowers," don't think fresh (unless it's part of a description of services provided); the permanent decorations are artificial, of varying levels of quality, though usually well dusted.

Chapel of Love   This is a friendly place largely run by women (men take the photos and are the limo drivers), featuring four different chapels. Good news came when the Divine Madness fantasy wedding chapel closed and brought all of their many costumes and props over here—along with their silly sensibility. The chapels herein have been remodeled as well, and while you won't get, say, fantasy hotel–level set design, this is the spot for Fun Weddings, for those who want Renaissance- or Egyptian-themed nuptials (to say nothing of Gangster, Tarzan & Jane, or Adam & Eve). None of the rooms is very big, and again, if they say "jungle," you should think "plastic plants." It's a hoot, anyway. There is also a reception room for a cold buffet or hot hors d'oeuvres. Their packages are quite reasonable, and they put all the "hidden" charges (such as suggested gratuities for the minister and so forth) right in their brochure, so there are no surprises.

1431 Las Vegas Blvd. S. **(** **800/922-5683** or 702/387-0155. www.chapelsoflove.com. Mon–Thurs 8am–10pm; Fri–Sat 8am–midnight; Sun 9am–9pm.

Chapel of the Bells   Sporting perhaps the largest and gaudiest sign on the Strip, this chapel also shares a parking lot with the bright pink Fun City Motel. We won't make any jokes. It is also probably the least helpful, most cranky of the wedding chapels we've dealt with—on such a special day, who needs it? The chapel has wood paneling, sage carpeting, and gilt trim up by the pulpit. Electric candles light the walls. It seats only about 25. They prefer advance booking but can do same-day ceremonies if called to.

2233 Las Vegas Blvd. S. **(** **800/233-2391** or 702/735-6803. www.chapelofthebellslasvegas.com. Mon–Thurs 9am–10pm; Fri–Sat 9am–1am. They stay open as late as needed on holidays.

Cupid's Wedding Chapel   "The little chapel with the big heart." Well, it just might be. The manager explains that, unlike other chapels on the Strip, they schedule weddings an hour apart; this gives them time for the full production number. The folks at Cupid's pride themselves on offering "a traditional church wedding at a chapel price." This includes a bridal processional, dimmed lights as the minister introduces the happy couple, and then a tape of the couple's favorite song so they can have their first dance right there at the pulpit after their "first" kiss. They also offer family weddings for those couples blending preexisting families; the children become a part of the service, and as their parents exchange rings with each other, the kids are given their own small token, to let them know the parents are marrying them as well. The chapel is pleasantly low-frills and down-to-earth, with white walls and pews, and modern stained glass with doves and roses. (Kitsch-phobes will be pleased to know that the cupids are only in the lobby.) It seats 60 to 70. They recently added a classic banquet hall (and by that we mean, think New Jersey banquet hall) so you can have your reception and wedding all in one place. And, yes, if they don't have something already scheduled, they will take walk-ups.

827 Las Vegas Blvd. S. (C) **800/543-2933** or 702/598-4444. www.cupidswedding.com. Sun–Thurs 10am–10pm; Fri–Sat 10am–1am.

Graceland Wedding Chapel   Housed in a landmark building that's one of the oldest wedding chapels in Vegas, the Graceland bills itself as "the proverbial mom and pop outfit. We offer friendly, courteous service, and are willing to go that extra step." No, Elvis never slept here (one of the owners was friends with Elvis and asked his permission to use the name). This is a tiny New England church building with a small bridge and white picket fence out front. Inside is a 33-seat chapel; the walls are burgundy and white, with a large, modern stained-glass window of doves and roses behind the pulpit. The pews are dark-blond wood. It's not the nicest of the chapels, but Catherine Oxenberg and Caspar Van Diem got married here. Jon Bon Jovi and Lorenzo Lamas did also, though not to each other.

619 Las Vegas Blvd. S. (C) **800/824-5732** or 702/382-0091. www.gracelandchapel.com. Sun–Thurs 9am–9pm; Fri–Sat 9am–midnight.

Little Chapel of the Flowers   Their current claim to fame is that Dennis Rodman and Carmen Electra exchanged their deathless vows here. Given that fact, it doesn't look the way you might think. This is actually the spiffiest wedding operation on the Strip, with another miniature old-fashioned church building with a very tiny garden and gazebo. They have two chapels off their pretty and comfortable lobby (mock-antique look). The Victorian chapel, which holds only 30, has white walls and dark wood pews and doesn't look very Victorian at all, but is the nicest of the lot. The Heritage Chapel holds 70 and adds rose-colored drapes and electric-candle chandeliers. They also offer a medium-size reception room and live organ music upon request. It's a pretty, friendly place that somehow manages to act as if every one of the many daily weddings they do is special. They do not allow rice or confetti throwing.

1717 Las Vegas Blvd. S. (C) **800/843-2410** or 702/735-4331. www.littlechapel.com. Mon–Thurs 9am–10pm; Fri–Sat 9am–11pm.

Little White Chapel   This is arguably the most famous of the chapels on the Strip, maybe because they have the big sign saying Michael Jordan and Joan Collins were married here (again, not to each other), maybe because they were the first to do the drive-up window. Or maybe because this is where Britney and that guy who isn't the guy from *Seinfeld* began their 51 hours of wedded bliss. (No, we will never, ever get tired of mocking that bit of bad decision making.) It is indeed little and white. However, it has a factory-line atmosphere, processing wedding after wedding after wedding, 24 hours a day. Move 'em in, and move 'em out. (No wonder they put in that drive-up window!) The staff, dressed in hot-pink smocks, is brusque, hasty, and has a bit of an attitude (though we know one couple who got married here and had no complaints). They do offer full

Fun Fact **Trivia: Viva Las Vegas**

1. Gambling was legalized in Nevada in:
   - a. 1931
   - b. 1918
   - c. 1877
   - d. 1849

2. Fremont Street was the site of Las Vegas's first:
   - a. elevator
   - b. paved street
   - c. streetlight
   - d. all of the above

3. McCarran International Airport is the nation's seventh-busiest airport. It averages how many flights a day?
   - a. 210
   - b. 540
   - c. 720
   - d. 980

4. Though Las Vegas is known for its casinos, it also has numerous churches, synagogues, and other places of worship. Approximately how many?
   - a. 1,200
   - b. 500
   - c. 140
   - d. 70

5. The Spanish words *las vegas* mean:
   - a. "the winners"
   - b. "the meadows"
   - c. "the sands"
   - d. "the losers"

6. Las Vegas is famous for its neon. How many miles of neon tubing are along the Strip and in Downtown?

wedding ceremonies, complete with candlelight service and traditional music. There are two chapels, the smaller of which has a large photo of a forest stream. They also have a gazebo for outdoor services, but since it's right on the Strip, it's not as nice as it sounds. If you want something special, there are probably better choices, but for a true Vegas wedding experience, this is Kitsch Wedding Central.

1301 Las Vegas Blvd. S. © **800/545-8111** or 702/382-5943. www.alittlewhitechapel.com. Open 24 hr.

Mon Bel Ami Wedding Chapel   Formerly the Silver Bells chapel, this is a spanking new redo, a pretty little churchlike building complete with a big gold and flower-bedecked chapel room (maybe the taller peaked ceiling gives that effect) fitted with surround-sound speakers, new wood fittings, carpet, and paint. The Cupid bas-relief is a bit much. They do frilly and fancy wedding receptions, as well as events where white doves are released. Perhaps because of this, the establishment seems to attract

a. 15,000 miles
b. 400 miles
c. 1,500 miles
d. 4 miles

7. There are how many hotel swimming pools in the Las Vegas area?
a. 17
b. 27
c. 35
d. 50+

ANSWERS

1: a

Gambling was legalized in 1931. In 1909, the state passed a no-gambling law, which forbade even flipping a coin for the cost of a drink; no one in Las Vegas, however, really paid much attention to the law.

2: d

Fremont Street was also the location of the city's first hotel, Hotel Nevada, opened in 1905.

3: d

On average, McCarran International Airport handles 980 flights a day at 94 gates.

4: b

Over 40 faiths are served at 500-plus places of worship.

5: b

6: a

Fifteen thousand miles of neon tubing make nighttime Las Vegas one of the most recognizable cityscapes in the world.

7: d

There are over 50 hotel pools; unfortunately, most close (or aren't heated) in the winter.

---

fewer walk-ins than prebooked weddings, so you should call in advance or you might be stuck in the Strip-side gazebo.

607 Las Vegas Blvd. S. (C) **866/503-4400** or 702/388-4445. www.monbelami.com. Sun–Thurs 9am–10pm; Fri–Sat 9am–2am.

San Francisco Sally's Victorian Chapel *(Finds* This is an extremely tiny wedding chapel bursting at the seams with Victorian frills (fringed lamps, swags of lace curtains). They basically offer "an Olde Tyme Parlor Wedding." This is perfect if you want a very intimate wedding—like you, your intended, and someone to officiate. It literally can't hold more than six people. (And the space at the back of the room opens for an even tinier reception area—it can barely fit the cake!) But if you love Victoriana or you want to play dress-up at your wedding, this is the place. The shop rents out dresses and costumes, so you can wear a Scarlett O'Hara antebellum outfit or some other period number for your big day. (It's all fantasy anyway, so why not go whole hog?) They specialize in extras without extra charges, like altering and whatnot. The women who run it refer to themselves as "a bunch of mother hens"; they're delightful and will pamper you to within an inch of your life. (One couple drops in every year just to say hi.) Some may find it a bit cutesy, but it really is quite charming and has its own distinct personality, unlike most of the other chapels in the area (where the interiors all start to blur together after a while). This is a decidedly special place that, depending on your wedding desires and fantasies, might be just right.

1304 Las Vegas Blvd. S. © 800/658-8677 or 702/385-7777. Mon–Sat 10am–6pm; Sun 10am–4pm.

A Special Memory Wedding Chapel   This is a very nice wedding chapel, particularly when compared to the rather tired facades of the classics on the Strip. This is absolutely the place to go if you want a traditional, big-production wedding; you won't feel it the least bit tacky. It's a New England church–style building, complete with steeple. The interior looks like a proper church (well, a plain one—don't think ornate Gothic cathedral) with a peaked roof, pews with padded red seats, modern stained-glass windows of doves and flowers, and lots of dark wood. It's all very clean and new, and seats about 87 comfortably. There is a short staircase leading to an actual bride's room; she can make an entrance coming down it or through the double doors at the back. The area outside the chapel is like a minimall of bridal paraphernalia stores. Should all this just be too darn nice and proper for you, they also offer a drive-up window (where they do about 300 weddings a month!). It'll cost you $25—just ring the buzzer for service. They have a photo studio on-site and will do receptions featuring a small cake, cold cuts, and champagne. There is a gazebo for outside weddings, and they sell T-shirts!

800 S. 4th St. (at Gass Ave.). © 800/962-7798 or 702/384-2211. www.aspecialmemory.com. Sun–Thurs 8am–10pm; Fri–Sat 8am–midnight.

Wee Kirk O' the Heather   This is the oldest wedding chapel in Las Vegas (it's been here since 1940; ah, Vegas, and its mixed-up view of age) and the one at the very end of the Strip, right before Downtown (and thus even closer to the license bureau). It would be declared a historic landmark, except some renovations in the past moved just enough of the interior walls to alter it sufficiently to keep it from being official. An even more recent face-lift invigorated it. The decor is entirely fresh, and while that means gold-satin-patterned wallpaper in the chapel, we still like it a great deal. Just the right balance between kitsch and classic, and that's what you want in a Vegas wedding chapel. After all, what else is the point?

231 Las Vegas Blvd. S. © 800/843-2566 or 702/382-9830. www.weekirk.com. Daily 10am–midnight.

3 Attractions in Nearby Henderson

About 6 miles from the Strip in the town of Henderson are two factories that offer free tours (there used to be more, but they recently closed), and if that's your kind of thing, well, you won't be entirely alone. It's best to see them on a weekday when they're fully operative.

To get to Henderson, drive east on Tropicana Avenue, make a right on Mountain Vista, then go 2 miles to Sunset Way; turn left into Green Valley Business Park. You will soon see Ethel M Chocolates, a good place to begin. Use the map in this section to find your way to the other facility.

Clark County Heritage Museum ⭒⭒ *(finds* Someday, one of these casino moguls (yeah, we're lookin' at you, Trump) is going to take just some of those mega-millions they are pouring into yet another Strip hotel and put it into the museum that this bizarre town, and its ridiculously rich 100-year history, deserves. Until then, this dear little place will have to do its best—and that best is actually pretty good. With everything from dioramas of dinosaurs to a small street filled with original buildings including the 1932 Boulder City train depot, and an exhibit of 100 years of Vegas (on display until Jan 2006), this is a throwback to ghost towns and other low-tech diversions. Sweet, informative, and you can't beat the price. Note that hot days will make the outdoor portions less than bearable.

1830 S. Boulder Hwy., East Las Vegas. ⓒ 702/455-7955. Admission $1.50 adults, $1 seniors and kids 3–15. Daily 9am–4:30pm.

Ethel M Chocolates ⭒ This tourist attraction draws about 2,000 visitors a day. Ethel Mars began making fine chocolates in a little candy kitchen around the early 20th century. Her small enterprise evolved to produce not only dozens of varieties of superb boxed chocolates, but some of the world's most famous candies: M&Ms, Milky Way, 3 Musketeers, Snickers, and Mars bars.

Alas, the tour lasts only about 10 minutes and consists entirely of viewing stations with an audiotape explaining the chocolate-baking process. You learn very little. But the place does look like a bakery rather than a factory, which is nice, as no one wants to see their chocolates handled without love. Even more sadly, you get only one small chocolate as a sample—delicious, but hardly satisfying. (Surely, this is by design; now overwhelmingly in the mood for sugar, you are more likely to buy some of their expensive chocolate.) *Note:* Come before 2:30pm, which is when the workers start to pack up and go home.

What's really worth seeing is outside: a lovely and extensive **2½-acre garden** ⊛ displaying 350 species of rare and exotic cacti with signs provided for self-guided tours. It's best appreciated in spring, when the cacti are in full bloom. There's a little gazebo in which to sit and enjoy the garden, which would be quite peaceful were it not for the busloads of tourists in the area. Behind the garden, also with a self-guided tour, is Ethel M's "Living Machine," a natural wastewater treatment and recycling plant that consists of aerated tanks, ecological fluid beds, a constructed wetlands, reed beds, and a storage pond.

2 Cactus Garden Dr. (just off Mountain Vista and Sunset Way in the Green Valley Business Park). © **702/433-2500** for recorded information, or 702/458-8864. www.ethelm.com. Free admission. Daily 8:30am–7pm. Closed Dec 25.

Ron Lee's World of Clowns   It's easy to give this one a miss, but you're here, so what the heck. This factory manufactures clown figurines (and other types, most notably Disney figures). The tour itself consists of simply looking in windows as people mold and paint. The real attraction (aside from a beautiful carousel) is the gift shop, with a nearly limitless amount of high-quality figurines, primarily with a clown motif.

330 Carousel Pkwy., Henderson. © **800/829-3928** or 702/434-3920. Free admission. Mon–Fri 8:30am–4:30pm.

4 Especially for Kids

Like much of the rest of the world, you may be under the impression that Las Vegas has evolved from an adults-only fantasyland into a vacation destination suitable for the entire family. The only explanation for this myth is that Las Vegas was referred to as "Disneyland for adults" by so many and for so long that the town became momentarily confused and decided it actually *was* Disneyland. Some of the gargantuan hotels then spent small fortunes on redecorating in an attempt to lure families, with vast quantities of junk food and a lot of hype. They now vehemently deny that any such notion ever crossed their collective minds, and, no, they don't know how that roller coaster got into the parking lot.

To put things simply, Las Vegas makes money—lots and lots of money—by promoting gambling, drinking, and sex. These are all fine pursuits if you happen to be an adult, but if you haven't reached the magical age of 21, you really don't count in this town. In any case, the casinos and even the Strip itself are simply too stimulating, noisy, and smoky for young kids.

Older progeny may have a tolerance for crowds and the incessant pinging of the slot machines, but they will be thoroughly annoyed with you when casino security chastises them if they so much as stop to tie their shoelaces anywhere near the gaming tables. Since you can't get from your hotel room to the parking lot without ambling through a casino, you can't reasonably expect a teenager to be in a good mood once you stagger outside. And those amusement parks and video halls that haven't yet been purged are very expensive places to park your kids for an afternoon or evening, assuming they are old enough to be left unsupervised.

Nevertheless, you may have a perfectly legitimate reason for bringing your children to Las Vegas (like Grandma was busy, or you were just stopping off on your way from somewhere else), so here are some places to take the children both on and off the Strip.

Circus Circus (p. 112) has ongoing circus acts throughout the day, a vast video-game-and-pinball arcade, and dozens of carnival games on its mezzanine level. Behind the hotel is the **Adventuredome,** detailed below.

Excalibur (p. 88) also offers video and carnival games, plus thrill cinemas and free shows (jugglers, puppets, and so on).

At **Caesars Palace** (p. 92), animated talking statues in the **Forum Shops** are also a kick.

Sin City Inverted

If you want to get away from the glitz and kitsch or just go where most of the tourists don't go, here are several "un-Vegasy" things to do, kindly supplied by James P. Reza, Geoff Carter, and the editors of the *Las Vegas Weekly.*

- **Double Down Saloon** (p. 288). Sin City's coolest bar, hands down. Enjoy cocktails, plug songs into the world's wildest jukebox, admire the bizarre mural work by Vegas artists, or just mingle with local characters and the occasional celebrity.

- **West Sahara Library Fine Arts Museum,** 9600 W. Sahara Ave. (© 702/507-3630). Don't laugh. Las Vegas has its very own gala art museum, ensconced in the most impressive building built in the valley since Wayne Newton set up residence. Built to Smithsonian specs, the museum is one of the few urban buildings in Vegas that lends a sense of space and quality to the surrounding stucco. Hours are Monday through Thursday from 9am to 9pm, Friday through Sunday from 10am to 6pm.

- **The Arts Factory** (see below). Las Vegas's premier artist collective maintains a gallery inside the "Arts Factory" art compound. The CAC's unique vision of this town is too good to miss. Open Monday, Tuesday, Thursday, and Friday from noon to 5pm.

- **Jazzed Cafe & Vinoteca** (p. 283). Run by professional dancers Kirk Offerle and Connie Chambers, this tiny, elegant bistro stays open until the wee hours, lit by candles and the brilliance of the clientele. Great java, terrific wine list.

- **Floyd Lamb State Park,** I-95 North; exit at Durango. This huge former working ranch once served as a forerunner of those trendy "desert spas" so popular in Scottsdale. Today you'll find acres and acres of grassy picnic areas; walking, hiking, biking, and horse trails; huge shade trees; and two lakes. Wanna be a true native? Always call it "Tule Springs."

- **Chinatown Mall,** 4255 Spring Mountain Rd. The Occident meets the Orient in a big way. A prodigious meeting of great restaurants, interesting shops, and unique amenities, all with roots buried deep in the Far East.

Star Trek: The Experience and Borg Invasion 4-D **attraction** (p. 202) deserve to draw families to the **Las Vegas Hilton,** but it may be a bit much for younger children.

The erupting volcano might divert them, as the Secret Garden of Siegfried and Roy and Dolphin Habitat at **The Mirage** (p. 200) surely will, and the **Shark Reef at Mandalay Bay** (p. 202) is worth a look. Ditto the various attractions at **Luxor Las Vegas** (the IMAX Theater, p. 196; King Tut's Tomb, p. 194; and simulator ride, p. 196), and **Cyber Speedway** and **Speed: The Ride** (p. 202) at the **Sahara.**

Children 10 and up will love the many options for play (from high-tech to low-tech, from video wonders to actual physical activity) offered at **GameWorks** (p. 193), as will their parents.

Of moderate interest to youngsters are the **factory tours in Henderson** (see "Attractions in Nearby Henderson," above), especially Ethel M Chocolates, though they will like the free sweets best. More educational is the **Marjorie Barrick Museum** at UNLV (p. 197), but only the reptile exhibit will really interest kids. The **Clark County Museum** is also a dear little throwback, and uncynical kids may enjoy wandering through the old buildings and checking out some of the dioramas.

Appropriate shows for kids include *Tournament of Kings* at Excalibur, **Lance Burton** at the Monte Carlo, **Mac King** at Harrah's, and Cirque du Soleil's *Mystère* at TI at the Mirage. As a general rule, early shows are less racy than late-night shows. All of these productions are reviewed in detail in chapter 10.

Beyond the city limits (see chapter 11 for details on all of these) is **Bonnie Springs Ranch/Old Nevada,** with trail and stagecoach rides, a petting zoo, old-fashioned melodramas, stunt shootouts, a Nevada-themed wax museum, crafts demonstrations, and more. **Lake Mead** has great recreational facilities for family vacations. Finally, organized tours (see the following section) to the Grand Canyon and other interesting sights in southern Nevada and neighboring states can be fun family activities. Check with your hotel sightseeing desk. Kids should also be entertained by the personalized tours offered by **Creative Adventures** (✆ **702/361-5565**); see p. 217.

Specifically kid-pleasing attractions are described below.

Adventuredome 🎡🎡   This isn't a half-bad place to spend a hot afternoon, especially now it's about all that remains of the great Vegas-Is-For-Kids-Too experiment. Plus, unlike most theme parks, it's indoors! The glass dome that towers overhead lets in natural light, a solace to those of us who look peaked under the glow of the artificial kind. A double-loop roller coaster careens around the simulated Grand Canyon, and there's the requisite water flume, a laser-tag area, some bouncy/twirly/stomach-churning type rides, and a modest number of other tamer rides for kids of all ages. A dinosaur-bone excavation area will provide a good time for preschoolers and a place to rest for the supervising adults. Video games and a carnival-style arcade are separate from the attractions, cutting down just a tad on the noise level. Jugglers and magicians provide impromptu entertainment. The newish SpongeBob SquarePants 4-D ride is disappointing, since the technology is about 10 years behind the times and the story hard to follow, thanks to bad acoustics. Our only suggestion is not to leave kids here alone; they could easily get lost.

2880 Las Vegas Blvd. S. (behind Circus Circus). ✆ **702/794-3939.** Free admission; pay per ride $4–$6; daily pass $23 adults, $15 children 33–47 in. AE, DC, DISC, MC, V. Park hours vary seasonally but are usually Mon–Thurs 10am–6pm; Fri–Sat 10am–midnight; Sun 10am–8pm.

Las Vegas Natural History Museum 🎡   Conveniently located across the street from the Lied Discovery Children's Museum (described below), this humble temple of taxidermy harkens back to elementary-school field trips circa 1965, when stuffed elk and brown bears forever protecting their kill were as close as most of us got to exotic animals. Worn around the edges but very sweet and relaxed, the museum is enlivened by a hands-on activity room and two life-size dinosaurs that roar at one another intermittently. A small boy was observed leaping toward his dad upon watching this display, so you might want to warn any sensitive little ones that the big tyrannosaurs aren't going anywhere. Surprisingly, the gift shop here is particularly well stocked with neat items you won't too terribly mind buying for the kids.

900 Las Vegas Blvd. N. (at Washington). ℂ 702/384-3466. www.lvnhm.org. Admission $6 adults; $5 seniors, students, and military; $3 children 3–11; free for children under 2. Daily 9am–4pm.

Lied Discovery Children's Museum 🕮🕮 (Finds)
A hands-on science museum designed for curious kids, the bright, airy, two-story Lied makes an ideal outing for toddlers and young children. With lots of interactive exhibits to examine, including a miniature grocery store, a tube for encasing oneself inside a soap bubble, a radio station, and music and drawing areas, you'll soon forget your video/poker losses. Clever, thought-inducing exhibits are everywhere. Learn how it feels to be handicapped by playing basketball from a wheelchair. Feed a wooden "sandwich" to a cutout of a snake and to a human cutout, and see how much nutrition each receives. See how much sunscreen their giant stuffed mascot needs to keep from burning. On weekend afternoons from 1 to 3pm, free drop-in art classes are offered, giving you a bit of time to ramble around the gift store or read the fine print on the exhibit placards. The Lied also shares space with a city library branch, so after the kids run around, you can calm them back down with a story or two.

833 Las Vegas Blvd. N. (½ block south of Washington, across the street from Cashman Field). ℂ 702/382-3445. www.ldcm.org. Admission $7 adults; $6 seniors, military, and children 1–17. Tues–Sun 10am–5pm.

Scandia Family Fun Center 🕮🕮
This family-amusement center, located just a few blocks off the Strip, is still the most viable alternative for those who need to amuse children not quite old enough for GameWorks, or for those on a tighter budget. Certainly, it's where local families come for outings, and they keep the batting cages hopping ($1.25 for 25 pitches). The arcade is a bit warm and stinky, and other parts (including miniature-car racing and bumper boats, $4 per ride; small children ride free with an adult) are a bit worn, but the miniature-golf course (three 18-hole courses, $5.50 per game, free for children under 6) is quite cute. Still, we do have to wonder about those 'round-the-clock weekend hours; we certainly hope those playing miniature golf at 4am are not parents occupied by children.

2900 Sirius Ave. (at Rancho Dr. just south of Sahara Ave.). ℂ 702/364-0070. Free admission, but there's a fee for each game or activity. Super Saver Pass $13 (includes 1 round of miniature golf, 2 rides, and 5 game tokens); Unlimited Wristband Package $18 (includes unlimited bumper-boat and car rides, unlimited miniature golf, and 10 tokens for batting cages or arcade games). Mar–Oct daily 24 hr.; Nov–Feb Sun–Thurs 10am–11pm, Fri–Sat 10am–midnight.

5 Organized Tours

Just about every hotel in town has a sightseeing desk offering a seemingly infinite number of tours in and around Las Vegas. You're sure to find a tour company that will take you where you want to go.

Gray Line Tours (ℂ **800/634-6579;** www.grayline.com) offers a rather comprehensive roster, including the following:

• A pair of 5-to 6-hour **city tours** (1 day, 1 night), with various itineraries, including visits to Ethel M Chocolates, the Liberace Museum, and the Fremont Street Experience

Mayor Oscar B. Goodman's Top 10 Places to Recapture Old Las Vegas

1. The proposed "Mob" Museum in the old U.S. Courthouse and Post Office (300 E. Stewart Ave.)
2. The "Bugsy" Suite at the Flamingo Hotel & Casino
3. Bob Taylor's Ranch House at 6250 Rio Vista (where the old-timers went)
4. Fellini's Restaurant at 5555 W. Charleston (ambience of yore)
5. Piero's Italian Cuisine at 355 Convention Center Dr. (characters eating pasta)
6. 200 feet at bottom of Lake Mead
7. 6 feet in desert near the state line
8. Howard Hughes's bungalow behind Channel 8
9. The WELCOME TO LAS VEGAS sign south of the Strip
10. The Huntridge Theater at 1208 E. Charleston

Oscar B. Goodman is the Mayor of Las Vegas through 2007.

- Half-day excursions to **Hoover Dam** and **Red Rock Canyon** (see chapter 11 for details)
- A half-day tour to **Lake Mead** and **Hoover Dam**
- Several full-day **Grand Canyon excursions**

Call for details or inquire at your hotel's sightseeing desk, where you'll also find free magazines with coupons for discounts on these tours.

GRAND CANYON TOURS

Generally, tourists visiting Las Vegas don't drive 300 miles to Arizona to see the Grand Canyon, but there are dozens of sightseeing tours departing from the city daily. In addition to the Gray Line tours described above, the major operator, **Scenic Airlines** (© **800/634-6801** or 702/638-3300; www.scenic.com), runs deluxe, full-day guided air-ground tours starting at $269 per person ($239 for children 2–11); the price includes a bus excursion through the national park, a flight over the canyon, and lunch. All scenic tours include flightseeing. The company also offers both full-day and overnight tours with hiking.

Scenic also offers tours to other points of interest and national parks, including Bryce Canyon and Monument Valley. Ask for details when you call.

UNIQUE DESERT TOURS

A totally different type of tour is offered by Char Cruze of **Creative Adventures** ★★★ (© **702/361-5565**). Char, a charming fourth-generation Las Vegan (she was at the opening of The Flamingo), spent her childhood riding horseback through the mesquite and cottonwoods of the Mojave Desert, discovering magical places you'd never find on your own or on a commercial tour. Char is a lecturer and storyteller as well as a tour guide. She has extensively studied southern Nevada's geology and desert wildlife, its regional history, and its Native American cultures. Her personalized tours, enhanced by fascinating stories about everything from miners to mobsters, visit haunted mines, sacred Paiute grounds, ghost towns, canyons, and ancient petroglyphs.

She also has many things to entertain and educate children, and carries a tote bag full of visual aids, like a board covered in labeled rocks to better illustrate a lecture on local geology. Char has certain structured tours, but she loves to do individual tours tailored to the group. This is absolutely worth the money—you are definitely going to get something different than you would on a conventional tour, while Char herself is most accommodating, thoughtful, knowledgeable, and prompt. Char rents transport according to the size of the group and can handle clients with disabilities.

Depending on your itinerary, the cost is about $100 a day if you use your own car (more, depending on the number of people, if rental transportation is required; however, it's even more of a bargain with a larger group). It's a good idea to make arrangements with her prior to leaving home.

6 Fore! Great Desert Golf

In addition to the listings below, there are dozens of local courses, including some very challenging ones that have hosted PGA tournaments. *Note:* Greens fees vary radically depending on time of day and year. Also, call for opening and closing times, as these change frequently.

If you're a serious golfer, you may want to contact **American Golf** (© 800/468-7918), a nationwide reservations service that's based in Arizona. They can help you arrange golf packages and book hard-to-get tee times.

Note also that the **Rio All-Suite Hotel** (p. 103) has an affiliated golf course. Also, Wynn Las Vegas has a state-of-the-art course, but we aren't including it for two reasons; as of this writing, it is for guests only—and they mean it. If anyone in your party is not also staying at the hotel, they can't play. And the greens fees? A mere $500 a person. Call when you get to town, to see if they've come to their senses.

Angel Park Golf Club   This 36-hole, par-70/71 public course is a local favorite. Arnold Palmer originally designed the Mountain and Palm courses (the Palm Course was redesigned several years later by Bob Cupp). Players call this a great escape from the casinos, claiming that no matter how many times they play it, they never get tired of it. The Palm Course has gently rolling fairways that offer golfers of all abilities a challenging yet forgiving layout. The Mountain Course has rolling natural terrain and gorgeous panoramic views. In addition to these two challenging 18-hole courses, Angel Park offers a night-lit Cloud 9 Course (12 holes for daylight play, 9 at night), where each hole is patterned after a famous par 3. You can reserve tee times up to 60 days in advance with a credit card guarantee.

Yardage: Palm Course 6,525 championship and 5,438 resort; Mountain Course 6,722 championship and 5,164 resort.

Facilities: Pro shop, night-lit driving range, 18-hole putting course, restaurant, snack bar, cocktail bar, and beverage cart.

100 S. Rampart Blvd. (between Summerlin Pkwy. and Alta St.; 20 min. northwest of the Strip). © 888/629-3929 or 702/254-0566. www.angelpark.com. Greens fees $95–$145. Discounted twilight rates available.

Bali Hai Golf Club   One of the newest and most exclusive golf addresses belongs to this multimillion-dollar course built in 2000 on the Strip just south of Mandalay Bay. Done in a wild South Seas theme, the par-71 course features over 7 acres of water hazards, plus an island green, palm trees, and tropical foliage everywhere you look. Not impressed yet? How about the fact that all of its golf carts are equipped with Global Positioning Satellite (GPS) tracking systems. Or that celeb chef Wolfgang Puck chose to open his newest Vegas eatery here. Okay, if that doesn't convince you of the upscale nature of the joint, check out the greens fees.

Even at those prices, tee times are often booked 6 months in advance.

Yardage: 7,002 championship.

Facilities: Pro shop, putting green, gourmet restaurant, grill, and lounge.

5150 Las Vegas Blvd. S. ℂ 888/397-2499. www.waltersgolf.com. Greens fees $175–$245.

Black Mountain Golf & Country Club   Two new greens have recently been added to this 27-hole, par-72 semiprivate course, which requires reservations 4 days in advance. It's considered a great old course, with lots of wildlife, including roadrunners. However, unpredictable winds may affect your game.

Yardage: 6,550 championship, 6,223 regular, and 5,518 ladies.

Facilities: Pro shop, putting green, driving range, restaurant, snack bar, and cocktail lounge.

In nearby Henderson, 500 Greenway Rd. ℂ 702/565-7933. www.golfblackmountain.com. Greens fees $50–$145.

Craig Ranch Golf Club (Value   This is a flat 18-hole, par-70 public course with many trees and bunkers; both narrow and open fairways feature Bermuda turf. The greens fees are a bargain, and you can reserve tee times 7 days in advance.

Yardage: 6,001 regular and 5,221 ladies.

Facilities: Driving range, pro shop, PGA teaching pro, putting green, and snack bar.

628 W. Craig Rd. (between Losee Rd. and Martin Luther King Blvd.). ℂ 702/642-9700. Greens fees $19 walking, $29 in golf cart.

Desert Rose Golf Club   This is an 18-hole, par-71 public course built in 1963 and designed by Dick Wilson and Joe Lee. Narrow fairways feature Bermuda turf. You can reserve tee times up to 7 days in advance.

Yardage: 6,511 championship, 6,135 regular, and 5,458 ladies.

Facilities: Driving range, putting and chipping greens, PGA teaching pro, pro shop, restaurant, and cocktail lounge.

5483 Clubhouse Dr. (3 blocks west of Nellis Blvd., off Sahara Ave.). ℂ 702/431-4653. Greens fees $33–$79; some packages include cart rentals.

Las Vegas National Golf Club   This is an 18-hole (about 8 with water on them), par-71 public course, and a classic layout (not the desert layout you'd expect). If you play from the back tees, it can really be a challenge. The 1996 Las Vegas Invitational, won by Tiger Woods, was held here. Discounted tee times are often available. Reservations are taken up to 60 days in advance; a $5 to $7 fee applies.

Yardage: 6,815 championship, 6,418 regular, and 5,741 ladies.

Facilities: Pro shop, golf school, driving range, restaurant, and cocktail lounge.

1911 Desert Inn Rd. (between Maryland Pkwy. and Eastern Ave.). ℂ 702/734-1796. www.lasvegasnational.com. Greens fees $35–$150, some including cart rental.

Royal Links Golf Club (Finds   More than just greens and water traps, Royal Links is an 18-hole, par-72 course designed to simulate play on some of the greatest courses in the British Open tour. St. Andrews Road Hole, the Postage Stamp at the Royal Troon in Scotland, and a dozen others are all faithfully re-created here for a unique game and an interesting history lesson.

Also fun is the clubhouse, designed (of course) to resemble a medieval castle, complete with an English pub inside.

Yardage: 7,029 championship, 6,602 regular, and 5,864 ladies.

Facilities: Pro shop, golf school, driving range, restaurant, and cocktail lounge.

5995 E. Vegas Valley Rd. (east of Boulder Hwy., between Flamingo Rd. and Sahara Ave.). © **702/450-8000.** Greens fees $135–$275.

7 Staying Active

You need not be a slot-hypnotized slug when you come to Vegas. The city and surrounding areas offer plenty of opportunities for active sports. In addition to many highly rated golf courses (described above), just about every hotel has a large swimming pool and health club, and tennis courts abound. All types of watersports are offered at Lake Mead National Recreation Area; there's rafting on the Colorado, horseback riding at Mount Charleston and Bonnie Springs, great hiking in the canyons, and much, much more. Do plan to get out of those smoke-filled casinos and into the fresh air once in a while. It's good for your health and your finances.

Note: When choosing a hotel, check out its recreational facilities, all listed in chapter 5.

BOWLING   Gold Coast Hotel, 4000 W. Flamingo Rd. (at Valley View; © **702/ 367-7111**), has a 72-lane bowling center open daily 24 hours.

The **Orleans,** 4500 W. Tropicana Ave. (© **702/365-7111**), has 70 lanes, a pro shop, lockers, meeting rooms, and more. Open daily 24 hours.

Out on the east side of town, you'll find 56 lanes at **Sam's Town,** 5111 Boulder Hwy. (© **702/456-7777**), plus a snack shop, cocktail lounge, video arcade, day-care center, pro shop, and more. Open daily 24 hours.

In 2005, **Sunset Station,** 1301 W. Sunset Rd. in Henderson (© **702/547-7777**) added a high-tech 72-lane facility called Strike Zone. It's got all the latest automated scoring gizmos, giant video screens, a full bar, a snack shop, a pro shop, a video arcade, and more.

Up north at **Santa Fe Station,** 4949 N. Rancho Rd. (© **702/658-4900**), you'll find a newly remodeled (as of 2005) 60-lane alley with the most modern scoring equipment, all new furnishings, a fun and funky bar, a small cafe, and much more.

Suncoast, 9090 Alta Dr., in Summerlin (© **702/636-7111**), offers 64 lanes divided by a unique center aisle. The high-tech center with touch-screen scoring has become a regular stop on the Pro Bowlers tours. Open daily 24 hours.

BUNGEE JUMPING   If you want to take a *real* gamble, this is the place to do it— the odds are stacked in your favor, but the thrill is nearly immeasurable. **A. J. Hackett Bungy,** 810 Circus Circus Dr., between Las Vegas Boulevard South and Industrial Road (© **702/385-4321**), is a worldwide chain; they've done more than one million jumps and they haven't lost anyone yet. The instructors are enthusiastic and do much to make you feel comfortable. Expect about an hour wait (there is a bar with a TV and pool table to keep you occupied), but given how meticulous and careful they are with each jumper, you'll be glad they aren't rushing people through.

An elevator in the shape of a rocket takes you to the top of a 171-foot tower, the base for an exhilarating plunge toward a large swimming pool below. During the ride up, you will receive your instructions (which basically amount to "stick your toes over the edge, arms out in front, and dive"). Our guinea pig needed a gentle shove. The whole jump lasts perhaps 3 minutes, but you will have enough adrenaline pumping through your veins to keep you up all night. (And then go gamble!) Dive at night, and you sail right into the lights of Vegas. The price is $59 for your first jump, but an extra

$10 will get you a T-shirt, and an extra $20 will snare you a video of yourself. Each subsequent jump is $25. Students and military with ID should inquire about discounts. If you're under 18, you must be accompanied by a parent. Call for hours.

HORSEBACK RIDING   **Cowboy Trail Rides** ⨂ (© **702/948-7061;** www.cowboy trailrides.com) offers a variety of rides and trails in Red Rock Canyon and on Mount Charleston (at the 12-mile marker), ranging in price from $69 to $139. The high end is for a Red Rock Canyon sunset trail ride; it's about 2 hours, with the canyon providing a glorious backdrop for the sunset. Riders then return to camp for a barbecue

---

⸤Tips⸥ Desert Hiking Advice

Except in summer, when temperatures can reach 120°F (49°C) in the shade, the Las Vegas area is great for hiking. The best hiking season is November to March. Great locales include the incredibly scenic Red Rock Canyon and Valley of Fire State Park (see chapter 11 for details on both).

Hiking in the desert is exceptionally rewarding, but it can be dangerous. Here are some safety tips:

1. Don't hike alone.
2. Carry plenty of water and drink it often. Don't assume spring waters are safe to drink. A gallon of water per person per day is recommended for hikers.
3. Be alert for signs of heat exhaustion (headache, nausea, dizziness, fatigue, and cool, damp, pale, or red skin).
4. Gauge your fitness accurately. Desert hiking may involve rough or steep terrain. Don't take on more than you can handle.
5. Check weather forecasts before starting out. Thunderstorms can turn into raging flash floods, which are extremely hazardous to hikers.
6. Dress properly. Wear sturdy walking shoes for rock scrambling, long pants (to protect yourself from rocks and cacti), a hat, sunscreen, and sunglasses.
7. Carry a small first-aid kit.
8. Be careful when climbing on sandstone, which can be surprisingly soft and crumbly.
9. Don't feed or play with animals, such as the wild burros in Red Rock Canyon. (It's actually illegal to approach them.)
10. Be alert for snakes and insects. Though they're rarely encountered, you'll want to look into a crevice before putting your hand into it.
11. Visit park or other information offices before you start out, and acquaint yourself with rules and regulations and any possible hazards. It's also a good idea to tell the staff where you're going, when you'll return, how many are in your party, and so on. Some park offices offer hiker-registration programs.
12. Follow the hiker's rule of thumb: Take only photographs and leave only footprints.

dinner (including a steak, salad, baked beans, and "all the fixin's"), joined by the cowboys for singalongs and marshmallow roasting. They also offer hourly rates of $25 and buses from the Excalibur hotel. Riding stables at **Bonnie Springs Ranch** (© **702/875-4191;** www.bonniesprings.com) also offer guided trail rides daily. Rates start at $30 per person per hour for a guided walking tour through Red Rock Canyon.

ROCK CLIMBING   Red Rock Canyon, just 19 miles west of Las Vegas, is one of the world's most popular rock-climbing areas. In addition to awe-inspiring natural beauty, it offers everything from boulders to big walls. If you'd like to join the bighorn sheep, Red Rock has more than 1,000 routes to inaugurate beginners and challenge accomplished climbers. Experienced climbers can contact the **visitor center** (© **702/515-5350**) for information.

If you're interested in learning or improving your skills, an excellent rock-climbing school and guide service called **Sky's the Limit** (© **800/733-7597** or 702/363-4533; www.skysthelimit.com) offers programs for beginning, intermediate, and advanced climbers. No experience is needed. The school is accredited by the American Mountain Guides Association.

TENNIS   Tennis buffs should choose one of the many hotels in town that have tennis courts.

Bally's (© **702/967-3380**) has eight night-lit hard courts. Fees per hour range from $10 per hour for guests, $15 per hour for nonguests. Facilities include a pro shop. Hours vary seasonally. Reservations are advised.

The Flamingo Las Vegas (© **702/733-3444**) has four outdoor hard courts (all lit for night play) and a pro shop. It's open to the public daily from 7am to 7pm. Rates are $12 per hour for guests, $20 per hour for nonguests. Lessons are available. Reservations are required.

Monte Carlo (© **702/730-7777**) has three night-lit courts available to the public for $15 per hour.

In addition to hotels, the **University of Nevada, Las Vegas (UNLV),** Harmon Avenue just east of Swenson Street (© **702/895-0844**), has a dozen courts (all lit for night play) that are open weekdays from 6am to 9:45pm, weekends 8am to 9pm. Rates are $5 per person per day. You should call before going to find out if a court is available.

8 Spectator Sports

Las Vegas isn't known for its sports teams. Except for minor-league baseball and hockey, the only consistent spectator sports are those at UNLV. For the pros, if watching Triple A ball (in this case, a Los Angeles Dodgers farm team) in potentially triple-degree heat sounds like fun, the charmingly named and even-better merchandized **Las Vegas 51's** (as in Area 51, as in alien-themed gear!) Triple A ball team's schedule and ticket info can be found at www.lv51.com, or call © **702/ 798-7825.** Ice hockey might be a better climate choice; info for the Las Vegas Wranglers can be reached at www.lasvegaswranglers.com or at © **702/471-7825.**

The **Las Vegas Motor Speedway** (p. 195) is a main venue for car racing and should draw major events to Las Vegas.

But since the city has several top-notch sporting arenas, there are important annual events that take place in Las Vegas, details for which can be found in the "Las Vegas Calendar of Events" in chapter 2. The **PGA Tour's Las Vegas Senior Classic** is held

For the Race Car Enthusiast

Race car fans are a very specific subset of sports fans, and Las Vegas has everything race car–themed you could want to get your kid revved up—from food to actual drivable scale models of NASCAR vehicles, virtual car races, an amazing auto museum, a tour of a race car factory, and more. Listed below are some of the best race car–related activities in town.

Eat at the NASCAR Cafe   Theme aplenty here, with autographed team jackets, actual cars, and a genuine love of NASCAR. *Tip:* Eat *after* the rides (Sahara Hotel, 2535 Las Vegas Blvd. S.; © **888/696-2121** or **702/737-2111**; www.saharavegas.com)!

Watch the Races at the Las Vegas Motor Speedway   Weekly events here include stock car races, Motocross, and hot rod races, but this is also a major stop on the NASCAR circuit. Some of the top races in the country are held here from March through December, with tickets at this 250,000-seat race course at times exceeding $100. But January and February, you can see races for under $10. There are tours available when races aren't on. The action takes place at 7000 Las Vegas Blvd. N. (© **800/644-4442**; www.lvms.com).

Tour the Shelby American Sports Car Museum and Assembly Area   Located next to the Las Vegas Motor Speedway, this free museum displays a dozen classic Shelby American cars (the Shelby Cobra is considered by enthusiasts to be the finest American sports car ever built—designer Carroll Shelby also worked for Ford and created the Mustang Cobra for that company), while the working auto assembly plant shows cars in every stage of production. The museum is located at 6755 Speedway Blvd. (© **702/942-7325**; www.shelbyamerican.com).

Visit the Liberace Museum   While the ladies ooh and aah over the world's largest rhinestone, check out the customized cars that Liberace collected (1775 E. Tropicana Ave.; © **702/798-5595**; www.liberace.com).

Explore the Auto Collections at the Imperial Palace   This constantly changing display features Duesenbergs, vintage commercial vehicles, cars owned by presidents, and, most impressively, a Tucker, one of the 51 manufactured before the company went out of business (Imperial Palace Hotel, 3535 Las Vegas Blvd. S.; © **702/794-3174**; www.autocollections.com).

Race on a Track   SportCenter, 121 E. Sunset Rd. (© **702/317-7777**; www. sportcenterlasvegas.com), offers a go-kart track, allowing kids over 58 inches to zip around. Those 33 inches and up can ride as passengers. **Las Vegas Mini Grand Prix**, 91401 N. Rainbow Blvd. (© **702/259-7000**; www.lvmgp.com), has go-karts and mini Grand Prix racers.

each April in nearby Summerlin, and the **Las Vegas Invitational** takes place in Las Vegas each October. The **National Finals Rodeo** is held in UNLV's Thomas and Mack Center each December. From time to time, you'll find NBA exhibition games, professional ice-skating competitions, or gymnastics exhibitions. Then there are the only-in-Vegas spectaculars, such as Evel Knievel's ill-fated attempt to jump the fountains in front of Caesars.

Finally, Las Vegas is well known as a major location for **boxing matches.** These are held in several Strip hotels, most often at Caesars or the MGM Grand, but sometimes at The Mirage. Tickets are hard to come by and quite expensive.

Tickets to sporting events at hotels are available either through **Ticketmaster** (℗ 702/893-3000; www.ticketmaster.com) or through the hotels themselves (why pay Ticketmaster's exorbitant service charges?).

MAJOR SPORTS VENUES IN HOTELS

Caesars Palace (℗ 800/634-6698 or 702/731-7110) has a long tradition of hosting sporting events, from Evel Knievel's attempted motorcycle jump over its fountains in 1967 to Grand Prix auto races. Mary Lou Retton has tumbled in gymnastic events at Caesars, and Olympians Brian Boitano and Katarina Witt have taken to the ice, as has Wayne Gretzky. And well over 100 world-championship boxing contests have taken place here since the hotel opened. In the spirit of ancient Rome, Caesars awards riches and honors to the "gladiators" who compete in its arenas.

The **MGM Grand's Garden Events Arena** (℗ 800/929-1111 or 702/891-7777) is a major venue for professional boxing matches, rodeos, tennis, ice-skating shows, World Figure Skating Championships, and more.

Mandalay Bay (℗ 877/632-7400) has been hosting a number of boxing matches in its 12,000-seat Events Center.

The Mirage (℗ 800/627-6667 or 702/791-7111) also features occasional championship boxing matches.

8

About Casino Gambling

What? You didn't come to Las Vegas for the Liberace Museum? We are shocked. Shocked.

Yes, there are gambling opportunities in Vegas. We've noticed this. You will too. The tip-off will be the slot machines in the airport as soon as you step off the plane. Or the slot machines in the convenience stores as soon as you drive across the state line. Let's not kid ourselves; gambling is what Vegas is about. The bright lights, the shows, the showgirls, the food—it's all there just to lure you in and make you open your wallet. (The free drinks certainly help ease the latter as well.)

You can disappoint them if you want, but what would be the point? *This is Las Vegas.* You don't have to be a high roller. You would not believe how much fun you can have with a nickel slot machine. You won't get rich, but neither will most of those guys playing the $5 slots, either.

Of course, that's not going to stop anyone from trying. Almost everyone plays in Vegas with the hopes of winning The Big One. That only a few ever do win doesn't stop them from trying again and again and again. That's how the casinos make their money, by the way.

It's not that the odds are stacked so incredibly high in their favor—though the odds *are* in their favor, and don't ever think otherwise. Rather, it's that if there is one constant in this world, it's human greed. Look around in any casino, and you'll see countless souls who, having doubled their winnings, are now trying to quadruple them, and are losing it all and then trying to recoup their initial bankroll and losing

still more in the process. See that chandelier up there? Enjoy it—you paid for it.

Which is not meant to dissuade you from gambling. Just be sure to look at it as recreation and entertainment, *not* as an investment or moneymaking opportunity. Spend only as much as you can afford to lose and not a penny more. It doesn't matter if that's $10 or $100,000. You can have just as good a time with either. (Though if you can afford to lose $100,000, we would like to meet you.)

Remember also that there is no system that's sure to help you win. We all have our own systems and our own ideas. Reading books and listening to others at the tables will help you pick up some tips, but if there were a surefire way to win, the casinos would have taken care of it (and we will leave you to imagine just what that might entail). Try to have the courage to walk away when your bankroll is up, not down. Remember, your children's college fund is just that, and not a gambling-budget supplement.

The first part of this chapter is a contribution from James Randi, a master magician, who looks at the four major fallacies people bring with them to the gaming tables in Las Vegas; it's fascinating, and we thank him for this contribution.

The second part tells you the basics of betting. Knowing how to play the games not only improves your odds but also makes playing more enjoyable. In addition to the instructions below, you'll find dozens of books on how to gamble at all casino hotel gift shops, and many casinos offer free gaming lessons on the premises.

Impressions

Stilled forever is the click of the roulette wheel, the rattle of dice, and the swish of cards.

—Shortsighted editorial in the *Nevada State Journal* after gambling was outlawed in 1910

The third part of this chapter describes all the major casinos in town. Remember that gambling is supposed to be entertainment. Picking a gaming table where the other players are laughing, slapping each other on the back, and generally enjoying themselves tends to make for considerably more fun than a table where everyone is sitting around in stony silence, morosely staring at their cards. Unless you really need to concentrate, pick a table where everyone seems to be enjoying themselves, and you will too, even if you don't win. Maybe.

1 The Four Most Pervasive Myths About Gambling

by James Randi

James Randi is a world-class magician (the Amazing Randi), now involved in examining supernatural, paranormal, and occult claims. He is the author of 11 books on these subjects and is the president of the James Randi Educational Foundation in Fort Lauderdale, Florida. The JREF offers a prize of $1.1 million to any person who can produce a demonstration of any paranormal activity. His website is www.randi.org, where details of the offer can be found.

Most of us know little, if anything, about statistics. It's a never-never land we can live without, something for those guys in white coats and thick glasses to mumble over. And because we don't bother to learn the basics of this rather interesting field of study, we sometimes find ourselves unable to deal with the realities that the gambling process produces.

I often present my audiences with a puzzle. Suppose that a mathematician, a gambler, and a magician are walking together on Broadway and come upon a small cluster of people who are observing a chap standing at a small table set up on the sidewalk. They are told that this fellow has just tossed a quarter into the air and allowed it to fall onto the table, nine times. And that has produced nine "tails" in a row. Now the crowd is being asked to bet on what the next toss of the coin will bring. The question: How will each of these three observers place their bets?

The mathematician will reason that each toss of the coin is independent of the last toss, so the chances are still exactly 50/50 for heads or tails. He'll say that either bet is okay and that it doesn't make any difference which decision is made.

The gambler will go one of two ways; either he'll reason that there's a "run" taking place here—and that a bet on another tail will be the better choice—or he'll opine that it's time for the head to come up, and he'll put his wager on that likelihood.

The magician? He has the best chance of winning because he knows that there is only 1 chance in 512 that a coin will come up tails nine times in a row—*unless there's something wrong with that coin!* He'll bet tails and he'll win!

The reasoning of the mathematician is quite correct, that of the gambler is quite wrong (in either one of his scenarios), but just as long as that isn't a double-tailed coin.

The point of view taken by the magician is highly specialized, but human nature being what it is, that view is probably the correct one.

In professional gambling centers such as Las Vegas, great care is taken to ensure that there are no two-tailed quarters or other purposeful anomalies that enable cheating to take place. The casinos make their percentages on the built-in mathematical advantage, which is clearly stated and available to any who ask, and though that is a very tiny "edge," it's enough to pay for the razzle-dazzle that lures in the customers. It's volume that supports the business. The scrutiny that is applied to each and every procedure in Vegas is evident everywhere.

So, **Fallacy Number One** is: Cheating of some sort is necessary for an operation to prosper. It isn't.

Fallacy Number Two: Some people just have "hunches" and "visions" that enable them to win at the slots and tables. Sorry folks, it just ain't so. The science of parapsychology, which has studied such claims for many decades now, has never come up with evidence that any form of clairvoyance ("clear-seeing," the supposed ability to know hidden data, such as the next card to come up in a deal or the next face on the dice) or telepathy ("mind reading") actually exists. It's remarkably easy for us to imagine that we have a hot streak going, or that the cards are falling our way, but the inexorable laws of chance prevail and always will.

Fallacy Number Three: There are folks who can give us systems for winning. Now, judicious bet placing is possible, and there are mathematical methods of minimizing losses, it's true. But the investment and base capital needed to follow through with these methods makes them a rather poor investment. The return percentage can be earned much more easily by almost any other form of endeavor, at less risk and less expenditure of boring hours following complicated charts and equations. The best observation we can make on the "systems" is: Why would the inventors of the "systems" sell something that they themselves could use to get rich, which is what they say you can do with it? Think about that!

Of course, the simplest of all the systems is bet doubling. It sounds great in theory, but an hour spent tossing coins in your hotel room, or at the gaming tables, will convince you that theory and practice are quite different matters. Bet doubling, as applied to heads or tails (on a fair coin!), consists of placing a unit bet on the first coin toss, then pocketing the proceeds if you win, but doubling your bet on the next toss if you lose. If you get a lose, lose, win sequence, that means you will have lost three units (one plus two) and won four. You're up one unit. You start again. If you get a lose, lose, lose, win sequence, you've put out 15 units and brought in 16. Again, you're up only one unit. And no matter how long your sequences go, you'll always be up only one unit at the end of a sequence. It requires you to make that "unit" somewhat sizable if you want to have any significant winnings at all, and that may mean going bankrupt by simply running out of capital before a sequence ends—and if you hang on, you'll have been able to end up only one unit ahead, in any case. Not a good investment at all.

Fallacy Number Four: Studying the results of the roulette wheels will provide the bettor with useful data. We're peculiar animals, in that we constantly search for meaning in all sets of observations. That's how subjects of Rorschach tests find weird faces, figures, and creatures in inkblots that are actually random patterns with single symmetry. Similarly, any sets of roulette results are, essentially, random numbers; there are no patterns to be found there that can give indications of probable future spins of the wheels. Bearing in mind that those wheels are carefully monitored to detect any biases or defects, we should conclude that finding clues in past performances is futile.

I recall that when I worked in Wiesbaden, Germany, just after World War II, I stuck around late one night after closing at the "Spielbank" and watched as an elderly gentleman removed all the rotors of the 12 wheels they had in operation, wrote out the numbers 1 to 12 on separate scraps of paper, and reassembled the wheels according to the random order in which he drew each slip of paper from a bowl. He was ensuring that any inconsistencies in the wheels would be essentially nullified. Yet, as he told me, the front desk at the casino continued to sell booklets setting out the results of each of the wheels because patrons insisted on having them and persisted in believing that there just had to be a pattern there, if only it could be found.

We're only human. We can't escape certain defects in our thinking mechanism, but we can resist reacting to them. When we see Penn & Teller, Ayala, Siegfried & Roy, or Lance Burton doing their wonders, we smile smugly and assure ourselves that those miracles are only illusions. But if we haven't solved those illusions, and we haven't, how can we assume that we aren't being fooled by our own self-created delusions? Let's get a grip on reality and enjoy Las Vegas for what it really is: a grand illusion, a fairyland, a let's-pretend project, but not one in which the laws of nature are suspended or can be ignored.

Enjoy!

2 The Games

As you walk through the labyrinthine twists and turns of a casino floor, your attention will likely be dragged to the various games and, your interest piqued, your fingers may begin to twitch in anticipation of hitting it big. Before you put your money on the line, it's imperative to know the rules of the game you want to play. Most casinos offer free gambling lessons at scheduled times on weekdays. This provides a risk-free environment for you to learn the games that tickle your fancy. Some casinos follow their lessons with low-stakes game play, enabling you to put your newfound knowledge to the test at small risk. During those instructional sessions, and even when playing on your own, dealers in most casinos will be more than happy to answer any questions you might have. Remember, the casino doesn't need to trick you into losing your money . . . the odds are already in their favor across the board; that's why it's called gambling. Another rule of thumb: Take a few minutes to watch a game being played in order to familiarize yourself with the motions and lingo. Then go back and reread this section—things will make a lot more sense at that point. Good luck!

BACCARAT

The ancient game of baccarat, or *chemin de fer,* is played with eight decks of cards. Firm rules apply, and there is no skill involved other than deciding whether to bet on the bank or the player. No, really—that's all you have to do. The dealer does all the other work. You can essentially stop reading here. Oh, all right, carry on.

Any beginner can play, but check the betting minimum before you sit down, as this tends to be a high-stakes game. The cards are shuffled by the croupier and then placed in a box called the "shoe." Players may wager on "bank" or "player" at any time. Two cards are dealt from the shoe and given to the player who has the largest wager against the bank, and two cards are dealt to the croupier, acting as banker. If the rules call for a third card, the player or banker, or both, must take the third card. In the event of a tie, the hand is dealt over. ***Note:*** The guidelines that determine whether a third card

---

---

must be drawn (by the player or banker) are provided at the baccarat table upon request.

The object of the game is to come as close as possible to the number 9. To score the hands, the cards of each hand are totaled and the *last digit* is used. All cards have face value. For example: 10 plus 5 equals 15 (score is 5); 10 plus 4 plus 9 equals 23 (score is 3); 4 plus 3 plus 3 equals 10 (score is 0); and 4 plus 3 plus 2 equals 9 (score is 9). The closest hand to 9 wins.

Each player has a chance to deal the cards. The shoe passes to the player on the right each time the bank loses. If the player wishes, he or she may pass the shoe at any time.

Note: When you bet on the bank and the bank wins, you are charged a 5% commission. This must be paid at the start of a new game or when you leave the table.

BIG SIX

Big Six provides pleasant recreation and involves no study or effort. The wheel has 56 positions on it, 54 of them marked by bills from $1 to $20. The other two spots are jokers, and each pays 40 to 1 if the wheel stops in that position. All other stops pay at face value. Those marked with $20 bills pay 20 to 1, the $5 bills pay 5 to 1, and so forth. The idea behind the game is to predict (or just blindly guess) what spot the wheel will stop at and place a bet accordingly.

BLACKJACK

The dealer starts the game by dealing each player two cards. In some casinos, they're dealt to the player face up, in others face down, but the dealer always gets one card up and one card down. Everybody plays against the dealer. The object is to get a total that is higher than that of the dealer without exceeding 21. All face cards count as 10; all other number cards, except aces, are counted at their face value. An ace may be counted as 1 or 11, whichever you choose it to be.

Starting at his or her left, the dealer gives additional cards to the players who wish to draw (be "hit") or none to a player who wishes to "stand" or "hold." If your count is nearer to 21 than the dealer's, you win. If it's under the dealer's, you lose. Ties are a push and nobody wins. After all the players are satisfied with their counts, the dealer exposes his or her face-down card. If his or her two cards total 16 or less, the dealer must "hit" (draw an additional card) until reaching 17 or over. If the dealer's total exceeds 21, he or she must pay all the players whose hands have not gone "bust." It is important to note here that the blackjack dealer has no choice as to whether he or she should stay or draw. A dealer's decisions are predetermined and known to all the players at the table.

If you're a novice or just rusty, do yourself a favor and buy one of the small laminated cards available in shops all over town that illustrate proper play for every possible hand in blackjack. Even longtime players have been known to pull them out every now and then, and they can save you from making costly errors.

HOW TO PLAY

Here are eight "rules" for blackjack:

1. Place the number of chips that you want to bet on the betting space on your table.
2. Look at the first two cards the dealer starts you with. If you wish to "stand," then wave your hand over your cards, palm down (watch your fellow players), indicating that you don't wish any additional cards. If you elect to draw an additional card, you tell the dealer to "hit" you by tapping the table with a finger (watch your fellow players).
3. If your count goes over 21, you are "bust" and lose, even if the dealer also goes "bust" afterward.
4. If you make 21 in your first two cards (any picture card or 10 with an ace), you've got blackjack. You will be paid 1½ times your bet, provided the dealer does not have blackjack, too, in which case it's a push and nobody wins.
5. If you find a "pair" in your first two cards (say, two 8s or two aces), you may "split" the pair into two hands and treat each card as the first card dealt in two separate hands. You will need to place an additional bet, equal to your original bet, on the table. The dealer will then deal you a new *second* card to the first split card and play commences as described above. This will be done for the second split card as well. *Note:* When you split aces, you will receive only one additional card per ace and must "stand."
6. After seeing your two starting cards, you have the option to "double down." You place an amount equal to your original bet on the table and you receive only one more card. Doubling down is a strategy to capitalize on a potentially strong hand against the dealer's weaker hand. *Tip:* You may double down for less than your original bet, but never more.
7. Anytime the dealer deals himself or herself an ace for the "up" card, you may insure your hand against the possibility that the hole card is a 10 or face card, which would give him or her an automatic blackjack. To insure, you place an amount up to one-half of your bet on the "insurance" line. If the dealer does have a blackjack, you get paid 2 to 1 on the insurance money while losing your original bet: You break even. If the dealer does not have a blackjack, he or she takes your insurance money and play continues in the normal fashion.
8. *Remember:* The dealer must stand on 17 or more and must hit a hand of 16 or less.

Tips Look, but Don't Touch!

1. *Never* touch your cards (or anyone else's), unless it's specifically stated at the table that you may. While you'll receive only a verbal slap on the wrist if you violate this rule, you *really* don't want to get one.
2. Players must use hand signals to indicate their wishes to the dealer. All verbal directions by players will be politely ignored by the dealer, who will remind players to use hand signals. The reason for this is the "Eye in the Sky," the casino's security system, which focuses an "eye" on every table and must record players' decisions to avoid accusations of misconduct or collusion.

PROFESSIONAL TIPS

Advice of the experts in playing blackjack is as follows:

1. *Do not* ask for an extra card if you have a count of 17 or higher, *ever.*
2. *Do not* ask for an extra card when you have a total of 12 or more if the dealer has a 2 through 6 showing in his or her "up" card.
3. *Ask* for an extra card or more when you have a count of 12 through 16 in your hand if the dealer's "up" card is a 7, 8, 9, 10, or ace.

There's a lot more to blackjack strategy than the above, of course. So consider this merely as the bare bones of the game. Blackjack is played with a single deck or with multiple decks; if you're looking for a single-deck game, your best bet is to head to a Downtown casino.

A final tip: Avoid insurance bets; they're sucker bait!

CRAPS

The most exciting casino action is usually found at the craps tables. Betting is frenetic, play fast-paced, and groups quickly bond while yelling and screaming in response to the action.

THE POSSIBLE BETS

The craps table is divided into marked areas (Pass, Come, Field, Big 6, Big 8, and so on), where you place your chips to bet. The following are a few simple directions.

PASS LINE   A "Pass Line" bet pays even money. If the first roll of the dice adds up to 7 or 11, you win your bet; if the first roll adds up to 2, 3, or 12, you lose your bet. If any other number comes up, it's your "point." If you roll your point again, you win, but if a 7 comes up again before your point is rolled, you lose.

DON'T PASS LINE   Betting on the "Don't Pass" is the opposite of betting on the "Pass Line." This time, you lose if a 7 or an 11 is thrown on the first roll, and you win if a 2 or a 3 is thrown on the first roll.

If the first roll is 12, however, it's a push (standoff), and nobody wins. If none of these numbers is thrown and you have a point instead, in order to win, a 7 will have to be thrown before the point comes up again. A "Don't Pass" bet also pays even money.

COME   Betting on "Come" is the same as betting on the Pass Line, but you must bet after the first roll or on any following roll. Again, you'll win on 7 or 11 and lose on 2, 3, or 12. Any other number is your point, and you win if your point comes up again before a 7.

DON'T COME   This is the opposite of a "Come" bet. Again, you wait until after the first roll to bet. A 7 or an 11 means you lose; a 2 or a 3 means you win; 12 is a push, and nobody wins. You win if 7 comes up before the point. (The point, you'll recall, was the first number rolled if it was none of the above.)

FIELD   This is a bet for one roll only. The "Field" consists of seven numbers: 2, 3, 4, 9, 10, 11, and 12. If any of these numbers is thrown on the next roll, you win even money, except on 2 and 12, which pay 2 to 1 (at some casinos 3 to 1).

BIG 6 AND 8   A "Big 6 and 8" bet pays even money. You win if either a 6 or an 8 is rolled before a 7. Mathematically, this is a sucker's bet.

ANY 7   An "Any 7" bet pays the winner 5 for 1. If a 7 is thrown on the first roll after you bet, you win.

Dice Probabilities

Number	Possible Combinations	Actual Odds	Percentage Probability
2	1	35:1	2.8%
3	2	17:1	5.6%
4	3	11:1	8.3%
5	4	8:1	11.1%
6	5	6.2:1	13.9%
7	6	5:1	16.7%
8	5	6.2:1	13.9%
9	4	8:1	11.1%
10	3	11:1	8.3%
11	2	17:1	5.6%
12	1	35:1	2.8%

"HARD WAY" BETS   In the middle of a craps table are pictures of several possible dice combinations together with the odds the casino will pay you if you bet and win on any of those combinations being thrown. For example, if double 3s or 4s are rolled and you had bet on them, you will be paid 7 to 1. If double 2s or 5s are rolled and you had bet on them, you will be paid 9 to 1. If either a 7 is rolled or the number you bet on was rolled any way other than the "Hard Way," then the bet is lost. In-the-know gamblers tend to avoid "Hard Way" bets as an easy way to lose their money.

ANY CRAPS   Here you're lucky if the dice "crap out"—if they show 2, 3, or 12 on the first roll after you bet. If this happens, the bank pays 7 to 1. Any other number is a loser.

PLACE BETS   You can make a "Place Bet" on any of the following numbers: 4, 5, 6, 8, 9, or 10. You're betting that the number you choose will be thrown before a 7 is thrown. If you win, the payoff is as follows: 4 or 10 pays at the rate of 9 to 5, 5 or 9 pays at the rate of 7 to 5, 6 or 8 pays at the rate of 7 to 6. "Place Bets" can be removed at any time before a roll.

SOME PROBABILITIES

The probability of a certain number being rolled at the craps table is not a mystery. As there are only 36 possible outcomes when the dice are rolled, the probability for each number being rolled is easily ascertained. See the "Dice Probabilities" chart in this section to help you, in case you decided it was more fun to pass notes or sleep during your math classes.

So 7 has an advantage over all other combinations, which, over the long run, is in favor of the casino. You can't beat the law of averages, but if you can't beat 'em, join 'em. (Play the "Don't Pass" bet.)

KENO

Originating in China, this is one of the oldest games of chance. Legend has it that funds acquired from the game were used to finance construction of the Great Wall of China.

Chinese railroad construction workers first introduced keno into the United States in the 1800s. Easy to play, and offering a chance to sit down and converse between bets, it is one of the most popular games in town—despite the fact that *the house percentage is greater than that of any other casino game!*

To play, you must first obtain a keno form, available at the counter in the keno lounge and in most Las Vegas coffee shops. In the latter, you'll usually find blank keno forms and thick black crayons on your table. Fill yours out, and a miniskirted keno runner will come and collect it. After the game is over, she'll return with your winning or losing ticket. If you've won, it's customary to offer a tip, depending on your winnings.

For those of you with state lotteries, this game will appear very familiar. You can select from 1 to 15 numbers (out of a total of 80) and if all of your numbers come up, you win. Depending on how many numbers you've selected, you can win smaller amounts if less than all of your numbers have come up. For example, if you bet a "3 spot" (selecting a total of three numbers) and two come up, you'll win something but not as much as if all three had shown up. A one-number mark is known as a 1-spot, a two-number selection is a 2-spot, and so on. After you have selected the number of spots you wish to play, write the amount you want to wager on the ticket, in the right-hand corner where indicated. The more you bet, the more you can win if your numbers come up. Before the game starts, you have to give the completed form to a keno runner, or hand it in at the keno lounge desk, and pay for your bet. You'll get back a duplicate form with the number of the game you're playing on it. Then the game begins. As numbers appear on the keno board, compare them to the numbers you've marked on your ticket. After 20 numbers have appeared on the board, the game is over, and if you've won, turn in your ticket to collect your winnings.

The more numbers on the board matching the numbers on your ticket, the more you win (in some cases, you get paid if *none* of your numbers comes up). If you want to keep playing the same numbers over and over, you can replay a ticket by handing in your duplicate to the keno runner; you don't have to keep rewriting it.

In addition to the straight bets described above, you can split your ticket, betting various amounts on two or more groups of numbers. It does get a little complex, as combination-betting options are almost infinite. Helpful casino personnel in the keno lounge can assist you with combination betting.

POKER

Poker is the game of the Old West. There's at least one sequence in every Western where the hero faces off against the villain over a poker hand. In Las Vegas, poker is just about the biggest thing going, thanks to the prevalence and popularity of celebrity poker TV shows, poker tours, books, magazines, and who knows what all. Just about every casino now has a poker room, and it's just a matter of time before the others catch up.

There are lots of variations on the basic game, but one of the most popular is **Hold 'Em.** Two cards are dealt face down to the players. After a betting round, five community cards (everyone can use them) are dealt face up on the table. Players makes the best five-card hand, using their own cards and the "board" (the community cards), and the best hand wins. The house dealer takes care of the shuffling and the dealing, and moves a marker around the table to alternate the start of the deal. The house rakes 1% to 5% (it depends on the casino) from each pot. Most casinos also provide tables for playing Seven-Card Stud, Omaha High, and Omaha Hi-Lo. A few will even have Seven-Card Stud Hi-Lo split. To learn how these variations are played, either read a book or take lessons.

Warning: If you don't know how to play poker, don't attempt to learn at a table. Card sharks are not a rare species in Vegas; they will gladly feast on fresh meat (you!). Find a casino that provides free gaming lessons and learn, to paraphrase Kenny Rogers, when to hold 'em, and when to fold 'em.

PAI GOW POKER

Pai gow poker (a variation on poker) has become increasingly popular. The game is played with a traditional deck plus one joker. The joker is a wild card that can be used as an ace or to complete a straight, a flush, a straight flush, or a royal flush. Each player is dealt seven cards to arrange into two hands: a two-card hand and a five-card hand. As in standard poker, the highest two-card hand is two aces, and the highest five-card hand is a royal flush. The five-card hand *must* be higher than the two-card hand (if the two-card hand is a pair of sixes, for example, the five-card hand must be a pair of sevens or better). Any player's hand that is set incorrectly is an automatic loser. The object of the game is for both of the players' hands to rank higher than both of the banker's hands. Should one hand rank exactly the same as the banker's hand, this is a tie (called a "copy"), *and the banker wins all tie hands.* If the player wins one hand but loses the other, this is a "push," and no money changes hands. The house dealer or any player may be the banker. The bank is offered to each player, and each player may accept or pass. Winning hands are paid even money, less a 5% commission.

CARIBBEAN STUD POKER

Caribbean stud poker is yet another variation of poker that is gaining in popularity. Players put in a single ante bet and are dealt five cards face down from a single deck; they play solely against the dealer, who receives five cards, one of them face up. Players are then given the option of folding, or may call by making an additional bet that is double their original ante. After all player bets have been made, the dealer's cards are revealed. If the dealer doesn't qualify with *at least an ace/king combination,* players are paid even money on their ante and their call bets are returned. If the dealer does qualify, each player's hand is compared to the dealer's. On winning hands, players receive even money on their ante bets, and call bets are paid out on a scale according to the value of their hands. The scale ranges from even money for a pair, to 100 to 1 on a royal flush, although there is usually a cap on the maximum payoff, which varies from casino to casino.

An additional feature of Caribbean stud is the inclusion of a progressive jackpot. For an additional side bet of $1, a player may qualify for a payoff from a progressive jackpot. The jackpot bet pays off only on a flush or better, but you can win on this bet even if the dealer ends up with a better hand than you do. Dream all you want of getting that royal flush and taking home the jackpot, but the odds of it happening are astronomical, so don't be so quick to turn in your resignation letter. Most veteran gamblers will tell you this is a bad bet (from a strict mathematical standpoint, it is), but considering that Caribbean stud already has a house advantage that is even larger than the one in roulette, if you're going to play, you might as well toss in the buck and pray.

LET IT RIDE

Let It Ride is another popular game that involves poker hands. You place three bets at the outset and are dealt three cards. The dealer is dealt two cards that act as community cards (you're not playing against the dealer). Once you've seen your cards, you can choose to pull the first of your three bets back or "Let It Ride." The object of this game is to get a pair of 10s or better by combining your cards with the dealer's. If you're holding a pair of 10s or better in your first three cards, you want to let your bets ride the whole way through. Once you've decided whether or not to let your first bet ride, the dealer exposes one of his or her two cards. Once again, you must make a decision to take back your middle bet or keep on going. Then the dealer exposes the last of his or her cards; your third bet must stay. The dealer then turns over the hands of the players and determines whether you've won. Winning bets are paid on a scale, ranging from even money for a single pair up to 1,000 to 1 for a royal flush. These payouts are for each bet you have in play. Like Caribbean Stud, Let It Ride has a progressive jackpot that you can win for high hands if you cough up an additional dollar per hand, but be advised that the house advantage on that $1 is obscene. But hey, that's why it's called gambling.

3-CARD POKER

3-Card Poker is rapidly gaining popularity, and now you'll find at least one table in most major Vegas casinos. It's actually more difficult to explain than to play. For this reason, we recommend watching a table for awhile. You should grasp it pretty quickly.

Basically, players are dealt three cards with no draw and have to make the best poker hand out of those three cards. Possible combinations include a straight flush (three sequential cards of the same suit), three of a kind (three queens for example), a straight (three sequential cards of any suit), a flush (three cards of the same suit), and a pair (two queens, for example). Even if you don't have one of the favored combinations, you can still win if you have cards higher than the dealer.

On the table you'll see three betting areas—the Ante, the Play, and the Pair Plus. There are actually two games in one on a 3-Card Poker table—"Pair Plus" and "Ante and Play." You can play only the Pair Plus or only the Ante or both. Place your chips in the areas you want to bet in.

In Pair Plus, you are betting only on your hand, not competing against anyone else at the table or the dealer. If you get a pair or better, depending on your hand, the pay-off can be pretty fab—Straight Flush: 40 to 1, Three of a Kind: 30 to 1, Straight: 6 to 1, Flush: 3 to 1, Pair: 1 to 1.

In Ante and Play, you are betting that your hand will be better than the dealer's but are not competing against anyone else at the table. You place an Ante bet, view your cards, and then if you decide you like your hand, you place a bet in the Play area equal to your Ante bet. If you get lousy cards and don't want to go forward, you can fold, losing only your Ante bet and your Pair Plus bet, if you made one. Once all bets are made, the dealer's hand is revealed—he or she must have at least a single queen for the bet to count; if not, your Ante and Play bets are returned. If you beat the dealer's hand, you get a 1 to 1 payoff, but there is a bonus for a particularly good winning hand: Straight Flush: 5 to 1, Three of a Kind: 4 to 1, Straight: 1 to 1.

Your three cards are dealt. If you played only Pair Plus, it doesn't matter what the dealer has—you get paid if you have a pair or better. If you don't, you lose your bet. If you played the Ante bet, you must then either fold and lose the Ante bet or match the Ante bet by placing the same amount on the Play area. The dealer's hand is revealed and payouts happen accordingly. Each hand consists of one fresh 52-card deck.

Meanwhile, as if all this wasn't enough, new variations on table games keep popping up. The latest is Crazy 4 Poker—similar to 3-Card poker, only with five cards dealt, no draw, make your best 4-card poker hand out of it.

ROULETTE

Roulette is an extremely easy game to play, and it's really quite colorful and exciting to watch. The wheel spins and the little ball bounces around, finally dropping into one of the slots, numbered 1 to 36, plus 0 and 00. You can place bets "Inside" the table and "Outside" the table. Inside bets are bets placed on a particular number or a set of numbers. Outside bets are those placed in the boxes surrounding the number table. If you bet on a specific number and it comes up, you'll be paid 35 to 1 on your bet. Bear in mind, however, that the odds of a particular number coming up are actually 38 to 1 (don't forget that 0 and 00!) so the house has an advantage the moment you place an Inside bet. For payoffs on Outside bets, such as Red/Black, Odd/Even, and so forth, see the table below. The methods of placing single-number bets, column bets, and others are fairly obvious. The dealer will be happy to show you how make many interesting betting combinations, such as betting on six numbers at once. Each player is given different-colored chips so that it's easy to follow the numbers you've bet on.

> **Impressions**
> If you aim to leave Las Vegas with a small fortune, go there with a large one.
> —Anonymous

Some typical bets are indicated by means of letters on the roulette layout depicted here. The winning odds for each of these sample bets are listed. These bets can be made on any corresponding combinations of numbers.

SLOTS

You put the coin in the slot and pull the handle. What, you thought there was a trick to this?

Actually, there is a bit more to it. But first, some background. Old-timers will tell you slots were invented to give wives something to do while their husbands gambled. Slots used to be stuck at the edges of the casino and could be counted on one hand, maybe two. But now they *are* the casino. The casinos make more from slots than from craps, blackjack, and roulette combined. There are 115,000 slot machines (not including video poker) in the county. Some of these are at the airport, steps from you as you deplane. It's a just a matter of time before the planes flying into Vegas feature slots that pop up as soon as you cross the state line.

But in order to keep up with the increasing competition, the plain old machine, where reels just spin, has become nearly obsolete. Now they are all computerized and have added buttons to push so you can avoid getting carpal tunnel syndrome from yanking the handle all night. (The handles are still there on many of them.) Many don't even have reels anymore but are entirely video screens, which offer a number of little bonus extras that have nothing to do with actual play. The idea is still simple: Get three (sometimes four) cherries (clowns, sevens, dinosaurs, whatever) in a row and you win something. Each machine has its own combination. Some will pay you something with just one symbol showing; on most, the more combinations there are, the more opportunities for loot. Some will even pay if you get three blanks. Study each machine to learn what it does. *Note:* The **payback** goes up considerably if you bet the limit (from 2 to as many as 45 coins).

Progressive slots are groups of linked machines (sometimes spread over several casinos) where the jackpot gets bigger every few moments (just as lottery jackpots build up). Bigger and better games keep showing up; for example, there's Anchor Gaming's much-imitated **Wheel of Gold,** wherein if you get the right symbol, you get to spin a roulette wheel, which guarantees you a win of a serious number of coins. **Totem Pole** is the Godzilla of slot machines, a behemoth that allows you to spin up to three reels at once (provided you put in the limit).

Players Clubs

If you play slots or video poker, or, indeed, just gamble quite a bit, or even just gamble, it definitely pays to join a players club. These so-called clubs are designed to attract and keep customers in a given casino by providing incentives: meals, shows, discounts on rooms, gifts, tournament invitations, discounts at hotel shops, VIP treatment, and (more and more) cash rebates. Join a players club (it doesn't cost a cent to sign up), and soon you, too, will be getting those great hotel-rate offers—$20-a-night rooms, affordable rooms at the luxury resorts, even free rooms. (This is one way to beat the high hotel rates.) Of course, your rewards are often greater if you play just in one casino, but your mobility is limited.

When you join a players club (inquire at the casino desk), you're given something that looks like a credit card, which you must insert into an ATM-like device whenever you play. Yes, many casinos even have them for the tables as well as the machines. (Don't forget to retrieve your card when you leave the machine, as we sometimes do—though that may work in your favor if someone comes along and plays the machine without removing it.) The device tracks your play and computes bonus points.

Which players club should you join? Actually, you should join one at any casino where you play because even the act of joining usually entitles you to some benefits. It's convenient to concentrate play where you're staying; if you play a great deal, a casino-hotel's players-club benefits may be a factor in your accommodations choice. Consider, though, particularly if you aren't a high roller, the players clubs Downtown. You get more bang for

Other gimmick machines include the popular **Wheel of Fortune** machines, slots that have a gorilla attempt to climb the Empire State Building, heading up as you win, and machines with themes like Elvis or the Three Stooges. And, of course, there are always those **giant slot machines,** gimmicky devices found in almost every casino. They may not win as often as regular slots (though there is no definite word on it one way or the other), but not only are they just plain fun to spin, they often turn into audience-participation gambling, as watchers gather to cheer you on to victory.

Nickel slots, which for a long time had been overlooked, relegated to a lonely spot somewhere by a back wall because they were not as profitable for the casinos as quarter and dollar slots, are making a comeback. Many machines now offer a 45-nickel maximum (meaning a larger bet on those machines than on the five-quarter-maximum slots), and gamblers have been flocking to them. As a result, more cash is pocketed by the casino (which keeps a higher percentage of cash off of nickel slots than it does off of quarter slots), which is happy to accommodate this trend by offering up more and more nickel slots. (See how this all works? Are you paying attention?) Ultra-tightwads will be pleased by the increased presence of the humble penny slot, but few, if any, allow for only a penny bet—in fact, the maximum bet is $3!

The biggest trend in Vegas, though, is the use of cashless machines. When gambling with these machines, players insert their money, they play, and when they cash your buck because you don't have to spend as much to start raking in the goodies.

Another advantage is to join a players club that covers many hotels under the same corporate umbrella. Caesars Entertainment (formerly Park Place) runs Caesars, The Flamingo Las Vegas, Paris, Bally's, and more, and their players club offers discounts and point awards at all of their properties. The same goes for the Harrah's hotels, which just purchased Caesars Entertainment, those in the MGM MIRAGE stable (The Mirage, Bellagio, MGM Grand, and so on), the locals' favorite Station Casinos (Palace, Sunset, Texas, and more), and the Carl Icahn properties, which include Arizona Charlie's and the Stratosphere Casino Hotel & Tower. Note that any minute now, the Mandalay Resorts (Mandalay Bay, Luxor, Circus Circus, Excalibur) will be added to the MGM MIRAGE banner, giving you still more possibilities.

One way to judge a players club is by the quality of service you receive when you enroll. Personnel should politely answer all your questions (for instance, is nickel play included, and is there a time limit for earning required points?) and be able to tell you exactly how many points you need for various bonuses.

Maximizing your players club profits and choosing the club that's best for you is a complex business. If you want to get into it in depth, order a copy of Jeffrey Compton's *The Las Vegas Advisor Guide to Slot Clubs* ($9.95 plus shipping), which examines just about every facet of the situation (© 800/ 244-2224). Compton gives high ratings to the clubs at Caesars Palace, The Mirage, TI at the Mirage, The Flamingo Las Vegas, Rio, Sahara, Sam's Town, Four Queens, Golden Nugget, and Lady Luck.

out, they get—instead of the comforting sound of coins cascading out into the tray—a little paper ticket with their total winnings on it. (Those of us who find the sound of the coins pouring out a comfort are only slightly pleased to learn that the same noise plays, as a computer-generated audio effect, when the ticket is disgorged.) Hand in your ticket at a cashier's window, and you get your winnings. It's not nearly as viscerally satisfying, but it is the wave of the future; many of the casinos are already entirely cashless, and the rest are on their way. Why take this cheap thrill from us? Because it saves gambling time (instead of waiting for the flow of coins to stop, you can grab your ticket and pop it into another machine) and maintenance time (keeping the machines stocked with coins), and the casinos no longer need worry about having enough quarters on hand. We are not pleased about this. *Note:* As a result of cashless machine trend, the casinos are much quieter, as many of the formerly chatty machines have been largely silenced, and that famous Vegas clang-clang is somewhat dimmed.

Are there surefire ways to win on a slot machine? No. But you can lose more slowly. The slot machines use minicomputers known as Random Number Generators (RNGs) to determine the winning combinations on a machine; depending on how many numbers have been programmed into the RNG, some machines are going to be "looser" than others. A bank of empty slots probably (but not certainly) means the machines are tight. Go find a line where lots of people are sitting around with trays full of money. (Of course, yours will be the one that doesn't hit.) A good rule of thumb is that if your slot doesn't hit something in four or five pulls, leave it and go find another. It's not as though you won't have some choice in the matter. Also, each casino has a bank of slots that they advertise as more loose or with a bigger payback. Try these. It's what they want you to do, but what the heck.

Note: Many slot machines no longer accept coins at all for bets. For these new machines, bets have to start with bills accepted into special slots. This will make all but extinct the famous change carts that used to roam the floors, helping people get rolls of quarters and the like.

SPORTS BOOKS

Most of the larger hotels in Las Vegas have sports-book operations, which look a lot like commodities-futures trading boards. In some, almost as large as theaters, you can sit comfortably, occasionally in recliners and sometimes with your own video screen, and watch ball games, fights, and, at some casinos, horse races on huge TV screens. To add to your enjoyment, there's usually a deli/bar nearby that serves sandwiches, hot dogs, soft drinks, and beer. As a matter of fact, some of the best sandwiches in Las Vegas are served next to the sports books. Sports books take bets on virtually every sport (and not just who'll win, but what the final score will be, who'll be first to hit a home run, who'll be MVP, who'll wear red shoes, you name it). They are best during important playoff games or big horse races, when everyone in the place is watching the same event—shrieking, shouting, and moaning, sometimes in unison. Joining in with a cheap bet (so you feel like you, too, have a personal stake in the matter) makes for bargain entertainment.

VIDEO POKER

Rapidly gaining on slots in popularity, video poker works the same way as regular poker, except you play against the machine. You are dealt a hand, you pick which cards to keep and which to discard, and then get your new hand. And, it is hoped, you collect your winnings. This is somewhat more of a challenge and more active than slots because you have some control (or at least the illusion of control) over your fate, and it's easier than playing actual poker with a table full of folks who probably take it very seriously.

There are a number of varieties of this machine, with **Jacks or Better, Deuces Wild,** and so forth. Be sure to study your machine before you sit down. (The best returns are offered on the **Bonus Poker** machines; the payback for a pair of Jacks or better is two times your bet, and three times for three of a kind.) The Holy Grail of video-poker machines is the 9/6 (it pays nine coins for a full house, six coins for a flush), but you'll need to pray a lot before you find one in town. Some machines offer **double down:** After you have won, you get a chance to draw cards against the machine, with the higher card the winner. If you win, your money is doubled and you are offered a chance to go again. Your money can increase nicely during this time, and you can also lose it all very quickly, which is most annoying.

Technology is catching up with video poker, too. Now they even have touch screens, which offer a variety of different poker games, blackjack, and video slots—just touch your screen and choose your poison.

3 The Casinos

Casino choice is a personal thing. Some like to find their lucky place and stick with it, while others love to take advantage of the nearly endless choices that Vegas offers. Everyone should casino-hop at least once to marvel (or get dizzy) at the decor/spectacle and the sheer excess of it all. But beyond decoration, there isn't too much difference. You've got your slot machines, your gaming tables, and your big chandeliers.

Virtually all casinos make sure they have no clocks or windows—they do not want you to interrupt your losing streak by realizing how much time has passed. Of course, we've all heard the legend that Vegas casinos pump in fresh oxygen to keep the players from getting tired and wanting to pack it in. The veracity of this is hard to confirm, but we can only hope it's true, especially when we think of that time we looked up after a long stretch of gambling and discovered it was Thursday.

Don't be a snob, and don't be overly dazzled by the fancy casinos. Sometimes you can have a better time at one of the older places Downtown, where stakes are lower, pretensions are nonexistent, and the clientele is often friendlier. Frankly, real gamblers—and by that we don't necessarily mean high rollers, but those who play to win regardless of the amount of said win—head straight for Downtown (and most often, straight for Binion's) for these precise reasons, caring not a whit about glitz and glamour. Even if you don't take your gambling as seriously as that, you may well want to follow their example. After all, it's getting harder and harder to find cheap tables (where you can play a hand of blackjack, for example, for less than $10) on the Strip—so take your hard-earned money to where you can lose it more slowly!

We would also call your attention to less glamorous, less readily accessible casinos, such as local favorites Sunset Station, Texas Station, the Cannery, Fiesta Rancho, Fiesta Henderson, and Fiesta Santa Fe, where payoffs are often higher than on the Strip, and the limits are lower.

You can expect to find in every casino the usual and expected assortment of games—slot machines, of course, video poker, blackjack, table poker (though less and less these days), a race and sports book, a keno lounge, a poker room, baccarat, mini-baccarat, Caribbean stud, Let It Ride, craps, roulette, pai gow poker, and more, more, more. If you want a particular game, and it's not one of the most obvious, you might want to call before heading over to a particular casino, just to make sure.

What follows is a description of most of the major casinos in Vegas, including their level of claustrophobia, whether they have a giant slot machine (it's a sucker's bet, but we love them), and a completely arbitrary assessment based on whether we won there.

SOUTH STRIP

Excalibur   As you might expect, the Excalibur casino is replete with suits of armor, stained-glass panels, knights, dragons, and velvet and satin heraldic banners, with gaming action taking place beneath vast iron-and-gold chandeliers fit for a medieval

Impressions

Tip Number 3: Win a bunch of money. I can't recommend this too highly. If it hasn't occurred to you, win $1,200 and see for yourself. It's very energizing and really adds to your Vegas fun.

—Merrill Markoe, Viva Las Wine Goddesses!

Memories of a Longtime Dealer

Lou has been a part of the gaming industry for 40 years, the first 20 of which he spent as a dealer in Las Vegas.

"My favorite places were The Flamingo, the Sands, and the Desert Inn. That's when the corporations weren't there. That's when the other folks were in. The mob guys—I never knew it, but that's what they were. I was just a kid. Bugsy had just gotten killed when I went to work at The Flamingo. The Sands was my very first favorite. That was the hotel of all hotels. They had the very best management team. They took care of their help. Their benefits were better than any union. It was the place.

"Years ago, you had great entertainment. You could go to a lounge and catch better acts than in the showroom. Major stars were in the lounges, or they would come in and sit in with the acts after the showroom closed. Don Rickles: Sinatra would get up with him once in a while. Sinatra gave me my first $100 tip. He was playing blackjack. Then he said, 'Do you want to play it or keep it?' I wanted to be polite, so I said, 'Bet it.' And he lost. In those days when the star would appear on stage, between shows they would come out into the casinos. Sinatra and Sammy would deal. They would blow money, but the casinos didn't care. It was a fun, fun place.

"The casinos were run the way they were supposed to be run—for the customer, not so corporate-minded. In those days, you could go to Vegas, get your room very reasonable, your food was practically free, your shows were practically free, you would spend $500 in the casino, but you would come back and be happy because gaming was a form of entertainment. When they ran the casinos, you would have a ball, come home, and be happy. They were very happy if the restaurants and shows lost money—you still lost that $500. Now it would cost you $100 to stay at a hotel, and food

castle fortress. This all makes it fine for kitsch-seekers, but anyone who hates crowds or is sensitive to noise will hate it. The overall effect is less like a castle and more like a dungeon. One of us won a lot of money here and refused to share it with the other, so our final judgment about the casino is, well, mixed. Excalibur is now part of Mandalay Resorts' One Club slot-reward program, which is also valid at Luxor, Mandalay Bay, Circus Circus, and others, and will most likely be integrated with the casinos of new corporate owner MGM MIRAGE, including MGM Grand, The Mirage, TI at the Mirage, and Bellagio. 3850 Las Vegas Blvd. S. ✆ 702/597-7777.

Luxor Las Vegas   More accessible than ever, thanks to the air-conditioned people mover from Excalibur and the monorail from Mandalay Bay, Luxor's casino was completely remodeled a few years back and, in our opinion, improved immeasurably. You enter through a giant temple gateway flanked by massive statues of Ramses. Gone is the space-wasting central area that used to contain the bathrooms, cashiers, and casino offices. This additional space gives the casino a much more airy feel, which produces a low claustrophobia level—in parts, you can see all the way up the inside of the pyramid. King Tut heads and sphinxes adorn slot areas. The One Club, a Mandalay is much more expensive, and to get a ticket to one of these shows is ridiculous. Now you gamble only $150 and you aren't as happy when you come home because you don't feel like you've been treated to anything. It all goes into the same pocket—what difference does it make? It gives the customer the same hours and more fun. They don't understand that. It's not the same industry as when they ran it. And it shows."

LOU THE DEALER'S GAMING TIPS
If you are a **craps** shooter, just look around at the tables where they have the most chips. Find the guy with the most chips, and do what he does. Follow him along.

For **blackjack,** everybody will tell you in all your books to try to play single and double decks. I don't agree with that, and I never will. The average player goes in to enjoy himself and to win a few dollars. So he is not a professional card counter. Play a shoe. If that shoe is going bad and you catch a run, you will make a lot more money than with a single deck.

Look at gaming as a form of entertainment. Look at that $100 that you might have spent on dinner or a club, where we laughed and had a few drinks and had a good time. Think of it that way.

If you double your money, quit. Not quit gambling, but quit that table. Go have a sandwich or watch a show. And *then* come back. The odds aren't that tremendously in favor of the casinos. How they make their money is through greed; gamblers doubling their money then trying to quadruple it and losing it all, and more.

Try to survive. Don't try to win the hotel. Just try to win a few dollars. Then stop and enjoy it.

Resorts slot-players club, also valid at sister properties such as Excalibur, Mandalay Bay, Circus Circus, and others, offers rewards of cash, merchandise, meals, and special services to slot and table players. Sports action unfolds on 17 large-screen TVs and 128 personalized monitors in Luxor's race and sports book. We already felt inclined to like this casino, thanks to a good run at blackjack, but the redesign has made it even more inviting. 3900 Las Vegas Blvd. S. ☎ 702/262-4000.

Mandalay Bay You'll find "elegant" gaming in a pre-fab, deliberate way, with a very high ceiling that produces a very low claustrophobia factor. It's definitely the right place to gamble if you're looking for less hectic, less gimmick-filled play. The layout makes it look airy, and it's marginally less confusing and certainly less overwhelming than many other casinos. Because it is so far down the Strip, there are fewer walk-in players, but the presence of the House of Blues and the increasing popularity of the rumjungle nightclub can mean a late-night influx of customers. There's a big, ultra-comfortable sports book (complete with armchairs that could well encourage a relaxed gambler to fall asleep), including a live daily sports-radio show. Players can sign up for the One Club, a Mandalay Resorts player-reward system also valid at sister properties like Luxor, Excalibur, Circus Circus, and others that will most likely be integrated with the casinos of new corporate owner MGM MIRAGE, including MGM Grand, The Mirage, TI at the Mirage, and Bellagio. 3950 Las Vegas Blvd. S. ℂ 702/632-7777.

MGM Grand   Las Vegas's largest casino (171,500 sq. ft.)—we've been to countries that were smaller!—is divided into four themed areas, in a futile attempt to make it seem smaller. Most of the *Wizard of Oz* decorations have been removed, but spend an hour in here and you may feel like Dorothy after she was whisked away by the twister. You will get lost at least once. One section features a high-roller slot area with machines that operate on coins valued at $100 and $500! The sports casino houses a big poker room, a state-of-the-art race and sports book, and the Turf Club Lounge. The French Riviera–themed Monte Carlo casino has a luxurious marble-columned and gold-draped private high-end gaming area. Carousels of progressive slots unique to the MGM Grand include the very popular Majestic Lions high-frequency $1 slot machines, which pay out more than $1 million daily, and the Lion's Share $1 slots, which are capable of jackpots exceeding $1 million each at any time. This hotel takes part in the MGM MIRAGE Players Club, which is also valid at sister properties like The Mirage, New York–New York, and others, and will probably be integrated with Mandalay Resorts casinos in the future. 3799 Las Vegas Blvd. S. ℂ 702/891-7777.

Monte Carlo Resort & Casino   This place is all huge ceilings and white-light interior: Obviously, they're trying to evoke gambling in Monaco. While the decor shows lots of attention, it perhaps had too much attention. Bulbs line the ceiling, and everywhere you look is some detail or other. It's busy on both your eyes and your ears. So despite the effort put in, it's not a pleasant place to gamble. However, there is a large and comfortable race and sports-book area, with its own cocktail lounge. This casino takes part in the One Club player-reward system, also valid at Mandalay Bay, Luxor, and others, and may be integrated with the MGM MIRAGE Players Club in the future now that they are all under the same corporate umbrella. 3770 Las Vegas Blvd. S. ℂ 702/730-7777.

New York–New York   Another theme-run-wild place: tuxes on the backs of gaming chairs and so forth, all set in a miniature New York City. It's all fabulous fun, but despite a low claustrophobia level (thanks to an unusually high ceiling), it is a major case of sensory overload. This may prove distracting. On the other hand, we won repeatedly here, so we love it. And in places, it is, if one can say this about anything in Vegas with a straight face, quite beautiful—or at least dazzling. Serious gamblers understandably may sniff at it all and prefer to take their business to a more seemly casino, but everyone else should have about the most Vegasy time they can. NY–NY participates in the MGM MIRAGE Player's Club, also valid at sister properties like the MGM Grand and The Mirage, and will probably be linked to Mandalay Resorts properties like Mandalay Bay and Luxor at some point in the future. 3790 Las Vegas Blvd. S. ℂ 702/740-6969.

Orleans   This is not a particularly special gambling space, though it does have a low claustrophobia level. Another plus is that they sometimes play Cajun and zydeco music over the sound system, so you can two-step while you gamble, which can make losing somewhat less painful. It has all the needed tables—blackjack, craps, and so forth—plus plenty of slots, including the popular Wheel of Fortune machine, which works like those other roulette-wheel slots, but in this case, actually plays the theme song from the TV show. It will even applaud for you if you win. Since Orleans is popular with locals, there are lots of video-poker options. And because it's not on the Strip, you'll find better odds for craps and cheaper table minimums. Their players' club card gains you points at all Coast Casinos, such as Gold Coast, Suncoast, and others, and may be linked in the future to new corporate owner Boyd Casinos at places like the Stardust and Main Street Station. 4500 W. Tropicana Ave. ✆ 702/365-7111.

Tropicana   Not quite as good-looking as it once was, and, yes, highly tropical, with gaming tables situated beneath a massive stained-glass archway and Art Nouveau lighting fixtures. In summer it offers something totally unique: swim-up blackjack tables located in the hotel's 5-acre tropical garden and pool area. Slot and table-game players can earn bonus points toward rooms, shows, and meals by obtaining an Island Winners Club card in the casino. A luxurious high-end slot area has machines that take up to $100 on a single pull. Numerous tournaments take place here, and free gaming lessons are offered weekdays. 3801 Las Vegas Blvd. S. ✆ 702/739-2222.

MID-STRIP

Aladdin   No telling what will happen to all the actual Moroccan tile (and other *Arabian Nights* touches) that makes us like this casino so much, when new owners, Planet Hollywood, complete their renovations sometime in 2006. But right now, it's just good and tacky. It's big, with high ceilings that help the claustrophobia index, but it's also confusingly laid out, though a recent revamping of the floor has helped alleviate the problem some. Still, we won with the giant slot machine, and one of our moms won there, so, hey, no complaints. Also, the big problem, from the hotel's standpoint, though not really from ours, is that it was planned so that one was not required to walk through it to get to other Aladdin goodies, but what that does mean is that, in some ways, it's kind of hard to find—which is not good for business. That may change, maybe even by the time you read this, as there are plans in the works to restructure the outside to make casino passage virtually mandatory. A bigger potential change to keep in mind is that plan Planet Hollywood has to remake the casino in its own image (what that means is hard to say, but we can all probably look to the Hard Rock for ideas). Do notice the European-style gaming salon that is operated by famed London Clubs International. It has its own private entrance and elevator, a gourmet restaurant, and 24-hour butler service in addition to the high-stakes tables and slots. Too rich for our blood, but perhaps not for yours. 3667 Las Vegas Blvd. S. ✆ 702/736-0111.

Bally's Las Vegas   Bally's casino is large (the size of a football field), with lots of colorful signage. The big ceiling makes for a low claustrophobia level. Their players club is valid at sister properties like Caesars Palace and Paris (and will most likely be linked

---

Tips   A Breath of Fresh Air

Las Vegas is one of the few cities in America that welcomes smokers with open arms. Smoking doesn't just exist in the casino hotels, it runs rampant. (Would you like some air with your smoke?) Which is why we were pleasantly shocked when Bellagio's poker room and The Mirage's keno lounge and poker room went completely smoke-free. It seems the hotels are doing their darnedest to attract those most rabid of antismokers—Californians. (Right across the border, California is one of Sin City's biggest markets.)

to new owners Harrah's Total Rewards), offering members cash rebates, room discounts, free meals and show tickets, and invitations to special events, among other perks. The casino hosts frequent slot tournaments, and free gaming lessons are offered. 3645 Las Vegas Blvd. S. ✆ 702/739-4111.

Barbary Coast   The Barbary Coast is an 1890s-style casino ornately decorated with $2 million worth of gorgeous stained-glass skylights and signs, as well as immense crystal-dangling globe chandeliers over the gaming tables. It's kind of small, dark, and cluttered, but it's also Old Las Vegas (and we mean "old" loosely), and small is rare on the Strip. The casino has a players club tied into the other Coast Casinos, such as Orleans and Suncoast, and may be linked to new owners Boyd Casinos at places like the Stardust and Main Street Station. 3595 Las Vegas Blvd. S. ✆ 702/737-7111.

Bellagio   The slot machines here are mostly encased in marble and fine woods. How's that for upping the ante on classy? In all fairness, Bellagio comes the closest to re-creating the feel of gambling in Monte Carlo (the country, not the next-door casino), but its relentless good taste means that this is one pretty forgettable casino. After all, we are suckers for a wacky theme that screams "Vegas," and European class just doesn't cut it. Then again, we brought a pal of more refined sensibility, and she adored it, finding it the perfect antidote to New York–New York. Sure, there are good touches—we always like a high ceiling to reduce the claustrophobia index, and the place is laid out in an easy-to-navigate grid with ultrawide aisles, so walking through doesn't seem like such a crowded collision-course maze. (*Tip:* The main casino path is identified with black carpets.) And we won big here, so there's that. Anyway, the cozy sports book has individual TVs and entirely denlike leather chairs—quite, quite comfortable. Bellagio is part of the MGM MIRAGE Players Club, earning you points that can be used for comps here or at sister properties like The Mirage, TI at the Mirage and, at some point in the future, new siblings Mandalay Bay and Luxor, among others. 3600 Las Vegas Blvd. S. ✆ 888/987-6667.

Caesars Palace   Caesars' casino is simultaneously the ultimate in gambling luxury and the ultimate in Vegas kitsch. Cocktail waitresses in togas parade about as you gamble under the watchful gaze of faux-marble Roman statues. The very high ceiling in certain areas of the casino makes for a very low claustrophobia level, especially thanks to the recent face-lift, which has lightened up the paint and made the area much brighter. Unfortunately, some spots in the casino are dark and entirely too claustrophobic. Although we love it, the casino has become somewhat confusing and unmanageable because of its size and meandering layout, like Caesars itself.

A notable facility is the state-of-the-art **Race and Sports Book,** with huge electronic display boards and giant video screens. (Caesars pioneered computer-generated wagering data that can be communicated in less than half a second, and has sophisticated satellite equipment that can pick up the broadcast of virtually any sporting event in the world.) The domed VIP slot arena of the Forum Casino (minimum bet is $5, but you can wager up to $1,500 on a single pull!) is a plush, crystal-chandeliered precinct with seating in roomy, adjustable chairs. Gamblers can accumulate bonus points toward cash back, gifts, gratis show tickets, meals, and rooms by joining the players club, also valid at sister properties like Bally's and Paris. Club membership also lets you in on grand-prize drawings, tournaments, and parties. There's a good chance their players club will be integrated with Harrah's Total Rewards since the two companies merged in 2005.

The most upscale of the Caesars gaming rooms is the intimate, European-style casino adjoining the **Palace Court** restaurant. It's a gorgeous and elegant place to gamble, but we've never won there, so we hate it. 3570 Las Vegas Blvd. S. © 702/731-7110.

The Flamingo Las Vegas If you've seen the movie *Bugsy*, you won't recognize this as Mr. Siegel's baby. We can't say for sure what their seemingly years-long casino renovation actually did. It all looks pretty much the same, but it might be marginally less confusing and tortuous a layout (trust us, anything is an improvement) with better, and most welcome, access to the street (before, you needed a trail of bread crumbs and a lot of stamina to find your way out). Still, the claustrophobia factor is moderately high. We have to say that of all the casinos that qualify as older, this is the most pleasant one in which to play. Unfortunately, the gambler seems to be paying for it; no more daytime $3 blackjack. One of our favorite slot machines is here, but we won't tell you which one, to save it for ourselves. Sorry. The Flamingo takes part in Caesars Entertainment players-reward club, also valid at sister properties such as Caesars and Paris, and will probably be linked into Harrah's Total Rewards eventually now that they all share the same corporate master as of 2005. 3555 Las Vegas Blvd. S. © 702/733-3111.

Gold Coast Adjacent to the Rio, this casino is not only well lit, but totally unique in Vegas: It has windows! It's a little thing, but it made us really excited. They also have a higher ratio of video-poker machines to slot machines, rather than the other way around. A remodeling made it much bigger, with high ceilings, and very bright overall. Nice job. The casino and their players club is tied to other Coast properties like Orleans and Barbary Coast, and may be linked to new corporate owner Boyd Casinos at places like Stardust and Main Street Station. 4000 W. Flamingo Rd. © 702/367-7111.

Harrah's A mixed bag of a casino, one that is both dated (low ceilings, old lighting, stuffy) and fun (parts have high-enough ceilings, and there are special attractions we will detail in a moment). The main reason to come here are the "party pits," gaming-table areas where dealers are encouraged to wear funny hats, celebrate wins, and otherwise break the usual stern dealer facade. Singing, dancing, and the handing out of party favors have all been known to erupt. (Gambling is supposed to be fun, so enjoy it!) Slot and table-game players can earn bonus points toward complimentary rooms, meals, and show tickets by joining Harrah's Total Rewards in the casino, which is also valid at sister hotel Rio (and eventually, most likely, new acquisitions Caesars Palace, Flamingo, and others). There are nonsmoking areas (fat lot of good that did, the place reeks of smoke), and free gaming lessons are offered on weekdays. 3475 Las Vegas Blvd. S. © 702/369-5000.

Imperial Palace The 75,000-square-foot casino here reflects the hotel's pagoda-roofed Asian exterior with a dragon-motif ceiling and giant wind-chime chandeliers. There is a Breathalyzer for voluntary alcohol-limit checks on your way to the parking lot (useful, since there are nine bars on the casino premises). The Imperial Palace boasts a 230-seat race and sports book, attractively decorated with oil murals of sporting events; the room is tiered like a grandstand, and every seat has its own color monitor. One giant slot machine is red, white, and blue; try singing the National Anthem to it, and see if you win more money. One kitsch feature of note is the casino's Legends Pit, where, on weekends after 6pm, celebrity impersonators aping everyone from Elvis to Madonna deal blackjack. This is also one of the few places on this part of the Strip where you might be able to find $5 table minimums. 3535 Las Vegas Blvd. S. © 702/731-3311.

The Mirage   Gamble in a Polynesian village in one of the prettiest casinos in town. It has a meandering layout, and the low ceiling makes for a medium claustrophobia level, but neither of these aspects is overwhelming. This remains one of our favorite places to gamble. Facilities include a plush European-style *salon privé* for high rollers at baccarat, blackjack, and roulette; an elegant dining room serves catered meals to gamblers there. Slot and table players can join the MGM MIRAGE Players Club, also valid at sister hotels such as TI at the Mirage and MGM Grand (and perhaps at new corporate siblings Mandalay Bay, Luxor, and others in the future), and work toward bonus points for cash rebates, special room rates, complimentary meals and/or show tickets, and other benefits. The elaborate race and sports book offers theater stereo sound and a movie theater–size screen. It's one of the most pleasant and popular casinos in town, so it's crowded more often than not. 3400 Las Vegas Blvd. S. Ⓒ 702/791-7111.

Palms Resort & Casino   Here's where this Desperately-Seeking-the-Hip hotel has a bit of an identity crisis because it also wants to be a place where locals feel comfortable gambling. You know, like Palace and Texas Station. Huh? That's right, the Palms wants to mirror those hotels off the Strip that offer loose slots and other incentives to make the locals feel at home. This rarely makes for a chic playing area (because locals don't want to have to get glammed up to go out and play some slots). On the other hand, the area is, especially on weekend nights, ringed with the beautiful and slender and aloof, desperate to get into Ghost Bar and Rain. If they aren't inside, they are surly about it. Let's hope everyone just keeps getting along. The gaming area covers most of the ground floor (it recently had part of its bulk diminished, in response to complaints that it was too crowded with tables and machines) and is replete with Miami tropical–inspired details. 4321 W. Flamingo Rd. Ⓒ 702/942-7777.

Paris Las Vegas Casino   Surrounded by a rather Disney-esque one-third-scale replica of the streets of Paris, this 83,000-square-foot casino is a very pleasant place to gamble, in that Vegas-gimmick kind of way. It's one of those kitschy places that "real" gamblers are appalled by. To heck with them, we say. A tall ceiling gives the illusion that you are trying to bust the bank while strolling outside and results in an airy effect. The place doesn't feel all that large, thanks to a meandering layout. There are over 2,000 slot machines and over 100 table games. A state-of-the-art race and sports book features live satellite feeds of sporting events from around the world. As of this writing, the Paris's players club is under the umbrella of Caesars Entertainment—owners of Paris, Bally's, Caesars, and The Flamingo—so you can rack up points at one casino and redeem them at any in the family, but it will most likely be pulled into Harrah's Total Rewards now that all the casinos are owned by the same company. 3655 Las Vegas Blvd. S. Ⓒ 702/946-7000.

Rio All-Suite Hotel & Casino   This Brazilian-themed resort's 85,000-square-foot casino is, despite the presence of plenty of glitter and neon, very dark. It has about the highest claustrophobia rating of the major casinos and seems very dated these days. Its sports book feels a little grimy. The waitresses wear scanty costumes (particularly in the back), probably in an effort to distract you and throw your game off (all the more so now that they are adding "Bev-entertainment"—those poor waitresses are going to have to burst into song and/or dance in between delivering your beer). Do not let them. The part of the casino in the Masquerade Village is considerably more pleasant (the very high ceilings help), though still crowded, and the loud live show here adds even more noise. In the high-end slot area ($5–$100 a pull), guests enjoy a private lounge and gratis champagne. There are nonsmoking slot and gaming table areas. The

Rio participates in the Harrah's Total Rewards players club, allowing gamers to earn points toward meals, cash back, rooms, and more, which can be used at any Harrah's-owned casino. 3700 W. Flamingo Rd. ℂ **702/252-7777.**

TI at the Mirage   We really loved it when this place was a casino set in Disneyland's Pirates of the Caribbean—or so it seemed. It doesn't seem like a big deal, the loss of those pirate chests dripping gold, jewels, and skulls with eye patches, but with the removal of the theme, this is now just a very nice casino. But it is that, so you should come here. Players club members can earn points toward meals, services, show tickets, and cash rebates at any of the MGM MIRAGE hotels, including The Mirage, MGM Grand, and more (with possible future additions of former Mandalay Resorts casinos like Mandalay Bay and Luxor).

There are nonsmoking gaming tables in each pit. A race and sports book boasts state-of-the-art electronic information boards and TV monitors at every seat, as well as numerous large-screen monitors. 3300 Las Vegas Blvd. S. ℂ **702/894-7111.**

The Venetian   "Tasteful" is the watchword in these days of classy Vegas gaming, and consequently, with the exception of more hand-painted Venetian art re-creations on parts of the ceiling, The Venetian's casino is interchangeable with those found at Mandalay Bay, the Monte Carlo, and, to a certain extent, Bellagio. All that gleaming marble, columns, and such is very nice, but after a while, it's also a bit ho-hum. Besides, this is Vegas, and we want our tacky theme elements, by gosh. The lack thereof, combined with poor signage, may be why this casino is so hard to get around—every part looks exactly the same. It's not precisely claustrophobic, but it can be confusing. Plus, there is no (at this writing) giant slot machine. On the other hand, we made a killing at blackjack and my editor struck it rich at the slots, so we have to love the place for those reasons. Another (less personal) plus is that you can access the casino directly from the St. Mark's Square re-creation out front. The smoke-sensitive report that the ventilation system here seems to be tops. 3355 Las Vegas Blvd. S. ℂ **702/414-1000.**

NORTH STRIP

Circus Circus   This vast property has three full-size casinos that, combined, comprise one of the largest gaming operations in Nevada (more than 100,000 sq. ft.). More important, they have an entire circus midway set up throughout, so you are literally gambling with trapeze stunts going on over your head. The other great gimmick is the slot machine carousel—yep, it turns while you spin the reels. The Mandalay Resorts One Club offers slot/video-poker and table players the opportunity to earn points redeemable for cash, discounted rooms and meals, and other benefits at Circus Circus or any of the sister properties, such as Mandalay Bay or Luxor (and probably new corporate sister properties like Bellagio, MGM Grand, and The Mirage in the future). The Circus Bucks progressive slot machines here build from a jackpot base of $500,000, which players can win on a $2 pull. Gaming facilities include a 10,000-square-foot race and sports book with 30 video monitors ranging from 13 to 52 inches, and 40-seat and 89-seat keno lounges. Unfortunately, the casino is crowded and noisy, and there are lots of children passing through (making it more crowded and noisy). That, plus some low ceilings (not in the Big Top, obviously), makes for a very high claustrophobia rating, though the current commedia dell'arte clown motif (as opposed to the old garish circus motif) has upgraded the decor. 2880 Las Vegas Blvd. S. ℂ **702/734-0410.**

The Riviera   The Riviera's 100,000-square-foot casino, once one of the largest in the world, offers plenty of opportunities to get lost and cranky. Especially if you, as one of us recently did, lose all your recent blackjack winnings at a table here. (What? Like you have fond memories of places where you've dropped a bundle?) A wall of windows lets daylight stream in (most unusual), but as the hotel gets shabbier, every inch of the casino smells like smoke and age. The casino's Slot and Gold (seniors) clubs allow slot players to earn bonus points toward free meals, rooms, and show tickets. Nickeltown is just that—nothin' but nickel slots and video poker. The race and sports book here offers individual monitors at each of its 250 seats, and this is one of the few places in town where you can play the ancient Chinese game of *sic bo.* 2901 Las Vegas Blvd. S. © 702/734-5110.

Sahara   This is one place where there seem to be more tables than slots and video-poker machines. It's also one of the few Strip casinos that offers low rollers good deals such as $1 craps and blackjack. But belligerent drunks and other fun-killing folks are often found at these $1 tables. Still, on a recent visit, the high ceilings and the unexpected *Arabian Nights* touches over the tables were nicer than we remembered from previous visits (maybe it all got dusted recently), and we made a killing at blackjack, so now we love this place again. (What? We told you it was entirely arbitrary!) The Sahara runs frequent slot tournaments and other events, and its slot club, Club Sahara, offers cash rebates and other perks. *Note:* This is the only Strip casino that offers *pan,* a card game. 2535 Las Vegas Blvd. S. © 702/737-2111.

Stardust   This once-popular casino features 90,000 square feet of lively gaming action, including a 250-seat race and sports book with a sophisticated satellite system and more than 50 TV monitors airing sporting events and horse-racing results around the clock. Adjacent to it is a sports handicapper's library offering comprehensive statistical information on current sporting events. Stardust Slot Club members win cash rebates, with credit piling up even on nickel machines; free rooms, shows, meals, and invitations to special events are also possible bonuses. We usually do well here, so even though it's a little loud, we like it. Check out those $1 slots just inside the front door—they've been very good to us. 3000 Las Vegas Blvd. S. © 702/732-6111.

Stratosphere Casino Hotel & Tower   Originally set up to evoke a world's fair but ending up more like a circus, Stratosphere redid its whole casino area to make it more appealing to the many adults who were staying away in droves. This should lure many of you because it is a nicer, and less crowded, place to play. They heavily advertise their high payback on certain slots and video poker: 98% payback on dollar slots and 100% payback on quarter video poker (if you bet the maximum on each). We can't say we noticed a difference, but other people around us were winning like crazy. There's a test area for new slot games, a Harley slot area with motorcycle-seat stools, and a high-roller slot room ($5 minimum bet) where chairs move up and down and can vibrate to give you a back massage while you play. The Stratosphere Players Club sponsors frequent tournaments, and its members can earn points toward gifts, VIP perks, discounted room rates, meals, and cash rebates—just a bit of play here, and you may be getting more free-room offers than you know what to do with. 2000 Las Vegas Blvd. S. © 702/380-7777.

Westward Ho Hotel & Casino   This small but centrally located Strip casino hosts many slot tournaments, and slot players who obtain Preferred Customer cards can amass credits toward complimentary rooms, meals, and shows, among other benefits. A new addition in 2005 is the amusingly named "The Ho," a glorified convenience store/snack shop/bar/minicasino at the back of the property along Industrial Road. It's tiny (a hundred or so slots, a couple of tables, and a sports-betting window), but great hot dogs! 2900 Las Vegas Blvd. S. ℂ 702/731-2900.

Wynn Las Vegas   Sprawling off the registration and conservatory/atrium/garden walkway, this looks like every other casino in a good-taste Vegas hotel (but most notably like Bellagio's, down to the little shade canopies over the tables, though without the marble on the side of the slot machines. Pity. We like that fancy touch.) and thus is instantly forgettable. Excessive geometric detailing on the ceiling gives it the illusion of lower height and so delivers a medium-high claustrophobia rating. It's also perhaps the quietest of the major casinos, which is kind of a good thing. Since this is a Grown-Up Place, playfulness is mostly missing—no machines squealing out "Wheel! Of! Fortune!" or other gimmicky (and never mind a Big Giant Slot Machine) and squeal-inducing sounds, though we did overhear at least one slap-happy craps dealer exhorting his customers in a party-hearty way. All the games you could want, plus a poker room and the rest, are here, though good luck finding a blackjack table under $15 a hand. And we aren't just saying that because we remain bitter about that losing streak at blackjack. 3131 Las Vegas Blvd. S. ℂ 702/770-7700.

EAST OF THE STRIP

Casino MonteLago   We are including this in case you find yourself staying in Lake Las Vegas (it's the only casino near the Ritz), or simply in the neighborhood, admiring the lake, or eating at Como's (all excellent uses of your time). It's only half the size of Strip casinos, but with exposed wood beams and stonework (in keeping with the location's Italian village theme, it's meant to evoke a 17th-c. Tuscan winery; PR stuff like that makes us laugh), it has its own style. The very high ceiling gives this an especially low claustrophobia rating, and overall, the absence of neon light madness continues to support the belief that this general area is for grown-ups. Also, we won a truckload of money here twice, so you know we might be a tad biased. There are all the latest slots and video poker, plus the usual mainstay tables, manned by a sometimes friendly, sometimes surly staff. 8 Strada di Villaggio, Henderson. ℂ 877/553-3555 or 702/939-8888.

Green Valley Ranch Resort   Probably too far for the average traveler to drive—after all, when there is a casino just steps (or floors) away from your hotel room (and between you and anywhere in the world apart from your hotel room), to say nothing of several dozen more within a few blocks of your hotel room, you may be disinclined to drive out to one that is isolated from many other decent casinos. But given that this is a swank resort (or at least, trying to be); that it's smallish and elegant; that it's got a happening, decadent bar with girls prancing in go-go boots right in the center; and that more bars attracting the young and beautiful and well-heeled are opening here, you might want to make a visit, just to see the scene. And they have penny slots. Go figure. 2300 Paseo Verde Dr. (at I-215), Henderson. ℂ 702/617-7777.

Hard Rock Hotel & Casino   Where Gen X goes to gamble. The Hard Rock has certainly taken casino decor to a whole new level. The attention to detail and the resulting playfulness is admirable, if not incredible. Gaming tables have piano keyboards at one end, some slots have Fender guitar fret boards as arms, gaming chips have band names and/or pictures on them, slot machines are similarly rock-themed (check out the Jimi Hendrix machine!), and so it goes. The whole thing is set in the middle of a circular room, around the outskirts of which are various rock memorabilia in glass cases. Rock blares over the sound system, allowing boomers to boogie while they gamble.

A bank of slots makes gambling an act of charity: Environmentally committed owner Peter Morton (the Hard Rock's motto is "Save the Planet") donates profits from specified slots to organizations dedicated to saving the rainforests. A Back Stage Pass allows patrons to rack up discounts on meals, lodging, and gift-shop items while playing slots and table games. The race and sports book here provides comfortable seating in leather-upholstered reclining armchairs. All this is genuinely amazing, but the noise level is above even that of a normal casino and we just hated it. We are in the minority, though; most people love it, so assume you will be one of them. 4455 Paradise Rd. ℭ 702/693-5000.

Las Vegas Hilton   The casino has two parts, thanks to the space-themed portion adjacent to *Star Trek: The Experience*. In an area designed to look like a spaceport, you find space-themed slot machines, many of which have no handles—just pass your hand through a light beam to activate. You'll find other gimmicks throughout the casino (though already some have been dropped since the opening), including urinals that give you an instant "urinalysis"—usually suggesting this is your lucky day to gamble. We do like a well-designed space in which to lose our money.

Over in the original casino section, Austrian-crystal chandeliers add a strong touch of class. The casino is actually medium-size, but it does have an enormous sports book—at 30,500 square feet, it's the world's largest race and sports book facility. It, too, is a luxurious precinct equipped with the most advanced audio, video, and computer technology available, including 46 TV monitors, some as large as 15 feet across. In fact, its video wall is second in size only to NASA's. The casino is adjacent to the lobby but is neither especially loud nor frantic. Especially plush is the vast 6,900-square-foot baccarat room—with gorgeous crystal chandeliers, silk-covered walls, and velvet-upholstered furnishings—and the VIP slot area where personnel are attired in tuxedos. Both areas offer gracious service to players.

The Las Vegas Hilton has a new owner as of 2004, so there will probably be some changes by the time you read this. 3000 Paradise Rd. ℭ 702/732-7111.

Sam's Town   On its two immense floors of gaming action (153,083 sq. ft., second only to the MGM Grand in size), Sam's Town maintains the friendly, just-folks ambience that characterizes the entire property. The casino is adorned with Old West paraphernalia (horseshoes, Winchester rifles, holsters, and saddlebags) and is looking a bit less dated, thanks to some recent sprucing up (it's subtle, but believe us, it's better). Sam's Town claims its friendliness extends to looser slots. Join the Sam's Town Slot Club to earn points toward rooms, meals, and cash rebates. Free gaming lessons are offered weekdays from 11am to 4pm, with poker lessons at other times. 5111 Boulder Hwy. (at Nellis Blvd.). ℭ 702/456-7777.

DOWNTOWN

Binion's *Finds*   Binion's has had quite the ride lately. Here's the back story: Professionals in the know say that "for the serious player, the Binions are this town." Benny Binion could neither read nor write, but, boy, did he know how to run a casino. His venerable establishment has been eclipsed over the years, but it claims the highest betting limits in Las Vegas on all games (probably in the entire world, according to a spokesperson). Unfortunately, its last couple of years read like a Vegas soap opera—you know, in-family fighting, murder of one scion at the (alleged) hands of his stripper girlfriend, another taking out many of the elements that made Binion's famous, and the whole thing getting shuttered in early 2004 thanks to nonpayment of bills. To

The World Series, Las Vegas–Style

Binion's Horseshoe was internationally known as the home of the **World Series of Poker**. It was "Nick the Greek" Dondolos who first approached Benny Binion in 1949 with the idea for a high-stakes poker marathon between top players. Binion agreed, with the stipulation that the game be open to public viewing. The competition, between Dondolos and the legendary Johnny Moss, lasted 5 months, with breaks only for sleep. Moss ultimately won about $2 million. As Dondolos lost his last pot, he rose from his chair, bowed politely, and said, "Mr. Moss, I have to let you go."

In 1970, Binion decided to re-create the battle of poker giants, which evolved into the annual World Series of Poker. Johnny Moss won the first year and went on to snag the championship again in 1971 and 1974. Thomas "Amarillo Slim" Preston won the event in 1972 and popularized it on the talk-show circuit. In 2002, there were more than 7,595 entrants from over 22 countries, each ponying up the $10,000 entrance fee, and total winnings were in excess of $19 million (the tournament was also televised on ESPN). During one memorable year, the participants included actors Matt Damon and Edward Norton, fresh from *Rounders,* a movie in which they played a couple of card sharks. They decided to try out their newly acquired moves against the pros, who were unhappy that these kids were barging in on their action and so, rumor has it, offered a separate, large bounty to whatever player took them out. Both actors got knocked out on the first day but took it with good grace and apparently had a blast. Matt's buddy Ben Affleck, an experienced player, tried in 2003—the line on him to win (he didn't) was 400:1. *Note:* In 2005, the World Series of Poker moved to the Rio under the auspices of Harrah's Entertainment, which bought the rights to the event in 2004.

everyone's relief, after 3 months, the casino reopened, thanks to its dual owners, one of which was Harrah's, which managed it for a year before running off with the Horseshoe name (and rumors are running wild over what that will mean, including speculation that they will build a new "Harrah's Horseshoe" on the spot currently occupied by the New Frontier) and the rights to Binion's famous World Series of Poker, which was moved to the Rio in 2005. MTR Gaming now runs Binion's and vows to continue to pump more money and new blood into the place. We'll see.

Do you care about any of this? Maybe. Binion's has about 400 fewer slot machines than it used to, in an effort to improve flow, and some parts got painted, so it looks less dingy (but still like an Old West bordello) but remains otherwise essentially the same. That includes the relatively high claustrophobia level. It offers single-deck blackjack and $2 minimums, 10-times odds on craps, and high progressive jackpots. Real gamblers still won't consider going anywhere else. 128 E. Fremont St. (between Casino Center Blvd. and 1st St.). ✆ **702/382-1600.**

California Hotel/Casino   The California is a festive place filled with Hawaiian shirts and balloons. This friendly facility actually provides sofas and armchairs in the casino area—an unheard-of luxury in this town. Players can join the Cal Slot Club and amass points toward gifts and cash prizes, or participate in daily slot tournaments. This is the first place we found our favorite Piggy Bankin' machines. 12 Ogden Ave. (at 1st St.). © 702/385-1222.

El Cortez   This casino is one of the last shreds of pre-1980s Las Vegas, which is either wonderful or horrible, depending on your view. It features frequent big-prize drawings (up to $50,000) based on your social security number. It's also popular for low limits (10¢ roulette and 25¢ craps). 600 Fremont St. (between 6th and 7th sts.). © 702/385-5200.

Fitzgeralds   This casino is done up in greens and golds, and the overall effect is not quite as tacky as you might expect, though the now near-total absence of any overt Irish theme means it's rather forgettable. In fact, it's rather friendly and with a medium-to-low claustrophobia level, thanks in part to some windows to the outside Fremont Street. The casino actually has two levels: From the upstairs part, you can access a balcony from which you get an up-close view of the Fremont Street Experience.

Blackjack, craps, and keno tournaments are frequent events here. Slot machines that paid out over 100% the previous week are marked with a MR. LUCKY sign. The Fitzgerald Card offers slot players gifts, meals, and other perks for accumulated points. Several slot machines have cars as prizes, fun books provide two-for-one gaming coupons, and there are $1-minimum blackjack tables. 301 Fremont St. (at 3rd St.). © 702/388-2400.

Four Queens   The Four Queens is New Orleans–themed, with late-19th-century-style globe chandeliers, which make for good lighting and a low claustrophobia level. It's small, but the dealers are helpful, which is one of the pluses of gambling in the more manageably sized casinos.

The facility boasts the world's largest slot machine: More than 9 feet high and almost 20 feet long, six people can play it at one time! It's the Mother of all giant slot machines, and frankly, it intimidates even us. Here is also the world's largest blackjack table (it seats 12 players). The Reel Winners Club offers slot players bonus points toward cash rebates. Slot, blackjack, and craps tournaments are frequent events, and there are major poker tournaments every January and September. The casino also offers exciting multiple-action blackjack (it's like playing three hands at once with separate wagers on each). 202 Fremont St. (at Casino Center Blvd.). © 702/385-4011.

Fremont Hotel & Casino   This 32,000-square-foot casino—it's much bigger than it initially looks—offers a relaxed atmosphere. In some ways, it's more comfortable gambling here than on the Strip, possibly in part because the beautiful people don't bother with places like this. Though lots of other people do, and so it can be more crowded than other Downtown casinos, even during the day. Low gambling limits ($2 blackjack, 25¢ roulette, though not as many tables with these as we would like) help. It's also surprisingly open and bright for a Downtown casino. Just 50¢ could win you a Cadillac or Ford Mustang here, plus a progressive cash jackpot. Casino guests can accumulate bonus points redeemable for cash by joining the players club, and take part in frequent slot and keno tournaments. No giant slot machine, though. 200 E. Fremont St. (between Casino Center Blvd. and 3rd St.). © 702/385-3232.

The Golden Gate   This is one of the oldest casinos in Downtown, and though its age is showing, it's still fun to go there. As you might expect from the name, old San

Francisco artifacts and decor abound (think earthquake time). At one end of the narrow casino is the bar, where a piano player performs ragtime jazz, which is better than the homogenized pop offered in most casino lounges. Unfortunately, the low ceiling, dark period wallpaper, and small dimensions give this a high claustrophobia level. 1 Fremont St. ℰ 702/382-3510.

Golden Nugget   While this is not the standout among casino properties developed by Steve Wynn (and recently sold by MGM MIRAGE to Internet entrepreneurs Thomas Breitling and Timothy Poster), it's still one of the nicest places to gamble, lookswise, in Downtown. (We prefer Main Street Station, but you might prefer the more obvious attempts at class that this place exudes.) That's because this looks like Old Vegas, but in the classy, gilded, glittery golden, cramped way, rather than the current dingy and depressing way. Some tables are only $5 minimum, at least during the day. And compared to most other Downtown properties, this is the most like the Strip. There's no word on what the new owners plan to do to the casino, but they've promised to bring back "Old Vegas" style to Downtown. Stay tuned. 129 E. Fremont St. (at Casino Center Blvd.). ℰ 702/385-7111.

The Gold Spike   Despite an updating (after a serious fire), The Gold Spike remains deliciously, or frighteningly (depending on your aesthetic views and desires), dated; it may no longer have that '70s-era shag carpeting and wood paneling, but it has the modern-day spiritual equivalent. It's still one of those dingy, forgotten Downtown spaces that we usually criticize. So what? Here, everyone is equal, and everyone is having a good time, or at least they can sincerely join you in your misery. Best of all, they have penny slots! (Not very many, to be sure, and getting a seat at one can require patience.) Hey tightwads, take a buck and spend a few hours. 400 Ogden Ave. (at Las Vegas Blvd.). ℰ 702/384-8444.

Jackie Gaughan's Plaza Hotel/Casino   This is Old Vegas, with an attempt at '60s glamour (think women in white go-go boots). It had gotten worn, but new owners, as of this writing, are making improvements. Cautious bettors will appreciate the $1 blackjack tables and penny slots here. 1 Main St. (at Fremont St.). ℰ 702/386-2110.

Lady Luck   A complete remodeling didn't do too much to change this old gal, who is still a bit more smoky and crowded than we prefer, but that doesn't mean she's not good for a few go-rounds. Plus, its liberal game rules are attractive to gamblers. You can play "fast-action hold 'em" here—a combination of 21, poker, and pai gow poker. 206 N. 3rd St. (at Ogden Ave.). ℰ 702/477-3000.

Main Street Station *Finds*   This is the best of the Downtown casinos, at least in terms of comfort and a pleasant environment. Even the Golden Nugget, nice as it is, has more noise and distractions. The decor here is, again, classic Vegas/old-timey (Victorian-era) San Francisco, but with extra touches (check out the old-fashioned fans above the truly beautiful bar) that make it work much better than other attempts at the same decor. Strangely, it seems just about smoke-free, perhaps thanks in part to a very high ceiling. The claustrophobia level is zero. 200 N. Main St. (between Fremont St. and I-95). ℰ 800/713-8933 or 702/387-1896.

9

Shopping

Shopping in Vegas—Nirvana or an endless Sisyphean repetition of every mall you've ever been to? Depends on your viewpoint. If you are looking for quaint, clever, unique stores, this isn't the town for you (with a few notable exceptions, most of which will require you to drive some blocks off the Strip). But if you are looking for general shop-till-you-drop fun, this is your kind of town. In addition to some extensive (and recently revamped) malls, many hotels have comprehensive, and sometimes highly themed, shopping arcades. The most notable of the arcades are in Caesars Palace, Aladdin, and The Venetian (details below).

In addition to exploring the malls, outlets, and shops listed below, you might consider driving **Maryland Parkway,** which runs parallel to the Strip on the east and has just about one of everything: Target, Toys "R" Us, several major department stores, Tower Records, major drugstores (in case you forgot your shampoo and don't want to spend $8 on a new bottle in your hotel's sundry shop), some alternative-culture stores (tattoo parlors and hip clothing stores), and so forth. It goes on for blocks.

1 The Malls

Boulevard Mall   The Boulevard was the largest mall in Las Vegas until the remodeled Fashion Show Mall trumped it in late 2003. Its 144-plus stores and restaurants are arranged in arcade fashion on a single floor occupying 1.2 million square feet. Geared to the average consumer, it has anchors like Sears, JCPenney, Macy's, Dillard's, and Marshalls. There's a wide variety of shops offering all sorts of items—moderately priced shoes and clothing for the entire family, books and gifts, jewelry, and home furnishings. There are also more than a dozen fast-food eateries. In short, you can find just about anything you need here. And there's free valet parking. The mall is open Monday through Saturday from 10am to 9pm and Sunday from 11am to 6pm. 3528 S. Maryland Pkwy. (between Twain Ave. and Desert Inn Rd.). © 702/732-8949. www.blvdmall.com.

Fashion Show Mall   What was a nondescript, if large, mall has now been revamped with a *yowsa* exterior much more fitting Las Vegas. It's capped by a giant . . . well . . . they call it a "Cloud" but we call it "that weird thingy that looks like a spaceport for UFOs, what in the heck were they thinking?" Inside, you will find the city's first Nordstrom, a Bloomingdale's, Saks Fifth Avenue, a Macy's, and other high-end retailers. The mall comprises more than 250 shops, restaurants, and services. And the Cloud/Alien Spaceport Thingy has giant LED screens, music, and other distractions—again, much more fitting for Vegas, where even the malls have to light up. Valet parking is available, and you can even arrange to have your car hand-washed while you shop. The Fashion Show is open Monday through Friday from 10am to 9pm, Saturday from 10am to

8pm, and Sunday from 11am to 6pm. 3200 Las Vegas Blvd. S. (at the corner of Spring Mountain Rd.). ✆ 702/369-0704. www.thefashionshow.com.

The Galleria at Sunset This is a 1-million-square-foot Southwestern-themed shopping center, 9 miles southeast of Downtown Las Vegas. Anchored by four department stores (Dillard's, JCPenney, Mervyn's California, and Robinsons-May), the Galleria's 140 emporia include branches of Gap/Gap Kids/Baby Gap, The Limited Too, Eddie Bauer, Ann Taylor, bebe, Caché, Lane Bryant, Victoria's Secret, The Body Shop, B. Dalton, and Sam Goody. In addition to shoes and clothing for the entire family, you'll find electronics, eyewear, gifts, books, home furnishings, jewelry, and luggage here. Dining facilities include an extensive food court and two restaurants. Open Monday through Saturday from 10am to 9pm and Sunday from 11am to 6pm. In nearby Henderson, 1300 W. Sunset Rd. (at Stephanie St., just off I-515). ✆ 702/434-0202. www.galleriaatsunset.com.

The Meadows Another immense mall, The Meadows is made up of more than 140 shops, services, and eateries, anchored by four department stores: Macy's, Dillard's, Sears, and JCPenney. In addition, there are 11 shoe stores, a full array of apparel for the entire family (including maternity wear, petites, and large sizes), an extensive food court, and shops purveying toys, books, CDs and tapes, luggage, gifts, jewelry, home furnishings (The Bombay Company, among others), accessories, and so on. Fountains and trees enhance The Meadows's ultramodern, high-ceilinged interior, and there are a few comfortable seating areas for resting your feet a moment. The Meadows Mall is open Monday through Saturday from 10am to 9pm and Sunday from 10am to 6pm. 4300 Meadows Lane (at the intersection of Valley View and U.S. 95). ✆ 702/878-3331. www.meadowsmall.com.

Showcase Mall Less traditional mall than an entertainment center, it has plenty of both shopping and fun—we rarely miss a chance to drop by M&M World. Other occupants include GameWorks, the World of Coca-Cola store, Grand Canyon Experience, and the United Artist Cinemas—the only regular movie theater complex on the Strip. Hours vary by store. 3785 S. Las Vegas Blvd (right next to the MGM Grand). ✆ 702/597-3122.

2 Factory Outlets

Las Vegas has a big factory-outlet center just a few miles past the southern end of the Strip (see below). If you don't have a car, you can take a no. 301 CAT bus from anywhere on the Strip and change at Vacation Village to a no. 303. You can see from the review below that it doesn't do much for us, which is why we usually head to Primm to drop more money than we do at the tables (Williams-Sonoma outlet, how we love you).

Fashion Outlet at Primm Dedicated bargain hunters may want to make the roughly 40-minute drive along I-15 (there's also a $13 shuttle from the MGM Grand or the mall at Planet Hollywood) to this big outlet complex, right on the border of California and Nevada. On your left is a large factory outlet with some designer names prominent enough to make that drive well worthwhile—Kenneth Cole, Gap, Banana Republic, Old Navy, even a rare Williams-Sonoma, among several others. Why so far out of town? Our guess is because all these designers have full-price boutiques in various hotels, and they don't want you ignoring those in favor of discounted items. Open daily from 10am to 8pm. 32100 Las Vegas Blvd. S. ✆ 888/424-6898. www.fashionoutletlasvegas.com.

Las Vegas Outlet Center Formerly Belz Outlet Center, this massive complex houses more than 150 air-conditioned outlets, including a few dozen clothing stores and shoe stores. It offers a range of merchandise, but even given our understanding of the hit-and-miss nature of outlets, we've never bought a thing here and feel nothing but apathy for the center. Among other stores (which you will perhaps find less disappointing than we have), you'll find Casual Corner, Liz Claiborne, Perry Ellis, Levi's, Nike, Dress Barn, Oshkosh B'Gosh, L'eggs/Hanes/Bali, Carter's, Reebok, Jockey, Springmaid, Danskin, Van Heusen, Tommy Hilfiger, Burlington, Royal Doulton, Waterford (crystal), Black & Decker (tools), and Geoffrey Beene. There are also a carousel and a food court. Open Monday through Saturday from 10am to 9pm, Sunday from 10am to 8pm. 7400 Las Vegas Blvd. S. (at Warm Springs Rd.). ℭ 702/896-5599. www.premiumoutlets.com.

Las Vegas Premium Outlets   We had such high hopes for this, the most conveniently located, and largest, outlet mall in Vegas. We can say that it looks nice, in that pretty outdoor mall kind of way. But the key here is "outdoor." It's fine on a regular day, but on a hot Vegas day—and there are plenty of those—this is an open oven of misery. Put a roof over the thing or at least install a whole bunch of misters. Roast away while shopping among disappointingly dull stores, some of which are "outlets" only because they aren't in regular malls (the Bath & Body Works shop, for example, consists mostly of regular products at regular prices). Maybe we are just feeling bitter about that pair of Bass shoes that were half a size too small. Or that we can't quite fit into the Dolce & Gabbana sample sizes. Still, bring a lot of water if you go during the summer. Stores include Armani, Bernini, Brooks Brothers, Calvin Klein, Coach, Crabtree & Evelyn, Dolce & Gabbana, Kenneth Cole, Lacoste, Nike, Perry Ellis, Ralph Lauren, Quicksilver, Samsonite, Timberland, Tommy Hilfiger, Wilson's Leather, and Zales. Open Monday through Saturday from 10am to 9pm, Sunday from 10am to 8pm. 875 S. Grand Central Parkway (at I-15). ℭ 702/474-7500. www.premiumoutlets.com.

3 Hotel Shopping Arcades

Just about every Las Vegas hotel offers some shopping opportunities. The following have the most extensive arcades. The physical spaces of these shopping arcades are always open, but individual stores keep unpredictable hours. For addresses and telephone numbers, see the hotels' listings in chapter 5.

Note: The Forum Shops at Caesars, the Grand Canal Shoppes at The Venetian, and the Desert Passage at Aladdin—as much sightseeing attractions as shopping arcades—are in the must-see category.

ALADDIN   The most recent Vegas "dazzle the tourists out of their money" shopping experience (the others being over at Caesars and The Venetian), the Desert Passage uses the mystical and romantic architecture (or re-creations thereof) of the Middle East (Egypt, Morocco, Turkey) as its theme, and the results are pretty swell. Even the ceiling overhead is painted to replicate sultry days and nights, with occasional thunderstorms hitting. There is a lot to look at beyond the shops, even more than usual, since, at this writing, they have frequent live entertainers—acrobats, jugglers, and belly dancers—to add to the visuals. And it's not just visual but odiferous: They pipe in spices and other evocative scents appropriate to those regions. The whole thing allows you to have that Middle Eastern souk-shopping experience without all the pesky touts trying to drag you into their stall for hours of haggling. You can even take a pedicab (that would be a bicycle-powered vehicle pedaled by some comely worker) for a tour of Morocco, kinda. The stores are the assortment of mid- and high-end name brands one would expect (so the gouging happens in a different way than in the souks!). It's one of our favorite shopping areas in Vegas, for sure. The thing that worries us the most about the purchase of the Aladdin by Planet Hollywood—and the shift of the hotel's thematic focus—is how that might affect this mall, which was sold shortly after the Aladdin to different owners.

BALLY'S   Bally's **Avenue Shoppes** consist of around 20 emporia offering, you know, stuff (kitschy card-shop knickknacks and the like). In addition, there are several gift shops, art galleries, and a pool-wear shop. There are blackjack and slot tournaments right in the mall, as well as a race and sports book. You can dispatch the kids to a video arcade here while you shop (or gamble). A recent addition of a walkway to neighboring hotel Paris features more stores and restaurants.

BELLAGIO   The Via Bellagio collection of stores isn't as big as some of the other megahotel shopping arcades, but here it's definitely quality over quantity. It's a veritable roll call of glossy magazine ads: Armani, Prada, Chanel, Tiffany, Hermès, Fred Leighton, Gucci, and Moschino. That's it. You need anything else? Well, yes—money. If you can afford this stuff, good for you, you lucky dog. (Actually, we've discovered affordable, good-taste items in every store here, from Tiffany's $30 silver key chains to $100 Prada business-card holders.) A nice touch is a parking lot by the far entrance to Via Bellagio, so you need not navigate the great distance from Bellagio's main parking structure; instead, you can simply pop in and pick up a little something.

CAESARS PALACE   Since 1978, Caesars has had an impressive arcade of shops called the **Appian Way,** highlighted by an immense white Carrara-marble replica of Michelangelo's *David* standing more than 18 feet high. All in all, a respectable grouping of hotel shops, and an expansion is in the works.

But in the hotel's tradition of constantly surpassing itself, in 1992 Caesars inaugurated the fabulous **Forum Shops** ⚘, an independently operated 250,000-square-foot Rodeo-Drive-meets-the-Roman-Empire affair complete with a 48-foot triumphal arch entranceway, a painted Mediterranean sky that changes as the day progresses from rosy-tinted dawn to twinkling evening stars, acres of marble, lofty Corinthian columns with gold capitals, and a welcoming goddess of fortune under a central dome. The architecture and sculpture span a period from 300 B.C. to A.D. 1700, so you've got all your ancient Italian cityscape clichés. Then there is the Festival Fountain, where some seemingly immovable "marble" animatronic statues of Bacchus (slightly in his cups), a lyre-playing Apollo, Plutus, and Venus come to life for a 7-minute revel with dancing waters and high-tech laser-light effects. The shows take place every hour on the hour. The whole thing is pretty incredible, but also very Vegas—particularly the Bacchus show, which is truly frightening and bizarre. Even if you don't like shopping, it's worth the stroll just to giggle.

There are more than 100 prestigious emporia here, including Louis Vuitton, Bernini, Christian Dior, A/X Armani Exchange, bebe, Gucci, Ann Taylor, and Gianni Versace, along with many other clothing, shoe, and jewelry stores.

In 1998 the Forum Shops added an extension. The centerpiece is a giant **Roman Hall,** featuring a 50,000-gallon circular aquarium and another fountain that also comes to life with a show involving fire (don't stand too close—it gets really hot), dancing waters, and animatronic figures, as the mythical continent of Atlantis rises and falls every hour. The production values are much higher than those of the Bacchus extravaganza, but this "performance" takes itself more seriously, so the giggle factor remains. In this shopping area, you'll find a number of significant stores, including a DKNY, Emporio Armani, Niketown, Fendi, Polo for Ralph Lauren, Guess, and Virgin Megastore. Do go see the latter, as it is fronted by a gigantic Trojan horse, in which you can clamber around, while its head moves and smoke comes out its nostrils. We love it. Also in the shops are Wolfgang Puck's Chinois and a Cheesecake Factory. A 2004 expansion upped an already high ante. The three-story addition tacked on a new Strip entryway complete with a deliriously audacious circular escalator and another 175,000 square feet of retail space. The multistoried extension tries to permanently move past "kitsch" and into "classy rich personal's shopping experience"—though any sort of movement, literal or metaphoric, is tricky, what with all the giant marbled pillars, statues and fountains, plus an atrium that actually admits sunlight. New tenants include Harry Winston jewelers, Brooks Brothers, Tommy Bahama, Juicy Couture, Taryn Rose, several new restaurants, a branch of famed barbershop to the Royal Family Truefitt and Hill, a Playboy store, Kiehl's cosmetics, MAC, Agent Provacateur lingerie, and Vosges Haut-Chocolat, the latter few of which get us more excited than the usual Vegas shopping experience, as those are stores with more limited availability.

The majority of Caesars Palace's shops are open Sunday to Thursday from 10am to 11pm, Friday and Saturday from 10am to midnight.

CIRCUS CIRCUS   There are about 15 shops between the casino and the Adventuredome (p. 214), offering a wide selection of gifts and sundries, logo items, toys and games, jewelry, liquor, resort apparel for the entire family, T-shirts, homemade fudge/candy/soft ice cream, and, fittingly, clown dolls and puppets. Adjacent to the Adventuredome, there's a shopping arcade (with the usual souvenir stores and such) themed as a European village, with cobblestone walkways, fake woods, and so forth, decorated with replicas of vintage circus posters.

ESPLANADE AT WYNN LAS VEGAS   Along the same rarified lines of the Bellagio shopping area, in that it's a Euro-style-esque (love those Vegas qualifiers!) shopping street lined with pricey places with famous names—Chanel, Cartier, Dior, Judith Leiber, Jean Paul Gaultier, Manolo Blahnik, Oscar de la Renta, La Flirt (a sort of mini-Sephora), Chocolat (excellent pastries and gourmet chocolates), and Jo Malone. We prefer it some to the one at Bellagio because it seems like it has just enough shops (like La Flirt) that nearly reach an average person's budget.

EXCALIBUR   For the most part, the shops of **"the Realm"** reflect the hotel's medieval theme. Dragon's Lair, for example, features items ranging from pewter swords and shields to full suits of armor, and Merlin's Mystic Shop carries crystals, luck charms, and gargoyles. Other shops carry more conventional wares—gifts, candy, jewelry, women's clothing, and Excalibur logo items. And most important, they have a branch of that medieval staple—Krispy Kreme Doughnuts!

THE FLAMINGO LAS VEGAS   The **Crystal Court** shopping promenade here accommodates men's and women's clothing/accessories stores, gift shops, and a variety of other emporia selling jewelry, beachwear, Southwestern crafts, fresh-baked goods, logo items, children's gifts, toys, and games.

HARRAH'S   Harrah's has a small outdoor shopping promenade called **Carnaval Court.** Among the store highlights is a Ghirardelli chocolate store, a branch of the famous San Francisco–based chocolate company. This store is remarkably like a smaller version of the one in San Francisco (alas, without the vats of liquid chocolate being mixed up), and in addition to candy, you can get a variety of delicious sundaes and other ice-cream treats. Other stores include the Carnaval Market and Wine and Spirits shops, perfect for creating your own outdoor picnic feast.

LUXOR   The **Giza Galleria** is a 20,000-square-foot shopping arcade with eight full shops. Most of the stores emphasize clothing. Adjacent is the Cairo Bazaar, a trinket shop.

MGM GRAND   The hotel's **Star Lane Shops** include more than a dozen upscale emporia lining the corridors en route from the monorail entrance. And it's here that you can still find the semibanished figures from the hotel's original *Wizard of Oz* diorama. **Studio Walk** is another shopping area adjacent to the main casino, featuring some upscale boutiques and several restaurants.

MONTE CARLO   An arcade of retail shops here includes several upscale clothing, timepiece, eyewear, and gift boutiques plus a Lance Burton magic-paraphernalia shop.

RIO   The 60,000-square-foot **Masquerade Village** is a nicely executed shopping arcade at Rio. It's done as a European village, and is two stories tall, featuring a wide variety of shops including the nation's largest Nicole Miller, Speedo, and the Nawlins store, which includes "authentic" voodoo items, Mardi Gras masks, and so forth.

THE RIVIERA   The Riviera has a fairly extensive shopping arcade comprising art galleries, jewelers, shops specializing in women's shoes and handbags, clothing for the entire family, furs, gifts, logo items, toys, phones and electronic gadgets, and chocolates.

STRATOSPHERE   The internationally themed (though in a high-school production kind of way, compared to what's over at Aladdin and The Venetian) second-floor **Tower Shops** promenade, housing more than 40 stores, is entered via an escalator from the casino. Some shops are in "Paris," along the Rue Lafayette and Avenue de l'Opéra (there are replicas of the Eiffel Tower and Arc de Triomphe in this section). Others occupy Hong Kong and New York City streetscapes.

TI AT THE MIRAGE   TI's shopping promenade, nowhere near as interesting since they took all the pirate-themed bits out. Emporia here include the TI Store (your basic hotel gift/sundry shop, also offering much pirate-themed merchandise) plus the new *Sirens of TI* themed lingerie shop. Cirque du Soleil and *Mystère* logo wares are also sold in a shop near the ticket office in the hotel.

THE VENETIAN ⊛   The **Grand Canal Shoppes** are a direct challenge to Caesars Palace's shopping eminence. As in the Forum Shops, you stroll through a re-created Italian village—in this case, more or less Renaissance-era Venice, complete with a painted, cloud-studded blue sky overhead, and a canal right down the center on which gondoliers float and sing. Pay them ($12) and you can take a lazy float down and back, serenaded by your boatman (actors hired especially for this purpose and with accents perfect enough to fool Roberto Benigni). As you pass by, under and over bridges, flower girls will serenade you and courtesans will flirt with you, and you may have an encounter with a famous Venetian or two, as Marco Polo discusses his travels and Casanova exerts his famous charm. The stroll (or float) ends at a miniature (though not by all that much) version of St. Mark's Square, the central landmark of Venice. Here, you'll find opera singers, strolling musicians, glass blowers, and other bustling marketplace activity. It's all most ambitious and beats the heck out of animatronic statues.

The Shoppes are accessible directly from outside (so you don't have to navigate miles of casino and other clutter), via a grand staircase whose ceiling features more of those impressive hand-painted art re-creations. It's quite smashing. The Venetian's

"Phase Two" hotel addition will eventually adjoin the Shoppes at the far end of St. Mark's Square.

Oh, the shops themselves? The usual high- and medium-end brand names: Jimmy Choo, Mikimoto, Movado, Davidoff, Kenneth Cole, Ann Taylor, BCBG, bebe, Banana Republic, Rockport, and more, plus Venetian glass and paper shops. Madame Tussaud's waxworks (p. 197) is also located here, and so is the Canyon Ranch Spa Club.

4 Vintage Clothing

The Attic   The Attic shares a large space with Cafe Neon, a coffeehouse that serves Greek-influenced cafe food (so you can raise your blood sugar after a long stretch of shopping), and a comedy-club stage; it's also upstairs from an attempt at a weekly club (as of this writing, the Sat-night Underworld). The store itself, former star of a Visa commercial, offers plenty of clothing choices on many racks. During a recent visit, a man came in asking for a poodle skirt for his 8-year-old. They had one. Open Monday through Thursday from 10am to 5pm, Friday from 10am to 6pm, Saturday from 11am to 6pm, and closed Sunday. 1018 S. Main St. © 702/388-4088. www.theatticlasvegas.com.

Buffalo Exchange   This is actually a branch of a chain of stores spread out across the western United States. If the chain part worries you, don't let it—this merchandise doesn't feel processed. Staffed by plenty of incredibly hip alt-culture kids (ask them what's happening in town during your visit), it is stuffed with dresses, shirts, pants, and so forth. You can easily go in one day and come out with 12 fabulous new outfits, but you can just as easily go in and come up dry. But it's still probably the most reliable of the local vintage shops. The store is open Monday through Saturday from 10am to 8pm, Sunday from 11am to 7pm. 4110 S. Maryland Pkwy. (at Flamingo Rd.). © 702/791-3960. www.buffaloexchange.com.

5 Souvenirs

The **Arts Factory Complex,** 103 E. Charleston Blvd. (© 702/382-3886), has a gift shop full of pink flamingos and Vegas-specific items. There should be something here for every camp fancy.

If you prefer your souvenirs to be less deliberately ironic, head over to the **Bonanza Gift and Souvenir Shop,** 2460 Las Vegas Blvd. S. (© 702/384-0005). It's the self-proclaimed "World's Largest Gift Shop" and it certainly is big. T-shirts, Native American "handicrafts," all kinds of playing cards both new and used (casinos have to change decks frequently, so this is where used packs go), dice, things covered in rhinestones, snowglobes—in short, something for everyone, provided "everyone" has a certain sensibility. We looked, and we felt the tackiest item available was the pair of earrings made out of poker chips. The coolest? Some inexpensive, old-fashioned styled dice.

For reverent camp, encrusted with sequins, do take a peek at the **Liberace Museum gift store,** 1775 E. Tropicana Ave. (© 702/798-5595). Encourage them to get even more out there (don't you think they should add Liberace mouse pads and screen savers?).

If you like your souvenirs with more style (spoilsports), **Cirque de Soleil's *O*** has a gift shop in Bellagio, 3600 Las Vegas Blvd. S. (© 702/693-7444), with Cirque-specific articles, but also fanciful pottery, masks, and other curiosities.

6 Reading Material: Used Books, Comics & Gambler Books

USED BOOKS

Albion Books *(Value)*   Six thousand square feet of used books, including first editions, vintage children's books, pop and sci-fi, pulp fiction, and bestsellers, both hard and paperback. You're welcome to take a seat and browse through your finds before purchasing. Open daily from 10am to 6pm. 2466 E. Desert Inn Rd. **702/792-9554.**

Dead Poet Books *(Finds)*   The dead poet in question was the man from whose estate the owners bought their start-up stock. He had such good taste in books that they "fell in love with him" and wanted to name the store in his memory. Just one problem— they never did get his name. So they just called him "the dead poet." His legacy continues at this book-lover's haven. Open 7 days a week from 10am to 6pm. 3874 W. Sahara Ave. (corner of Valley View, near Raley's Supermarket). (C) **702/227-4070.**

LAS VEGAS SPECIALTY BOOKSTORES

Gambler's Book Shop   Here you can buy a book on any system ever devised to beat casino odds. Owner Edna Luckman carries more than 4,000 gambling-related titles, including many out-of-print books, computer software, and videotapes. She describes her store as a place where "gamblers, writers, researchers, statisticians, and computer specialists can meet and exchange information." On request, knowledgeable clerks provide on-the-spot expert advice on handicapping the ponies and other aspects of sports betting. The store's motto is "knowledge is protection." Open Monday through Saturday from 9am to 5pm, closed Sunday. 630 S. 11th St. (just off Charleston Blvd.). (C) **800/522-1777** or 702/382-7555. www.gamblersbook.com.

Gamblers General Store   A gambler's paradise stocked with a massive book collection, both antique and current slot machines, gaming tables (blackjack, craps, and so on), roulette wheels, collectible chips, casino dice, classic Vegas photos, and a ton of gaming-related souvenirs. Open daily from 9am to 5pm. 800 S. Main St. (Downtown). (C) **800/322-2447** or 702/382-9903. www.gamblersgeneralstore.com.

COMIC BOOKS

Alternate Reality Comics   The best place in Vegas for all your comic-book needs. They have a nearly comprehensive selection, with a heavy emphasis on underground comics. But don't worry—the superheroes are here, too. Open Monday through Saturday from 11am to 7pm, Sunday from noon to 6pm. 4800 S. Maryland Pkwy, Suite D. (C) **702/736-3673.**

7 Candy

M&M World *(Kids)*   What can one do when faced with a wall of M&Ms in colors never before seen by man or woman (Purple! Teal! Lime green!)? Overpriced? Yeah! Who cares? There are doodads galore, replete with the M&M logo, and a surprisingly enjoyable short film and comedy routine, ostensibly about the "history" of the candy, but really just a cute little adventure with a decent budget behind it. Open Sunday through Thursday from 9am to midnight, Friday and Saturday from 9am to 1am. In the Showcase Mall, 3785 Las Vegas Blvd. S. (just north of the MGM Grand Hotel). (C) **702/736-7611.**

8 Antiques

Antiques in Vegas? You mean really old slot machines, or the people playing the really old slot machines?

Actually, Vegas has quite a few antiques stores—nearly two dozen—of consistent quality and price, nearly all located within a few blocks of each other. We have one friend, someone who takes interior design very seriously, who comes straight to Vegas for most of her best finds (you should see her antique chandelier collection!).

To get to this antiquing mecca, start in the middle of the 1600 block of **East Charleston Boulevard** and keep driving east. The little stores, nearly all in old houses dating from the '30s, line each side of the street. Or you can stop in at **Silver Horse Antiques,** 1651 E. Charleston Blvd. (✆ **702/385-2700**), and pick up a map to almost all of the locations, with phone numbers and hours of operation.

Antiques at the Market   A newer antiques minimall (for lack of a better phrase) with a number of individuals operating stalls under one roof. Open Monday through Saturday from 10am to 6pm, Sunday from noon to 5pm. 6663 S. Eastern Ave. (between Sunset and Warm Springs Rd.). ✆ 702/307-3960.

Antique Square   A cruddy-looking collection of stores in several remodeled houses arranged in a square. But every good antiques shopper knows that these kinds of crammed junk stores are the places to find real treasures and to do real antiques hunting (because once they've been really picked through and prettily displayed by pros, you can kiss bargains and real finds goodbye). Individual store hours vary, but most are closed on Sunday and Monday. 2014–2034 Charleston Blvd. (at Eastern Ave.). ✆ 702/471-6500.

Red Rooster Antique Mall   Sort of a combination of the two preceding entries; older and battered, but also featuring those individual stalls. Individual store hours vary, but most are open Monday through Saturday 10am to 6pm, Sunday from 11am to 5pm. 1109 Western Ave. (at Charleston and I-15). ✆ 702/382-5253.

9 Wigs

Serge's Showgirl Wigs   Oh, you probably thought all those showgirls just naturally had bountiful thick manes. Sorry to burst your bubble. Actually, we aren't—if you don't know it's all illusion, you ought to. Meanwhile, if you have a desire to look like a showgirl yourself (and why not?), come to Serge's, which for 23 years has been supplying Vegas's wiggy needs, with more than 2,000 wigs to choose from. This, by the way, is not just for showgirls or the similarly delusional. Not only can wigs be fun for everyone (we treasure our own turquoise number), but at least one sassy gal we know with thinning hair issues recently bought two natural-looking models and reports that the sales staff was as nice and helpful as could be. Wigs range in price from $130 to over $1,500, depending on quality and realness, and you can pick from Dolly Parton's wig line or get something custom-made. They also make hairpieces and toupees and carry hair-care products. Open Monday through Saturday from 10am to 5:30pm.

And, if the prices at Serge's are too rich to bring your fantasy alive, right across the way is **Serge's Showgirl Wigs outlet,** with prices running from a more reasonable $60 to $70. 953 E. Sahara Ave. no. A-2. ✆ 702/732-1015. www.showgirlwigs.com.

10

Las Vegas After Dark

You will not lack for things to do at night in Vegas. This is a town that truly comes alive only after dark. Don't believe us? Just look at the difference between the Strip during the day, when it's kind of dingy and nothing special, and at night, when the lights hit and the place glows in all its glory. Night is when it's happening in this 24-hour town. In fact, most bars and clubs don't even get going until close to midnight. That's because it's only around then that all the restaurant workers and people connected with the shows get off the clock and can go out and play themselves. It's extraordinary. Just sit down in a bar at 11pm; it's empty. You might well conclude it's dead. Return in 2 hours and you'll find it completely full and jumping.

But you also won't lack for things to do before 11pm. There are shows all over town, ranging from traditional magic shows to cutting-edge acts such as *Mystère*. The showgirls remain, topless and otherwise; Las Vegas revues are what happened to vaudeville, by the way, as chorus girls do their thing in between jugglers, comics, magicians, singers, and specialty acts of dubious category. Even the topless shows are tame; all that changes is that the already scantily clad showgirls are even more so.

Every hotel has at least one lounge, usually offering live music. But the days of fabulous Vegas lounge entertainment, when the lounge acts were sometimes of better quality than the headliners (and headliners like Sinatra would join the lounge acts on stage between their own sets), are gone. Most of what remains is homogeneous and bland, and serves best as a brief respite or background noise. On the other hand, finding the most awful lounge act in town can be a rewarding pursuit of its own.

Vegas still does attract some dazzling headliner entertainment in its showrooms and arenas. Madonna's 2001 show commanded the top prices on her tour; Bruce Springsteen played his first Vegas show ever in early 2000; Bette Midler did an HBO special from the MGM Grand in early 1997 (and her *Millennium* show at Mandalay Bay); U2 started their Pop-Mart tour at UNLV's stadium; the Rolling Stones played both the MGM Grand and the Hard Rock Hotel's The Joint; Pavarotti inaugurated Mandalay Bay's Arena, with Bob Dylan doing the same for the House of Blues; and Cher opened up The Venetian with a rare live performance. The Red Hot Chili Peppers gave a free concert to celebrate the city's centennial. It is still a badge of honor for comedians to play Vegas, and there is almost always someone of marquee value playing one showroom or the other.

Admission to shows runs the gamut, from about $20 for *Mac King* (comedy magic show at Harrah's) to $200 and more for top headliners or Céline Dion. Prices occasionally include two drinks or, in rare instances, dinner.

To find out who'll be performing during your stay and for up-to-date listings of shows (prices change, shows close), you can call the various hotels, using their toll-free numbers. Or call the **Las Vegas Convention and Visitors Authority** (© 877/VISIT-LV) and ask them to send you a free copy of *Showguide* or *What's On in Las Vegas* (one or both of which will probably be in your hotel room). You can also check out what's playing at **www.visitlasvegas.com**. It's best to plan well ahead if you have your heart set on seeing one of the most popular shows or catching a major headliner.

The hotel entertainment options described below include information on ticket prices, what's included in that price (drinks, dinner, taxes, and/or gratuities), showroom policies (whether it's preassigned or maitre d' seating, and smoking policies), and how to make reservations. Whenever possible, reserve in advance, especially on weekends and holidays. If the showroom has **maitre d' seating** (as opposed to preassigned seats), you may want to tip him to upgrade your seat. A tip

of $15 to $20 per couple will usually do the trick at a major show, less at a small showroom. An alternative to tipping the maitre d' is to wait until the captain shows you to your seat. Perhaps it will be adequate, in which case you've saved some money. If not, you can offer the captain a tip for a better seat. If you do plan to tip, have the money ready; maitre d's and captains tend to get annoyed if you fumble around for it. They have other people to seat. You can also tip with casino chips (from the hotel casino where the show is taking place only) in lieu of cash. Whatever you tip, the proper etiquette is to do it rather subtly—a kind of palm-to-palm action. There's really no reason for this, since everyone knows what's going on, but being blatant is in poor taste. Arrive early at maitre d' shows to get the best choice of seats.

If you buy tickets for an assigned-seat show in person, you can look over a seating chart. Avoid sitting right up by the stage, if

---

(*Moments* Lounge Lizard Supreme

All those faux-hipster artists doing woeful lounge-act characters in Hollywood and New York only wish they could be Mr. Cook E. Jarr, whose sincerity and obvious drive to entertain puts mere performance artists to shame. With George Hamilton's tan, Cher's first shag haircut (it's certainly not his factory-original coif), and a bottomless, borderless catalog of rock, pop, soul, swing, and standard favorites, he's more Vegas than Wayne Newton.

Cook has a cult following of blue-collar casino denizens and the youthful cocktail set, who listen enraptured as he plays human jukebox, complete with karaoke-style backing recordings, terrible jokes, an array of disco-era lights, and (his favorite) a smoke machine. He's actually a solid, throaty singer, with a gift for vocal mimicry as he moves from Ben E. King to Bee Gees to Tony Bennett turf. And his tribute the night Sinatra died—a version of "My Way" in which he voiced, alternately, Sammy, Dino, and Elvis welcoming Ol' Blue Eyes to Heaven—was priceless.

He moves around a lot, but lately you can often catch him on Friday and Saturday nights, late, at **Harrah's Carnaval Court Lounge,** at 3475 Las Vegas Blvd. S. (© **702/369-5222**). Don't miss him! (And if he has left there by the time you read this, try to track him down.)

possible, especially for big-production shows. Dance numbers are better viewed from the middle of the theater. With headliners, you might like to sit up close.

Note: All of these caveats and instructions aside, most casino-hotel showrooms offer good visibility from just about every seat in the house.

If you prefer alternative or real rock music, your choices used to be limited, but that's all changing. More rock bands are coming to town, attracted to the House of Blues or the Hard Rock Hotel's The Joint, so that means you can actually see folks like Marilyn Manson and Beck in Vegas. But otherwise, the alternative club scene in town is no great shakes. Check out the listings below for bars and coffeehouses, several of which offer live alternative or blues music. If you want to know what's playing during your stay, consult the local free alternative papers: the *Las Vegas Weekly,* formerly *Scope*

magazine (biweekly, with great club and bar descriptions in their listings), and *City Life* (weekly, with no descriptions but comprehensive listings of what's playing where all over town). Both can be picked up at restaurants, bars, record and music stores, and hip retail stores. Or you can call *Las Vegas Weekly* directly; act nice and they just might give you a tip on the spot. If you're looking for good alt-culture tips, try asking the cool staff at the **Buffalo Exchange** vintage-clothing store (© 702/791-3960); they have their fingers right on the pulse of the underground.

In addition to the listings below, consider the **Fremont Street Experience,** described on p. 193.

Be aware that there is a curfew law in Vegas: Anyone under 18 is forbidden from being on the Strip without a parent after 9pm on weekends and holidays. In the rest of the county, minors cannot be out without parents after 10pm on school nights, and midnight on weekends.

1 What's Playing Where

It used to be that a show was an essential part of the Vegas experience. Back in those days, a show was pretty simple: A bunch of scantily (and we mean scantily) clad showgirls paraded around while a comedian engaged in some raunchy patter. The showgirls are still here and still scantily clad (though not as often topless; guess cable TV has taken some of that thrill away), but the productions around them have gotten impossibly elaborate. And they have to be because they have to compete with a free dancing water fountains show held several times nightly right on the Strip. Not to mention a volcano, a Mardi Gras parade in the sky, lounge acts galore, and the occasional imploding building. All free.

The big resort hotels, in keeping with their general over-the-top tendencies, are pouring mountains of money into high-spectacle extravaganzas, luring big-name acts into decades-long residencies and surrounding them with special effects that would put some Hollywood movies to shame. Which is not to say the results are Broadway quality—they're big, cheesy fun. Still, with the exception of the astonishing work done by the Cirque du Soleil productions, most of what passes for a "show" in Vegas is just a flashier revue, with a predictable lineup of production number/magic act/production number/acrobatics/production number.

Unfortunately, along with big budgets and big goals come big-ticket prices. Sure, you can still take the whole family of four to a show for under $100, but you're not going to get the same production values that you'd get by splurging on a Cirque du Soleil show. Which is not to say you always get what you pay for: There are some reasonably priced shows that are considerably better values than their more expensive counterparts.

Tips Our Favorites

Our vote for **best show?** It's a toss-up between *O* at Bellagio and *Mystère* at Treasure Island, both by Cirque du Soleil. Either must be seen to be believed—and even then you may not believe it, but you won't be forgetting the experience anytime soon. **Most intelligent show** is put on by Penn & Teller, and we are grateful. The **best magic show,** and one of the most reasonably priced productions (and thus the overall **best value for the money**), is Lance Burton at Monte Carlo. **Best classic Vegas topless revue** is *Jubilee!* at Bally's. **Best we aren't sure what the heck to call it but you should really try to see it** is Blue Man Group, at their new home at The Venetian.

Note: Although every effort has been made to keep up with the volatile Las Vegas show scene, keep in mind that the following reviews may not be indicative of the actual show you'll see, but the basic concept and idea will be the same. What's more, the show itself may have closed, so it's a good idea to always call the venue and check.

The following section describes each of the major production shows currently playing in Las Vegas, arranged alphabetically by the title of the production. But first, here's a handy list arranged by hotel:

- **Bally's:** *Jubilee!* (Las Vegas–style revue)
- **Bellagio:** Cirque du Soleil's *O* (unique circus-meets-performance-art theatrical experience)
- **Caesars Palace:** *Céline Dion* (music and variety)
- **Excalibur:** *Tournament of Kings* (medieval-themed revue)
- **The Flamingo Las Vegas:** *Second City Improv* (improvisational comedy)
- **Harrah's:** *Clint Holmes* (music and variety) and *Mac King* (comedy and magic)
- **Imperial Palace:** *Legends in Concert* (musical impersonators)
- **The Las Vegas Hilton:** Barry Manilow: *Music & Passion* (he writes the songs)
- **Mandalay Bay:** *Mamma Mia!* (a musical that features ABBA songs and was a great hit in London and on Broadway)
- **The Mirage:** *Danny Gans* (impressions)
- **MGM Grand:** Cirque du Soleil's *KA* (astounding marital arts and acrobatics); *La Femme* (adults-only topless dancers)
- **Monte Carlo:** Lance Burton: *Master Magician* (magic show and revue)
- **New York–New York:** Cirque du Soleil's *Zumanity* (adults-only provocative revue)
- **Paris Las Vegas:** *We Will Rock You* (rock musical featuring songs from Queen)
- **Rio All-Suite Hotel & Casino:** *Penn & Teller* (illusions) and *Chippendales* (male strippers)
- **The Riviera:** *An Evening at La Cage* (female impersonators), *Crazy Girls* (sexy Las Vegas–style revue), and *Splash* (aquatic revue)
- **Stratosphere Casino Hotel & Tower:** *American Superstars* (an impression-filled production show) and *Viva Las Vegas* (Las Vegas–style revue)
- **TI at the Mirage:** Cirque du Soleil's *Mystère* (unique circus performance)
- **Tropicana:** *Folies Bergère* (Las Vegas–style revue) and *Rick Thomas* (magic)
- **The Venetian:** *Blue Man Group* (hilarious performance art)
- **Wynn Las Vegas:** *Le Rêve* (water-themed production show)

2 The Major Production Shows

This category covers all of the major Las Vegas production shows and a few of the minor ones as well. In addition to the following, we recommend **Rita Rudner**'s stand-up comedy at New York–New York, and we urge you to stay away from the musical family the **Scintas** at the Rio—a fossilized Vegas act full of near-parody-level lounge singing and jokes at the expense of every ethnicity, handicap, and sexual orientation out there. Meanwhile, here are some shows that may be running by the time you read this, though we couldn't get any details about them by deadline time (for some reason, this is a remarkably closed-mouth town, even the publicists; seriously, guys, Bugsy is long gone and squealers aren't punished as sharply anymore): There will be a new Beatles/Yellow Submarine–themed Cirque du Soleil show at The Mirage opening in 2006. The former Guggenheim space at The Venetian is being converted into a theater, with plans to bring *Phantom of the Opera* there by early 2006. The charming hit musical *Hairspray!*, based on the John Waters movie about 1950s Baltimore and those crazy kids who just want to dance, has taken over the theater at Luxor now that the Blue Man Group has moved up the street to The Venetian. Speaking of Broadway hits, the raunchy and wonderful Tony-winning puppet show *Avenue Q* will be up and running at Wynn Las Vegas by the time you read this. All three will likely be in somewhat truncated forms to allow for their new settings.

Note: Shows can close without warning, even ones that have been running just shy of forever, so please call first. Note also that some ticket prices may not include tax or drinks, so you might also check for those potential hidden costs.

American Superstars One of a number of celebrity-impersonator shows (well, it's cheaper than getting the real headliners), *American Superstars* is one of the few shows where the impersonators actually sing live. Five performers do their thing; the celebs impersonated vary depending on the evening.

A typical Friday night featured Gloria Estefan, Charlie Daniels, Madonna, Michael Jackson, and Diana Ross and the Supremes. (And they recently added Christina Aguilera and Ricky Martin.) The performers won't be putting the originals out of work any time soon, but they aren't bad. Actually, they were closer in voice than in

---

Value Hot Tip!

Tickets2Nite is a newish daily service that puts any unsold seats for that evening on sale, starting at 2pm, for—get this!—*half price*. Hot diggity! Of course, there are some drawbacks. It's rare and downright unlikely that really ultra super-duper shows are ever going to have unsold seats (because the hotel will just sell them to the always-waiting-and-happy-to-pay-full-price standby line), but you'd be shocked at the range otherwise, from basic crap to stuff that we would recommend even at full price (they aren't allowed to say on the record which shows' tickets often come up for sale). Alas, the very nature of the service means you can't plan; you have to stand in line and take your chances starting at 2pm (we advise getting in line even earlier than that). So if you have your heart set on white tigers, don't rely on Tickets2Nite, but, if like a good gambler, you like taking chances, head for 3785 Las Vegas Blvd. S. (in the Showcase Mall booth).

looks to the celeb in question (half the black performers were played by white actors), which is an unusual switch for Vegas impersonators. The "Charlie Daniels" actually proved to be a fine fiddler in his own right and was the hands-down crowd favorite. The live band actually had a look-alike of their own: Kato Kaelin on drums (it's good that he's getting work). The youngish crowd (by Vegas standards) included a healthy smattering of children and seemed to find no faults with the production. The action is also shown on two large, and completely unnecessary, video screens flanking the stage, so you don't have to miss a moment. Sunday to Tuesday 7pm; Wednesday, Friday, and Saturday 6:30 and 8:30pm; dark Thursday. In the Stratosphere Casino Hotel & Tower, 2000 Las Vegas Blvd. S. ⓒ 800/99-TOWER or 702/380-7711. Tickets $39 adults, $28 children 5–12; show and buffet package $44 (includes taxes and fees).

Blue Man Group ⓕⓕⓕ   Are they blue? Indeed they are—three hairless, nonspeaking men dipped in azure paint (you may have seen them on a commercial or two and wondered what in the heck they were all about), doing decidedly odd stunts with marshmallows, art supplies, audience members, tons of paper, and an amazing array of percussion instruments fashioned fancifully from PVC piping. If that doesn't sound very Vegas, well, it's not. It's a franchise of a New York–born performance-art troupe that seems to have slipped into town through a side door opened by Cirque du Soleil's groundbreaking successes. Don't get the wrong idea: This is no Cirque clone. There are no acrobatics or flowing choreography, no attempt to create an alternate universe—just a series of surreal, unconnected bits. But even if the whole is no greater than the sum of the parts, the parts are pretty great themselves. It's funny in the weirdest and most unexpected ways, and the crowd is usually roaring by the end. Fans of typical Vegas shows may leave scratching their heads, but we are glad there is another color in the Vegas entertainment spectrum. At The Venetian (no ticket nor show times available at press time).

Céline Dion ⓕⓕ   Still a hot ticket in town, proving wrong the naysayers, which included us, we must admit. It was genuinely unprecedented for a star of this magnitude to take up a 3-year residency in a Vegas show—not to mention a Vegas show designed, theater and all, just for her, and a show with a subsequent $150-million price tag, and ticket prices that seem nearly that high. For those of you with (understandable) sticker shock, you can take some comfort in the fact that the money is all on the stage here. Some of that cost is represented by Our Star's salary, certainly, but the rest is present in one magnificent theater (battling it out with *O*'s home at Bellagio for finest in town), where, thanks to steep stadium seating, no seat is less than 150 feet from the stage. (Though in some cases, that means straight up, so you decide if that's really a good thing.) And the rest is quite evident in stunning staging, including a heralded enormous LED screen that allows for the most extraordinary special effects in town. Along with the sweeping landscapes, storms, and occasional video close-ups of the action brought to you on the screen, you can add the usual Cirque du Soleil touches (the show's director/producer is Franco Dragone, who previously brought this town *O* and *Mystère*), which means dancers (the finest of any show in Vegas) moving enigmatically, plus blooming trees, flying pianos, giant chandeliers, and other artistic touches straight out of Chagall or Magritte.

None of it even remotely relates to whichever song they occur during, but no matter. The Diva herself silences early negative predictions by appearing on stage at least 90% of the time, and generally working her tail off when she's there. Her pearly tones are right on the money. Are they live? Probably not always, but such issues are no

---

> **Tips** **Coolest House in Town?**
>
> The Ice House, a $5-million, two-story, 12,800-square-foot restaurant, bar, and gaming facility, is the latest sign of Downtown's upswing. Opened in summer 2003, the Art Deco–inspired building evokes images of South Beach rather than a Downtown dive, with an interior accented by retrospective photos of Old Vegas and '60s-style furniture. Both of the Ice House's two lounges sport frozen bar tops made of solid ice to keep drinks cold. Down a drink, grab a bite, and then play video poker or watch some sports.

---

longer relevant in the context of modern pop concerts where so many of today's performers rely on tape. More to the point, no matter how visually stunning or remarkably staged, this is nonetheless a Céline Dion concert, and nothing else. That's great news if you are a fan, but not if you aren't. (It's worth noting that in an effort to make this appeal to audience members beyond her fan base, she's included covers ranging from Sinatra to Stevie Wonder, and that these songs are the least successfully performed.) This won't convert anyone, probably, despite her genuine best efforts—she's got a heck of a voice and she is a true entertainer, in the best sense of the tradition, if not the most charismatic one. And perhaps also not the most thoughtful one; did she notice that the Wonder song begins "Looking back on when I was a little nappy-headed boy?" Wednesday through Sunday 8:30pm. In Caesars Palace, 3570 Las Vegas Blvd. S. ℂ 877/CELINE-4, or through www.ticketmaster.com. Tickets $75–$200 (excluding tax).

Cirque du Soleil's KA ✪✪✪   Our initial reaction to the opening of this was "Does Vegas really need *another* Cirque show?" And, for that matter, "Is there anything else Cirque can possibly *do*?" The answer to the latter is "Apparently, yes" and to the former "Certainly, as long as it's this one." To begin with, *KA* subverts expectations by largely eschewing the usual Cirque format—wide-eyed innocent is taken on surreal adventure, beautiful but aimless, complete with acrobats and clowns and lots of weird floaty things—in favor of an actual plot, as a brother and sister from some mythical Asian kingdom are separated by enemy raiders and have to endure various trials and tribulations before being reunited. Gleefully borrowing imagery from magical realist martial arts movies such as *Hero* and *Crouching Tiger, Hidden Dragon,* the production makes use of a technically extraordinary set that shifts the stage not just horizontally but vertically, as the action moves from under the sea to the side of a steep cliff and beyond. The circus elements—acrobats, clowns—are for once incorporated into the show in a way that makes some loose narrative sense, though this does mean that the physical stunts are mostly pretty much that rather than feats of daring-do, and between the stage's antics and the clever lighting effects, the show is more about hydraulics than humans. Except not; there really is a story, and it is by turns funny, tragic, and whimsical. There are at least two moments that are nothing but simple stagecraft and yet are exquisite, among the most memorable of any current Vegas show. The theater is cavernous, but extensive catwalks and other staging tricks mean that those in the back won't feel cheated or that far from the action. It might be a little long and intense for younger children, but older ones will be enthralled—and so will you. Don't sit here reading this any longer; go see it. Friday through Tuesday at 7:30 and 10pm. In the MGM Grand, 3799 Las Vegas Blvd. S. ℂ 877/880-0880. Tickets $99–$150.

Cirque du Soleil's *Mystère* 😊😊😊 (Kids)   The in-house ads for *Mystère* (Miss-*tair*) say "Words don't do it justice," and for once, that's not just hype. The show is so visual that trying to describe it is a losing proposition. And simply calling it a circus is like calling the Hope Diamond a gem, or the Taj Mahal a building. It's accurate but, as the ad says, doesn't begin to do it justice.

Cirque du Soleil began in Montréal as a unique circus experience, not only shunning traditional animal acts in favor of gorgeous feats of human strength and agility, but also adding elements of the surreal and the absurd. The result seems like a collaboration between Salvador Dalí and Luis Buñuel, with a few touches by Magritte and choreography by Twyla Tharp. MGM MIRAGE has built the troupe its own theater, an incredible space with an enormous dome and superhydraulics that allow for the Cirque performers to fly in space. Or so it seems.

While part of the fun of the early Cirque was seeing what amazing stuff they could do on a shoestring, seeing what they can do with virtually unlimited funds is spectacular. Cirque took full advantage of MGM MIRAGE's largesse, and their art only rose with their budget. The show features one simply unbelievable act after another (seemingly boneless contortionists and acrobats, breathtakingly beautiful aerial maneuvers), interspersed with Dadaist/commedia dell'arte clowns, and everyone clad in costumes like nothing you've ever seen before. All this and a giant snail!

The show is dreamlike, suspenseful, funny, erotic, mesmerizing, and just lovely. At times, you might even find yourself moved to tears. For some children, however, it might be a bit too sophisticated and arty. Even if you've seen Cirque before, it's worth coming to check out, thanks to the large production values. It's a world-class show, no matter where it's playing. That this arty and intellectual show is playing in Vegas is astonishing. Wednesday through Saturday 7:30 and 10:30pm, Sunday 4:30 and 7:30pm. In TI at the Mirage, 3300 Las Vegas Blvd. S. © 800/288-7206 or 702/894-7722. www.cirque dusoleil.com. Tickets $60–$95 (excluding tax).

Cirque du Soleil's *O* 😊😊😊   How to describe the seemingly indescribable wonder and artistry of Cirque du Soleil's latest and most dazzling display? An Esther Williams–Busby Berkeley spectacular on peyote? A Salvador Dalí painting come to life? A stage show by Fellini? The French troupe has topped itself with this production—and not simply because it's situated its breathtaking acrobatics in, on, around, and above a 1.5-million-gallon pool (*eau*—pronounced *O*—is French for "water"). Even without those impossible feats, this might be worth the price just to see the presentation, a constantly shifting dreamscape tableau that's a marvel of imagination and staging. If you've seen *Mystère* at TI at the Mirage or other Cirque productions, you'll be amazed that they've once again raised the bar to new heights without losing any of the humor or stylistic trademarks, including the sensuous music. If you've never seen a Cirque show, prepare to have your brain turned inside out. We know—those ticket prices—*ouch*. We want to say that we can guarantee it's worth it, but that's a decision only you can make. (Though no one we've personally sent has come back regretting that they went.) But we can say this: Watch this show, and you know where a good chunk of the money is going (in other words, they spend a bundle nightly to mount this thing). Note that no tank tops, shorts, or sneakers are allowed. Wednesday through Sunday 7:30 and 10:30pm. In Bellagio, 3600 Las Vegas Blvd. S. © 888/488-7111 or 702/693-7722. Tickets $99–$150 (excluding tax).

Cirque du Soleil's *Zumanity* (Overrated)   If we really need to tell you one more time, Las Vegas is not for kids. And here is the final proof: Cirque du Soleil, long considered the smartest family entertainment around, now produces this, an adult show dedicated to celebrating human sexuality. Or celebrating how they can shamelessly empty your pockets, but hold on—more cynicism to come. Staunch warnings tell audience members this is 18-and-over, and you know it as ushers dressed, and we feel terrible for them, in comic T-shirts designed to make them look naked, escort you to seats as the usual pre-show Cirque business gets under way, this time in the form of a self-loving, well-muscled male egoist who oozes and seduces gullible patrons. And thus begins the least subtle show on the Strip (appropriately for the least subtle hotel on the Strip), an erotic cabaret of the sort that stopped being shocking in fin-de-siècle Paris, not that that stops the crowd from eating it up. A rhinestone-bedecked transvestite hostess (former club kid Joey Arias, at this writing) introduces a bevy of acts which are all meant to be lewd or alluring or both. But if you pay attention, they are mostly just basic Cirque acts (and worse, just basic striptease acts, which you can see anywhere in town for a great deal less money), though instead of giving the illusion of near-nakedness, they give the illusion of total nakedness (an illusion that works better the farther you sit from the stage). As they contort and writhe and feign pleasure or apathy, we feel sympathy for all the parents who spent money on gymnastics and ballet lessons over the years, only to have their poor kids end up in this. See, Cirque is naturally sexy and erotic, so all this is gilding the lily until it chokes from lack of oxygen and dies. But if you were feeling sexy despite this stuff, the comic antics of the clowns, as they beat each other with blow-up dolls and faux phalli, should quench your ardor, while a triple-jointed contortionist should put you off sex—and your lunch—for good. (Remember when he would have been safely confined to freak shows?) There are some visually stunning moments (two women splashing about in a large glass, a woman performing with a dozen hula hoops), and at least one sketch (involving a woman and a muscled dwarf) that actually says something about love, romance, and tenderness. But overall, this is an endeavor of such cynicism that it makes our own look faint-hearted. Save your money for *La Femme* across the street, or just go to Sapphire and tip the best dancer there. Friday through Tuesday 7:30 and 10:30pm. 3790 Las Vegas Blvd. S. (in New York–New York). ✆ **702/740-6969**. www.zumanity.com. Tickets $125 (sofas), $85–$95 (theater seats), $65–$85 (cabaret stools), all including tax.

Clint Holmes ⚘⚘ Who? "My name is Michael, I've got a nickel." Oh, right. So why should you go? Because you miss, or simply still long for, the days of pure Vegas *entertainers*—you know, guys who sang (competently), told jokes and self-deprecating stories (competently), and dared the audience to love him with great confidence and, well, competence. No tigers, no magic, just a strong band and a strong sense of self—which is interesting, as it's been hard to market this guy because he doesn't offer magic, tigers, or any other kind of flashy gimmick, and has a bit of talent to back up his confident and

---

⌢**Kids Family-Friendly Shows**

Appropriate shows for kids, all described in this chapter, include the following:
- ***Tournament of Kings*** at Excalibur (p. 278)
- **Lance Burton** at the Monte Carlo (p. 274)
- **Cirque du Soleil's *Mystère*** at TI at the Mirage (p. 270)

Vegas on the Upswing

Vegas: Everything old is new again, and again. Whereas once it was the thing to do—to have a regular Vegas act, back in the Frankie and the Rat Pack days, and then again in the Elvis days—so it went that such acts became cornball and cheese. Then you couldn't get a performer with any critical or commercial legitimacy to touch the place with a 10-foot roll of quarters. And now? Miss Céline Dion has made it safe again, and here comes **Elton John,** filling Dion's spot on some of her off nights with his *The Red Piano* 🎭🎭 show. It's a gorgeously mounted production, featuring Elton and his lacquered piano, plus artistic video installations and other touches that have earned the show critical raves. Too bad he does it only a few weeks a year. Oh, and that the prices make even Dion's look cheap. ✆ **888/ 4ELTONJ** (435-8665). Tickets $110 to $275 plus Ticketmaster surcharge (no charge for box office walk-ups). Less technical pizzazz, but no less show-manship (not to mention more frequent dates and lower ticket prices) comes from **Barry Manilow:** *Music & Passion* 🎭🎭, who, bless him, knows just who he is and how to use it. In the Las Vegas Hilton, 3000 Paradise Rd., ✆ **800/222-5361.** Tickets $85 to $145. Wednesday to Friday at 9pm, Satur-day at 7:30 and 10pm.

We really wish these guys, in making Vegas safe again for legit perform-ers, also made it safe again for those on budgets. Oh, well, there's always Wayne Newton! Meanwhile, look for more performers to follow suit—if the rumors play out, Mötley Crüe will be getting their own venue at the new Planet Hollywood. The mind boggles, and really, really wants to go.

competent stage manner. You will hear some originals, some covers ("Banana Boat Song," "What Kind of Fool Am I?"), in addition to stories of how Holmes was influ-enced by Sammy Davis, Jr., which explains a lot, and we mean that in a positive way. He's good, but you need to want to see this kind of retro entertainment, and we mean that in a positive way as well. Monday through Saturday 7:30pm. In Harrah's, 3475 Las Vegas Blvd. S. ✆ 800/392-9002. Tickets $60 (excluding tax).

Crazy Girls   *Crazy Girls,* presented in an intimate theater, is probably the raciest revue on the Strip. It features sexy showgirls with perfect bodies in erotic song-and-dance numbers enhanced by innovative lighting effects. Think of *Penthouse* poses coming to life. Perhaps it was best summed up by one older man from Kentucky: "It's okay if you like boobs and butt. But most of the girls can't even dance." Wednesday through Monday 9:30pm. In The Riviera Hotel & Casino, 2901 Las Vegas Blvd. S. ✆ 877/892-7469 or 702/794-9433. Tickets $35 (excluding tax).

Danny Gans: *The Man of Many Voices* 🎭🎭   In a town where the consistent sell-outs are costly, elaborate extravaganzas, it's a tribute to Danny Gans's charisma and appeal that his one-man variety act can draw the same crowds with nothing more than a backup band and a few props. Gans is "the man of many voices"—more than 400 of them—and his show features impressions of 80 different celebrities, usually a dif-ferent mix each night, depending on audience demographics.

The emphasis is on musical impressions (everyone from Sinatra to Springsteen), with some movie scenes (Hepburn and Fonda from *On Golden Pond,* Tom Hanks in *Forrest Gump*) thrown in. A standout (though he doesn't always do it) is "The Twelve Months of Christmas" sung by 12 different celebrities (Paul Lynde, Clint Eastwood, Woody Allen, and so on). Gans's vocal flexibility is impressive, though his impersonations are hit-or-miss (his Springsteen needs work). That said, when we last saw him, he did a dead-on impression of comedian Jeff Foxworthy that had the crowd rolling, a hilarious bit involving George Burns imitating MC Hammer, and a somewhat freaky but totally on-target impression of Macy Gray. Truth be told, he's better than his current material (particularly if the mood strikes and he improvises), which is padded with obvious jokes and mawkish sentimentality. Still, he's a consistent crowd-pleaser, and the lack of bombast can be a refreshing change of pace. Tuesday through Thursday and Saturday through Sunday 8:00pm. In The Mirage, 3400 Las Vegas Blvd. S. ℂ 800/963-9634 or 702/792-7777. Tickets $100 (including tax).

An Evening at La Cage   No, it wasn't inspired by the French movie or the recent American remake, or even the Broadway musical. Actually, it's more like the stage show derived from the movie *Priscilla, Queen of the Desert.* Female impersonators dress up as various entertainers (with varying degrees of success) to lip-sync to those celebrity entertainers' greatest hits (with varying degrees of success). The celebs lampooned can include Cher, Bette Midler, Judy Garland, Whitney Houston, Dionne Warwick, and, intriguingly, Michael Jackson. A Joan Rivers impersonator, looking not unlike the original but sounding not at all like her (even with the aid of an odd constant echo), is the hostess, delivering scatological phrases and stale jokes. They do make the most of a tiny stage with some pretty stunning lighting, though the choreography is bland. Still, it's a crowd-pleaser—one couple was back for their fourth visit (all comped, but still). Wednesday through Monday at 7:30pm. In The Riviera Hotel & Casino, 2901 Las Vegas Blvd. S. ℂ 877/892-7469 or 702/794-9433. Tickets $55 (excluding tax).

Folies Bergère 👫👫   The longest-running production show in town has recently undergone a "sexier than ever" face-lift, but the result is far from that. It's more like tamed-down burlesque, as done by a college drama department. Bare breasts pop up (sorry) at odd moments (late shows only): not during the cancan line, but rather during a fashion show and an *en pointe* ballet sequence. The effect is neither erotic nor titillating, suggesting only that absent-minded dancers simply forgot to put their shirts on. The dance sequences (more acrobatics than true dance) range from the aforementioned ballet and cancan to jazz and hoedown, and are only occasionally well costumed. A coyly cute '50s striptease number on a *Hollywood Squares*–type set is more successful, as is a clever and funny juggling act (don't miss his finale with the vest and hat). Monday, Wednesday, Thursday, and Saturday 7:30 (covered), and 10pm (topless). Tuesday and Friday 8:30pm (topless). In Tropicana Resort & Casino, 3801 Las Vegas Blvd. S. ℂ 800/829-9034 or 702/739-2411. Tickets $45–$55 (excluding tax).

Jubilee! 👫👫👫   A classic Vegas spectacular, crammed with singing, dancing, magic, acrobats, elaborate costumes and sets, and, of course, bare breasts. It's a basic revue, with production numbers featuring homogenized versions of standards (Gershwin, Cole Porter, some Fred Astaire numbers) sometimes sung live, sometimes lip-synced, and always accompanied by lavishly costumed and frequently topless showgirls. Humorous set pieces about Samson and Delilah, and the sinking of the *Titanic* (!) show off some pretty awesome sets. (They were doing the *Titanic* long before a certain movie, and recent attendees claimed the ship-sinking effect on stage here was better than the one in the movie.) The finale features aerodynamically impossible feathered and bejeweled costumes and headpieces designed by Bob Mackie. So what if the dancers are occasionally out of step, and the action sometimes veers into the dubious (a Vegas-style revue about a disaster that took more than 1,000 lives?) or even the inexplicable (a finale praising beautiful and bare-breasted girls suddenly stops for three lines of "Somewhere Over the Rainbow"?). Note that *Jubilee!* offers a marvelous backstage walking tour in the afternoons. Saturday through Thursday 7:30 and 10:30pm. In Bally's Las Vegas, 3645 Las Vegas Blvd. S. ℂ 800/237-7469 or 702/739-4567. Tickets $55–$74 (excluding tax).

La Femme! ⭐⭐   Further proof that Vegas is trying to distance itself from the "Vegas Is for Families" image, "Classy Adult Entertainment" are the new watchwords in several hotels, with *La Femme!* leading the pack. Allegedly the same show that has been running for years in a famous racy French nightclub, this show is just a bunch of pretty girls taking their clothes off. Except that the girls are smashingly pretty, with the kind of bodies just not found on real live human beings, and they take their clothes off in curious and, yes, artistic ways, gyrating on pointe shoes while holding on to ropes or hoops, falling over sofas while lip-syncing to French torch songs—in short, it's what striptease ought to be, and by gosh, if strip clubs were this well staged, we'd go to them all the time. But $60 a ticket is a great deal to pay for arty nudie fun, especially when the routines, no matter how clever or how naked (the girls get down to a postage-stamp-size triangle soul patch covering the naughtiest of their bits, so they aren't "nude," but talk about a technicality), start to seem alike after a while. Wednesday through Monday 8 and 10:30pm. In the MGM Grand, 3799 Las Vegas Blvd. S. ℂ 800/929-1111 or 702/891-7777. Tickets $59 (excluding tax).

Lance Burton: *Master Magician* ⭐⭐⭐ *Kids*   Magic acts are a dime a dozen in Vegas of late. Along with impersonator acts, they seem to have largely replaced the

12 Inaccuracies in the Movie *Showgirls*

By the showgirls in *Jubilee!*

1. Nomi Malone wouldn't be in a Las Vegas production because she can't sing (or act).
2. Showgirls do not live in trailers.
3. Showgirls aren't discovered in strip bars.
4. Showgirls do not pimp themselves at conventions or trade shows.
5. Hotel owners do not throw lavish cast parties.
6. A lead dancer does not become a celebrity.
7. No one learns a show in a day.
8. Pushing someone down the stairs doesn't get you a lead role—it gets you fired.
9. Ice is used backstage to treat injuries, not to erect nipples.
10. Leaving rehearsal to go to Spago to drink champagne is generally frowned upon.
11. Showgirls are not coke-sniffing, champagne-drinking lesbians.
12. Anyway, showgirls do not drink champagne backstage—we prefer Jack Daniels!

topless showgirls of yore. Most magic shows seem more than a little influenced by the immeasurable success of Siegfried & Roy. So when someone pops up who is original—not to mention charming and, yes, actually good at his job—it comes as a relief. Handsome and folksy (he hails from Lexington, Kentucky), Burton is talented and engaging, for the most part shunning the big-ticket special effects that seem to have swamped most other shows in town. Instead, he offers an extremely appealing production that starts small, with "close-up" magic. These lovely, precise tricks, he tells us, are what won him a number of prestigious magic competitions. They are truly extraordinary, we are told by other professional magicians. (We swear that he tossed a bird up in the air, and the darn thing turned into confetti in front of our eyes. Really.) Burton doesn't have patter, per se, but his dry, laconic, low-key delivery is plenty amusing and contrasts nicely with other performers in town, who seem as if they have been spending way too much time at Starbucks. He does eventually move to bigger illusions, but his manner follows him—he knows the stuff is good, but he also knows the whole thing is a bit silly, so why not have fun with it? His longtime support act is comedian/juggler Michael Goudeau, who is not only perhaps the only genuinely funny and talented support act on the Strip, but can also juggle a beanbag chair, a chainsaw, and a peanut M&M all at once. His presence is just further proof of how right Burton's show is overall.

All this and extremely comfortable movie theater–style plush seats with cup holders. Tuesday and Saturday at 7 and 10pm. Wednesday through Friday at 7pm. In the Monte Carlo Resort & Casino, 3770 Las Vegas Blvd. S. ℂ 877/386-8224 or 702/730-7160. Tickets $60–$65 (excluding tax).

Legends in Concert ℛ   This is a crowd-pleaser, which is probably why it's been running since May 1983. Arguably the best of the Vegas impersonator shows (though it's hard to quantify such things), *Legends* features performers singing live rather than lip-syncing. And the performers look remarkably like the originals; free use of video cutting between action on stage and the real performer generally shows what a good simulation the former is. Acts vary from night to night (in a showroom that could use a face-lift) on a nice, large stage with modern hydraulics, but twinkle lighting that is stuck in a *Flip Wilson Show* time warp. The personal touches here include scantily clad (but well-choreographed) male and female dancers, and an utterly useless green laser. When we went, the performers included a carbon copy (at least in looks) of the early Little Richard, a crowd-pleasing Shania Twain, an energetic Prince, an appropriately flamboyant Liberace, a striking Bette Midler, and one helluva Elvis impersonator. Monday through Saturday 7:30 and 10:00pm. In Imperial Palace, 3535 Las Vegas Blvd. S. ℂ 888/777-7664. Tickets $40–$60 adults (includes 1 drink, tax, and gratuity), $25–$45 children 12 and under.

Le Rêve: *A Small Collection of Imperfect Dreams* ℛ   Note to Dragone, former Cirque impresario, the man behind both *O* and Céline Dion's show down the street, and the producer of this it's-not-Cirque-even-though-it-looks-just-like-it production: If you must subtitle shows, be careful when doing so, because calling something "a small collection of imperfect dreams" is just begging for a reviewer to seize upon the latter adjective and write things like "and boy is it ever." And while we are at it, why invite still more comparisons with Bellagio by setting this production, like *O*, in, around, and above a stage made of water?

But that is *Le Rêve,* named for the most significant of the paintings in the Wynn Art Gallery, a Cirque-like and, specifically, *O*-evoking extravaganza featuring all the usual elements: gorgeously sculpted athletic performers who twist, contort and mostly pose in filmy tattered outfits before and after diving in and splashing out of a giant pool. Intermittently funny clowns do their thing. Magritte figures float by. Fountains rise out of the stage. The result is pure spectacle, and that is the problem; were this a genuine Cirque show, there would be skill acts built into the proceedings—tiny Chinese contortionists, aerialists, and so on. Here, the performers do very little, apart from some synchronized swimming and diving, and some balance work, until about 15 minutes from the end, when more traditional (but not all that challenging) skit stunts appear, along with Cocteau-inspired sets and scenes that are the most striking of the entire show. It's like the biggest, most impressive Esther Williams production you can imagine, beautiful and devoid of any content, plus some casual references to sexual violence and homophobia. And, not to take away from the performers' abilities, a lot of what they do is passive—they are pulled, hoisted, and flown every which way, as they are called upon merely to spin, stretch, and gaze enigmatically at the audience. Speaking of which, you may wish to avoid sitting in the front rows, unless you don't mind spending 90 minutes huddling under the provided towels—not only does the in-the-round staging mean the performers routinely splash water, but long, filmy costumes, when hauled out of said water and lifted high in the air, drip most impressively and most wetly on the first couple rows. Since no seat is that far from the stage, and since the farther back the more of the complex imagery you can take it, there really isn't a bad seat, so stay back and stay dry. Tuesday through Monday 8pm. In Wynn Las Vegas, 3131 Las Vegas Blvd. S. ℂ 888/320-7110. Tickets $121.

Mac King ⭐⭐⭐ *Value*   One of the best entertainment values in Vegas, this is an afternoon comedy-magic show—and note order of precedence in that introduction. King does magic, thankfully, as far as we are concerned, emphasizing the only kind that's really mind-blowing these days—those close-up tricks that defy your eyes and mind. But he surrounds his tricks with whimsy and wit, and sometimes gut-busting guffaws, which makes you wonder how someone else can still perform stunts with a straight face. (Check out how he takes a $100 bill and—wait, we don't want to give it away, but suffice it to say it involves an old shoe, a Fig Newton, and several other unexpected props.) Perfect for the kids, perfect for the budget, perfect timing if you need something in the afternoon before an evening of gambling, dining, and cavorting. Then again, we are rather surprised he's still just an afternoon gig. One day, someone is going to wise up and move him to the big time, and his ticket prices will move up, too. So catch him while he's still a bargain. Tuesday through Saturday 1 and 3pm. 3475 Las Vegas Blvd. S (in Harrah's). ℂ 800/427-7247. Tickets $19.95 (plus tax).

Mamma Mia! ⭐⭐   We applaud Mandalay Bay for continuing to try to offer genuine theater options for Vegas patrons. Their first attempt was a production of the revival of *Chicago* (we can only imagine the business it would have done post-2003 Oscars!), and this charming and fluffy show is their second. It seems even better suited for Vegas audiences, since it's all-ages, innocuous, and promotes much clapping and dancing. There is little of substance in the story, a loose narrative created solely for the purposes of bringing the many, many hit songs of the Swedish '70s wonder group ABBA to the stage. Don't get us wrong; it's quite cute, as a young woman on the eve of her wedding, longing for the father she never knew to be a part of her present happiness, brings the three men who are the most likely biological daddy to her Greek island home, forcing her long-independent mother to face up to her past and make choices for the future. Some of the songs fit better than others, but all are sung with the appropriate breezy joy. We want to shake the director when we witness all too

Penn & Teller's Top 10 Things One Should NEVER Do in a Vegas Magic Show

Penn & Teller have been exercising their acerbic wit and magical talents in numerous forums together for more than 25 years, and their show at the Rio is one of Vegas's best and most intelligent. We must confess that we couldn't get the quieter half of the duo, Teller, to cough up a few words, but the more verbose Penn Jillette was happy to share.

1. Costume yourself in gray business suits totally lacking in rhinestones, animal patterns, Mylar, capes, bell-bottoms, shoulder pads, and top hats.
2. Wear your hair in any style that could NOT be described as "feathered" or "spiked."
3. Use really good live jazz music instead of canned sound-alike cheesy rip-off fake pop "music."
4. Cruelly (but truthfully) make fun of your siblings in the magic brotherhood.
5. Do the dangerous tricks on each other instead of anonymous show women with aftermarket breasts, and/or endangered species.
6. Toss a cute little magic bunny into a cute little chipper shredder.
7. Open your show by explaining *and* demonstrating how other magicians on the Strip do their most amazing tricks, and then do that venerable classic of magic "The Cups and Balls," with transparent plastic cups.
8. Treat the audience as if they had a brain in their collective head.
9. Allow audience members to sign real bullets, load them into real guns, and fire those bullets into your face.
10. Bleed.

(You will find **all 10** of these "don'ts" in the *Penn & Teller* show at the Rio All-Suite Hotel and Casino.)

many broad gestures and pointless scamperings during the rare moments of dialogue, but the cast is earnest and those darn Swedes wrote songs that we have to admit, 30 years on, are still mighty infectious. Monday through Thursday 7pm, and Saturday and Sunday 6 and 10pm. 3950 Las Vegas Blvd. S. (in Mandalay Bay). © 877/632-7400. www.mandalaybay.com. Tickets $45–$100 (plus tax).

Penn & Teller ★★★ *Moments*   The most intelligent show in Vegas, as these two— magicians? illusionists? truth-tellers? BS artists? Tell you what, let's settle on geniuses—put on 90 minutes of, yes, magic and juggling, but also acerbic comedy, mean stunts, and great quiet beauty. Looking like two characters out of Dr. Seuss, big, loud Penn and smaller, quiet Teller (to reduce them to their basic characteristics) perform magic, reveal the secrets behind a few major magic tricks, discuss why magic is nothing but a bunch of lies, and then turn around and show why magic is as lovely an art form as any other. We won't tell you much about the various tricks and acts, for fear of ruining punch lines, but watching Teller fish money out of an empty glass aquarium or play with shadows is to belie Penn's earlier caveats about learning how tricks are done—it doesn't ruin the wonder of it, not at all, nor the serenity that settles in your Vegas-sensory-overloaded brain. Wednesday through Monday 9pm. 3700 W. Flamingo (in the Rio Hotel). ℭ 888/746-7784. Tickets $75, plus tax.

Second City Improv 𝕣𝕣   Second City is the Chicago-based comedy group that spawned not only *SCTV* but some of the best modern-day comics (such as Gilda Radner, John Belushi, Martin Short, and Mike Myers). This is an improv and sketch-comedy show, with cast members performing stunts similar to those you might have seen on *Whose Line Is It Anyway?*—you know, taking suggestions from the audience and creating bizarre little skits and such out of them, all of it done at lightning speed with wit and a wink. Some of it can turn R-rated, so be careful bringing the kids, but do not hesitate to see it yourself. And join in—any improv group is only as good as the material fed it (so remember, there's only so much a group can do with jokes about sex and vomiting, especially if every single audience thinks that would be funny material with which to work). One of the best values and highest-quality shows in Vegas. Sunday through Thursday 8pm, and Friday through Saturday 8 and 10:30pm. In The Flamingo Las Vegas, 3555 Las Vegas Blvd. S. ℭ 800/732-2111. Tickets $33 (excluding tax).

Splash   Newly redesigned to celebrate the 20th anniversary of *Splash,* the 50th anniversary of The Riviera, and the 100th anniversary of Las Vegas itself, we fully expected to remain underwhelmed by this dated piece of old-style Vegas entertainment. And yet, while it remains solidly old-style Vegas entertainment, we have to admit that sometimes, much as we love the artistic daring of Cirque et al, we kind of also love old-style Vegas entertainment, at least when it's done right. And now, oddly, *Splash* has kind of done it right. They kept some of the last makeover's ice-skating numbers—frozen water, don't you know, implemented originally 'cause *O* made any other water skits look even stupider, thus the death knell for *Splash's* mermaids—plus the usual variety acts (nutty gauchos, jugglers, an acrobat, the motorcycle ball of death). What makes it particularly fun now are bits of connecting video footage using Vegas's past—montages of performers (Sammy! Elvis! Liza!) who played The Riviera, and odes to Vegas history—plus some particularly good dancing, all wrapped up in a more wink-wink attitude that makes you think they are in on the joke. Tuesday through Sunday 7pm; additional show Saturday 9:30pm. In The Riviera Hotel & Casino, 2901 Las Vegas Blvd. S. ℭ 877/892-7469 or 702/734-9301. Tickets $65–$80 (excluding tax).

Tournament of Kings 𝕣 *Kids*   If you've seen the Jim Carrey movie *The Cable Guy,* you probably laughed at the scene in which the two protagonists go to a medieval dinner and tournament. Perhaps you thought it was satire, created just for the movie. You would be wrong. It's actually part of a chain, and something very like it can be found right here in Vegas, though in a new and improved version. Those of us who shuddered at the former incarnation find this new one to be, at worst, highly tolerable, and at times downright entertaining.

For a fixed price, you get a dinner that's better than you might expect (Cornish game hen, very fine baked potato, and more), which you eat with your hands (in keeping with the theme), while Merlin (or someone like him) spends too much time trying to work the crowd up with a singalong. This gives way to a competition among the kings of various medieval countries, competing for titles in knightly contests (jousting, horse races, and such) that are every bit as unrehearsed and spontaneous as a professional wrestling match. Eventually, good triumphs over evil and all that.

Each section of the arena is given a king to be the subjects of and to root for, and the audience is encouraged to hoot, holler, and pound on the tables, which kids love but teens will be too jaded for (though we know some from whom a spontaneous "way cool" slipped out a few times unchecked). Many adults might find it tiresome, particularly when they insist you shout "huzzah!" and other period slang. Acrobatics are terrific, and certain buff performers make for a different sort of enjoyment. Daily at 6 and 8:30pm. In Excalibur, 3850 Las Vegas Blvd. S. © 800/933-1334 or 702/597-7600. Tickets $48.

We Will Rock You ⟨ Inevitably compared to *Mamma Mia!*, in that the hits of a beloved group of the '70s have been gathered around a loose plot line and are presented on stage as a conventional, if winking, musical. The narrative here is even thinner than

Afternoon Delight?

By now, it will not have escaped your attention that most of the nighttime shows in Vegas, at least the ones of any quality, cost a lot. Except for the ones that cost a whole heck of a lot. And that we tend to prefer the latter. "Isn't there *any* cheap entertainment in this town?" you may have begun to wonder, and trust us, even if we are awfully liberal with the contents of your wallets, we feel your pain.

So, barring the possibility that you might be the kind of gambler we wish to be, the sort who gets comped free tickets to expensive shows (that you could probably afford anyway, in typical Vegas irony), there are some alternatives. Several Vegas hotels offer afternoon shows, at much more reasonable prices—that, of course, being a relative term. Here are a couple of the better offerings (note that Mac King, because he's quite a bit better, gets his own full review above). **Ronn Lucas** ⟨⟨ (in the Rio, 3700 W. Flamingo Rd.; © 888/746-7784; Sat–Thurs 3pm; $30, including drink and program) seems like a throwback to corny vaudeville days—after all, he's a ventriloquist. But his puppets are maladjusted (why not?) with bite and wit, and he is fearless in the same manner of Penn & Teller; he gleefully deconstructs his art form, confident that after he shows you how it all works, he can still bamboozle you. Watch if you don't suddenly start thinking of those puppets as real characters, even though you know exactly how it all works. He's clever, funny, and weird. And if the price seems too high (even with drink and souvenir program as part of the package), look for discount coupons in the free magazines in your hotel room.

Rick Thomas ⟨ (Stardust Resort & Casino, 3000 Las Vegas Blvd S.; © 866/888-3427 or 702/732-6325; Thurs–Tues 2 and 4pm; $25) is an entertaining magician, though one wonders why he merits his own afternoon show but not his own nighttime show, or a part of one of the big nighttime production revues. *Viva Las Vegas* (in the Stratosphere Casino Hotel & Tower, 2000 Las Vegas Blvd. S.; © 800/99-TOWER or 702/380-7777; Mon–Sat 2 and 4pm; $17, including tax), an everything-but-the-kitchen-sink Vegas variety show, is good only if you really need an hour's respite from the slots in the afternoon.

Note: Discount coupons for the afternoon shows are often found in those free magazines in your hotel room. Sometimes the discount gets you in free, with just the price of a drink.

MM: Some time in the future, evil corporations control everything and have banned rock music because it's rebellious and independent and can't be corporately marketed as tidily as prefab boy and girl pop bands. It's up to a ragtag bunch of punk-rock-clothed rebel "bohemians" to find the music that they've only heard rumors about and bring back Rock'n'Roll. This leads to one of those curious paradoxes: a rock musical that features a bunch of people singing rock songs about how there is no rock music any more. Also, the music that will revive rock is that of . . . Queen. That's right. Not the Stones. Not Sabbath. Queen. Bless them, they wrote fantastic songs that work excellently as show tunes, but no one delivers them like Freddy. The cast all sing fine and overact to an inch of their lives. The show itself has some funny moments, but not enough to make the 2 hours (without intermission) go by quickly enough to get to what everyone came for the first place, "Bohemian Rhapsody." But there is no justification at all for the decision that gave the single most rocking line in the single most rocking song to the one character in the musical who does not sing rock. Monday through Wednesday and Friday 8:30pm; Saturday 7:00 and 10:30 pm; Sunday at 2:00 and 8:30pm. In Paris Las Vegas, 3655 Las Vegas Blvd. S. © **877/ROCK-SHOW.** Tickets $45–$100.

3 Headliner Showrooms

Vegas entertainment made its name with its showrooms, though its glory days are somewhat behind it, gone with the Rat Pack themselves. For a long time, Vegas headliners were something of a joke; only those on the downhill side of fame were thought to play here. But with all the new performance spaces—and high fees—offered by the new hotels, Vegas suddenly has some respect again, especially, on (of all things) the rock scene. Both the Hard Rock Hotel's The Joint and the House of Blues are attracting very current and very popular acts who find it hip, rather than humiliating, to play Sin City. However, the classic Vegas showroom itself does seem headed the way of the dinosaurs; many of the hotels have shuttered theirs. As for the remainder, one is pretty much like the other, with the exception of the Hard Rock and HOB (hence their detailed descriptions), and in any case, audiences go based on the performer rather than the space itself. Check with your hotel, or those free magazines in your room, to see who is in town when you are.

Hard Rock Hotel's The Joint ⓖ   Formerly just about the only game in town in terms of good rock bookings, The Joint, with its 1,400-seat capacity, now faces some stiff competition from the House of Blues. For example, when Alanis Morrisette came to town, she played the Hard Rock, but her opening act, Garbage, played the House of Blues. On the other hand, it was here the Rolling Stones chose to do a show during their arena tour—this was the smallest venue the band had played in years, and, as you can imagine, it was one hot ticket. When the Hard Rock Hotel opened in 1995, the Eagles were the first act to appear. Since then the facility has presented Bob Dylan, Ziggy Marley, Marilyn Manson, Hootie and the Blowfish, the Black Crowes, Donna Summer, Stephen Stills, Jimmy Cliff, Tears for Fears, Johnny Cash, Lyle Lovett, and James Brown.

The venue is not a preferred one, however; it's worth going only if a favorite performer is playing or if it's an opportunity to see a big artist play a smaller-than-usual room. Though there's sometimes table seating, it's usually festival style, making personal space at a premium during a crowded show; and though the floor is slightly raked, this still makes for poor sightlines. The balconies upstairs, if you can get to them, aren't much better, as once the bodies are packed in about two deep, the stage is completely obscured. Unless you want to brave the crush at the very front (sure, you should—it's a rock show!), we suggest standing at the rail toward the back, which not only elevates you slightly above the crowd (improving those sightlines), but at least protects one side of your body from the crowd. *Note:* As of this writing, the Hard Rock announced plans to close The Joint sometime in the near future and totally redo it as part of their own ongoing billion-dollar upgrade.

Showroom Policies: Smoking permitted for some shows; seating is either preassigned or general, depending on the performer. **Price:** $20 to $250, depending on the performer (tax and drinks extra). **Showtimes:** 8:30pm (nights of performance vary). **Reservations:** You can reserve up to 30 days in advance. In the Hard Rock Hotel & Casino, 4455 Paradise Rd. ℂ **800/693-7625** or 702/693-5000.

House of Blues ⚂⚂   With its entry into Las Vegas, the House of Blues is going head to head with The Joint at the Hard Rock Hotel, and the prospects for some great bookings due to competition are high. On its own merits, the House of Blues is a good, intimate room with a cozy floor surrounded by a bar area, and an upstairs balcony area that has actual theater seating. (The balcony might actually be a better place to see a show since the sightlines are unobscured, unlike down below, where posts and such can obstruct the view.) It's probably the most comfortable and user-friendly place to see a rock show in Vegas.

The heavy theme decor (a constant evocation of the Delta region and New Orleans) is a bit too Disneyland-meets-Hearst-Castle, with corrugated-tin this and weathered-wood

---

(Fun Fact) **Wayne Newton's Top 10 Favorite Lounge Songs**

Wayne Newton is the consummate entertainer. He has performed more than 25,000 concerts in Las Vegas alone, and in front of more than 25 million people worldwide. Wayne has received more standing ovations than any other entertainer in history. Along with his singing credits, his acting credits are soaring—one of his more recent credits is *Vegas Vacation*. Make sure you catch him. No trip to Vegas is complete without seeing the "King of Las Vegas."

1. "You're Nobody, Til Somebody Loves You" (You don't have a body unless somebody loves you!)
2. "Up a Lazy River" (or "Up Your Lazy River!")
3. "Don't Go Changing (Just the Way You Are)" (The clothes will last another week!)
4. "Having My Baby" (Oh God!)
5. "The Windmills of My Mind" (A mind is a terrible thing to waste!)
6. "The Wind Beneath My Wings" (Soft and Dry usually helps!)
7. "Copacabana"
8. "When the Saints Go Marching In"
9. "I Am, I Said" (Huh?!)
10. "The Theme from the Love Boat" (or "Would a Dinghy Do?")

Headliner Stadiums

Three arenas are worth a special mention since they often feature major entertainers. **Sam Boyd Stadium,** the outdoor stadium at the University of Nevada, Las Vegas (UNLV), has been host to such major acts as Paul McCartney, U2, the Eagles, and Metallica. **Thomas and Mack Center,** the university's indoor arena, has a more comprehensive concert schedule, including such names as Van Halen and Michael Bolton, as well as such shows as *Disney on Ice* and the Ringling Bros. Circus. Both are located on the **UNLV campus** at Boulder Highway and Russell Road (© **702/ 895-3900**). **Ticketmaster** (© **702/474-4000**) handles ticketing for both arenas.

that, plus walls covered in outsider/primitive/folk art from various Southern artists. But it annoys us less in Vegas than it does in New Orleans; here it's sort of a welcome touch of the genuine amid the artificial, while in the actual Big Easy, it comes off as pre-fab.

The House of Blues has rock and blues shows just about every night, and, as mentioned, nationally recognized acts are already flocking to the place, starting with Bob Dylan on opening night and continuing with shows by Seal, X, Garbage, Taylor Dane, Al Green, James Brown, the Go-Go's, the Neville Brothers, and even spoken word by Henry Rollins.

Showroom Policies: Smoking permitted; seating is either preassigned or general, depending on the performer (some shows are all general admission, with everyone standing on the floor). **Price:** $18 to $250, depending on the performer. **Showtimes:** Vary, but usually 8pm. **Reservations:** You can buy tickets as soon as shows are announced; lead time varies with each artist. In Mandalay Bay, 3950 Las Vegas Blvd. S. © **877/ 632-7400** or 702/632-7600.

Other major headliner showrooms in Vegas include the following:

- **Aladdin Center for the Performing Arts**   In the Aladdin Resort & Casino, 3667 Las Vegas Blvd. S. (© **877/333-WISH** [333-9474] or 702/785-5555)
- **Las Vegas Hilton Showroom**   In the Las Vegas Hilton, 3000 Paradise Rd. (© **800/222-5361** or 702/732-5755)
- **Mandalay Bay Events Center**   In Mandalay Bay, 3950 Las Vegas Blvd. S. (© **877/632-7400** or 702/632-7580)
- **MGM Grand Garden Events Arena**   In the MGM Grand Hotel & Casino, 3799 Las Vegas Blvd. S. (© **800/929-1111** or 702/891-7777)
- **MGM Grand Hollywood Theatre**   In the MGM Grand Hotel & Casino, 3799 Las Vegas Blvd. S. (© **800/929-1111** or 702/891-7777)
- **Orleans Showroom**   In the Orleans, 4500 W. Tropicana Ave. (© **800/ORLEANS**)

4 Comedy Clubs

Comedy Club   The Riviera's comedy club, on the second floor of the Mardi Gras Plaza, showcases four comedians nightly. Once a month, usually on the last weekend, the club hosts a late-night *XXXTREME Comedy Showcase* for shock and X-rated comedians. Other special events include the *All Gay Comedy Revue* and R-rated hypnotist Frank Santos. Daily 8:30 and 10:30pm, with occasional Friday and Saturday late-night shows at 11:45pm. In The Riviera Hotel & Casino, 2901 Las Vegas Blvd. S. © **800/634-6753** or 702/734-9301. Tickets $18.

Comedy Stop   Similar to the other comedy clubs in town, the Comedy Stop features three nationally known comedy headliners nightly. Daily 8 and 10:30pm. In Tropicana Resort & Casino, 3801 Las Vegas Blvd. S. ✆ **800/468-9494** or 702/739-2411. Tickets $20 (includes tax, tip, and 1 drink).

The Improv ★★   This offshoot of Budd Friedman's famed comedy club (the first one opened in 1963 in New York City) presents about four comedians per show in a 400-seat showroom. These are talented performers—the top comics on the circuit, who you're likely to see on Leno and Letterman. You can be sure of an entertaining evening. Tuesday through Sunday 8:30 and 10:30pm. In Harrah's Las Vegas, 3475 Las Vegas Blvd. S. ✆ **800/392-9002** or 702/369-5111. Tickets $25.

5 Coffeehouses

It could be a sign of how stagnant local Vegas culture is, that as we went to press, all of the local coffeehouses had closed. There may be others open by the time you read this, and if you are looking for a break from the usual Vegas glitter, it would be worth dropping by one to see what passes for local alt culture. They should offer live music and/or poetry readings; check the listings in *Las Vegas Weekly* and *City Life* for details (or just call the place in question).

Jazzed Cafe & Vinoteca ★★★ *(Finds)*   This genuine European-style cafe (well, by way of California) is owned and operated by the charming and friendly Kirk, a choreographer who lived in Italy for 10 years. Originally just an itty-bitty location on Flamingo, it's now a larger but still intimate venue (seating only 40) on Sahara, an even farther drive for the average tourist, but well worth it if you want something less Vegas. Featuring candlelight and cool jazz most nights, with hot art on the walls, they try to serve eclectic and unusual wines, along with multiple coffee drinks (be sure to try the terrific Illy, a renowned Italian brand). There's a small but satisfying food menu featuring inexpensive authentic Italian specialties—simple pastas, focaccia bread, and so forth, all made by Kirk on the spot. It's a great respite from the maddening crowds (and a cheap place to eat well), though it fills up with the owner's show-and-dance pals after the shows let out. A sign warns you not to order lemon peel with your espresso—if you do, be prepared to be sworn at (sweetly) in Italian. Open Sunday from 5pm until they feel like closing, Tuesday through Thursday from 5pm to midnight, and Friday and Saturday from 5pm to 1am. 8615 W. Sahara (at Durango). ✆ **702/233-2859.** www.jazzedcafe.com.

6 Piano Bars

The Bar at Times Square ★   If you're looking for a quiet piano bar, this is not the place for you. It's smack in the middle of the Central Park part of the New York–New York casino. Two pianos are going strong every night, and the young hipster, cigar-smoking crowd overflows out the doors. It always seems to be packed with a singing, swaying, drinking throng full of camaraderie and good cheer—or at least, full of booze. Hugely fun, provided you can get a foot in the door. And yes, every night, right outside, the ball on top drops at midnight, for a little *Auld Lang Syne.* Shows daily from 8pm to 2:15am. In New York–New York, 3790 Las Vegas Blvd. S. ✆ **702/740-6969.** Cover Fri–Sat $10.

Recording Vegas

A funny thing happened in connection with the 2005 emergence of the band the Killers: People started talking about the notion of a hip, hot band in conjunction with Las Vegas.

Now, that seems odd, given the association of such unimpeachable icons as Frank Sinatra and Elvis Presley with the town. But even the Rat Pack chic at the core of Vegas's musical legacy carries a taint of finger-snapping camp. And let's not forget that when *American Idol* inquisitor Simon Cowell wants to zing a particularly withering remark about a performance, one of his favorite methods is to say it reminds him of something he'd see "in a Las Vegas lounge."

Maybe it would behoove Cowell to sit down and hear some of the things that actually have been in Las Vegas lounges (and showrooms) over the years, though. To that end, there are plenty of documents he could explore. One nice byproduct of the Vegas-baby revival running from *Swingers* through the "what happens in Vegas" campaign is a proliferation of CDs collecting some of the great music associated with and, often, made on the strip.

Arguably, the definitive set is the 1965 live recording *Sinatra at the Sands.* Accompanied by Count Basie and his Orchestra, Ol' Blue Eyes is at his Vegas best—in both great voice and sassy mood. The mix of signature songs, some intriguing side trips and at times salty (or to some ears, truly offensive) banter with the band and audience more or less makes for the archetype of what a Vegas artist does. And Sinatra was clearly the master. It was this album that a local radio station played in its entirety during the key afternoon drive time on the day Sinatra died.

Capitol Records' *Vegas Baby,* an entry in its ongoing "Ultra-Lounge" series, is not a bad place to start for an overview, with selections from Bobby Darin, Vic Damone, Wayne Newton, Tom Jones, Louis Prima, Dean Martin, and others, all emphasizing upbeat, high-roller themes. Many of these artists themselves released full albums recorded in Vegas along the way in

Napoleon's ★★ A formerly nice but rather sedate space near the back of the Paris Las Vegas shopping gallery has been transformed into a rollicking good-time venue with the addition of dueling piano performances. The bar is a mixture of French old-world charm and Las Vegas showmanship, done all in reds and dark browns with lots of comfy seating scattered about. The pianists play Tuesday through Thursday and Sunday between 8pm and midnight, and Friday and Saturday between 9pm and 1am. In Paris Las Vegas, 3570 Las Vegas Blvd. S. ☎ 702/946-7000.

PJ Mcraes ★ This low-key, sophisticated piano bar—its walls lined with oil paintings of icons such as Elvis, Bogart, James Dean, and Marilyn Monroe (not to mention Rodney Dangerfield, finally getting respect)—is a romantic setting for cocktails and classic piano-bar entertainment every night except Sunday and Monday. There's a small dance floor. On Friday and Saturday a talented vocalist is on hand as well. Far their careers, and a "Live at Caesars Palace" series in recent years added some new picks from the vaults.

But with the 2005 Vegas Centennial celebration, a tie-in set of releases from Capitol might offer the best audio picture of the neon city thus far. Sinatra is captured in the twilight at a 1986 Golden Nugget concert. Dean Martin is represented at his loosest and raciest in a 1967 late show at the Sands. Wayne Newton never recorded a live album in Vegas (go figure), but Capitol has put together a representative collection for the town's official "Mr." And there is an Elvis Presley disc compiling live performances from 1970 and 1972—not Elvis at his best, but maybe Elvis at his most Vegas.

The revelatory albums in the series, however, come from Bobby Darin, Nancy Wilson, and the amazing Louis Prima & Keely Smith team. The latter (captured in concert at the Sahara in the mid-'50s, with most of the material previously unreleased) is the quintessential lounge act, he the Italian jester, she the brassy dame with the gifted pipes and the wit to keep the lugs she worked with in their place. (If only Cowell was to be faced with anything on this level!) Wilson's rescued-from-the-vaults 1968 concert at the Sands is atypical for what is perceived as Vegas style, but her soulful dignity is never less than mesmerizing.

And the Darin set may well do a better job of encapsulating the enigma that somewhat escaped the Kevin Spacey bio-pic *Beyond the Sea*, as he splish-splashes his way from Dino-esque crooner to stand-up comic (some pretty so-so impersonations of Cagney, Grant, Brando, and others, to be honest, in a long interlude) to earnest folky in the course of this one performance, recorded in 1963 at The Flamingo. It does not counter the impression of Darin as someone who wanted to both be and do everything, yet had no idea what he really wanted to do, but it's a fascinating trip all the way.

Oh, and per a search of the All Music Guide website, there are currently 85 available recorded versions of "Viva Las Vegas." Simon, what are you waiting for?

from a meat market, but it's a relaxed atmosphere in which to meet people, with an over-30 crowd. A menu offers salads, burgers, steak sandwiches, pastas, and gourmet appetizers such as oysters Rockefeller and escargot-stuffed mushrooms. Open daily 24 hours. 1487 E. Flamingo Rd. (between Maryland Pkwy. and Tamarus St.; on your right as you come from the Strip; look for the La-Z-Boy Furniture Gallery). ✆ 702/737-6212.

7 Gay Bars

Hip and happening Vegas locals know that some of the best scenes and dance action can be found in the city's gay bars. And no, they don't ask for sexuality ID at the door. All are welcome at any of the following establishments—as long as you don't have a problem with the people inside, they aren't going to have a problem with you. For women, this can be a fun way to dance and not get hassled by overeager Lotharios. (Lesbians, by the way, are just as welcome at any of the gay bars.)

If you want to know what's going on in gay Las Vegas during your visit, pick up a copy of the *Las Vegas Bugle,* a free gay-oriented newspaper that's available at any of the places described below. Or call them at ℂ **702/369-6260.**

The Buffalo ℱ   Close to both Icon (formerly Angles) and Gipsy, this is a leather/Levi's bar popular with motorcycle clubs. It features beer busts (all you can drink for a small cover) and other drink specials throughout the week. There are pool tables and darts, and music videos play in this not-striking environment. It's very cheap, however, with longnecks going for a few bucks, and it gets very, very busy, very late (3 or 4am). Open daily 24 hours. 4640 Paradise Rd. (at Naples St.). ℂ **702/733-8355.**

The Eagle   Off the beaten track in just about every sense of the phrase, The Eagle is the place to go if well-lit bars make you nervous. It's dark and slightly seedy, but in that great '70s gay bar kind of way. All in all, it's a refreshing change from the over-processed slickness that is Las Vegas. The crowd, tending toward middle age, is mostly male and of the Levi's/leather group. There is a small dance area (calling it a dance floor would be generous), a pool table, video poker, and a nice-size bar. Drinks are inexpensive, and special events make them even more so. For instance, The Eagle is rapidly becoming famous for its twice-weekly underwear parties (if you check your pants, you receive draft beer and drinks for free—that's right: free). The 20-minute drive from the Strip makes it a questionable option, but try it out if you've got a sense of adventure. Open daily 24 hours. 3430 E. Tropicana Ave. (at Pecos Rd.). ℂ **702/458-8662.**

Gipsy ℱℱ   For years, Gipsy reigned supreme as the best gay dance place in the city, and for good reason: great location (Paradise Rd. near the Hard Rock), excellent lay-out (sunken dance floor and two bars), and very little competition. A few years ago, some fierce competition stole some of its spotlight, along with a good portion of the clientele, and so the Gipsy fought back with a $750,000 renovation that seemed to recapture past glories. The drink specials, along with special events, shows, male dancers, and theme nights, make this place a good party bar. Open daily from 10pm to 6am. 4605 Paradise Rd. (at Naples St.). ℂ **702/731-1919.** Cover varies but is usually $5 and up on weekends, less or even free on weekdays.

Good Times ℱ   This quiet neighborhood bar is located (for those of you with a taste for subtle irony) in the same complex as the Liberace Museum, a few miles due east of the MGM Grand. There's a small dance floor, but on a recent Friday night, nobody was using it, the crowd preferring instead to take advantage of the cozy bar area. A small conversation pit is a perfect spot for an intimate chat. Of course, there's the omnipresent pool and video poker if you're not interested in witty repartee. We remember this place as being a lot more crowded than it was during our most recent visit (but perhaps we were there on an off night). It makes a nice respite after the Liberace Museum (after which you may very well need a stiff drink). Open daily 24 hours. In the Liberace Plaza, 1775 E. Tropicana Ave. (at Spencer St.). ℂ **702/736-9494.**

Krave ℱℱ   Most notably the first gay club on the Strip, not that anyone's admitting it's a gay club anymore, using "alternative" as the winking buzzword. The result is a more mixed crowd than you might get at other, openly gay clubs. The interior is a well-crafted Gothic explosion, with a dance floor and some go-go cages that can fea-ture dancers of either gender. Overall, a toss-up; clearly, more money is going into the place, and the Strip access is important since most other local gay bars take some doing to get to. On the other hand, it has limited hours and a possibly even more competitive crowd. Note that if you don't pay the club valet, you have to park in the regular hotel parking, and that calls for a long job through the evening-deserted Desert Passage shopping mall, which might be uncomfortable in club togs—limited access may well explain why there have already been two failed nightclubs in this space. Open daily except Monday from 8pm until late (after hours until dawn Fri and Sat). At Planet Hollywood Hotel & Casino, 3667 Las Vegas Blvd. S. (entrance on Harmon). ℂ **702/836-0830**. Cover varies.

8 Other Bars

In addition to the venues listed below, consider hanging out, as the locals quickly began doing, at **Aureole** ⭐⭐, **Red Square** ⭐⭐, and the **House of Blues** ⭐⭐, all in **Mandalay Bay** (see chapter 6). There's a separate bar at Aureole facing the wine tower, where your wish for wine sends comely lasses flying up four stories, courtesy of *Peter Pan*–style harnesses, to fetch your desired bottle. At Red Square, keep your drink nicely chilled all night long on the ice bar, created by water that's freshly poured and frozen daily. Or hang out and feel the blues at the small bottle-cap-bedecked bar in the corner of the House of Blues restaurant, which gets quite lively with off-duty locals after midnight.

You might also check out the incredible nighttime view at the bar atop the **Stratosphere Casino Hotel & Tower**—nothing beats it.

There's also the **Viva Las Vegas Lounge** at the Hard Rock Hotel, which every rock-connected person in Vegas will eventually pass through.

And the **Petrossian Bar** ⭐⭐⭐ in Bellagio offers class along with its cocktails (to say nothing of caviar and other delicacies)—but come for the cocktails, as those in the know claim it's not only the best bar in Vegas for such matters, but maybe the best bar in the West.

Caramel ⭐⭐ It's small, but worlds away from the Bellagio-business-as-usual just outside its doors. How happy the 20-somethings are that there is this hip-hop spinning, glowing, caramel-and-chocolate-coated drink glasses, glowing bar, nonthreatening (and non-Euro-stodgy), scene-intensive hangout in the middle of Bellagio. How much does this prove Bellagio is trying to lure the Ghost Bar crowd away from the Palms? Not that this will do it, but if you are here and young, it's where you should be. Open daily 5pm to 4am. 3600 Las Vegas Blvd. S. (in the Bellagio Hotel). ℂ **702/693-7111**.

Champagnes Café ⭐⭐ Wonder where Old Vegas went? It ossified right here. Red- and gold-flocked wallpaper and other such trappings of "glamour" never die—in fact, with this ultralow lighting, they will never even fade. A seedy old bar with seedy old scary men leering away. They even serve ice-cream shakes spiked with booze—two indulgences wrapped into one frothy package, and quite a double addiction delight. Some might run screaming from the place, while others will think they've died and gone to heaven. Just remember—this is the kind of place director Quentin Tarantino, or this year's alt-cult hit movie, will make famous. It can't be long. And then it will be overrun with hipsters. Beat the rush, go there now, and brag that you knew about it back before it was so cool it became passé. Again. Open daily 24 hours. 3557 S. Maryland Pkwy. (between Twain Ave. and Desert Inn Rd.). ℂ **702/737-1699**.

Coyote Ugly ⭐ You've seen the movie, now go have some of that prepackaged fun for yourself. Oh, come on—you don't think those bartender girls really dance on the bar and hose down the crowd just because they are so full of spontaneous rowdy high sprits, now do you? Not when the original locale built a reputation (and inspired a bad movie) on just such behavior, creating a success strong enough to start a whole chain of such frat-boy fun places? By the way, sarcastic and cynical as we are, can we say, totally fun place? Open daily from 6pm to 4am. In New York–New York, 3790 Las Vegas Blvd. S. (at Tropicana Ave.). ℂ 702/740-6969. Cover varies, usually $10 and up on weekends.

The Dispensary ℛ   Stuck in a '70s time warp (the water wheel and the ferns are the tip-off, though the Muzak songs confirm it), this is a fine place for a nice, long, quiet drink. One that lasts decades, perhaps. It's very quiet, low-key, and often on the empty side. Things pick up on weekends, but it still isn't the sort of place that attracts raucous drunks. (Of course, if it were on the Strip instead of being tucked away, it probably would.) "We leave you alone if you don't want to be bothered," says the proprietor. (We still worry about what happens if you sit here long enough.) If you are a hep cat, but one on the mild side, you'll love it. Open 24 hours. 2451 E. Tropicana Ave. (at Eastern Ave.). ℂ 702/458-6343.

Double Down Saloon ℛℛℛ *Finds*   "House rule: You puke, you clean." Okay, that about sums up the Double Down. Well, no, it doesn't really do the place justice. This is a big local hangout, with management quoting an old *Scope* magazine description of its clientele: "Hipsters, blue collars, the well-heeled lunatic fringe." Rumored to have been spotted here: director Tim Burton and Dr. Timothy Leary. Need to know more? Okay, trippy hallucinogenic graffiti covers the walls, the ceiling, the tables, and possibly you if you sit there long enough. Decor includes Abby Rents–type chairs, thrift-store battered armchairs and sofa, a couple of pool tables, and a jukebox that holds everything from the Germs and Frank Zappa to Link Wray, Dick Dale, and the Rev. Horton Heat. On Wednesday night, they have a live blues band, while other nights might find local alternative, punk, or ska groups performing. On some Sundays, the Blue Man Group plays, but under another name, as a percussion band. Call about that, for sure. There's no cover unless they have some out-of-town band that actually has a label deal. Open daily 24 hours. 4640 Paradise Rd. (at Naples St.). ℂ 702/791-5775. www.doubledownsaloon.com.

Drop Bar ℛ   Smack in the middle of the Green Valley Resort Casino, with '60s-inspired go-go girls dancing away. Open daily 24 hours. In the Green Valley Ranch Resort, 2300 Paseo Verde Pkwy., Henderson. ℂ 702/221-6560. Cover varies, usually $10 and up.

Eiffel Tower Bar ℛ   From this chic and elegant room, in the restaurant on the 11th floor of the Eiffel Tower, you can look down on everyone (in Vegas)—just like a real Parisian! (Just kidding, Francophiles.) But really, this is a date-impressing bar, and, since there's no cover or minimum, it's a cost-effective alternative to the overly inflated food prices at the restaurant. Drop by for a drink, but try to look sophisticated. And then you can cop an attitude and dismiss everything as *gauche*—or *droit*, depending on which way you are seated. Open daily 5:30 to 11:30pm. In Paris Las Vegas, 3655 Las Vegas Blvd. S. ℂ 702/948-6937.

40 Deuce ℛℛ   The brainchild of Los Angeles club impresario Ivan Kane, this is a supremely hot combo bar/nightclub/burlesque review, a modern take on the classic girlie shows, featuring va-va-voom clever dancers (with shows every 90 min. for at least 15 min.—longer if there are more dancers) who strip down to little pasties, short shorts and g-strings. Drinks are obscenely expensive, and tables are entirely bottle service, and naturally, the view of the show is better from those seats. DJs spin between sets, and you can't fit a piece of paper inside on the weekends. The beautiful people love it, and we kind of do, too. Open Sunday and Wednesday 10pm to 4am, Friday and Saturday 1pm to 6am. Shows start at 11pm. In Mandalay Bay, 2950 Las Vegas Blvd. S. © 702/632-7000. Cover varies.

Ghost Bar 🌟🌟 Probably the most interesting aspect of this desperate-to-get-into-the-gossip-pages-as-the-trendy-bar-of-the-moment place (decorated with a '60s Mod/futuristic silver-gleam look) is that though much is made of the fact that it's on the 55th floor, it's really on the 42nd. Something about the number 4 being bad luck in Asian cultures. Whatever. The view still is fabulous, which is the main reason to come here, that and to peer at those tousled-hair beauties copping an attitude on the couches and see if any of them have the kind of names that will make tomorrow's gossip pages. This may be the hot bar of the moment by the time you get there (dress up), or everyone may have moved on. Who knows? Open daily 8pm until dawn. In the Palms Resort & Casino, 4321 W. Flamingo Rd. (just west of the Strip). © 702/942-7778. Cover varies, usually $10 and up.

Gordon-Biersch Brewing Company 🌟 This is part of a chain, and while it does feel like it, it's better than the average lounge chain. The interior is both contemporary and rustic, and warmer than its semi-industrial look sounds like it would be. It's roomy, so you don't feel stacked up on top of other customers. The house lager (they specialize in German brews) was tasty and the noise level acceptable. A good place to go hoist a few. Open daily 11am to 2am or later. 3987 Paradise Rd. (just north of Flamingo Rd.). © 702/312-5247.

Peppermill's Fireside Lounge 🌟 *Finds* Walk through the classic Peppermill's coffee shop (not a bad place to eat, by the way) on the Strip, and you land in its dark, plush, cozy 24-hour lounge. A fabulously dated view of hip, it has low, circular banquette seats, fake floral foliage, low neon, and electric candles. But best of all is the water and fire pit as the room's centerpiece—a piece of kitsch thought to be long vanished from the earth, and attracting nostalgia buffs like moths to a flame. It all adds up to a cozy, womblike place, perfect for unwinding a bit after some time spent on the hectic Strip. The enormous, exotic froufrou tropical drinks (including the signature bathtub-size margaritas) will ensure that you sink into a level of comfortable stupor. Open daily 24 hours. 2985 Las Vegas Blvd. S. © 702/735-7635.

Pink E's 🌟 Sick of the attitude at Club Rio? Escape directly across the street to Pink E's, where the theme is pink. (You were expecting maybe seafoam?) Anyway, at least one regular described this as "the only place to go if you are over 25 and have a brain." And like pink. Because everything at this 24-hour joint is: the many pool tables, the Ping-Pong tables, the booths, the lighting, the lava lamp on the bar, and even the people. In its own way, it's as gimmick-ridden as The Beach dance club (see below), but surely no one would put out a pink pool table in all seriousness? Yeah, it's a ludicrous heresy, but don't you want to play on one? Pink E's offers retro diner food and a DJ on weekends. The dress code basically translates to "no gangsta-wannabe wear." Go, but wear all black (and no pink), just to be ornery. Open daily 24 hours. 3695 W. Flamingo Rd. © 702/252-4666.

Risque 🌟🌟 Ready to put the *ooh la la* back in Vegas (like it needed it, but never mind), this is Paris Las Vegas's most recent lounge (a bar with a dance floor, in this case), which has '80s lingerie-clad girls, as reconceived in the Cirque du Soleil world, practicing lurid versions of their yoga poses, with a detached and yet erotic attitude, perched on a ledge for you to gawk at as soon as you walk in the door. More scantily dressed gals work the top of the bar, while a DJ spins discs in this industrial-nightclub-meets-modern-day-strip-bar. Fancy constructed desserts are for sale, and there are dark nooks everywhere (including balconies that fit no more than four), where the desserts can be consumed and we don't want to know what else could go on. Of course, for every dipped-in-black club kid beauty there is a denim-wearing tourist, but still, you can get your jollies. Open Thursday through Sunday from 10pm to 4am. 3655 Las Vegas Blvd. S. (in the Paris Hotel). ℂ 702/946-7000. Cover varies, but usually men $20, women $10.

Sand Dollar Blues Lounge   Reopened after a brief sprucing up, in part to get rid of a "bad element" (think too many bikers), this is the kind of funky, no-decor (think posters and beer signs), atmosphere-intensive, slightly grimy, friendly bar you either wish your town had or wish it had something other than. Just up the road from TI at the Mirage this is a great antidote to artificial Vegas. Attracting a solid mix of locals and tourists (employees claim the former includes everything from bikers to chamber of commerce members), the Sand Dollar features live blues (both electric and acoustic, with a little Cajun and zydeco thrown in) every night. We wondered how Vegas had enough blues bands to fill out a whole weekly bill. The answer? All the musicians play in multiple bands in different configurations. The dance floor is tiny and often full. The minimal cover always goes to the band. Drinks are happily affordable ($2.50 for a beer!). Depending on your desires, it's either refreshingly not Las Vegas or just the kind of place you came to Vegas to escape. Go before someone has the idea to build a theme hotel based on it. Open 24 hours. 3355 Spring Mountain Rd. (at Polaris Ave.). ℂ 702/871-6651. Cover varies but is usually no more than a few bucks.

Sky Lounge ⚘   It may not be the view offered by the Stratosphere's bar, but it's pretty darn good and a lot easier to get to. You don't see quite enough of the MGM Grand to the left, but otherwise there are no complaints. The decor is too modern (heavy on '80s black and purple), but overall the place is quiet (especially during the day) and civil. Occasional jazz/piano acts perform at night, when the views are, naturally, the best. The atmosphere produced by all this is classic Vegas in the best sense (with only a slight touch of necessary kitsch). Worth a trip for an escape from the mob, though you won't be the only tourist fighting for window seats. Open daily 8:30am until whenever they feel like closing. At the Polo Towers, 3745 Las Vegas Blvd. S. ℂ 702/261-1000.

Tangerine ⚘   Vegas just keeps giving us reasons to remind you about that whole "not for families" thing anymore, and here's another one. Taking up the space once occupied by the Battle Bar—where patrons could watch the pirate battle, back in the days before it featured girls in lingerie—now it actually features more girls in lingerie by way of the ever-increasingly popular modern burlesque show. If you hated the '60s and its use of orange sherbet as a color scheme, you won't be pleased by this interior. The show is nothing compared to 40 Deuce or Pussycat Dolls, so your main reason

---

Impressions

"It's a wonderful town all right!" a stick man at the Thunderbird told me. *"Where else can a fellow gamble all day, get drunk, go to sleep, get up at four in the morning, and find plenty of company when he walks into the lobby?"*
                                                    Daniel Lang, *Blackjack and Flashes*

Tips Bathroom Break

When you gotta go, you gotta go, particularly if you've tried drinking at every bar listed here, and so when you do, do try to do so in the unisex, free-standing Space Age pods at **Mandalay Bay's China Grill.**

---

for coming here will be the enormous outdoor patio lounge where personal space is at a premium, and you know what that means . . . well, *that,* plus an up, party-vibe atmosphere, provided that the sight of dancing female pirates (it still overlooks the renamed Sirens of TI) doesn't ruin your groove. Open Tuesday through Saturday 10pm to 4am. Outside bar also open Sunday through Monday 5pm to midnight. In TI at the Mirage, 3300 Las Vegas Blvd. S. ℭ 702/894-7111. Cover varies.

Tommy Rocker's Mojave Beach ℛ Tommy Rocker is the owner—surely he wasn't born with that name—and he plays his club every Friday and Saturday night, mixing bar-band standards with '80s and '90s hits. It's a one-man show, with Strip musicians dropping by after their own shifts are done. (Occasionally, local bands are permitted to play as well.) Sort of like the inside of a Quonset hut painted black, his vaguely beach frat party–themed club has become the home for local and out-of-town Parrot Heads (Jimmy Buffet fans, for those not in the know), with the result that the crowd is 5 to 10 years past their heavy college-drinking days. A large bar dominates the middle of the room; there are two pool tables and a grill for ordering food, plus an espresso machine. Open daily 24 hours. 4275 Dean Martin Dr. (at Flamingo Rd.). ℭ 702/261-6688.

Triple 7 Brew Pub ℛ *Finds* Yet another of the many things the Main Street Station hotel has done right. Stepping into its microbrew pub feels like stepping out of Vegas. Well, except for the dueling-piano entertainment. The place has a partially modern warehouse look (exposed pipes, microbrew fixtures visible through exposed glass at the back, and a very high ceiling), but a hammered-tin ceiling continues the hotel's Victorian decor; the overall effect seems straight out of San Francisco's North Beach. It's a bit on the yuppified side but escapes being pretentious. And frankly, it's a much-needed modern space for the Downtown area. This place has its own brew master and a number of microbrews ready to try, and if you want a quick bite, there's also an oyster-and-sushi bar, plus fancy burgers and pizzas. It can get noisy during the aforementioned piano-duel act, but otherwise casino noise stays out. Since all of Downtown is too heavy on the Old Las Vegas side (which is fine, but not *all* the time), this is good for a suitable breather. Open daily from 11am to 7am. In Main St. Station, 200 Main St. ℭ 702/387-1896.

Whiskey Sky ℛℛ Probably your best bet for a trendy place that might actually have either beautiful locals or out-of-town celebs looking for a cool time but wanting a lower profile. This cool, low-key vibe is due to the bar's off-the-Strip location, and also its creator, hip-bar-master Rande Gerber (Cindy Crawford's hubby). Think beds instead of couches, and you've got a sense of the gestalt. Open daily at 8pm until late. In the Green Valley Ranch Resort, 2300 Paseo Verde Pkwy., Henderson. ℭ 702/617-7560. Cover varies, usually $10 and up.

Zuri ℛ This is the best of the casino-hotel free bars (free as in no admission price), probably because of its construction, a semicurtained enclave just off the elevators (as opposed to a space just plunked down right off or right in the middle of a casino). With swooping wood and red-velvet couches, the drinks are expensive, but at least you can hear your partner's whispered sweet nothings. A rare thing in a Vegas hotel. Open 24 hours. In the MGM Grand, 3799 Las Vegas Blvd. S. ⓒ 702/891-7777.

9 Dance Clubs

In addition to the options listed below, country-music fans might want to wander on over to **Dylan's,** 4660 Boulder Hwy. (ⓒ 702/451-4006). They offer country music (live and otherwise) and line dancing, with free dance lessons. Dylan's is casual and basic, with a definite roadhouse vibe.

Note: As far as a dress code is concerned, you are going to go further with more obviously expensive clothes, but you may not have the budget or fashion sense for that (and who travels with really good clothes, anyway?). When in doubt, all black should do it, and showing skin helps. Otherwise, just dress as nicely as you can. But do avoid sports team–affiliated jerseys and baseball hats, baggy pants, and other things that might fall under the heading "gangsta-wear" because that's one sure way of not getting past the velvet rope.

The Beach 🐸🐸   If you're a fan of loud, crowded, 24-hour party bars filled with tons of good-looking fun-seekers, then bow in this direction, for you have found mecca. This huge tropical-themed (hence the whole "Beach" thing) nightclub is right across the street from the Convention Center and is, according to just about anyone you ask, the hottest club in the city. It's a two-story affair with five separate bars downstairs and another three up.

Just in case walking the 20 feet to the closest bar is too much of an effort, they also have bikini-clad women serving beer out of steel tubs full of ice (they also roam the floor with shot belts). The drinks are on the pricey side ($4.25 for an 8-oz. domestic beer), but the unfailingly gorgeous, 4% body-fat bartenders (both men and women) are friendly and offer rotating drink specials that might keep you from busting your budget.

Downstairs is the large two-story dance floor, which dominates the center of the room and is built around a full-service bar at one end. The sound system is top of the line, as is the lighting design (but the wash from the rest of the bar made it a little too bright on the floor to appreciate). Nobody really seemed to care, though—there wasn't 1 square inch of space available on a recent Friday night. Upstairs, there are balconies overlooking the dance floor, pool tables, darts, foosball, pinball, and various other arcade games—plus slot machines, video poker, and a sports book. Other neat touches include tarot-card readings by the stairs and hot-pizza vendors. And let's not forget those Jell-O-shot contests where club-goers try to eat shaky cubes of alcohol-spiked gelatin off each other's partially bared bodies.

The crowd is aggressively young and pretty, more men than women (70/30 split), and about 60% tourist, which is probably why the place can get away with charging a $10 cover. Party people look no further: There's free valet parking, and if you've driven here and become intoxicated, they'll drive you back home at no charge. Open daily 24 hours. 365 S. Convention Center Dr. (at Paradise Rd.). ⓒ 702/731-1925. www.beachlv.com. Cover $5 and up.

Bikinis 🐸   By now, you should be getting the format for the most recent trend in clubs and lounges in Vegas: liberal use of dancing girls who wear very, very little. What makes this different from an honest strip bar, we don't know (you can read some thoughts on the matter later in this chapter in our review of Sapphire), but it does show how mainstream strip bars have become. How else to explain the go-go dancers here, who wear thong bikinis and little wisps of gauze as they dance, with varying degrees of enthusiasm and talent, on stages with strippers' poles, and then sometimes get into tanks of water to gyrate? How else to explain the gaggle of male customers who watch them with studied blank expressions, and the female customers who end up congregating toward the back, studiously ignoring the floor show, except to say things like "I wish I had her legs"? Expect also occasional pillow fights and lingerie shows. In between this is a dance floor for you to shake your thang to hip-hop and house, while the interior Lava Lounge plays old-school funk. Open Thursday to Sunday from 10pm to late into the night. 3700 W. Flamingo Rd. (in the Rio). Ⓒ 702/777-7777. Cover varies.

Body English ⓇⓇ   To our way of thinking, this is exactly what a Las Vegas club should be—because all the other hot nightclubs in town look exactly like a hot nightclub in any old town, and so we always want Vegas places to be *Vegas*—over the top and just a little bit wrong. So this clash of Anne Rice and Cher Gothic–themed whacky decadence, with fabrics on top of wood on top of mirrors, not to mention the sort of layout that allows for intimate corners and voyeuristic balcony viewing of the dance floor, is just the sort of overly rich dessert of a place we crave. So do many others; it's one of the hottest spots in town, and the wait in line is so long you might well polish off a Rice novel while standing in it. Well, you gotta pass the time somehow. Expect a hefty cover charge, too. Open Friday through Sunday 1:30pm to "late." In the Hard Rock Hotel, 4455 Paradise Rd. Ⓒ 702/693-5000. Cover varies.

Cleopatra's Barge Nightclub Ⓡ   This is a small, unique nightclub set in part on a floating barge—you can feel it rocking. The bandstand, a small dance floor, and a few (usually reserved) tables are here, while others are set around the boat on "land." It's a gimmick, but one that makes this far more fun than other, more pedestrian, hotel bars. Plenty of dark makes for romance, but blaring volume levels mean you will have to scream those sweet nothings. Check out the bare-breasted figurehead on the ship's prow, who juts out over the hallway going past the entrance. She could put someone's eye out. Open nightly from 10:30pm to 4am. In Caesars Palace, 3570 Las Vegas Blvd. S. Ⓒ 702/731-7110. 2-drink minimum.

Club Rio   Still a hot nightspot as of this writing, but apparently made so by people who don't mind long lines, restrictive dress codes, attitudinal door people, hefty cover charges, and bland dance music. Waits can be interminable and admittance denied thanks to the wrong footwear or shirt. The dress code (no sneakers, and shirts must have a collar) is supposed to make the clientele look more sophisticated than grungy; the effect is the opposite, as most of the men end up in combinations of chinos and button-down shirts. Of course, it's so dark you can't tell if someone is wearing sneakers. For pity's sake, there are lots more interesting places now. But then again, those have even longer lines, so what the hey.

Once inside, you find a large, circular room, with a spacious dance floor taking up much of the space. Giant video screens line the upper parts of the walls, showing anything from shots of the action down below to catwalk footage. Comfy circular booths fill out the next couple of concentric circles; these seem mostly reserved, and when empty, they leave the impression that the place isn't very full—so why the wait? Music on a recent visit included a Madonna medley and the perennial "Celebration," not the most *au courant* of tunes. The total effect is of a grown-up, not terribly drunken frat and sorority mixer. The club opens at 11pm on Thursday and 11:30pm on Friday and Saturday, and stays open until about 4am each of these nights. In the Rio All-Suite Hotel & Casino, 3700 W. Flamingo Rd. ℭ 702/252-7777. Advertised cover $10 for men, local women free, out-of-state women $5 (but frequently when we went by on a weekend night, the cover was $20 for everyone).

Drai's After Hours ✿   Young Hollywood film execs and record-company types are likely to be found here, schmoozing and dancing it up to house, techno, and tribal music. Open Wednesday through Sunday from midnight until dawn. In Barbary Coast, 3595 Las Vegas Blvd. S. ℭ 702/737-0555. Cover varies, usually $20.

Ice ✿✿   Housed in the former Drink space (one of our favorite Vegas clubs; we miss it), this is along the same lines (hence, doubtless, the linked name); though there is one main multistory dance floor, there are also several themed rooms, so the effect is of several clubs rolled into one massive space. Very good for the conflicted or a group where someone wants to hear house music in all its many varieties and someone else wants acid jazz and someone else wants R&B. It's all state-of-the-art and very chic. The intimate smaller rooms include the "Fur Room," where S&M fantasies are teased. There are even platforms for performance artists. The new hot (or cool) destination, it's far more interesting than most of the fabled clubs at the big hotels. Open Tuesday and Thursday through Sunday from 11pm to 5am. 200 E. Harmon Ave. ℭ 702/699-9888. Cover $20.

La Bete ✿✿   From the Cocteau-inspired big beast feet that frame the entrance to the fuchsia-pink fabric that swathes the walls, this is one fun seductive atmosphere. The exterior leads to a narrow patio overlooking a waterfall ("I hate the fake waterfall out front, but I love it in a disco," said one admiring patron) and a statue of three Griffin-like mythological creatures. They could do more with this place, and probably will. Open Thursday through Saturday 10pm to 4am. 3131 Las Vegas Blvd. S. (in the Wynn hotel). Cover $20.

Light ✿✿   In contrast to the metallic high gloss that characterizes most trendy nightspots, this is a grown-up nightclub (sister to an establishment in NYC)—fitting, since it's in the grown-up Bellagio—all wood and velvet and polite attitudes from the staff. Music tends toward both modern and old-school hip-hop and pop, with dancers (real ones) clad in rather modest costumes. Sometimes there are other touches, such as a live sax player jamming along to the music. Guests are probably all tourists, but tourists of the heir-to-the-hotel-fortune sort; yet the club doesn't feel exclusive, but rather like one big open party—a nifty and tricky feat to pull off. Open Thursday through Sunday from 10:30pm to 4am. In Bellagio, 3600 Las Vegas Blvd. S. ℭ 702/693-8300. Cover varies, usually $25.

Monte Carlo Pub & Brewery ✿ *Finds*   After 9pm nightly, this immense warehouselike pub and working microbrewery (details on p. 144) turns from a casual restaurant into something of a dance club. Rock videos blare forth from a large screen and 40 TV monitors around the room, while on stage, dueling pianos provide music and audience-participation entertainment. The pub is cigar-friendly and maintains a humidor. There's a full bar, and, of course, the house microbrews are featured. You can also order pizza. Open until 2am Sunday to Thursday, until 4am Friday and Saturday. In the Monte Carlo Resort & Casino, 3770 Las Vegas Blvd. S. ℭ 702/730-7777.

Pure ✿✿   The biggest club on the Strip (it occupies the former home of the late, lamented, and much more family-friendly Caesar's Magical Empire), Pure is everything a big loud nightclub ought to be. The theme is reflected in the decor—or lack of it, since just about everything is as white as Ivory Soap (get the name?)—which is either minimalist brilliant or reflects the fact that even Vegas designers get tired. In any event, the noise and lack of cushy corners means this is a definite get-your-booty-in-motion kind of place, though there is ample space (seriously, there are airline hangers that are smaller) for just standing around watching other booties in motion. There is also a rooftop club, itself bigger than most regular Vegas clubs, with views of the Strip, for those who need a little fresh air. Open Friday through Tuesday 10:30pm to 4am. In Caesars Palace, 3570 Las Vegas Blvd. S. ℂ **702/731-7110.** Cover varies.

Ra 𝒜 The futuristic Egyptian-themed Ra was one of the first of the new generation of Vegas nightclubs, and it's gotten popular all over again. It has that Vegas "we're a show and an attraction" vibe but is still not overly pretentious. The staff is friendly, which is a rare thing for a hot club. It might be worth it to go just to gawk at the heavy gilt decor. You'll also find a major light show, cigar lounges off the disco, draped VIP booths, and plenty of little nooks and crannies. Current dance music (mostly techno) is on the soundtrack. The later you go, the more likely the mid- to upper-20s clientele will be entirely local. Wednesday ("Pleasuredome" night, a blend of house music) and Friday ("Empire," a blend of house, rock, '80s, and hip-hop) are the current hot nights, so expect lines to start early. Open Wednesday through Saturday from 10pm to 4am. In Luxor Las Vegas, 3900 Las Vegas Blvd. S. ℂ **702/262-4000.** Cover $10–$30.

Rain 𝒜𝒜 At press time, still just about the hottest nightclub in Vegas. Which means you (and us—don't think we aren't standing there with you, shoulder to shoulder in solidarity) probably will spend most of your time trying to convince someone, anyone, to let you in. You and a couple of thousand of size-2 Juicy Couture jeans–clad 20-somethings who feel they will simply cease to exist if they don't get inside. We smirk and snicker at their desperation because it makes us feel superior. But we also have to be honest; if you can brave the wait, the crowds, and the attitude, you will be inside a club that has done everything right, from the multilevel layout that allows them to pack the crowds in and allows those crowds to peer up and down at their brethren, to DJs who play the right house and techno cuts (at a pulse-thumping tempo, so don't expect for your good pickup lines to be overheard), to the scaffolding that holds pyrotechnic and other mood-revvers, to the ubiquitous-of-late go-go girls dressed like strippers. You will have more fun here than at, say, Bikinis (see above) because this is bigger and more crowded, but then again, you can get in there more readily, so you decide what's more important to you. If this is your choice, then note that they start lining up way before the 11pm opening time. Open Thursday to Saturday from 11pm until dawn. 4321 W. Flamingo Rd. ℂ **702/940-7246.** Cover $20 and up.

rumjungle 𝒜 Now, normally our delicate sensibilities wince at such overkill, and we tend to write off such efforts as just trying a bit too hard. But surprisingly, rumjungle really delivers the great fun it promises. The fire-wall entrance gives way to a wall of water; the two-story bar is full of the largest collection of rum varieties anywhere, each bottle illuminated with a laser beam of light; go-go girls dance and prance between bottles of wine to dueling congas; and the food all comes skewered on swords. It's all a bit much, but it works, it really does. A great deal of thought went into the various clever designs and schemes, and it's paid off. Almost instantly, rumjungle became and stayed one of the hottest clubs in Vegas, with lines of partiers out the door every night, ready to dance to live world-beat music. Get there early (before 10pm) to avoid lines/guest lists/the cover charge, and consider having dinner (served till 11pm); it's costly, but it's a multicourse, all-you-can-eat feast of flame pit–cooked Brazilian food. For the amount of food and the waiving of the cover charge, dinner is a good deal. Then dance it all off all night long (the club is open 'til 2am on weeknights, 'til 4am Thurs–Sat nights). In Mandalay Bay, 3950 Las Vegas Blvd. S. ℂ **702/632-7408.** Cover $10–$20.

Studio Club 🎤 In the main rotunda of the MGM Grand, which once housed the *Wizard of Oz* walk-through diorama, this is the biggest and best of the free hotel lounges, which are these days otherwise best known for their enthusiastic but not notably talented cover bands (you just know most of the singers are the sort who didn't get past the first couple audition rounds for American Idol). It has an enormous and elaborate stage and band, but since it's in the middle of an area you have to cross if you are passing through from the Strip, it can be hard to navigate through on a busy weekend night. Open daily 4pm to 4am. In the MGM Grand, 3799 Las Vegas Blvd. S. ℂ **702/ 891-1111.**

Studio 54 The legendary Studio 54 has been resurrected here in Las Vegas, but with all the bad elements and none of the good ones. Forget Truman, Halston, and Liza doing illegal (or at least immoral) things in the bathroom stalls; that part of Studio 54 remains but a fond memory. The snooty, exclusive door attitude has been retained, however. Hooray. Red-rope policies are all well and good if you're trying to build mystique in a regular club, but for a tourist attraction, where guests are likely to be one-time-only (or, at best, once a year), it's obnoxious. Oddly, this doesn't lead to a high-class clientele; of all the new clubs, this is the trashiest (though apparently the hot night for locals is Tues, so if you do go, go then). The large dance floor has a balcony overlooking it, the decor is industrial (exposed piping and the like), the music is hip-hop and electronic, and there is nothing to do other than dance. If the real Studio 54 were this boring, no one would remember it today. Open Tuesday through Saturday from 10pm until dawn. In the MGM Grand, 3799 Las Vegas Blvd. S. ℂ **702/891-1111.** Cover varies, but usually $10–$40.

Tabu 🎤 A little by-the-numbers for a nightclub but still, despite the name, less stripper saucy than the other new "ultra lounges" (which here means "noisy, high-priced bar"), and consequently is more grown up, and just as loud. With an interior of late '90s high tech/industrial meets cheesy '80s bachelor's den, it's nothing aesthetically special, though there are some nice spots for canoodling. But do find a wall or the circular couch if you want to hear yourself think. Open Tuesday through Sunday 10pm to "early morning." At MGM Grand, 3799 Las Vegas Blvd. S. ℂ **702/891-7183.** Cover varies, but about $10 for men and free for women.

Voodoo Lounge 🎤 Occupying, along with the Voodoo Cafe, two floors in the newer addition to the Rio, the Lounge almost successfully combines Haitian voodoo and New Orleans Creole in its decor and theme. There are two main rooms: one with a large dance floor and stage for live music, and a disco room, which is filled with large video screens and serious light action. Big club chairs in groups form conversation pits, where you might actually be able to have a conversation. The big seller? The bartenders put on a show, a la Tom Cruise in *Cocktail*. They shake, jiggle, and light stuff on fire. Supposedly, the live music includes Cajun acts, but when it comes down to it, rock seems to rule the day. The mid- to late-20s crowd is more heavily local than you might expect; the dress code calls for "business casual," with no shorts, jeans, or shirts without collars for men. It's open nightly from 5pm to 3am. In the Rio All-Suite Hotel & Casino, 3700 Las Vegas Blvd. S. ℂ **702/252-7777.** Cover $10 and up.

10 Strip Clubs

No, we don't mean entertainment establishments on Las Vegas Boulevard South. We mean the other kind of "strip." Yes, people come to town for the gambling and the wedding chapels, but the lure of Vegas doesn't stop there. Though prostitution is not legal within the city, the sex industry is an active and obvious force in town. Every other cab carries a placard for a strip club, and a walk down the Strip at night will have dozens of men thrusting fliers at you for clubs, escort services, phone-sex lines, and more. And some of you are going to want to check it out.

And why not? An essential part of the Vegas allure is decadence, and naked flesh would certainly qualify, as does the thrill of trying something new and daring. Of course, by and large, the nicer bars aren't particularly daring, and if you go to more than one in an evening, the thrill wears off, and the breasts don't look quite so bare.

In the finest of Vegas traditions, the "something for everyone" mentality extends to strip clubs. Here is a guide to the most prominent and heavily advertised; there are plenty more, of increasing seediness, out there. You don't have to look too hard. The most crowded and zoolike times are after midnight, especially on Friday and Saturday nights. Should you want a "meaningful" experience, you might wish to avoid the rush and choose an off-hour for a visit.

Cheetah's ℛ   This is the strip club used as the set in the movie *Showgirls,* but thanks to the magic of Hollywood and later renovations by the club, only the main stage will look vaguely familiar to those few looking for Nomi Malone. There's also a smaller stage, plus three tiny "tip stages" so that you can really get close to (and give much money to) the woman of your choice. Eight TVs line the walls; the club does a brisk business during major sporting events. The management believes "If you treat people right, they will keep coming back," so the atmosphere is friendlier than at other clubs. They "encourage couples—people who want to party—to come here. We get a 21- to 40-aged party kind of crowd," the manager told us. And indeed there is a sporty, frat-bar feel to the place. (Though on a crowded Sat night, some unescorted women were turned away, despite policy.) Lap dances are $20. Open daily 24 hours. 2112 Western Ave. ℂ **702/384-0074.** Topless. Cover $10.

Club Paradise ℛ   Until the new behemoths moved into town, this was the nicest of the strip clubs. Which isn't to say it isn't still nice; it's just got competition. The outside looks a lot like the Golden Nugget; the interior and atmosphere are rather like that of a hot nightclub where most of the women happen to be topless. The glitzy stage looks like something from a miniature showroom: The lights flash and the dance music pounds, there are two big video screens (one featuring soft porn, the other showing sports!), the chairs are plush and comfortable, the place is relatively bright by strip-club standards, and they offer champagne and cigars. Not too surprisingly, they get a very white-collar crowd here. The result is not terribly sleazy, which may please some and turn others off. The women ("actual centerfolds") are heavy (and we do mean heavy) on the silicone. They don't so much dance as pose and prance, after which they don skimpy evening dresses and come down to solicit lap dances, which eventually fills the place up with writhing females in thongs. The club says it is "women-friendly," and indeed there were a few couples, including one woman who was receiving a lap dance herself—and didn't seem too uncomfortable. Occasionally, the action stops for a minirevue, which ends up being more like semi-naked cheerleading than a show. Lap dances are $20. Open Monday to Friday from 4pm to 6am, and Saturday and Sunday from 6pm to 6am. 4416 Paradise Rd. © 702/734-7990. Cover $10–$20, 2-drink minimum (drinks are $4.50 and up). Unescorted women allowed. Topless.

Crazy Horse, Two *(Overrated)*   We've omitted the address of this place on purpose. It's full of so much obnoxious jerk attitude, with overly aggressive girls soliciting lap dances, that even the other clubs in town sneer at them. Yeah, yeah, Jenna Jamieson got her start dancing here. Whatever. There are plenty of strip bars—pass this one by.

Déjà vu Showgirls 🟊🟊   Owned by the same people as Little Darlings (see below), this place both deeply perturbs us and amuses the heck out of us. The latter because it's one of the rare strip clubs where the women actually perform numbers. Instead of just coming out and taking off an article or two of clothing and then parading around in a desultory manner before collecting a few tips and running off to solicit lap dances, each stripper comes out and does an actual routine—well, okay, maybe not so much, but she does remove her clothes to personally chosen music, shedding an outfit tailored to her music selection. And so it happened that we have now seen a punk-rock chick strip to "Anarchy in the UK" and a Ramones tune. But it also distresses us because it's the kind of place where guys bring their buds the night before their wedding to make sure they get photographed with a naked girl (yes, the girls get totally naked here) performing something raunchy with a sex toy—that's the kind of fun that leaves a bad taste in the mouth. Open Monday through Saturday from 11am to 6am and Sunday from 6pm to 4am. 3247 Industrial Rd. © 702/894-4167. Cover $5–$25. $20–$30 lap dances. Totally nude. Unescorted women allowed.

Glitter Gulch 🟊   Right there in the middle of the Fremont Street Experience, Glitter Gulch is either an eyesore or the last bastion of Old Las Vegas, depending on your point of view. The inside is modern enough: black light and bubble fountains, arranged around a runway strip. The shows are basic—the women take off sequined gowns to reveal G-strings. Customers sit in comfortable booths, and the dancers then come around and offer up-close and personal table dances, often chatting merrily away while they expose themselves. As you enter, you are assigned your own (overly clothed) waitress who escorts you to your table. They also offer limo service to the hotels and even a line of souvenir clothing. Given such services and its convenient location, this is the perfect place for the merely curious—you can easily pop in, check things out, goggle and ogle, and then hit the road. Open daily from 1pm to 4am. 20 Fremont St. © 702/385-4774. Topless. 2-drink minimum (drinks $7.75 and up). Table dances $20.

Little Darlings 🟊   They call themselves the "Pornocopia of Sex," and given the number of services they offer, you can see why. In addition to a fully stocked adult store, they have private nude dances in booths (dancers must stay 6 in. from the customer at all times). This is one of the few clubs where the women are not allowed any physical contact with the customers. There are also rooms where you can watch a nude woman take a shower (in theory, doing erotic things with soap), and "Fantasy Rooms" where a glass pane separates you from a woman performing still more erotic stunts. The women are all healthy and athletic, including some who do impressive work with the poles on stage (using their legs to climb all the way to the rafters). Despite all the nude offerings, the resultant atmosphere is not especially dirty, just rowdy. (Tellingly, they do promotions with a local radio station.) That's not surprising when you consider that alcohol is not served on the premises. At least one late-20s customer felt it was all too much like high school and that the cover was prohibitively expensive. A totally nude private dance in a booth is $20, Fantasy Rooms are $100 to $300. Open

Monday to Saturday from 11am to 6am, Sunday from 6pm to 4am. 1514 Western Ave. © 702/366-0145. No unescorted women. Totally nude. Cover $20 (includes sodas and juice).

Olympic Gardens Topless Cabaret 𝕲 Once the largest of the strip clubs, this almost feels like a family operation, thanks to the middle-aged women often handling the door—maybe they're the reason for the equal-opportunity male strippers on special nights. They also have a boutique selling lingerie and naughty outfits. (Because they get a lot of couples coming in, perhaps this is in case someone gets inspired and wants to try out what they learned here at home.) There are two rooms: one with large padded tables for the women to dance on, the other featuring a more classic strip runway. The girls all seemed really cute—perhaps the best-looking of the major clubs. The crowd is a mix of 20s to 30s blue-collar guys and techno geeks. As the place fills up and the chairs are crammed in next to each other, it's hard to see how enjoyable, or intimate, a lap dance can be when the guy next to you is getting one as well. That didn't seem to stop all the guys there, who seemed appropriately blissed out. Lap dances are $20, more in the VIP room. Open daily 24 hours. 1531 Las Vegas Blvd. S. © 702/385-8987. Unescorted women allowed. Topless. Cover $20.

The Palomino 𝕲 This used to be a classy, proper strip bar, the way perhaps some of you, who haven't experienced them lately, imagine such establishments to be. Now, however, it edges into the seedy end of things. It's also a bit out of the way. On the other hand, it does offer total nudity in a classic red-walled setting. And its location outside of the Vegas city limits means that it's one of the only clubs that offers both total nudity *and* alcohol. It's two levels, with the downstairs consisting of a large stage where featured dancers ("all have appeared in *Playboy* or *Penthouse* or some kind of publication") do themed dances with specific music, costumes, and props (one healthy blonde surfer gal used a big white bed and satin nightie in her set), which can result in some incongruous sights, like an essentially interpretive dance with pauses for gynecological shots. Upstairs has two or three small stages with dancers doing their thing up close and personal. There is also a large room off to the side where they take you

---

Tips Two Strippers Offer Nine Strip-Bar Etiquette Tips

Brittany and Kitty each have several years' experience working in strip bars, so they know what they're talking about. And they both really are sweet girls, honest.

1. Bathe.
2. Don't lie and say you never go in these places.
3. Don't take off your wedding ring. We can still see the mark it leaves.
4. Don't ask if we take credit cards. Bring cash!
5. Don't fall asleep. Just because we are open 24 hours, we aren't a hotel.
6. Don't wear wool pants. They scratch.
7. Don't ask for our phone numbers.
8. Don't lick us. We're not Popsicles.
9. Don't forget: We aren't dumb strippers. We are a lot smarter than you think.

for lap dances, ensuring a small measure of privacy. Topless lap dances are $20, totally nude dances are $40. Open daily 24 hours. 1848 Las Vegas Blvd. N. © **702/642-2984**. Totally nude. Cover $15–$30.

Sapphire 👁👁👁 Ladies and gentlemen, particularly the latter, Las Vegas, home of the largest everything else, now brings you—drum roll—the largest strip club *in the world!* That's right, 71,000 square feet of nakedity. Of course, you have to see it—and of course, that's what they are counting on. But let's say this: While really it's nothing you haven't seen before strip-club-wise, if you haven't seen a strip club, this is the place to start (though the size and looks are atypical, to say the least; it's all downhill from here) because it's modern and clean, and, frankly, it's not all that different, lookswise, from Rain, the super-hot nightclub over at the Rio, except that here you can actually hear yourself think, and the girls sometimes wear more clothes than at Rain. It's also more friendly and less attitudinal. Expect three stages in a bridge shape (including one where gawkers who paid for the privilege can watch the action from below, thanks to a glass floor), and a fourth in a separate, and still large, room, with several poles and strippers all working it at the same time. Giant video screens occasionally act as a Jumbotron for the action on the other side of the cavernous room. Upstairs are incredibly posh and incredibly expensive rooms for wealthy sports and movie figures to utilize. Lap dances are $20. Open daily 24 hours. 3025 S. Industrial © **702/796-0000**. Topless. Cover $20 after 6pm.

Spearmint Rhino 👁 Did you know that even strip bars come in chains? They do, and this is a familiar brand to those in the know, or who read billboards close to airports. The runway (where some of the dancers get a little personal with each other) is actually in a separate back area, so it is possible to have a drink at the front (where there are many TVs and other manly accouterments) and never see a naked girl (save for the smaller stage and pole nearby). On a busy night, it's crammed with grown-up frat boys enjoying a clubby space. There can be a veritable factory assembly line of lap dances during these busy periods, which frankly, seems the opposite of a turn-on to us. Unescorted women should also note that while normally they are permitted, lately it seems that they might also be taken for hookers and turned away from the door (lest they come inside and lure customers away). Lap dances are $20. Open daily 24 hours. 3444 Highland Dr. © **702/796-3600**. Unescorted women allowed. Topless. Cover $10.

Striptease Cabaret 👁👁 This club has been redone to eliminate the rather disturbing "fantasy rooms" (where lap dances could occur in private), replacing them with a generic "classy" gentlemen's-club look, all shiny runways and stages (three total, plus the "shower" stage, where periodically two girls will soap each other up). One of the bouncers was in the film *Ocean's Eleven* as a thug menacing George Clooney. With live DJs and girls far more interested in working the lap-dance angle than dancing, it's a fine, safe first-time strip-bar experience, but not one to make you see what all the fuss is about. Lap dances are $20 and up. Courtesy limo pickup. Open daily from 11am to 6am. 3750 S. Valley View Blvd. © **702/253-1555**. Unescorted women allowed, couples encouraged. Topless. Cover $10–$20.

Treasures 👁👁👁 Right now, along with Sapphire, our favorite of the strip clubs, for several reasons. From the outside, this looks like one of the new fancy casino-hotels (if considerably smaller), but inside it's straight out of a Victorian sporting house (that's a brothel, by the way), down to replicas of 19th-century girlie pictures on the walls. On stage, the performers actually perform; anyone who has witnessed the desultory sway-ing of the hips and vacant stare of a bored, can't-be-bothered stripper will appreciate not just the bump-and-grind (some of which gets on the raunchy side) dance routines, but the special effects, from hair-blowing fans to smoke machines to a neon pole, that makes it all the more memorable. We are suckers for this combination of period-inspired style and contemporary approach to the business at hand. However, and we don't mean this in an off-putting way, "suckers" is a word to bear in mind; this is a place of commerce, and any adult-industry operation this professional knows it. Try not to forget that, especially couples and first-timers, for whom this is still an excellent and comfortable venue. *Note:* The entrance to the parking lot can be hard to spot after dark. Go down Highland and keep your eyes peeled. Open daily noon to 7am. 2801 Westwood Dr. Ⓒ 702/257-3030. No unescorted women. Cover $20. Lap dances $20 "and up."

11

Side Trips from Las Vegas

Though all of Vegas is designed to make you forget that there is an outside world, it might do you and your pocketbook much good to reacquaint yourself with the non-Vegas realm. Actually, if you're spending more than 3 days in Vegas, this may become a necessity; 2 days with kids, and it absolutely will.

Plus, there is such a stark, startling contrast between the artificial wonders of Sin City and the natural wonders that, in some cases, lie just a few miles away. Few places are as developed and modern as Vegas; few places are as untouched as

some of the canyons, desert, and mountains that surround it. The electrical and design marvel that is the Strip couldn't exist without the extraordinary structural feat that is Hoover Dam. Need some fresh air? (My heavens, don't you!) There are plenty of opportunities for outdoor recreation, all in a landscape like no other.

The excursions covered in this chapter, with the exception of Area 51 and the Grand Canyon trips mentioned below, will take you from 20 to 60 miles out of town. Every one of them offers a memorable travel experience.

GRAND CANYON TOURS

Generally, tourists visiting Las Vegas don't drive 300 miles to Arizona to see the Grand Canyon, but there are dozens of sightseeing tours departing from the city daily. In addition to the Gray Line tours described in chapter 7, a major operator, **Scenic Airlines** (© **800/634-6801** or 702/638-3300; www.scenic.com), runs several tours, including their most popular: a deluxe, full-day guided air-ground tour for $269 per person ($239 for children 2–11); the price includes a bus excursion through the national park, a flight over the canyon, and lunch. All scenic tours include flightseeing. The company also offers both full-day and overnight tours with hiking.

Scenic Airlines also offers tours to other points of interest and national parks, including Bryce Canyon and Monument Valley. Ask for details when you call.

1 Hoover Dam & Lake Mead

30 miles SE of Las Vegas

This is one of the most popular excursions from Las Vegas. Hoover Dam is visited by 2,000 to 3,000 people daily. Why should you join them? Because it's an engineering and architectural marvel and it changed the Southwest forever. Without it, you wouldn't even be going to Vegas. Kids may be bored, unless they like machinery or just plain big things, but expose them to it anyway, for their own good. (Buy them ice cream and a Hoover Dam snow globe as a bribe.) Obviously, if you are staying at Lake Mead, it's a must.

The tour itself is a bit cursory, but you do get up close and personal with the dam. Wear comfortable shoes; the tour involves quite a bit of walking. Try to take the tour

Excursions from Las Vegas

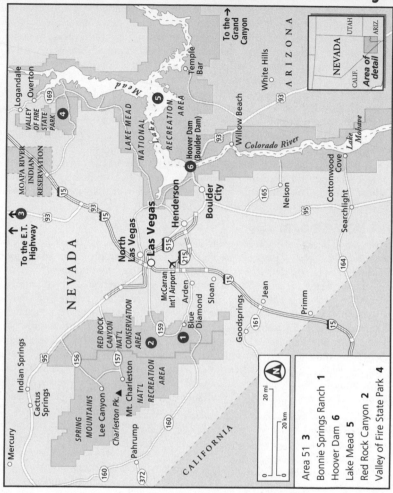

Area 51 **3**
Bonnie Springs Ranch **1**
Hoover Dam **6**
Lake Mead **5**
Red Rock Canyon **2**
Valley of Fire State Park **4**

in the morning to beat the desert heat and the really big crowds. You can have lunch out in Boulder City, and then perhaps drive back through the **Valley of Fire State Park** (a landscape of wind and water-hewn formations of red sandstone), which is about 60 magnificently scenic miles from Lake Mead (purchase gas before you start!). Or you can spend the afternoon on Lake Mead–centered pursuits such as hiking, boating, even scuba diving in season, or perhaps a rafting trip down the Colorado River.

GETTING THERE

Drive east on Flamingo Road or Tropicana Avenue to U.S. 515 South, which automatically turns into I-93 South and takes you right to the dam. This will involve a rather dramatic drive as you go through Boulder City and come over a rise, and Lake

Mead suddenly appears spread out before you. It's a beautiful sight. At about this point, the road narrows down to two lanes and traffic can slow considerably. On normal busy tourist days, this drive would take about an hour. But because the bridge bypass won't be completed until 2007, thanks to new security measures that call for most trucks and many other vehicles to be stopped and searched, during peak hours the drive is taking longer than ever. Plan accordingly.

Go past the turnoff to Lake Mead. As you near the dam, you'll see a five-story parking structure tucked into the canyon wall on your left. Park here ($5 charge) and take the elevators or stairs to the walkway leading to the new visitor center.

If you would rather go on an **organized tour,** Gray Line (© **800/634-6579;** www.grayline.com) offers a Hoover Dam package that includes a buffet lunch and a side trip to the Ethel M Chocolate factory. When you're in Las Vegas, look for discount coupons in the numerous free publications available at hotels. The 7½-hour **Deluxe Hoover Dam Tour** departs daily at 7:45am; the price is $45, with admission to the dam's Discovery Tour an additional $10.

THE HOOVER DAM 🐾🐾🐾

There would be no Las Vegas as we know it without the Hoover Dam. Certainly, the neon and glitz that we know and love would not exist. In fact, the growth of the entire Southwest can be tied directly to the electricity that comes from the dam.

Until the Hoover Dam was built, much of the southwestern United States was plagued by two natural problems: parched, sandy terrain that lacked irrigation for most of the year, and extensive flooding in spring and early summer when the mighty Colorado River, fed by melting snow from its source in the Rocky Mountains, overflowed its banks and destroyed crops, lives, and property. On the positive side, raging unchecked over eons, the river's turbulent, rushing waters carved the Grand Canyon.

In 1928, prodded by the seven states through which the river runs during the course of its 1,400-mile journey to the Gulf of California, Congress authorized construction of a dam at Boulder Canyon (later moved to Black Canyon). The Senate's declaration of intention stated, "A mighty river, now a source of destruction, is to be curbed and put to work in the interests of society." Construction began in 1931. Because of its vast scope and the unprecedented problems posed in its realization, the project generated significant advances in many areas of machinery production, engineering, and construction. An army of more than 5,200 laborers was assembled, and work proceeded 24 hours a day. Completed in 1936, 2 years ahead of schedule and $15 million under budget (it is, no doubt, a Wonder of the Modern Fiscal World), the dam stopped the annual floods and conserved water for irrigation, industrial, and domestic use. Equally important, it became one of the world's major electrical-generating plants, providing low-cost, pollution-free hydroelectric power to a score of surrounding communities. Hoover Dam's $165-million cost has been repaid with interest by the sale of inexpensive power to a number of California cities and the states of Arizona and Nevada. The dam is a government project that paid for itself—a feat almost as awe-inspiring as its engineering.

The dam itself is a massive curved wall, 660 feet thick at the bottom, tapering to 45 feet where the road crosses it at the top. It towers 726 feet above bedrock (about

> **Impressions**
>
> Everybody knows Las Vegas is the best town by a dam site.
>
> —Masthead slogan of the *Las Vegas Review-Journal*

the height of a 60-story skyscraper) and acts as a plug between the canyon walls to hold back up to 9.2 trillion gallons of water in Lake Mead, the reservoir created by its construction. Four concrete intake towers on the lake side drop the water down about 600 feet to drive turbines and create power, after which the water spills out into the river and continues south.

All the architecture is on a grand scale, and the design has beautiful Art Deco elements, unusual in an engineering project. Note, for instance, the monumental 30-foot bronze sculpture, *Winged Figures of the Republic,* flanking a 142-foot flagpole at the Nevada entrance. According to its creator, Oskar Hansen, the sculpture symbolizes "the immutable calm of intellectual resolution, and the enormous power of trained physical strength, equally enthroned in placid triumph of scientific achievement."

The dam has become a major sightseeing attraction along with Lake Mead, America's largest artificial reservoir and a major Nevada recreation area.

Seven miles northwest of the dam on U.S. 93, you'll pass through **Boulder City,** which was built to house managerial and construction workers. Sweltering summer heat (many days it is 125°F/52°C) ruled out a campsite by the dam. The higher elevation of Boulder City offered lower temperatures. The city emerged within a single year, turning a desert wasteland into a community of 6,000. By 1934 it was Nevada's third-largest town.

TOURING THE DAM

The very nice **Hoover Dam Visitor Center,** a vast three-level circular concrete structure with a rooftop overlook, opened in 1995. You'll enter the Reception Lobby (bags were not allowed inside after the Sept 11 terrorist attacks, but ask about current security measures as they may have changed), where you can buy tickets; peruse informational exhibits, photographs, and memorabilia; and view three 12-minute video presentations (about the importance of water to life, the events leading up to the construction of Hoover Dam, and the construction itself, as well as the many benefits it confers). Exhibits on the Plaza Level include interactive displays on the environment, habitation, and development of the Southwest, the people who built the dam, and related topics.

Yet another floor up, galleries on the Overlook Level demonstrate, via sculpted bronze panels, the benefits of Hoover Dam and Lake Mead to the states of Arizona, Nevada, and California. The Overlook Level additionally provides an unobstructed view of Lake Mead, the dam, the power plant, the Colorado River, and Black Canyon. (There are multiple photo opportunities throughout this trip.)

You can visit an exhibit center across the street where a 10-minute presentation in a small theater focuses on a topographical map of the 1,400-mile Colorado River. It also has a cafeteria. Notice, by the way, how the restrooms in the exhibition center have only electric dryers, no paper towels. A tribute?

The center closes at 5pm, and 4:45pm is the last admission time. Admission is $10 for adults, $8 for seniors and military personnel and their dependents, $4 for children 7 to 16, and free for children under 7. There is no need to call ahead to reserve a place but for more information, call ✆ **866/291-TOUR** or 702/597-5970.

At this writing, because of post–September 11 security measures, tours of the dam are highly restricted. It's no longer the quite nifty, and lengthy, experience it once was because access is so limited. Currently, visitors go to the center, see a movie, and, best of all, get to walk on top of the dam, using a self-guided tour aided by the occasional information kiosk or guide/docent planted at intervals along the way. Guests should also be able to view one of the engine rooms. Obviously, this current set-up could at any moment be increased, or further tightened, though the latter is sadly more likely than the former.

Some fun facts you might hear along the way: It took 6½ years to fill the lake. Though 96 workers were killed during the construction, contrary to popular myth, none were accidentally buried as the concrete was poured (it was poured only at a level of 8 in. at a time). Look for a monument outside dedicated to the workers who were killed—"they died to make the desert bloom"—along with a tombstone for their doggy mascot who was also killed, albeit after the dam was completed. Compare their wages of 50¢ an hour to their Depression-era peers, who made 5¢ to 30¢.

For more information on the dam, surf over to its website at **www.usbr.gov/lc/ hooverdam**.

LAKE MEAD NATIONAL RECREATION AREA ✸✸

Under the auspices of the National Park Service, 1.5-million-acre Lake Mead National Recreation Area was created in 1936 around Lake Mead (the reservoir lake that is the result of the construction of Hoover Dam) and later Lake Mohave to the south (formed by the construction of Davis Dam). Before the lakes emerged, this desert region was brutally hot, dry, and rugged—unfit for human habitation. Today it's one of the nation's most popular playgrounds, attracting about nine million visitors annually. The two lakes comprise 291 square miles. At an elevation of 1,221 feet, Lake Mead itself extends some 110 miles upstream toward the Grand Canyon. Its 550-mile shoreline, backed by spectacular cliff and canyon scenery, forms a perfect setting for a wide variety of watersports and desert hiking.

The **Alan Bible Visitor Center,** 4 miles northeast of Boulder City on U.S. 93 at Nevada 166 (✆ 702/293-8990), can provide information on all area activities and services. You can pick up trail maps and brochures here, view informative films, and find out about scenic drives, accommodations, ranger-guided hikes, naturalist programs and lectures, bird-watching, canoeing, camping, lakeside RV parks, and picnic facilities. The center also sells books and videotapes about the area. It's open daily from 8:30am to 4:30pm except Thanksgiving, Christmas, and New Year's Day.

For information on accommodations, boat rentals, and fishing, call **Seven Crown Resorts** (✆ 800/752-9669; www.sevencrown.com).

You can also find info on the Web at **www.nps.gov/lame**.

In May 2000 the park service began to charge **entry fees** for the first time. Fees are $5 per vehicle, which covers all passengers, or $3 per person if you're walking or biking in.

OUTDOOR ACTIVITIES

This is a lovely area for scenic drives amid the dramatic desert landscape. One popular route follows the Lakeshore and Northshore Scenic drives along the edge of Lake Mead. From these roads there are panoramic views of the blue lake set against a backdrop of the browns, blacks, reds, and grays that make up the desert mountains. Northshore Scenic Drive also leads through areas of brilliant red boulders and rock formations, and you'll find a picnic area along the way.

BOATING & FISHING   A store at **Lake Mead Resort and Marina,** under the auspices of Seven Crown Resorts (✆ **800/752-9669** or 702/293-3484), rents fishing boats, ski boats, personal watercraft, and patio boats. It also carries groceries, clothing, marine supplies, sporting goods, water-skiing gear, fishing equipment, and bait and

Lake Mead & Vicinity

tackle. You can get a fishing license here ($69 for a year, $18 for 1 day plus $7 for each additional day; discounts for children under 15 are available; additional fees apply for special fishing classifications). The staff is knowledgeable and can apprise you of good fishing spots. Largemouth bass, striped bass, channel catfish, crappie, and bluegill are found in Lake Mead; rainbow trout, largemouth bass, and striped bass in Lake Mohave. You can also arrange here to rent a fully equipped houseboat at **Echo Bay,** 40 miles north.

Other convenient Lake Mead marinas offering similar rentals and equipment are **Las Vegas Boat Harbor** (© 702/565-9111), which is even closer to Las Vegas, and **Callville Bay** (© 702/565-8958), which is the least crowded of the five on the Nevada Shore.

CAMPING   Lake Mead's shoreline is dotted with campsites, all of them equipped with running water, picnic tables, and grills. Available on a first-come, first-served basis, they are administered by the **National Park Service** (© 702/293-8990; www. nps.gov). There's a charge of $10 per night at each campsite.

CANOEING   The **Alan Bible Visitor Center** (see above) can provide a list of outfitters who rent canoes for trips on the Colorado River. There's one catch, however: A canoeing permit ($10 per person) is required in advance for certain areas near the dam and is available from the **Bureau of Reclamation** (Attn.: Canoe Launch Permits), Box 60400, Boulder City, NV 89006-0400 (© **702/293-8204**). You can apply for and receive the permit on the same day that you plan to canoe.

HIKING   The best season for hiking is November to March (it's too hot the rest of the year). Some ranger-guided hikes are offered via the **Alan Bible Visitor Center** (see above), which also stocks detailed trail maps. Three trails, ranging in length from .75 mile to 6 miles, originate at the visitor center. The 6-mile trail goes past remains of the railroad built for the dam project. Be sure to take all necessary desert-hiking precautions (see details in chapter 7).

LAKE CRUISES   A delightful way to enjoy Lake Mead is on a cruise aboard **Lake Mead Cruises'** *Desert Princess* (© **702/293-6180;** www.lakemeadcruises.com), a Mississippi-style paddle-wheeler. Cruises depart year-round from a terminal near **Lake Mead Lodge** (see below). It's a relaxing, scenic trip (enjoyed from an open promenade deck or one of two fully enclosed, climate-controlled decks) through Black Canyon and past colorful rock formations known as the "Arizona Paint Pots" en route to Hoover Dam, which is lit at night. Options include narrated midday cruises ($20 adults, $9 children), cocktail/dinner cruises ($44 adults, $21 children), sunset dinner/dance cruises with live music ($54 adults, children not permitted), and Sunday Brunch cruises ($33 adults, $15 children). Dinner is served in a pleasant, windowed, air-conditioned dining room. There's a full onboard bar. Call for departure times.

SCUBA DIVING   October to April, there's good visibility, lessened in summer months when algae flourishes. A list of good dive locations, authorized instructors, and nearby dive shops is available at the **Alan Bible Visitor Center** (see above). There's an underwater, designated diving area near Lake Mead Marina.

BOULDER CITY

You might want to consider poking around Boulder City on your way back to Vegas. Literally the company town for those building Hoover Dam, it was created by the wives who came with their husbands and turned a temporary site into a real community, since aided by the recreational attractions and attendant businesses of Lake Mead. It doesn't look like much as you first approach it, but once you are in the heart, you'll discover that it's quite charming. There are some antiques and curio shops, and a number of family-style restaurants and burger and Mexican joints, including **Toto's,** a reasonably priced Mexican restaurant at 806 Buchanan Blvd. (© **702/293-1744**); it's in the Von's shopping center. Or you could try the **Happy Days Diner,** 512 Nevada Hwy. (© **702/293-4637**), which is right on the road to and from the dam. A '50s diner in looks and menu, it has the usual burgers, shakes, and fries, plus complete breakfasts, and is quite inexpensive ($3 for a turkey burger on a recent visit), friendly, and a good place to take the kids.

WHERE TO STAY

In addition to the hotel below (the only place to stay right on Lake Mead itself, aside from campsites), there are a number of little hotels in Boulder City.

Lake Mead Lodge *Value*   If camping isn't your bag, spend your night or nights at this rustic and comfortable bungalow-style lodge. It's an easy drive from Hoover Dam and is right on the lake, but also right on the desert, so don't picture it as a wooded resort. The rooms are pleasant, with wood-paneled ceilings and walls of white-painted brick or rough-hewn pine. All offer full private bathrooms. There is a suite with three rooms and a small kitchen, which might be good for families staying a few days. (There are plans to add a second suite.) The pool is rudimentary, but you might want to relax with a good book in one of the gazebos on the property. About ½ mile down the road is the marina, where you can while away a few hours over cocktails on a lakeside patio. The marina (the Lake Mead Resort and Marina) is the headquarters for boating, fishing, and watersports; it also houses a large shop (see marina details above, under "Boating & Fishing").

There's a nautically themed restaurant called **Tale of the Whale** (© 702/293-3484) at the marina, its rough-hewn pine interior embellished with various seafaring iconography. It's open from 7am to 8pm Sunday to Thursday, and until 9pm Friday and Saturday (it closes an hour later during the summer). The restaurant serves hearty breakfasts; sandwiches, salads, and burgers at lunch; and steak-and-seafood dinners. And Boulder Beach, also an easy walk from the lodge, has waterfront picnic tables and barbecue grills.

322 Lakeshore Rd., Boulder City, NV 89005. © **800/752-9669** or 702/293-2074. 42 units. Apr–Oct $85 and up double; rest of the year $70 and up double. Extra person $10. Children under 5 stay free in parent's room. DISC, MC, V. Pets accepted, $10 per pet. **Amenities:** Restaurant; outdoor pool; watersports equipment; picnic area w/barbecue pit. *In room:* A/C, TV w/basic cable.

2 Valley of Fire State Park ★★

60 miles NE of Las Vegas

Most people visualize the desert as a vast expanse of undulating sands punctuated by the occasional cactus or palm-fringed oasis. But the desert of America's Southwest bears little relation to this Lawrence of Arabia image. Stretching for hundreds of miles around Las Vegas in every direction is a seemingly lifeless tundra of vivid reddish earth, shaped by time, climate, and subterranean upheavals into majestic canyons, cliffs, and ridges.

The 36,000-acre Valley of Fire State Park typifies the mountainous red Mojave Desert. It derives its name from the brilliant sandstone formations that were created 150 million years ago by a great shifting of sand and that continue to be shaped by the geologic processes of wind and water erosion. These are rock formations like you'll never see anywhere else. There is nothing green, just fiery flaming red rocks, swirling unrelieved as far as the eye can see. No wonder various sci-fi movies have used this place as a stand-in for another planet—it has a most otherworldly look. The whole place is very mysterious, loaded with petroglyphs, and totally inhospitable. It's not hard to believe that for the Indians it was a sacred place, where men came as a test of their manhood. It is a natural wonder that must be seen to be appreciated.

Although it's hard to imagine in the sweltering Nevada heat, for billions of years these rocks were under hundreds of feet of ocean. This ocean floor began to rise some 200 million years ago, and the waters became more and more shallow. Eventually the sea made a complete retreat, leaving a muddy terrain traversed by ever-diminishing streams. A great sandy desert covered much of the southwestern part of the American continent until about 140 million years ago. Over eons, winds, massive fault action, and water erosion sculpted fantastic formations of sand and limestone. Oxidation of iron in the sands and mud—and the effect of groundwater leaching the oxidized iron—turned the rocks the many hues of red, pink, russet, lavender, and white that can be seen today. Logs of ancient forests washed down from faraway highlands and became petrified fossils, which can be seen along two interpretive trails.

Human beings occupied the region—a wetter and cooler one—as far back as 4,000 years ago. They didn't live in the Valley of Fire, but during the Gypsum period (2000 B.C.–300 B.C.), men hunted bighorn sheep (a source of food, clothing, blankets, and hut coverings) here with a notched stick called an *atlatl* that is depicted in the park's petroglyphs. Women and children caught rabbits, tortoises, and other small game. In the next phase, from 300 B.C. to A.D. 700, the climate became warmer and drier. Bows and arrows replaced the atlatl, and the hunters and gatherers discovered farming. The Anasazi people began cultivating corn, squash, and beans, and communities began replacing small nomadic family groups. These ancient people wove watertight baskets, mats, hunting nets, and clothing. Around A.D. 300, they learned how to make sun-dried ceramic pottery. Other tribes, notably the Paiutes, migrated to the area. By A.D. 1150, they had become the dominant group. Unlike the Anasazi, the Paiutes were still nomadic and used the Valley of Fire region seasonally. These were the inhabitants whom white settlers found when they entered the area in the early to mid-1800s. The newcomers diverted river and spring waters to irrigate their farmlands, destroying the nature-based Paiute way of life. About 300 descendants of those Paiute tribespeople still live on the Moapa Indian Reservation (about 20 miles northwest) that was established along the Muddy River in 1872.

GETTING THERE

From Las Vegas, take I-15 north to exit 75 (Valley of Fire turnoff). However, the more scenic route is to take I-15 north, then travel Lake Mead Boulevard east to Northshore Road (Nev. 167) and proceed north to the Valley of Fire exit. The first route takes about an hour, the second 1½ hours.

There is a $5-per-vehicle admission charge to the park, regardless of how many people you cram inside.

Plan on spending a minimum of an hour in the park, though you can spend a great deal of time more. It can get very hot in there (there is nothing to relieve the sun beating down on all that red and reflecting off it) and there is no water, so be certain to bring a liter, maybe two, with you in the summer. Without a guide, you must stay on paved roads, but don't worry if they end; you can always turn around and come back to the main road again. You can see a great deal from the car, but there are also hiking trails.

Numerous **sightseeing tours** go to the Valley of Fire. **Gray Line** (© 800/634-6579; www.grayline.com) offers tours, although at press time none to Valley of Fire, but that could change by the time you read this. Inquire at your hotel tour desk. Char Cruze of **Creative Adventures** (p. 216) also offers a fantastic tour.

The Valley of Fire can also be visited in conjunction with Lake Mead. From **Lake Mead Lodge** (see above), take Nevada 166 (Lakeshore Scenic Dr.) north, make a right turn on Nevada 167 (Northshore Scenic Dr.), turn left on Nevada 169 (Moapa Valley Blvd.) West—a spectacularly scenic drive—and follow the signs. The Valley of Fire is about 65 miles from Hoover Dam.

WHAT TO SEE & DO

There are no food concessions or gas stations in the park; however, you can obtain meals or gas on Nevada 167 or in nearby **Overton** (15 miles northwest on Nev. 169). Overton is a fertile valley town replete with trees, agricultural crops, horses, and herds of cattle—quite a change in scenery. On your way in or out of the teeming metropolis, do stop off at **Inside Scoop** 🍦, 395 S. Moapa Valley Blvd. (© 702/397-2055), open Monday through Saturday from 10am to 8pm and Sunday from 11am to 7pm.

It's a sweet, old-fashioned ice-cream parlor run by extremely friendly people, with a proper menu that, in addition to classic sandwiches and the like, features some surprising options—a vegetarian sandwich and a fish salad with crab and shrimp, for example. Everything is quite tasty and fresh. They also do box lunches, perfect for picnicking inside the park. We strongly recommend coming by here on your way in for a box lunch, and then coming by afterward for a much-needed cooling ice cream.

At the southern edge of town is the **Lost City Museum** *(R)*, 721 S. Moapa Valley Blvd. (© **702/397-2193**), a sweet little museum, very nicely done, commemorating an ancient Anasazi village that was discovered in the region in 1924. Artifacts dating back 12,000 years are on display, as are clay jars, dried corn and beans, arrowheads, seashell necklaces, and willow baskets from the ancient Pueblo culture that inhabited this region between A.D. 300 and 1150. Other exhibits document the Mormon farmers who settled the valley in the 1860s. A large collection of local rocks—petrified wood, fern fossils, iron pyrite, green copper, and red iron oxide, along with manganese blown bottles turned purple by the ultraviolet rays of the sun—are also displayed here. The museum is surrounded by reconstructed wattle-and-daub pueblos. Admission is $3 for adults, $2 for seniors over 65, free for children under 18. It's open daily from 8:30am to 4:30pm. Closed Thanksgiving, December 25, and January 1.

Information headquarters for the Valley of Fire is the **visitor center** on Nevada 169, 6 miles west of Northshore Road (© **702/397-2088**). It's open daily from 8:30am to 4:30pm and is worth a quick stop for information and a bit of history before entering the park. Exhibits on the premises explain the origin and geologic history of the park's colorful sandstone formations, describe the ancient peoples who carved their rock art on canyon walls, and identify the plants and wildlife you're likely to see. Postcards, books, slides, and films are for sale here, and you can pick up hiking maps and brochures. Rangers can answer your park-related questions. For Web information on the park, surf over to **http://parks.nv.gov/vf.htm**.

There are **hiking trails, shaded picnic sites,** and **two campgrounds** in the park. Most sites are equipped with tables, grills, water, and restrooms. A $12-per-vehicle, per-night camping fee is charged for use of the campground; if you're not camping, it costs $5 per vehicle to enter the park.

Some of the notable formations in the park have been named for the shapes they vaguely resemble—a duck, an elephant, seven sisters, domes, beehives, and so on. Mouse's Tank is a natural basin that collects rainwater, so named for a fugitive Paiute called Mouse who hid there in the late 1890s. And Native American petroglyphs etched into the rock walls and boulders—some dating from as long as 3,000 years ago—can be observed on self-guided trails. **Petroglyphs** at Atlatl Rock and Petroglyph Canyon are both easily accessible. In summer, when temperatures are usually over 100°F (38°C), you may have to settle for driving through the park in an air-conditioned car.

3 Red Rock Canyon *(R)(R)(R)*

19 miles W of Las Vegas

If you need a break from the casinos of Vegas, with their windowless, claustrophobic, noisy interiors, Red Rock Canyon is balm for your overstimulated soul. Less than 20 miles away—but a world apart—this is a magnificent unspoiled vista that should cleanse and refresh you (and if you must, a morning visit should leave you enough time for an afternoon's gambling). You can drive the panoramic 13-mile **Scenic Drive** (daily 7am–dusk) or explore it in more depth on foot, making it perfect for both athletes and armchair types. There are many interesting sights and trail heads along the drive itself. The wider **National Conservation Area** offers hiking trails and internationally acclaimed rock-climbing opportunities. Especially notable is 7,068-foot Mount Wilson, the highest sandstone peak among the bluffs; for information on climbing, contact the **Red Rock Canyon Visitor Center** at ✆ **702/363-1921.** There are picnic areas along the drive and in nearby **Spring Mountain Ranch State Park,** 5 miles south, which also offers plays in an outdoor theater during the summer. Since Bonnie Springs Ranch (see the next section) is just a few miles away, it makes a great base for exploring Red Rock Canyon.

GETTING THERE
Just drive west on Charleston Boulevard, which becomes Nevada 159. As soon as you leave the city, the red rocks will begin to loom around you. The visitor center will appear on your right.

You can also go on an **organized tour.** Gray Line (✆ **800/634-6579;** www.grayline. com), among other companies, runs bus tours to Red Rock Canyon. Inquire at your hotel tour desk.

Finally, you can go **by bike.** Not very far out of town (at Rainbow Blvd.), Charleston Boulevard is flanked by a bike path that continues for about 11 miles to the visitor center/scenic drive. The path is hilly but not difficult if you're in reasonable shape. However, exploring Red Rock Canyon by bike should be attempted only by exceptionally fit and experienced bikers.

Just off Nevada 159, you'll see the **Red Rock Canyon Visitor Center** (✆ **702/363-1921;** www.redrockcanyon.blm.gov), which marks the actual entrance to the park. There, you can pick up information on trails and view history exhibits on the canyon. The center is open daily from 8:30am to 4:30pm. Red Rock Canyon can be combined with a visit to Bonnie Springs Ranch.

ABOUT RED ROCK CANYON
The geological history of these ancient stones goes back some 600 million years. Over eons, the forces of nature have formed Red Rock's sandstone monoliths into arches, natural bridges, and massive sculptures painted in a stunning palette of gray-white limestone and dolomite, black mineral deposits, and oxidized minerals in earth-toned sienna hues ranging from pink to crimson and burgundy. Orange and green lichens add further contrast, as do spring-fed areas of lush foliage. And formations like Calico Hill are brilliantly white where groundwater has leached out oxidized iron. Cliffs cut by deep canyons tower 2,000 feet above the valley floor.

During most of its history, Red Rock Canyon was below a warm, shallow sea. Massive fault action and volcanic eruptions caused this seabed to begin rising some 225 million years ago. As the waters receded, sea creatures died and the calcium in their bodies combined with sea minerals to form limestone cliffs studded with ancient fossils. Some 45 million years later, the region was buried beneath thousands of feet of windblown sand. The landscape was as arid as the Sahara. As time progressed, iron oxide and calcium carbonate infiltrated the sand, consolidating it into cross-bedded rock.

Shallow streams began carving the Red Rock landscape, and logs that washed down from ancient highland forests fossilized, their molecules gradually replaced by quartz and other minerals. These petrified stone logs, which the Paiute Indians believed were weapons of the wolf god Shinarav, can be viewed in the **Chinle Formation** at the base of the Red Rock Cliffs. About 100 million years ago, massive fault action began dramatically shifting the rock landscape here, forming spectacular limestone and sandstone cliffs and rugged canyons punctuated by waterfalls, shallow streams, and serene oasis pools. Especially notable is the **Keystone Thrust Fault,** dating back about 65 million years when two of the earth's crustal plates collided, forcing older limestone and dolomite plates from the ancient seas over younger red and white sandstones. Over the years, water and wind have been ever-creative sculptors, continuing to redefine this strikingly beautiful landscape.

Red Rock's valley is home to more than 45 species of mammals, about 100 species of birds, 30 reptiles and amphibians, and an abundance of plant life. Ascending the slopes from the valley, you'll see cactus and creosote bushes, aromatic purple sage, yellow-flowering blackbrush, yucca and Joshua trees, and, at higher elevations, clusters of forest-green pinyon, juniper, and ponderosa pines. In spring, the desert blooms with extraordinary wildflowers.

Archaeological studies of Red Rock have turned up pottery fragments, stone tools, pictographs (rock drawings), and petroglyphs (rock etchings), along with other ancient artifacts. They show that humans have been in this region since about 3000 B.C. (some experts say as early as 10,000 B.C.). You can still see remains of early inhabitants on hiking expeditions in the park. (As for habitation of Red Rock, the same Anasazi-to-Paiutes-to-white-settlers progression related in the Valley of Fire section above occurred here.)

In the latter part of the 19th century, Red Rock was a mining site and later a sandstone quarry that provided materials for many buildings in Los Angeles, San Francisco, and early Las Vegas. By the end of World War II, as Las Vegas developed, many people became aware of the importance of preserving the canyon. In 1967 the secretary of the interior designated 62,000 acres as Red Rock Canyon Recreation Lands under the auspices of the Bureau of Land Management, and later legislation banned all development except hiking trails and limited recreational facilities. In 1990, Red Rock Canyon became a National Conservation Area, further elevating its protected status. Its current acreage is 197,000.

WHAT TO SEE & DO

Begin with a stop at the **visitor center;** not only is there a $5 per-vehicle fee to pay, but you can pick up a variety of helpful literature: history, guides, hiking trail maps, and lists of local flora and fauna. You can also view exhibits that tell the history of the canyon and depict its plant and animal life. You'll see a fascinating video here about Nevada's thousands of wild horses and burros, protected by an act of Congress since 1971. Furthermore, you can obtain permits for hiking and backpacking. Call ahead to find out about ranger-guided tours as well as informative guided hikes offered by groups like the Sierra Club and the Audubon Society. And if you're traveling with children, ask about the free *Junior Ranger Discovery Book* filled with fun family activities. Books and videotapes are for sale here, including a guidebook identifying more than 100 top-rated climbing sites.

The easiest thing to do is to **drive the 13-mile scenic loop** ⭐⭐. It really is a loop and it only goes one way, so once you start you are committed to driving the whole thing. You can stop the car to admire any number of fabulous views and sights along the way, or have a picnic, or take a walk or hike. As you drive, observe how dramatically the milky-white limestone alternates with iron-rich red rocks. Farther along, the mountains become solid limestone, with canyons running between them, which lead to an evergreen forest—a surprising sight in the desert.

If you're up to it, however, we can't stress enough that the way to really see the canyon is by **hiking.** Every trail is incredible—glance over your options and decide what you might be looking for. You can begin from the visitor center or drive into the loop, park your car, and start from points therein. Hiking trails range from a .7-mile-loop stroll to a waterfall (its flow varying seasonally) at Lost Creek to much longer and more strenuous treks. Actually, all the hikes involve a certain amount of effort, as you have to scramble over rocks on even the shortest hikes. Unfit or undexterous people should beware. Be sure to wear good shoes, as the rocks can be slippery. You must have a map; you won't get lost forever (there usually are other hikers around to help you out, eventually), but you can get lost. It is often tough to find a landmark, and once deep into the rocks, everything looks the same, even with the map. Consequently, give yourself extra time for each hike (at least an additional hour), regardless of its billed length, to allow for the lack of paths, getting disoriented, and simply to slow down and admire the scenery.

A popular 2-mile round-trip hike leads to **Pine Creek Canyon** and the creek-side ruins of a historic homesite surrounded by ponderosa pine trees. Our hiking trail of choice is the **Calico Basin,** which is accessed along the loop. After an hour walk up the rocks (which is not that well marked), you end up at an oasis surrounded by sheer walls of limestone (which makes the oasis itself inaccessible, alas). In the summer, flowers and deciduous trees grow out of the walls.

As you hike, keep your eyes peeled for lizards, the occasional desert tortoise, herds of bighorn sheep, birds, and other critters. But the rocks themselves are the most fun, with many minicaves to explore and rock formations to climb on. (Relive childhood with a politically incorrect game of Cowboys and Indians!) On trails along Calico Hills and the escarpment, look for "Indian marbles," a local name for small, rounded sandstone rocks that have eroded off larger sandstone formations. Petroglyphs are also tucked away in various locales.

Biking is another option; riding a bicycle would be a tremendous way to travel the loop. There are also terrific off-road mountain-biking trails, with levels from amateur to expert.

After you tour the canyon, drive over to Bonnie Springs Ranch (details in the next section) for lunch or dinner. See chapter 7 for further details on biking and climbing.

4 Bonnie Springs Ranch/Old Nevada ⊛⊛

About 24 miles W of Las Vegas, 5 miles past Red Rock Canyon

Bonnie Springs Ranch/Old Nevada is a kind of Wild West theme park with accommodations and a restaurant. If you're traveling with kids, a day or overnight trip to Bonnie Springs is recommended, but it is surprisingly appealing for adults, too. It could even be a romantic getaway, as it offers horseback riding, gorgeous mountain vistas, proximity to Red Rock Canyon, and temperatures 5 to 10 degrees cooler than on the Strip.

For additional information, you can call **Bonnie Springs Ranch/Old Nevada** at ℂ **702/875-4191** or visit them on the Web at **www.bonniesprings.com**.

If you're **driving,** a trip to Bonnie Springs Ranch can be combined easily with a day trip to Red Rock Canyon; it is about 5 miles farther on. But you can also stay overnight.

For those without transportation, jeep tours to and from Las Vegas are available through **Action Tours** (© **888/288-5200;** http://actiontours.com).

WHAT TO SEE & DO IN OLD NEVADA

Old Nevada ☆☆ (© **702/875-4191**) is a re-creation of an 1880s frontier town, built on the site of a very old ranch. As tourist sights go, this is a good one; it's a bit cheesy, but knowingly, perhaps even deliberately, so. It's terrific for kids up to about the age of 12 or so (before teenage cynicism kicks in), but not all that bad for adults fondly remembering similar places from their own childhoods. Many go expecting a tourist trap, only to come away saying that it really was rather cute and charming.

Certainly, Old Nevada looks authentic, with rustic buildings made entirely of weathered wood. And the setting, right in front of beautiful mountains with layered red rock, couldn't be more perfect for a Western film fantasy. You can wander the town (it's only about a block long), taking peeps into well-replicated places of business, such as a blacksmith shop, a working mill, a saloon, and an old-fashioned general store (cum gift shop) and museum that has a potpourri of items from the Old West and Old Las Vegas: antique gaming tables and slot machines, typewriters, and a great display of old shoes, including lace-up boots. There is also a rather lame wax museum; the less said about it, the better.

Country music is played in the saloon during the day, except when **stage melodramas** take place (at frequent intervals between 11:30am and 5pm). These are entirely tongue-in-cheek—the actors are goofy and know it, and the plot is hokey and fully intended to be that way. Somehow, it just heightens the fun factor. It's interactive with the audience, which, in response to cue cards held up by the players, boos and hisses the mustache-twirling villain, sobs in sympathy with the distressed heroine, and laughs, cheers, and applauds. It's hugely silly and hugely fun, provided you all play along. Kids love it, though younger ones might be scared by the occasional gunshot.

Following each melodrama, a **Western drama** is presented outside the saloon, involving a bank robbery, a shootout, and the trial of the bad guy. A judge, prosecuting attorney, and defense attorney are chosen from the audience, the remainder of whom act as the jury. The action always culminates in a hanging. None of this is a particularly polished act, but the dialogue is quite funny and the whole thing is performed with enthusiasm and affection.

Throughout the area, cowboys continually interact with visiting kids, who, on the weekends, are given badges so that they can join a posse hunting for bad guys. There are also ongoing **stunt shootouts** (maybe not at the level found at, say, Universal Studios) in this wild frontier town, and some rather unsavory characters occasionally languish in the town jail.

In the **Old Nevada Photograph Shoppe** you can have a tintype picture taken in 1890s Wild West costume (they have a fairly large selection) with a 120-year-old camera. There are replicas of a turn-of-the-20th-century church and stamp mill; the latter, which has original 1902 machinery, was used for crushing rocks to separate gold and silver from the earth. Movies (one about nearby Red Rock Canyon, one a silent film) are shown in the **Old Movie House** throughout the day from 10:30am to 5pm. You can tour the remains of the **old Comstock lode silver mine,** though there isn't much to see there. You can also shop for a variety of "Western" souvenirs (though to us, that's when the tourist-trap part kicks in). Eateries in Old Nevada are discussed below. There's plenty of parking; on weekends and holidays a free shuttle train takes visitors from the parking lot to the entrance.

Admission to Old Nevada is charged by vehicle—$7 per car weekdays, for up to six people in the car, and $10 per car on the weekend. The park is open daily from 10:30am to 5pm November to April, and until 6pm the rest of the year.

WHAT TO SEE & DO AT BONNIE SPRINGS RANCH

There are several things to do here free of charge, and it's right next door to Old Nevada. It's quite a pretty place, in a funky, Western kind of way, and in season, there are tons of flowers everywhere, including honeysuckle and roses. The main attraction is the small **zoo** 🐾 on the premises. Now, when we say "zoo," unfortunately we mean that in addition to a petting zoo with the usual suspects (deer, sheep, goats, and rabbits) and some unusual animals (potbelly pigs and snooty, beautiful llamas) to caress and feed, there is also a mazelike enclosure of a series of wire-mesh pens that contain a variety of livestock, some of which should not be penned up (though they are well taken care of), including wolves and bobcats. Still, it's more than diverting for kids.

Less politically and ecologically distressing is the aviary, which houses peacocks, Polish chickens, peachface and blackmask lovebirds, finches, parakeets, ravens, ducks, pheasants, and geese. Keep your eyes peeled for the peacocks roaming free; with luck, they will spread their tails for a photo op. With greater luck, some of the angelic, rare white peacocks will do the same. It may be worth dropping by just in the hopes of spotting one in full fan-tailed glory. (And the ranch also sells peacocks, for $25. Now *there's* a souvenir!)

Riding stables offer guided trail rides into the mountain area on a continuous basis throughout the day (9am–3:15pm spring–fall, until 5:45pm in summer). Children must be at least 6 years old to participate. Cost is $30 per person. For more information, call ✆ **702/875-4191.**

WHERE TO STAY & DINE

In Old Nevada, the **Miner's Restaurant** is a snack bar located in quite a large room that looks great thanks to Western-motif accessories. Inexpensive fare is served (sandwiches, decent burgers, pizza, and hot dogs), along with fresh-baked desserts. There are tables out on the porch. In summer you can also get beer and soft drinks in a similarly old-fashioned **Beer Parlor.**

Bonnie Springs Motel 🐾 This is really a hoot; a funky, friendly little place in the middle of nowhere—except that nowhere is a gorgeous setting. The motel is in two double-story buildings and offers regular rooms, "Western" rooms, "specialty theme" rooms, and kitchen suites.

Where to begin? Here, the theme is expressed mostly through the use of fabrics, personally decorated by the owner, who did a pretty nice job. The "gay 1890s" room is done in black and pink, with a lace canopy over the bed, an old-fashioned commode, and liberal use of velvet. The American Indian room uses skins and feathers, and has a bearskin-covered burl-wood chair. You get the idea. The "Western" rooms have more burl-wood furniture and electric-log fireplaces that blow heat into the room.

All special theme rooms (aka fantasy suites) have mirrors over the beds and big whirlpool tubs in the middle of the room (not in the bathrooms), and come with bottles of champagne (the empties of which you can see littering the road on your way out). All the rooms are quite large, though long and narrow, and have private balconies or patios, and mountain views. There are also large family suites with fully equipped kitchens, bedrooms, living rooms (with convertible sofas), and dressing areas; these are equipped with two phones and two TVs, and are available for long-term rentals (many of the people who work at Old Nevada actually rent these as apartments). Videotapes and players are available for rental, and there is even a tiny train that takes you around the grounds and on a short tour of the desert.

The **Bonnie Springs Ranch Restaurant** has a lot of character and is a perfect family place. It's heavily rustic (stone floors, log beams, raw wooden chairs made from tree branches, lanterns, a roaring fire in winter, and plenty of dead animals adorning the walls). It's a bit touristy, but small-town touristy. The food is basic—steak, ribs, chicken, burgers, and potato skins; pancakes and eggs for breakfast; it's all greasy but good. There is a cozy bar attached to the restaurant, its walls covered with thousands of dollar bills with messages on them—a classic neighborhood bar, if it were actually in a neighborhood.

1 Gunfighter Lane, Old Nevada, NV 89004. *©* **702/875-4400.** Fax 702/875-4424. www.bonniesprings.com/motel.html. 50 units. Double Sun–Thurs $60–$70, Fri–Sat $70–$80; fantasy suite Sun–Thurs $120, Fri–Sat $135; family suite Sun–Thurs $95, Fri–Sat $100. Extra person $5. AE, MC, V. **Amenities:** Restaurant; outdoor pool; nonsmoking rooms. *In room:* A/C, TV w/pay movies, coffeemaker.

5 Mount Charleston & Lee Canyon Ski Area

Mount Charleston: 40 miles NW of Las Vegas; Lee Canyon: 47 miles NW of Las Vegas

You may have noticed that most of the time, when we suggest getaways from Las Vegas, we point you in the direction of the desert. That's understandable—it's where Vegas is located, after all. But some of you may be saying, "Er, I don't actually *like* the desert. It's kind of . . . sparse. I mean, I don't mind it when I can sit in a really nice hotel, but otherwise, I frankly prefer . . . foliage." Good news! Just a short drive away are mountains and trees, real mountains, unlike the one in front of Wynn Las Vegas. And what's more? During the winter, there is skiing and snowboarding nearby. It's just a matter of time before some Vegas casino hotel installs year-round skiing on man-made snow, but until then, take a day or even overnight trip to Mount Charleston. Bonus: In summertime, the mountains that encircle Toiyabe National Forest are as much as 30 to 40 degrees cooler than the sweltering desert city. These mountains, once an island in an ancient sea, are today a cool oasis in the desert. The highest peak towers 11,918 feet above sea level, and it's a beautiful drive. Nevada 157 winds up for about 21 miles through gorgeous canyon scenery, and, as you ascend, desert vegetation—cactus, yucca, creosote bush, and Joshua trees—gives way to stands of juniper, dense ponderosa forest, aspen firs, and bristlecone pine. ("Ahhhh . . . " some of you are saying.) The highway ends at the picturesque Mount Charleston Lodge. You can plan a day around lunch here, with activities like hiking, camping, bird-watching, and horseback riding. In winter, there can be sleigh rides, and you can ski at nearby Lee Canyon (though note that an avalanche during the 2005 heavy winter has left the area fairly damaged. They do hope to be back in operation by Thanksgiving 2005). In summer, there are hayrides, scenic chairlift rides in the ski area, barbecues, and more.

It's a twilight-zone feeling to come from hot and air-conditioned Las Vegas to this sometimes snowy region where you can sit in front of a blazing fire sipping hot buttered rum. Both the Mount Charleston Lodge and the Mount Charleston Hotel serve as information centers for area activities. In addition to the attractions listed below, see "Staying Active" in chapter 7.

ESSENTIALS
GETTING THERE BY CAR
Take I-15 north and stay in the Reno Lane to U.S. 95 North. Make a left on Nevada 157. During ski season you can catch a bus to the Lee Canyon Ski Area. Departure

points vary each year. For details, call © **702/645-2754.** There is no bus transportation to Mount Charleston.

WHAT TO SEE & DO

There are numerous hiking trails, ranging from short panoramic walks to waterfalls near the restaurant/lounge to more difficult hikes father afield. A popular 5-mile trail beginning at Lee Canyon Highway takes you through a canyon of aspen and into forested areas of ponderosa, white fir, and bristlecone pine. There are picnic areas and campsites along some trails. For information on camping and hiking trails, contact the U.S. Forest Service, 2881 S. Valley View Blvd., Suite 16, Las Vegas, NV 89102 (© **702/873-8800**). For camping information and reservations, you can also call 800/280-CAMP. Both the Mount Charleston Lodge and the Mount Charleston Hotel can provide trail maps.

The Las Vegas Ski and Snowboard Resort, in Lee Canyon, at the end of Nevada 156, has a base elevation of 8,510 feet, which, along with an extensive snow-making system, provides an almost ideal climate and snow cover for skiing Thanksgiving Day through Easter Day. Facilities include a lodge, a complete ski school, an extensive ski-rental shop, a snowboard park, a coffee shop, and a lounge with blazing fireplace and sun deck. Chair lifts carry skiers over 40 acres of well-maintained slopes, with runs that carry Vegas-evoking names like Blackjack, Slot Alley, and so on. There is also a half-pipe and a snowboard park. They do have all levels of runs but reserve the big runs for those with some experience. The lodge, useful mostly as a place to spend the night before you go ski (so you can hit the slopes early), is open year round. *Note:* At the beginning of 2005, a major avalanche caused the first death of a skier in a U.S. ski resort in years. The entire area was damaged (Lee Canyon residents were without phone service for weeks), though there remains the intent to have the resort repaired and running again by the start of the ski season. 3620 N. Rancho Rd. (mailing only); © **702/872-5462;** www.skilasvegas.com. Lift tickets $38 full-day pass, $28 for half-day; $25 all-day child and seniors pass, $18 half-day child and seniors.

WHERE TO STAY

The Mount Charleston Hotel ✦   Nestled in the mountains, this three-story property offers lodgings in a rustic log-and-stone building. Its lobby, with massive stone fireplaces, mounted deer heads, and a lofty beamed pine ceiling, resembles a ski lodge. The accommodations are standard hotel boring, which doesn't mean they aren't attractive (earth tones and forest green), but the views out the window are far more impressive. Cathedral ceilings, balconies, and VCRs make third-floor rooms (they call 'em "mini-suites"—we just call them "bigger rooms") especially desirable. Nicer, as is often the case, are the suites with convertible sofas in the living rooms, larger balconies, and wood-burning stone fireplaces. Expect a new cafe (called, intriguingly, Café Chocolat!) and fitness room open by the time you read this.

The hotel's hexagonal Alpine Dining Room has a lot of charm, with two working fireplaces, windows all around overlooking beautiful mountain scenery, and heavy wrought-iron chandeliers suspended from a cathedral pine ceiling. At night it's romantically candlelit. All meals are available here, including full and continental breakfasts. Lunch includes moderately priced burgers, sandwiches, and salads, while dinner entrees bring fancier food. Look for live music in the lounge on the weekend, plus activities like horseback riding arranged by the hotel.

2 Kyle Canyon Rd. (on Nev. 157). ℭ **702/872-5500.** www.mtcharlestonhotel.com. 57 units. Double $105–$115; mini-suite $125; suite $229. Extra person $10. Children stay free in parent's room. Inquire about ski packages. AE, DC, DISC, MC, V. **Amenities:** Restaurant; lounge; Jacuzzi; sauna.

Mount Charleston Lodge ⋆⋆   These charmingly rustic pine log cabins, built right into, and almost at the top of, the mountainside to ensure stunning scenic views, are a delight. Beautifully decorated with southwestern and Native American artifacts (Paiute drums and decorative blankets, sheepskin rugs, steer horns), they have peaked ceilings beamed with rough-hewn logs, oak parquet floors, and lots of windows. Knotty-pine furnishings are complemented by oversize king-size beds and attractively upholstered armchairs and sofas, each room has a working gas fireplace and a whirlpool tub big enough for two, and in-room amenities include fan chandeliers and coffeemakers (coffee, tea, and cocoa are provided). A big plus: Each cabin has a furnished mountain-view terrace that would be a good place to enjoy the sunset. The construction of additional lodging is under way and may be complete by the time you read this. The restaurant serves game (including elk!) and other intriguing dishes. Expect polka music on the weekends. This serene (well, apart from the polka music) getaway is the perfect antidote to Las Vegas glitz and glitter, and, for couples, it would be hard to come by a more romantic setting.

1200 Old Park Road. (end of Nev. 157). ℭ **800/955-1314** or 702/872-5408. www.mtcharlestonlodge.com. 24 cabins. Honeymoon Cabin (for 1 or 2) $125–$200; Family Cabin (for up to 4) $155–$240. Extra person $10. AE, DC, DISC, MC, V. **Amenities:** Restaurant; lounge; heated pool (under construction). *In room:* TV w/DVD/VCR, coffeemaker.

6 Outdoor Activities & Tour Companies

CYCLING

Downhill Bicycle Tours (ℭ **702/897-8287**) can take you on tours that span 18 miles and three different environments through areas surrounding Las Vegas. **Escape Adventures** (ℭ **702/383-6966** or 800/596-2953; www.escapeadventures.com) rents bikes and biking equipment, starting at $30 per day, as well as providing guided and self-guided tours of Red Rock Canyon and Mount Charleston, which begin at $89 for a half-day self-guided tour and include the bike rental. These tours range from 7 to 23 miles and span experience and age levels, depending on your children's abilities. One that is definitely suited to children is a summer tour that's 18 miles and all downhill from the top of Mount Charleston (a shuttle takes you up the mountain).

HIKING

Desert hiking trails in the region include marked trails in both Red Rock Canyon and Valley of Fire. Keep in mind that in the summer, temperatures can soar to 120°f (49°C); the best time for exploring the beauty of the desert is November through March. If you'd prefer a guided hiking adventure in Red Rock, an experienced guide from **Grand Canyon Tours** (ℭ **800/222-6966** or 702/655-6060; www.grand-canyontourcompany.com) will pick up at your hotel and drive you into Red Rock for lunch and an up-close walking tour of the formations for $160 to $215 per person (no discount for children). **Sky's the Limit** (ℭ **800/733-7597** or 702/363-4533; www.skysthelimit.com) offers a tour called Hike of the Day, in either the morning or afternoon, where you'll explore a portion of Humboldt–Toiyabe National Forest, which includes Mount Charleston and Red Rock Canyon. The half-day hike includes lunch. You should be fundamentally fit and able to walk several miles to enjoy this excursion, which costs $100 per person. **Escape Adventures** (ℭ **702/383-6966;**

www.escapeadventures.com) offers a half-day guided hike through Red Rock for $89 per person. Guided tours are offered on a limited basis through the Red Rock Canyon visitor center, but reservations must be made in advance. There is a website specifically devoted to hiking in the Las Vegas area, www.hikinglasvegas.com, which provides an overview of local hiking sights. Also see the "Desert Hiking Advice" box, on p. 220, for more information on hiking in the desert.

HORSEBACK RIDING

Cowboy Trail Rides (© 702/948-7061; www.cowboytrailrides.com) offers a variety of rides and trails in Red Rock Canyon and on Mount Charleston (at the 12-mile marker), ranging in price from $89 to $139. The high end is for a Red Rock Canyon sunset trail ride; it's about 2 hours, with the canyon providing a glorious backdrop for the end of the day. Riders then return to camp for a barbecue dinner (including a 16-oz. T-bone steak), joined by the cowboys for singalongs and marshmallow roasting. They also offer hour-and-a-half rides at $70. There are also riding stables at **Bonnie Springs Ranch** (© 702/875-4191; see section earlier in this chapter) that offer guided trail rides daily through the area close to Red Rock. Rates are $25 per person per hour. Wear tennis shoes, riding boots, or hiking boots and jeans for riding.

For children 11 years and up a real *City Slickers* experience is available at **Sandy Valley Ranch** (© 877/726-3998; www.sandyvalleyranch.com), located 45 minutes southwest of the Strip. Isolated from towns, roads, and just about everything else, you can follow existing trails or blaze new ones in 300 square miles (yes, that's square *miles*) of sage and mesquite rangeland. The terrain varies from flat valleys to foothills to canyons and mountains. Guest horses are carefully screened for responsiveness, gentleness, patience, and compatibility with other horses. The ranch offers overnight camping in sturdy, platform-mounted tents; excellent dinners in a modern but rustic dining hall; buckboard rides; and guided trail rides. Most fun of all, however, is playing with cattle (you'll want to take some home!). You can participate in an actual round-up where you scour the plains and canyons in search of cattle to herd back to the corral, or you can join friendly competitions in the rodeo arena. Partial day outings run from $60 to $138. All include preliminary training, a trail ride, and working with the cattle. The more expensive outings include a meal, cowboy skills games, and, in the evening, a campfire. The ranch also provides transportation from Las Vegas hotels.

ROCK CLIMBING

If you or your children are interested in learning to rock climb or in improving your skills, an excellent rock-climbing school and guide service called **Sky's the Limit** (© 800/733-7597 or 702/363-4533; www.skysthelimit.com) offers programs for beginning, intermediate, and advanced climbers. No experience is needed. The school is accredited by the American Mountain Guides Association. The beginning program ($200 per person) is a 1-day, entry-level experience suitable for those of all ages who are mobile and basically athletic. You are taken to Red Rock Canyon where you'll receive your guide's personalized attention and instruction in this challenging sport. You'll learn to climb and rappel; and by the end of the day, you'll not only have the terminology and basic skills of a rock climber, but you'll have a sense of accomplishment, plus be able to tie a really strong knot. For locations to practice rock climbing, check out some of the places listed on p. 221.

SKIING & SNOWBOARDING

From roughly Thanksgiving through Easter, depending on weather conditions, you can ski and snowboard at the **Las Vegas Ski and Snowboard Resort** (© 702/593-9500; www.skilasvegas.com). It rents equipment and clothing as well as provide lessons. Adult all-day passes are $33; children 12 and under $25; afternoon passes good from 1 to 4pm are $6 less. For more information see p. 318.

7 A Close Encounter with Area 51 ⍟

150 miles N of Las Vegas

Want to feel like an extra on the *X-Files*? Just want to get an idea of the kind of spots the government picks when it needs a place in which to do secret things? Take the drive from Vegas out to the **"E. T. Highway,"** where folks were spotting aliens years before it became fashionable. This is about a 150-mile trip one-way, so it's probably not something to do on a whim, but even for non–alien buffs, it can be a long, strange—and oddly illuminating—trip indeed.

Area 51 is a secret military facility, containing a large air base that the government will not discuss. The site was selected in the mid-1950s for the testing of the U2 spy plane and is supposedly the current testing ground for "black budget" aircraft before their public acknowledgment. (Oh, heck, who are they trying to kid? *Of course* that's where they are testing high-tech gadgets.) But its real fame comes with the stories of aliens, whose bodies and ships were supposedly taken there when they "crashed" at Roswell.

Mind you, the only thing alien you are guaranteed to see is the landscape. Only fans of desert topography will find the scenery attractive. It's a desolate area, but that's part of the inexplicable charm. There is absolutely a weird vibe in the air; something is going on out here. And one thing's for sure: If you need a place for covert, or at least private, activities, you couldn't find a better location for it. Alien bodies? Shoot, you could hide an entire alien fleet.

But don't come looking for monuments, historical markers, or good shopping—with a few exceptions, there's a whole lot of nothing out there. You'd think the tourist possibilities would have led to more development, but even in Vegas, despite the presence of plenty of alien merchandise in the gift shops and an entire Area 51–themed shopping area at the airport expansion, there is not as much awareness as you might think. One waitress, when asked if she'd been there, responded, "Not since they remodeled."

All we know for sure is that you turn down one of the most well-maintained dirt roads you will ever encounter, drive a few miles, and come upon a fence with a sign that warns you against going any farther in the utmost of strict terms (though the language has been toned down from "use of deadly force authorized" to threats of fines and jail time). Along the way down that road, notice how there is absolutely no wildlife other than grasshoppers, that the Joshua trees suddenly turn to an enormous size and monstrous shape, and that the few cattle grazing around don't seem like any cattle you've seen before. Then notice those blasted-out craters in the earth, with the core sample holes in the center. When you realize you are looking at nuclear test sites, the desolation and mutations suddenly make sense. Wave hi at the guys in the military vehicles who are making damn sure you don't go through that gate, and hightail it out of there.

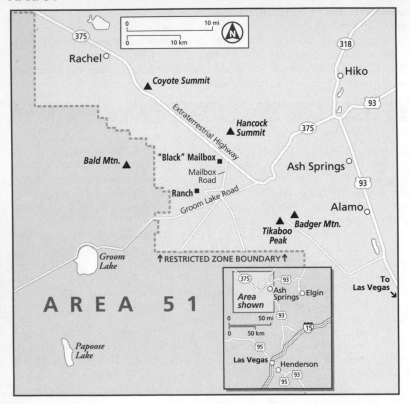

The other hot spot is the "town" of **Rachel** (**www.rachel.dreamlandresort.com**), really just a collection of trailer homes. Here's where you'll find the **Little A'Le'Inn** diner and gift shop ("Earthlings Welcome")—where a very funny *X-Files* episode was filmed—and, in theory, chat with fellow E. T.–spotters, who often gather at night to search the skies. The owners don't play along as much as one would like, though they do feel they were "called there for a special purpose," but their gift shop makes up for it with fine humorous souvenirs (we liked the alien-head-shaped guitar pick). Plus, they serve up satisfying diner food. You can also drop in at the **Area 51 Research Center** (just look for the big yellow trailer), which was opened after its founder (Glenn Campbell, who is largely responsible for Area 51's recent cultural icon status, and who wrote the definitive book *Area 51 Viewer's Guide*) got kicked out of the Little A'Le'Inn. Their headquarters is now in Las Vegas, and their store is open only during spring and summer but stocks all manner of Area 51 logo items and a number of related books.

There is no place to stay out here, so unless you want to camp (which could be fun; aliens usually show up at night), plan this as a lengthy day trip. Be sure to fill your tank before you head out, as there are few opportunities to do so once you leave Vegas. If you'll be doing this drive in the heat of the summer, bring water, for your car and yourself. Along the way, keep your eyes peeled for little green men (or weather balloons, jackrabbits, tumbleweeds, broken-down cars . . .), and should you spot one, don't forget to write us all about it.

By the way, word is starting to spread of a *really* mysterious secret base even farther out in the desert. Just mention Area 58 and watch people go nuts.

To start, you take I-15 north to U.S. 93 North (paying close attention—it's an easy exit to miss; if you do, you can take State Rte. 168 at Moapa west back to U.S. 93), and then get off at the E. T. Highway, a 98-mile stretch of State Route 375. The town of Rachel is approximately 43 miles away; the "black mailbox" (it's now white) road, which leads you to Area 51, actually comes first, about 17 miles down the highway. (We strongly suggest going to Rachel first, to get your bearings, chat with knowledgeable locals and other alien-spotters, and pick up some literature, including a good local map.) Turn left and keep driving; any of the dirt roads that lead off of it will get you to the Area 51 fence and gates. Veer right at the fork in the road (not the ranch turnoff, which you come to first) if you want to go to the most commonly talked about entrance, the one at Groom Lake (though you can't see the lake from where you are forced to stop.)

For more information, call the **Nevada Commission on Tourism** (℗ **800/ NEVADA-8**), and ask them to send you their *Pioneer Territory* brochure and a list of E. T. Highway services (gas stations, chambers of commerce, restaurants, and more). On the Internet, check out **www.ufomind.com** (this is a huge site maintained by the Area 51 Research folks, and contains countless links and all sorts of information) and **www.ufo-hyway.com**.

Appendix:
Las Vegas in Depth

There has rarely been a time in Vegas's post-Bugsy history when the city wasn't booming, but it seems on a particular roll right now. A new megaresort seems to go up every other week, and each brings something new to the party, sometimes things hitherto never invited: great works of art, five-star world-renowned chefs, rock clubs and arenas that attract significant and still-current acts—you get the idea. In other words, everything old is new again, and Vegas glamour is back.

1 A Look at the Past

THE EIGHTH WONDER OF THE WORLD

For many years after its creation, Las Vegas was a mere whistle-stop town. That all changed in 1928 when Congress authorized the building of nearby Boulder Dam (later renamed Hoover Dam), bringing thousands of workers to the area. In 1931, gambling once again became legal in Nevada, and Fremont Street's gaming emporiums and speak-easies attracted dam workers. Upon the dam's completion, the Las Vegas chamber of commerce worked hard to lure the hordes of tourists who came to see the engineering marvel (it was called "the Eighth Wonder of the World") to its casinos. But it wasn't until the early years of World War II that visionary entrepreneurs began to plan for the city's glittering future.

LAS VEGAS GOES SOUTH

Contrary to popular lore, developer Bugsy Siegel didn't actually stake a claim in the middle of nowhere—he just built a few blocks south of already-existing properties.

And in 1941, El Rancho Vegas, ultra-luxurious for its time, was built on the same remote stretch of highway (across the street from where the Sahara now stands). Scores of Hollywood stars were invited to the grand opening, and El Rancho Vegas soon became the hotel of choice for visiting film stars.

Dateline

- **1831–48** Artesian spring waters of Las Vegas serve as a watering place on the Old Spanish Trail.
- **1855** Mormon colony of 30 missionaries establishes settlement just north of today's Downtown. Unsuccessful in its aims, the colony disbands in 1858.
- **1864** President Lincoln proclaims Nevada the 36th state of the Union. Las Vegas, however, is still part of the Territory of Arizona.
- **1865** Gold prospector Octavius D. Gass builds Las Vegas Ranch, the first permanent settlement in Las Vegas, on the site of the old Mormon fort.
- **1880s** Due to the past 2 decades' mining fever and the fervor for westward migration, the population of Nevada soars to more than 60,000 in 1880. The Paiutes are forced onto reservations.
- **1895** San Francisco inventor Charles Fey creates a three-reel gambling device—the first slot machine.
- **1907** Fremont Street, the future "Glitter Gulch," gets electric lights.
- **1909** Gambling is made illegal in Nevada, but Las Vegas pays little heed.
- **1928** Congress authorizes construction of Boulder Dam

Beginning a trend that continues today, each new property tried to outdo existing hotels in luxurious amenities and thematic splendor. Las Vegas was on its way to becoming the entertainment capital of the world.

Las Vegas promoted itself in the 1940s as a town that combined Wild West frontier friendliness with glamour and excitement. As chamber of commerce president Maxwell Kelch put it in a 1947 speech, "Las Vegas has the impact of a Wild West show, the friendliness of a country store, and the sophistication of Monte Carlo." Throughout the decade, the city was Hollywood's celebrity playground. The Hollywood connection gave the town glamour in the public's mind. So did the mob connection (something Las Vegas has spent decades trying to live down), which became clear when notorious underworld gangster Bugsy Siegel built the fabulous Flamingo, a tropical paradise and "a real class joint."

A steady stream of name entertainers came to Las Vegas. In 1947, Jimmy Durante opened the showroom at The Flamingo. Other headliners of the 1940s included Dean Martin and Jerry Lewis, tap-dancing legend Bill "Bojangles" Robinson, the Mills Brothers, skater Sonja Henie, and Frankie Laine. Future Las Vegas legend Sammy Davis, Jr., debuted at El Rancho Vegas in 1945.

While the Strip was expanding, Downtown kept pace with new hotels such as the El Cortez and the Golden Nugget. By the end of the decade, Fremont Street was known as "Glitter Gulch," its profusion of neon signs proclaiming 'round-the-clock gaming and entertainment.

THE 1950s: BUILDING BOOMS & A-BOMBS

Las Vegas entered the new decade as a city (no longer a frontier town) with a population of about 50,000. Hotel growth was phenomenal. The Desert Inn, which opened in 1950 with headliners Edgar Bergen and Charlie McCarthy, brought country-club elegance (including an 18-hole golf course and tennis courts) to the Strip.

In 1951 the Eldorado Club Downtown became Benny Binion's Horseshoe Club, which would gain fame as the home of the annual World Series of Poker. In 1954 the Showboat sailed into a new area east of Downtown. The Showboat not only introduced buffet meals, but it also offered 'round-the-clock bingo and a bowling alley (106 lanes to date).

In 1955 the Côte d'Azur–themed Riviera became the ninth big hotel to open on the Strip. Breaking the ranch-style

---

30 miles away, bringing thousands of workers to the area. Later, Las Vegas will capitalize on hundreds of thousands who come to see the engineering marvel.

- **1931** Gambling is legalized once again.
- **1932** The 100-room Apache Hotel opens Downtown.
- **1933** Prohibition is repealed. Las Vegas's numerous speakeasies become legit.

- **1934** The city's first neon sign lights up the Boulder Club Downtown.
- **1941** The luxurious El Rancho Vegas becomes the first hotel on the Strip. Downtown, the El Cortez opens.
- **1942** Last Frontier opens 2 miles south of El Rancho Vegas.
- **1946** Benjamin "Bugsy" Siegel's Flamingo extends the boundaries of the Strip. Sammy Davis, Jr., debuts at

the El Rancho Vegas. Downtown (dubbed "Glitter Gulch") gets two new hotels: the Golden Nugget and the Eldorado.

- **1947** United Airlines inaugurates service to Las Vegas.
- **1948** The Thunderbird becomes the fourth hotel on the Strip.
- **1950** The Desert Inn adds country club panache to the Strip.

continues

mode, it was, at nine stories, the Strip's first high-rise. Liberace, one of the hottest names in show business, was paid the unprecedented sum of $50,000 a week to dazzle audiences in The Riviera's posh Clover Room.

Elvis appeared at the New Frontier in 1956 but wasn't a huge success; his fans were too young to fit the Las Vegas tourist mold. In 1958 the $10-million, 1,065-room Stardust upped the spectacular stakes by importing the famed *Lido de Paris* spectacle from the French capital. It became one of the longest-running shows ever to play Las Vegas.

Throughout the 1950s, most of the Vegas hotels competed for performers whose followers spent freely in the casinos. The advent of big-name Strip entertainment tolled a death knell for glamorous nightclubs in America; owners simply could not compete with the astronomical salaries paid to Las Vegas headliners. Two performers whose names have been linked to Las Vegas ever since—Frank Sinatra and Wayne Newton—made their debuts there. Mae West not only performed in Las Vegas, but also cleverly bought up ½ mile of desolate Strip frontage between the Dunes and the Tropicana.

Competition for the tourist dollar also brought nationally televised sporting events such as the PGA's Tournament of Champions. In the 1950s the wedding industry helped make Las Vegas one of the nation's most popular venues for "goin' to the chapel." Celebrity weddings of the 1950s that sparked the trend included singer Dick Haymes and Rita Hayworth, Joan Crawford and Pepsi chairman Alfred Steele, Carol Channing and TV exec Charles Lowe, and Paul Newman and Joanne Woodward.

On a grimmer note, the '50s also heralded the atomic age in Nevada, with nuclear testing taking place just 65 miles northwest of Las Vegas. A chilling 1951 photograph shows a mushroom-shaped cloud from an atomic bomb test visible over the Fremont Street horizon. Throughout the decade, about one bomb a month was detonated in the nearby desert (an event, interestingly enough, that often attracted loads of tourists).

THE 1960s: THE RAT PACK & A PACK RAT

The very first month of the new decade made entertainment history when the Sands hosted a 3-week "Summit Meeting" in the Copa Room that was presided over by "Chairman of the Board" Frank Sinatra with Rat Pack cronies Dean Martin; Sammy Davis, Jr.; Peter Lawford; and Joey Bishop (all of whom happened to be in town filming *Ocean's Eleven*).

- **1951** The first of many atom bombs is tested in the desert just 65 miles from Las Vegas.
- **1952** The Club Bingo (opened in 1947) becomes the desert-themed Sahara. The Sands's Copa Room enhances the city's image as an entertainment center.
- **1954** The Showboat pioneers buffet meals and bowling alleys in a new area of Downtown.

- **1955** The Strip gets its first high-rise hotel, the nine-story Riviera, which pays Liberace the unprecedented sum of $50,000 to open its showroom.
- **1957** The Dunes introduces bare-breasted showgirls in its *Minsky Goes to Paris* revue. The most luxurious hotel to date, the Tropicana, opens on the Strip.
- **1958** The 1,065-room Stardust opens as the world's

largest resort complex with a spectacular show from France, the *Lido de Paris*.
- **1959** The Las Vegas Convention Center goes up, presaging the city's future as a major convention city.
- **1960** A championship boxing match, the first of many, takes place at the Convention Center. El Rancho Vegas, the Strip's first property, burns to the ground.

The building boom of the '50s took a brief respite. Most of the Strip's first property, the El Rancho Vegas, burned down in 1960. And the first new hotel of the decade, the first to be built in 9 years, was the exotic Aladdin in 1966.

During the '60s, negative attention focused on mob influence in Las Vegas. Of the 11 major casino hotels that had opened in the previous decade, 10 were believed to have been financed with mob money. Then, like a knight in shining armor, Howard Hughes rode into town and embarked on a $300-million hotel- and property-buying spree, which included the Desert Inn itself (in 1967). Hughes was as "bugsy" as Benjamin Siegel any day, but his pristine reputation helped bring respectability to the desert city and lessen its gangland stigma.

Las Vegas became a family destination in 1968, when Circus Circus burst onto the scene with the world's largest permanent circus and a "junior casino" featuring dozens of carnival midway games on its mezzanine level. In 1969, Elvis made a triumphant return to Las Vegas at the International's showroom and went on to become one of the city's all-time legendary performers. His fans had come of age.

Hoping to establish Las Vegas as "the Broadway of the West," the Thunderbird Hotel presented Rodgers and Hammerstein's *Flower Drum Song*. It was a smash hit. Soon The Riviera picked up *Bye, Bye, Birdie*, and, as the decade progressed, *Mame* and *The Odd Couple* played at Caesars Palace. While Broadway played the Strip, production shows such as the Dunes's *Casino de Paris* became ever more lavish, expensive, and technically innovative.

THE 1970s: MERV & MAGIC

In 1971 the 500-room Union Plaza opened at the head of Fremont Street on the site of the old Union Pacific Station. It had what was, at the time, the world's largest casino, and its showroom specialized in Broadway productions. The same year, talk-show host Merv Griffin began taping at Caesars Palace, taking advantage of a ready supply of local headliner guests. He helped popularize Las Vegas even more by bringing it into America's living rooms every afternoon.

The year 1973 was eventful: Over at the Tropicana, illusionists extraordinaire Siegfried & Roy began turning women into tigers and themselves into legends in the *Folies Bergère*.

Two major disasters hit Las Vegas in the 1970s. First, a flash flood devastated the Strip, causing more than $1 million in damage. Second, gambling was legalized in Atlantic City. Las Vegas's hotel business slumped as fickle tourists

---

- **1963** McCarran International Airport opens.
- **1966** The Aladdin, the first new hotel on the Strip in 9 years, is soon eclipsed by the unparalleled grandeur of Caesars Palace. The Four Queens opens Downtown. Howard Hughes takes up residence at the Desert Inn. He buys up big chunks of Las Vegas and helps erase the city's gangland stigma.

- **1967** Elvis Presley marries Priscilla Beaulieu at the Aladdin.
- **1968** Circus Circus gives kids a reason to come to Las Vegas.
- **1973** The ultraglamorous 2,100-room MGM Grand assumes the mantle of "world's largest resort." Siegfried and Roy, debut at the Tropicana.
- **1976** Pioneer aviator Howard Hughes dies aboard

a plane en route to a Houston hospital. Dean Martin and Jerry Lewis make up after a 20-year feud.
- **1979** A new international arrivals building opens at McCarran International Airport.
- **1980** McCarran International Airport embarks on a 20-year, $785-million expansion program. Las Vegas celebrates its 75th birthday. A

continues

decided to check out the new East Coast gambling mecca.

As the decade drew to a close, an international arrivals building opened at McCarran International Airport, and dollar slot machines caused a sensation in the casinos.

THE 1980s: THE CITY ERUPTS

As the '80s began, Las Vegas was booming once again. McCarran Airport began a 20-year, $785-million expansion program.

Siegfried & Roy were no longer just the star segment of various stage spectaculars. Their own show, *Beyond Belief,* ran for 6 years at the Frontier, playing a record-breaking 3,538 performances to sellout audiences every night. It became the most successful attraction in the city's history.

In 1989, Steve Wynn made Las Vegas sit up and take notice. His gleaming white-and-gold The Mirage was fronted by five-story waterfalls, lagoons, and lush tropical foliage—not to mention a 50-foot volcano that dramatically erupted regularly! Wynn gave world-renowned illusionists Siegfried & Roy carte blanche (and more than $30 million) to create the most spellbinding show Las Vegas had ever seen.

THE 1990s THROUGH TODAY: KING ARTHUR MEETS KING TUT

The 1990s began with a blare of trumpets heralding the rise of a turreted medieval castle fronted by a moated drawbridge and staffed by jousting knights and fair damsels. Excalibur reflected the '90s marketing trend to promote Las Vegas as a family-vacation destination.

More sensational megahotels followed on the Strip, including the *new* MGM Grand hotel, backed by a full theme park (it ended Excalibur's brief reign as the world's largest resort), Luxor Las Vegas, and Steve Wynn's Treasure Island.

In 1993 a unique pink-domed 5-acre indoor amusement park, Grand Slam Canyon, became part of the Circus Circus hotel. In 1995 the Fremont Street Experience was completed, revitalizing Downtown Las Vegas. Closer to the Strip, rock restaurant magnate Peter Morton opened the Hard Rock Hotel, billed as "the world's first rock 'n' roll hotel and casino." The year 1996 saw the advent of the French Riviera–themed Monte Carlo and the Stratosphere Casino Hotel & Tower, its 1,149-foot tower the highest building west of the Mississippi. The unbelievable New York–New York arrived in 1997.

But it all paled compared with 1998 and 1999. As Vegas hastily repositioned itself from "family destination" to "luxury resort," several new hotels, once again eclipsing anything that had come before, opened. Bellagio was the latest from

devastating fire destroys the MGM Grand, leaving 84 dead and 700 injured.

- **1981** Siegfried and Roy begin a record-breaking run in their own show, *Beyond Belief,* at the Frontier.
- **1982** A Las Vegas street is named Wayne Newton Boulevard.
- **1989** Steve Wynn makes headlines with his spectacular Mirage, fronted by an erupting volcano.

- **1990s** The family-friendly medieval Arthurian realm of Excalibur opens as the new "world's largest resort" title-holder with 4,032 rooms, a claim it relinquishes when the MGM Grand's new 5,005-room megaresort/theme park opens in 1993, with a *Wizard of Oz* theme. Other properties geared toward families opened in the 1990s, most notably Luxor, with its pyramid and Egyptian motifs, and

the pirate-themed Treasure Island. The rock-'n'-roll Hard Rock, Mandalay Bay, Bellagio, The Venetian, and Paris Las Vegas carried concept gaming resorts to new heights, while New York–New York was built with a roller coaster running around it.

- **2004** Strip Monorail debuts.
- **2005** Wynn Las Vegas, the first major new casino resort to open in 5 years, debuts on the Strip.

Vegas visionary Steve Wynn, an attempt to bring grand European style to the desert, while at the far southern end of the Strip, Mandalay Bay charmed. As if this weren't enough, The Venetian's ambitious detailed re-creation of everyone's favorite Italian city came along in May 1999, and was followed in short order by the opening of Paris Las Vegas in the fall of 1999.

The 21st century opened up with a bang as the Aladdin blew itself up and gave itself a from-the-ground-up makeover, while Steve Wynn blew up the Desert Inn and replaced it with the $2.7-billion showstopper Wynn Las Vegas. Along the way, everyone has expanded, with first the Luxor, then Caesars, and lately, Mandalay Bay, The Venetian, and Bellagio all adding new towers and hundreds more rooms each. Clearly, no one can rest on their laurels in Vegas, for this is not only a city that never sleeps, but one in which progress never stops moving, even for a heartbeat.

For the latest shake-ups on the Strip, see "What's New in Las Vegas," at the beginning of this guide.

Index

See also Accommodations and Restaurant indexes, below.

RESTAURANTS

FROMMER'S® COMPLETE TRAVEL GUIDES

Alaska
Alaska Cruises & Ports of Call
American Southwest
Amsterdam
Argentina & Chile
Arizona
Atlanta
Australia
Austria
Bahamas
Barcelona
Beijing
Belgium, Holland & Luxembourg
Bermuda
Boston
Brazil
British Columbia & the Canadian
  Rockies
Brussels & Bruges
Budapest & the Best of Hungary
Calgary
California
Canada
Cancún, Cozumel & the Yucatán
Cape Cod, Nantucket & Martha's
  Vineyard
Caribbean
Caribbean Ports of Call
Carolinas & Georgia
Chicago
China
Colorado
Costa Rica
Cruises & Ports of Call
Cuba
Denmark
Denver, Boulder & Colorado Springs
Edinburgh & Glasgow
England
Europe
Europe by Rail
European Cruises & Ports of Call
Florence, Tuscany & Umbria

Florida
France
Germany
Great Britain
Greece
Greek Islands
Halifax
Hawaii
Hong Kong
Honolulu, Waikiki & Oahu
India
Ireland
Italy
Jamaica
Japan
Kauai
Las Vegas
London
Los Angeles
Madrid
Maine Coast
Maryland & Delaware
Maui
Mexico
Montana & Wyoming
Montréal & Québec City
Munich & the Bavarian Alps
Nashville & Memphis
New England
Newfoundland & Labrador
New Mexico
New Orleans
New York City
New York State
New Zealand
Northern Italy
Norway
Nova Scotia, New Brunswick &
  Prince Edward Island
Oregon
Ottawa
Paris
Peru

Philadelphia & the Amish Country
Portugal
Prague & the Best of the Czech
  Republic
Provence & the Riviera
Puerto Rico
Rome
San Antonio & Austin
San Diego
San Francisco
Santa Fe, Taos & Albuquerque
Scandinavia
Scotland
Seattle
Seville, Granada & the Best of
  Andalusia
Shanghai
Sicily
Singapore & Malaysia
South Africa
South America
South Florida
South Pacific
Southeast Asia
Spain
Sweden
Switzerland
Texas
Thailand
Tokyo
Toronto
Turkey
USA
Utah
Vancouver & Victoria
Vermont, New Hampshire & Maine
Vienna & the Danube Valley
Virgin Islands
Virginia
Walt Disney World® & Orlando
Washington, D.C.
Washington State

FROMMER'S® DOLLAR-A-DAY GUIDES

Australia from $50 a Day
California from $70 a Day
England from $75 a Day
Europe from $85 a Day
Florida from $70 a Day
Hawaii from $80 a Day

Ireland from $80 a Day
Italy from $70 a Day
London from $90 a Day
New York City from $90 a Day
Paris from $90 a Day
San Francisco from $70 a Day

Washington, D.C. from $80 a Day
Portable London from $90 a Day
Portable New York City from $90
  a Day
Portable Paris from $90 a Day

FROMMER'S® PORTABLE GUIDES

Acapulco, Ixtapa & Zihuatanejo
Amsterdam
Aruba
Australia's Great Barrier Reef
Bahamas
Berlin
Big Island of Hawaii
Boston
California Wine Country
Cancún
Cayman Islands
Charleston
Chicago
Disneyland®
Dominican Republic

Dublin
Florence
Frankfurt
Hong Kong
Las Vegas
Las Vegas for Non-Gamblers
London
Los Angeles
Los Cabos & Baja
Maui
Miami
Nantucket & Martha's Vineyard
New Orleans
New York City
Paris

Phoenix & Scottsdale
Portland
Puerto Rico
Puerto Vallarta, Manzanillo &
  Guadalajara
Rio de Janeiro
San Diego
San Francisco
Savannah
Vancouver Island
Venice
Virgin Islands
Washington, D.C.
Whistler

FROMMER'S® NATIONAL PARK GUIDES

Algonquin Provincial Park
Banff & Jasper
Family Vacations in the National
  Parks

Grand Canyon
National Parks of the American West
Rocky Mountain

Yellowstone & Grand Teton
Yosemite & Sequoia/Kings Canyon
Zion & Bryce Canyon

FROMMER'S® MEMORABLE WALKS

Chicago
London

New York
Paris

San Francisco

FROMMER'S® WITH KIDS GUIDES

Chicago
Hawaii
Las Vegas
New York City

Ottawa
San Francisco
Toronto

Vancouver
Walt Disney World® & Orlando
Washington, D.C.

SUZY GERSHMAN'S BORN TO SHOP GUIDES

Born to Shop: France
Born to Shop: Hong Kong, Shanghai
  & Beijing

Born to Shop: Italy
Born to Shop: London

Born to Shop: New York
Born to Shop: Paris

FROMMER'S® IRREVERENT GUIDES

Amsterdam
Boston
Chicago
Las Vegas
London

Los Angeles
Manhattan
New Orleans
Paris
Rome

San Francisco
Seattle & Portland
Vancouver
Walt Disney World®
Washington, D.C.

FROMMER'S® BEST-LOVED DRIVING TOURS

Austria
Britain
California
France

Germany
Ireland
Italy
New England

Northern Italy
Scotland
Spain
Tuscany & Umbria

THE UNOFFICIAL GUIDES®

Beyond Disney
California with Kids
Central Italy
Chicago
Cruises
Disneyland®
England
Florida
Florida with Kids
Inside Disney

Hawaii
Las Vegas
London
Maui
Mexico's Best Beach Resorts
Mini Las Vegas
Mini Mickey
New Orleans
New York City
Paris

San Francisco
Skiing & Snowboarding in the West
South Florida including Miami &
  the Keys
Walt Disney World®
Walt Disney World® for
  Grown-ups
Walt Disney World® with Kids
Washington, D.C.

SPECIAL-INTEREST TITLES

Athens Past & Present
Cities Ranked & Rated
Frommer's Best Day Trips from London
Frommer's Best RV & Tent Campgrounds
  in the U.S.A.
Frommer's Caribbean Hideaways
Frommer's China: The 50 Most Memorable Trips
Frommer's Exploring America by RV
Frommer's Gay & Lesbian Europe

Frommer's NYC Free & Dirt Cheap
Frommer's Road Atlas Europe
Frommer's Road Atlas France
Frommer's Road Atlas Ireland
Frommer's Wonderful Weekends from
  New York City
Retirement Places Rated
Rome Past & Present

THE NEW TRAVELOCITY GUARANTEE

**EVERYTHING YOU BOOK WILL BE RIGHT, OR WE'LL WORK
WITH OUR TRAVEL PARTNERS TO MAKE IT RIGHT, RIGHT AWAY.**

*To drive home the point,
we're going to use the word "right" in every single sentence.*

Let's get right to it. Right to the meat! Only Travelocity guarantees everything about your booking will be right, or we'll work with our travel partners to make it right, right away. Right on!

Here's a picture taken smack dab right in the middle of Antigua, where the guarantee also covers you.

The guarantee covers all but one of the items pictured to the right.

For example, what if the ocean view you booked actually looks out at a downright ugly parking lot? You'd be right to call – we're there for you. And no one in their right mind would be pleased to learn the rental car place has closed and left them stranded. Call Travelocity and we'll help get you back on the right track.

Now, you may be thinking, "Yeah, right, I'm so sure." That's OK; you have the right to remain skeptical. That is until we mention help is always right around the corner. Call us right off the bat, knowing that our customer service reps are there for you 24/7. Righting wrongs. Left and right.

Now if you're guessing there are some things we can't control, like the weather, well you're right. But we can help you with most things – to get all the details in righting,* visit **travelocity.com/guarantee**.

*Sorry, spelling things right is one of the few things not covered under the guarantee.

I'd give my right arm for a guarantee like this, although I'm glad I don't have to.

travelocity
You'll never roam alone.

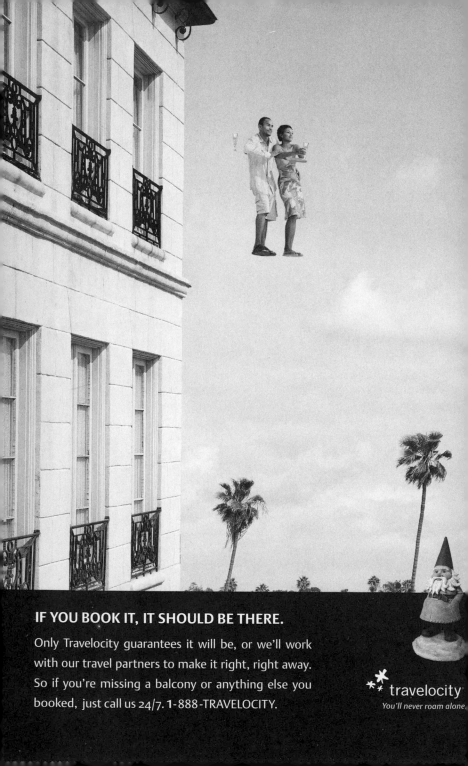

IF YOU BOOK IT, IT SHOULD BE THERE.

Only Travelocity guarantees it will be, or we'll work with our travel partners to make it right, right away. So if you're missing a balcony or anything else you booked, just call us 24/7. 1-888-TRAVELOCITY.

travelocity

You'll never roam alone.

My, what an inefficient
way to fish.

Ring toss, good. Horseshoes, bad.

Faster! Faster! Faster!

We take care of the fiddly bits, from
providing over 43,000 customer reviews
of hotels, to helping you find our best
fares, to giving you 24/7 customer service.
So you can focus on the only thing
that matters. Goofing off.

travelocity®
You'll never roam alone.℠

PAYIN' HIGH RATES IN
SIN CITY
WOULD BE A SIN

For our absolute lowest rates in Las Vegas, there's just one place to go.

Book Smart.℠

 Get our **Lowest Rate** online.
Or call **1.800.THRIFTY**® or your professional travel agent.